Microsoft® SQL Server® Reporting Services Recipes

FOREWORD xxiii

PREFACE xxv

INTRODUCTION xxvii

CHAPTER 1   Business Reporting Paradigms 1

CHAPTER 2   Basic Report Design Concepts 29

CHAPTER 3   Report Design Essentials 45

PART I   Columnar and Grouped Reports 83

PART II   BI Dashboards and Elements 129

PART III   Chart and Gauge Reports 233

PART IV   Interactive Reporting 297

PART V   Integrated Reporting Applications 339

PART VI   Enhanced Report Content 373

PART VII   Filtering and Parameterization 479

PART VIII   Custom and Dynamic Data Sources 551

PART IX   Games 583

INDEX 601

Microsoft® SQL Server®
Reporting Services Recipes

for Designing Expert Reports

Paul Turley
Robert M. Bruckner

Wiley Publishing, Inc.

QL Server® Reporting Services Recipes: for Designing Expert Reports

ng, Inc.
oint Boulevard
IN 46256
.com

© 2010 by Paul Turley and Robert M. Bruckner

d by Wiley Publishing, Inc., Indianapolis, Indiana

ed simultaneously in Canada

978-0-470-56311-3

ufactured in the United States of America

9 8 7 6 5 4 3 2 1

For general information on our other products and services please contact our Customer Care Department within the United States at (877) 762-2974, outside the United States at (317) 572-3993 or fax (317) 572-4002.
Wiley also publishes its books in a variety of electronic formats. Some content that appears in print may not be available in electronic books.

Library of Congress Control Number: 2010920661

This book is dedicated to every database professional, developer, and report designer who has gone beyond the call of duty, worked ridiculous hours obsessing over that perfect report — so their business leaders can know what's going on in their organizations.

— Paul Turley and Robert M. Bruckner

CREDITS

EXECUTIVE EDITOR
Robert Elliott

PROJECT EDITOR
Tom Dinse

TECHNICAL EDITORS
Paul S. Waters
Rob Boek

PRODUCTION EDITOR
Kathleen Wisor

COPY EDITORS
Christopher Jones
Maryann Steinhart
Kim Cofer

EDITORIAL DIRECTOR
Robyn B. Siesky

EDITORIAL MANAGER
Mary Beth Wakefield

**ASSOCIATE DIRECTOR
OF MARKETING**
David Mayhew

PRODUCTION MANAGER
Tim Tate

**VICE PRESIDENT AND
EXECUTIVE GROUP PUBLISHER**
Richard Swadley

**VICE PRESIDENT AND
EXECUTIVE PUBLISHER**
Barry Pruett

ASSOCIATE PUBLISHER
Jim Minatel

PROJECT COORDINATOR, COVER
Lynsey Stanford

PROOFREADER
Word One, New York

INDEXER
Johnna VanHoose Dinse

COVER DESIGNER
Mike E. Trent

COVER IMAGE
© Mark Evans

ABOUT THE AUTHORS

 PAUL TURLEY, MVP, MCTS-BI, MCITP-BI, MCT, MCDBA, MCSD, MSF Practitioner

Paul is a BI Solution Architect / Manager for Hitachi Consulting and a Microsoft Most Valuable Professional (MVP). He is part of Hitachi Consulting's national Business Intelligence and Process Management team and works on occasion from Hitachi's regional office in Portland, Oregon.

He has been architecting, managing, and developing applications and business intelligence solutions for large and small businesses since 1992. He has developed custom database, BI, and reporting solutions for many companies including Microsoft, Nike, Disney, Hewlett-Packard, and Boeing. He teaches, develops training courseware, speaks at industry conferences, and has authored and co-authored several technical books. He has presented at the Professional Association for SQL Server (PASS) global summit since 2004.

He is an MSDN forum moderator for SQL Server Reporting Services and has been a Microsoft Certified Solution Developer (MCSD) since 1996 and maintains certifications in software architecture and development, database administration (MCDBA), and project management methodologies (MSF & IT Project+.) He holds the current MCTS and MCITP certifications for SQL Server BI.

Paul has authored and co-authored eleven books including *Beginning Transact-SQL for SQL Server 2005 and 2008*, *Beginning Transact-SQL for SQL Server 2000 and 2005*, *Professional SQL Server 2008 Reporting Services*, *Professional SQL Server 2005 Reporting Services*, *Microsoft Press SQL Server 2005 Integration Services Step by Step*, *Beginning SQL Server 2005 Administration*, and *Professional SQL Server Reporting Services* (2000).

 ROBERT M. BRUCKNER, Technical Lead, Microsoft

Robert is a developer and technical lead with the Microsoft SQL Server product team. His core area of responsibility is the development of the scalable report processing engine, hosted in server and client components that ship in SQL Server Reporting Services and Visual Studio ReportViewer.

Prior to joining Microsoft and the Reporting Services development team in 2003, Robert researched, designed, and implemented database and business intelligence systems for several years as a research assistant at Vienna University of Technology, Austria, and as a system architect at T-Mobile Austria. Robert holds a master's degree and a PhD with highest distinctions in Computer Science from Vienna University of Technology, and holds several patents.

Anyone good with a search engine can find several thousands of Robert's past postings on public newsgroups and MSDN forums sharing his insights, tips, tricks, and expert advice related to Reporting Services, RDL, and other SQL Server technologies. Robert regularly speaks at industry conferences and also maintains a popular blog at: http://blogs.msdn.com/robertbruckner. In his spare time, Robert enjoys mountain biking, skiing, and playing foosball.

ABOUT THE CONTRIBUTORS

ROB BOEK, MCITP, MCDBA, MCPD, MCSD, MSCE, MCT

Rob is a Sr. Database Developer for Smarsh, Inc. He has been a database administrator, developer, consultant, and Microsoft Certified Trainer for over 12 years. Rob has supported environments with hundreds of SQL Servers and databases as large as 35 TB.

Rob is a co-founder of the Oregon SQL Developers group. He has presented at the Professional Association for SQL Server (PASS) global summit, and is a frequent presenter at user groups, code camps, and SQL Saturday events. Rob participated in the development of the SQL Server 2008 certification exams as a Subject Matter Expert.

C. RYAN CLAY, Senior Architect, Hitachi Consulting

Ryan specializes in business intelligence, data management, portal and collaboration, and integration/interoperability solutions employing Microsoft technologies. Ryan has implemented Microsoft Business Intelligence solutions for a variety of Fortune 500 clients in the retail, construction, finance, and consumer goods industries. Ryan holds degrees in computer science, is a published author, and is active in the Microsoft community through speaking engagements and presentations at regional and national events. He lives in the Dallas area with his wife and daughter.

RISHI JARIWALA, Senior Consultant, Hitachi Consulting

Rishi has been working as a consultant specializing in Microsoft platforms and implementing enterprise-level applications for over six years. Over the last two years, he has been concentrating on the Microsoft BI Platform and has designed and implemented end-to-end BI solutions using the full Microsoft BI Stack, ranging from data warehouse to performance management. Within the Microsoft BI space, Rishi's interests are aligned with SQL Server Reporting Services, SQL Server Analysis Services, and PerformancePoint Server. He has gained several Microsoft certifications including MCDBA, MCTS in SQL Server 2005 BI, and MCTS PerformancePoint Server 2007.

DAN KISTING, Senior Consultant, Dynamics National Team of Hitachi Consulting

Dan specializes in software development, business intelligence, and ERP solution implementation featuring Field Service Automation for Microsoft Dynamics AX (FSA) and other Microsoft technologies. Dan has implemented FSA and Dynamics AX in both functional and technical positions for many Fortune 500 clients in the material testing services, food sorting machine manufacturing, and the heating and air conditioning industries. Dan holds degrees in both computer science and graphic communication, as well as a MBA in Global Management. He lives in the Portland, Oregon area with his wife, son, and two pugs, Chi-Chi Guey and Mariposa.

GRANT PAISLEY, Founder Angry Koala Pty Ltd, SQL Server MVP

Grant has over 15 years of experience in Business Intelligence and in using Reporting Services and Analysis Server since SQL 2000. Currently he designs, develops, and implements business intelligence solutions using the Microsoft BI stack with David Lean, Geoff Orr, Glyn Llewellyn, Lesley Llewellyn, Mark Fitzpatrick, Praveen Chand, Shaun Bliss, and Sue Fitzpatrick. Grant runs the Sydney SQL Server User Group (sqlserver.org.au). He also founded the reporting community (reportsurfer.com), and is a regular speaker at SQL Code Camp, Usergroups, and TechEd Australia. Any spare time he has he spends mountain biking or kitesurfing, and he loves Hawaiian stopovers.

EF ROMERO, Senior Consultant, Hitachi Consulting

Ef is a Senior Consultant at Hitachi Consulting where he specializes in business intelligence development with SQL Server. His work with SQL Server is concentrated in ETL, data warehouse development, database optimization, and reporting. He received his bachelor's and master's degrees, both in pure mathematics, from UTEP, and has worked as a mathematician and BI developer for the past four years.

JOE SALVATORE, Business Intelligence Architect, MicroLink, LLC.

Joe has been a database architect, business intelligence and database developer for more than 12 years, specializing in data access architecture, ETL, data quality profiling, and business intelligence development. Serious about successful business intelligence solutions that incorporate best practices, he has attended many of Ralph Kimball's classes and regularly attended professional conferences such as the Microsoft Business Intelligence Conference and Professional Association for SQL Server (PASS) Summits. Joe also is an accomplished SQL Server author who has contributed to Wrox's *Professional SQL Server 2005 Administration*, content relicensed for *Professional SQL Server 2008 Administration*, and he has contributed articles for *Information Management* and *SQL Server Standard* magazines. Joe is also a Microsoft Certified IT Professional - Microsoft SQL Server 2005 and 2008 Business Intelligence Developer as well as a Microsoft Certified Technical Specialist - Microsoft SQL Server 2005 and 2008 Business Intelligence Development.

THIAGO SILVA, MCAD, MCTS (ASP.NET), MCPD-Web Developer, Software Architect and Manager of Specialized Services, Hitachi Consulting

Thiago has been developing custom .NET and Reporting Services solutions since the early days of .NET and SQL Server 2000. He is a part of the Microsoft practice within Hitachi Consulting, where he helps create, manage, and deliver solutions for clients around the Microsoft technology stack. Thiago is co-author of *Professional SQL Server 2008 Reporting Services*, and has been featured on the tech podcast .NET Rocks. He is an active member of the .NET development community, where he presents at local user groups. He writes tech articles for his blog "Silvaware," found at http://silvaware.blogspot.com. Thiago holds a bachelor's degree in Information and Operations Management from Texas A&M University. He is also a Microsoft Certified Professional with the following titles: MCAD, MCTS (ASP.NET), and MCPD Web Developer.

PAUL S. WATERS, Business Intelligence Architect, AMECO (www.paulswaters.com)

During Paul's 16 years of working in IT, he has held a variety of positions including help desk manager, application developer, network administrator, and Director of IT. For the past several years, he has been focused on business intelligence and data warehouse design and development. Currently he designs, develops, and implements business intelligence solutions using the Microsoft BI stack with his two co-workers Jason S. Burton and Todd Sibley.

Paul is the Founder and President of the SQL Server Innovators Guild (www.ssig.org), a founding board member of the GSA Technology Council (www.gsatc.org), a member of Greenville Tech's Program Advisory Council, and was Co-Chairman of the South Carolina Code Camp 2.0 (www.sccodecamp.com). He is also a presenter at local user groups and conferences.

ACKNOWLEDGMENTS

I THANK MY LEADERS at Hitachi Consulting for their support and tolerance during this long project. I would especially recognize Hilary Feier, Patrick Bolin, and John Lauer for allowing this book to materialize. My thanks go to Thierry D'Hers and the entire Reporting Services product team who have provided direct support and have been responsive to my questions and feedback; to Sean Boon, Bob Meyers, Lukasz Pawlowski, Chris Baldwin, Chris Hays and Carolyn Chau for building an incredible product and helping us take it up a notch or two.

Thanks to my family. To my wonderful wife, Sherri, who is the toughest, most selfless, and most caring woman on the planet. To my daughters Rachael, Sara, and Krista for supporting their dad. To my son Josh for doing the right thing to serve his country, and to Angel for being there with him. Thank you especially to Sara for being strong and teaching us about love.

Thank you to my Lord and Savior, for providing for my family and for challenges to make us stronger and better people.

— PAUL TURLEY

I WOULD LIKE TO thank in particular Paul Turley and Bob Elliott for initially envisioning and approaching me about this project, and the great collaboration throughout. Furthermore, I would like to express a big "thank you" to all co-authors contributing to this book, and the invaluable editorial work of Tom Dinse, Rob Boek, and Paul Walters to ensure accuracy.

— ROBERT M. BRUCKNER

THANKS TO THE MANY people who contributed to this material — far too many to name here, but you know who you are. And a very special thanks to my wonderful, beautiful wife, Donna. She is the one who truly inspires me in every aspect of our lives.

— C. RYAN CLAY

IN ADDITION TO THE constant support from my wife, I would really like to thank Paul Turley for this great opportunity. I would also like to thank Bob Elliott, Tom Dinse, Paul S. Waters, and Rob Boek for reviewing and editing our work and, last but not least, I would like to thank my co-authors for contributing to this special book.

— RISHI JARIWALA

THANKS TO THE DIFFERENT people who contributed to this effort, including the technical editors, Paul T., Paul W., and Tom D. on the team, Steve Svoboda for giving me the opportunity to learn FSA and AX, and Angela Garcia and Erin Gray for reviewing my material. Most importantly, however, thank you to my incredibly beautiful (and patient) wife Rosa "Cuca" and my equally beautiful son Alejandro for the patience, support, and for doing everything they do on a daily basis to make my life complete.

— DAN KISTING

I WISH TO THANK MY wife Sue (who put up with the 3am Skype calls) and our three kids Megan, Lisa, and Zoe for their patience while writing these recipes ("Dad, you're writing recipes? You don't cook!").

— GRANT PAISLEY

AN INESTIMABLE MEASURE of love and gratitude is deserved of both my beautiful wife Dawn and my precious daughter Phoebe. Their love, support, and patience were vital not only throughout this project but in every day of my life. I would also like to thank all co-authors for their inspiration during this endeavor, especially Paul Turley for providing the opportunity to work on this project.

Additionally, I would like to express my thanks to our editors Tom Dinse, Rob Boek, and Paul Walters whose hard work provided for content of the highest fidelity.

— EF ROMERO

I WISH TO RECOGNIZE THE love and support of my wife, Linda, and my two boys, Andrew and Matthew, for their inspiration and motivation behind great endeavors such as professional writing. I am always grateful for the examples and encouragement supplied by both my parents and my extended family. Thanks especially to the top-notch efforts of all the managers, editors, and reviewers without whom our efforts would be less than the stellar results that have been achieved.

— JOE SALVATORE

THANKS TO MY BEAUTIFUL, loving wife Michelle who supports me and inspires me to be the man that I am, and to my kids, Gabriella and baby boy Silva (who will be joining us soon after we complete this book). They are the most precious gifts from God.

I would like to thank the Lord God for endurance, provision, and inspiration during the writing of these recipes, and throughout the long nights and weekends.

I also acknowledge:

My colleagues and peers at Hitachi Consulting, for challenging and encouraging me throughout this adventure;

The folks from the Reporting Services team at Microsoft, who have been helpful in answering our questions and getting us to the bottom line of the features discussed in this book;

My co-authors for assisting with ideas and insightful discussions (and for all their collaboration);

Bob Elliott, Tom Dinse, Paul Waters, and Rob Boek, the editors and reviewers of this book, for their input and guidance, as well as patience and fantastic job of testing and keeping this book consistent and legible.

— THIAGO SILVA

I WOULD LIKE TO thank my beautiful wife Sarah, and my children, Megan, Laura, Michaela, and Trevor for their love, patience, and support while writing this book.

Thanks to Paul Turley and Robert Bruckner for the opportunity to participate in this project, and to Tom Dinse and Bob Elliott for their guidance through the process.

— ROB BOEK

I WISH TO THANK my beautiful wife Jennifer and our two wonderful children Emma and Ian for their love, support, patience, and understanding while working on this book.

— PAUL S. WATERS

CONTENTS

FOREWORD   *xxiii*

PREFACE   *xxv*

INTRODUCTION   *xxvii*

CHAPTER 1: BUSINESS REPORTING PARADIGMS   1

Process and Operational Support   2

Report Types   2

Sales Orders, Invoices, Manifests, and Inventory Forms   2

Template Forms   3

Tabular and List Reports   4

Catalogs   6

Labels   6

Activity Summaries   7

Status Reports   8

Analytical Reporting   8

Report Types   9

Dashboards and Scorecards   9

Pivot Table and Matrix Reports   9

Charts   10

Maps   14

Interactive Reports   15

Application Integration   17

Report Integration into Applications   18

Desktop Applications   18

Web Applications   19

Portal Content   19

ReportViewer Control   20

Installing the Reporting Services Samples and SQL Server
Sample Databases   21

Server Reports   22

HTML Viewer   23

Report Viewer Control   23

Reporting Services Processors and Extensions   23

Report Caching   24

The HTML Rendering Extension   25

The CSV-Rendering Extension   25

The XML-Rendering Extension	25
The Image-Rendering Extension	26
The PDF-Rendering Extension	26
The Excel-Rendering Extension	26
The Word-Rendering Extension	26
Summary	**26**

CHAPTER 2: BASIC REPORT DESIGN CONCEPTS	**29**

Using Report Builder	**30**
Formatting and Sample Values	31
Data Sources	31
Datasets and Queries	**32**
Designing Queries	33
Dataset Best Practices	36
Filtering Data	**37**
Using Stored Procedures	38
Reports and Report Objects	**39**
Report Body	39
Headers and Footers	40
Aggregate Functions and Totals	41
Adding Totals to a Table or Matrix Report	42
The Tablix	**43**
Static and Dynamic Columns and Rows	43
Summary	**44**

CHAPTER 3: REPORT DESIGN ESSENTIALS	**45**

Tabular and Matrix Reports	**45**
Defining Table Groups	45
Group Expressions and Options	46
Formatting Table Values	48
Matrix Reports	51
Sorting Options	51
Sorting in the Query	51
Sorting in a Group	52
Interactive Sort	53
Adding Headers and Footers	53
The Low Down on Drill-Down	54
Report Navigation Essentials	54
Reports with Multi-Level Groups and Drill-Down Actions	54
Standard Terminology	54
Drill-Down	55

Creating a Drill-Down Report 59
Drill-Through Reports 60
   Navigating to a URL 62
   Report Navigation Summary 62
Charting Basics 63
   Series and Category Axes 63
   Polar and Radar Charts 65
   Shape Charts 65
   Bar Charts 65
Gauges 67
   Scales 67
   Pointers and Markers 67
   Ranges 67
   Radial Gauges 68
   Linear Gauges 68
Maps 69
   Map Gallery 69
   ESRI Shape Files 69
   SQL Server Spatial Data 69
Using Parameters 69
   Creating a Parameter List 70
   Modifying and Formatting MDX Queries 72
   Multi-Value Parameters 73
   Cascading Parameters 74
   Report Parameters 75

Expressions and Custom Code **75**
Calculated Fields 76
Conditional Expressions 76
Using Custom Code 78
   Using Custom Code in a Report 78
   Using a Custom Assembly 79

Formatting Report Data **80**
Introduction to Dynamic Formatting 81
Designing Multicolumn Reports 81

Summary **82**

PART I: COLUMNAR AND GROUPED REPORTS

Green Bar Reports **85**
Designing the Report 85
Alternate Row Colors in an SSRS 2000 or 2005 Matrix 90
Final Thoughts 92
Credits and Related References 92

Alternate Background Shading for Table Groups   **93**
  Designing the Report   93
  Designing the Report for Reporting Services 2005   98
  Final Thoughts   98
  Credits and Related References   99
Nested Group Green Bar Effect   **100**
  Designing the Report   100
  Final Thoughts   104
  Credits and Related References   104
Creating Dynamic Groups   **105**
  Designing the Report   105
  Final Thoughts   114
  Credits and Related References   114
Hiding and Showing Columns in a Table   **115**
  Designing the Report   115
    Showing and Hiding Group Headers   120
  Final Thoughts   120
Horizontal Table   **121**
  Designing the Report   121
  Designing the Report for Reporting Services 2005   124
  Final Thoughts   124
  Credits and Related References   124
Resetting the Page Number Based on Groups   **125**
  Designing the Report   125
  Final Thoughts   127

PART II: BI DASHBOARDS AND ELEMENTS

Creating Sparklines   **131**
  Designing the Report   131
    Sales Trends   131
  Final Thoughts   137
  Credits and Related References   138
Cube Dynamic Rows   **139**
  Designing the Report   140
  Final Thoughts   147
  Credits and Related References   147
Cube Metadata   **148**
  Designing the Report   148
    Adding MeasureGroups (for Cube/Perspective) 151
    Adding Other Cube Metadata   153
  Final Thoughts   161
  Credits and References   162

Cube Browser   **163**

  Anatomy of the Reports   165
    Cube Browser   165
    Cube Browser Metadata   166
    Cube Browser Member   167
  Behind the Scenes   167
    Cube Browser   167
    Report Body   173
    Restricting Rows and Columns   174
    Swap Actions   175
    Titles   176
    Footer Information   179
  Final Thoughts   182
  Credits and Related References   184

Australian Sparklines   **185**

  Designing the Report   186
    Preparing the Data and Adding Extra Controls   187
    Building a Full-Sized Australian Sparkline   197
    Adding the Australian Sparkline to a Table   201
  Final Thoughts   203
  Credits and Related References   203

Angry Koala Cube Browser   **204**

  Anatomy of the Reports   205
    r100 - Angry Koala Cube Browser   206
    r101 - Angry Koala Graph   207
    r102 - Angry Koala Driver   208
    r103 - Angry Koala Member   210
  Behind the Scenes   210
    Angry Koala Cube Browser   210
    Report Body   219
    Restricting the Number of Rows and Columns   220
    Swap Actions   220
    Titles   220
    Report Footer Info   220
  Final Thoughts   221
  Credits and Related References   221

Bullet Charts   **222**

  Designing the Report   222
  Final Thoughts   226
  Credits and Related References   227

Synchronizing Groups, Charts, and Sparklines   **228**

  Designing the Report   228
  Final Thoughts   232
  Credits and Related References   232

PART III: CHART AND GAUGE REPORTS

Chart Custom Color Palette   **235**
Designing the Report   236
    Custom Legends   237
Final Thoughts   238
Credits and Related References   238

Chart Keywords   **239**
Designing the Report   239
Final Thoughts   241
Credits and Related References   242

Column Chart with Goal Threshold Line   **244**
Designing the Report   244
    Adding Dynamic Color   249
Final Thoughts   249

Creating a Personal Report Card   **250**
Designing the Report   250
Final Thoughts   259

Customizing Gauges with Images   **260**
Designing the Report   260
Final Thoughts   263
Credits and Related References   263

Exception Highlighting with Gauges/Bullet Graphs   **264**
Designing the Report   264
Final Thoughts   267
Credits and Related References   267

Grouped Pie Chart Slices   **268**
Designing the Report   268
Final Thoughts   271

Growing Bar and Column Charts   **272**
Designing the Report   272
Final Thoughts   275
Credits and Related References   275

Histogram Chart   **276**
Designing the Report   276
Final Thoughts   278
Credits and Related References   278

Linear Regression Line   **279**
Designing the Report   279
Final Thoughts   285

Creating a Multi-Series Multi-Y Axis Chart   **286**
Designing the Report   286
Credits and Related References   292

Pareto Chart   293
  Designing the Report   293
  Final Thoughts   296
  Credits and Related References   296

PART IV: INTERACTIVE REPORTING

Conditional Linking   299
  Designing the Report   299
  Final Thoughts   304
  Credits and Related References   304
Drill-Through for a Multi-Level Matrix Report   305
  Designing the Drill-Through Target Report   305
  Designing the Drill-Through Source Report in 2005   309
  Designing the Drill-Through Source Report in 2008   315
  Final Thoughts   317
  Credits and Related References   317
Drill-Through Report Link Breadcrumbs   318
  Designing the Report   319
  Final Thoughts   325
Dynamic Pivoting as a Matrix Replacement   326
  Designing the Report   326
  Final Thoughts   330
Using a Document Map Table for Navigation   331
  Designing the Report   331
  Final Thoughts   337
  Credits and Related References   337

PART V: INTEGRATED REPORTING APPLICATIONS

Creating a Report Server Usage Report   341
  Designing the Report   343
  Final Thoughts   346
Rotating Report Dashboard   347
  Designing the Report   347
  Final Thoughts   351
  Credits and Related References   351
Updating Data From a Report   352
  Designing the Report   352
  Final Thoughts   358
Offline Reporting Using the Report Viewer Control   359
  Designing the Report   359
    Computer Requirements and Prerequisites   362
    Wiring Up the Report   363

Programming the Code-Behind 365
Final Thoughts 372

PART VI: ENHANCED REPORT CONTENT

Creating a Calendar Report 375
Designing the Report 375
Final Thoughts 382
Credits and Related References 382

Creating Mailing Labels 383
Designing the Report 383
Final Thoughts 390
Credits and Related References 390

Barcodes 391
Designing the Report 391
Fonts 392
Custom Report Items (Barcode Components) 393
Final Thoughts 399
Credits and Related References 399

Currency Translation 400
Designing the Report 400
Final Thoughts 406

Custom Aggregation 407
Designing the Report 407
Designing the Median Report in SSRS 2005 407
Implementing the Report in SSRS 2008 409
Final Thoughts 414
Credits and Related References 414

Dynamic (Conditional) Page Breaks 415
Designing the Report 415
Designing the Report for Previous Versions of Reporting
Services without the PageBreak.Disabled Property 418
Final Thoughts 419

Excel Worksheet Naming And Page Naming 420
Designing the Report 420
Final Thoughts 424

External Image Sources 425
Designing the Report 425
Creating the ASP.NET External Image Source 430
Final Thoughts 438

Language Localization 439
Multi-cultural Considerations 439
Designing the Report 440

Creating the External Resource Lookup with .NET | 441
Final Thoughts | 446
Credits and Related References | 446

Page Running Total | **447**
Designing the Report | 447
Final Thoughts | 453

Renderer-Dependent Layout and Formatting | **454**
Designing the Report | 454
Final Thoughts | 459

Creating a Checkbox List to Show Existing Records | **460**
Designing the Report | 460
Final Thoughts | 463

Using a Checkbox List to Select and Deselect Records | **464**
Designing the Report | 464
Using the Checkbox Report for Parameter Selection | 472
Final Thoughts | 473

Using the Map Wizard | **474**
Designing the Report | 474
Final Thoughts | 478
Credits and Related References | 478

PART VII: FILTERING AND PARAMETERIZATION

Multiple Criterion Report Filtering | **481**
Designing the Report | 481
Filtering in the Query | 484
Using Code to Build the Query String | 485
Filtering in the Dataset | 487
Samples | 488
Final Thoughts | 488
Credits and Related References | 489

Using Multi-Value Parameters with a Stored Procedure | **490**
Designing the Report | 490
Final Thoughts | 495

Using Multi-Value Parameters with a Subscription Report | **496**
Designing the Report | 496
Final Thoughts | 505

Parameterized Top Values Report | **506**
Designing the Report | 506
Top Value Reports for Cubes | 510
Final Thoughts | 512

Cube Restricting Rows | **513**
Designing the Report | 513

A Better Way to Interact With a Report Parameter 518

Final Thoughts 521

Creating Custom Sorting Reports **522**

Parameterizing Custom Sorted Queries 523

Designing the Report 523

Parameterizing the Order By Clause 530

Custom Sorting in Tablix Groups 533

Using the Interactive Sort Feature 535

Creating a Custom Interactive Sort 536

Final Thoughts 542

Credits and Related References 543

Filtering User-Specific Report Data **544**

Designing the Report 544

Final Thoughts 550

PART VIII: CUSTOM AND DYNAMIC DATA SOURCES

Using a Web Service as a Data Source **553**

Designing the Report 553

Final Thoughts 560

Credits and Related References 560

Reporting on SharePoint List Data **561**

Preparing the Sample Data 562

Designing the Report 564

Designing the Report in 2008 R2 570

Final Thoughts 573

Credits and Related References 573

Dynamics AX Report Wizard **574**

Designing the Report 574

Final Thoughts 581

PART IX: GAMES

Hangman Game **585**

Reviewing the Report 585

Final Thoughts 589

Credits and Related References 590

Sea Battle Game **591**

Reviewing the Report 592

How It Works 593

Final Thoughts 599

Credits and Related References 599

INDEX *601*

FOREWORD

When we started work on the Reporting Services 2008 R2 release back in summer 2008 (at the time it was codenamed Kilimanjaro), we set out to focus on end users: on enabling business users and traditional report consumers to serve their own needs by authoring their own reports. Given our goals, I was curious about the type of books that would be authored about this release. I thought the only thing that would be relevant and appropriate would be user- and solution-oriented books. When Paul first talked to me about his project, I was intrigued with the recipe-style chapters idea. It departed from the traditional Administrator-oriented books that attempt to cover all aspects and components of the product. The reason for my interest was not just that it was a newer, fresher approach to authoring a book on our product, it also reflected the spirit and the theme of Reporting Services 2008 R2: self-service and end-user oriented.

Later, while talking with Robert Bruckner, a senior developer in the Reporting Services processing and rendering engine team, I discovered that he also was involved with this project. I was feeling good: that was a solid project well under way. A couple of months later, at TechEd US, I am in a meeting with Brian Larson who is in the middle of a book signing session. Brian is well known for having authored among the most popular Reporting Services best-sellers. As we are discussing various things, we come to talk about book projects for R2, and to my great surprise, I learn that he, too, has contributed material to this recipe book project. I am exultant. Later that day, I am due to have lunch with Grant Paisley to talk about one of his rather unique reports, known, among other names, as the "Australian Sparkline" (If you are curious about it, go to the Cube browser report recipe). It turns out that at the table with Grant and me are Paul and a couple other SSRS MVPs. Inevitably at some point the conversation turns to books, and Grant drop the news that he, too, is on this project. Needless to say, for a second I believe he is teasing me, but he is not. But this is not the end of it; Thiago, Joe, and about 10 other MVPs and book authors contributed to this book. This is unprecedented. Never before have we seen such a concentration of knowledge and experience coming together to author what will probably be one of the most memorable books ever written on Reporting Services.

It is probably not the kind of book you will read front to back, but it is likely to be the one you keep on your desk at all times, close at hand and ready to open at the right time — when your business needs will require a specific report design. You are likely to find a chapter right on topic in this book. You might ask, "Thierry, how can you be so confident that this book will give me just what I need just when I need it?"

Well, the answer is that not only are the authors of this book all practitioners, they are also some of the most actives posters on the Reporting Services forums and some of the most active participants in other Microsoft events, and as such they have a deep knowledge about the most commonly discussed topics and questions asked by users. They are experts whose experience I deeply admire and whose judgment I fully trust. They are considered by the product team as a panel of experts whose advice our team seeks when we need opinions about product direction or validation of product feature prioritization. For us, the product group, they represent the voice of the customers. With you, they become an extension of the product team, showing you some of the best ways to solve real business problems and take full advantage of Reporting Services.

You are in great hands; I hope you will enjoy the book as much as I enjoyed working with its authors.

— THIERRY D'HERS
Group Program Manager
Microsoft SQL Server Reporting Services team

PREFACE

With rapidly increasing data volumes in every organization, the real challenge today is presenting data efficiently in a format that is easy to digest. The Reporting Services platform provides a lot of flexibility and an extensible architecture, which can help you adapt and extend the out-of-the-box experience if needed and implement solutions that fit your specific needs.

If you are looking for examples of interactive reports that you probably never imagined you could accomplish with Reporting Services reports, I recommend you attend the BI Power Hour session at big conferences such as Tech Ed, BI Conference, or SQL PASS. The BI Power Hour session is about demonstrating, in perhaps unusual and fun ways, the power of business intelligence tools. For the most recent conference seasons I built demos for the Reporting Services part of the BI Power Hour that included a multi-player Sea Battle report game (included in this book), and an artificial intelligence Sales Strategy/Risk Assessment reporting game, which will be published to my blog soon.

Some people say I know a lot about available Reporting Services report features. Probably because I implemented many of those, I'm using Reporting Services every day, and I have been answering questions and sharing my insights and advice for many years in various Microsoft internal discussion groups, private early adopter newsgroups, public Reporting Services newsgroups, as well as MSDN forums. Anyone good with a search engine can find several thousands of my postings.

Nonetheless, what continues to fascinate me since the early days of Reporting Services 2000 is seeing the amazing things that people are doing with the Reporting Services product leveraging its flexibility and extensibility, and pushing it in ways that we in the product team may not have thought of originally. I also frequently observe that people realize they could accomplish solutions with Reporting Services that they initially didn't think were feasible, and become curious about what else is possible. I hope the report design recipes in this book will provide you with answers and new ideas.

This reminds me of a related conversation I had with Paul Turley sometime during the fall of 2009. At the time, Paul was preparing a new conference presentation with Reporting Services contents. We had been exchanging frequent emails, in which I explained how to accomplish particular report designs in the best way. At some point in that conversation, Paul pointed out that several aspects of a proposed report design are rather complex to accomplish in Reporting Services 2005. I responded by saying that this is absolutely true and that we in the product team specifically monitor that kind of customer feedback. We consequently decided to introduce the "tablix" in Reporting Services 2008, which simplified that scenario tremendously. Furthermore, I mentioned in that same conversation that I had just finished the implementation for one of the new features in Reporting Services 2008 R2 that enables renderer-dependent layout decisions in reports (another frequent customer request). Paul humorously responded that this was "not being fair," because there are many consultants out there who make a good living from extending the out-of-the-box experience of Reporting Services. So the next thing the product team does is to close a bunch of these gaps, making it really simple to accomplish those scenarios easily in the next release.

Well, this book is truly special! It draws from the experience of many Reporting Services industry experts and brings together best practices, report design patterns. The recipes provide inspiration on what is possible today, and provide clear steps on how to implement them successfully. Each recipe calls out the versions of Reporting Services it applies to, and as a bonus we included several recipes that specifically target new features enabled in the upcoming Reporting Services 2008 R2 release. Examples include naming worksheets from within the report on Excel export, dynamic page breaks, resetting the page number based on groups, rendering format dependent layout decisions.

Good luck and happy reporting!

— ROBERT M. BRUCKNER
Redmond, WA

INTRODUCTION

AS A REPORTING SERVICES USER AND REPORT DESIGNER, you and I have something in common. We both appreciate the power and simplicity of SQL Server Reporting Services. You may have used SSRS to design common table and matrix reports. Perhaps you have designed reports that use parameters to let your users filter data and you want to help them gain more insight into their business. Like an artist, you've discovered some interesting techniques for using this tool to solve business problems in creative ways, and now you'd like to take the next step and create compelling and dynamic reporting solutions so your users can get more meaningful value from their data. Perhaps you'd like to learn about techniques developed by others who also appreciate this exciting tool.

We've brought together a team of creative and experienced report designers to showcase their recipes for unique report designs. Most of these designs have been tested and used in large organizations with real business data, and for consulting clients who have unique problems to solve and high expectations. Every one of us is passionate about technology, data, and SQL Server Reporting Services, which is why we created this unique book.

This is not a beginning-level book to teach the essentials of basic report design, but it's not exclusively an advanced-level book either. If you understand the basics of report design and have a cursory knowledge of Reporting Services, you should be able to use the recipes in this book to learn more advanced techniques and build useful business reports.

WHO THIS BOOK IS FOR

Before using this book to design reports with these recipes, you should know how to do the following:

- ➤ Use Report Builder 2.0 or 3.0 to create a simple report.

- ➤ Use Business Intelligence Development Studio or Visual Studio to create a report project.

- ➤ Design a data source and connect to a SQL Server database.

- ➤ Create a dataset and use the query builder to design a simple database query.

- ➤ Add a data region to a report. This may include designing a simple table or matrix.

- ➤ Add a group to a table or matrix.

- ➤ Create report parameters.

If you can master these essentials on your own, we'll show you how to apply these basic skills to create useful business reports. With these skills, you'll learn to apply more advanced design techniques to take your report designs to the next level.

If you are familiar with Report Builder 2.0, 3.0, or Business Intelligence Development Studio report designer, you'll find that the differences between these report design tools are subtle, and you should be able to easily make the necessary adjustments to follow a recipe while using a report designer other than the one the recipe was written for.

We don't provide beginning-level, step-by-step instructions for every task; rather, we summarize the essentials and focus on design techniques. For example, in nearly every recipe you will be instructed to create a data source for a particular database, add a dataset, add parameters, and design a simple report data region. You should be able to create a dataset and build a query. The recipe author will provide the query script for you to type or enter into the query design window.

WHAT THIS BOOK COVERS

This is a book of report recipes — instructions for designing specific report styles and solutions. It will help an experienced Reporting Services report designer create specific types of reports for solving unique business problems. The complexity and difficulty of these recipes ranges from 200 to 400 level. If you possess basic skills, as you work through these recipes, you may learn to improve your report design skills and advance to more complex recipes. However, to get started, you will need a working knowledge of fundamental report design using SQL Server Reporting Services.

You will find chapters and report recipes organized into categorized sections. The introductory chapters in this book are comprised, in part, from previous writings of the same authors, in order to be a comprehensive reference guide for experienced report authors. They are designed to get you started in a high-level overview of the Reporting Services architecture, design principles, deployment strategies, and basic report design techniques. This overview is provided as a refresher course and a quick reference guide for experienced Reporting Services report design users.

If you need help getting started with report design, before you use this book, we recommend that you first read *Professional SQL Server 2008 Reporting Services* (Wrox, 2008).

HOW THIS BOOK IS STRUCTURED

The book is organized in two main sections. We begin with three chapters that introduce the SSRS product, architecture, and design tools. These chapters cover report design essentials at a high-level to help fill-in gaps for moderately skilled report authors. These chapters also provide a reference for the essential techniques required to design and build basic reports. These techniques are the building blocks for most of the recipes in the sections that follow.

The bulk of the materials in this book are several short report recipes, grouped by category. Each recipe begins with a brief description of its purpose and provides a business case for its use and the problems that it solves. The versions of Reporting Services for which the design techniques apply are listed, followed by a list of skills or other resources you will need to design the recipe report. This is like a list of ingredients in a cookbook.

This is followed by an illustration of the finished report, followed in turn by a set of step-by-step instructions, fully-illustrated, that will lead you through the process to create the recipe report. In most cases, the author will instruct the reader to use well-known techniques, rather than the detailed steps, to perform common design tasks — tasks like creating a data source, adding a dataset, adding a parameter, or drawing a table. The recipes are written in plain language to address the skill level of a moderately experienced SSRS report design user. At the end of each recipe, you will see and experience a functioning example of the completed recipe design.

In most cases, the author concludes by discussing similar applications for the technique and different ways that the report may be adapted to address different reporting needs.

WHAT YOU NEED TO USE THIS BOOK

To use the techniques in the book, you will need a report design and report hosting environment running on SQL Server Developer, Standard or Enterprise Edition. The majority of the examples and instructions are written for SSRS 2008 using Report Builder 2.0. All of these recipes may also be applied using SQL Server 2008 R2 with Report Builder 3.0. These are the tools we recommend that you use. Some of the recipes showcase new features introduced in SSRS 2008 R2 and will only work with that version, forward. Each recipe indicates the version(s) of Reporting Services that it supports and the database you will need.

If you are using an older version of Reporting Services, several of the recipes will also work with SSRS 2000 and 2005, as indicated. Some include alternate instructions for the earlier report designers. Some, but not all, of the techniques written for the newer report designers may be adapted to earlier versions, but in order to do so, you will need to be familiar with the differences and make these adaptations yourself.

The databases used in these recipes may be downloaded from the book companion site at www.wrox.com. These databases include AdventureWorks2008, AdventureWorksDW2008, Northwind, and the Adventure Works DW database for Analysis Services. For those recipes that support earlier SSRS versions, you may also use the AdventureWorks and Adventure Works DW databases for SQL Server 2005, which may be obtained from Microsoft at www.codeplex.com. Any of the recipes that use specialized databases, other than the standard samples, will include these in the download files provided for that recipe.

CONVENTIONS

To help you get the most from the text and keep track of what's happening, we've used a number of conventions throughout the book.

Boxes like this one hold important, not-to-be forgotten information that is directly relevant to the surrounding text.

Notes, tips, hints, tricks, and asides to the current discussion are offset and placed in italics like this.

As for styles in the text:

- ➤ We *highlight* new terms and important words when we introduce them.
- ➤ We show keyboard strokes like this: Ctrl+A.
- ➤ We show file names, URLs, and code within the text like so: `persistence.properties`.
- ➤ We present code in a special monofont typeface:

```
We use a monofont type with no highlighting for most code examples.
```

SOURCE CODE

As you work through the examples in this book, the necessary expressions, function code, and query scripts are provided for you. You can either type in all the code manually, or use the completed report files that accompany the book. All of the finished reports and source code used in this book are available for download at `http://www.wrox.com`. Once at the site, simply locate the book's title (either by using the Search box or by using one of the title lists) and click the Download Code link on the book's detail page to obtain all the sample files for the book.

 Because many books have similar titles, you may find it easiest to search by ISBN; this book's ISBN is 978-0-470-56311-3.

Once you download the code, just decompress it with your favorite compression tool. Alternately, you can go to the main Wrox code download page at `http://www.wrox.com/dynamic/books/download.aspx` to see the code available for this book and all other Wrox books.

ERRATA

We make every effort to ensure that there are no errors in the text or in the code. However, no one is perfect, and mistakes do occur. If you find an error in one of our books, like a spelling mistake or faulty piece of code, we would be very grateful for your feedback. By sending in errata you may save another reader hours of frustration and at the same time you will be helping us provide even higher quality information.

To find the errata page for this book, go to `http://www.wrox.com` and locate the title using the Search box or one of the title lists. Then, on the book details page, click the Book Errata link. On this page you can view all errata that has been submitted for this book and posted by Wrox editors. A complete book list including links to each book's errata is also available at `www.wrox.com/misc-pages/booklist.shtml`.

If you don't spot "your" error on the Book Errata page, go to `www.wrox.com/contact/techsupport.shtml` and complete the form there to send us the error you have found. We'll check the information and, if appropriate, post a message to the book's errata page and fix the problem in subsequent editions of the book.

P2P.WROX.COM

For author and peer discussion, join the P2P forums at p2p.wrox.com. The forums are a Web-based system for you to post messages relating to Wrox books and related technologies and interact with other readers and technology users. The forums offer a subscription feature to e-mail you topics of interest of your choosing when new posts are made to the forums. Wrox authors, editors, other industry experts, and your fellow readers are present on these forums.

At http://p2p.wrox.com you will find a number of different forums that will help you not only as you read this book, but also as you develop your own applications. To join the forums, just follow these steps:

1. Go to p2p.wrox.com and click the Register link.

2. Read the terms of use and click Agree.

3. Complete the required information to join, as well as any optional information you wish to provide, and click Submit.

4. You will receive an e-mail with information describing how to verify your account and complete the joining process.

 You can read messages in the forums without joining P2P, but in order to post your own messages, you must join.

Once you join, you can post new messages and respond to messages other users post. You can read messages at any time on the Web. If you would like to have new messages from a particular forum e-mailed to you, click the Subscribe to this Forum icon by the forum name in the forum listing.

For more information about how to use the Wrox P2P, be sure to read the P2P FAQs for answers to questions about how the forum software works, as well as many common questions specific to P2P and Wrox books. To read the FAQs, click the FAQ link on any P2P page.

1

Business Reporting Paradigms

In the world of business, we use a lot of different styles and types of reports. To appreciate how pervasive reports are in the world of business, in different organizations, and in our day-to-day lives, we must first define what a report is. Any formatted output of data from a database or any other type of data source could be called a report. Some types are obvious and may include sales reports, end-of-period summaries, trend analysis, and comparisons. These are some traditional report styles. Reports are used in all areas of business and practically every business function involves printing, displaying, browsing, or using some other method to present data to business leaders, workers, service providers, customers, inspectors, analysts, and others for a variety of reasons. Reports, in many different forms, are everywhere.

Less traditional report types that may be used in different business scenarios include things like product labels, name badges, routing tags, invoices, claim forms, request forms, government documents, and shipping manifests. You probably have types of reports that are unique to your specific business or industry that outsiders aren't even aware of. To provide a better understanding about the various functions that reports perform, this chapter explores different types of reports. Chapters 2 and 3 will review the basic building blocks of report design and development that you will need to know to apply the report design recipes in this book. We expect that you already have some hands-on experience with SQL Server Reporting Services but we will review the basics as a quick refresher.

For the purpose of simplicity, we will group all of these report types into general categories. You will no doubt be able to identify some of your own unique reporting requirements but they generally fall into one of the following major categories:

- ➤ Process and operational support
- ➤ Business intelligence and analytical reports
- ➤ Application integration
- ➤ Forms, labels, and letters

PROCESS AND OPERATIONAL SUPPORT

Day-to-day business processes require reporting solutions to keep business working. Nearly all businesses and organizations today rely on operational data stored in some kind of database. Although there are some proprietary, special-purpose databases used to support certain types of business, more than ninety percent of all data is stored in a relational database system on a standard product platform such as Oracle, SQL Server, IBM DB2, or SyBase. These systems capture transactions as they occur, and records are stored at the detailed transactional level to support real-time processes.

Consumer business has many common examples. A point-of-sale transaction is captured in a local database at the store or POS terminal and may be replicated to a regional or central database. Of course, the sales receipt is a report generated directly from this transactional data. Similarly, banking transactions record every debit, credit, and adjustment made to an account. Transactional records may be recorded every time you use your cellular phone, swipe your key card at work, go to the gym, send a tweet, post a comment on Facebook, or visit a secure web site.

Report Types

Operational reports are some of the most commonplace in the business and consumer world but they also exist in many specialized scenarios. In working with several different consulting clients to migrate their reporting solutions to a new platform or toolset, we often ask them to identify the operational reports from analytical and decision-support reports. Inevitably we identify a gray area of reports in each category. These may be reports that aggregate and group details for analysis from operational data stores or analytical reports that include some level of operational detail.

Putting the exceptions aside for the time being, let's take a look at some of the more common and a few of the less common types of operational reports.

Sales Orders, Invoices, Manifests, and Inventory Forms

The items in this category are usually not referred to — or even thought of — as reports. Specialized software is typically used to input and process orders. These may be for general use in a retail or commercial wholesale operation or they may be for specialized applications, such as a medical laboratory or an electronics assembly plant. Although the basic structure of an order or invoice may be similar, the specific components may be adapted to meet specific business needs. An invoice usually contains a header, specific sections for the seller and customer's contact, and billing and shipping information, followed by a tabular section of line items. Each item typically has a product code, description, price, quantity, and other information that may be specific to the business process or industry, such as weight, cost, discounts, freight, tax, or shipping cost.

These types of reports have a relatively simple design but are also usually integrated into a custom application, rather than selected from a report menu on a central server. Some order forms may be printed on stock forms and other companies may print the entire form on blank paper. Figure 1-1 shows a typical sales order report with a customer and shipping details header, repeating line items, summary totals, and a footer area containing contact information.

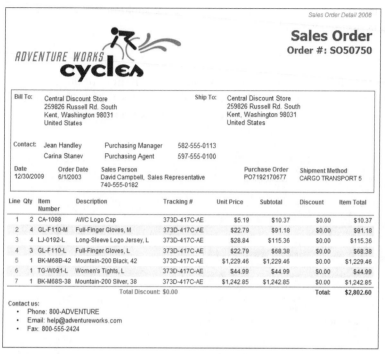

FIGURE 1-1

Template Forms

In the past, most forms were preprinted with blank lines for typed or hand-written information. Modern printers have made it much easier to produce highly formatted forms all at once on blank paper rather than using fill-in-the-blank forms with preprinted logos, borders, and detail lines. However, certain applications call for printing on standard forms for a variety of reasons. It may be cheaper to use lesser-quality printers or black ink/toner printers with multi-colored forms. Some forms require duplicate copies produced with impact printers. Or, perhaps the process has yet to be modernized. In the medical insurance claim business, for example, some of these traditional standards were highly influenced by a thriving pre-printed forms industry.

Whatever the reason, these forms can be quite challenging because each character must be printed in a specific location. Often, getting the report character spacing and size to line up is only half the battle because these forms are highly-dependent on the printer and paper dimensions such as the margins and gripper space. Reports that are designed to provide some latitude for margins and character positioning make it easier to adjust the report itself rather than to rely on printer settings.

In recent years, most of the industry-standard preprinted forms have been replaced by all-at-once reports that print on standard sized blank paper. Less expensive, high quality printers have made this more feasible for small businesses but it has created more demand for sophisticated reporting tools capable of producing pixel-perfect reports and forms.

Tabular and List Reports

Tabular, row-based reports have been common for so long and many variations of this design have become commonplace. The green bar-style report, shown in Figure 1-2, uses a shaded background for every other row to make it easier for users to differentiate and follow each row visually.

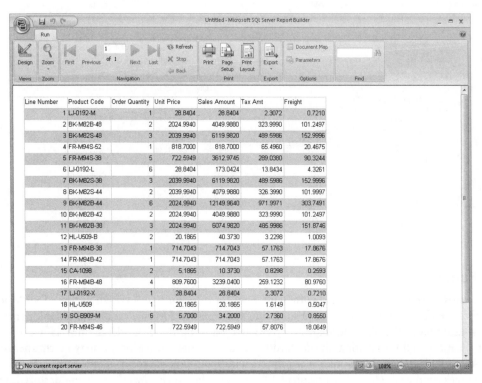

FIGURE 1-2

Grouped reports add more information to the tabular layout with grouped bands, headers, and footers. Color has become more important in report design, and different background colors are often used to differentiate not only each row but the group bands and other related elements. This report type uses different background colors for the table header and two group bands, and then a light color for alternate row shading. A simple example is shown in Figure 1-3.

Sometimes it may be more important to differentiate group values rather than the detail rows. In the example shown in Figure 1-4, the Category values use alternating shading bands.

Category	Subcategory	Product Number	Product	Description	List Price
Accessories	Bike Racks	RA-H123	Hitch Rack - 4-Bike	Carries 4 bikes securely; steel construction, fits 2" receiver hitch.	$120.00
	Bike Stands	ST-1401	All-Purpose Bike Stand	Perfect all-purpose bike stand for working on your bike at home. Quick-adjusting clamps and steel construction.	$159.00
	Bottles and Cages	BC-M005	Mountain Bottle Cage	Tough aluminum cage holds bottle securly on tough terrain.	$9.99
		BC-R205	Road Bottle Cage	Aluminum cage is lighter than our mountain version; perfect for long distance trips.	$8.99
		WB-H098	Water Bottle - 30 oz.	AWC logo water bottle - holds 30 oz; leak-proof.	$4.99
	Cleaners	CL-9009	Bike Wash - Dissolver	Washes off the toughest road grime; dissolves grease, environmentally safe. 1-liter bottle.	$7.95
	Fenders	FE-6654	Fender Set - Mountain	Clip-on fenders fit most mountain bikes.	$21.98

FIGURE 1-3

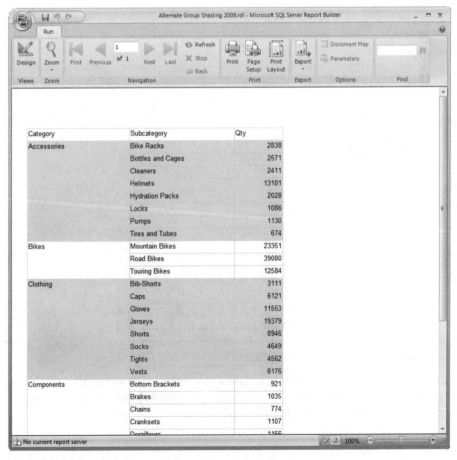

FIGURE 1-4

Catalogs

A product catalog is a common layout used to group categories of products and then provide details in an ordered list. A catalog report must be easy to read with bold headings and group descriptive text. Figure 1-5 shows a continuous report using a repeating list area for product category and subcategory groups and containing a description block and product image in the group header. The groups include a tabular region for product details.

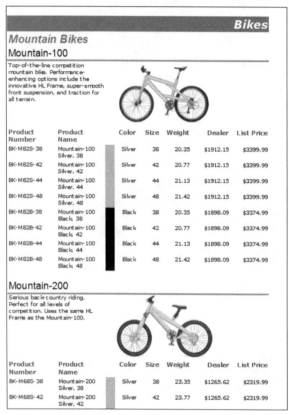

FIGURE 1-5

Labels

Label reports are usually simple in layout but have a few unique characteristics. A rectangular data region is repeated across rows and columns on the printed page. The size and position of the data region must be aligned to the standard label sheet with relatively precise margins and column spacing. Figure 1-6 shows a multi-column list report formatted to fit a standard label sheet.

The greatest challenge is to easily produce labels in a variety of standard sizes and dimensions. The label industry, led by a few well-known companies and influenced by dozens of generic label form producers, has managed to produce hundreds of "standard" sheet label formats.

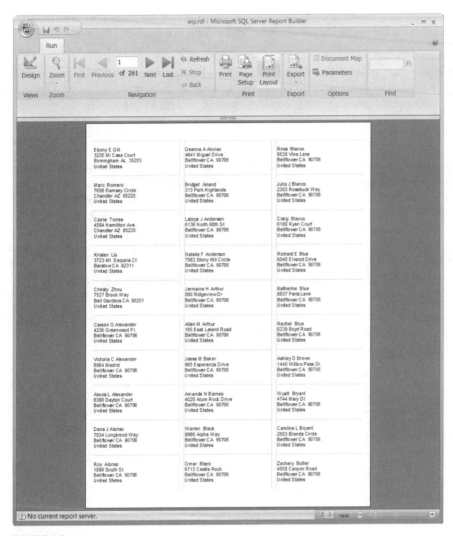

FIGURE 1-6

Activity Summaries

The line between operational and analytical reporting is not simply that one is at the detail level and the other includes groups and summaries. There is a lot of business value in rolling up details into groups and aggregating measures into summary totals. Even when these summaries are compared across different business dimensions, such as time or geography, these comparisons can be performed appropriately using operational data. The most significant difference between operational and analytical reporting is the approach taken to get to the result. If these summaries are performed within an operational scope (such as a single manufacturing plant or within a finite period of time) and the results should be easy reconciled back to the details, then this is an extension of operational reporting. However, if the results are for enterprise-wide comparisons, long-term trend analysis, and corporate decision support, you will be met with significant challenges trying to run these reports with operational data sources.

Summary reports on occasion will evolve to include components of truly analytical reports and, when that happens, it's important to consider whether they should be migrated to a business intelligence reporting model. The paramount question to consider is whether the report exists to support a specific business operation within the scope of that group, department, and leadership.

Status Reports

The term "status report" means different things to different people but the common theme is that this type of report is used to provide concise results that are comparable over periods of time. It's important to understand the needs of the person who will use the report and the message it should convey. A common report may be for a team leader to get the status for a project or task. This should typically summarize data points to a standard indicator at the end of a time period or project phase, relative to some goal or objective. For example, is the project on schedule, behind schedule, or ahead of schedule? Is the application component development completed or incomplete? These simplified results are typically broken down by tasks, stages, or responsibilities for comparison over each reporting period to measure progress.

Status reports can vary in sophistication but most are fairly simple. Figure 1-7 shows an example of a Top 10 report of ranked values, which is common in many business scenarios where leaders may want to see the best producing items.

Top Customers | 10 | View Report

Top 10 Customers by Total Sales Amount

Customer Name	Sales Amount
Jordan Turner	$15,999.10
Willie Xu	$13,490.06
Nichole Nara	$13,295.38
Kaitlyn Henderson	$13,294.27
Margaret He	$13,269.27
Randall Dominguez	$13,265.99
Adriana Gonzalez	$13,242.70
Rosa Hu	$13,215.65
Brandi Gill	$13,195.64
Brad She	$13,173.19

FIGURE 1-7

ANALYTICAL REPORTING

The concept and purpose of business intelligence (BI) is much more than just reporting. BI solutions help business leaders make critical decisions. A complete BI strategy involves financial forecasting and strategic approaches to the way resource investments are planned, managed, and measured. A business intelligence methodology prescribes the rules and standards for defining business targets and the success factors for measuring actual metrics against those targets. Reporting is a big part of that process. After defining business metrics and the rules for measuring success — and of course, gathering all of the necessary data, different report types are used to analyze current and historical data to evaluate correlations and trends.

Analytical reports tend to be more concise and graphical than operational reports. Traditionally, column and line charts dominated the desktops of business analysts but a new breed of reports plays the role of BI dashboard components. There are a variety of standard metaphors for indicating goals, status, and trends. Sometimes an array of simple pie charts or needle gauges is an effective method to convey the state of things in the business enterprise. However, as user reporting needs have become more sophisticated (as have many business users) there is an ever-increasing need to add more useful information to business reports while keeping reports easy to read and manageable.

Report Types

The style of reports used in a BI solution range from common tabular and chart reports to particular report styles with graphical indicators, symbols, arrows, and progress bars. BI defines a lot more than just a style of reports; other types of business data systems can include dashboard and scorecard report styles.

Dashboards and Scorecards

By definition, a dashboard is a collection of reports or report elements and gauges that convey the state of related key metrics. At a glance, a dashboard reflects the health of the business. Report actions allow users to drill down or drill through to more specific details and assess the status of each metric across different dimensions, such as time periods or geographic regions. A business scorecard is a specific style of dashboard-type report that helps business leaders measure key performance and success values relative to goals and business plans. Aside from the style and layout of reports, business scorecards conform to a standard process for planning business growth and measuring success.

Although dashboards and scorecards may not be limited to business intelligence solutions, the need for them may suggest that eventually a full BI solution should be developed to support all the business reporting requirements.

Dashboard design is often a balancing act between simplicity and usability. The goal is to give business users the information that they need, based on universally understood metrics, measures, and performance indicators. That information must be delivered at the right level of detail so the users can make important decisions and take action on the most critical issues affecting business performance.

Pivot Table and Matrix Reports

Known within different products as a cross-tab, pivot table, or matrix, this type of report groups data on both the rows and columns axis, showing aggregated values at each intersect point. Pivot reports are very useful for ad-hoc analysis. For larger volume result sets, drill-down features can allow results to be aggregated at higher group levels within axis hierarchies and allow users to expand each branch to expose more detail at lower group levels. See Figure 1-8.

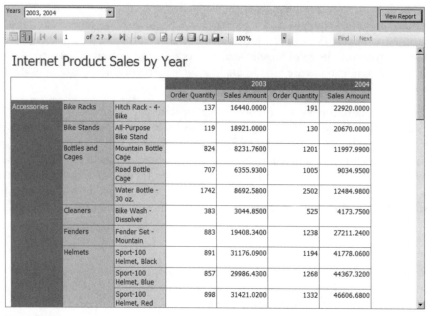

FIGURE 1-8

Charts

Chart reports provide a varied range of visualization options. Aggregated data is presented graphically and plotted on a linear two-dimensional or three-dimensional grid, in circular pie slices, or a radial plot space. Combinations of chart types may be combined to make comparisons and to correlate graphical data displays. In Figure 1-9, a Pareto chart employs a column chart type to range categories in descending order while a line chart type shows cumulative values.

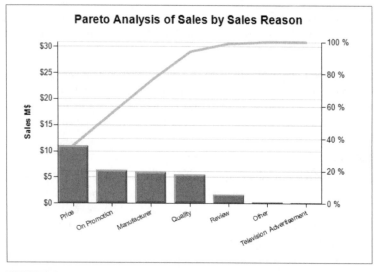

FIGURE 1-9

Simplicity is often the best choice. A basic pie chart displays proportional values with an optional legend (see Figure 1-10). Pie charts can also display data point values and/or point labels over each slice or with callout labels. Pie or donut charts can have bold visual impact when exploded, extruded, or embossed 3-D options are added.

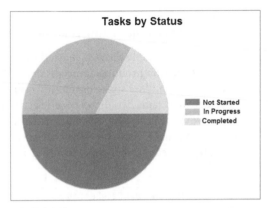

Although common chart types like the pie and donut display data in a simple, easily readable format, they may not be the best choice when more sophisticated users need a lot of information presented with the most effective use of screen space.

FIGURE 1-10

Charting data values provides an effective means for seeing whether a measured data point or aggregated total is more or less than another but at times it's important to apply some conclusive business logic to a measurement and show whether a certain value is "good," "bad," "acceptable," or otherwise. Business data should be actionable; and for leaders to take action, they must be able make a judgment. That's why decision makers measure results against goals, targets, and quotas.

Figure 1-11 shows variations of column and line charts that put more information into a relatively small space. This "report card" report groups axis labels in a two-level hierarchy — showing both years and quarters, and then plots quotas and actual values using two different chart types in the same chart area. Columns not only show relative aggregate values by column height but apply conditional logic to display the meaningful results in red, yellow, or green bars.

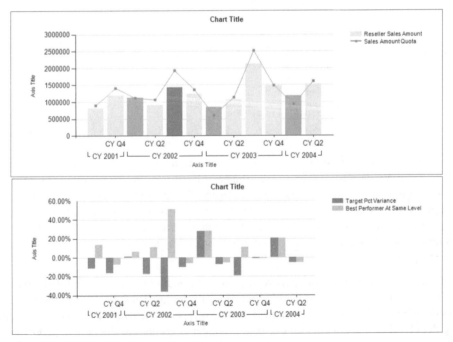

FIGURE 1-11

The lower column chart plots time relative values above or below a target or threshold line. Bars are also colored to add qualitative context.

The previous example showed charted values on a scaled grid with detailed labeling. Often times, too much information produces unnecessary noise and defeats the purpose of a report. The example in Figure 1-12 combines sparkline charts in-line with tabular details. It is a report pattern that provides a balance of specific detail and high-level trend analysis that can help a report consumer get the big picture without becoming overwhelmed and lost in the details. This simple example uses sparklines to show the annual sales trend. If this visual is interesting to the reader, he can click the chart and drill through to a detail chart report showing a measured and scaled view of the same data.

Combined Internet and Reseller Sales
by Year

Year	Product Category	Sales Total	Trend
2001			
	Accessories	$20,239.66	
	Bikes	$10,665,953.45	
	Clothing	$34,467.29	
	Components	$615,474.98	
2002			
	Accessories	$93,796.84	
	Bikes	$26,664,534.04	
	Clothing	$489,820.19	
	Components	$3,611,041.24	
2003			
	Accessories	$594,999.24	
	Bikes	$35,186,943.67	
	Clothing	$1,022,601.53	
	Components	$5,486,723.33	
2004			
	Accessories	$569,710.18	
	Bikes	$22,597,735.69	
	Clothing	$591,688.92	
	Components	$2,091,051.85	

FIGURE 1-12

Different users need more or less information than others and one report may not provide the appropriate level of detail for every data consumer. One of the great challenges in report design is tuning the detail and presentation of important data facts to the audience. For example, a simple gauge or trend line may be an appropriate graphical metaphor for a poster or advertisement for a donation campaign. But a production plant or robotic assembly line operating engineer will spend most of his or her time watching an operating console and may need to monitor a lot of detailed information in a relatively small area of screen space.

The example in Figure 1-13 takes a comprehensive approach, providing more useful information in a smaller space. This report is the result of many generations of design. The line chart at the top of the report shows detailed trend lines on a scaled grid with axis labels. The large chart acts as a zoom feature, showing details when a user clicks on one of the smaller sparklines in the tabular report area below. Line segments are colored to indicate status and the last segment has a heavier line weight to draw attention to the current period value and trend. The lighter trend line displays data from a prior period for comparison.

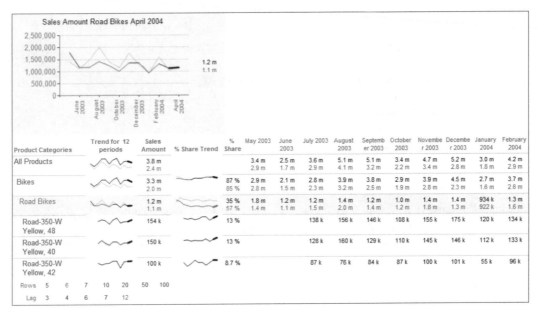

FIGURE 1-13

Detailed values are displayed in tubular form with conditional text formatting to conserve screen space. The first column shows indented group labels to indicate hierarchal groupings of summaries and detail with clickable drill-down paths.

The report also contains controls in the footer area allowing the user to adjust the report volume and level of detail displayed in each of the sparklines.

By combining report data region elements with different report types, users benefit by reading meaningful data in context. Figure 1-14 shows a column sparkline chart embedded within a pivot table report.

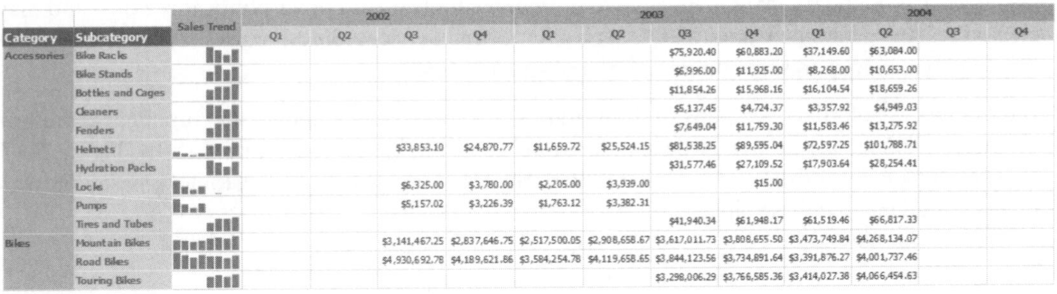

FIGURE 1-14

Bullet charts (see Figure 1-15) exemplify a compact reporting element capable of displaying several relative values in a small space. A single bullet chart, constructed from a linear gauge report item, plots four separate values in a single thermometer or progress bar line.

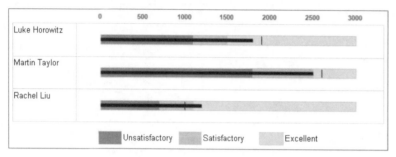

FIGURE 1-15

Combining a bullet chart or other variations of gauges or charts with a table, list, or matrix is an effective way to create intuitive reports. Graphics and icons can be used with standard bars to separate different types of data elements. Figure 1-16 uses a graphic dot to plot goals and a bar to show grade scores.

FIGURE 1-16

Maps

Geographical reporting has become a mainstream requirement for many reporting solutions. Map reports can include data and visual elements from several sources. Geospatial data may be stored in standard formats such as SQL Server spatial objects and data types, ESRI map objects, and map files. Geographical boundary maps are available for many countries and other political regions, and may be created for any geographical unit. SQL Server Reporting Services (SSRS) maps may be combined with the Bing map service to show online aerial and street views.

Data points are plotted over maps to show address locations, regional data measurements, and points of interest. These may be standard shapes, variable size bubbles, or customized icons. Figure 1-17 shows a Bing map of the Los Angeles area with the locations plotted for customers, based on data points stored in a database table.

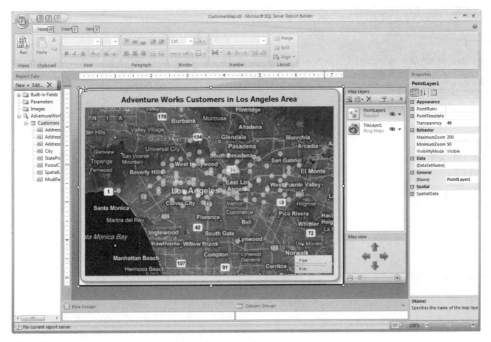

FIGURE 1-17

Interactive Reports

Reporting is no longer just about printing information on paper. Reports can be used to gather information from users, to update records, and to perform actions. A common request in Reporting Services solutions is to customize the parameter bar and provide a richer prompting interface for report parameters and other user input. The best way to prompt a user for report parameters may be to use a report. Because a report can call a report action when a user clicks text, images, or other report items, an action may be used to send parameter information back to the same report.

With a little creativity, parameters, and expression code, users can benefit from a customized navigation experience. Figure 1-18 shows a report that uses checkbox icons to identify selected or related records with a checkmark. An interactive version of this report allows users to check list items and then click a button or image to update, delete, or pass the selected items to another report as parameter selections.

Figure 1-19 shows an example of how report items may be used to track a user's report navigation history and provide links to each report in a breadcrumb list. Reports can be used to create custom menus and launch screens for reports and other applications.

Figue 1-20 shows another example of a report with custom navigation. The box on the left acts as a table of contents for groups in the report body. Links in that list may be used to navigate within the report.

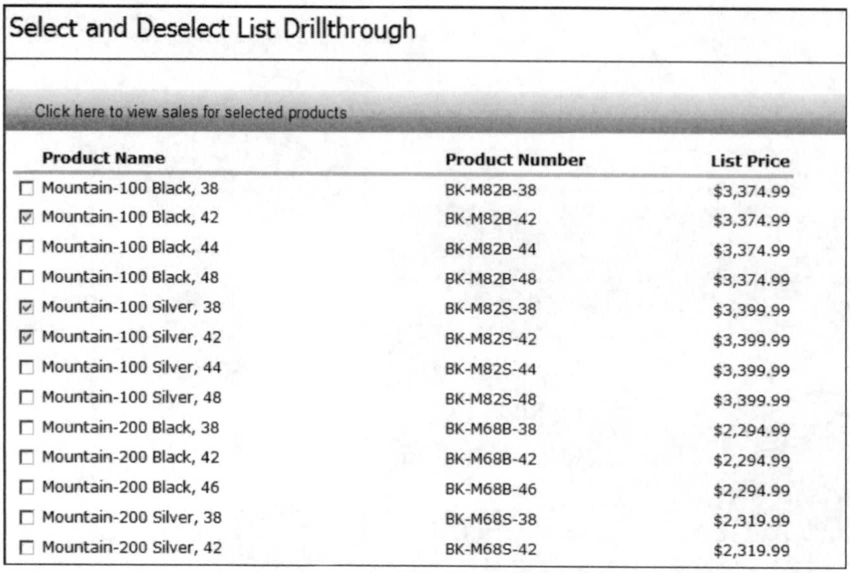

Select and Deselect List Drillthrough

Click here to view sales for selected products

Product Name	Product Number	List Price
☐ Mountain-100 Black, 38	BK-M82B-38	$3,374.99
☑ Mountain-100 Black, 42	BK-M82B-42	$3,374.99
☐ Mountain-100 Black, 44	BK-M82B-44	$3,374.99
☐ Mountain-100 Black, 48	BK-M82B-48	$3,374.99
☑ Mountain-100 Silver, 38	BK-M82S-38	$3,399.99
☑ Mountain-100 Silver, 42	BK-M82S-42	$3,399.99
☐ Mountain-100 Silver, 44	BK-M82S-44	$3,399.99
☐ Mountain-100 Silver, 48	BK-M82S-48	$3,399.99
☐ Mountain-200 Black, 38	BK-M68B-38	$2,294.99
☐ Mountain-200 Black, 42	BK-M68B-42	$2,294.99
☐ Mountain-200 Black, 46	BK-M68B-46	$2,294.99
☐ Mountain-200 Silver, 38	BK-M68S-38	$2,319.99
☐ Mountain-200 Silver, 42	BK-M68S-42	$2,319.99

FIGURE 1-18

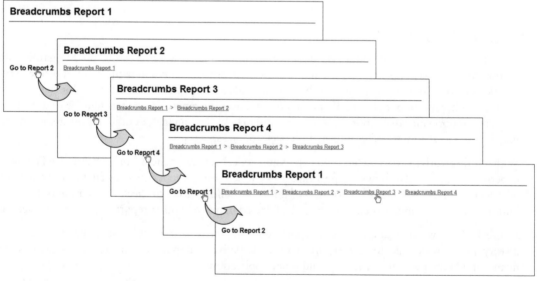

FIGURE 1-19

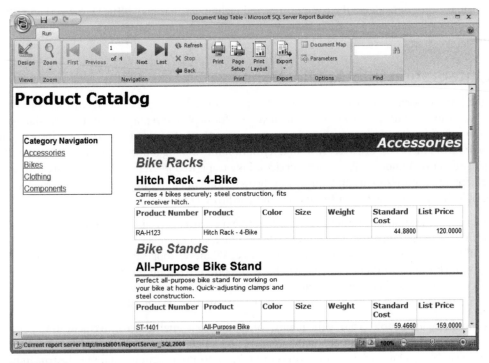

FIGURE 1-20

APPLICATION INTEGRATION

The title of this category could really mean two different things. First of all, any kind of report could be integrated into an application of some kind. For example, a web page could include, among other content, a chart report or a gauge dashboard placed in a frame or panel next to the menus and navigation buttons coded using programming tools that make up a standard web application page. The other definition of an integrated application report is a report that contains the menu functionality and buttons, rather than simply sharing the page with these controls. Because online reports can include navigation links and programming logic, where do reports end and applications start? Conversely, where do applications end and reports start? That's a very good question, and one that doesn't always have a simple answer.

Using powerful capabilities in SQL Server Reporting Services, a lot of the programming logic typically created using traditional application development tools can now be designed into reports. As a moderator on the MSDN support forum for Reporting Services, I hear users constantly asking how to extend reports to make them behave more like applications. And, although it's possible to achieve a lot of this behavior through advanced features and custom programming, an important question comes to mind: is this the right tool for the job? Like using a pair of pliers to pound in a nail (rather than taking the time to go to the garage to get the hammer), always consider using the best tool for the job.

The following section introduces the components and techniques that may be used to enable reports to be integrated into applications. After that, we'll discuss some ways that reports can behave like applications.

Report Integration into Applications

Out-of-the-box, Reporting Services installs a web application called Report Manager to serve as both a report server management console and a menu system for deployed reports. With Report Manager, users make use of familiar web navigation links to open folders, select parameter options, display, and print reports from their web browser. A secondary option for running reports is integration with Office SharePoint Server or Windows SharePoint Services. Like using Report Manager, reports are displayed in SharePoint site libraries by using built-in web browser functionality. In either instance, the user experience is that they navigate to a specific site in their browser to view and run reports.

In many cases, we may want to offer users a different experience, more in line with their business processes. Rather than going to a special web site or address to get their reports, the users simply use controls within their business application or device. Whatever tool, screen, program, or other mechanism the business workers use, they will have an option to obtain the information they need to more effectively perform their job function — using a report. Sometimes users may not even perceive that they are using a report at all. They simply see the information they need.

Reports should be actionable. That is the mantra of the business intelligence movement in the business community today. What is an actionable report? One might say that it is a report that delivers information enabling a business leader or worker to take appropriate action. That may be true in many cases but an actionable report can also be a user interface designed using a sophisticated reporting tool where the report may be used to take the action. Imagine a report containing links labeled "click here to place an order" or "click here to resolve this issue." When the user clicks the link, the appropriate application dialog opens to complete the necessary task or a record is simply updated with no further action required.

Desktop Applications

Desktop applications usually contain rich functionality and are responsive to user interaction because the processing takes place on the desktop computer. On the Microsoft Windows platform, each dialog or window contains a variety of controls for gathering user input or performing a task of some kind. Windows programs developed on the .NET Framework utilize Windows forms (Win Forms) to design each application dialog. Win Forms applications have the most sophisticated, easiest to program controls because using the Visual Studio integrated development environment allows you to directly utilize Windows' capabilities through objects exposed in the .NET Framework namespaces and common language runtime (CLR).

Like developing most visual functionality in Win Forms programming, adding reports is as simple as dropping a control onto a form and setting a few properties. The Win Forms ReportViewer control uses properties and methods to abstract all of the major functionality of Reporting Services with as little or as much programming and control as you like. Most all report functions that can be performed through the Report Manager interface can be performed using the ReportViewer control, either visually using toolbar options or programmatically, using methods of the control object in custom code.

Web Applications

With the expansion of business applications throughout distributed business enterprises, many desktop applications have been replaced with web applications to reduce maintenance and support costs, and to make applications more accessible. If you have worked with both Windows forms desktop applications and web applications, either as a user or programmer, you know that there are usually some differences in the look, feel, and responsiveness of the application. Web applications are hosted on a central web server and viewed in the user's web browser. Most user requests require a postback to the server, which takes more time to process than a typical desktop application. Since web-based applications became a reality in the late 1990s, programmers and technology architects have developed a variety of techniques and technologies to make them behave more like desktop programs, including Java applets, ActiveX controls, Flash, AJAX, and Silverlight.

Microsoft's web development platform is ASP.NET which, like Win Forms, is an extension of the .NET Framework and CLR. Web Forms projects may also be developed with Visual Studio and there are many similarities in the development environment and some of the programming objects. The similarities can be deceiving because there are significant differences in the capabilities and behavior of the objects and the subsequent user experience.

Fortunately, Reporting Services is a web technology and is in fact based in the ASP.NET programming platform. SSRS reports are easily added to ASP.NET applications using the WebForms version of the ReportViewer control, which is almost identical to the WinForms version.

Because Reporting Services is a web technology, it also can be integrated into web applications developed using non-Microsoft programming tools. A report may be added to a web page using simple HTML tags, embedded frames, JavaScript, or an HTTP address with query string parameters. They may not offer the same level of convenience or sophistication as the .NET ReportViewer controls but most report functionality can be accessed using these simple techniques.

Portal Content

Corporate intranet portals have become an important component in the way we communicate and collaborate with our business associates. Simply storing documents and other content in network folders is not a sufficient method for managing important business content. The most significant challenges we typically face when allowing a group of people access to shared content are how to keep that content accessible only to the right people and keep it synchronized and consistent as it is shared. Shared file stores only make it possible to copy the content to the desktop, where it may be changed and pushed back to the file system. In a shared environment, this means that different users could overwrite each other's changes. Users download their own copies of spreadsheets and reports, creating different versions of the truth. And if changes are made, change tracking and version control may be important. Many documents and components requiring maintenance and testing may need to progress through a workflow and signoff process.

Reports can be used in a collaborative portal environment. Whether the objective is to manage the design and testing phases of report development or to give users access to a completed report in a consistent interface with other shared content, an intranet, web-based portal as an excellent platform for this type of collaboration. SharePoint server technologies have become the de facto standard for managing collaborative content for many organizations. Reporting Services integrates effectively with SharePoint in several different ways. Because different organizations and development groups have different needs and objectives, here are some of the ways SSRS may be used within a SharePoint site:

➤ For development teams, reports may be deployed to document or report libraries to manage the development cycle. Workflow processes may be used to manage and graduate a report definition as it is designed, validated, tested, and deployed for production use. The report can remain in a single library and use a workflow to manage the progress and sign-off through these stages or it may be migrated from one library to another for design and development, unit testing, user acceptance, integration, and release to production.

➤ For self-service reporting, business users can save their reports to a personal or team library or site. By isolating user reports from IT production reports, the needs of business users and business leaders are both met while maintaining a standard method of validation for mission-critical data reporting.

➤ SharePoint server enables version control for reports and other content. Like other documents, reports must be checked out and then checked back into the library to maintain ownership and change control. With version control enabled, each check-in creates an assessable version of the file so a report may be reverted to a prior version.

➤ Because site content is stored in a SQL Server database, all documents, files, and reports are backed up and may be restored using a conventional disaster recovery plan.

➤ Report content and security may be fully integrated and managed through SharePoint using the SharePoint integrated mode. This places all content, security, and deployment management into the hands of SharePoint administrators. Reports deployed to SharePoint site libraries may be managed with integrated workflow and version control.

➤ SharePoint pages and dashboards may be used to surface reports using a ReportViewer web part. The content or report server folders may be added to pages using the ReportList web part to create simple report menus. Report content may appear alongside Excel and PerformancePoint reports to create interactive pages and complex reporting dashboards. This type of report integration is possible in SharePoint integrated or SSRS native mode.

ReportViewer Control

All of the functionality of Reporting Services is exposed through a web service that provides multiple SOAP endpoints. This was exciting news for developers because they could have access to every capability through a low-level programming interface and automate reports within their custom applications. However, this approach to report integration removes much of the convenience and efficiency that are part of the inherent user experience. For example, capabilities like user authentication, page caching, drill-through, drill-down, and prompt interaction are normally part of the standard browser-based UI. By handling the report rendering through SOAP calls, the developer must manage rendering, report and image content streaming, and any dynamic report features themselves. The advantage of the SOAP-based API is that developers can integrate reports into custom applications using any programming platform that speaks SOAP, such as Java, PERL, or C++.

The ReportViewer control allows report execution to be managed through a self-contained user interface while still preserving programmable objects for more advanced control. Two versions exist: the Win Forms control is used to place a report on a Windows form application developed in Visual Studio with the .NET Framework and common language runtime. The Web Forms control is exactly the same but used to add a report to an ASP.NET web form. Both of these controls can render reports on the report server using the remote processing mode, or reports may be rendered locally within the application using local processing mode. For Win Forms, reports are actually processed on the desktop and for Web Forms; the report is processed on the web server hosting the web forms application.

The ReportViewer SharePoint web part is an ASP.NET wrapper around the Web Forms ReportViewer control. It has the same behavior as the web form control but processes reports only on the report server in remote processing mode.

Installing the Reporting Services Samples and SQL Server Sample Databases

The report recipes in this book use a variety of sample databases. With the exception of those that have special requirements, most of our recipes use the sample databases provided by Microsoft. You can download working samples of all the reports and the specialized databases from Wrox.com.

The standard SQL Server sample databases primarily consist of two databases containing data related to a fictional bicycle manufacturer, Adventure Works Cycles. The OLTP sample database contains structures typical of a transactional system, whereas the DW sample database contains structures typical of an analytical system. Together, these will assist you in gaining familiarity with both operational and analytical reporting. To work through all of the SSRS 2008 recipes that depend on a SQL Server data source, download and install the AdventureWorks2008 transactional database, the AdventureWorksDW2008 sample data warehouse, and the Adventure Works DW Analysis Services sample database and project.

The Reporting Services samples and SQL Server sample databases are available on the CodePlex web site at www.CodePlex.com/SqlServerSamples. For each sample database and the Reporting Services samples, you will need to download an installation file appropriate to your hardware platform. These files are identified in the following table. Each recipe will tell you what version of SQL Server is supported. Many of the recipes will work with the sample databases from either SQL Server 2005 or 2008.

CPU	MSI	SAMPLE
32-bit	SQL2008.Reporting_Services.Samples.x86.msi	Reporting Services Samples
	SQL2008.AdventureWorks_OLTP_DB_v2008.x86.msi	AdventureWorks2008 Sample Database
	SQL2008.AdventureWorks_DW_BI_v2008.x86.msi	AdventureWorks2008DW Sample Database
x64 64-bit	SQL2008.Reporting_Services.Samples.x64.msi	Reporting Services Samples
	SQL2008.AdventureWorks_OLTP_DB_v2008.x64.msi	AdventureWorks2008 Sample Database
	SQL2008.AdventureWorks_DW_BI_v2008.x64.msi	AdventureWorks2008DW Sample Database
IA64 64-bit	SQL2008.Reporting_Services.Samples.ia64.msi	Reporting Services Samples
	SQL2008.AdventureWorks_OLTP_DB_v2008.ia64.msi	AdventureWorks2008 Sample Database
	SQL2008.AdventureWorks_DW_BI_v2008.ia64.msi	AdventureWorks2008DW Sample Database

Before starting the sample installations, verify that the SQL Server Database Engine and Reporting Services are running. Then, launch each downloaded MSI and follow the instructions provided to install the samples.

The installation procedure and specific files you may need are subject to change. Please refer to information on the CodePlex web site for the most up-to-date installation instructions for these files.

SERVER REPORTS

The new generation of Report Builder provides true ad-hoc reporting tools that allow users to create reports directly on the server without using the local file system. This capability is not enabled in the initial RTM release of SQL Server 2008 but was added in Service Pack 1. The functionality is enabled by default in SQL Server 2008 R2 with Report Builder 3.0.

With server reports enabled on the report server, any standard reports to which the user has access can be opened directly in Report Builder using the standard Open dialog. To open a report on the server, local, or network file system, click the "orb" Office start button in the top left corner and select Open from the menu. You can navigate to a folder using the most recent items or other folder shortcuts on the Open Report dialog window.

In this book we will not discuss any specific differences between reports deployed in native mode and SharePoint integrated mode. For our purposes, you will simply use the appropriate URL to target the report server or the SharePoint library used to manage your reports. If your report server is in native mode, you may use the Report Manager web application to access and manage reports. If you are using SharePoint integrated mode, you will use SharePoint to manage reports and then deploy and view them in a document or report library.

HTML Viewer

Web browsers, such as Microsoft Internet Explorer, are the most popular tools for viewing Reporting Services reports. In most cases, when a report is rendered to HTML, Reporting Services adds JavaScript to provide several interactive features. These features include a toolbar, document maps, fixed table headers, and table sorting. Collectively, these script-based features are referred to as the HTML Viewer.

To ensure compatibility with the HTML Viewer, it is recommended that you use the latest version of Internet Explorer. Currently, Microsoft guarantees full HTML Viewer functionality in Internet Explorer version 8.0 with up-to-date service packs and scripting enabled.

Other web browsers can be used to view Reporting Services reports rendered to HTML, but many of the HTML Viewer features will not be available. Refer to Books Online for more details on which features are supported by which browsers if you plan to distribute reports to users employing browsers other than current versions of Internet Explorer.

Report Viewer Control

The Report Viewer control allows Reporting Services reports to be displayed within custom applications. The Report Viewer control is actually two controls — one for use in web applications and the other for Win Forms applications. Each supports the same functionality.

The Report Viewer control runs in one of two modes. In the default Remote Processing mode, reports are rendered by a Reporting Services instance and displayed through the control. This is the preferred mode as the full feature set of Reporting Services is available and the processing power of the Reporting Services server can be employed.

In situations in which a Reporting Services server is not available or retrieving data directly through the client system is required, the Report Viewer control can be run in the Local Processing mode. In this mode, the application retrieves data and couples it with the report definition to produce a rendered report on the host system without the support of a Reporting Services server. Not all Reporting Services features are available when the control is executed in Local Processing mode.

Reporting Services Processors and Extensions

What exactly is Reporting Services? The core processing engine is a Windows service whose functionality is performed by several processing extensions. Theses .NET assemblies perform security authentication, data processing, format-specific report rendering, and report delivery. These processing extensions can be extended by developers by registering additional assemblies on the server and in the development tools.

Microsoft's Windows Management Instrumentation (WMI) technology provides a mechanism for the consistent management of devices and applications running on Windows platforms. The Reporting Services Windows service exposes itself to WMI by registering two classes with the local WMI

Windows service. These classes expose properties and methods that the WMI service makes available to administrative applications.

The first of the two classes registered by Reporting Services, MSReportServer_Instance, provides basic information about the Reporting Services installation, including edition, version, and mode.

The second class, MSReportServer_ConfigurationSetting, provides access to many of the settings in the RSReportServer.config configuration file and exposes a host of methods supporting critical administrative tasks. Administrative interfaces such as the Reporting Services Configuration tool leverage this provider for their functionality.

A Remote Procedure Call (RPC) interface provided by the Reporting Services service acts as a bridge between the WMI and Reporting Services Windows services. Through this bridge, calls against the registered classes received by the WMI service are relayed to Reporting Services.

All server functionality is exposed through the Reporting Services Windows service endpoints. The service's core processing features were introduced as an application domain whose functionality is provided through a collection of components. You will now explore those components to gain a deeper understanding of just how Reporting Services delivers its primary functionality and where that functionality can be extended.

Before jumping into the specific components, you should be aware of the difference between extensions and processors. Processors are the coordinators and facilitators in Reporting Services' component architecture. They are responsible for calling the extensions as needed and providing mechanisms for data exchange between them. Although configuration settings may alter their behavior, the processors cannot be extended through custom code.

Extensions are components registered with Reporting Services to provide specific functionality. They expose standardized interfaces, which provide the mechanism by which Reporting Services engages them.

Report Caching

When a report is initially rendered, a session is established. Requests from a specific user are made within the context of a specific session until that session expires.

During a session, users will often request that the same report be rendered multiple times, possibly in differing formats. Reporting Services anticipates this by storing the intermediate format report in its Session cache. The cached copy is recorded with Session identifiers so that when an end-user repeats a request for a report as part of his or her session, the cached copy can be leveraged. This feature of Reporting Services, known as report session caching, is always enabled.

If a deployed report is configured for instance caching, and data is retrieved using the requestor's credentials, the report may contain data only appropriate for that specific user. The intermediate report contains this data so that if it is cached and made available to another requestor, that user may be exposed to data that he or she otherwise should not see.

For this reason, only reports that do not use the requestor's credentials to retrieve data from external data sources can be configured for report execution caching. With report execution caching, the intermediate report generated from a report request is cached for some period of time and used to render reports for other users until the cached copy expires.

With both report session and report execution caching, the end-user requests a report, and the Report Processor checks for a cached copy. If none exists, the Report Processor must assemble the intermediate format report, store it in a cache for subsequent requests, and then render the requested final report. While later requests may take advantage of the cached copy, the first request does not have this option. This can lead to an inconsistent end-user experience.

To address this, snapshots may be scheduled to populate the cache in advance of an end-user request. Snapshots are recorded in the same intermediate format and have the same security requirements as report execution caching.

The HTML Rendering Extension

HTML is highly accessible and a generally good format for interactive reports. For these reasons, HTML 4.0 is the default rendering format for Reporting Services reports.

The downside to HTML is that web pages have never been very good for printing. The HTML Viewer, a JavaScript-based application embedded in most HTML-rendered reports discussed earlier in this chapter, provides client-side printing that overcomes some of the challenges experienced when printing from a web browser. (Client-side printing is accessed through the HTML Viewer toolbar.)

The HTML rendering extension can be instructed to return MIME-HTML (MHTML) as an alternative to the HTML 4.0 default. With MHTML, images, style sheets, and other referenced items are embedded in the HTML document. This allows a report to be delivered without dependencies on external resources. That can be very useful in certain scenarios such as the e-mail delivery of a report to a user. (Not all e-mail products support MHTML, so check with your user community before selecting this format for e-mail delivery.)

The CSV-Rendering Extension

The comma-separated values (CSV)–rendering extension renders the data portion of a report to a comma-delimited flat-file format accessible by spreadsheets and other applications. With the 2008 release of Reporting Services, this extension has been improved to keep formatting elements out of the resulting data file.

The 2008 CSV-rendering extension operates in two modes. In the default, Excel-optimized mode, each data region of the report is rendered as a separate block of comma-delimited values. In CSV-compliant mode, the extension produces a single, uniform block of data accessible to a wider range of applications.

The XML-Rendering Extension

XML is another format commonly used for rendering reports. The XML-rendering extension incorporates both data and layout information in the XML it generates.

One of the most powerful features of the XML-rendering extension is its capability to accept an XSLT document. XSLT documents provide instructions for converting XML to other text-based formats.

These formats may include HTML, CSV, XML, or a custom file format. The Reporting Services team recommends attempting to leverage the XML-rendering format with XSLT for specialized rendering needs before attempting to implement a custom rendering extension.

The Image-Rendering Extension

Through the Image-rendering extension, reports are published to one of seven image formats, the default of which is Tagged Image File Format (TIFF). TIFF is a widely used format for storing document images. Many facsimile (fax) programs use TIFF as their transfer standard, and many organizations make use of it for document archives.

The PDF-Rendering Extension

Reporting Services comes with a rendering extension for Adobe's Portable Document Format (PDF). The PDF format is one of the most popular for document sharing over the Internet. It produces clean, easy-to-read documents with exceptional printing capabilities. In addition, PDF documents are not easily altered.

Although not as interactive as an HTML report with the HTML Viewer, PDFs do support document maps. This functionality enables the creation of a table of contents-like feature, which is invaluable with large reports. Adobe Acrobat Reader 6.0 or higher is required for viewing the PDF documents produced by Reporting Services. It is available for free download from the Adobe web site.

The Excel-Rendering Extension

Rendering reports to Excel is another option supported by Reporting Services. Rendering to Excel is highly useful if additional analysis is to be performed on the data by the end-user.

Not all report elements translate to Excel. While many features not available in prior versions of the Excel-rendering extension (such as nested data regions and sub-reports) are supported in this release, other features continue to render poorly or not at all. It is a good idea to review your reports rendered to this format prior to publication if Excel rendering is a critical requirement. Reporting Services Books Online provides details of how each report feature is handled when rendered to Excel.

The Word-Rendering Extension

The Word-rendering extension is new for Reporting Services 2008. The extension renders reports in Microsoft Word 97 format with many of the same features and limitations as rendering in PDF. Unlike PDF, the Word format allows reports to be more easily edited by the end-user following rendering.

SUMMARY

Most all reports will fit into the categories introduced in this chapter. There will be other variations of these basic themes and you'll likely develop a set of designs that work best for you, your users, project sponsors, or clients. We encourage you to leverage successful report designs others have created. Following proven design patterns provides a reliable starting point. After you discover what does and doesn't work for you, you can make necessary adjustments to create your own brand of reports.

Reporting Services developers enjoy strong community support because creative individuals share their ideas and feedback for the benefit of the community. When you discover a pattern that works well (or doesn't), please share it with the community by participating in the MSDN forum or contact the authors through their blog sites.

We've introduced report categories and report design concepts at a high level. The next two chapters review essential report design components and the specific skills necessary to apply these patterns to create many of the reports introduced in this chapter.

2

Basic Report Design Concepts

The purpose of this chapter is to lay the foundation for the techniques you will use as you apply report design recipes in the later sections. This chapter is designed to be a short refresher course on techniques with which you should already have some experience. We expect that you already have solid foundation of basic report design in your skill set, but this might help to fill some gaps. You can use this as a reference for applying the basic techniques of report design that you will need to know when using the recipes. At the very least you should already know how to:

➤ Create a new report in the Business Intelligence Development Studio (BIDS) or Report Builder 2.0/3.0 report designer

➤ Deploy or save the report to the report server

➤ Create an embedded or shared data source

➤ Create a dataset and common data sources like SQL Server or Analysis Services databases

➤ Understand basic T-SQL query syntax

➤ Add a simple table data region to a report

➤ Define groups with a report data region

➤ Define and use parameters for basic query or dataset filtering

Portions of this chapter were borrowed from our previous book; *Professional SQL Server 2008 Reporting Services*. In this abbreviated version, we do not include the tutorial instructions for using all of these features. You will find some hands-on instructions for applying many of these techniques in the recipes that follow. Most recipes will provide high-level directions for performing these basic report design tasks since we assume you already know how to perform them. Because this chapter is not an exhaustive lesson on designing reports for beginners, if you are new to SQL Server Reporting Services, we recommend that you use the *Professional* series book to learn the basics before you continue. For the experienced report designer, this chapter should serve as a reference and reminder for the essential skills you've already developed.

USING REPORT BUILDER

During the history of Reporting Services the term *Report Builder* has been used to refer to a few different report design tools. Many of our recipes can be used in SSRS 2005 and if you are using this version of Reporting Services, you should use Business Intelligence Development Studio (BIDS) and not the old Report Builder 1.0 tool that came with this version of the product. The original Report Builder tool was very lightweight and could not be used to design standard RDL reports. Most of the recipes in this book were written using SSRS 2008 and Report Builder 2.0. To demonstrate new features introduced in SSRS 2008 R2, some recipes were written using Report Builder 3.0, which is very similar in design, and you should be able to follow the RB 2.0 directions with very little or no modification.

The basic theme in Report Builder is simplicity. To this end, designer and wizard dialogs will automatically open when a required object (such as a data source, dataset, or report data region) must be defined. Although I do a lot of report design in Visual Studio projects, I often prefer to start designing new reports with Report Builder 2.0 or 3.0 because it's so much more convenient.

A new addition to Report Builder 2.0 was a set of data region-specific design wizards. When a new report is opened (or you simply open Report Builder), icons are displayed in the center of the new report design surface. Click any of these to launch the appropriate design wizard that will lead you through the process of adding a data source and dataset query, and organizing data fields and groups in a table, matrix, or chart. After defining a query, fields are simply dragged into row or column groups, or into the data area of a table or matrix report.

In Report Builder 3.0 for SSRS 2008 R2, an opening dialog (shown in Figure 2-1) is displayed, prompting the user to choose from a number of report styles.

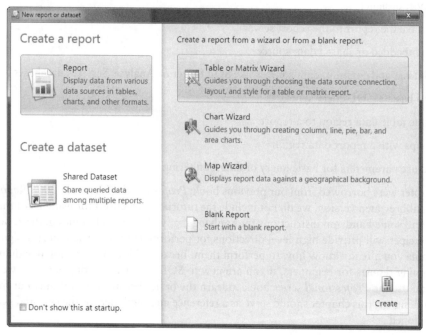

FIGURE 2-1

Most of the recipes that were written using Report Builder 2.0 will have you select and remove the new report wizard placeholder and then explicitly add and design each report item. This placeholder is displayed in the center of a new report when the designer is opened. To adapt these recipes for Report Builder 3.0, just choose the Blank Report option in the opening dialog.

Formatting and Sample Values

Numeric formatting can be applied very easily using the ribbon. This is another convenient design feature and a significant improvement over previous versions of the report designer. Not only can you apply a variety of predefined format options to a field on the report, but you can also preview the format at design time. Figure 2-2 shows the Sample Values preview feature. Select the field value textbox in the designer. A format can be applied using the Number group on the Home tab ribbon. A convenient feature was added in Report Builder 2.0 that allows you to preview a formatted value while designing the report. Choose Sample Values from the numbers drop-down list to view a representative formatted numerical value in the textbox. This option is shown in Figure 2-2.

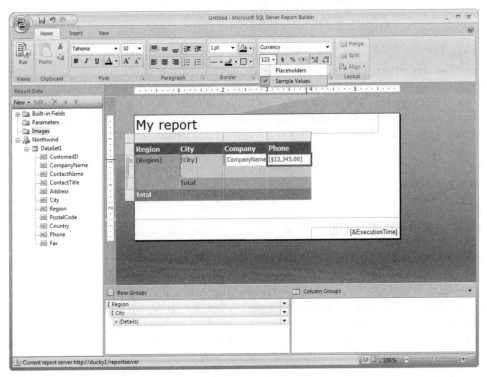

FIGURE 2-2

Data Sources

A *data source* encapsulates connection information used to access databases or other resources that return data to a report. A data source can be either embedded into a report definition, or stored as a separate definition file and shared among multiple reports once deployed to the report server. Shared data sources are easier to maintain in formal business environments where you have several reports using multiple database servers. Even if you don't have several reports that need to share a central data source, it takes no additional effort to create a shared data source. This may still be advantageous in this case, as the data source is managed separately from each report and can be easily updated if necessary. Then, as you add new reports, the shared data source will already be established and deployed to the report server.

A data source references a data provider installed on the report designer's computer and on the report server. Data providers enable connectivity to database products and may include .NET native providers, OLE DB providers, and ODBC drivers. SQL Server 2008 installs several data providers for Microsoft and third-party products that will allow reports to retrieve data from different versions of SQL Server, SQL Server Analysis Services, Microsoft Access, Oracle, XML data, and other third-party sources. Additional or custom-developed data processing extensions can be added to the report designers and report server using the respective configuration files.

Creating a data source is usually a simple task, but be mindful that each type of data source is a little different and may require some unique properties or other information specific to the data provider or storage technology.

The usual best practice for reports designed with Report Builder is to create a shared data source with stored credentials and deploy this to the report server. When designing reports with Report Builder 2.0 or 3.0, the paradigm for using shared data sources changes compared to BIDS. You must store user credentials in the data source. The best approach is to typically use an application user account, rather than a human user. If you haven't already established an application user for your reporting database, work with your system administrator or database administrator to have a database or network account created with minimal read permissions to the appropriate database and restrictive permissions to any unnecessary network resources. This data source must be stored on the report server before it can be used in the report designer.

DATASETS AND QUERIES

A *dataset* is typically a query or database object reference used to retrieve a set of records for reporting. SSRS reports can consume data from a variety of data sources. The query language used for a dataset is specific to the data provider or processing extension specified in the data source. A dataset must have only one data source, but a data source, whether embedded or shared, can serve any number of datasets. Because the query command text is processed by the data provider, queries must be in the native query language of the data source. For example, a dataset for SQL Server uses the T-SQL query language.

Nearly all relational database products are queried using a form of Structured Query Language (SQL), which means that a query created for one database product (say, IBM DB2) may be somewhat portable to a different data source (perhaps Oracle, MySQL, SyBase, or Microsoft SQL Server). Most database products implement a form of SQL conforming to the ANSI SQL standard. Microsoft SQL Server, for example, conforms to the ANSI 92 SQL standard, and other products may conform to other revisions (like ANSI 89 SQL or ANSI 99 SQL). Beyond the most fundamental SQL statements, most dialects of SQL are not completely interchangeable and will require some understanding of their individual idiosyncrasies.

Regardless of the language compatibility, technical users of many database platforms typically apply a convention that is common within their communities. For example, in Oracle circles, it's considered proper form to use non-ANSI joins by matching key columns in the WHERE clause, rather than in the FROM clause. Using the JOIN and ON operators is more common in the Microsoft realm. The query syntax is interpreted by the data provider and target database engine, so you are free to use the syntax appropriate for that particular data platform. For SQL Server Analysis Services, queries are written using the MDX query language. For the casual user, designing reports for SSAS cubes requires little or no knowledge of MDX.

Report Builder 3.0 now allows datasets to be shared and stored as separate objects much like a shared data source. This is a useful way for multiple reports that use similar data to share a reusable design object and simplify the overall report design process. A shared dataset definition file has an RSD extension and may be saved directly to the report server to be referenced and reused by multiple reports.

Designing Queries

When creating reports for SQL Server relational databases, you have the option to design queries using a graphical design environment or a generic text editor. This is one of only a few areas where the Report Builder 2.0 and 3.0 design tools offer less functionality than BIDS. In BIDS or Visual Studio, when you design a query for any modern version of SQL Server, the Graphical Query Editor is available, allows you to add and use tables; drag-and-drop columns to create joins; a design grid to define column aliases; and sorting and filtering logic. The GQE tool has been part of the SQL Server client tools suite for more than a decade and has seen incremental improvements and enhancements along the way. For example, the GQE can handle query structures like subqueries and unions. Although many "real" database professionals refuse to use graphical design tools, this is a very capable interface that can save time and simplify the process of creating simple or complex T-SQL queries. The BIDS query designer shares UI components with the SQL Server Management Studio query designer so you can open an implementation of the GQE from either application.

The Report Builder designers do not include this query editor. This is because the GQE components are part of the SQL Server client tools application stack, which the Business Intelligence Development Studio is part of. Because Report Builder 2.0 and 3.0 do not have this dependency, it was necessary for the product team to create a new query design tool with the business user, rather than the IT professional, in mind — and the new tool simply hasn't had over ten years to evolve and improve with age. For our purposes, we generally recommend that if you are using RB, you design advanced reports like most of our recipe examples; and that you use the SSMS query editor to design and test your T-SQL queries, then paste them into the dataset query window. To launch the GQE in a Management Studio query window, right-click over the cursor to add a new query, or select a query and right-click to modify it in the graphical designer. You can see this menu option in Figure 2-3, and the graphical query editor interface in Figure 2-4.

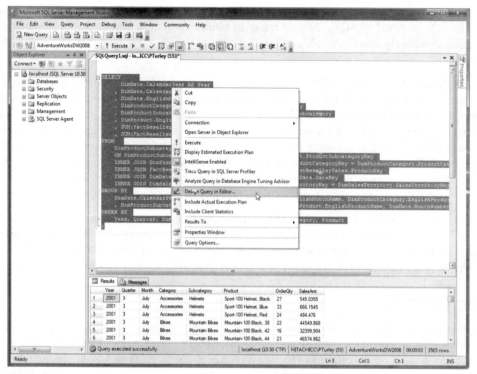

FIGURE 2-3

Unlike the SSRS query editor, if you run a parameterized T-SQL query in SSMS, it will fail because it doesn't have the same ad-hoc parameter support. This is easily remedied in one of two ways. T-SQL variables follow the same syntax convention as a query parameter in Reporting Services. Just add a variable declaration and set a value for the variable above the SELECT statement. For example, the following simple query example will run in the SSRS query editor:

```
SELECT EnglishProductName, ListPrice
FROM DimProduct
WHERE Color = @Color
```

The report designer parses this query and automatically generates a report parameter named Color to match the query parameter. This query will not run in SSRS, but making the following changes will work:

```
DECLARE @Color VarChar(20)
SET @Color = 'Blue'
```

```
SELECT EnglishProductName, ListPrice
FROM DimProduct
WHERE Color = @Color
```

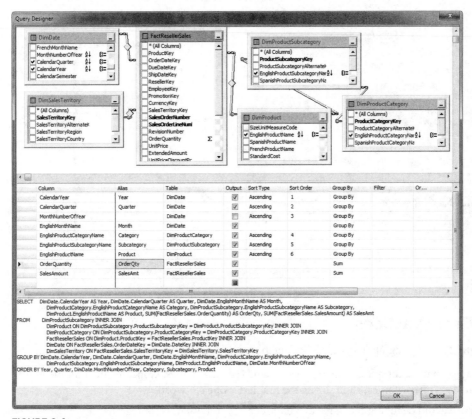

FIGURE 2-4

After testing and debugging the query script in SSMS, copy and paste it into the report designer query editor excluding the DECLARE and SET statements.

To query cube structures in Analysis Services, a specialized query language called *Multidimensional Expressions* (MDX) is used. The graphical MDX editor is shown in Figure 2-5.

For most of the recipes we will provide the T-SQL or MDX query script for you to type or paste into the dataset query editor.

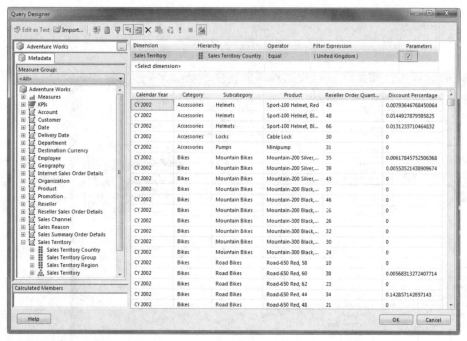

FIGURE 2-5

Dataset Best Practices

When creating and managing datasets, following best practices and suggestions may be useful:

➤ Dataset names cannot contain spaces. Use mixed-case names. Concatenate multiple words and descriptive names, capitalizing the first letter of each word.

➤ Try to avoid changing the name of a dataset after you use it. Data regions have a `DatasetName` property that must be manually updated if you change a dataset's name.

➤ Independent report items that are bound to a field reference a dataset name in the second argument of the aggregate function used in the `Value` property to define the function scope. For example, if the CustomerName field is dragged from Dataset1 to the report body, it produces a textbox with the Value expression: =FIRST(Fields!CustomerName.Value, "Dataset1")

➤ Use the T-SQL graphical query builder to design simple queries. For more advanced queries, design them in the SSMS query designer, which has a richer set of code validation and debugging tools. Copy and paste the resulting query into the report designer query editor using text mode.

➤ For MDX datasets, use the graphical editor to generate the field metadata, parameters, and parameter drop-list datasets. If you modify or enhance a MDX query, make sure it conforms to the same metadata signature and the result returns the same fields in the same order. Always make a backup copy of the report before modifying a MDX query.

➤ For complex, parameterized datasets: consider building the SQL or MDX command string in an expression or custom function. Write and execute a simple form of the query first to generate the field's metadata.

FILTERING DATA

SSRS offers two different mechanisms for filtering data in a report. The most common approach is to use the dataset query WHERE clause and filter records at the source. Consider the following example where the data is filtered for a specified range of hard-coded dates in the query:

```
SELECT
   D.CalendarYear
   , D.CalendarQuarter
   , D.MonthNumberOfYear
   , D.DateKey
   , ST.SalesTerritoryCountry
   , ST.SalesTerritoryRegion
   , F.OrderQuantity
   , F.SalesAmount
FROM
   DimDate D INNER JOIN FactResellerSales F ON D.DateKey = F.OrderDateKey
   INNER JOIN DimSalesTerritory ST ON F.SalesTerritoryKey = ST.SalesTerritoryKey
WHERE
   D.FullDateAlternateKey BETWEEN '2004-01-15' AND '2004-01-31'
ORDER BY
   D.CalendarYear
   , D.CalendarQuarter
   , D.MonthNumberOfYear
   , D.DateKey
   , ST.SalesTerritoryCountry
   , ST.SalesTerritoryRegion
;
```

By passing selection criteria parameters at the database object level, network traffic can be greatly reduced and the report is rendered more efficiently. The next example replaces the static date values with named parameters:

```
SELECT
   D.CalendarYear
   , D.CalendarQuarter
   , D.MonthNumberOfYear
   , D.DateKey
   , ST.SalesTerritoryCountry
   , ST.SalesTerritoryRegion
   , F.OrderQuantity
   , F.SalesAmount
FROM
   DimDate D INNER JOIN FactResellerSales F ON D.DateKey = F.OrderDateKey
   INNER JOIN DimSalesTerritory ST ON F.SalesTerritoryKey = ST.SalesTerritoryKey
WHERE
   D.FullDateAlternateKey BETWEEN @ShipDateFrom AND @ShipDateTo
ORDER BY
   D.CalendarYear
   , D.CalendarQuarter
   , D.MonthNumberOfYear
   , D.DateKey
   , ST.SalesTerritoryCountry
   , ST.SalesTerritoryRegion
;
```

When the query parser encounters these two query parameters as the query is parsed, corresponding report parameters are added and then these parameters can be fine-tuned in the Report Parameter Properties to provide a better user experience.

Using this filtering technique, if the user provides different parameter values to render several views of the same report within a session, the database will be queried repeatedly, perhaps resulting in longer overall wait times and much of the same data moving across the network multiple times. The dataset filtering feature, which is defined on the Filter page of the Dataset dialog, screens data in the report after it reaches the report server. This means that more data may be retrieved from the database than actually appears in the report. This may not be the most efficient way to filter data for a single report execution, but it can speed things up after the initial query runs and a user continues to interact with a report and provide different parameter values during a session. Because all the data is cached (held in memory), reports will render much faster after the report cache has been loaded. This technique can reduce the overall network traffic and rendering time. The report can also be configured so that the cached data is saved to disk, usually for a specific period of time.

Using Stored Procedures

Several advantages exist to using stored procedures rather than verbose T-SQL queries in a report. Complex queries can be stored as reusable database objects. Stored procedures can run more efficiently and provide greater security and control.

The following T-SQL script is used to create a stored procedure in SQL Server Management Studio. Once created, the procedure is simply referenced and executed by name from the report.

```
CREATE PROCEDURE spGet_ResellerSalesByRegion
  @ShipDateFrom Date
 ,@ShipDateTo   Date
AS
SELECT
  D.CalendarYear
  , D.CalendarQuarter
  , D.MonthNumberOfYear
  , D.DateKey
  , ST.SalesTerritoryCountry
  , ST.SalesTerritoryRegion
  , F.OrderQuantity
  , F.SalesAmount
FROM
  DimDate D INNER JOIN FactResellerSales F ON D.DateKey = F.OrderDateKey
  INNER JOIN DimSalesTerritory ST ON F.SalesTerritoryKey = ST.SalesTerritoryKey
WHERE
  D.FullDateAlternateKey BETWEEN @ShipDateFrom AND @ShipDateTo
ORDER BY
  D.CalendarYear
  , D.CalendarQuarter
  , D.MonthNumberOfYear
  , D.DateKey
  , ST.SalesTerritoryCountry
  , ST.SalesTerritoryRegion
;
```

The best way to query a data source will depend mainly on your requirements. Filtering techniques when processing parameters (on the database server, the client, or both) affects performance, efficiency, and the flexibility of your reporting solution. Handling parameters on the database server will almost always be more efficient, whereas processing parameters on the client will give you the flexibility of handling a wider range of records and query options without needing to go back to the database every time you need to render the report. As a general rule, it's a good idea to filter data on the database server unless you have a good reason to do otherwise.

Using a parameterized stored procedure is typically going to provide the most efficient means for filtering relational data because it returns only the data matching your criteria. Stored procedures are compiled to native processor instructions on the database server. When any kind of query is processed, SQL Server creates an execution plan, which defines the specific instructions that the server uses to retrieve data. In the case of a stored procedure, the execution plan is prepared the first time it is executed, and then it is cached on the database server. In subsequent executions, results will be returned faster since some of the work has already been done.

REPORTS AND REPORT OBJECTS

A specific hierarchy of objects is used to manage all the items and properties within a report. Keep in mind that a report definition is stored in an XML file and all the objects accessed in the Properties window relate to nested XML element tags in the XML structure of a Report Definition Language (RDL) file. All of the objects within a report are defined by nested XML elements. The `Report` object contains properties related to the report itself but not the data regions on the report. These data regions are contained within the `Report Body` object.

The `Report` object also contains the following advanced properties used for adding custom internal or externally referenced programming code, which can be used to extend a report's capabilities:

➤ **Code** — Custom Visual Basic functions can be written and stored in the report and then called from expressions on any of the properties for this report.

➤ **References** — Like custom functions stored in the Code element, external code libraries may be referenced and also used in property expressions. The advantage of this approach is that a single code library may be used by multiple reports.

➤ **Variables** — Custom variables may be defined and used within the report to enable dynamic and advanced functionality. These variables are typically set and used within expressions or custom code functions in the report.

➤ **Page Properties** — Page attributes and properties consist of the page scale units, page orientation, height, width, and margins.

Report Body

The `Body` object contains just a few properties and serves as a container for all the data ranges and report items within the report. In the designer, the report body really is a blank canvas on which you place report items and data ranges. This is a unique approach when comparing Reporting Services with most other reporting products. This is a very flexible approach to report design that encourages free-form report formatting and unconstrained layout. Rather than being constrained to placing items at specific rows or columns, you have the freedom to place items anywhere within the report body. Later, you see how the List data region extends this pattern by repeating a free-form region for each record.

Headers and Footers

As a result of the free-form approach, there is no need to designate a specific area to be the report header or footer. Essentially, the *report header* is all the space at the top of the report body before the first data range. Likewise, the space between the last data range and the end of the report body is the *report footer*.

This is because of the way a report is rendered. Like the carriage of a typewriter (or inkjet printer, for those of you who might have no idea what a typewriter is), the report is rendered from the top left-hand corner, from left to right, and then down the page until it reaches the bottom-right corner of the report body. Any report items, like textboxes and images, are rendered once. Data ranges, like tables and matrices, cause rows and columns to be repeated, making the report body grow. It's really quite an elegant approach — and the area of the report body above and below these data ranges is the report header and footer, respectively.

A report, however, does have a specific area defined for the page header and page footer. In the designer, these areas are enabled using the Header & Footer group on the Home ribbon or the Report menu in the BIDS designer.

The report body will act as a header or footer, depending on where you place data region items. If you were to place a table an inch below the top of the report body, this would give you a report header 1-inch tall. Because there is no set limit to the number of data regions or other items you can add to a report (and you can force page breaks at any location), all of the space above, below, and in-between these items is essentially header and footer space.

You have a lot of flexibility for displaying header and footer content. In addition to the standard report and page headers and footers, data region sections can be repeated on each page, creating additional page header and footer content. Figure 2-6 shows a table report with each of the header and footer areas labeled.

Figure 2-7 shows the first rendered page of this report.

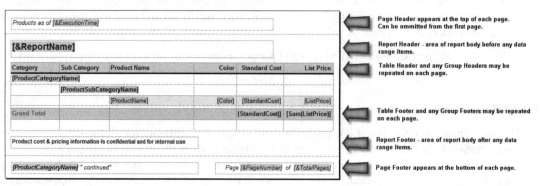

FIGURE 2-6

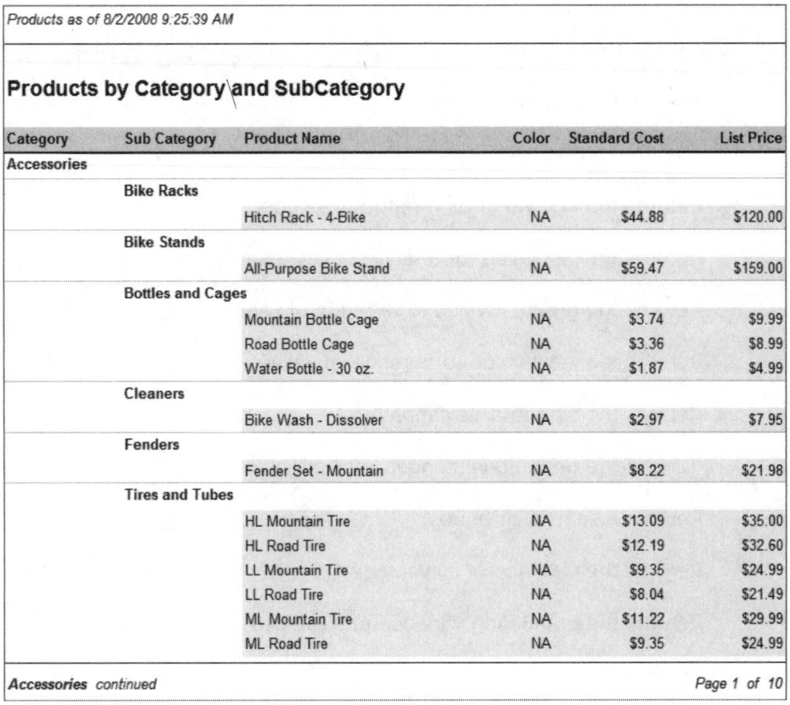

Category	Sub Category	Product Name	Color	Standard Cost	List Price
Accessories					
	Bike Racks				
		Hitch Rack - 4-Bike	NA	$44.88	$120.00
	Bike Stands				
		All-Purpose Bike Stand	NA	$59.47	$159.00
	Bottles and Cages				
		Mountain Bottle Cage	NA	$3.74	$9.99
		Road Bottle Cage	NA	$3.36	$8.99
		Water Bottle - 30 oz.	NA	$1.87	$4.99
	Cleaners				
		Bike Wash - Dissolver	NA	$2.97	$7.95
	Fenders				
		Fender Set - Mountain	NA	$8.22	$21.98
	Tires and Tubes				
		HL Mountain Tire	NA	$13.09	$35.00
		HL Road Tire	NA	$12.19	$32.60
		LL Mountain Tire	NA	$9.35	$24.99
		LL Road Tire	NA	$8.04	$21.49
		ML Mountain Tire	NA	$11.22	$29.99
		ML Road Tire	NA	$9.35	$24.99

Products as of 8/2/2008 9:25:39 AM

Products by Category and SubCategory

Accessories continued — Page 1 of 10

FIGURE 2-7

In earlier versions of Reporting Services, you were restricted from placing fields in the page headers and footers because these areas were added to the final report output after the data was processed and before pagination was applied by the rendering extension. This restriction is no longer in place. You also have access to several resources such as global variables, parameters, and report items.

Aggregate Functions and Totals

Reporting Services supports several aggregate functions similar to those supported by the T-SQL query language. Each aggregate function accepts one or two arguments. The first is the field reference or expression to aggregate. The second, optional, argument is the name of a dataset, report item, or group name to indicate the scope of the aggregation. If not provided, the scope of the current data region or group is assumed. For example, suppose a table contains two nested groups based on the Category and Subcategory fields. If you were to drag the SalesAmount field into the Subcategory group footer, the SUM(SalesAmount) expression would return the sum of all SalesAmount values within the scope of each distinct Subcategory group range. The following table lists the aggregate functions:

Function	Description
AVG()	The average of all non-null values
COUNT()	The count of values

continues

(continued)

Function	Description
COUNTDISTINCT()	The count of distinct values
COUNTROWS()	The count of all rows
FIRST()	Returns the first value for a range of values
LAST()	Returns the last value for a range of values
MAX()	Returns the greatest value for a range of values
MIN()	Returns the least value for a range of values
STDEV()	Returns the standard deviation
STDEVP()	Returns the population standard deviation
SUM()	Returns a sum of all values
VAR()	Returns the variance of all values
VARP()	Returns the population variance of all values

In addition to the aggregate functions, special-purpose functions exist that behave in a similar way to aggregates but have special features for reports:

Function	Description
LEVEL()	Returns an integer value for the group level within a recursive hierarchy. The group name is required.
ROWNUMBER()	Returns the row number for a group or range.
RUNNINGVALUE()	Returns an accumulative aggregation up to this row.

You can find examples of aggregate function expressions and recursive levels in the following sections for table and matrix report items.

Adding Totals to a Table or Matrix Report

The grouping paradigm has remained consistent in all versions of Reporting Services. However, the technique for grouping tables and matrices changed in SSRS 2008 with the introduction of the new tablix data region. The drag-and-drop grouping method used in the SSRS 2008 and SSRS 2008 R2 designers is far more intuitive and flexible than in SSRS 2005 and has an improved interface with the row group and column group panes.

Adding a total to a group adds a new row (for row groups) or column (for column groups) that applies an aggregate function to all the members of *that* group. If you think about this, you're actually adding a total that applies to the *parent* of the group. Think about it using this example: if columns are grouped by Quarter and then by Year, and if you were to add a total to the Quarter column group, the total would be for all of the Quarters adding into the Year. This means that a total applied to the top-most group will always return the grand total for all records in the data region. We've included a report with the samples to help make this point.

Adding a total to a group displays total values for all fields in the data area of the matrix. Defining a total for a group at a lower level would create a subtotal break. Totals can be placed before or after group values. For a column group, adding totals after the group inserts a total column to the right of the group. Inserting a total before the group places totals to the left of the group columns. By default, group totals are aggregated like the data cells in the same group, using a sum by default.

THE TABLIX

Reporting Services 2000 and 2005 have three different data range items that can be used to group data across rows or columns. The list, table, and matrix have some similar characteristics and capabilities but are three distinctly different objects, each with its own design goals, capabilities, and limitations. Shortly after the release of SQL Server 2005 Reporting Services, the product team began an effort to combine all these capabilities to create a super data-region item to replace the former list, table, and matrix items. In SSRS 2008 and beyond, the tablix (named for the combined features of a "table" and a "matrix") serves this purpose.

Combinations of properties will cause an instance of the tablix to behave and exhibit the characteristics of a list, a table, or a matrix. The advantage of this design is that you are no longer bound by the limitations of any one of these objects. For example, the characteristic of a table is that it has static columns that are typically bound to individual fields in the dataset. You will often define dynamic row groups that expand with each distinct field value according to the row group definition. But, if you decide, after the original design, to add a dynamic column group, this is now a possibility without having to start over with a different data range item.

Chapter 3 demonstrates the essential design steps for building a table type report data region.

Static and Dynamic Columns and Rows

An additional concept introduced with the tablix is that of static and dynamic columns and rows. A static column or row is a band of cells with an associated field expression. Take a row group, for example; for records in the dataset, as long as the group expression's field value remains the same, this causes only one instance of the row group to be rendered. All detail rows below this grouping can either be displayed as lower-level detail rows or as field values that can be aggregated at the group level. Previous versions of the matrix have always treated columns in this way. Now, in the tablix, a column may be inserted at any position and designated to behave as a static column (without grouping) or as a dynamic (or grouped) column. By taking this approach, the tablix has more flexibility than the previous table, list, or matrix data regions.

When the row group encounters a new distinct value, a new row for the group will be rendered, perhaps with lower-detail rows under it, or with values to be rolled up and aggregated for inclusion in the row.

By far, the majority of report designers will not concern themselves with adding dynamic columns to change the natural order of things and contend with the delicate balance of a happily working table or matrix, which is why each of these fine, preconfigured items — the table, matrix, and list — stands alone in both designers. For advanced report design when the tablix will be customized, you can add either a table or a matrix to the report body as a starting point. Static and dynamic groups can be added or removed to modify the table or matrix to behave as you like.

SUMMARY

Report design is a matter of using the essential building blocks. As an experienced report designer, you should be familiar with most of the basic techniques. This chapter, and the chapter that follows, are a quick refresher course and may serve as a reference guide as you build upon these basic techniques to design more advanced and specialized reporting solutions. In the report recipes that follow, you will use report and page headers and footers, data regions and report items to manage and manipulate the report layout. You will use parameters to filter data and provide some basic conditional logic.

In SSRS 2008 and 2008 R2, you will use Report Builder 2.0 and 3.0 to design data access, data regions, and report items. If you are working with earlier versions of SSRS or in a team development environment, you may use a BIDS solution development shell to create integrated reporting solutions and custom developed applications. The report recipes that follow will primarily demonstrate techniques using the Report Builder 2.0 and 3.0 report design tools. For SSRS 2000 and 2005, you can use the BIDS report designer with some minor adaptations.

3

Report Design Essentials

Reporting Services is a highly adaptable and customizable reporting platform. Unlike many other reporting products, Reporting Services reports are composed of individual report items and data region components. The report itself doesn't consume data but acts as a container or canvas for the objects that do visualize the data. Each of these components consumes data from report datasets. Data regions and report items may be embedded at multiple levels. This design approach provides a great deal of flexibility and opportunity when it comes to building creative business reporting solutions.

TABULAR AND MATRIX REPORTS

Tabular, or table-like, reports have a fixed number of columns that typically correspond to static fields in the underlying data source — like a spreadsheet or grid. Beyond a simple list of records, tabular reports can be grouped with headers, footers, and subtotals for each band of grouped records. Grouping is performed on one or more column values, with group values either repeated on each row, appearing only once in the grouped field column, or appearing only in the group header. Aggregated values for numeric columns can be displayed in the group header or footer. Aggregation is performed using one of several aggregate functions, such as SUM or AVG. Some aggregations can be used with non-numeric columns, such as COUNT or COUNTDISTINCT.

This section reviews the essential techniques for designing table reports. The same techniques are used for creating list and matrix reports in Reporting Services 2008.

Defining Table Groups

Groups are used throughout Reporting Services and are useful in many ways. The SQL Server 2008 report design environment now uses field drop zones to define groups located at the bottom of the Designer pane. When any part of the table is selected in the designer, separate list boxes are displayed for Row Groups and Column Groups.

In earlier product versions, each table group was used to define a separate group header row or footer row. Although this pattern is still possible, multiple groups can now be defined on the same row with separate headers that don't take up additional row space.

In this example, we've grouped the rows of this table on the CalendarYear and then the SalesTerritoryRegion fields. Note that, by default, a DetailsGroup item is displayed in the Row Groups list. This is a placeholder for fields to include at the detail level of this table. To add the CalendarYear field as a group at a level above the details row, you drag and drop this field from the Data window to above the DetailsGroup item in the Row Groups list, as shown in Figure 3-1.

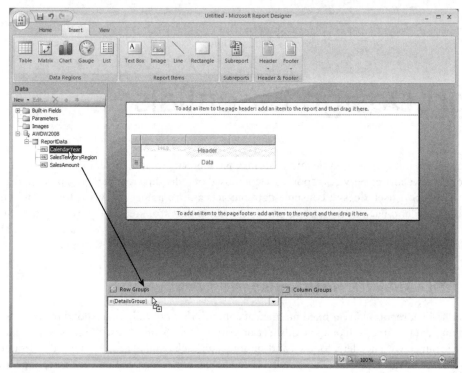

FIGURE 3-1

Measure values typically appear on each detail row and are then summarized in header or footer rows. In this example, the SalesAmount field will serve this purpose. When designing this report, you would drag the SalesAmount field from the Data window to the third column in the details row, as shown in Figure 3-2.

Group Expressions and Options

By dragging and dropping fields into the Row Groups list, you automatically add group definitions to the tablix. If you have used the table data region in prior versions of Reporting Services, you'll recall that this required a few more steps. If you need to modify a group or define specific properties, you can do so using the Tablix Group Properties dialog. To do this, in the Designer, select any part of the table to enable the Row Groups list. Clicking the down arrow on any row group enables the menu. From this menu, you would select Edit Group to display the Tablix Group Properties dialog, as shown in Figure 3-3.

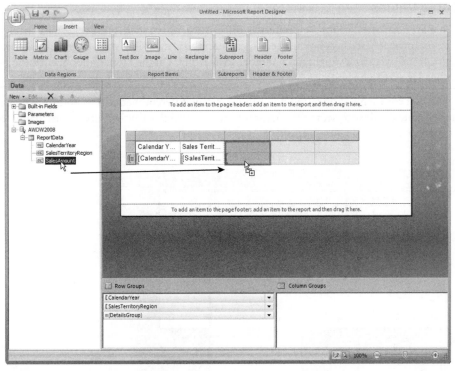

FIGURE 3-2

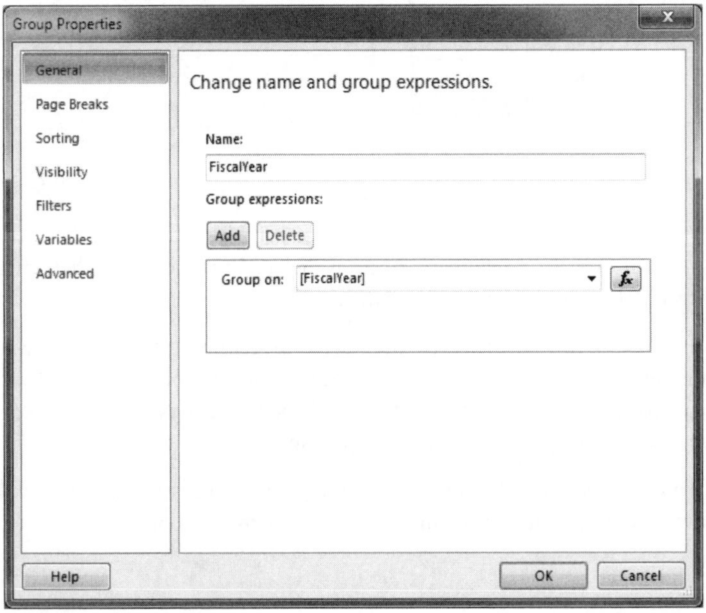

FIGURE 3-3

Formatting Table Values

Values in a table are formatted using the properties of constituent report items. Because each cell contains a textbox, property settings are applied to each textbox, including the background color, foreground color, font style, size, weight, and number formatting. On the Home ribbon, click the Bold icon to set the header text to be bold.

Text formatting is set for each textbox, and you can use a few different methods to do this. You can use the Properties pane window to set the Format property or open the Textbox Properties dialog from the right-click menu (shown in Figure 3-4).

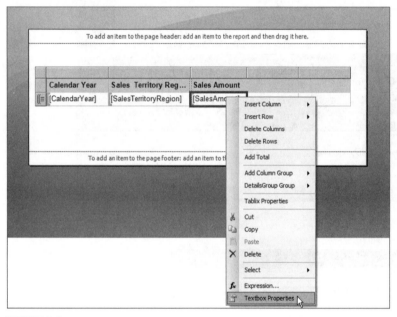

FIGURE 3-4

The Text Box Properties dialog, shown in Figure 3-5, contains a list of property categories on the left side. Selecting Number displays several numeric formatting options. Select Currency, and then check the box indicating that you want to include a thousands separator.

The report shows a detail record for every row returned by the query. By grouping the detail rows of the table, the size of the report will be reduced by summarizing the Sales Amount for each record within the group in the Row Groups pane located on the bottom-left side of the report designer. To do this, click the down arrow next to the Details group and choose Group Properties.

In the Group Properties dialog, you can use the Add button to add a group expression and select the appropriate field. Figure 3-6 shows a simple table report in the report designer Preview window.

FIGURE 3-5

FIGURE 3-6

Switching back to Design view (Figure 3-7), two different design methods can be used to add totals to the end of a group break with the same result. These include adding an explicit row to the group and choosing the Add Totals menu option. The first technique is more convenient, but the latter provides a little more flexibility.

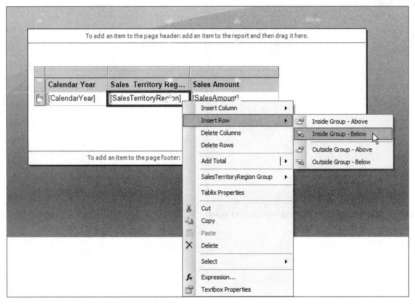

FIGURE 3-7

The new row is added below the group values. A fields list can be accessed by hovering the mouse pointer over a cell. This displays a list of fields like you see in Figure 3-8. Simply select a field to bind it to the cell. Using this feature in a group header or footer total cell automatically applies the SUM aggregate function to numeric fields.

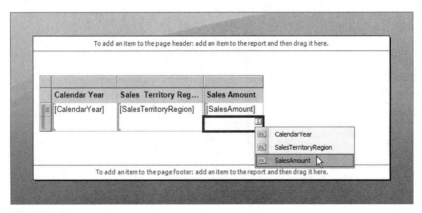

FIGURE 3-8

Optionally, you can apply formatting to the field value, as shown in Figure 3-9. As you see, for demonstration purposes, we have changed the number format of the textbox. We've also changed the font size and weight.

Matrix Reports

Prior to SQL Server 2008, the SSRS matrix data region was a separate design object from the table and list. Each of these three components included some redundant functionality but exhibited slightly different behavior and design characteristics. Each of these data regions applied data groups and aggregate functions to data fields, and could be used as a container for other data regions and report items. In SSRS 2008, these three components were combined into the Tablix data region and the list, table, and matrix are now implementations of the Tablix based upon templated property settings.

Calendar Year	Sales Territory Region	Sales Amount
2001	Canada	$1,513,359.46
	Central	$951,240.65
	Northeast	$568,545.52
	Northwest	$1,689,790.14
	Southeast	$1,448,921.51
	Southwest	$1,893,578.02
		$8,065,435.31
2002	Canada	$4,822,999.20
	Central	$2,625,639.72
	France	$857,123.18
	Northeast	$2,443,901.73
	Northwest	$3,471,099.54
	Southeast	$2,815,903.10
	Southwest	$6,266,005.43
	United Kingdom	$841,757.76
		$24,144,429.65

FIGURE 3-9

Designing a matrix is much the same as designing a table except the matrix is grouped on both rows and columns, consisting of row groups and column groups in the report designer. With groups defined on both axes, the cells at the intersect point of each normally define an aggregate, rather than a detail row. Totals can also be added to each column or row group, much like you would in the grouped rows in a table.

Sorting Options

You have a few different options for sorting the data displayed in a table. The best method to choose depends on your needs and any interactive features you may want to support. When the report is executed, after making a connection to the data source, the first thing that happens is that queries are executed by the data source, and records are presented to the report items in their natural order or the order specified in the query. A dataset is more than just a fancy name for a query. It's actually an object managed by the report execution engine that holds a cache of the report data. As the dataset records flow to a data region, it can group and reorder the records before the report is rendered.

In short, you have three options: if you always want records to be displayed in a specific order, you should use a query or database object to sort them. In case you use a data provider that doesn't allow sorting or you need to reorder records after a query runs, you also have the option to reorder records in the report. If you need to provide some dynamic data reordering using a parameter selection or some other creative report design, you can sort records in the report using more advanced methods.

Sorting in the Query

It's important to realize that the SQL Server database engine, like many other relational database products, doesn't guarantee that records will be returned from the database tables in a particular order unless you specify this in a query. To be on the safe side, it's a good idea to be specific and use an ORDER BY clause in your T-SQL queries when records should always appear in a specific order.

The query feeding data to this report table includes an ORDER BY clause. In the following example, this query will always return records sorted by the CalendarYear and then the SalesTerritoryRegion field values:

```
SELECT
    DimDate.CalendarYear, DimSalesTerritory.SalesTerritoryRegion,
    SUM(FactResellerSales.SalesAmount) AS SalesAmount
FROM FactResellerSales INNER JOIN DimDate
    ON FactResellerSales.OrderDateKey = DimDate.DateKey
    INNER JOIN DimSalesTerritory
    ON FactResellerSales.SalesTerritoryKey =
        DimSalesTerritory.SalesTerritoryKey
ORDER BY DimDate.CalendarYear, DimSalesTerritory.SalesTerritoryRegion
```

To optimize report performance, if you intend to use dynamic features in the report to reorder these records, it might be best to leave off the ORDER BY clause so that your report isn't working against the database engine. Another option would be to parameterize the query to dynamically change the ORDER BY clause, letting the database engine do the reordering, rather than the reporting engine. To keep things simple, I will typically specify a natural ORDER BY in a query and then use other sorting features to apply exceptional rules, unless I have good reason to do otherwise.

Sorting in a Group

Part of the Tablix's job is to apply groups and sorting options. Any group can be sorted in any order using any combination of data fields and expressions.

Figure 3-10 shows the Row Groups pane in the designer. To set the sort order for a group, click the down arrow on the group listed in the Row or Column Groups list when the Tablix is selected in the designer, and then select Edit Group from the dropdown menu.

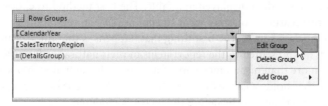

FIGURE 3-10

The Tablix Group Properties dialog is displayed with a list of pages on the left side (shown in Figure 3-11). Select Sorting and click the Add button to add a new sorting expression. Complex expressions and combinations of fields can be used for sorting and grouping. This simple example shows a typical sorting expression based on one of the fields displayed in the report. In a more complex report, you might add multiple sorting definitions based on different column/field values or other expressions.

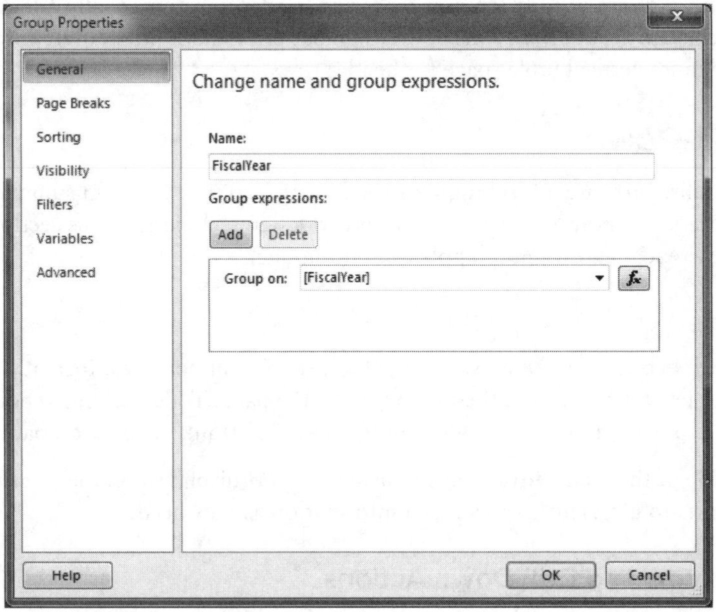

FIGURE 3-11

Interactive Sort

The Interactive Sort feature was added to the table in the 2005 product and now works much the same way in the Tablix. Interactive sorting is applied after the groups are processed, so the entire report doesn't need to be re-rendered each time a user clicks the column header to reorder column values. This is actually a feature of a textbox located in a header.

To add interactive sorting, right-click the cell for the field column header and choose Textbox Properties. On the Interactive Sort page of this dialog, choose the group name and Sort by field. By specifying this group, rows within this group will be sorted within their parent group. In other words, when a user clicks the column header textbox, the rows will be resorted in either ascending or descending order, while the parent group heading values will remain the same. Before resorting the column, a pair of up and down arrows is displayed. Hovering over these arrows changes the mouse pointer to indicate that each is a hyperlink. Click the up button to sort in descending order or the down arrow to sort in ascending order. After sorting, the arrows pair changes to a single up or down arrow to indicate a toggled state for the sort order.

Adding Headers and Footers

By combining the table, list, and matrix reports from previous product versions into the Tablix data region, the grouping paradigm has changed slightly in SQL Server 2008 Reporting Services, enabling a more flexible reporting interface. In previous versions, inserting a group into a table would add two additional rows by default: one header row and one footer row. This same pattern is still possible, but the Tablix now works differently out-of-the-box. The default behavior for a group is more akin to the old matrix data region. When a group is added, a non-repeating header is automatically added to the same row rather than a separate header row. This new design pattern looks a little different from the old method, which required more vertical table space for header rows.

The Low Down on Drill-Down

Drill-down, drill-through, and subreports are all techniques for allowing a user to get from summary data to details, but these are different concepts that require different design techniques. This section will help you understand the differences and when to apply each technique.

Report Navigation Essentials

Printed reports were the norm for decades. When a user wanted to get some important information, they would use their software to print a report and then read it from the page. Today, online reports are used to give users access to important information without the need to put ink or toner on paper.

Aside from saving the forests, one of the many advantages of using a report displayed on the screen is that users can interact with reports to get as little or as much information as they need.

Reports with Multi-Level Groups and Drill-Down Actions

Multi-level grouped reports are one of the most fundamental report designs. A natural extension of this style of report has each subgroup collapsed, with the ability to click a toggle item to expand or collapse each group to view detail at a lower level.

Using Reporting Services, this is a straight-forward design pattern, but it's not well documented for the novice report designer.

There are also a number of options to consider when you design multi-level drill-down reports, such as:

➤ Multi-level grouped reports with subtotals

➤ Drill-down reports on a single dataset

➤ Drill-down reports with dynamic details

➤ Embedded drill-through targets

Standard Terminology

I spend a good deal of time answering questions and moderating the Microsoft Developer Network (MSDN) forum for Reporting Services. New SSRS users tend to use terms inconsistently to describe report design elements and concepts — for example, "I want to click a drill-down link to open a sub-report in a new window to view the details for the item I clicked on." Although this probably makes sense to the user who wrote it, it may not make sense to those familiar with standard Reporting Services concepts. Before we can discuss these design concepts, it's important that we're on the same page, using the same words and phrases to describe the same concepts. The discussion in this section is limited to designing reports using a table data region.

Groups

A table data region can have one or more row groups. A *group* may be created by dragging a field into the Row Groups list in the lower-left area of the report designer while the table is selected. A group may optionally have numeric subtotals in the group header (above the details) or the group footer (below the details). Each group has one or more group field expressions. A table with two nested groups might have sales records grouped first by the year and then subgrouped by the month.

Figure 3-12 shows a typical multi-level grouped table report design in Report Builder 2.0. Note the inline group headers in the table row which correspond to row groups, which are displayed in the left-side pane of the groups panel below the report design window.

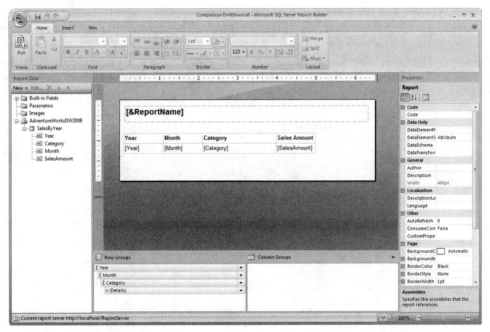

FIGURE 3-12

This example uses a table data region with grouped rows. The drill-down functionality in the next section will work just as well with matrix style reports with column groups.

Drill-Down

A dynamic reporting experience is created by hiding and showing report elements. Various techniques can be used to show and hide fields, groups, rows, columns, and entire data regions using conditional expressions and toggle items. All report items and group definitions have a `Visibility` property that can be set either permanently or conditionally.

A common use for the `Visibility` property is to create drill-down reports, where table or matrix group headers are used to toggle, or expand and collapse, details. Typically, a plus [+] or minus [−] icon is displayed next to the toggle item row or column header.

Beyond the basic drill-down report design, where a multi-level grouped table has group header rows which may be expanded and collapsed using a toggle item, certain details could also be hidden and shown using a toggle item as well. For example, a product name could be displayed in the detail row with a toggle item used to show a description or order details.

Toggle Items

The name of a report item existing in a row at a level above the current group is a *toggle item*. In typical reports, a toggle item is a textbox in the header of a parent group used to expand (show all) or collapse (or hide) a set of rows. By default, a plus or minus icon is displayed to the left of the toggle item to indicate the expanded or collapsed state. When a user clicks this icon, the plus icon [+] is used to expand the level and the minus icon [−] is used to collapse and hide details in the lower-level group for that parent value. Figure 3-13 shows a drill-down report with toggle items set for the group header rows of a table.

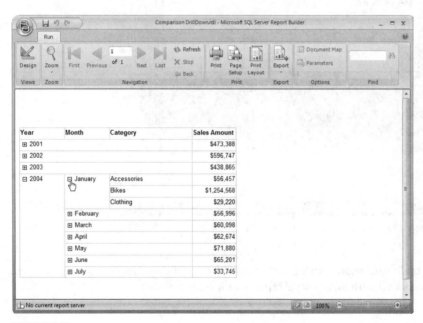

FIGURE 3-13

Drill-Through

Drill-through refers to a type of report action that navigates from a specific report item to a different report. Optionally, one or more field values in the context of the current row are passed to parameters in the target report to filter records related to the row or item in the source report. By default, the target report is displayed in the same browser or viewer window as the source report. Optionally, the drill-through target report can be displayed in a secondary window. In HTML report rendering, drill-through is implemented using a hyperlink and anchor tag to navigate to the target report. A drill-through report may be implemented using a Report action or a URL action, or using an expression to specify the server path, folder name, report name, parameters, and optional query string commands.

Drill-Through Source

The report containing one or more report items having a Report or URL action is known as the *drill-through source*. A user navigates from a source report to a drill-through target report.

Drill-Through Target

The report that a user navigates to in a drill-through report or URL action is the *drill-through target*. Any report on the report server may be used as a drill-through target using a relative folder path. When using Business Intelligence Development Studio to design a Report action for a textbox or other report item, all reports in the same project (which are deployed to the same folder) are listed as available target reports.

In Figure 3-14, the target source report contains a table data region. The textbox for the Year field has a drill-through action that opens a drill-through target report. The corresponding Year field value is passed to a parameter on the target report that filters data in the query for the specified year. In the example shown in Figure 3-14, that is the product category sales for 2004.

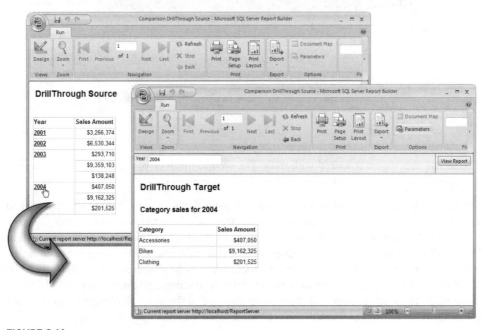

FIGURE 3-14

Subreports

A *subreport* is a report embedded inside another report. Subreports can simply be independent reports or master/detail reports that show detail records related to a group header or master record. Independent subreports are often used to display standardized header and footer information, such as legal statements and disclaimers. To filter and correlate master/detail records, the subreport should be designed with parameters used to filter records in each instance of the subreport related to the master record in the parent report. In Figure 3-15, you can see the parent report in the report designer which shows a dark gray placeholder labeled with the path and name of the child subreport.

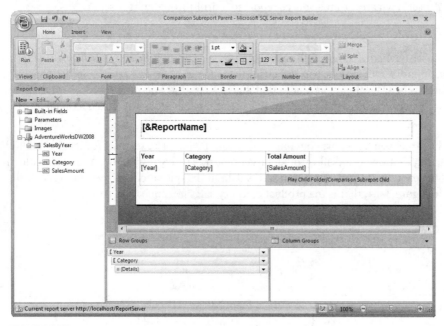

FIGURE 3-15

Figure 3-16 shows this report rendered with data. The second instance of the subreport is called out, which displays subcategory sales details related to the Bikes category.

One of the advantages of using a subreport to display master/detail records is that each report is based on a separate data source and dataset query. As such, this technique may be used to federate and correlate related data from two different data sources. Even the database platforms and query languages can be different. Conversely, one of the disadvantages of this technique is that by opening multiple data connections and running separate queries, report processing may be slower and less efficient. However, if the data truly resides in different locations and in different database platforms, this may be the best method to bring it into a single view. Subreports are also one of the more challenging report elements to render or export into different formats with the same fidelity as a single table or matrix.

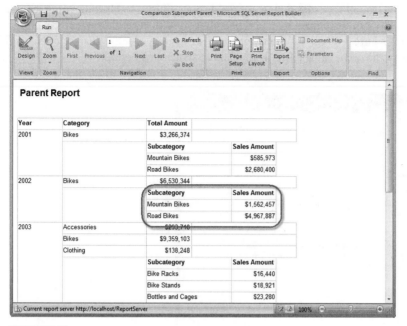

FIGURE 3-16

Creating a Drill-Down Report

Figure 3-17 shows a drill-down report with toggle items set for the group header rows of a table.

Creating a drill-down report is a simple matter of hiding a group and setting its `ToggleItem` property to refer to a report item, usually a textbox, in a higher-level group. In our example report, records are grouped by Calendar Year and then Sales Territory Region. The properties for the latter group are set using the group pane in the lower part of the Design window, as shown in Figure 3-18.

Reseller Sales by Year and Territory

Calendar Year	Sales Territory Region	Sales Amount
2001	Canada	$1,513,359.46
	Central	$951,240.65
	Northeast	$568,545.52
	Northwest	$1,689,790.14
	Southeast	$1,448,921.51
	Southwest	$1,893,578.02
⊞ 2002		$4,822,999.20
⊞ 2003		$847,430.96
⊞ 2004		$746,904.41

FIGURE 3-17

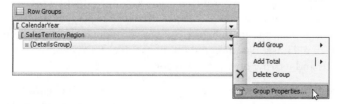

FIGURE 3-18

In the Visibility page of the Group Properties dialog, set the display options to Hide the group contents, check the box labeled Display can be toggled by this report item, and then select the textbox bound to a field in the parent group. Figure 3-19 shows the toggle item set to the CalendarYear field. Note that this textbox may not always have the same name as the field to which it is bound.

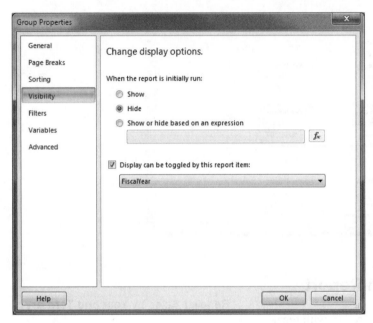

FIGURE 3-19

Dynamic visibility can also be used to hide and show areas of a report based on parameters or field threshold values. With a little creativity and some basic programming skills, some very interesting things are possible.

Drill-Through Reports

Links and drill-through reports are powerful features that enable a textbox or image to be used as a link to another report by passing parameter values to the target report. The target report can consist of a specific record or multiple records, depending on the parameters passed to the target report. In the following example, the Product Name textbox is used to link to a report that will display the details of a single product record. The Product Details report, shown in Figure 3-20, is very simple. It contains only textboxes and an image bound to fields of a dataset based on the Products table. This report accepts a `ProductID` parameter to filter the records and narrow down to the record requested.

Any textbox or image item can be used for intra-report or inter-report navigation, for navigation to external resources like web pages and documents, and also to send e-mail. All these features are enabled by using navigation properties that can be specified in the Text Box Properties or Image Properties dialog. In the Text Box Properties dialog, use the Actions page to set the drill-through destination and any parameters you would like to pass. Figure 3-21 shows the Text Box Properties dialog Action page.

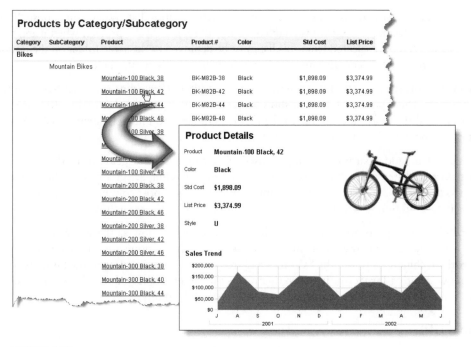

FIGURE 3-20

FIGURE 3-21

Note the navigation target selections under the Enable as a action option list. When you choose "Go to report," the report selection dropdown is enabled, listing all reports in the project, when using the BIDS report designer. A report selected from this list must be deployed to the same folder on the Report Server as the source report. You can also just type a report name in this combo box.

A drill-through report is typically used to open the report to a filtered record or result set based on the value in this textbox. The typical pattern is to show a user-friendly caption in the textbox (the product name in this case) and then pass a key value to the report parameter to uniquely identify records to filter in the target report. In this case, the ProductID value is passed.

To enable this behavior, add a parameter mapping used when running the target report. All parameters in the target report are listed in the Name column. In the Value column, select a field in the source report to map to the parameter. A new feature is apparent in the right-most column. An expression can be used to specify a condition in which the parameter is not passed to the target report.

By default, drill-through reports are displayed in the same browser window as the source report. A few techniques exist for opening the report in a secondary window, but none are out-of-the-box features. My favorite technique is to use the "Go to URL" navigation option and open the target report using a URL request with a JavaScript function that opens the target report in a new browser window. Although this is a little more involved, it provides a great deal of flexibility.

Navigating to a URL

The "Go to URL" option can be used to navigate to practically any report or document content on your Report Server; files, folders, and applications in your intranet environment; or the World Wide Web. With some creativity, this can be used as a powerful, interactive navigation feature. It can also be set to an expression that uses links stored in a database, custom code, or any other values. It's more accurate to say that any URI (Uniform Resource Identifier) can be used, because a web request is not limited only to a web page or document. With some creative programming, queries, and expressions, your reports could be designed to navigate to a web page, document, e-mail address, Web Service request, or a custom web application, directed by data or custom expressions.

A word of caution: Reporting Services does not make any attempt to validate a URL passed in an expression. If a malformed URL is used, the Report Server will return an error, and there is no easy way to trap or prevent this from occurring. The most effective way to handle this issue is to validate the URL string before passing it to the "Go to URL" property.

Report Navigation Summary

As a general rule, if data tables or entities can be combined in the server or query using joins or a cube, it is best to use a single dataset to bring this into a single view to visualize the data in a report data region. When data cannot be unified on the server or query, you should use a subreport with a limited number of master records.

For more information about report navigation design options, see Report Bruckner's blog post titled Report Performance Optimization Tips (Subreports, Drilldown): `http://blogs.msdn.com/robertbruckner/archive/2009/01/08/report-performance-optimization-tips-subreports-drilldown.aspx`.

Paul Turley's blog contains a post with the same title as this section, with similar posts on the related topics: http://www.sqlserverbiblog.com/post/The-Low-Down-on-Drill-Down.aspx.

Charting Basics

Reporting Services includes several different types of charts that consume and visualize data in a variety of different ways. Regardless of the specific charting representation, all charts apply the same basic concepts. Using the chart design, interface data is grouped in the same way that groups are defined in a matrix. Within these groups, numeric values are aggregated using the SUM() function by default, but any aggregate function can be applied manually. Like a matrix, aggregated values represent the intersection points of distinct group values. The difference is that a chart plots or visualizes the values rather than displaying the number in a cell.

Series and Category Axes

The *series* is the axis associated with the chart's legend, if you choose to include it. In a column chart, for example, series values are displayed in the legend and/or column clusters.

Category groups are the labeled group values that are usually represented with a single column, point, or bar. In a column chart, categories are plotted along the *X*-axis with labels typically along the bottom of the chart.

Many different types of charts are now available. Probably the most common and most recognizable chart type is the column chart. The example in Figure 3-22 shows sales data for a given year, grouped by quarter and the sales territory country. The total sales amount is plotted on the category or *Y*-axis (columns) of the chart.

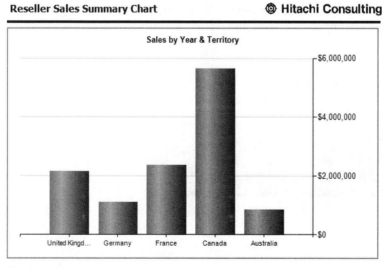

FIGURE 3-22

Adding a group to the series axis can cause the column chart to show a cluster of columns side-by-side. The columns are color-coded with a color key shown in the legend. Figure 3-23 shows a category group based on the CalendarYear field with a cluster of two columns. Column clusters can be displayed in a flattened, two-dimensional view like this, or arranged along the Z-axis when three-dimensional (3D) visualizations are enabled.

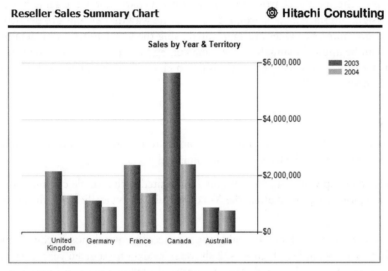

FIGURE 3-23

One of the powerful features of the chart item is the ability to group data within each axis. Figure 3-24 shows a simple column chart with two field groups on the X-axis, representing related categories. In this example, columns are grouped by calendar year and then by the sales territory country.

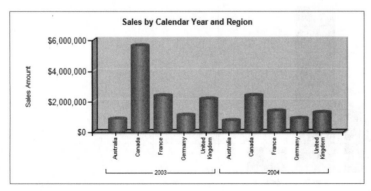

FIGURE 3-24

A number of these features — including multiple axes, clustering, and nested groups — can be combined to create some interesting and compelling chart visualizations.

Some charts require only one axis group. For example, a pie chart uses only a series group. Pie charts put proportional values into perspective. Values are presented visually as a percentage of the total for all values in a series. Pie and doughnut chart views can be either *simple* or *exploded*. The exploded presentation may help to visually separate values, especially the smaller slices. These types of charts can be useful for placing values into comparative perspective.

Polar and Radar Charts

Figure 3-25 shows one of the new chart types introduced in SSRS 2008. This is a radar chart, one of the new and polar chart types in the new product. This is an interesting visualization that combines elements of a line chart with a pie chart-like format.

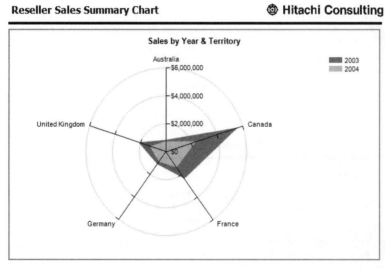

FIGURE 3-25

Shape Charts

Some special-purpose charts are commonly used to visualize data for certain vertical applications. For example, the funnel chart, shown in Figure 3-26, is commonly used as an illustration of customer sales leads "flowing down" through the funnel in customer relationship management (CRM) solutions, to help manage a sales opportunity pipeline.

Bar Charts

Bar charts and column charts are pretty much the same in functionality. You can tilt your head to the side to get the same view as the other. Figure 3-27 shows the same data from the previous column chart, in a bar chart. When this chart type is chosen, category group values are visualized with values plotted on the Y-axis and the value scale along the X-axis — a 90-degree rotation of the same column chart.

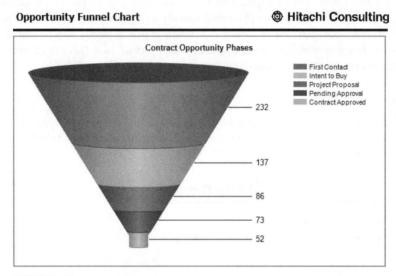

FIGURE 3-26

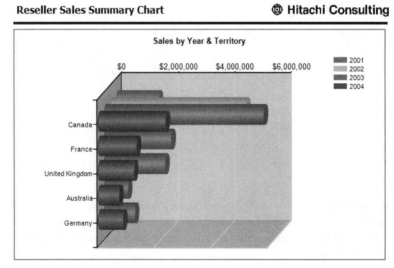

FIGURE 3-27

In addition to the standard, single-bar view, the stacked view provides a consolidated look at a series of values by using fewer bars or columns. Each bar is like a mini pie chart, where each value in the bar's range is in proportion to the others. A series of related values is stacked in the column to show the aggregate sum of values and their proportional values. A variation, the 100 percent stacked bar or chart, displays each bar with the same height or length as others, regardless of the total values. This type of chart is useful for comparing values within the bar's range, but not for comparing the aggregates represented by each bar.

Many chart variations and special chart types are not pictured here. In addition to the standard report items that ship with the product, application developers and third-party companies can create custom report items (CRI) that can be installed and used in the Designer. You are likely to see more CRI suites for Reporting Services that will add even more capabilities to your reports.

Gauges

The new gauge report items introduced in Reporting Services 2008 enable you to control virtually every aspect of gauges, including background colors and shading, borders, scales, pointers, and markers. Practically any characteristic you've seen in a physical gauge or meter is possible. Although there are many properties, most are fairly easy to work with and to discover with just a little bit of guidance.

The basic principles of gauge design are quite simple because most of the properties pertain to a single scale, pointer, range, and marker used to plot a value. However, the application of all these simple properties can be a bit overwhelming at times. Like the new chart data range, a single gauge can contain several gauge areas. This essentially lets you create an entire dashboard with one gauge item. Each gauge area has its own scales, pointers, ranges, and markers, and a single gauge can have multiple gauge areas. Like looking at the world through a microscope, it's helpful to keep track of where you are and where you've been. I find it useful to diagram the anatomy of the gauge elements on paper and keep track of the properties I've set.

Scales

The *scale* is the set of markers and reference numbers around the dial of a radial gauge or along the range of a linear gauge. Any number of scales can be added to a single gauge.

Pointers and Markers

In a radial gauge, pointers are typically needles and arrows or small "tick" marks that can extend from the center of the gauge and point to a scale, or simply indicate certain points on a scale. Several preset pointers and markers are available in different shapes. Each can be resized and, like every other element, can be set with solid or gradient shading.

Ranges

Ranges typically are used to provide some sort of context and are typically displayed on or near the scale, behind pointers and markers. A range can be used to indicate that a value is within acceptable or exceptional boundaries. Ranges can be color-coded, tapered, or shaded with solid or gradient fills.

Radial Gauges

Radial gauges can be circular or partially circular, with one or more pointers extending from a central fulcrum. The simplest form of gauge, shown in Figure 3-28, has a single scale and pointer. The maximum scale value in this example is set with an expression to indicate the total number of sales units for a calendar year. The pointer value gets its value from an expression to show the total units in a quarter, thus showing the proportion of the quarter units to the year.

Linear Gauges

Linear gauges can be arranged vertically or horizontally in a variety of formats. Markers are typically used in the place of radial pointers but behave in much the same way. The example in Figure 3-29 shows a linear gauge with a single marker. This gauge has three color-coded ranges, which are used to indicate threshold values along the scale.

Gauges can have any number of pointers and markers that can be used to create unique visual components like bullet graphs and multi-range indicators. These report items become very useful when they are used to compare a group of related values side-by-side within a grouped data region, such as a table, list, or matrix. For example, Figure 3-30 shows a composite report designed by embedding a single gauge into a Tablix with repeating columns.

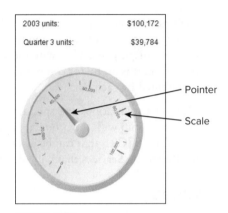

FIGURE 3-28

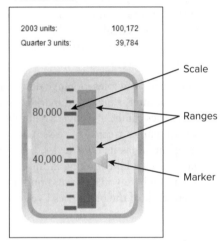

FIGURE 3-29

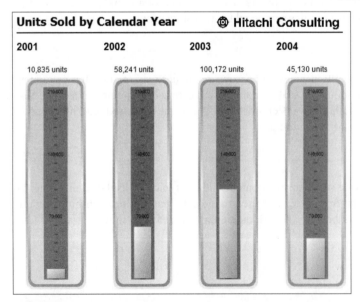

FIGURE 3-30

Maps

SSRS 2008 R2 introduces the map report item, which is based on components acquired from the Dundas Map geospatial visualization controls and enhanced to include new industry standards and SQL Server capabilities. A map can consist of multiple layers, which can include a vector-based map with boundaries, borders, and fills; and the data visualizations consisting of plotted markers, images, or bubbles. A map can also include a Bing map layer using any of the views available from the live Bing map service. Bing maps can be superimposed over a standard report map. The map item has the capability to visualize geographic data in one of three different ways, as described in the following sections.

Map Gallery

The map gallery is a set of predefined maps for any common geographic unit such as countries, states, provinces, counties, and municipalities. This is an extensible model that can be adapted to fit any geographic standard. Each map is encapsulated in an RDL file. The RDL specification was expanded to include support for embedded vector polygons and standard map coordinates stored as meridians and parallels. Additional maps will be available as they're developed by Microsoft and third parties.

ESRI Shape Files

Shape files store geospatial information in a standard file format established by ESRI (formerly known as the Environmental Systems Research Institute) for its suite of ArcGIS Geographical Information System software products. This is a de facto industry standard capable of storing polygon and vector objects with attributes and properties.

SQL Server Spatial Data

Spatial data is stored using new object data types introduced in SQL Server 2008. This advanced standard is unique to SQL Server but based on standards from the Open Geospatial Consortium. Spatial types can define simple polygons and complex geographical objects using the Geodetic (round earth) model or Planar (flat earth) models. As a native SQL Server standard, spatial data can be indexed and optimized to support large data volumes and integration with other Microsoft technologies.

Using Parameters

Creating and using parameters in report design usually isn't difficult, but until you have a chance to do some creative things with them in both queries and report expressions, you might not fully appreciate the power of parameters. Categorically, two different types of parameters exist: dataset parameters and report parameters. Dataset parameters can be derived from database objects, such as stored procedures and user-defined functions, or they can be derived from a parameterized query statement. Most commonly, report parameters will be derived from parameters defined in an ad hoc query, but you don't have to have a parameterized query to use parameters in a report.

When using SQL Server as the data source, parameters are defined in the SQL syntax by prefixing the names with a single @ symbol. Other query languages may use different characters such as ?, :, and # to prefix parameters. In a stored procedure, these parameters are defined first and then used in the procedure body much as you would in an ad hoc query. The Report Designer automatically parses the query and generates corresponding report parameters. If you use the Graphical Query Builder or generic Query Designer to write a T-SQL statement, the Report Designer will resolve dataset parameters and database object parameters and prompt for the parameter values when running the query. Dataset parameters are mapped to report parameters in the Dataset Properties dialog. This dialog is accessible when editing the dataset in the Report Data pane of the Report Designer.

For most basic queries, the Report Designer will match the query and report parameters for you automatically. But if have created a very complex or unusual dataset query, you may need to match the dataset and report parameters manually. Parameter resolution is performed when you test a query in the Query Designer, click the Refresh Fields button, or close the Dataset Properties dialog.

Regardless of the matching column data types, auto-generated parameters will be a character type and the report user will be prompted to enter a value in the parameter bar with a common textbox. You can use the Report Parameter Properties dialog to modify the data type and make this a more convenient experience. Using the previous query example, if the `ShipDateFrom` and `ShipDateTo` parameters were modified to have a Date data type, the user will be prompted to select a date using a more appropriate date picker control.

Over time, reports tend to grow and expand. Users will inevitably ask for more fields, more totals, and other features. Allowing the requirements to evolve in this manner can make your reports unruly and difficult to support — especially when you have different people involved in this haphazard and incremental style of design. Writing well-designed queries will go a long way in achieving efficient, maintainable reports. Carefully consider whether functionality should be built into the query or the report design. Often, handling business challenges in the query will make the report design much easier.

Creating a Parameter List

When a report is designed with a relational data source and with a parameterized query, by default the user is prompted to type a parameter value into a textbox in the parameter bar above the report. Although this works, it's not very convenient. You can provide a list of values for the user to select from by creating a new dataset that returns two columns. These will correspond to the `Value` and `Label` attributes of the parameter. In simple terms, the `Label` is the field value that the users sees in the parameter dropdown list and the `Value` is the internal field value, typically a key column, presented to the query or expression that references the parameter. In some cases, if you are not using a lookup table with a key, only one column may suffice and can be mapped to both the `Value` and `Label`. Use the Report Parameter Properties dialog to map the appropriate fields to these attributes as you see in Figure 3-31.

For SSAS cube-based reports, the MDX Query Designer will create the parameter lookup dataset and map the parameter attributes for you. If you choose a user hierarchy in the filtering pane of the graphical MDX Query Designer and check the Parameters box on the right side, the designer will auto-generate a new dataset and a report parameter. The MDX Query Designer is shown in Figure 3-32.

The auto-generated dataset includes five separate fields that are used to build a multi-level, multi-select parameter list. The parameter uses this dataset for the available values list. It maps the `ParameterValue` field to the `Value` attribute and the `ParameterCaptionIndented` field to the `Label` attribute. The `ParameterCaptionIndented` field uses the following expression to indent the level members according to the dimensional hierarchy:

```
=Space(3*Fields!ParameterLevel.Value) + Fields!ParameterCaption.Value
```

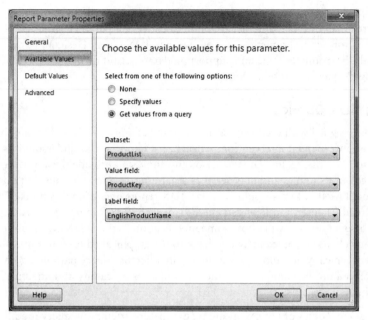

FIGURE 3-31

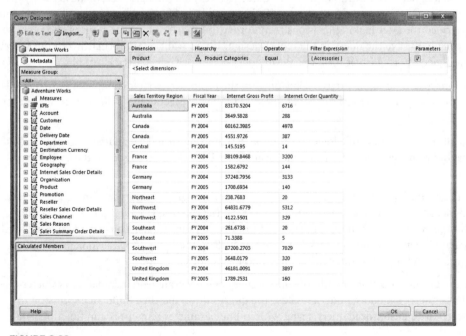

FIGURE 3-32

These auto-generated datasets, field expressions, and parameters have several moving parts, and it would be cumbersome to re-create all of this manually. If you need to write a parameterized MDX query outside of the graphical editor, we recommend that you use the MDX Query Designer to design the original query with the built-in parameter logic and supporting datasets, and then make modifications to the query logic, leaving the parameter logic alone.

Modifying and Formatting MDX Queries

The MDX Query Designer was designed with the business user in mind and is a very capable tool, but it was not designed to easily support manual intervention. As such, it's important to understand its idiosyncrasies before you venture into this realm. The recipes on this topic will provide the appropriate level of instruction to reproduce our examples and may serve as a pattern for your solutions, but don't attempt to cover everything you'll need to know about writing MDX report queries in this book. We strongly recommend that you read Chapter 9 in *Professional SQL Server 2008 Reporting Services* to learn more about this topic. The query editor will allow some modification to the MDX syntax in text mode, but once you've made any changes, you can't switch back to the graphical editor without losing those changes. The designer will typically not allow you to manually reference query parameters. As a rule, measures can only be placed on the columns axis and all dimension hierarchy and attribute members are typically placed in the rows axis.

Be meticulous about making backup copies of your working reports before attempting query modifications. If you switch the Query Designer from graphical to text mode, any modification you make will be lost if you switch back to the graphical editor. Once you've made changes, keep a master copy of the query in a separate file. You can manage your MDX script files in SSMS and paste the query text into the report query editor after making revisions. Any formatting, such as carriage returns and tabs, will also be lost when you save the query in the report design. If you want retain formatting in the Query Designer, you'll need to re-paste it from the SSMS query editor or your master script file.

You can use four general design patterns depending on the business need and complexity of your MDX queries. You can apply these patterns in order, moving to the next technique if the former doesn't meet the need:

1. Add all of the business rule logic to the cube design using stored calculated members and KPIs. Build the dataset query using the Graphical MDX Query Designer in the SSRS report designer.

2. Build an initial query in the Graphical MDX Query Designer. Allow the editor to generate field metadata, parameters, and parameter list dataset queries. Use the Edit as Text toolbar option to switch to text mode and make appropriate modifications. You can add query-based calculated members and in-line MDX function calls to the query script as long as the query returns a result with the same field names and metadata signature.

3. Use the graphical editor to build the initial query and generate field metadata, parameters, and parameter list dataset queries. Close the query editor and then build an expression to concatenate a customized query string with in-line parameter references and function calls.

Write and test the working query in the SSMS query editor and then copy-and-paste portions into the expression editor. Variations of this technique include writing an embedded custom function in the report or referencing an external custom assembly to return the MDX query string.

4. Build and test the MDX query in the SSMS query editor. After saving a backup copy of the report, open the RDL file in Visual Studio using the View Code right-click menu option in Solution Explorer. Find the CommandText element tag within the appropriate dataset definition element. Replace the CommandText content with the new query script. Save and open the report in the report designer. Do not attempt to edit this query in the report designer.

Multi-Value Parameters

Using the Report Parameter Properties dialog, you can configure parameters so that a user has the option to select a combination of values. Enabling the Multi-select setting changes the behavior of the parameter dropdown list, but it doesn't enable the SQL Server database engine to deal with the changes. A simple modification is required in the query syntax. Making the report parameter multi-valued changes it to an array type object. When the report parameter value(s) is mapped to the corresponding query parameter value (which is not an array), the value is converted to a string value containing a comma-separated list. Both T-SQL and MDX contain parsing functions that know how to deal with comma-delimited values. In T-SQL, the IN function will match a field value against items in such a list.

The following example demonstrates the technique in a T-SQL query. The Year report parameter is mapped to the query parameter named @Year. Internally, SSRS parses the array and creates a string with comma-separated values. Using the T-SQL IN() function is the logical equivalent to several OR statements testing the parameter's equality to a column.

```
SELECT
    D.CalendarYear
  , D.CalendarQuarter
  , ST.SalesTerritoryCountry
  , ST.SalesTerritoryRegion
  , SUM(F.OrderQuantity) AS QtySum
  , SUM(F.SalesAmount) AS AmtSum
FROM
  DimDate D INNER JOIN FactResellerSales F ON D.DateKey = F.OrderDateKey
  INNER JOIN DimSalesTerritory ST ON F.SalesTerritoryKey = ST.SalesTerritoryKey
WHERE
  D.CalendarYear IN ( @Year )
GROUP BY
    D.CalendarYear
  , D.CalendarQuarter
  , ST.SalesTerritoryCountry
  , ST.SalesTerritoryRegion
ORDER BY
    D.CalendarYear
```

```
    , D.CalendarQuarter
    , ST.SalesTerritoryCountry
    , ST.SalesTerritoryRegion
  ;
```

Cascading Parameters

A parameter can depend on another parameter so that the list of available values for a parameter is filtered based on another parameter selection. For example, if you offer users a list of product categories and another list of product subcategories, the subcategory list would only show subcategories for a selected category.

The Report Data pane shows the objects defined in the finished report. Two parameters are defined for the user to select the product category (named *CatKey* in this example) and the product subcategory (named *SubcatKey*). A dataset query corresponds to each parameter.

The most logical way to define these objects is to work backward through the process from the user's perspective. That is, a user will select a product category to see a filtered list of subcategories. After he or she selects a subcategory, the report will be filtered, based on the subcategory selection. To design this, you would add the subcategory filtering to the main dataset query and then create the filtered subcategory query and corresponding parameter. Finally, you would define the category query and parameter.

Following is an example of a query that would be used to generate the dropdown list items for the Subcategory parameter:

```
SELECT     ProductSubcategoryKey, EnglishProductSubcategoryName
FROM       DimProductSubcategory
WHERE      ProductCategoryKey = @CatKey
ORDER BY   EnglishProductSubcategoryName
```

Note the @CatKey query parameter used to filter product subcategory records in the query for a selected product category. This is tied to the CatKey report parameter used to return a selected product category from the following dataset query:

```
SELECT     ProductCategoryKey, EnglishProductCategoryName
FROM       DimProductCategory
ORDER BY   EnglishProductCategoryName
```

The cascading effect is automatic as long as the parameters are arranged in the logical order of their dependency. In this case, the user must select a product category first. After the category selection, a filtered list of subcategories is presented in the next dropdown list. After selecting a product subcategory, the report will run with data filtered by the selected subcategory. Parameters are ordered in the Report Data pane, located on the left side of the report designer. To change the parameter order, just select a parameter and move it up or down using the arrow buttons in the toolbar.

Report Parameters

In addition to report parameters derived from dataset parameters, you can explicitly add report parameters of your own. These report parameters (that do not have corresponding query parameters) can be added to support additional report functionality, such as hiding and showing report sections, page numbers, and dynamic formatting.

Several of our recipes utilize report parameters to extend report capabilities and create a dynamic user experience. Report parameters can be used to pass values into expressions and set property values. A report action can be used to modify a parameter value and pass it back to the same report. Report parameters used in conjunction with expressions and custom code are a powerful combination and can be used in very creative ways.

EXPRESSIONS AND CUSTOM CODE

Any textbox bound to a dataset field or built-in field actually contains an expression. You can build simple composite expressions in a textbox by dragging items from the Report Data pane into the textbox. For example, if you want to display the page number and total number of report pages in the page footer, insert a textbox into the page footer and then drag the `PageNumber` built-in field from the Report Data pane into the textbox. Place the cursor at the end of this text, hit the space bar, type the word "**of,**" hit the space bar, and then drag the `TotalPages` built-in field to the end of the text.

This produces an expression that appears like this in the Report Designer:

```
[&PageNumber] of [&TotalPages]
```

After the cursor leaves the textbox, the Report Designer displays the following non-descriptive label in gray:

```
<<Expr>>
```

To view or modify the actual expression in the textbox, right-click and choose Expression from the menu. This opens the Expression Builder dialog to reveal the Visual Basic expression code. The expression built by doing the drag-and-drop thing in the Designer is really just a simplified shorthand representation of this VB expression that Reporting Services stores in the RDL file:

```
="Page " & Globals!PageNumber & " of " & Globals!TotalPages
```

In addition to the Designer's drag-and-drop expressions and the Expression Editor's expression syntax differences, the built-in fields in the Report Data pane are referred to as members of the Globals collection within true report expressions. The term *built-in fields* is just a friendly term and not a syntax convention.

Expressions are used to create dynamic values based on a variety of built-in fields, dataset fields, and programming functions. Expressions can be used to set most property values based on a variety of conditions, parameters, field values, and calculations. You have two different ways to enter the expression. One method is to select and paste items from the object tree and member lists. You can either double-click an item or click Paste to add items to the expression. The other method is to simply type text into the expression text area. This uses the IntelliSense Auto List Members feature to provide dropdown lists for known items and properties.

The term *globals* (or *built-in fields*) applies to a set of variables built into Reporting Services that provide useful information like page numbers. You can find a list of available global variables, fields, and parameters in the Expression Builder.

Calculated Fields

Custom fields can be added to any report and can include expressions, calculations, and text manipulation. This might be similar in functionality to alias columns in a query or view, but the calculation or expression is performed on the Report Server after data has been retrieved from the database. Calculated field expressions can also use Reporting Services global variables and functions that may not be available in a SQL expression.

In the Fields page of the Dataset Properties dialog, click the Add button to add a new item to the Fields collection. Type the new field name, and then click the expression button (*fx*) next to the Field Source box on this new row. When the Expression dialog opens, simply type or build the same expression as before.

Using the calculated field is no different from using any other field derived from the dataset query. Just drag and drop the new field from the Report Data pane to the textbox on the report. You can use the expression button to invoke the Expression Builder to use any functionality available within the design environment in addition to the database fields exposed by the dataset query. These calculations will be performed on the Report Server rather than on the database server.

Conditional Expressions

Nearly all report and report item properties may be replaced with an expression. Exceptions are properties related to object size and placement, which can only be set at design time. The following example is used to modify the `Color` property for a textbox in the detail row of a table. By setting this property to an expression containing conditional logic instead of set to a value, the color of the text dynamically changes depending on the value of these two fields.

```
=IIF(Fields!Quantity.Value < Fields!ReorderPoint.Value, "Red", "Black")
```

In several of the recipes, you will see examples that modify the `Hidden` property of different objects. Because report items and data regions are only executed in the rendered report if they are visible, setting the `Hidden` property to `True` essentially removes it from the report. The report execution and rendering engine is smart enough not to execute a dataset if it is not referenced from a visible data region. Therefore, you can build entire data regions and report sections and then conditionally hide them based upon parameters and other conditional expressions.

The expression language for Reporting Services is Visual Basic .NET, which also supports many of the old-style VBScript and VB 6.0 functions. This means that there may be more than one way to perform the same action. The following table contains a few Visual Basic functions that may prove to be useful in basic report expressions:

FUNCTION	DESCRIPTION	EXAMPLE
FORMAT()	Returns a string value formatted using a regular expression format code or pattern. Similar to the Format property but can be concatenated with other string values.	=FORMAT(Fields!TheDate.Value, "mm/dd/yy")
MID() LEFT() RIGHT()	Returns a specified number of characters from a specified position [if using MID()] and for a specific length. You can also use the .SUBSTRING() method.	=MID(Fields!TheString.Value, 3, 5) =LEFT(Fields!TheString.Value, 5) = Fields!TheString.Value.SUBSTRING(2, 5)
INSTR()	Returns an integer for the first character position of one string within another string. Often used with MID() or SUBSTRING() to parse strings.	=INSTR(Fields!TheString.Value, ",")
CSTR()	Converts any value to a string type. Consider using the newer TOSTRING() method.	=CSTR(Fields!TheNumber.Value) =Fields!TheNumber.Value.TOSTRING()
CDATE() CINT() CDEC() ...	Type conversion function similar to CSTR (). Used to convert any compatible value to an explicit data type. Consider using the newer CTYPE() function to convert to an explicit type.	=CDATE(Fields!TheString.Value) =CTYPE(Fields!TheString.Value, Date)
ISNOTHING()	Tests an expression for a null value. May be nested within an IIF() to converts nulls to another value.	=ISNOTHING(Fields!TheDate.Value) =IIF(ISNOTHING(Fields!TheDate.Value), "n/a", Fields!TheDate.Value)
CHOOSE()	Returns one of a list of values based on a provided integer index value (1, 2, 3, and so on).	=CHOOSE(Parameters!FontSize.Value, "8pt" , "10pt", "12pt", "14pt")

Hundreds of Visual Basic functions can be used in some form, so this list is just a starting point. For additional assistance, view the Online Help index in Visual Studio, under Functions [Visual Basic]. This information is also available in the public MSDN library at `http://msdn.Microsoft.com`.

Using Custom Code

When you need to process more complex expressions, it may be difficult to build all the logic into one expression. In such cases, you can write your own function to handle different conditions and call it from a property expression.

Two different approaches exist for managing custom code. One is to write a block of code to define functions that are embedded into the report definition. This technique is simple, but the code will be available only to that report. The second technique is to write a custom class library compiled to an external .NET assembly, and reference this from any report on your Report Server. This approach has the advantage of sharing a central repository of code, which makes updates to the code easier to manage. The downside of this approach is that the configuration and initial deployment are a bit tedious.

Using Custom Code in a Report

A report can contain embedded Visual Basic .NET code that defines a function you can call from property expressions. The Code Editor window is very simple and doesn't include any editing or formatting capabilities. For this reason, you might want to write the code in a separate Visual Studio project to test and debug it before you place it into the report. When you are ready to add code, open the Report Properties dialog. You can do this from the Report menu. The other method starts from the Report Designer right-click menu. Right-click the Report Designer outside of the report body and select Properties. On the Properties window, switch to the Code tab, and write or paste your code in the Custom Code box.

The following example starts with a new report. Here is the code along with the expressions that you will need to create a simple example report on your own. The following Visual Basic function accepts a phone number or Social Security Number (SSN) in a variety of formats and outputs a standard U.S. phone number and properly formatted SSN. The `Value` argument accepts the value, and the `Format` argument accepts the values Phone or SSN. You're only going to use it with phone numbers, so you can leave the SSN branch out if you wish.

```
'***************************************************************
'    Returns properly formatted Phone Number or SSN
'    based on Format & length of Value argument.
'    PT
'***************************************************************
Public Function CustomFormat(Value as String, Format as String) _
  as String
       Select Case Format
       Case "Phone"
            Select Case Value.Length
            Case 7
                Return Value.SubString(0, 3) & "-" _
                    & Value.SubString(3, 4)
            Case 10
                Return "(" & Value.SubString(0, 3) & ") " _
```

```
                    & Value.SubString(3, 3) _
                    & "-" & Value.SubString(6, 4)
            Case 12
                Return "(" & Value.SubString(0, 3) & ") " _
                    & Value.SubString(4, 3) & "-" _
                    & Value.SubString(8, 4)
            Case Else
                Return Value
            End Select
        Case "SSN"
            If Value.Length = 9 Then
                Return Value.SubString(0, 3) & "-" _
                    & Value.SubString(3, 2) & "-" _
                    & Value.SubString(5, 4)
            Else
                Return Value
            End If
        Case Else
            Return Value
        End Select
    End Function
```

This function is called in an expression for the `Value` property of a textbox. For example, in a table, the Phone column uses an expression that calls the custom function preceded by a reference to the `Code` object:

```
=Code.CustomFormat(Fields!Phone.Value, "Phone")
```

Using a Custom Assembly

Rather than embedding code directly into each report, using a custom assembly can be a central repository of reusable code to extend the functionality of multiple reports. In Reporting Services, custom assembly support is enabled by default. However, the code in the assembly will have restricted access to system resources. If you intend for the assembly to interact with the file system or perform data access, you will need to modify some configuration settings in order to grant the appropriate level of access to your code. We discuss these conditions after a simple walk-through to create an assembly that won't require any special settings.

To begin, create a class module project. You can write this code in any .NET language because it's going to be built into an assembly. The methods you create can be either static or instanced. It's a little easier to use static methods so that you don't have to manage the instancing and life of each object. This simply means that you will declare public functions in your class using the `Static` keyword in C# or the `Shared` keyword in Visual Basic. Using the same code logic as in the previous example, the Visual Basic class code would look like this:

```
Public Class Report_Formats
    '**************************************************************
    '      Returns properly formatted Phone Number or SSN
    '      based on Format arg & length of Value arg
    '      PT
    '**************************************************************
    Public Shared Function CustomFormat(Value as String _
                                , Format as String) as String
```

```
        Select Case Format
        Case "Phone"
            Select Case Value.Length
            Case 7
                Return Value.SubString(0, 3) & "-" _
                        & Value.SubString(3, 4)
            Case 10
                Return "(" & Value.SubString(0, 3) & ") " _
                        & Value.SubString(3, 3) _
                        & "-" & Value.SubString(6, 4)
            Case 12
                Return "(" & Value.SubString(0, 3) & ") " _
                        & Value.SubString(4, 3) & "-" _
                        & Value.SubString(8, 4)
            Case Else
                Return Value
            End Select
        Case "SSN"
            If Value.Length = 9 Then
                Return Value.SubString(0, 3) & "-" _
                        & Value.SubString(3, 2) & "-" _
                        & Value.SubString(5, 4)
            Else
                Return Value
            End If
        Case Else
            Return Value
        End Select
    End Function
End Class
```

After debugging and testing the code, save and build the class library project in Release configuration, and then copy the assembly (DLL) file to the ReportServer\bin folder. The default path to this folder is C:\Program Files\Microsoft SQL Server\MSRS10.MSSQLSERVER\Reporting Services\ReportServer\bin.

In the Report Properties dialog (this is where you entered the code in the previous example), select the References page, and add the reference by browsing to the assembly file. The reference line shows metadata from the assembly, including the version number.

To use a custom method in an expression, reference the namespace, class, and method using standard code syntax. The expression for the CustomFormat method should look like this:

```
=Reporting_Component.Report_Formats.CustomFormat(Fields!Phone.Value
, "Phone")
```

FORMATTING REPORT DATA

Nearly as important as the data displayed on the report are the layout and the visual elements that make the data readable. For reports to be functional, data must be presented in a format that makes sense to the user and conforms to a standard that is both readable and visually appealing. Reports can be static in design, or certain elements can be set to dynamically adapt to user requests. Report elements can be designed to change or to appear only under specific conditions.

All formatting features are based on property settings. Static formatting involves the use of several properties, such as background color to apply shading, the font, font size, weight, style, foreground color, and borders.

In Report Builder 2.0 and 3.0, formatting properties are applied to selected items using the Format ribbon. In Business Intelligence Development Studio, formatting can be applied using the Report Format toolbar.

Background colors, font sizes, weights, and borders are added using either the formatting options on the Report Builder 2.0 Home ribbon or the Report Formatting toolbar in BIDS. The ribbon and toolbar buttons are used to set properties that can also be changed using the Properties window.

Introduction to Dynamic Formatting

You've seen how a report can be formatted using simple features and properties. Totals can be added to groups; sections can be made to expand or collapse using drill-down toggle items; values can be formatted; and areas of the report can be dressed up using borders, shading, font sizes, weights, and colors.

Expressions are the heart and soul of dynamic reports. You can design simple reports without special coding, but if you want to take your reports to the next level, you'll need to know some simple programming. Chapters 8 and 10 in the *Professional* series book demonstrate how to use expressions to incorporate more advanced report design techniques.

As the reports grow and evolve in a business, often different reports are just variations of other reports. You can define unique behaviors, such as dynamic sorting, filtering, or visual subsets of report data, by using a single report to include all the features, and then using expressions to modify the report's behavior and to enable or disable certain features.

An example is a table report designed for use by two different groups of users. A parameter is used to indicate whether the report should display retail or wholesale sales information. Using dynamic formatting expressions to hide and show relevant report items and to modify grouping, sorting, and field mapping expressions, you can create one report to meet the reporting requirements for multiple users.

Designing Multicolumn Reports

Tabular reports can be designed to display continuous data in snaking columns. To create a multicolumn report, add a table to the report body that occupies a fraction of the report width, allowing for column margin spacing. The `Columns` and `ColumnSpacing` properties are set for the `Report` object in the Properties window. For example, a report with two columns should contain a table that is less than one-half of the report width plus the `ColumnSpacing`. Use the following formula to calculate the width of a multicolumn report:

```
Report Width = (Body Width x # Columns) + (ColumnSpacing x # Margins between
    columns) + Left Margin + Right Margin
```

SUMMARY

You should already be familiar with the main concepts and techniques demonstrated in these introductory chapters. The purpose of this brief introduction was to provide a simple reference for the building blocks of report design.

This chapter reviewed the fundamental report design building blocks. The Tablix data region component is used to create table, matrix, and list reports with groups, aggregate summaries, and details from a dataset. We reviewed the use of expressions and custom code in a report. If you are comfortable with the concepts and techniques presented in Chapters 2 and 3, you should be prepared to apply the design patterns in the recipes presented in the rest of the book. For detailed instructions and tutorials on the techniques briefly reviewed, see *Professional SQL Server 2008 Reporting Services* (Wrox, 2008).

PART I
Columnar and Grouped Reports

- ▶ Green Bar Reports

- ▶ Alternate Background Shading for Table Groups

- ▶ Nested Group Green Bar Effect

- ▶ Creating Dynamic Groups

- ▶ Hiding and Showing Columns in a Table

- ▶ Horizontal Table

- ▶ Resetting the Page Number Based on Groups

GREEN BAR REPORTS

When you're dealing with large amounts of detailed information in a tabular report, it can be easy to lose track of the line you are reviewing. A common approach to enhance the readability of the report is to add a visual clue to differentiate one row from the next. This is typically accomplished by alternating the background color, or shading, of each row. Reports of this type are commonly referred to as *green bar* reports.

The concept of the green bar report has been around for quite some time. It originated many years ago when impact and dot-matrix printers would output line after line of data to stock, pin-fed paper that had alternating green and white stripes.

Green bar reports help you read detailed information quickly and accurately. And although those impact and dot-matrix printers are mostly a thing of the past, the need to present detailed information using the green bar style still exists with the electronic reports of today.

This recipe provides you with detailed instructions for applying the green bar effect to your Reporting Services reports.

Product Versions

➤   Reporting Services 2000

➤   Reporting Services 2005

➤   Reporting Services 2008

What You'll Need

➤   Report Builder or Business Intelligence Development Studio

➤   AdventureWorksDW sample database (2005 or 2008)

➤   A tabular report

➤   An understanding of expressions in Reporting Services

Designing the Report

This recipe demonstrates the concepts required for a green bar report. You will create a report using Report Builder 2.0 that displays the detail for a particular sales order from the AdventureWorksDW database. You will then modify the behavior of the report so that every other line is displayed with a shaded background. Figure P1-1 shows an example of the finished report.

While there are many different approaches to achieve this behavior, the basic pattern is to create a table-based report and apply an expression to the background color property of the detail row, altering the background color based on the current execution context.

1.   Start by creating a new, blank report using Report Builder 2.0.

2.   Design a new data source based on the Microsoft SQL Server provider that connects to either the AdventureWorksDW or AdventureWorksDW2008 sample database.

3.   Add a new dataset associated with this data source.

4. Construct the following query using the query designer or by entering the query as text into the query editor.

```
SELECT
    Sales.SalesOrderNumber
    ,Sales.SalesOrderLineNumber AS LineNumber
    ,Sales.OrderQuantity
    ,Sales.UnitPrice
    ,Sales.SalesAmount
    ,Sales.TaxAmt
    ,Sales.Freight
    ,Product.ProductAlternateKey AS ProductCode
FROM
    dbo.FactResellerSales AS Sales
    INNER JOIN dbo.DimProduct AS Product
        ON Product.ProductKey = Sales.ProductKey
WHERE
    Sales.SalesOrderNumber = 'SO43902'
ORDER BY
    Sales.SalesOrderLineNumber ASC
```

5. Execute the query to ensure there are no errors.

6. Click OK until you return to the report design surface.

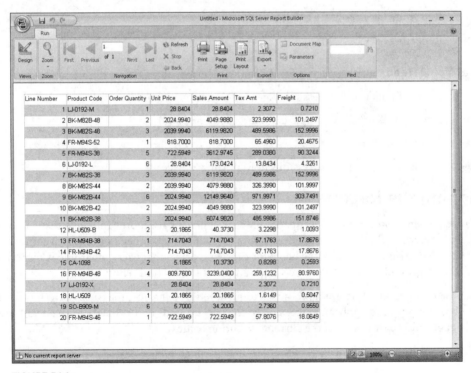

FIGURE P1-1

This query returns the sales order detail for a single sales order, SO43902. With the data source complete, it is now time to focus on the presentation. This will consist of a simple report that displays each of the sales order detail lines in a table.

1. Insert a Table data region to the body of the report design surface. This creates a simple table layout comprised of one header row, one data row, and three columns.

2. From the Report Data window, drag the LineNumber field to the first column of the data row in the table.

3. Repeat this process for the remaining fields in the dataset, placing the fields in the following order: LineNumber, ProductCode, OrderQuantity, UnitPrice, SalesAmount, TaxAmt, and Freight. When complete, the report design surface should appear as displayed in Figure P1-2.

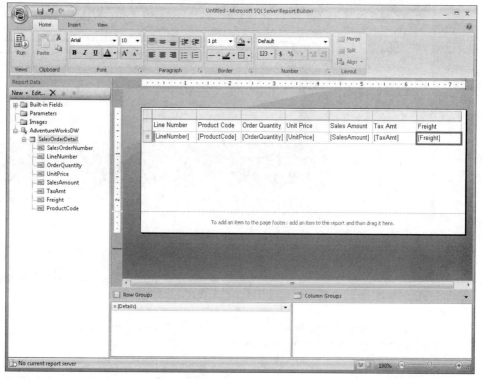

FIGURE P1-2

Run the report and review the results, which you saw in Figure P1-1. Notice how the data becomes difficult to read and follow as you move across the page. When trying to correlate a specific value from a column on the right side of the page, you may find yourself using your finger or mouse to trace the row back to the Line Number or Product Code on the left side of the page — I know I do. You may witness a similar behavior with a printed version of the report, where a ruler or some other straight edge is typically used.

In the following steps, you will make the report easier to read by adding the green bar effect to the sales order detail.

1. Return to design mode and highlight the detail row. Be sure to highlight the entire detail row and not just a single cell within the table. This is demonstrated in Figure P1-3.

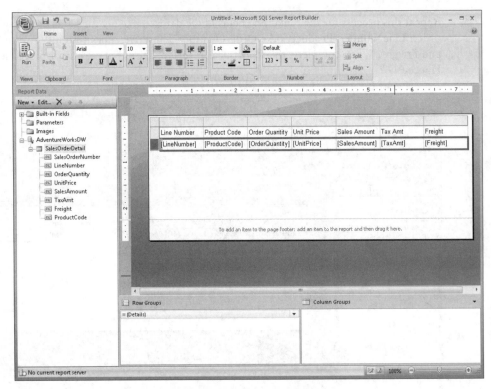

FIGURE P1-3

2. Using the Properties window, locate and select the BackgroundColor property for the detail row. Notice the current value is No Color.

The default value for the BackgroundColor property is No Color, which actually translates to the named color reference Transparent. Using the Properties window, you can change this value to be any other named color reference, RGB (Red, Green, and Blue), or HSB (Hue, Saturation, and Brightness) color value. However, simply changing the value from No Color to Red, for example, changes the background color for every detail row in the table, which is not the desired result.

In addition to a fixed color value, the BackgroundColor property can also be set using an expression. Simple or complex logic can be applied within the expression in order to determine the appropriate color value. And since the expression is evaluated for each detail row in the report, you can exploit this functionality to toggle the background color and create the green bar effect.

Applying this concept to the report, the background color should be shaded for every other detail row. That is, every odd row should be one color and every even row should be another color.

The Visual Basic IIf function, which is short for "Immediate If," can be used to achieve this:

```
=IIf(Expression As Boolen, TruePart As Object, FalsePart As Object)
```

The IIf function provides if-then-else functionality encapsulated within a single function call. The IIf function accepts three parameters. The first parameter, Expression, can be any simple or complex expression that evaluates to a Boolean value of True or False. The next parameter, TruePart, is the value to be used when Expression evaluates to True. Finally, the last parameter, FalsePart, is the value to use when Expression evaluates to False.

For this recipe, the expression should evaluate to True for odd rows and False for even rows. Likewise, the TruePart should indicate the background color for odd-numbered rows and the FalsePart indicates the background color for even-numbered rows.

The following expression uses the IIf function to return the color value Gainsboro (a light grey) if the row number is odd; otherwise it returns the color value Transparent (No Color):

```
=IIf((RowNumber(Nothing) MOD 2) = 1,
"Gainsboro", "Transparent")
```

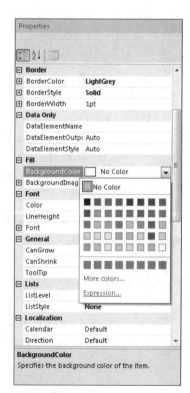

The RowNumber function and modulo operator, MOD, are used to determine if the current row is an even or odd. The RowNumber function returns the running count of the number of rows in the dataset. The modulo operator, which divides two numbers and returns the remainder, can then be used to determine if the result returned by the RowNumber function is an odd or even number.

Armed with this information, you are now ready to modify the background color to achieve the green bar effect on your report.

3. With the BackgroundColor selected in the Properties window, click the dropdown button to display the color selection window.

4. Click the Expression link at the bottom of the color selection window, as demonstrated in Figure P1-4, to open the Expression Editor.

FIGURE P1-4

5. As shown in Figure P1-5, enter the following expression using the expression editor:

```
=IIf((RowNumber(Nothing) MOD 2) = 1, "Gainsboro", "Transparent").
```

FIGURE P1-5

6. Click OK to accept the change and return to the Properties window.

7. Run the report to review the results shown in Figure P1-6. You can use the Line Number field in the first column to verify the behavior is as expected. Notice that it is much easier to follow the information on each row as you read across the page from Line Number to Freight.

Alternate Row Colors in an SSRS 2000 or 2005 Matrix

The previous technique works with the newer tablix-style matrix in SSRS 2008, but the matrix data region in SSRS 2000 and 2005 doesn't support the RowNumber function so it requires a different approach. This can be accomplished by using a simple embedded custom code function in the report.

1. Open the Report Properties dialog and create a Visual Basic.NET function in the code page by entering the following code:

```
Private bOddRow As Boolean

Function AlternateColor (ByVal OddColor As String, ByVal EvenColor As String, _
                         ByVal Toggle As Boolean) As String
    If Toggle Then bOddRow = Not bOddRow
```

```
    If bOddRow Then
        Return OddColor
    Else
        Return EvenColor
    End If
End Function
```

This function takes three arguments: the name or numeric string for the odd color rows, the name or numeric string for the even color rows, and a Boolean (for instance, True or False) flag used to switch between odd and even row modes. This function is called in an expression for the BackgroundColor property for every detail cell in the matrix and at least one row header cell.

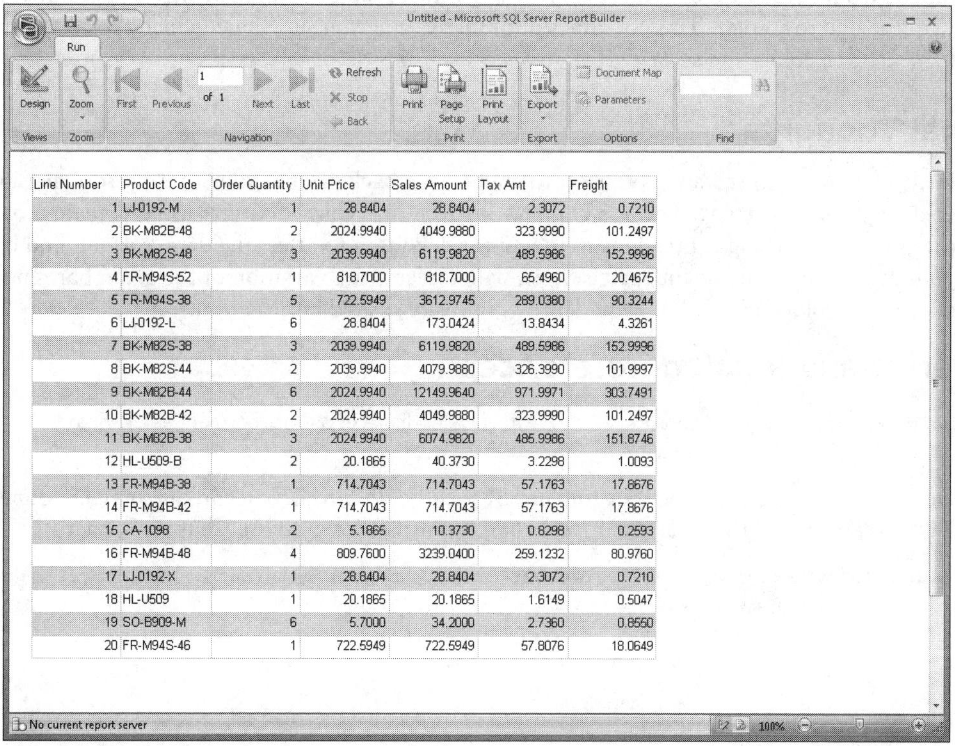

Line Number	Product Code	Order Quantity	Unit Price	Sales Amount	Tax Amt	Freight
1	LJ-0192-M	1	28.8404	28.8404	2.3072	0.7210
2	BK-M82B-48	2	2024.9940	4049.9880	323.9990	101.2497
3	BK-M82S-48	3	2039.9940	6119.9820	489.5986	152.9996
4	FR-M94S-52	1	818.7000	818.7000	65.4960	20.4675
5	FR-M94S-38	5	722.5949	3612.9745	289.0380	90.3244
6	LJ-0192-L	6	28.8404	173.0424	13.8434	4.3261
7	BK-M82S-38	3	2039.9940	6119.9820	489.5986	152.9996
8	BK-M82S-44	2	2039.9940	4079.9880	326.3990	101.9997
9	BK-M82B-44	6	2024.9940	12149.9640	971.9971	303.7491
10	BK-M82B-42	2	2024.9940	4049.9880	323.9990	101.2497
11	BK-M82B-38	3	2024.9940	6074.9820	485.9986	151.8746
12	HL-U509-B	2	20.1865	40.3730	3.2298	1.0093
13	FR-M94B-38	1	714.7043	714.7043	57.1763	17.8676
14	FR-M94B-42	1	714.7043	714.7043	57.1763	17.8676
15	CA-1098	2	5.1865	10.3730	0.8298	0.2593
16	FR-M94B-48	4	809.7600	3239.0400	259.1232	80.9760
17	LJ-0192-X	1	28.8404	28.8404	2.3072	0.7210
18	HL-U509	1	20.1865	20.1865	1.6149	0.5047
19	SO-B909-M	6	5.7000	34.2000	2.7360	0.8550
20	FR-M94S-46	1	722.5949	722.5949	57.8076	18.0649

FIGURE P1-6

2. For the group value that will be used to alternate row colors, edit that row group cell textbox properties and use the following expression for the BackgroundColor property.

```
=Code.AlternateColor("AliceBlue", "White", True)
```

Of course, you can use whatever colors you want for the odd and even background colors. These can either be standard web color names, like those you see in the SSRS color property list, or a six-character hexadecimal color value preceded by a pound sign.

3. For each cell textbox in the data region of the matrix, enter the same expression for the BackgroundColor property, only change the third argument to `False`:

```
=Code.AlternateColor("AliceBlue", "White", True)
```

That's it. When you run the report, the background color will change every time the group value changes.

How does it work? The matrix is rendered like a typewriter (for those of you born after the dawn of the Information Age, that's a device we used to use to fill out forms and send text messages). The cells are rendered from top to bottom and from left to right; returning to the left-most cell on the next row after it's done with the row above. When the renderer encounters a new group value, it creates a new instance of the row group cell which toggles the private `bOdd` Boolean variable. On the first row, it gets flipped from `False` to `True` (you're on row #1, which is an odd number.) Each cell on that row gets set with the odd row color. This continues until there's a new group value, which flips `bOdd` to `False` (row #2 is an even color) and so on.

Final Thoughts

In this recipe, you used an expression to control the background color of each row in a table and create a green bar report. This is a common pattern that you will utilize as you create more sophisticated reports — using expressions in the report definition to affect the data, format, and behavior of your report. In a subsequent exercise, you will implement a variation of the green bar report in which alternating colors are used to help identify groups of related information.

Credits and Related References

MDSN: Report Design Tips and Tricks (http://msdn.microsoft.com/en-us/library/bb395166(SQL.90).aspx)

Detailed step-by-step instructions for the SSRS 2000/2005 Matrix technique may be found in: *Professional SQL Server 2005 Reporting Services* (Wrox, 2006), Chapter 7, pages 272-277.

Paul Turley's blog: http://www.sqlserverbiblog.com/post/Alternate-Row-Colors-in-an-SSRS-2000-or-2005-Matrix.aspx

ALTERNATE BACKGROUND SHADING FOR TABLE GROUPS

Displaying every other row with an alternating background color can help the reader follow the contents of a tabular report, but sometimes it may be more important to differentiate between groups of data rather than just the rows. This variation of the green bar report creates bands of rows with alternating colors by group level. This technique displays all of the cells for every other grouped value in a different color.

Product Versions

➤ Reporting Services 2000

➤ Reporting Services 2005

➤ Reporting Services 2008

What You'll Need

➤ A grouped table

➤ An inline expression to set the `BackgroundColor` property for textbox cells in the table

Designing the Report

This example uses the AdventureWorksDW or AdventureWorksDW2008 sample database and a simple grouped query to return the product category, subcategory, and aggregated business measure. The first example uses the Reporting Services 2008 designer, with an example of the Reporting Services 2005 designer at the end. The final result of this recipe is shown in Figure P1-7.

1. Start by designing a data source for the AdventureWorksDW or AdventureWorksDW2008 sample databases.

2. Add a new blank report named Alternate Background Shading.rdl to your project.

3. Create a dataset query to include the FactResellerSales, DimProduct, DimProductSubcategory, and DimProductCategory tables.

```
SELECT
    DimProductCategory.EnglishProductCategoryName AS Category,
    DimProductSubcategory.EnglishProductSubcategoryName AS Subcategory,
    SUM(FactResellerSales.OrderQuantity) AS Qty
FROM
    DimProduct INNER JOIN DimProductSubcategory
      ON DimProduct.ProductSubcategoryKey
      = DimProductSubcategory.ProductSubcategoryKey
    INNER JOIN DimProductCategory
      ON DimProductSubcategory.ProductCategoryKey
      = DimProductCategory.ProductCategoryKey
    INNER JOIN FactResellerSales
      ON DimProduct.ProductKey = FactResellerSales.ProductKey
```

```
GROUP BY
    DimProductCategory.EnglishProductCategoryName,
    DimProductSubcategory.EnglishProductSubcategoryName
ORDER BY
    Category, Subcategory
```

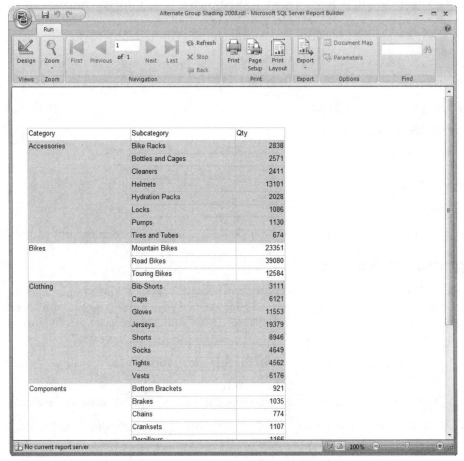

FIGURE P1-7

4. Add a table report item to the report body.

5. Drag the Category field into the Row Groups list above the Details row. This creates a row group header textbox for the Category field.

6. Drag the Subcategory and Qty fields to the second and third columns, respectively, in the Details row.

7. If you have an empty column at the end of your table, delete it.

The query is already grouped by Subcategory, so there is no need to define a group expression for the Details group.

This simple example uses the Category group for altering the background shading. In production, any group at any level within all the groups may be used for this purpose.

The report designer should look like Figure P1-8.

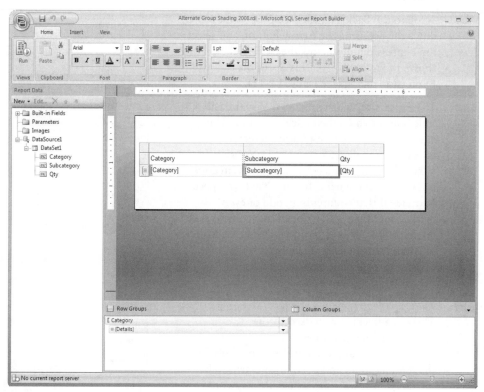

FIGURE P1-8

Note the name of the field used for grouping and to start a new background color. You will be referring to the field name and not the group name in the expression. In this example, they are both named Category.

8. Next, select all the cells in the row by clicking the row handle (Figure P1-9.)

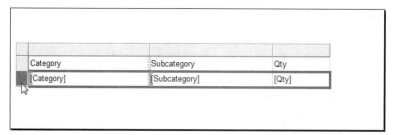

FIGURE P1-9

If you intend to alternate the background shading for the rows of a group below the top-level group defined in the table, you may want to exclude the parent group header cells in the selection.

Take a look at the properties window to see the common properties for all selected textboxes.

9. Scroll to the BackgroundColor property, drop down the list using the Arrow button, and select the Expression link below the color picker, shown in Figure P1-10. This opens the Expression dialog (see Figure P1-11).

The expression calls two nested Visual Basic functions and a mathematical operator. The RunningValue function returns an incremental integer for the distinct count of Category field values. This means that for each new Category, this counter increments by one. Next, you need to decide if that counter is an odd or even number and then assign one of two colors based on that result. This is performed using the MOD or Modulus operator, which returns the divisional remainder of two numbers. If the MOD of a counter divided by 2 returns 1, the counter is an odd number.

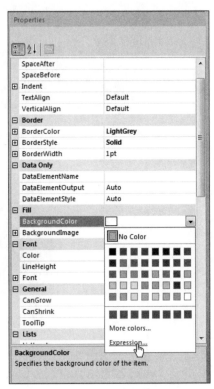

FIGURE P1-10

Three arguments are passed to the RunningValue function: the field value expression, the aggregate function to apply for the running total, and a scope argument to limit the range of rows. In this case, the keyword Nothing or the name of the dataset will apply the function to all rows returned by the dataset query. The IIF or immediate IF function is used to make a decision based on the outcome of the first statement and return the appropriate color value. Essentially, this expression can be translated to read "If the distinct count of unique Category field values is 1 (and is therefore an odd number), return the color "Gainsboro"; otherwise return the color "white." The following expression achieves this goal:

```
=IIF(RunningValue(Fields!Category.Value, CountDistinct, Nothing) MOD 2 = 1,
    "Gainsboro", "White")
```

10. Type this code as one line without carriage returns into the Expression window. Use the code completion, color coding, and parentheses-matching IntelliSense features to validate this expression, as shown in Figure P1-11.

11. Click the OK button when complete.

12. Preview the report to test the results.

As you can see in Figure P1-12, rows in the table are now grouped with alternating background colors.

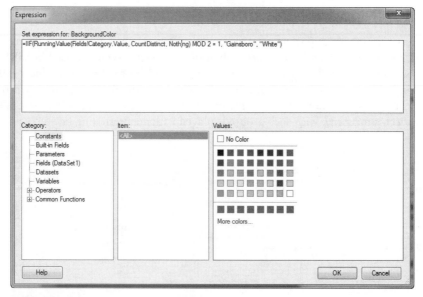

FIGURE P1-11

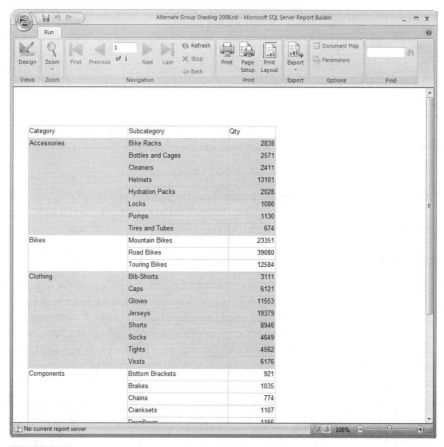

FIGURE P1-12

Designing the Report for Reporting Services 2005

In Reporting Services 2000 or 2005, the pattern is relatively the same. A grouped table in SSRS 2005 uses a separate row for the group header rather than the inline style typically used in SSRS 2008. Selecting the row in the report designer using the row handle selects the TableRow object rather than a collection of individual textboxes (see Figure P1-13). Simply set the BackgroundColor property for both the group header and/or footer row and the detail row to the same expression used in the 2008 example. The effect is the same, with each group displayed with an alternating background color.

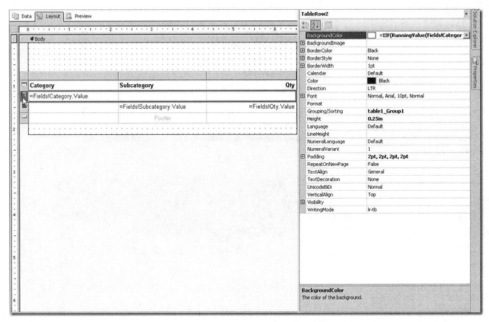

FIGURE P1-13

Many additional enhancements are possible by applying the same or similar expression to modify other visual elements. For example, you could separate the gray detail rows with a white border and the white rows with a gray border by setting the bottom border color for the detail row cells.

Final Thoughts

Aesthetic report design is more than just a matter of style and artistry. When all the reports in an organization are laid out in a regular and predictable manner, users are far less likely to misread data, making mistakes and bad decisions which could have costly effects. This is one of a few simple techniques that can make a big difference with little effort. The appropriate use of fonts, character size and weight, borders and colors are important design considerations not only to make reports simply look better but to make them more useful, people-friendly and to promote an image of professionalism and uniformity across your organization.

Publish report templates and samples of different standard report styles for your report designers to use when modeling new reports. Involve someone with a formal background in graphic design when defining these standards and carefully consider elements like on-screen and print report use, color-blind and sight-impaired users, black-and-white print and page size restrictions, margins for printer gripper space, punch holes and bindings.

Credits and Related References

A similar technique is demonstrated on Chris Hays' blog titled *Greenbar Matrix*, located at:
`http://blogs.msdn.com/chrishays/archive/2004/08/30/GreenBarMatrix.aspx`

NESTED GROUP GREEN BAR EFFECT

The green bar effect in reports originated long ago when data was typically printed on green bar paper (alternating green and white lines) by line printers. The visual effect made it easier to read a line of data within a long list.

The green bar effect is still popular for reports today, even though the color choices are not necessarily restricted to green and white.

This recipe is about demonstrating a technique applicable to nested groups in a table or matrix, where you want to ensure that the green bar effect continues across disparate row group instances. The implementation of this utilizes the new feature of read-write report variables in Reporting Services 2008 R2. The recipe works the same way for table and matrix layouts.

Product Versions

➤ Reporting Services 2008 R2

What You'll Need

➤ AdventureWorks2008 sample database

Designing the Report

This example uses the AdventureWorks2008 sample database and a grouped query to return detailed information about all products available in a product catalog. The final result of this recipe is shown in Figure P1-14. Note the consistent green bar effect across multiple nested subcategory groups in the table.

Category	Subcategory	Product Number	Product	Description	List Price
Accessories	Bike Racks	RA-H123	Hitch Rack - 4-Bike	Carries 4 bikes securely; steel construction, fits 2" receiver hitch.	$120.00
	Bike Stands	ST-1401	All-Purpose Bike Stand	Perfect all-purpose bike stand for working on your bike at home. Quick-adjusting clamps and steel construction.	$159.00
	Bottles and Cages	BC-M005	Mountain Bottle Cage	Tough aluminum cage holds bottle securly on tough terrain.	$9.99
		BC-R205	Road Bottle Cage	Aluminum cage is lighter than our mountain version; perfect for long distance trips.	$8.99
		WB-H098	Water Bottle - 30 oz.	AWC logo water bottle - holds 30 oz; leak-proof.	$4.99
	Cleaners	CL-9009	Bike Wash - Dissolver	Washes off the toughest road grime; dissolves grease, environmentally safe. 1-liter bottle.	$7.95
	Fenders	FE-6654	Fender Set - Mountain	Clip-on fenders fit most mountain bikes.	$21.98

FIGURE P1-14

1. Start by designing a data source for the AdventureWorks2008 sample database.

2. Create a new dataset named ProductCatalog with a query that returns product sales information by product category and subcategory, as well as by quarter and year.

```
SELECT
    PC.Name AS Category, PS.Name AS Subcategory, PM.Name AS Model,
    PD.Description, PP.LargePhoto, PP.LargePhotoFileName, P.Name AS Product,
    P.ProductNumber, P.Color, P.Size, P.Weight, P.StandardCost,
    P.Style, P.Class, P.ListPrice
FROM Production.Product P INNER JOIN
    Production.ProductSubcategory PS INNER JOIN
    Production.ProductCategory PC ON PS.ProductCategoryID = PC.ProductCategoryID
        ON P.ProductSubcategoryID = PS.ProductSubcategoryID INNER JOIN
    Production.ProductProductPhoto PPP ON P.ProductID = PPP.ProductID INNER JOIN
    Production.ProductPhoto PP
        ON PPP.ProductPhotoID = PP.ProductPhotoID LEFT OUTER JOIN
    Production.ProductDescription PD INNER JOIN
    Production.ProductModel PM INNER JOIN
    Production.ProductModelProductDescriptionCulture PMPDCL
        ON PM.ProductModelID = PMPDCL.ProductModelID
        ON PD.ProductDescriptionID = PMPDCL.ProductDescriptionID
        ON P.ProductModelID = PM.ProductModelID
WHERE (PMPDCL.CultureID = 'en')
```

3. Add a table using the Table wizard to display product details grouped by product category and subcategory.

a. Insert a new table from the Ribbon and use the Table wizard.

b. In Step 1 of the wizard, chose the ProductCatalog dataset.

c. In Step 2, group by the Category, Subcategory, and ProductNumber. Then add the following fields to the Values section as shown in Figure P1-15: Product, Description, ListPrice.

d. In Step 3, select a simple table layout by deselecting Show Subtotals and deselecting Expand/Collapse Groups.

e. Finish the wizard.

f. Adjust the table column widths to provide more room for the Description field.

g. Select the ListPrice column and apply currency formatting using the corresponding Ribbon button with the $ sign.

4. Add a writable report variable for the sequential group index calculation.

a. Right-click into the free space outside the report body area, and open the Report Properties dialog.

b. On the Variables page, create a new writeable (i.e., non read-only) report variable called GroupIndex and initialize it with =0, as shown in Figure P1-16.

This creates an overall counter, which you will sequentially increment in the next recipe step for each innermost group created for the ProductNumber group.

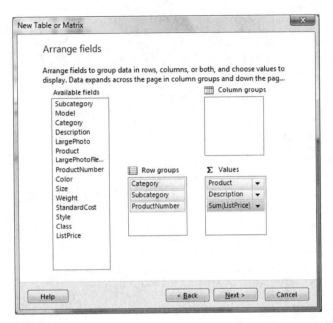

FIGURE P1-15

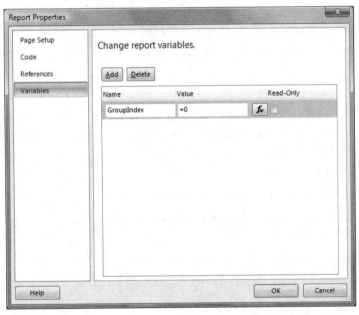

FIGURE P1-16

c. On the Code page, add the following custom Visual Basic code snippet to make the increment operation more convenient. Note that line breaks were added below for formatting reasons; when typing in this code, make sure to type the entire function declaration (the initial three lines) as one line without line breaks:

```
Public Function IncrementVariable(var As
Microsoft.ReportingServices.ReportProcessing.OnDemandReportObjectModel.
  Variable)
As Double
  var.Value = var.Value + 1
  return var.Value
End Function
```

5. Create a group variable on the innermost table group.

a. Select the table on the design surface. In the grouping pane under Row Groups, right-click on the ProductNumber group, and open the group properties.

b. On the Variables page, create a new group variable called BGColor, which you will use to calculate and store the background color for this particular group instance. This is accomplished by incrementing the overall group index counter and then calculating the background color based on whether the global group index counter value is even or odd. Define the BGColor group variable with the following calculation expression (also shown in Figure P1-17):

```
=iif(Code.IncrementVariable(Variables!GroupIndex) mod 2, "#e6eefc", "White")
```

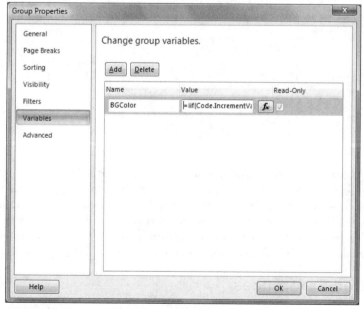

FIGURE P1-17

6. Set the background color of table row cells based on the calculated group variable BGColor.

   a. Select the textboxes that display ProductNumber, Product, Description, and ListPrice.

   b. In the Properties Window, set the BackgroundColor property based on the calculated group variable:

      ```
      =Variables!BGColor.Value
      ```

7. Preview the final report.

Figure P1-18 shows the final report with the green bar effect applied consistently across multiple levels of outer grouping hierarchies.

Category	Subcategory	Product Number	Product	Description	List Price
Accessories	Bike Racks	RA-H123	Hitch Rack - 4-Bike	Carries 4 bikes securely; steel construction, fits 2" receiver hitch.	$120.00
	Bike Stands	ST-1401	All-Purpose Bike Stand	Perfect all-purpose bike stand for working on your bike at home. Quick-adjusting clamps and steel construction.	$159.00
	Bottles and Cages	BC-M005	Mountain Bottle Cage	Tough aluminum cage holds bottle securly on tough terrain.	$9.99
		BC-R205	Road Bottle Cage	Aluminum cage is lighter than our mountain version; perfect for long distance trips.	$8.99
		WB-H098	Water Bottle - 30 oz.	AWC logo water bottle - holds 30 oz; leak-proof.	$4.99
	Cleaners	CL-9009	Bike Wash - Dissolver	Washes off the toughest road grime; dissolves grease, environmentally safe. 1-liter bottle.	$7.95
	Fenders	FE-6654	Fender Set - Mountain	Clip-on fenders fit most mountain bikes.	$21.98

FIGURE P1-18

Final Thoughts

Writable report variables are a new feature in Reporting Services 2008 R2. The lifetime, persistence, and session isolation of report variables is automatically managed by Reporting Services. You can assign any complex object that is *Serializable* to a report variable. This recipe shows a technique for using writable report variables in combination with group variables (already introduced in Reporting Services 2008) to create a green bar effect that continues across disparate inner nested groups in a table or matrix. This was very difficult to accomplish in previous releases of Reporting Services.

Credits and Related References

Documentation for more simple outer group or detail row green bar effects in earlier versions of Reporting Services is available on MSDN at `http://msdn.microsoft.com/en-us/library/ms156400.aspx`. For tables or matrices with one level of grouping, see blog postings such as Chris Hays' blog at `http://blogs.msdn.com/chrishays/archive/2004/08/30/GreenBarMatrix.aspx`.

CREATING DYNAMIC GROUPS

Groups help to organize data on a report or to calculate aggregate summaries. But allowing users to control the groups gives them the ability to organize the data to their liking. Rather than creating multiple reports with similar datasets grouped on different fields, dynamically grouped reports provide greater flexibility. Using this technique, one report can be used to do the job of multiple reports with different grouping criteria. This example shows how to create dynamic groups.

Product Versions

➤ Reporting Services 2000

➤ Reporting Services 2005

➤ Reporting Services 2008

What You'll Need

➤ A grouped matrix

➤ Parameters to indicate which field to group the data on

➤ An inline expression to set the Group On property of row and column groups to the selected parameter values

Designing the Report

This example uses the AdventureWorksDW for SQL Server 2005 or 2008 sample database and a simple query to return the product category, subcategory, product name, country, state, and sales amount. This example uses ReportBuilder 2.0. Figure P1-19 shows the finished report.

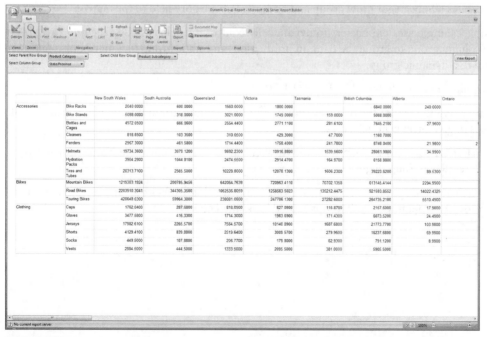

FIGURE P1-19

1. Start by designing a data source for the AdventureWorksDW or AdventureWorksDW2008 sample databases.

2. Enter the following code to create a dataset query that includes the FactInternetSales, DimProduct, DimProductSubcategory, DimProductCategory, DimCustomer, and DimGeography tables.

```
SELECT
PC.EnglishProductCategoryName AS Category
,PSC.EnglishProductSubcategoryName AS Subcategory
,P.EnglishProductName AS ProductName
,G.EnglishCountryRegionName AS Country
,G.StateProvinceName AS State
,FIS.SalesAmount
FROMdbo.FactInternetSales FIS
INNERJOINdbo.DimProduct P
ONFIS.ProductKey = P.ProductKey
INNERJOINdbo.DimProductSubcategory PSC
ONP.ProductSubcategoryKey = PSC.ProductSubcategoryKey
INNERJOINdbo.DimProductCategory PC
ONPSC.ProductCategoryKey = PC.ProductCategoryKey
INNER JOINdbo.DimCustomer C
ONFIS.CustomerKey = C.CustomerKey
INNER JOINdbo.DimGeography G
ONC.GeographyKey = G.GeographyKey
```

3. Using the Insert Tab, add a Matrix report item to the report body.

4. Select Category field into the Row Groups list, Country field into the Column Groups list, and SalesAmount field into the Data cell.

5. Drag the Subcategory field into the Row Groups list below the Category row group. This creates a Subcategory row group and adds the Subcategory field to the matrix.

This simple example uses parameters to dynamically control the fields used by the two row groups and one column group to group the data. In production, any static group in a matrix or a table can be converted to a dynamic group.

The report designer should look like Figure P1-20.

As you are going to convert the two row groups and one column group into dynamic groups, follow these steps to give them generic names.

1. Select Category row group from the Row Groups list and change the Name property to ParentRowGroup (Figure P1-21).

2. Similarly, change Subcategory row group name to ChildRowGroup and Country column group to ColumnGroup (Groups should look like Figure P1-22).

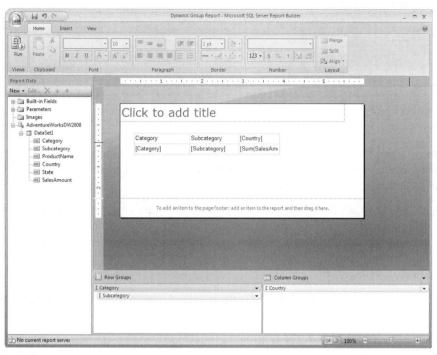

FIGURE P1-20

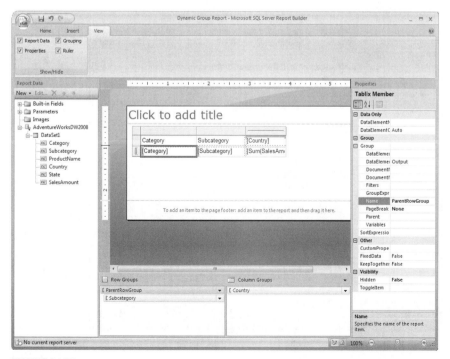

FIGURE P1-21

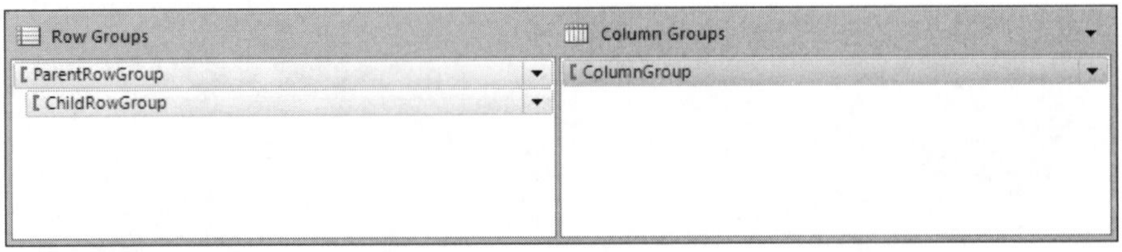

FIGURE P1-22

It is a good practice to rename the textboxes in the matrix to match the group names. For example, rename the Category textbox to ParentRowGroup, the Subcategory textbox to ChildRowGroup, and the Country textbox to ColumnGroup.

At this point, you have created a basic matrix report with Category and Subcategory as row groups and Country as the column group. Next, follow the steps below to convert these three groups into dynamic groups. For each dynamic group created, there needs to be a corresponding parameter that takes user input on which field to group the data. In this case, you create three parameters corresponding to each group you have in your report.

1. Add a parameter by right-clicking the Parameters folder in Report Data and clicking Add Parameter.

2. The first parameter is related to the ParentRowGroup row group. Enter ParentRowGroup-Param in the Name field and Select Parent Row Group in the Prompt field of the Report Parameter Properties dialog box and Click OK (Figure P1-23).

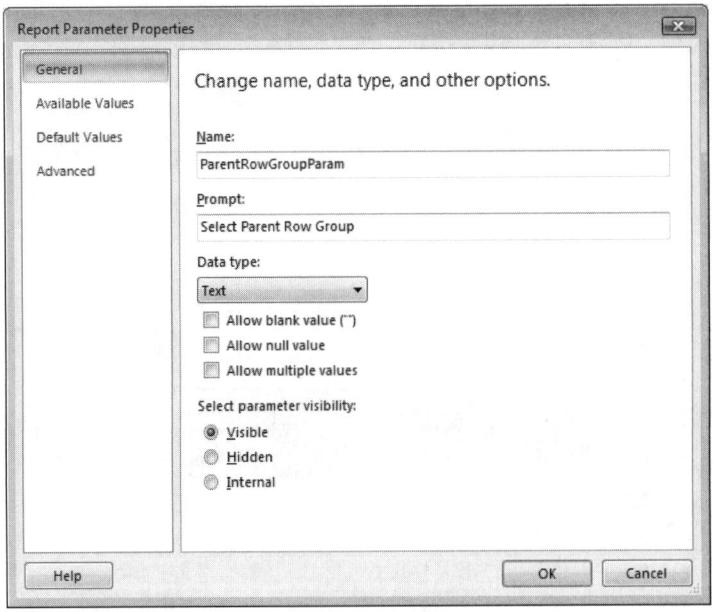

FIGURE P1-23

3. Similarly, create two more parameters for the ChildRowGroup and ColumnGroup groups with the name and prompt shown in the following table.

NAME	PROMPT
ChildRowGroupParam	Select Child Row Group
ColumnGroupParam	Select Column Group

Once the parameters are created, you need to think about what values should be available for users to select for each parameter. By following the steps below, you are going to allow users to select either Category or Subcategory for the ParentRowGroupParam, Subcategory or Product Name for the ChildRowGroupParam, and Country or State for the ColumnGroupParam. The key thing to keep in mind when adding available values to the parameters is that the Label can be descriptive, but the Value has to match the field name on which to group the data.

1. Double-click the ParentRowGroupParam parameter and select Available Values on the Report Parameter Properties dialog box.

2. Select the Specify values radio button and add the following values by clicking the Add button (see Figure P1-24).

LABEL	VALUE
Product Category	Category
Product Subcategory	Subcategory

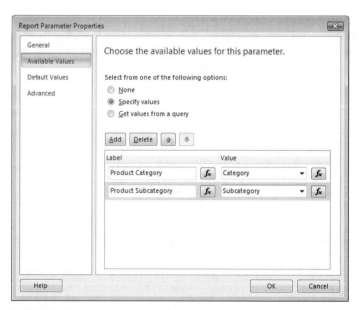

FIGURE P1-24

3. Click the OK button when completed.

4. Similarly, add the following values for ColumnGroupParam.

LABEL	VALUE
Country	Country
State/Province	State

Initially, you wanted to add the subcategory and product name to the ChildRowGroupParam parameter. But you can't just add those values, because you need to consider that ParentRowGroupParam also gives an option of selecting the subcategory. So, when it comes to adding values for the ChildRowGroupParam, you need to add the logic for displaying both subcategory and product name when the user selects Product Category from the ParentRowGroupParam, but to display only the product name when the user selects Product Subcategory from the ParentRowGroupParam parameter.

In other words, this logic can be stated using the following IF statement: If ParentRowGroupParam equals Category, add Subcategory as a valid available value or else do nothing. You can use the IIF (immediate IF) function to satisfy the logic. The following IIF statement first evaluates whether the ParentRowGroupParam equals the Category condition. If the condition is true, it returns Subcategory; otherwise, it returns Nothing.

```
=IIF(Parameters!ParentRowGroupParam.Value="Category","Subcategory",Nothing)
```

The logic will obviously have to be applied to both the label and the value of a parameter. The only thing that will change between the Label and Value expression would be the return value when the condition evaluates to true. For Label, you return Product Subcategory, whereas for Value, you return the field name called Subcategory.

As you did for the ParentRowGroupParam parameter, add the values for the ChildRowGroup parameter shown in the following table. After adding the values, the Report Parameter Properties dialog box will look like Figure P1-25.

LABEL	VALUE
`=IIF(Parameters!ParentRowGroupParam.Value= "Category","ProductSubcategory", Nothing)`	`=IIF(Parameters!ParentRowGroupParam.Value= "Category","Subcategory", Nothing)`
Product Name	ProductName

Let's briefly recap what you've done so far. In your quest to create dynamic groups, you created a basic matrix report with two row groups and one column group. You also created a parameter corresponding to each group that will capture the field we would like to group the data by. Now you need to connect the parameters to the groups so the groups can group on the field selected within the parameters.

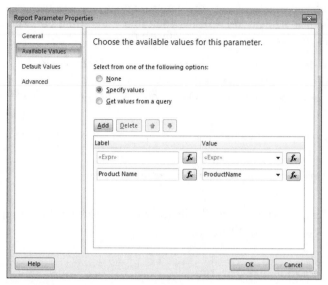

FIGURE P1-25

Somehow, you need to update the Group By clauses of your row and column groups to get the input from the parameters. Before we get into the details of updating the group by clauses, let's view the current values. Open the ParentRowGroup group properties and click the Expression button (*fx*) next to the Group On property (see Figure P1-26).

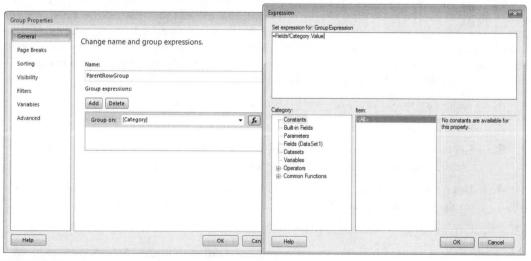

FIGURE P1-26

Normally, static group expressions are in this format: `Fields!FieldName.Value`. In this case, the ParentRowGroup Group By clause is `Fields!Category.Value` as shown in Figure P1-15. But the items in the Fields collection can also be accessed using an alternate string-based syntax such as `Fields("FieldName").Value`. Since the field name is just a string, you can use any string sub expression. Thus, you can use the parameters you just created to pass in the field names.

Using the string-based syntax, the `Fields!Category.Value` Group on clause in Figure P1-26 can be replaced with the `Fields(Parameters!ParentRowGroupParam.Value).Value`. This enables the group to dynamically group on the field that was selected in the parameter. Follow these steps to apply this change to all of groups:

1. Open the ParentRowGroup group properties and click the Expression button next to the Group On property.

2. Update the Group On expression to `=Fields(Parameters!ParentRowGroupParam.Value).Value`.

3. Similarly, update the Group On expression for the ChildRowGroup and ColumnRowGroup groups to the values shown in the following table.

GROUP	GROUP ON EXPRESSION
ChildRowGroup	=Fields(Parameters!ChildRowGroupParam.Value).Value
ColumnRowGroup	=Fields(Parameters!ColumnGroupParam.Value).Value

Now that you have connected the parameters to the groups, you need to update the fields in the matrix related to the groups. Currently, you have Category and Subcategory on the row and Country on the column of the matrix. Since the Category textbox field is related to the ParentRowGroup, you need to update the textbox expression to match the Group On expression for ParentRowGroup. Similarly, the Subcategory textbox field expression needs to be updated to match the ChildRowGroup Group On expression and Country textbox field expression to match the ColumnGroup Group On expression. Complete the following steps to perform the updates:

1. Right-click the Category textbox field and click Expressions.

2. Enter the ParentRowGroup Group On expression you used earlier.

3. Similarly, update the Subcategory and Country textbox field expressions to match the ChildRowGroup and ColumnGroup Group On expressions, respectively.

4. Delete the Category and Subcategory row header text (if you wish, you may add expressions for the row headers that will indicate the field name that was selected).

The final report design should look like Figure P1-27.

As you can see in Figure P1-28, the matrix report is grouped on Category, Subcategory, and State.

Preview the report to test the results. Select Product Category as the parent row group, Product Subcategory as the child row group, and State as the column row group.

You can further customize the report by adding drilldown functionality and optional grouping, and by formatting the data cell values.

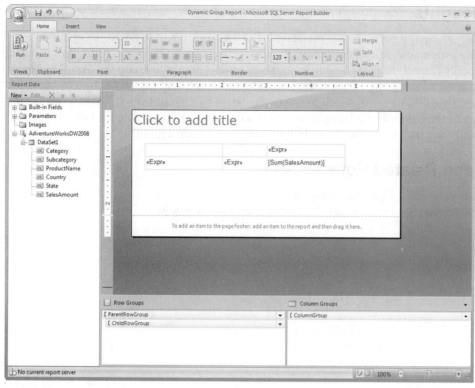

FIGURE P1-27

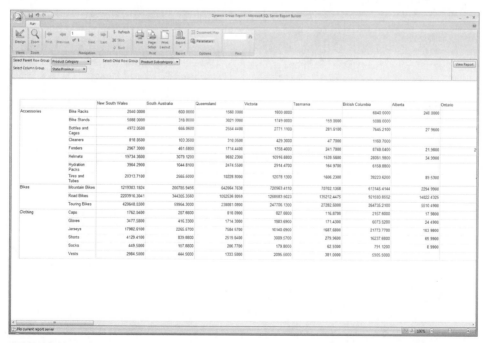

FIGURE P1-28

Final Thoughts

Dynamically grouped reports provide the flexibility of using one report to do the job of multiple reports by allowing users to use different grouping criteria. The technique used in this recipe uses parameters to dynamically control the fields used by row and/or column groups to group the data. The key thing to keep in mind when adding values to the parameter is that the label can be descriptive, but the value has to match the field name on which to group the data. Once parameters are added, connect the parameters to the groups by updating group expressions. And finally, update the fields in your table and/or matrix to match the group expression of their corresponding groups.

Credits and Related References

Chris Hays' blog titled Dynamic Grouping (`http://blogs.msdn.com/chrishays/archive/2004/07/15/DynamicGrouping.aspx`) also talks about optional grouping.

HIDING AND SHOWING COLUMNS IN A TABLE

Traditionally, when users wanted to see a different set of fields or columns than exist in another report based on a similar dataset, this requirement drove the design of a new report. Over time, several reports might have similar queries with only slight variations in the columns they include. In a scenario where multiple users need to see different columns from the same query, you can create a "super report" which returns all of the columns requested by a collective group of users. Logic within the report can be used to either hide or show certain columns in a table data region or to change the field binding for table columns.

The simple table data region in SSRS 2000 and 2005 makes it easy to hide and show columns because it has a collection of column objects. Using the Properties window in the report designer, it is a simple matter to select a table column and then use an expression to manipulate the Hidden property based on a parameter value or some other conditional logic. In SSRS 2008, the same technique may be used but it's a little more challenging to find these objects in the report designer. In this recipe, you learn about hiding and showing table columns and then see how to do the same for group header columns, using the somewhat less-intuitive elements of the tablix report data region.

Product Versions

➤   Reporting Services 2008

What You'll Need

➤   Table report with multiple columns

➤   Multi-level row group headers

➤   A parameter to indicate which columns to hide/show

➤   Visual Basic.NET expression

Designing the Report

You start with a typical grouped table. You can build this with any dataset you like, but, for demonstration purposes, you have a set of steps so you can follow along.

1.   Create a data source that connects to the AdventureWorksDW2008 database.

2.   Create a SQL Server dataset and use the following query. You can copy this from the completed sample report if you prefer to save yourself the typing.

```sql
SELECT
    DimDate.CalendarYear AS Year
  , DimDate.EnglishMonthName AS Month
  , DimReseller.ResellerName AS Reseller
  , DimEmployee.LastName AS SalesRep
  , DimProductCategory.EnglishProductCategoryName AS Category
  , DimProductSubcategory.EnglishProductSubcategoryName AS SubCategory
  , SUM(FactResellerSales.SalesAmount) AS Amount
  , SUM(FactResellerSales.TotalProductCost) AS Cost
```

```
  , SUM(FactResellerSales.OrderQuantity) AS Quantity
FROM
  DimProductSubcategory
  INNER JOIN DimProduct
  ON DimProductSubcategory.ProductSubcategoryKey
      = DimProduct.ProductSubcategoryKey
  INNER JOIN DimProductCategory
  ON DimProductSubcategory.ProductCategoryKey
      = DimProductCategory.ProductCategoryKey
  INNER JOIN FactResellerSales
  ON DimProduct.ProductKey = FactResellerSales.ProductKey
  INNER JOIN DimEmployee
  ON FactResellerSales.EmployeeKey = DimEmployee.EmployeeKey
  INNER JOIN DimDate
  ON FactResellerSales.OrderDateKey = DimDate.DateKey
  INNER JOIN DimSalesTerritory
  ON FactResellerSales.SalesTerritoryKey = DimSalesTerritory.SalesTerritoryKey
  INNER JOIN DimReseller
  ON FactResellerSales.ResellerKey = DimReseller.ResellerKey
GROUP BY
    DimDate.CalendarYear
  , DimDate.EnglishMonthName
  , DimReseller.ResellerName
  , DimEmployee.LastName
  , DimProductCategory.EnglishProductCategoryName
  , DimProductSubcategory.EnglishProductSubcategoryName
  , DimDate.MonthNumberOfYear
  , DimProductCategory.ProductCategoryKey
HAVING
  (DimDate.CalendarYear IN ('2003', '2004'))
ORDER BY
  Year, DimDate.MonthNumberOfYear, Reseller, SalesRep, Category, SubCategory
```

The report you're using is the same one you will use for a few related recipes, so you will see some additional design elements that don't pertain directly to this topic. Since the purpose of this recipe is to demonstrate hiding and showing a column, creating the row groups you will see in the screen captures is not crucial.

3. Add a table data region to the report body.

4. Drag the following fields into the Row Groups pane:

➤ Year

➤ Month

➤ SalesRep

➤ SubCategory

5. Select or drag the following fields into the cells in the detail row:

➤ Cost

➤ Quantity

6. Using the Row Groups pane below the report designer, right-click each row group and add a total after the group.

7. Add background shading and font adornments to suit your taste.

Your report should look similar to Figure P1-29.

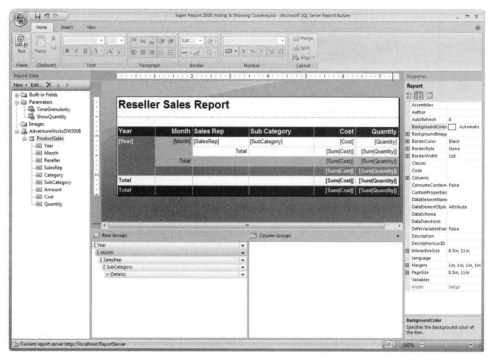

FIGURE P1-29

8. Add a report parameter named ShowQuantity.

9. Set the Data type to Boolean and set the Prompt as shown in Figure P1-30.

10. Use the Default Values dialog to add a default and set the value to True.

Alright, here comes the tricky part: In SSRS 2005, you would just click to select the column header at this point and use the Properties window to set the Visibility.Hidden property. You will set the same property to an expression in SSRS 2008 but the column object isn't available in the visual designer in this view. If you were to use the column header to choose a column, you would actually be selecting all of the individual cells in that column but not the column itself. This would result in leaving a blank column of white space in the rendered report. Instead, you need to find the static tablix member that represents the column.

11. To the right of the Column Groups pane header, you will see a small down arrow. Click this arrow and select Advanced Mode (shown in Figure P1-31).

FIGURE P1-30

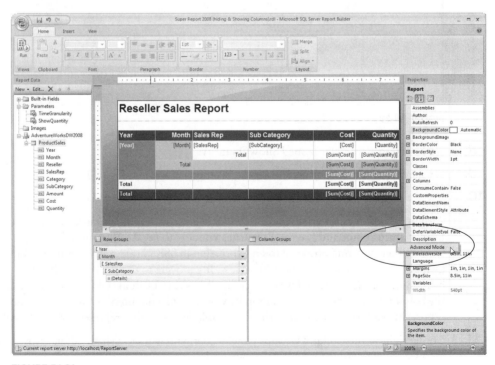

FIGURE P1-31

In Advanced Mode, you will see several tablix items in the Row Groups and Column Groups panes labeled (Static). The items in the Row Groups pane represent cells in the table and group headers and footers. Changing the Hidden property for any of these items will result in hiding the corresponding rows. The (Static) items in the Column Groups pane represent each of the columns to the right of the group column headers. As you see in Figure P1-32, there are two static columns to the right of the last group header labeled Sub Category.

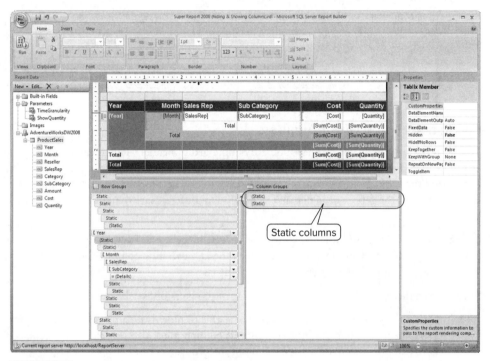

FIGURE P1-32

12. Enable the Properties Window in the report designer.

13. Select the second item, which represents the Quantity static column, in the Column Groups pane and find the Hidden property.

14. Drop down the list and choose <Expression . . . >

15. In the Expression window, build or type the following expression:

```
=NOT (Parameters!ShowQuantity.Value)
```

The NOT operator reverses the Boolean result of this expression and since you chose to call the parameter ShowQuantity, your user will intend to Show rather than Hide the column. This operator flips a True to a False when you go to Hide the column, rather than to show it.

16. Test the report by switching to Preview mode.

17. Use the radio buttons in the parameter toolbar to set the ShowQuantity parameter to False and then click View Report to see the Quantity column vanish. It's just like magic!

Many novice report designers tend to use the IIF() *function to test the parameter expression for a True or False result and then explicitly return a True or False result from the function. Since all expressions can return Boolean results, although this technique will work, it's redundant to use the* IIF() *function for this purpose. For example, the following expression could be used in place of the previous example:*

```
=IIF(Parameters!ShowQuantity.Value = True, False, True)
```

The following example would be used to test the result of a non-Boolean value. By wrapping an expression containing a comparison operator in parentheses, the expression returns a Boolean result.

```
=(Parameters!ReportView.Label="Retail")
```

Showing and Hiding Group Headers

The bottom line is that you cannot hide a dynamic group header. This means that if you created group headers by dragging and dropping a field into a row or column group pane, you'll have to restructure the table a bit. Fortunately, this is easy to do. Before you do this, I'd like to point out a subtle feature in the report designer that will help you differentiate dynamic group headers form static headers.

Go back and take a close look at Figure P1-32. When a cell in a Table data region is selected in the designer, a double-broken line appears between the last dynamic column and the first static column. This is how you can tell the difference between the two.

In order to hide and show these group columns, the conversion is relatively simple:

1. Delete the group columns you want to be able to hide using a parameterized expression. Any group header columns to the right of this column must also be deleted and replaced. Make sure you only delete the column and not the group.

2. Add a static column, which will appear to the right of the double-broken line.

3. Add the field, column header text and aggregate expressions, just as before.

4. Select the field cell and set the HideDuplicates property to True.

The table will look exactly the same in the designer, except the double-broken line will be to the left of the new column.

Final Thoughts

Any report item may be hidden or shown using a parameterized expression. In SSRS 2008, use the Advanced Mode option to show the static tablix members and then you can manipulate the Hidden property of any static columns using an expression, based on a parameter or any other condition.

To hide or show a group column header you must first replace the dynamic group header columns with static columns. You can use the HideDuplicates property to reproduce the same behavior as the default dynamic group headers.

HORIZONTAL TABLE

Displaying data rows utilizing the horizontal space available first, before adding a vertical row, can help in creating compact list representations of data.

Although there is no native "horizontal table" report item in Reporting Services, a horizontal table can be simulated with a matrix. This technique uses nesting of data regions and grouping.

Product Versions

➤ Reporting Services 2000

➤ Reporting Services 2005

➤ Reporting Services 2008

What You'll Need

➤ AdventureWorksDW sample database

Designing the Report

This example uses the AdventureWorksDW for SQL Server 2005 or 2008 sample database and a simple grouped query to return the product category, subcategory, and an aggregated business measure. The first example uses the Reporting Services 2008 designer. The second example uses Reporting Services 2005 and is nearly the same as the Reporting Services 2008 example, differing in only four steps, which are discussed in the "Designing the Report for Reporting Services 2005" section later in this recipe. Figure P1-33 shows the finished report.

Bike Racks	Bottles and Cages	Cleaners	Helmets
(Accessories)	(Accessories)	(Accessories)	(Accessories)
2838	2571	2411	13101

Hydration Packs	Locks	Pumps	Tires and Tubes
(Accessories)	(Accessories)	(Accessories)	(Accessories)
2028	1086	1130	674

Mountain Bikes
(Bikes)
23351

FIGURE P1-33

1. Start by designing a data source for the AdventureWorksDW or AdventureWorksDW2008 sample databases.

2. Create a dataset query to include the FactResellerSales, DimProduct, DimProductSubcategory and DimProductCategory tables.

```
SELECT
     DimProductCategory.EnglishProductCategoryName AS Category
   , DimProductSubcategory.EnglishProductSubcategoryName AS Subcategory
```

```
      , SUM(FactResellerSales.OrderQuantity) AS Qty
FROM
      DimProduct INNER JOIN DimProductSubcategory
         ON DimProduct.ProductSubcategoryKey
           = DimProductSubcategory.ProductSubcategoryKey
      INNER JOIN DimProductCategory
         ON DimProductSubcategory.ProductCategoryKey
           = DimProductCategory.ProductCategoryKey
      INNER JOIN FactResellerSales
         ON DimProduct.ProductKey = FactResellerSales.ProductKey
GROUP BY
      DimProductCategory.EnglishProductCategoryName,
      DimProductSubcategory.EnglishProductSubcategoryName
ORDER BY
      Category, Subcategory
```

3. Add a new matrix to represent the fixed layout for each set of data to repeat (in this example, product information).

Figure P1-34 shows a new empty matrix on the report design surface in Reporting Services 2008 and later.

FIGURE P1-34

4. Prepare the matrix report item layout.

Right-click into the Rows header, select Row Group ⇨ Delete Group, and then chose the Delete group and related rows and columns option. That deletes the row header and the dynamic group, and this particular matrix will only repeat its — now static — rows horizontally.

5. Prepare record layout.

In this case, you want to show a record layout with three rows. Using the field selector in report designer, select Subcategory for the Columns header textbox and Category for the textbox beneath it. Then click on the row left of the Category textbox and select Insert Row, to add a third (static) layout row that is used to display the Qty field. Figure P1-35 shows the result of this step.

FIGURE P1-35

6. Perform layout steps to repeat the record layout for each dataset row.

Right-click on the Subcategory column header and edit the group properties by selecting Column Group - Group Properties. Replace the current group expression with the following expression: =RowNumber(Nothing)

This causes the matrix to give you one column per row of data. Since horizontal tables can end up rather wide, you probably want your table to wrap around to the next "line" after a specific number of columns.

7. Put the matrix into a list.

Add a list to your report and drag the table into it.

8. Group by the number of records to be shown horizontally.

Select the details group of the list, and open the group properties. On the group dialog, add a new group expression and enter this: =Ceiling(RowNumber(Nothing)/5)

This will cause the list to group on every five rows. So you'll get a separate table for every five rows. The divisor (in this case, five) determines how many records are shown next to each other horizontally before a row break occurs.

9. Adjust the group expression of the matrix from Step 6 due to the matrix now being embedded inside the list.

Edit the column group expression in your matrix and change the RowNumber argument to be the list group name; for example: =RowNumber("Details")

Figure P1-36 shows the final report layout with additional textbox formatting and styling applied.

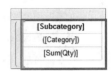

FIGURE P1-36

10. Preview the report to test the results.

Figure P1-37 shows the result of five records shown horizontally before a new row is added to the rendered layout.

Bike Racks	Bottles and Cages	Cleaners	Helmets	Hydration Packs
(Accessories)	(Accessories)	(Accessories)	(Accessories)	(Accessories)
2838	2571	2411	13101	2028
Locks	Mountain Bikes	Pumps	Road Bikes	Tires and Tubes
(Accessories)	(Bikes)	(Accessories)	(Bikes)	(Accessories)
1086	23351	1130	39080	674
Bib-Shorts	Caps	Gloves	Jerseys	Touring Bikes
(Clothing)	(Clothing)	(Clothing)	(Clothing)	(Bikes)
3111	6121	11553	19379	12584
Bottom Brackets	Shorts	Socks	Tights	Vests
(Components)	(Clothing)	(Clothing)	(Clothing)	(Clothing)
921	8946	4649	4562	6176
Brakes	Chains	Cranksets	Derailleurs	Forks
(Components)	(Components)	(Components)	(Components)	(Components)
1035	774	1107	1166	634
Handlebars	Headsets	Mountain Frames	Pedals	Road Frames
(Components)	(Components)	(Components)	(Components)	(Components)
3950	1009	11620	3931	11747
Saddles	Touring Frames	Wheels		
(Components)	(Components)	(Components)		
2145	3725	5263		

FIGURE P1-37

Designing the Report for Reporting Services 2005

In Reporting Services 2005, the pattern is nearly the same. The minor differences are in Steps 4, 5, 8, and 9:

4. Prepare the matrix report item layout.

Since the row header area of a matrix cannot be entirely removed in Reporting Services 2005, make it as small as possible by dragging the vertical divider to left. Then right-click into the matrix data cell and add a new row.

5. Prepare the record layout.

Drag fields into the corresponding areas of the matrix shown in Figure P1-38 and apply textbox formatting and styling.

FIGURE P1-38

8. Group by the number of records to be shown horizontally.

Right-click on the list and select Properties. Then click on Edit Details Group. On the group dialog, add a new group expression and enter this for the group expression:
`=Ceiling(RowNumber(Nothing)/5)`

This will cause the list to group on every five rows. So you'll get a separate table for every five rows. The divisor (in this case, five) determines how many records are shown next to each other horizontally before a row break occurs.

9. Adjust the group expression in the matrix.

Edit the column group expression in your matrix and change the RowNumber argument to be the list group name, which has a different default name in Reporting Services 2005; for example: `=RowNumber("list1_Details_Group")`

Final Thoughts

Nesting of data regions in Reporting Services is a powerful technique, as demonstrated in this recipe, to achieve the horizontal table effect.

Credits and Related References

A similar technique is demonstrated on Chris Hays' blog titled "Horizontal Tables" that may be found at `http://blogs.msdn.com/chrishays/archive/2004/07/23/HorizontalTables.aspx`.

RESETTING THE PAGE NUMBER BASED ON GROUPS

One of the frequent feature requests for Reporting Services is to add the ability to reset page numbers within the report based on, for example, a change in the group value.

Reporting Services 2008 R2 adds this capability through a more general feature to name pages, define dynamic page breaks and optionally reset page numbers.

Product Versions

➤   Reporting Services 2008 R2

What You'll Need

➤   AdventureWorks2008 sample database

➤   Product Catalog 2008 AdventureWorks sample report

Designing the Report

The goal of this recipe is to take an existing report that displays product information by categories, and modify it to show page number information for each product category, including restarting page numbers at 1 for each new category, as shown in Figure P1-39.

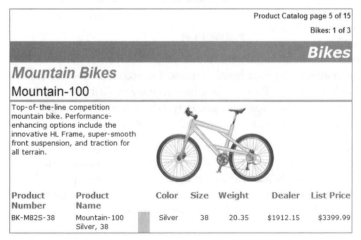

FIGURE P1-39

1.   Open the Product Catalog 2008 sample report in Report Builder 3.0 of SQL Server Reporting Services 2008 R2.

If you haven't downloaded the AdventureWorks sample reports yet from CodePlex, use the following link: http://www.codeplex.com/MSFTRSProdSamples.

2. Remove the PageBreakAtEnd from the product catalog cover page rectangle (Rectangle2), by changing the page break location property value from End to None.

3. Prepare the tablix (Tablix1) in the report body.

a. Open the Tablix Properties dialog for Tablix1, which shows the product catalog details, and ensure that the Keep together on one page if possible option is deselected.

b. While Tablix1 is selected, in the grouping pane select the Category row grouping. In the Properties window for the Category tablix member, expand the Group properties, and set the following page break-related properties as shown in Figure P1-40:

FIGURE P1-40

PageName: =Fields!Category.Value
BreakLocation: StartAndEnd
ResetPageNumber: True

Thereby, the PageName for a given report page is set to the current product category shown on that page, and each product category starts on a new page and the page numbers reset.

4. Create a page header to show overall page numbers as well as page numbers per section by applying the following steps:

a. In the page header, delete the existing textbox that shows the report name.

b. Add two new textboxes as shown in Figure P1-41. The first textbox uses two new global properties added in Reporting Services 2008 R2:

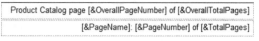

FIGURE P1-41

OverallPageNumber and OverallTotalPages. Those properties refer to the overall page counts and are unaffected by page number resets. The second textbox refers to the current PageNumber and TotalPages, taking into account explicit page number resets. In addition, it refers to the PageName property, which represents the product category shown on the current page, as set previously in Step 3.

c. On the second textbox, in the page header which references the PageName property, set conditional visibility based on the current PageName value. If the current page name is Null (as might be the case if the first page of the report only contains a product catalog cover page) then the textbox can be hidden using the following expression for the textbox Visibility.Hidden property:

```
=(Globals!PageName is Nothing)
```

5. Preview the report to test the results.

Verify by navigating through the report that the first page only shows the page information for the product catalog and the cover page. Subsequent pages with product details show product category-based pagination information, with the category-based page number resetting for each new category, as shown in Figure P1-39.

Final Thoughts

Reporting Services 2008 R2 adds page-break enhancements that are very powerful yet subtle and could be easily overlooked. This recipe demonstrated how to use new built-in fields that are added to the Globals collection. The OverallPageNumber and OverallTotalPages objects allow you to have greater control and visibility to page counts within groups and report sections. The new ResetPageNumber property enables you to reset page numbers with each group page break, changing the behavior of the PageNumber and TotalPages objects to operate within the context of the group or section. The addition of the new objects and the enhanced behavior of the existing objects provide greater flexibility for managing page series and totals in both simple reports and complex report solutions.

PART II
BI Dashboards and Elements

- ▶ Creating Sparklines

- ▶ Cube Dynamic Rows

- ▶ Cube Metadata

- ▶ Cube Browser

- ▶ Australian Sparklines

- ▶ Angry Koala Cube Browser

- ▶ Bullet Charts

- ▶ Synchronizing Groups, Charts, and Sparklines

CREATING SPARKLINES

Edward Tufte, one of the most recognized experts on the subject of data visualization, presents the idea of sparklines. As Tufte describes it in his book *Beautiful Evidence* (Graphics Press, 2006), sparklines are "small, high-resolution graphics embedded in a context of words, numbers, and images." These are simple, word-sized graphics that are an alternative to large, busy charts used to communicate a simple trend or series of measurements. In order to be meaningful, sometimes charts need to have annotated gridlines, point labels, and legends. However, some charts can effectively serve their purpose without the use of supporting text labels. To illustrate observations like "sales are improving," "a product is profitable," or that a trend is cyclical, a simple trend chart needs little or no labeling. Sparklines are best used when embedded in text or other report formats.

Product Versions

➤ Reporting Services 2008

What You'll Need

➤ A query expression used to return trend data

➤ A small, simplified line or area chart item

➤ A table item to display master rows

Although the instructions in this recipe are targeting the 2008 version of Reporting Services, the concept of creating sparkline reports can be applied to earlier versions as well, by simply changing how we create tables, groups, and datasets. In other words, the main goal can be achieved with all versions of Reporting Services, though the exact steps might be slightly different.

Designing the Report

Column and line charts are best suited for this type of presentation. In the example, you'll use a line chart to show sales trends data from the AdventureWorksDW2008 database. You'll design a sales trend report that will contain sparkline charts for each product category broken down by year. The final result is shown in Figure P2-1.

Sales Trends

This example shows product category sales on each row and sales by year in an associated line chart, plotting sales totals by month. This report's dataset is based on a query that returns aggregated reseller and Internet sales by year and month, and then by product category.

Let's begin by setting up your data source and dataset for the report. You'll create a dataset with a connection string to the AdventureWorksDW2008 database, as shown in Figure P2-2.

Combined Internet and Reseller Sales
by Year

Year	Product Category	Sales Total	Trend
2001			
	Accessories	$20,239.66	
	Bikes	$10,665,953.45	
	Clothing	$34,467.29	
	Components	$615,474.98	
2002			
	Accessories	$93,796.84	
	Bikes	$26,664,534.04	
	Clothing	$489,820.19	
	Components	$3,611,041.24	
2003			
	Accessories	$594,999.24	
	Bikes	$35,186,943.67	
	Clothing	$1,022,601.53	
	Components	$5,486,723.33	
2004			
	Accessories	$569,710.18	
	Bikes	$22,597,735.69	
	Clothing	$591,688.92	
	Components	$2,091,051.85	

FIGURE P2-1

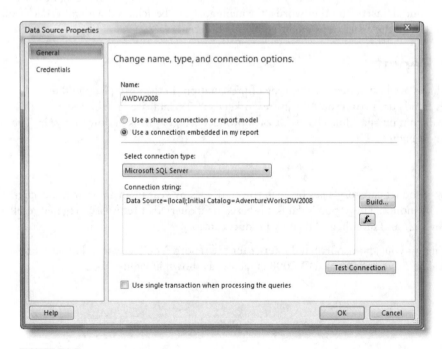

FIGURE P2-2

Next, you'll add a new dataset and configure it to use the data source we set up in the last step. For this sample, you'll use a query of type text and enter the following SQL in the query text box of the dataset:

```sql
SELECT
    SUM(t.ExtendedAmountSum) AS ExtendedAmountSum
    , t.EnglishProductCategoryName
    , t.CalendarYear
    , t.MonthNumberOfYear
FROM
(
    SELECT
        SUM(FactInternetSales.ExtendedAmount) AS ExtendedAmountSum
        , DimProductCategory.EnglishProductCategoryName
        , DimDate.CalendarYear
        , DimDate.MonthNumberOfYear
    FROM
        FactInternetSales
    INNER JOIN
        DimProduct ON FactInternetSales.ProductKey = DimProduct.ProductKey
    INNER JOIN
        DimProductSubcategory ON DimProduct.ProductSubcategoryKey =
            DimProductSubcategory.ProductSubcategoryKey
    INNER JOIN
        DimProductCategory ON DimProductSubcategory.ProductCategoryKey =
            DimProductCategory.ProductCategoryKey
    INNER JOIN
        DimDate ON FactInternetSales.OrderDateKey = DimDate.DateKey
    GROUP BY
        DimProductCategory.EnglishProductCategoryName
        , DimDate.CalendarYear
        , DimDate.MonthNumberOfYear
    UNION ALL
    SELECT
        SUM(FactResellerSales.ExtendedAmount) AS ExtendedAmountSum
        , DimProductCategory.EnglishProductCategoryName
        , DimDate.CalendarYear
        , DimDate.MonthNumberOfYear
    FROM
        FactResellerSales
    INNER JOIN
        DimProduct ON FactResellerSales.ProductKey = DimProduct.ProductKey
    INNER JOIN
        DimProductSubcategory ON DimProduct.ProductSubcategoryKey =
            DimProductSubcategory.ProductSubcategoryKey
    INNER JOIN
        DimProductCategory ON DimProductSubcategory.ProductCategoryKey =
            DimProductCategory.ProductCategoryKey
    INNER JOIN
        DimDate ON FactResellerSales.OrderDateKey = DimDate.DateKey
    GROUP BY
        DimProductCategory.EnglishProductCategoryName
        , DimDate.CalendarYear
        , DimDate.MonthNumberOfYear
) t
```

```
GROUP BY
        t.EnglishProductCategoryName
      , t.CalendarYear
      , t.MonthNumberOfYear
ORDER BY
    CalendarYear, EnglishProductCategoryName
```

This SQL query will give you the sum of both reseller and Internet sales amounts by year and category. It also provides data for the months so you can create the trend graph. This data should give you a good sampling for a trend analysis report.

Now, let's create the data regions:

1. If you started from scratch with a blank report body, remove the data region placeholder from the report body, since you do not wish to use the wizards to add more datasets. You'll manually add the table as follows.

2. From the Insert menu, select the table item and then the Insert table option. Click and drag the table element over the report body to create a table so you can place our data fields on it.

3. Delete the original Details row group and associated rows.

4. Now you need to create your own row groups with the following data fields in this order: (1) Calendar Year, and (2) English Product Category. To do that, simply drag each of the respective dataset fields onto the Row Groups window. Notice that when you drop the Category Name field in the row group window, it will become a child row group of Calendar Year.

5. You will display your tabular data in three columns, corresponding to the year, category, and sales aggregate values. By default, when you added the row groups, Report Builder also added respective columns to your table layout using the same table row. You may choose to keep this layout, or break the rows up into a header row for the parent group (year) and another row for the child row group (product category), shown in the following figures. The aesthetics are up to you, as you likely have a basic understanding of report layout design and customizations.

6. Finally, add one more column to the far right of the table, which will serve as the container for our trending lines later on. Add a header text to the column such as "Sales Trends."

Now you need to create the chart that will provide the trending sparkline. The chart's dataset should be the same used by the table, since you'll nest the chart into the table. "Smooth Line" is used here, but the normal "Line" type will work as well. Also, if you would prefer to have a gradient look instead of simple lines, you can choose the "Area" or "Smooth Area" chart types.

The goal of the sparkline is to keep it simple and clean while showing relative sales trends instead of specific values and points. To achieve that goal, you must remove all "noise" from the chart by getting rid of borders, labels, gridlines, and so on. The only thing you're interested in is the actual line graph.

If you are using one of the area chart types and want the gradient effect, then go to the Series properties, and change the fill type to Gradient. The final result of this recipe (see Figure 6), shows an example with the gradient fill and uses a lighter shade of blue and yellow for primary and secondary colors, respectively (although that's not obvious, since the figure is in black and white).

Also, it may be visually more appealing to set the border of the series to a solid line and a contrasting color like blue (to match our theme). This will give the area gradient a nice contour line, defining the perimeter of the shape.

In Figure P2-3, you can see that the table and chart are added and set up in separate areas of the report body. You need to assign data fields to the chart, so follow the steps below.

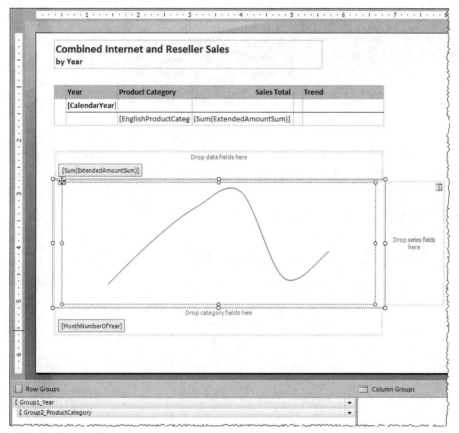

FIGURE P2-3

1. Drag the field MonthNumberOfYear on the category region.

2. Drag the field ExtendedAmountSum on the data fields region, which automatically is aggre-gated in that region with the SUM() expression.

After the chart is configured, add it to the table by dragging and dropping it in the appropriate cell. Since the chart will be displayed for each given year and product category group, you will include it in a group header row instead of the detail row.

In a production reporting solution, you might create a separate chart report, similar to the sparkline chart but with more detail. Figure P2-4 shows this report in design view after placing the chart inside the table.

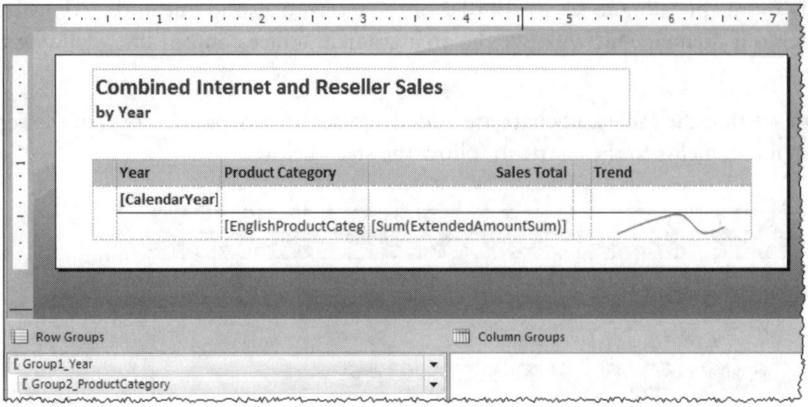

FIGURE P2-4

Finally, Figure P2-5 shows the finished report. The trend line shows sales totals over the course of the year. Whether data points represented days, weeks, or months, the effect would be the same.

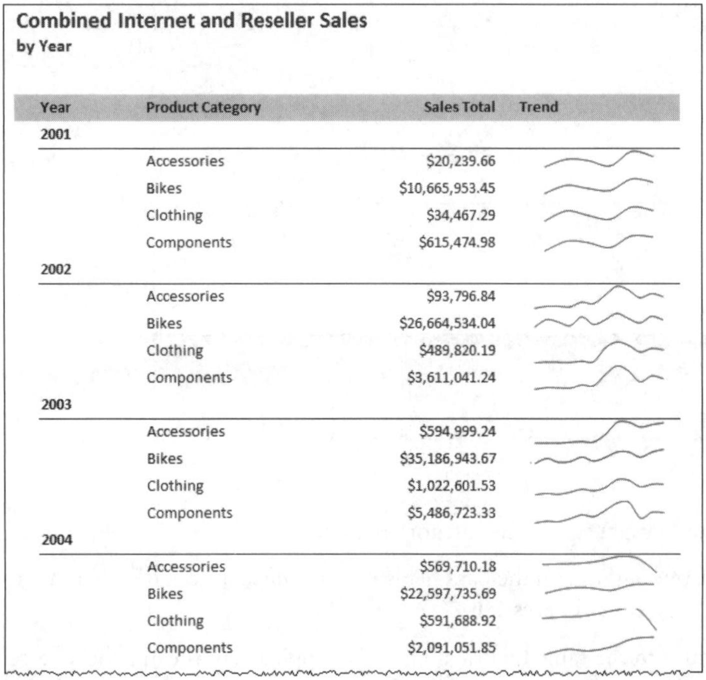

FIGURE P2-5

If you use the Smooth Area chart type with a gradient fill effect for the series, as previously mentioned in this recipe, the report will look like Figure P2-6.

Combined Internet and Reseller Sales
by Year

Year	Product Category	Sales Total	Trend
2001			
	Accessories	$20,239.66	
	Bikes	$10,665,953.45	
	Clothing	$34,467.29	
	Components	$615,474.98	
2002			
	Accessories	$93,796.84	
	Bikes	$26,664,534.04	
	Clothing	$489,820.19	
	Components	$3,611,041.24	
2003			
	Accessories	$594,999.24	
	Bikes	$35,186,943.67	
	Clothing	$1,022,601.53	
	Components	$5,486,723.33	
2004			
	Accessories	$569,710.18	
	Bikes	$22,597,735.69	
	Clothing	$591,688.92	
	Components	$2,091,051.85	

FIGURE P2-6

As a final note, it is worthwhile to mention that for the SQL Server 2008 R2 release of Reporting Services (slated for 2010), the designer will introduce a few new report item controls, one of which will simplify the creation of sparkline reports (Figure P2-7 shows the new toolbox item). These new menu items will simplify the process for creating common visualizations by automating some of the steps introduced in this recipe; however, the approach and techniques remain the same.

FIGURE P2-7

The new Sparkline report item will provide a simple drag-and-drop control and reduce the number of steps required for creating eye-catching sparkline reports.

Final Thoughts

In this recipe you saw the use of sparklines as a great way to represent trending data within your reports. You also walked through the steps to create your very own sparkline report using SQL Server 2008 Reporting Services.

The charting components in Reporting Services 2008 provide a rich design-time experience, full of configurable options that enable you to create charts to match your style preferences. In the upcoming 2008 R2 release of Reporting Services, we look forward to sparklines as first-class citizens of the report designer toolbox.

Credits and Related References

Beautiful Evidence, Edward Tufte (Graphics Press, 2006).

Professional SQL Server 2008 Reporting Services, Turley, et al. (Wrox, 2008).

Sean Boon's blog: `http://blogs.msdn.com/seanboon/archive/2008/10/10/how-to-build-sparkline-reports-in-sql-server-reporting-services.aspx`.

CUBE DYNAMIC ROWS

I have often observed when I'm creating reports for clients that the reports they want are very similar: the columns stay fairly static, with values like Amount, Amount Last Year, Growth, Growth Percent, Gross Profit, etc., with the only difference being the data shown on rows. So two reports could have identical columns, but one has Products on rows and another, Regions.

One of the neat things about Analysis Server is that it provides us with the capability to move up and down through hierarchies, selecting what we are interested in. In the Product dimension, for instance, we can select Product Category Bikes, or Product Sub-Category Mountain Bikes, or even select a single Product Model.

This recipe uses a parameter to allow for changing which hierarchy is displayed on rows, and allow drilling up or down within that hierarchy. It also uses a parameter for the measure to display. The final report will behave as shown in Figure P2-8: simply clicking a hierarchy member allows us to drill down to more and more detail, or similarly drill back up.

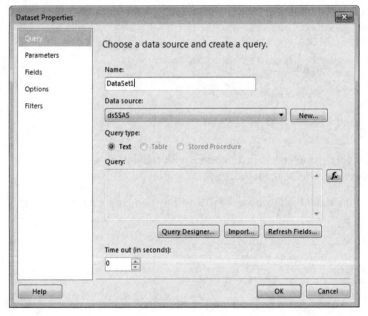

FIGURE P2-8

The Cube Browser recipe (an extension of this concept) calls a modified version of the Cube Metadata report that allows users to dynamically change what measure to display and what hierarchy to display on rows without the need to type a value into the parameter.

Product Versions

➤   Reporting Services 2005

➤   Reporting Services 2008

What You'll Need

➤   Ability to read MDX

Designing the Report

This recipe utilizes custom MDX, mainly calculated measures, to present consistent column names to Reporting Services, and therefore facilitate dynamically changing rows and measures.

First let's set up the data and parameters.

1.   From BIDS create a new report called Cube Dynamic Rows.

2.   Create a string report parameter called pMeasure with the default value [Measures].[Gross Profit] and the following expression values:

LABEL	VALUE
Gross Profit	[Measures].[Gross Profit]
Sales Amount	[Measures].[Sales Amount]

3.   Create another string report parameter called pRowMbr with the default value [Product].[Product Categories].[Subcategory].&[1].

4.   Create a dataset against the shared datasource dsSSAS as shown in Figure P2-9.

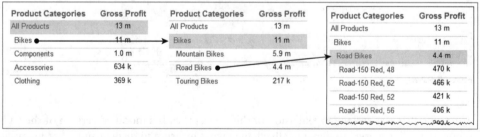

FIGURE P2-9

5. Click the Query Designer button, then select Design Mode in the toolbar and enter the following code into the Query Designer as shown in Figure P2-10. (The code is available in sample report or the CubeDynamicRows.MDX file on this book's page at Wrox.com.)

```
-----------------------------------------------------------------------------
-- Cube Dynamic Rows and Measure
--
-- Grant Paisley
-- Angry Koala
-- http://angrykoala.com.au
-- 28 Nov 2008
--
-- Note: certain attributes commented out as not needed
-- but may be of use in other reports
-----------------------------------------------------------------------------

WITH
-- The measure of interest
MEMBER [Measures].[Measure_Value] AS StrToValue(@pMeasure)

-- the friendly name of the measure
MEMBER [Measures].[Measure_Label] AS StrToValue(@pMeasure + ".Member_Name")

MEMBER [Measures].[Row_Key]
    AS StrToValue( @pRowMbr + ".Hierarchy.Currentmember.Uniquename" )
MEMBER [Measures].[Row_Label]
    AS StrToValue( @pRowMbr + ".Hierarchy.CurrentMember.Member_Caption" )
MEMBER [Measures].[Row_Level]
    AS StrToValue( @pRowMbr + ".Hierarchy.CurrentMember.Level.Ordinal" )

--MEMBER [Measures].[Row_Level_Name]
--   AS StrToValue( @pRowMbr + ".Hierarchy.Level.Name" )
MEMBER [Measures].[Row_Hierarchy_Name]
    AS StrToValue( @pRowMbr + ".Hierarchy.Name" )
--MEMBER [Measures].[Row_Hierarchy_UniqueName]
--   AS StrToValue( @pRowMbr + ".Hierarchy.UniqueName" )
MEMBER [Measures].[Row_Dimension_Name]
    AS StrToValue( @pRowMbr + ".Dimension.Name" )
--MEMBER [Measures].[Row_Dimension_UniqueName]
--   AS StrToValue(@pRowMbr + ".Dimension_Unique_Name" )

SELECT NON EMPTY {
 -- display the measure and rowmbr attributes on columns

 [Measures].[Row_Key],
 [Measures].[Row_Label],
 [Measures].[Row_Level],
 --[Measures].[Row_Level_Name],
 [Measures].[Row_Hierarchy_Name],
 --[Measures].[Row_Hierarchy_UniqueName],
 --[Measures].[Row_Dimension_Name],
 --[Measures].[Row_Dimension_UniqueName],

 [Measures].[Measure_Label] ,
 [Measures].[Measure_Value]
```

```
} ON COLUMNS,

NON EMPTY
    -- if want to display row member parent, self and children
    -- un-comment following code
    --STRTOSET("{" + @pRowMbr + ".parent, "
    --            + @pRowMbr + ", "
    --            + @pRowMbr + ".children}" )

    -- show the current hierarachy member with its ascendants
    -- together with its children on rows
    STRTOSET(
        "{Ascendants(" + @pRowMbr + " ), "
        + @pRowMbr + ".children}"
    )

ON ROWS

FROM [Adventure Works] -- must hard code the cube :(
-- the cube name, together with the default values are the only
-- things required to point this report at a different cube
```

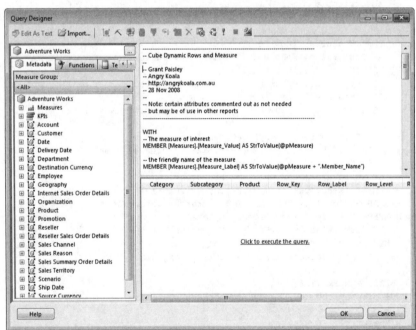

FIGURE P2-10

6.   Select the parameters icon from toolbar and add the following parameters:

PARAMETER	VALUE
pMeasure	[Measures].[Gross Profit]
pRowMbr	[Product].[Product Categories].[Subcategory].&[1]

Figure P2-11 shows this.

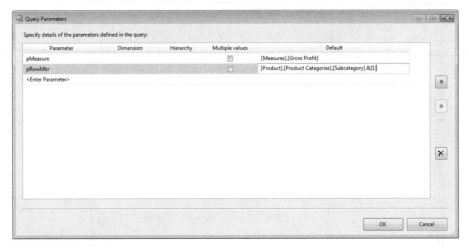

FIGURE P2-11

7. Execute the query to check that it runs properly before returning to the data set properties.

8. Click OK again to return to the design surface. Your Report Data should look like Figure P2-12.

Now that you have some data, let's build and format a table to hold it, and add a neat trick to better display numbers.

Add a table based on the Row_Label and Measure_Value data fields. Sort it and do the following basic formatting.

1. Add a new table to the report body.

2. Remove one column (leaving two).

3. Drag Row_Label and drop it on the data cell in the first column of the table.

4. Change Header value to show name of current hierarchy by setting it to [Row_Hierarchy_Name].

5. Drag Measure_Value and drop it on the data cell in the second column of the table.

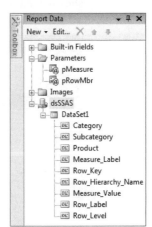

FIGURE P2-12

6. Change Header in second column to show the name of current measure by setting it to [Measure_Label].

7. Right click on the =(Details) group in the Row Groups pane and select Group Properties. Then add a group expression to group on Row_Key, as shown in Figure P2-13.

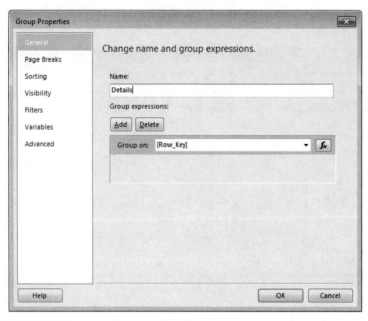

FIGURE P2-13

8. Go to the Sorting tab and add both Row_Level and Measure_Value data fields to sort as shown in Figure P2-14.

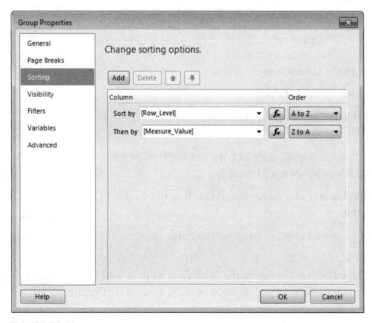

FIGURE P2-14

9. Select both header cells and both data cells and set BorderStyle Default from Solid to None.

10. Select both header cells and set the font to 8pt and bold, and the color to DimGray.

11. Select both data cells and set the font to 8pt.

12. Select both data cells and set BorderStyle Top and Bottom both to Solid, as shown in Figure P2-15.

13. Select the Row_Label textbox and set its format to the following expression:

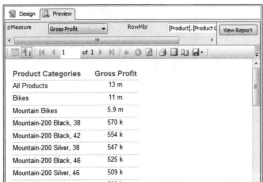

FIGURE P2-15

```
=iif(last(abs(Fields!Measure_Value.Value)) > 10000000,
    "#,, m;(#,, m)",
  iif(last(abs(Fields!Measure_Value.Value)) > 1000000,
    "#,,.0 m;(#,,.0 m)",
  iif(last(abs(Fields!Measure_Value.Value)) > 10000,
    "#, k;(#, k)",
  iif(last(abs(Fields!Measure_Value.Value)) > 1000,
    "#,.0 k;(#,.0 k)",
    "#,#;(#,#)"
))))
```

This is a pretty neat trick, as you now have the ability to succinctly display values that range from 1 into the millions without needing extra wide cells or having so many digits that it's hard to read.

Now preview it. You now have rows driven by the pRowMbr parameter, and for each row, the value for the measure specified in pMeasure, as shown in Figure P2-16.

You can test changing the report content by changing the value of the pMeasures parameter combo box from Gross Profit to Sales Amount.

Finally you need to create the self-drill-through action and add some formatting to indent rows by level and highlight the currently selected row.

FIGURE P2-16

1. Indent based on what level you are in the hierarchy. Open the Texbox Properties for Row_Label.

2. In the Alignment page, Padding Options, set Left to the following expression:

```
=str( (Fields!Row_Level.Value * 4) + 2 ) + "pt"
```

3. In the Action page, select Go to report and set the report name to Built-in field [&ReportName] and add these two parameters:

NAME	VALUE
pRowMbr	[Row_Key]
pMeasure	[@pMeasure]

Figure P2-17 shows this.

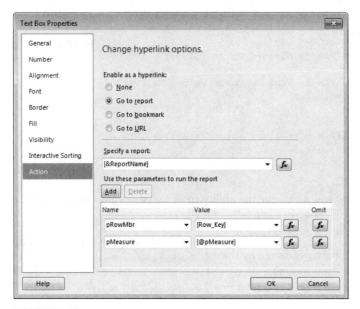

FIGURE P2-17

4. Highlight the row currently selected and indicate to users that they can select a row by setting its color to blue (users can't help but click on something that is blue).

5. In the detail row for both the Row_Label and Measure_Value cells, set the property BackgroundColor to the following expression:

```
=iif(Fields!Row_Key.Value=Parameters!pRowMbr.Value,
  "LemonChiffon",
  "None"
  )
```

and the font color to this expression:

```
=iif(Fields!Row_Key.Value=Parameters!pRowMbr.Value,
"DimGray",
"Blue")
```

Select the preview tab as shown in Figure P2-18 and play with drilling up and down the product hierarchy.

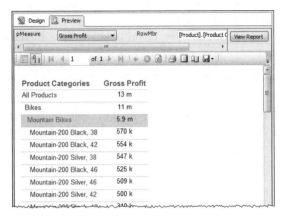

FIGURE P2-18

Final Thoughts

The recipe you have just created is the fundamental content presentation and navigation technique employed by the Cube recipes in this book. It allows any dimension hierarchy to be displayed, and enables you to navigate up and down through that hierarchy.

In the Cube Browser recipe you add columns, a filter, and a date, then hook it up to a modified version of the Cube Metadata report, thus allowing the user to change what is displayed in the report.

So you effectively have the start of a mini OLAP browser build in SSRS. By creating linked reports with different parameters you can provide an infinite number of reports for your users, everything from a profit and loss report to a salesperson profitability report.

In the Cube Restricting Number of Rows recipe later in this book, you will learn a technique to dynamically adjust the number of rows (or columns) displayed in a report.

Credits and Related References

http://angrykoala.com.au/_blog/Blog

http://cubesurfer.codeplex.com

http://reportsurfer.com

http://cubesurfer.com

CUBE METADATA

Wouldn't it be nice to have all your cube documentation up-to-date and available to your users? Wouldn't it be even better if you could create completely generic reports and, just by creating a linked report in Report Manager and changing a few parameters, you could generate a completely new report?

So how do we do this? The report in this recipe requires that we combine a few techniques, but to start with we need access to Analysis Services metadata.

This report could also be developed in Report Builder 2. However, the report calls itself (using a drill-through report action) and actions are disabled in Report Builder 2.0 when previewing report, which means that to test the report, you have to keep deploying to reporting services.

Product Versions

➤   Reporting Services 2005 (with CodePlex project Analysis Server Stored Procedures)

➤   Reporting Services 2008

What You'll Need

➤   An open mind

➤   Experience with VB expressions

Designing the Report

This solution is about tricking Reporting Services into talking nicely to Analysis Services and taking advantage of the new Dynamic Management Views (DMVs) in SQL Server 2008. The DMVs we utilize are:

➤   MDSCHEMA_CUBES

➤   MDSCHEMA_MEASUREGROUPS

➤   MDSCHEMA_MEASURES

➤   MDSCHEMA_MEASUREGROUP_DIMENSIONS

➤   MDSCHEMA_HIERARCHIES

➤   MDSCHEMA_LEVELS

There are others you might want to explore — that won't be needed in this recipe — such as:

➤   DBSCHEMA_CATALOGS

➤   DBSCHEMA_DIMENSIONS

To get the full list of DMVs, run the command

```
SELECT * FROM $SYSTEM.DBSCHEMA_TABLES
```

Figure P2-19 shows how the finished report will look.

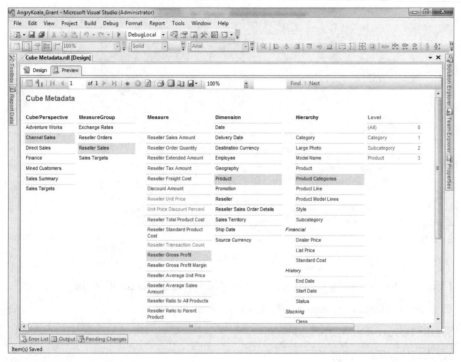

FIGURE P2-19

Add the DMV datasets.

1. From Business Intelligence Development Studio create a new report.

2. Add a data source for the AdventureWorksDW2008_AS database, named dsSSAS.

3. Enter the following DMV script as an expression to add a dataset and press Refresh Fields:

```
SELECT * FROM $System.MDSCHEMA_CUBES WHER CUBE_SOURCE =1
```

Your dataset properties should look those shown in Figure P2-20.

4. Insert a table on the design surface. To list the cubes/perspectives, follow these steps:

a. Add a new table to the report body.

b. Remove two columns (leaving one).

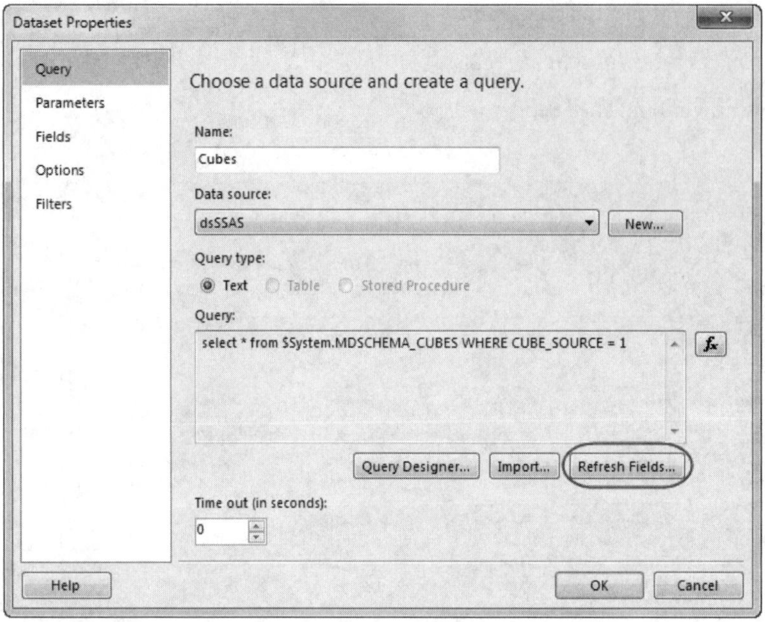

FIGURE P2-20

c. Drag and drop or select the cube name and drop it on the data cell in the table.

d. Change the Header value text to Cubes/Perspectives.

e. Set the Header font to 8pt and bold.

f. Set the Data font to 8pt.

g. Select both cells. In properties window expand BorderStyle and set the default to None.

h. Select just the CUBE_NAME text box and set the BorderStyle Top and Bottom both to Solid.

Figure P2-21 shows the Border Style properties.

Note that if you had left the BorderStyle Default set as Solid and then set Left and Right to None, you would have a problem. It would display perfectly in BIDS, with just a line at the top and bottom, but when you deploy it, lines would appear also on the left and right, forming a box. It might take you days to figure out what happened and correct it. (Vertical lines aren't needed because the columns of numbers line up.)

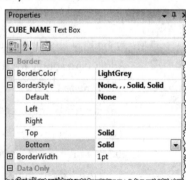

FIGURE P2-21

When you preview it you will see the cube metadata, as shown in Figure P2-22.

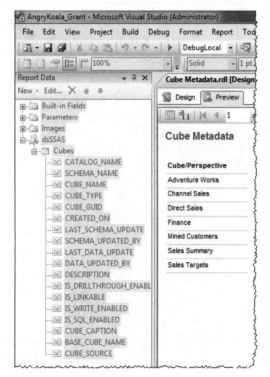

FIGURE P2-22

Adding MeasureGroups (for Cube/Perspective)

Follow these steps to insert a table named MeasureGroups and filter the data by CUBE_NAME using a self-calling drill-through action (when you click on a cube or perspective name on a row in the Cube table we just created).

1. Create a report parameter called pCube and set default value as Channel Sales.

2. Create a new dataset called MeasureGroups , set the query to

    ```
    SELECT * FROM $System.MDSCHEMA_MEASUREGROUPS
    ```

3. Add this filter: [CUBE_NAME] = [@pCube].

    A slightly more efficient approach is to add a pCube parameter to the dataset and then modify the query to the expression (but with the small amount of data there is little difference in response time):

```
="SELECT * FROM $System.MDSCHEMA_MEASUREGROUPS"
& " WHERE CUBE_NAME = '" & Parameters!pCube.Value & "'"
```

The Dataset Properties dialog in Figure P2-23 shows the filter condition.

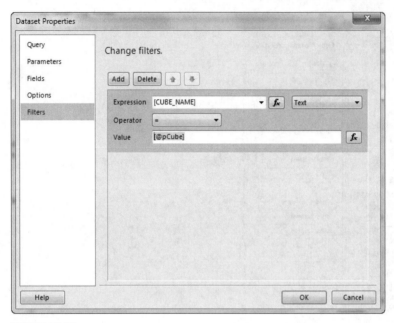

FIGURE P2-23

4. Highlight the currently selected cube and MeasureGroup and add the self-calling drill-through action.

5. For the CUBE_NAME text box in the properties window set the BackgroundColor expression to

```
=iif(Fields!CUBE_NAME.Value=Parameters!pCube.Value,"LemonChiffon","White")
```

6. Open the CUBE_NAME Text Box Properties dialog. In the Action page, select the Go to report radio button.

7. Set Specify a report to Cube Metadata. That is the name of the report you are building, so it is calling itself.

8. Add a parameter named pCube with a value of [CUBE_NAME] as shown in Figure P2-24.

9. Click OK.

10. Preview the report. You can see that clicking on a Cube/Perspective to select it displays the associated MeasureGroups, as shown in Figure P2-25.

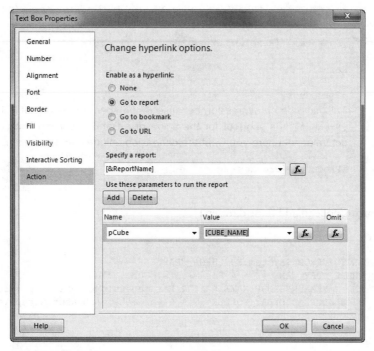

FIGURE P2-24

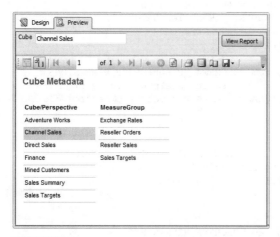

FIGURE P2-25

Adding Other Cube Metadata

You can also add metadata for measures, dimensions, hierarchies, and levels by following these steps:

1. Add the following report parameters and set their default values to the following:

PARAMETER	VALUE
pMeasure	[Measures].[Reseller Gross Profit]
pMeasureGroup	Reseller Sales
pDimension	="[Product]" This must be an expression because of the special meaning of [ ] in SSRS. [Product] is a shortcut for the value of a DataSet column such as Product.Value, but here you want the dimension unique name [Product].
pHierarchy	[Product].[Product Categories]

2. Enter the following code to add these datasets:

a. Measures

```
="SELECT * FROM $System.MDSCHEMA_MEASURES"
+ " WHERE CUBE_NAME = '" & Parameters!pCube.Value & "'"
+ " AND ( MEASUREGROUP_NAME = '" & Parameters!pMeasureGroup.Value & "'"
+ " OR MEASURE_DISPLAY_FOLDER = '" & Parameters!pMeasureGroup.Value & "' )"
```

Example:

```
SELECT * FROM $System.MDSCHEMA_MEASURES
WHERE CUBE_NAME = 'Channel Sales'
AND ( MEASUREGROUP_NAME = 'Reseller Sales'
OR MEASURE_DISPLAY_FOLDER = 'Reseller Sales' )
```

b. MeasureGroupDimensions

```
="SELECT * FROM $System.MDSCHEMA_MEASUREGROUP_DIMENSIONS "
+ " WHERE CUBE_NAME = '" & Parameters!pCube.Value & "'"
+ " AND MEASUREGROUP_NAME = '" & Parameters!pMeasureGroup.Value & "'"
```

Example:

```
SELECT * FROM $System.MDSCHEMA_MEASUREGROUP_DIMENSIONS
WHERE CUBE_NAME = 'Channel Sales'
AND MEASUREGROUP_NAME = 'Reseller Sales'
```

c. Hierarchies

```
="SELECT * FROM $System.MDSCHEMA_HIERARCHIES"
+ " WHERE CUBE_NAME = '" & Parameters!pCube.Value & "'"
+ " AND [DIMENSION_UNIQUE_NAME] = '" & Parameters!pDimension.Value & "'"
```

Example:

```
SELECT * FROM $System.MDSCHEMA_HIERARCHIES
 WHERE CUBE_NAME = 'Channel Sales'
 AND [DIMENSION_UNIQUE_NAME] = '[Product]'
```

d. Levels

```
="SELECT * FROM $System.MDSCHEMA_LEVELS "
+ " WHERE CUBE_NAME = '" & Parameters!pCube.Value & "'"
+ " AND [DIMENSION_UNIQUE_NAME] = '" & Parameters!pDimension.Value & "'"
+ " AND [HIERARCHY_UNIQUE_NAME] = '" & Parameters!pHierarchy.Value & "'"
```

Example:

```
SELECT * FROM $System.MDSCHEMA_LEVELS
WHERE CUBE_NAME = 'Channel Sales'
AND [DIMENSION_UNIQUE_NAME] = '[Product]'
AND [HIERARCHY_UNIQUE_NAME] = '[Product].[Product Categories]'
```

e. Datasets for databases and dimensions could also be included with this code:

```
select * FROM $System.DBSCHEMA_CATALOGS

="select * FROM $System.MDSCHEMA_DIMENSIONS WHERE CUBE_NAME = '" &
    Parameters!pCube.Value & "'"
```

Example:

```
SELECT * FROM $System.MDSCHEMA_DIMENSIONS
WHERE CUBE_NAME = 'Channel Sales'
```

You should now see the Report Data shown in Figure P2-26.

Now you add a table for each dataset, an expression to highlight the field when it's selected, and create a self-calling drill-through action.

1. MeasuresGroups

You have already created the MeasureGroup table, now you need to highlight the currently selected MeasureGroup row and create a self-calling drill-though action to allow for selecting a MeasureGroup on a different row. (You will also add new parameters to the CUBE_NAME drill-through action.)

a. Open the text box properties for MEASUREGROUP_NAME and in the Fill page set Fill Color to the following expression:

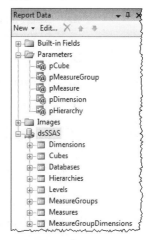

FIGURE P2-26

```
=iif(Fields!MEASUREGROUP_NAME.Value=Parameters!pMeasureGroup.Value,
"LemonChiffon","White")
```

b. On the Action page set the Enable action as a hyperlink radio button to Go to report, set Specify a report to [&ReportName], and add the following Report Parameter names and values:

PARAMETER	VALUE
pCube	[@pCube]
pMeasureGroup	[MEASUREGROUP_NAME]
pMeasure	[@pMeasure]

c. Now that you have added the extra parameters, go back to the CUBE_NAME Text Box properties and add to the Action page the following parameters:

PARAMETER	VALUE
pMeasureGroup	[@pMeasureGroup]
pMeasure	[@pMeasure]

2. Measures

In the following steps, you set the Measure text box to Gray if the metadata is not visible and you create a Tooltip to display additional information. Alternatively, you can add columns to show other metadata.

a. Insert a table and delete one column, leaving two. Drag the field [MEASURE_NAME] on to the data cell.

b. Set all cells in table to be 8pt.

c. Rename the header from MEASURE_NAME to Measure.

d. In the Text Box Properties dialog for MEASURE_NAME, add a self-calling drill-through action by setting Specify a report to [&ReportName] with the following parameter names and values:

PARAMETER	VALUE
pCube	[@pCube]
pMeasureGroup	[@pMeasureGroup]
pMeasure	[MEASURE_UNIQUE_NAME]

e. Set BackgroundColor to LemonChiffon when the field is selected:

```
=iif(Fields!MEASURE_UNIQUE_NAME.Value=Parameters!pMeasure.Value,
"LemonChiffon","White")
```

f. Set the font color to Gray when MEASURE is not visible:

```
=iif(Fields!MEASURE_IS_VISIBLE.Value,"Blue","Gray")
```

g. Add a Tooltip with the measure's description and an expression for calculated measures:

```
="Measure described as '" + Fields!DESCRIPTION.Value
+ "' with format " + Fields!DEFAULT_FORMAT_STRING.Value
+ " " + Fields!EXPRESSION.Value
```

h. Add a group based on the field [MEASURE_DISPLAY_FOLDER] by following these steps:

i. Highlight the detail row in the table, right-click, and select Add Group ➪ Parent Group as shown in Figure P2-27.

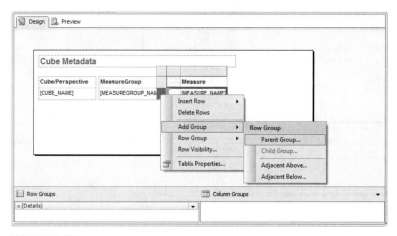

FIGURE P2-27

ii. Select [MEAURE_DISPLAY_FOLDER] in the option box and check Add group Header. Click OK. The Tablix group dialog box should look like Figure P2-28.

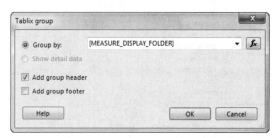

FIGURE P2-28

iii. Highlight the first column and delete it as shown in Figure P2-29.

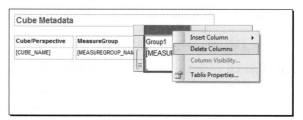

FIGURE P2-29

    iv. Select the two cells in the second row and right click, then select Merge cells as shown in Figure P2-30.

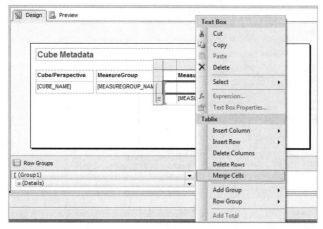

FIGURE P2-30

    v. Click on the field selection icon in the new merged cell and select MEASURE_DISPLAY_FOLDER, as shown in Figure P2-31.

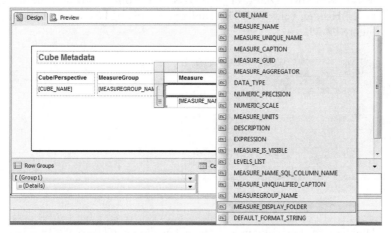

FIGURE P2-31

vi. Set FontStyle to Italic.

The design surface should resemble Figure P2-32 and preview like Figure P2-33.

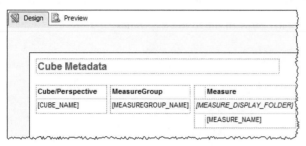

FIGURE P2-32

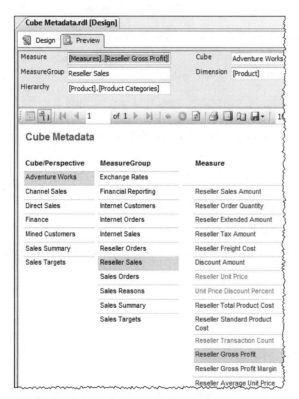

FIGURE P2-33

3. Dimensions

List the dimensions for the selected MeasureGroup and highlight the current dimension.

a. Add a table with the field [DIMENSION_UNIQUE_NAME] from the Measure-GroupDimensions dataset.

b. Change the value to an expression to remove the [ ]. (Unfortunately, the dimension-friendly name is not available in the MeasureGroupDimensions dataset.)

```
=Replace(Replace(Fields!DIMENSION_UNIQUE_NAME.Value,"[",""),"]","")
```

c. Add a self drill-through action with the following values:

PARAMETER	VALUE
pCube	[@pCube]
pMeasureGroup	[@pMeasureGroup]
pMeasure	[MEASURE_UNIQUE_NAME]

d. Set BackgroundColor to LemonChiffon when the field is selected:

```
=iif(Fields!DIMENSION_UNIQUE_NAME.Value=Parameters!pDimension.Value,
"LemonChiffon","White")
```

e. Set the font color to Gray if Measure is not visible:

```
=iif(Fields!DIMENSION_IS_VISIBLE.Value,"Black","Gray")
```

f. Add a row group based on the field [MEASURE_DISPLAY_FOLDER].

g. Set FontStyle to Italic.

4. Hierarchies

List the hierarchies for the selected dimension and highlight the current hierarchy.

a. Add a table with the field [HIERARCHY_NAME].

b. Add a self-calling drill-through action with the following parameter names and values. (The report is [&ReportName]):

PARAMETER	VALUE
pCube	[@pCube]
pDimension	[@pDimension]

c. Set BackgroundColor to LemonChiffon when the field is selected:

```
=iif(Fields!HIERARCHY_UNIQUE_NAME.Value=Parameters!pHierarchy.Value,
"LemonChiffon","White")
```

d. Set the font color to Gray if Hierarchy is not visible.

```
=iif(Fields!HIERARCHY_IS_VISIBLE.Value,"Blue","Gray")
```

e. Add a group based on the field [HIERACHY_DISPLAY_FOLDER] using the same technique you used for Measures previously.

f. Set FontStyle to Italic.

5. Levels

To provide complete information, show the level name and number for the selected hierarchy.

a. Add a table with the field [LEVEL_NAME].

b. Add a second details column with the value [LEVEL_NUMBER].

c. Set all fields to `DimGray`.

Figures P2-34 and P2-35 show the design surface and preview for Dimensions, Hierarhies, and Levels.

Dimension	Hierarchy	Level	Hea der
«Expr»	[HIERACHY_DISPLAY_FOLDER]	[LEVEL_NAME]	[LEVI
	[HIERARCHY_NAME]		

FIGURE P2-34

Dimension	Hierarchy	Level	
Date		(All)	0
Delivery Date	Category	Category	1
Destination Currency	Large Photo	Subcategory	2
Employee	Model Name	Product	3
Geography	Product		
Product	Product Categories		
Promotion	Product Line		
Reseller	Product Model Lines		
Reseller Sales Order Details	Style		
Sales Territory	Subcategory		
Ship Date	*Financial*		
Source Currency	Dealer Price		
	List Price		
	Standard Cost		
	History		
	End Date		
	Start Date		

FIGURE P2-35

Final Thoughts

You now have a way to discover information about the structure of your cubes so that, if you also populate the description fields within Analysis Server, you can provide users with up-to-date documentation, such as a measure's meaning. You can also enable users to search for a measure by name or you can add a help button on a standard report to display details of a dimension or measure.

The Cube Browser and the Angry Koala Cube Browser recipes in this book use this report. With some modifications, it will enable users to dynamically change the rows, columns, and filters in their Cube Browser reports.

Credits and References

http://angrykoala.com.au/_blog/Blog

http://cubesurfer.codeplex.com

http://reportsurfer.com

CUBE BROWSER

You can build a fully functional OLAP browser in Reporting Services by using drill-through actions to link the Cube Dynamic Rows report, where you can change what you see in Rows, to the Cube Metadata report where you can interrogate the cube to report on its structure. The steps to build a simple OLAP browser are:

1. Extend the Cube Dynamic Rows recipe to include dynamic columns.

2. Add a date filter.

3. Add a dynamic filter.

4. Allow users to change the measure.

5. Link the new report with a modified version of the Cube Metadata report to allow users to:

   ➤ Select the measure to display.

   ➤ Change content of rows and columns.

   ➤ Change the filter.

With these features, developers or power users can create a report with any combination of Rows, Columns, Filter, Date, and Measure by creating a linked report and setting the parameters appropriately. Also, once a report is running, users can slice and dice their data, and, if using the native reporting services manager, they can also create their own version of a report by simply saving the current report as a favorite in Internet Explorer.

This cube browser report is also *fast*. In a traditional report, when you add parameters in the MDX query window, behind the scenes an MDX query is generated for each parameter. This means that when a report is run, there can be 10-20 MDX queries running before the report is rendered. In the Cube Browser Report there is only the MDX query to bring back data for the grid (plus a very basic SQL union statement to generate a list of numbers for the row count and column count). You go to other supporting reports to collect parameters. Consequently when you drill up and down the response time is fantastic.

Figure P2-36 displays a Sales report and Figure P2-37 a Profit and Loss report. Both are examples of a finished Cube Browser report, just with different parameters.

Product Versions

➤ Reporting Services 2008

What You'll Need

➤ A basic understanding of and ability to read MDX

Gross Profit for April 2004 Product Categories by Sales Territory Promotions : All Promotions						columns
Swap rows with						5
Columns | Filter	All Sales Territories	North America	Europe	Pacific	NA	6
All Products	667 k	273 k	216 k	178 k		7
Bikes	583 k	219 k	197 k	167 k		10
Mountain Bikes	310 k	151 k	99 k	60 k		20
Mountain-200 Silver, 38	54 k	29 k	15 k	9.5 k		50
Mountain-200 Black, 38	50 k	24 k	16 k	9.4 k		100
Mountain-200 Black, 42	46 k	19 k	13 k	14 k		
Mountain-200 Silver, 42	41 k	20 k	14 k	6.3 k		
Mountain-200 Black, 46	40 k	19 k	15 k	6.3 k		
Mountain-200 Silver, 46	37 k	16 k	12 k	8.4 k		
Mountain-400-W Silver, 46	7.7 k	3.1 k	3.1 k	1.4 k		

Rows   5   6   7   10   20   50   100

run by platypus\grantp in < 1 second
11:00:25 PM Monday, December 07, 2009

Cube Browser
Page 1 of 1

FIGURE P2-36

Amount for February 2004 Accounts by Departments Organizations : North America Operations						columns
Swap rows with					Executive	columns
Columns | Filter	Corporate	Research and Development	Manufacturing	Quality Assurance	General and Administration	5
Net Income	241 k	788 k	(23 k)	(18 k)	(9.3 k)	6
Operating Profit	345 k	891 k	(23 k)	(18 k)	(9.3 k)	7
Operating Expenses	942 k	396 k	23 k	18 k	9.3 k	10
Labor Expenses	757 k	276 k	20 k	16 k	8.2 k	20
Commissions	63 k	63 k				50
Telephone and Utilities	33 k	21 k	555	435	196	100
Depreciation	31 k	11 k	960	656	404	
Travel Expenses	26 k	10 k	789	586	184	
Rent	12 k	4.5 k	347	277	139	
Office Supplies	6.0 k	2.3 k	175	132	50	

Rows   5   6   7   10   20   50   100

run by platypus\grantp in < 1 second
11:46:48 PM Monday, December 07, 2009

Cube Browser
Page 1 of 1

FIGURE P2-37

Anatomy of the Reports

Rather than a step-by-step approach to building the reports in this suite, let's run through the architecture and then the necessary techniques (recipes) utilized within the reports.

The reports are:

➤ Cube Browser

➤ Cube Browser Metadata

➤ Cube Browser Member

First, take a look at the roles of these reports.

Cube Browser

This Cube Browser is the main report and the only report directly visible to your users. You can have multiple linked reports based on this physical report showing different data on rows, columns, and filters by simply creating a linked report and changing the parameters.

The following list explains what users can do in this report and any linked reports, and how to do it. The key action for each item is in parentheses, as are any supporting parameter settings.

➤ Change the measure to display. Click on Measure Name in the title to drill-through to the Cube Browser Metadata report (driver = Measure).

➤ Change what hierarchy to display on rows. Click on Hierarchy Name in title to drill-through to Cube Browser Metadata (driver = Rows).

➤ Change what hierarchy to display on columns. Click on the Column Hierarchy Name to drill-through to Cube Browser Metadata (driver = Columns).

➤ Change what hierarchy to use for a filter. Click on the Filter Hierarchy Name to drill-through to Cube Browser Metadata (driver = Filter).

➤ Change the Filter value (member). Click on the Filter Member Name to drill-through to Cube Browser Member (driver = Filter).

➤ Change the date period (it can be year, quarter, month or day). Click on the Date Member in the title to drill-through to Cube Browser Member (driver = Date).

➤ Drill up and down the hierarchy displayed on rows or columns. Click on a row member to drill-to-self with new selection.

➤ Change the number of rows or columns to display. Click on row number to drill-to-self with new selection.

➤ Swap rows with filter. Click on the Swap Filter textbox to drill-to-self with `Row` and `Filter` parameters swapped.

➤ Swap rows and columns. Click on the Swap Column textbox to drill-to-self with `Row` and `Column` parameters swapped.

Figure P2-38 shows the key navigation paths from the Cube Browser to the Cube Browser Metadata, and the Cube Browser Member.

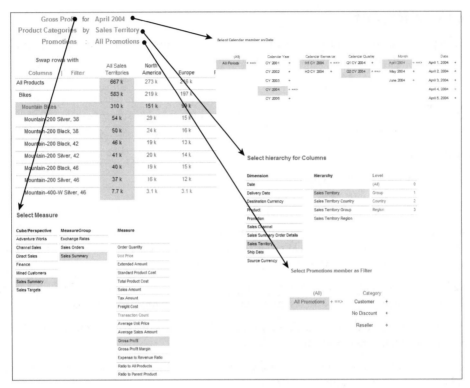

FIGURE P2-38

Cube Browser Metadata

The Cube Browser Metadata report is called from the Cube Browser report and returns a measure or a hierarchy. It is based on the Cube Metadata report and is called when the user wants to:

➤ Change the measure.

➤ Select what hierarchy to display on rows or columns.

➤ Select what hierarchy to filter by.

It therefore has two distinct behaviors. The following list explains what users can do if the driver parameter is Measure, and how to do it. The key action for each item is in parentheses, as are any supporting parameter settings.

➤ Select a cube/perspective. Click on the MeasureLabel to initiate drill-to-self action to display measures available in selected cube.

➤ Select a measure from the cube/perspective. Click on a measure to fire it as a drill-back action to the Cube Browser report passing the selected Measure.

The following list explains what users can do if the driver parameter is Row, Column, or Filter, and how to do it. The key action for each item is in parentheses, as are any supporting parameter settings.

➤ Select a dimension. Drill-to-self to display hierarchies.

➤ Choose a hierarchy for a selected dimension. Drill-back to Cube Browser with selected hierarchy: (driver = rows, columns, or filter).

Note that you do not hard code the report you *drill back* to. One of the parameters is the calling report and that allows this report to be called from different linked reports.

Cube Browser Member

The Cube Browser Member report is called from the Cube Browser report and returns a hierarchy member. It is called when the user wants to:

➤ Select a period of time to filter the report by (a specific year, quarter, month, or day).

➤ Select a member to filter the report by.

Behind the Scenes

Now let's look at the details and the recipes utilized.

Cube Browser

The Cube Browser report is based on the Cube Dynamic Rows recipe. It uses the same basic concept but extends the idea to columns. Date and dynamic filters are added. To do that you need the following parameters (I have included an example default value):

➤ pCube = Sales Summary (the name of the cube or perspective)

➤ pMeasureGroup = Sales Summary (the name of the MeasureGroup)

➤ pMeasure = [Measures].[Gross Profit] (the UniqueName of the measure)

➤ pDateMbr = [Date].[Calendar].[Month].&[2004]&[4] (the UniqueName of the Date member)

➤ pRowMbr = [Product].[Product Categories].[Subcategory].&[1] (the UniqueName of the member from which ascendants and children are shown on rows)

➤ pRowCount = 10 (the number of rows to show)

➤ pColMbr = [Sales Territory].[Sales Territory].[All Sales Territories] (the Unique-Name of the member from which ascendants and children are shown on columns)

➤ pColCount = 5 (the number of columns to show)

➤ pFilterMbr = [Promotion].[Promotions].[All Promotions] (the UniqueName of the member acting as filter)

If you open the DataSet1 query and select the parameters icon from toolbar, you'll see the list of parameters together with their default values, as shown in Figure P2-39.

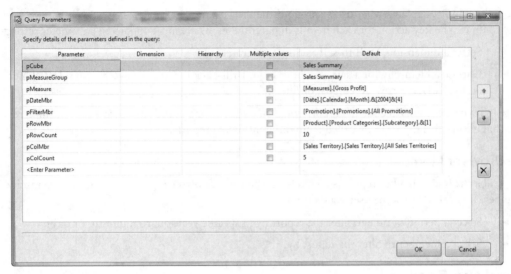

FIGURE P2-39

Here is the required MDX query including the necessary additions for extra functionality:

```
---------------------------------------------------------------------------
-- Cube Browser
--
-- Grant Paisley
-- Angry Koala
-- http://angrykoala.com.au
-- 10 Dec 2010
--
--
-- Note: certain attributes commented out as not needed
-- but may be of use in other reports
---------------------------------------------------------------------------

WITH
-- The measure of interest
MEMBER [Measures].[Measure_Value] AS StrToValue(@pMeasure)

-- the friendly name of the measure
MEMBER [Measures].[Measure_Label] AS StrToValue(@pMeasure + ".Member_Name")

-- Row metadata
MEMBER [Measures].[Row_Key]
    AS StrToValue( @pRowMbr + ".Hierarchy.Currentmember.Uniquename" )
MEMBER [Measures].[Row_Label]
    AS StrToValue( @pRowMbr + ".Hierarchy.CurrentMember.Member_Caption" )
MEMBER [Measures].[Row_Level]
    AS StrToValue( @pRowMbr + ".Hierarchy.CurrentMember.Level.Ordinal" )
MEMBER [Measures].[Row_Level_Name]
    AS StrToValue( @pRowMbr + ".Hierarchy.Level.Name" )
```

```
MEMBER [Measures].[Row_Hierarchy_Name]
   AS StrToValue( @pRowMbr + ".Hierarchy.Name" )
MEMBER [Measures].[Row_Hierarchy_UniqueName]
  AS StrToValue( @pRowMbr + ".Hierarchy.UniqueName" )
MEMBER [Measures].[Row_Dimension_Name]
   AS StrToValue( @pRowMbr + ".Dimension.Name" )
MEMBER [Measures].[Row_Dimension_UniqueName]
   AS StrToValue(@pRowMbr + ".Dimension_Unique_Name" )

-- Column metadata
MEMBER [Measures].[Col_Key]
   AS StrToValue( @pColMbr + ".Hierarchy.Currentmember.Uniquename" )
MEMBER [Measures].[Col_Label]
   AS StrToValue( @pColMbr + ".Hierarchy.CurrentMember.Member_Caption" )
MEMBER [Measures].[Col_Level]
   AS StrToValue( @pColMbr + ".Hierarchy.CurrentMember.Level.Ordinal" )
MEMBER [Measures].[Col_Level_Name]
   AS StrToValue( @pColMbr + ".Hierarchy.Level.Name" )
MEMBER [Measures].[Col_Hierarchy_Name]
   AS StrToValue( @pColMbr + ".Hierarchy.Name" )
MEMBER [Measures].[Col_Hierarchy_UniqueName]
  AS StrToValue( @pColMbr + ".Hierarchy.UniqueName" )
MEMBER [Measures].[Col_Dimension_Name]
   AS StrToValue( @pColMbr + ".Dimension.Name" )
MEMBER [Measures].[Col_Dimension_UniqueName]
   AS StrToValue(@pColMbr + ".Dimension_Unique_Name" )

-- Filter metadata
MEMBER [Measures].[Filter_Key]
   AS StrToValue( @pFilterMbr + ".Hierarchy.Currentmember.Uniquename" )
MEMBER [Measures].[Filter_Label]
   AS StrToValue( @pFilterMbr + ".Hierarchy.CurrentMember.Member_Caption" )
MEMBER [Measures].[Filter_Level]
   AS StrToValue( @pFilterMbr + ".Hierarchy.CurrentMember.Level.Ordinal" )
MEMBER [Measures].[Filter_Level_Name]
   AS StrToValue( @pFilterMbr + ".Hierarchy.Level.Name" )
MEMBER [Measures].[Filter_Hierarchy_Name]
   AS StrToValue( @pFilterMbr + ".Hierarchy.Name" )
MEMBER [Measures].[Filter_Hierarchy_UniqueName]
  AS StrToValue( @pFilterMbr + ".Hierarchy.UniqueName" )
MEMBER [Measures].[Filter_Dimension_Name]
   AS StrToValue( @pFilterMbr + ".Dimension.Name" )
MEMBER [Measures].[Filter_Dimension_UniqueName]
   AS StrToValue(@pFilterMbr + ".Dimension_Unique_Name" )

-- Date metadata
MEMBER [Measures].[Date_Key]
   AS StrToValue( @pDateMbr + ".Hierarchy.Currentmember.Uniquename" )
MEMBER [Measures].[Date_Label]
   AS StrToValue( @pDateMbr + ".Hierarchy.CurrentMember.Member_Caption" )
MEMBER [Measures].[Date_Level]
   AS StrToValue( @pDateMbr + ".Hierarchy.CurrentMember.Level.Ordinal" )
MEMBER [Measures].[Date_Level_Name]
   AS StrToValue( @pDateMbr + ".Hierarchy.Level.Name" )
```

```
MEMBER [Measures].[Date_Hierarchy_Name]
   AS StrToValue( @pDateMbr + ".Hierarchy.Name" )
MEMBER [Measures].[Date_Hierarchy_UniqueName]
  AS StrToValue( @pDateMbr + ".Hierarchy.UniqueName" )
MEMBER [Measures].[Date_Dimension_Name]
   AS StrToValue( @pDateMbr + ".Dimension.Name" )
MEMBER [Measures].[Date_Dimension_UniqueName]
   AS StrToValue(@pDateMbr + ".Dimension_Unique_Name" )


SELECT NON EMPTY {
 -- display the measure and rownumber attributes on columns

 [Measures].[Row_Key],
 [Measures].[Row_Label],
 [Measures].[Row_Level],
 [Measures].[Row_Level_Name],
 [Measures].[Row_Hierarchy_Name],
 [Measures].[Row_Hierarchy_UniqueName],
 [Measures].[Row_Dimension_Name],
 [Measures].[Row_Dimension_UniqueName],

 [Measures].[Col_Key],
 [Measures].[Col_Label],
 [Measures].[Col_Level],
 [Measures].[Col_Level_Name],
 [Measures].[Col_Hierarchy_Name],
 [Measures].[Col_Hierarchy_UniqueName],
 [Measures].[Col_Dimension_Name],
 [Measures].[Col_Dimension_UniqueName],

 [Measures].[Filter_Key],
 [Measures].[Filter_Label],
 [Measures].[Filter_Level],
 [Measures].[Filter_Level_Name],
 [Measures].[Filter_Hierarchy_Name],
 [Measures].[Filter_Hierarchy_UniqueName],
 [Measures].[Filter_Dimension_Name],
 [Measures].[Filter_Dimension_UniqueName],

 [Measures].[Date_Key],
 [Measures].[Date_Label],
 [Measures].[Date_Level],
 [Measures].[Date_Level_Name],
 [Measures].[Date_Hierarchy_Name],
 [Measures].[Date_Hierarchy_UniqueName],
 [Measures].[Date_Dimension_Name],
 [Measures].[Date_Dimension_UniqueName],

 [Measures].[Measure_Value],
 [Measures].[Measure_Label]


} ON COLUMNS,
```

```
    -- returns the top n number of rows based on current measure

    TOPCOUNT(

        -- show the current hierarachy member with its ascendants
        -- together with its children on rows

        STRTOSET(
            "{Ascendants(" + @pRowMbr + " ), "
            + @pRowMbr + ".children}"
        )

        ,StrToValue(@pRowCount)
        ,[Measures].[Measure_Value]
    )

*   -- cross product

    -- returns the top n number of Columns based on current measure

    TOPCOUNT(

        -- show the current hierarachy member with its ascendants
        -- together with it's children on Columns

        STRTOSET(
            "{Ascendants(" + @pColMbr + " ), "
            + @pColMbr + ".children}"
        )

        ,StrToValue(@pColCount)
        ,[Measures].[Measure_Value]
    )


ON ROWS

FROM [Adventure Works] -- must hard code the cube :(
-- the cube name, together with the default values are the only
-- things required to point this report at a different cube

WHERE STRTOTUPLE( "(" +@pFilterMbr +"," + @pDateMbr + ")" )
```

Much like how you created calculated measures for the metadata on rows, you now get the same metadata for the Date, Filter, and Column members. For each you collect:

➤ Key

➤ Label

➤ Level

➤ Level_Name

➤ Hierarchy_Name

➤ Hierarchy_UniqueName

➤ Dimension_Name

➤ Dimension_UniqueName

Notice that you have:

➤ added extra measures to display metadata for columns, date, and filter.

➤ created a cross product between rows and columns.

➤ added a tuple in the WHERE clause based on the Date member and the Filter member.

As shown in Figure P2-40, when you run the MDX query you see all the metadata together with the Measure value you want to display: Measure_Value.

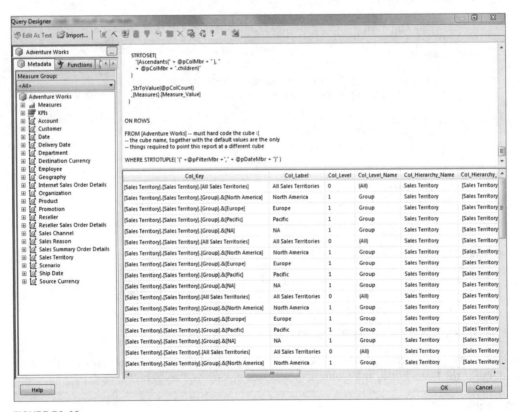

FIGURE P2-40

Report Body

The main tablix, shown in Figure P2-41, is a matrix with:

➤ columns grouped by `Col_Key` and displaying `Col_Label`.

➤ rows grouped by `Row_Key` and displaying `Row_Label`.

➤ the `Measure_Value` in the details cell.

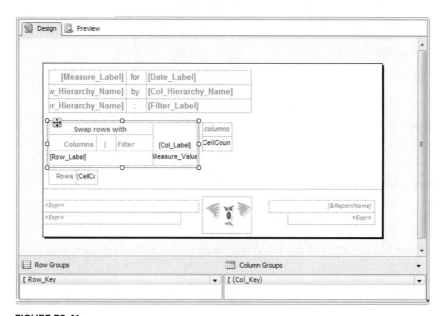

FIGURE P2-41

In the columns, similarly to the rows, the group is by `Col_Key` and sorted by the `Col_Level` (the level in the hierarchy) and within the level, descending by `Measure_Value`. You could enhance the report by adding a parameter to control whether sorting is ascending or descending (see Figure P2-42).

The `Measure_Value` textbox is tweaked to highlight the current member (LemonChiffon) for rows and columns.

The BackgroundColor is set as follows:

```
=iif(Fields!Row_Key.Value=Parameters!pRowMbr.Value, "LemonChiffon",
 iif(Fields!Col_Key.Value=Parameters!pColMbr.Value, "LemonChiffon",
 Nothing
 ))
```

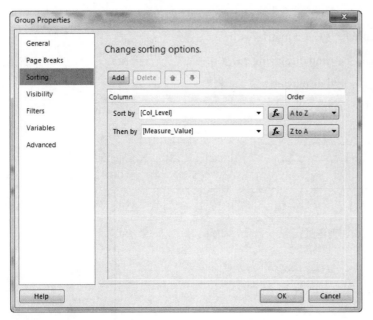

FIGURE P2-42

Similarly the font is set to Black if this cell corresponds to the current member; otherwise it is set to DimGray.

```
=iif(Fields!Row_Key.Value=Parameters!pRowMbr.Value, "Black",
 iif(Fields!Col_Key.Value=Parameters!pColMbr.Value, "Black",
  "DimGray"
  ))
```

On the labels for rows and columns the same background color is set (LemonChiffon), but the text color is DimGray if they correspond to the current member; otherwise it is Blue, indicating you can click on it to drill up and down the hierarchy.

```
=iif(Fields!Row_Key.Value=Parameters!pRowMbr.Value,
"DimGray",
"Blue")
```

Restricting Rows and Columns

The parameter pRowCount restricts the number of rows displayed in this report.

You simply use the TOPCOUNT function in MDX to restrict the number of row members returned in the query driven by the parameter pRowCount. However, instead of the user having to select the parameter with a fiddly option box in the parameters, the user just clicks on the number of rows they want. The TablixRowCount table displays these selectable values from the CellCount dataset. The clickable values are colored Blue except for the numeric matching the current parameter value and it is DimGray.

Clicking invokes a self-drill-though action with all parameters set as their existing values except for pRowCount, and that is set to the value of the TexboxRowCount cell clicked on. Figure P2-43 shows the parameter values for this action.

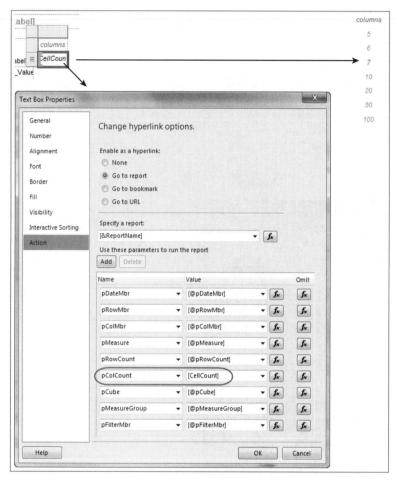

FIGURE P2-43

Restricting columns works in the same way as with the parameter pColCount. See the "Cube Restricting Rows" recipe later in this book.

Swap Actions

In the top left cell of the main tablix is the TablixSwap. It contains two blue cells that allow the user to swap the rows with columns or swap the rows with the filter. Again, all that happens is a self-drill-though action takes place. For instance, for the rows and columns swap, we set up Tooltip:

```
="Swap rows ("
+ Fields!Row_Hierarchy_Name.Value
+ ") with columns ("
+ Fields!Col_Hierarchy_Name.Value
+ ")"
```

and set up a self-drill-though action. Notice the swapping of row and column parameters. Figure P2-44 shows this.

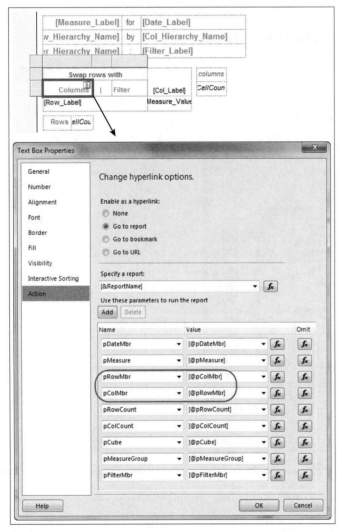

FIGURE P2-44

Titles

The titles in the report work both as titles and as places where users get to change what they see in the report.

Changing the Measure (TextboxMeasureName)

The first textbox in the Titles table includes the Measure to display in the report. When users click on it, they are taken to the Cube Browser Metadata report to select a different measure from the same cube, or even a measure from a completely different cube. All parameters are passed to the Cube Browser Metadata report plus the following:

➤ pCallingReport = is set by the report calling this report. This allows drill-through textbox action to return to the calling report.

➤ pDriver = Measure indicating that the user wants to select a cube and measure. Other values are Rows, Columns, Date, Filter.

Figure P2-45 illustrates the action, and Figure P2-46 illustrates selecting a measure.

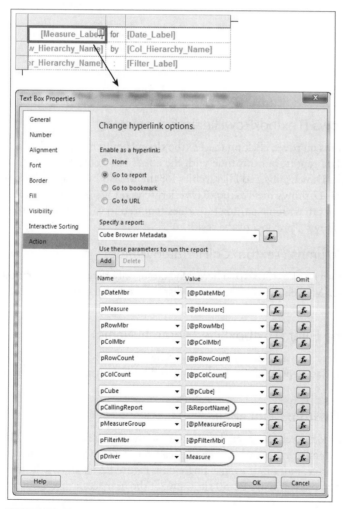

FIGURE P2-45

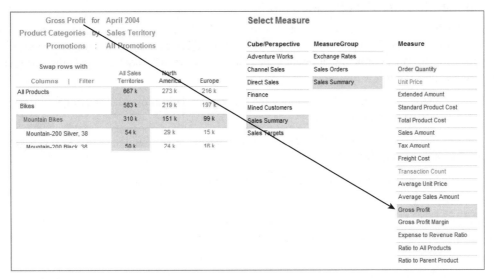

FIGURE P2-46

Changing the Hierarchy on Rows (TextboxRowHierarchyName)

Similarly, if you want to change what is on rows, click on the TextboxRowHierarchyName. The action calls the same Cube Browser Metadata report, but this time with the pDriver = Rows. Now the Cube Browser Metadata report displays the Dimensions and Hierarchies for the Measure Group corresponding to the current measure. Figure P2-47 shows the TextboxRowHierarchy on the design surface and the textbox properties window Action tab with the parameter values required to call the Cube Browser Metadata report, and Figure P2-48 shows a preview of the result.

Changing the Hierarchy on Columns (TextboxColHierarchyName)

Changing Columns works the same way as TextBoxRowHierarchyName, only the pDriver parameter is set to Columns so the Cube Browser Metadata report knows to display, and later return, the pColMbr parameter.

Changing the Hierarchy for the Filter (TextboxFilterHierarchyName)

Changing the filter also works the same way as TextBoxRowHierarchyName, only the pDriver is set to Filter so the Cube Browser Metadata report knows to display, and later return, the pFilterMbr parameter.

Changing the Date Member (TextboxDateLabel)

The user can change the period of time the report covers by clicking on the TextboxDateLabel. This drills-through to the Cube Browser Member report where the user can select another Date member in the hierarchy. This can be a year, quarter, month, or even a single day. Figure P2-49 shows the action parameters. This time pDriver is set to Date. (Figure P2-50 shows what the user sees.)

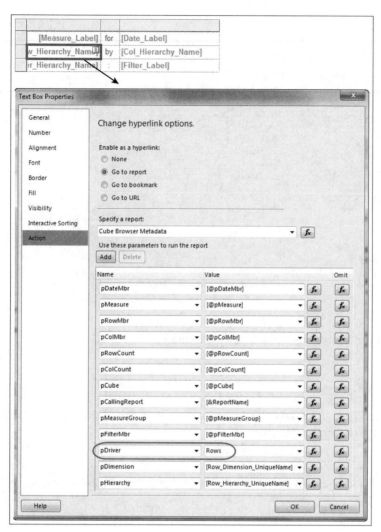

FIGURE P2-47

Footer Information

To round out the report, we have added some interesting information to the footer, including:

➤ Who ran it

➤ How long it took to execute

➤ Page numbers in 1 of *n* format

➤ The name of the report

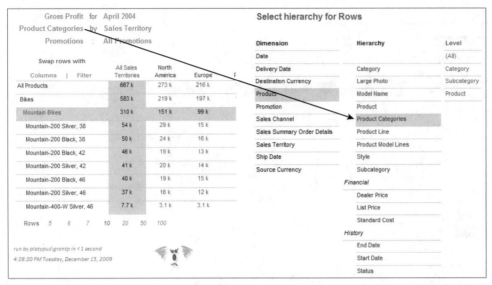

FIGURE P2-48

In production we always number our reports in the following format:

pnnn - <meaningful name>

For example: p012 - Channel Sales

So in the footer we would display the full number and name of the report, but in title we would strip out the number and just leave the report name.

Figure P2-51 shows a formatted footer.

The following is the code for the first textbox, which displays who ran the report and how long it took to run.

```
="run by " & User!UserID + " in " +

IIf(
 System.DateTime.Now.Subtract(Globals!ExecutionTime).TotalSeconds<1,
    "< 1 second",
(

IIf(System.DateTime.Now.Subtract(Globals!ExecutionTime).Hours >0,
    System.DateTime.Now.Subtract(Globals!ExecutionTime).Hours
    & " hour(s), ", "") +

IIf(System.DateTime.Now.Subtract(Globals!ExecutionTime).Minutes >0,
    System.DateTime.Now.Subtract(Globals!ExecutionTime).Minutes
    & " minute(s), ", "") +

IIf(System.DateTime.Now.Subtract(Globals!ExecutionTime).Seconds >0,
```

```
System.DateTime.Now.Subtract(Globals!ExecutionTime).Seconds
& " second(s)", ""))
```

```
)
```

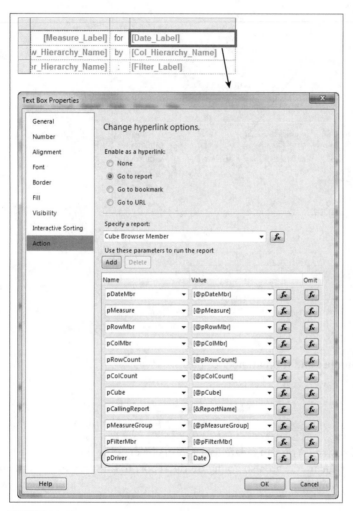

FIGURE P2-49

The next textbox shows the time the report was run.

```
= FormatDateTime(Globals!ExecutionTime,3)
& " "
& FormatDateTime(Globals!ExecutionTime,1)
```

Then, at the right of the footer comes the name of the report:

```
=Globals!ReportName
```

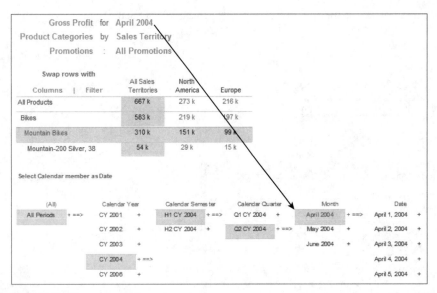

FIGURE P2-50

FIGURE P2-51

The final textbox holds the page number and total number of pages.

```
= "Page "
& Globals!PageNumber
& " of "
& Globals!TotalPages
```

So you now have a simple OLAP browser. You can create user reports by creating linked reports with different parameters. Interestingly, your users can also configure the report to one they like and then just save it as a favorite in Internet Explorer.

Final Thoughts

This is a great starting point for creating your own variation on an OLAP Cube Browser. For instance, the Angry Koala Cube Surfer report (shown in Figure P2-88) uses the same basic concept as the Cube Browser, but instead of showing a single measure in each data cell it shows:

➤   The measure for the current period (bold).

➤   The measure for the same period in a comparison period (driven by a lag number — for example, 12 means 12 months, and so would mean the same month last year.

➤   An Australian Sparkline (it has a line down under).

➤ Figure P2-52 shows the Cube Surfer comparing the last three periods to the previous periods - six, five, and four (lag = 3).

➤ Figure P2-53 shows the same report with a lag of 12 for a year on year comparison.

The Australian Sparkline report is covered in another recipe.

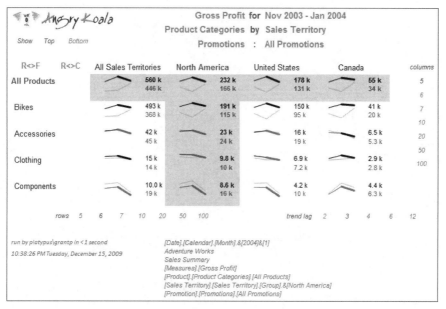

FIGURE P2-52

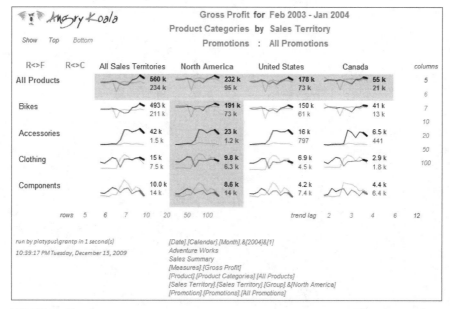

FIGURE P2-53

Credits and Related References

http://angrykoala.com.au/_blog/Blog

http://cubesurfer.codeplex.com

http://reportsurfer.com

AUSTRALIAN SPARKLINES

"In a project, we do not spend enough time on the final reporting and in particular on data visualization." That is one of the key points in my popular Extreme Reporting Services presentation. The Australian Sparkline (the sparkline with the line down under) is my attempt at getting richer information in a smaller space. Sparklines will be released with SQL2008 R2, can be built in SQL2005 based on the line chart (see Sparkline recipe), and can pack a lot of information into a single lineheight. After all, users usually just want to know the sales, profit, and so on for the current week or month or day, and the general trend (that is, is it going up, going down, or staying constant).

The Australian Sparkline visualizes both trend and rolling comparisons to prior periods. If you select Jun 2009 and Lag 3, you can compare that quarter's rolling 3 months with previous quarter. If you select Jun 2009 and Lag 12, you can compare 12 month rolling periods with the previous year. If you select an individual day, say 30 Aug 2009 and Lag 7, then you get to compare the daily trend of the week ending 30 Aug 2009 with the week ending 23 Aug 2009.

The Australian Sparkline's characteristics include the following:

➤ Up to double the height of a standard sparkline

➤ Includes two lines, comparing two consecutive rolling periods of time, for example, 12 months with last year, 7 days with last week

➤ The current period trend line is

   ➤ black when higher than the corresponding comparison period; red when lower

   ➤ a single-pixel-wide line, but a two-pixel-wide line for the last/current period

➤ The comparison period trend line is a single pixel width silver line

Figure P2-54 shows a year on year sales trend for Road Bikes. April 2004 sales of 1.2m (in black) are up from 1.1m in April 2003 (in gray), but Road Bikes as a percentage share of Bikes is down from 57% to 35%. Observe that even though the sales trend is looking better than last year, the percentage share has been significantly lower for a while.

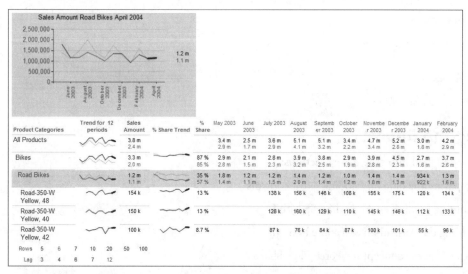

FIGURE P2-54

Figure P2-55 shows gross profit over three months compared to the prior three months before that. The April 2004 gross profit of 139k (in black) is up from 112k in January 2004 (in gray). Gross profit as percentage share is up from 23% to 24%.

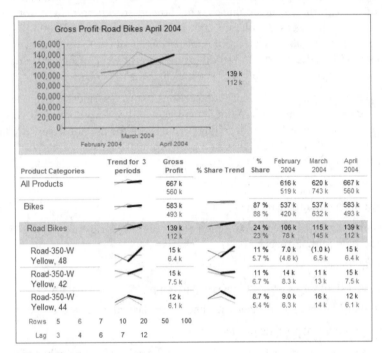

FIGURE P2-55

This recipe is an extension of the Cube Restricting Rows recipe in Part 7 of this book.

Product Versions

➤ Reporting Services 2008

What You'll Need

➤ Ability to read MDX

Designing the Report

This recipe is divided into several key sections:

➤ Preparing the data and adding extra controls

➤ Building a full sized Australian Sparkline

➤ Adding the Australian Sparkline to a table

➤ Extending the concept for Percentage Share

Preparing the Data and Adding Extra Controls

To create the Australian Sparkline you need more data than the Cube Restricting Rows recipe. Specifically you need to add a new parameter for the current period, and then modify the MDX query to return values of both the rolling periods and values for the period you are comparing to. You could create an Australian Sparkline based on SQL data but in this recipe you will use an MDX source.

First add the pLag parameter, for controlling the number of rolling periods in the trend, and the pDate parameter, for setting the current date period.

1. In BIDS make a copy of the report "Cube Restricting Rows" by copying and pasting it (Ctrl+C, Ctrl+V). Name it Australian Sparkline.

2. Create a new dataset called LagCount with the following SQL Query. See Figure P2-56.

```
Select 3 as LagCount union all
select 4 union all
select 6 union all
select 7 union all
select 12
```

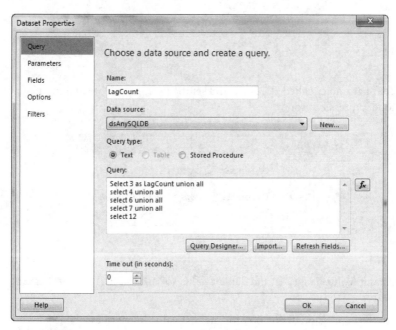

FIGURE P2-56

3. Create an integer parameter named pLag, and set the prompt to Lag and the following values from the LagCount dataset you just created (as shown in Figure P2-57):

➤ Dataset: LagCount

➤ Value field: LagCount

➤ Label field: LagCount

On the Default Values page, set the default value to= 12.

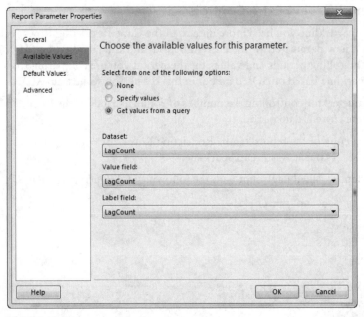

FIGURE P2-57

4.   Create a text parameter called pDateMbr and set the prompt to Date and the available values (Label/Value Expression) to:

LABEL	VALUE
30 Aug 2003	="[Date].[Calendar].[Date].&[20030830]"
April 2004	="[Date].[Calendar].[Month].&[2004]&[4]"
Q1 CY 2004	="[Date].[Calendar].[Calendar Quarter].&[2004]&[1]"

On the Default Values page, set the default value to [Date].[Calendar].[Month].&[2004]&[4]

Figure P2-58 shows the expression dialog box for the first value in list of available values.

Next, follow these steps to modify the MDX query in DataSet1 to utilize the pLag and pDate parameters to generate the set of date periods required by the Australian Sparkline to graph the trend values.

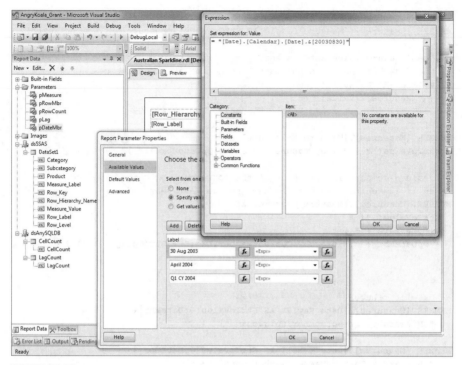

FIGURE P2-58

1. Open the query for DataSet1, and make the MDX modifications shown in bold in the following code.

```
-----------------------------------------------------------------------------

-- Grant Paisley
-- Angry Koala
-- http://angrykoala.com.au
-- 18 Dec 2008
--
-- Australian Sparkline
--
-- Note: certain attributes commented out as not needed
-- but may be of use in other reports
-----------------------------------------------------------------------------


WITH

-- The measure of interest
MEMBER [Measures].[Measure_Value] AS StrToValue(@pMeasure)
```

```
-- the friendly name of the measure
MEMBER [Measures].[Measure_Label] AS StrToValue(@pMeasure + ".Member_Name")

-- the [Measure_ValueLast] is set up to always return the value for
-- the date hard coded to the last time period in the sequence
-- eg MEMBER [Measures].[Measure_ValueLast] AS
-- ( [Measures].[Value],
--    [Time].[by Financial Year].[Financial Month].&[2009-04-01T00:00:00]
--  )
MEMBER [Measures].[Measure_ValueLast] AS
  strToValue( " ( " + @pMeasure + " , " + @pDateMbr + " )"  )

-- measure compare is the value of the corresponding compare period
-- eg if 12 months then with be same period last year
MEMBER [Measures].[Measure_Compare] AS
  StrToValue( "( "
  + @pMeasure + " , "
  + @pDateMbr + ".Hierarchy.CurrentMember.Lag(" + Str(@pLag)  + ") ) "
  )


-- date attributes
MEMBER [Measures].[Date_Key]   AS StrToValue(@pDateMbr +
   ".Hierarchy.Currentmember.Uniquename")

MEMBER [Measures].[Date_Label] AS StrToValue(@pDateMbr +
   ".Hierarchy.CurrentMember.Member_Caption")

MEMBER [Measures].[Date_Sort]   AS StrToValue(@pDateMbr +
   ".Hierarchy.Currentmember.Key")


-- row attributes
MEMBER [Measures].[Row_Key]
   AS StrToValue( @pRowMbr + ".Hierarchy.Currentmember.Uniquename" )

MEMBER [Measures].[Row_Label]
   AS StrToValue( @pRowMbr + ".Hierarchy.CurrentMember.Member_Caption" )

MEMBER [Measures].[Row_Level]
   AS StrToValue( @pRowMbr + ".Hierarchy.CurrentMember.Level.Ordinal" )

--MEMBER [Measures].[Row_Level_Name]
--   AS StrToValue( @pRowMbr + ".Hierarchy.Level.Name" )

MEMBER [Measures].[Row_Hierarchy_Name]
   AS StrToValue( @pRowMbr + ".Hierarchy.Name" )

--MEMBER [Measures].[Row_Hierarchy_UniqueName]
--   AS StrToValue( @pRowMbr + ".Hierarchy.UniqueName" )

MEMBER [Measures].[Row_Dimension_Name]
   AS StrToValue( @pRowMbr + ".Dimension.Name" )

--MEMBER [Measures].[Row_Dimension_UniqueName]
```

```
--   AS StrToValue(@pRowMbr + ".Dimension_Unique_Name" )

-- gives the ratio of member on row with its parent for the current period

MEMBER [Measures].[Measure_ValuePct] AS
  IIF(
  ([Measures].[Measure_Value], StrToMember([Measures].[Row_Key] + ".parent"))=0,

    Null,
    [Measures].[Measure_Value] /
   ([Measures].[Measure_Value], StrToMember([Measures].[Row_Key] + ".parent"))
  )

-- gives the ratio of member on row with its parent for the comparison period

MEMBER [Measures].[Measure_ComparePct] AS
  IIF(
  ([Measures].[Measure_Value], StrToMember([Measures].[Row_Key] + ".parent"))=0,

    Null,
    [Measures].[Measure_Compare] /
   ([Measures].[Measure_Compare], StrToMember([Measures].[Row_Key] + ".parent"))

  )


SELECT NON EMPTY {

-- date member info

 [Measures].[Date_Key],
 [Measures].[Date_Label],
 [Measures].[Date_Sort],

 -- display row member attributes

 [Measures].[Row_Key],
 [Measures].[Row_Label],
 [Measures].[Row_Level],
 --[Measures].[Row_Level_Name],
 [Measures].[Row_Hierarchy_Name],
 --[Measures].[Row_Hierarchy_UniqueName],
 --[Measures].[Row_Dimension_Name],
 --[Measures].[Row_Dimension_UniqueName],

-- measure value and other attributes

 [Measures].[Measure_Label] ,
 [Measures].[Measure_ValueLast],
 [Measures].[Measure_Value],
 [Measures].[Measure_ValuePct],
 [Measures].[Measure_Compare],
 [Measures].[Measure_ComparePct]
} ON COLUMNS,
```

```
{
  -- returns the number of periods back (lag) from current date member

  STRTOMEMBER(@pDateMbr) : STRTOMEMBER(@pDateMbr + ".lag(" + Str(@pLag - 1) + ")" )

*
    -- returns the top n number of rows based on current measure

    TOPCOUNT(

      -- show the current hierarachy member with its ascendants
      -- together with its children on rows

      STRTOSET(
        "{Ascendants(" + @pRowMbr + " ), "
        + @pRowMbr + ".children}"
      )

      ,StrToValue(@pRowCount)
      ,[Measures].[Measure_ValueLast]
    )
}
ON ROWS

FROM [Adventure Works] -- must hard code the cube :(
-- the cube name, together with the default values are the only
-- things required to point this report at a different cube
```

2. Select the Parameters icon from toolbar and, as shown in Figure P2-59, add:

   ➤ pLag with a default value of 12

   ➤ pDateMbr with a default value of [Date].[Calendar].[Month].&[2004]&[4]

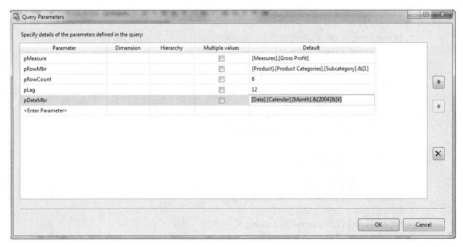

FIGURE P2-59

3. Execute the query to check that it runs properly before returning to the dataset properties. (See Figure P2-60.)

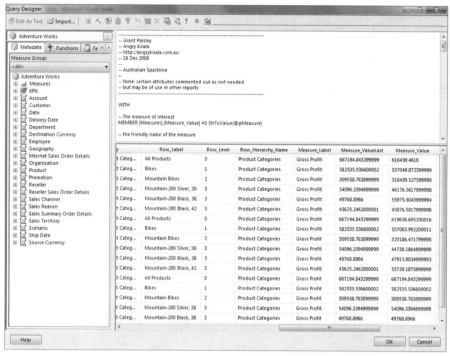

FIGURE P2-60

4. Click OK to return to the design surface. Your report data should look like Figure P2-61.

Notice that the values in the matrix are now overinflated. This is because each cell is now summing the 12 periods of data. You want to show the value for only the last period. To do this, change the expression for Measure_Value Text Box from =Sum(Measure_Value) to =Last(Measure_Value)

Now create a tablix on the design surface for changing the Lag. Set up a self-calling drill-through action similar to changing the number of rows to display. A neat trick is to copy and paste the existing Row-Count tablix and modify it. That saves a lot of time because it already contains the self-calling drill-through action.

First, though, before you copy it, follow these steps to add the new parameters:

1. Open the properties of the CellCount textbox in the RowCount tablix.

2. On the Action page (shown in Figure P2-62), add the two new parameters shown in the following table:

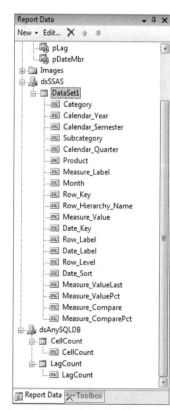

FIGURE P2-61

NAME	VALUE
pLag	[@pLag]
pDateMbr	[@pDateMbr]

Click OK.

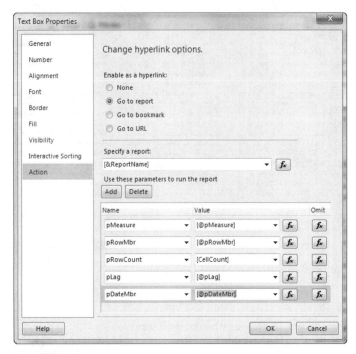

FIGURE P2-62

3. Select the RowCount tablix, copy and paste it (Ctrl+C, Ctrl+V), and then drag it immediately below the original tablix.

4. Open the new Tablix Properties and, as shown in Figure P2-63, set:

➤ Name to `TablixLagCount`

➤ Dataset name to `LagCount`

5. On the newly created matrix highlight the cell labeled Rows and change it to Lag.

6. Open the properties of the CellCount2 textbox and, as shown in Figure P2-64, set:

➤ Name to `LagCount`

➤ Value to `[LagCount]`

➤ ToolTip to Select the number of periods to display in Australian Sparkline

FIGURE P2-63

FIGURE P2-64

7. In the Action page, change the following parameter values, as shown in Figure P2-65:

NAME	VALUE
pRowCount	[@pRowCount]
pLag	[LagCount]

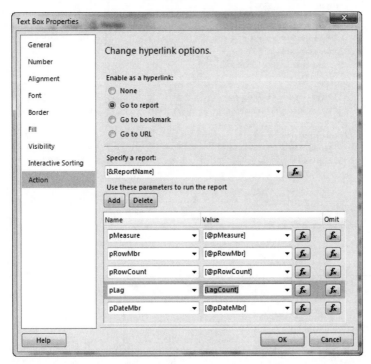

FIGURE P2-65

8. Change the color of the cell for the currently set lag. In the Font page, change the Color expression to the following:

```
=iif(
Fields!LagCount.Value = Parameters!pLag.Value,
"DimGray",
"Blue"
)
```

9. Click OK and return to the design surface.

10. As you did in Step 2, add new parameters to the Row action in the RowCount tablix by opening properties of TextBox Row_Label and adding the following:

NAME	VALUE
pLag	[@pLag]
pDateMbr	[@pDateMbr]

11. Finally, click on the LagCount tablix and open the properties of ColumnGroup2 and change Group on to [LagCount] as shown in Figure P2-66.

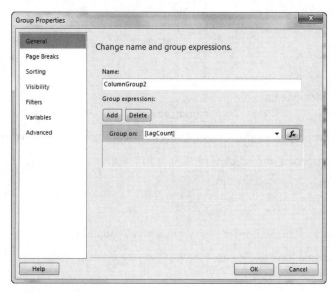

FIGURE P2-66

You should now have a design surface that looks like Figure P2-67. When previewed, the report looks like Figure P2-68.

Building a Full-Sized Australian Sparkline

Now that you have the navigation and data sorted out, you can build the Australian Sparkline. First add a full-sized Australian Sparkline chart representation showing its unique characteristics. Later you will "put it on a diet" before adding it to your table.

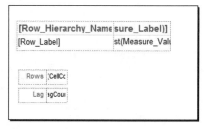

FIGURE P2-67

1. On the design surface move the tablixes down to make room at the top of the report and insert a line chart.

2. Drag `Measure_Value` and `Measure_Compare` from DataSet1 as data to the line chart you just inserted and change the function for each from `Sum()` to `Last()`.

3. Drag Date_Label to the line chart as the category.

4. Delete the legend.

5. Delete the X and Y axis titles.

6. Set chart property BorderStyle to `None`.

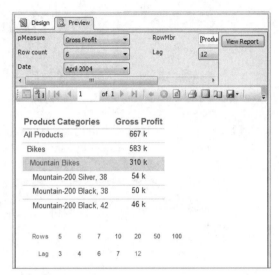

FIGURE P2-68

7. Open the Y chart access properties and set the Number Format to the custom format of `#,0`.

8. Open the Chart title properties and set the Title text as follows:

```
= First(Fields!Measure_Label.Value)
 + " " + Fields!Row_Label.Value
 + " " + Last(Fields!Date_Label.Value)
```

9. Open the chart properties. On the Border page set Line style: dropdown to `None`.

Your design surface should look like Figure P2-69.

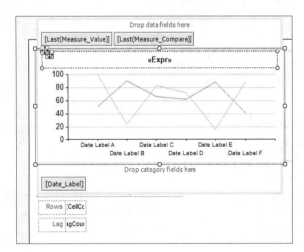

FIGURE P2-69

If you preview the report (shown in Figure P2-70), you will notice the values are too high and the title says All Products.

FIGURE P2-70

You now have to filter the data to display values for the current row member (highlighted Mountain Bikes in Figure P2-70). You will also add conditional formatting to the series: black if greater than the comparison period, red if less.

Open the chart properties. On the Filters tab add a filter with the following property:

EXPRESSION	OPERATOR	VALUE
[Row_Key]	=Value	[@pRowMbr]

Preview the report again and you will notice it now shows data just for the current row member, that is, Mountain Bikes, as shown in Figure P2-71.

FIGURE P2-71

The final change for the large version of the Australian Sparkline is to add the conditional formatting on the lines for the color and width, as follows:

1. Open the Measure_Value series properties and on the Fill page, set Color to this expression:

```
=iif(
  Fields!Measure_Value.Value >=
  Fields!Measure_Compare.Value,
    "Black",
    "Red"
        )
```

2. On the Border page set the Line width to this expression:

```
=iif(
  Fields!Date_Key.Value =
  Parameters!pDateMbr.Value,
    "2pt",
    "0.5pt"
        )
```

Preview the report and click on Bikes to confirm the formatting is working, as shown in Figure P2-72.

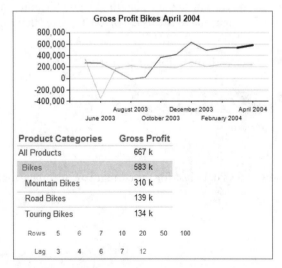

FIGURE P2-72

Adding the Australian Sparkline to a Table

The following steps lead you through creating the true Australian Sparkline ready for pasting in to the existing table. Essentially it is going on a diet.

1. Copy the current chart and paste it at the bottom of the design surface.

2. Right-click the X and Y Chart Axis and uncheck Show Axis.

3. Delete the chart title.

4. Open the chart properties and in the Filters tab, delete the filter.

If you preview the report, the new "slimmer" chart will look like Figure P2-73.

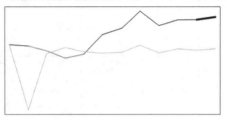

FIGURE P2-73

You now need to prepare the tablix. Add another column and row, insert the Australian Sparkline, and add the value for the comparison period.

1. Highlight the second row in the tablix, right-click and select Insert Row ⇨ Inside Group - Below (see Figure P2-74).

2. Select the first column in the matrix, right-click, and select Insert Column ⇨ Inside Group - Right (see Figure P2-75).

3. Select the second chart, and cut and then paste it into the data cell in the center column of the matrix.

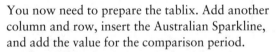

FIGURE P2-74

4. Set the header cell value to Trend.

5. Set the second row data cell in the third column expression to =Last(Fields!Measure_Compare.Value).

6. Set the cell Text Color to DimGray.

7. Set the Number format to the following expression:

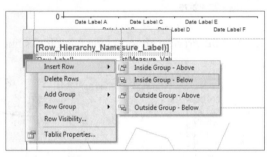

FIGURE P2-75

```
=iif(last(abs(Fields!Measure_Compare.Value)) >
   10000000,"#,, m;(#,, m)", iif(last(abs(Fields!Measure_Compare.Value)) >
   1000000,"#,,.0 m;(#,,.0 m)", iif(last(abs(Fields!Measure_Compare.Value)) >
   10000,"#, k;(#, k)", iif(last(abs(Fields!Measure_Compare.Value)) >
   1000,"#,.0 k;(#,.0 k)","#,
       #;(#,#)"
))))
```

8. Set the BorderStyle Top to None.

The completed design surface should look like Figure P2-76.

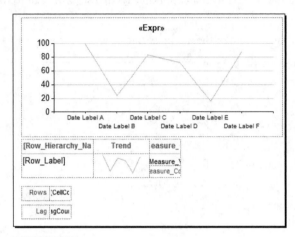

FIGURE P2-76

And the preview after clicking Bikes looks like Figure P2-77.

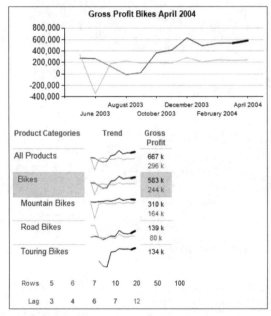

FIGURE P2-77

I have shown you how to create the Australian Sparkline and how to include it in an existing table of data. The other measure I included in the dataset is for showing percent share. Often the Sparkline is overwhelmed with seasonal data, particularly if it is showing retail data around Christmas time, which makes it difficult to spot the relative trend between products, for instance. By adding the percentage share of parent as an Australian Sparkline you can get a better idea of an individual product's or region's performance.

Final Thoughts

The "Australian Sparkline with Share of Parent" report is included as an example of how to implement this functionality. It also shows the individual monthly values.

The Angry Koala Browser is also included in this book. It is a full OLAP browser, and it includes the Australian Sparkline.

It is interesting that as part of the development process, I set the lag to only 3 periods to help with speed. As it turns out, I think this gives a very useful visualization for the recent trend — a bit like a KPI trend arrow but having three points instead of two. The thicker part of the line also acts a bit like an arrow. Sometimes the traditional 12 month trends are a bit overwhelming by comparison. What do you think? The Australian Sparkline with Lag = 3 is shown in Figure P2-78.

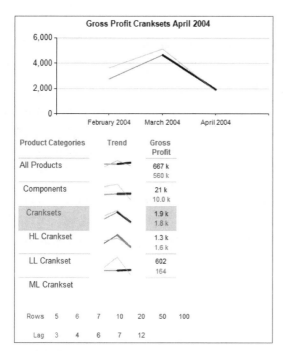

FIGURE P2-78

Credits and Related References

http://angrykoala.com.au/_blog/Blog

http://cubesurfer.codeplex.com

http://reportsurfer.com

http://cubesurfer.com

ANGRY KOALA CUBE BROWSER

The Angry Koala Cube Browser report suite is an OLAP client for Analysis Server featuring the Australian Sparkline (the Sparkline with the line down under) for trend analysis. It is simply a combination of the following recipes in this book:

➤   Cube Browser

➤   Cube Metadata

➤   Cube Dynamic Rows

➤   Cube Restricting Rows

➤   Australian Sparkline

Angry Koala Cube Browser report uses the same basic concept as the Cube Browser, but instead of showing a single measure in each data cell it shows:

➤   The measure value for the current period (bold)

➤   The measure value for the same period in the comparison period (driven by a lag number — for example, 12 means 12 months, and so would mean the same month last year)

➤   An Australian Sparkline (it has a line down under)

Users can change what they see on rows and columns, change the filter value, and see trend information based on a selected period of time. You can also drill-in on an Australian Sparkline to see the full details.

With the Angry Koala Cube Browser report, developers or power users can create a report with any combination of rows, columns, filters, dates, and measures as a linked report. Also, once a report is running, users can slice and dice their data (change what is shown in rows and columns), and if using the native reporting services manager, they can also create their own version of a report by simply saving the current report as a favorite in Internet Explorer.

Figure P2-79 displays a Sales report and Figure P2-80 a Profit and Loss report. Both are examples of the Angry Koala Cube Browser report, just with different parameters.

Product Versions

➤   Reporting Services 2008

What You'll Need

➤   A basic understanding of and ability to read MDX

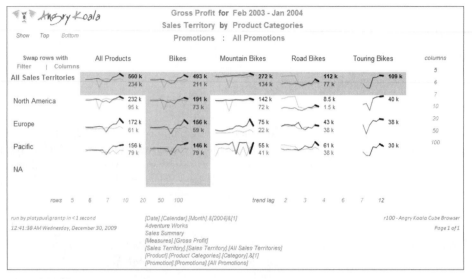

FIGURE P2-79

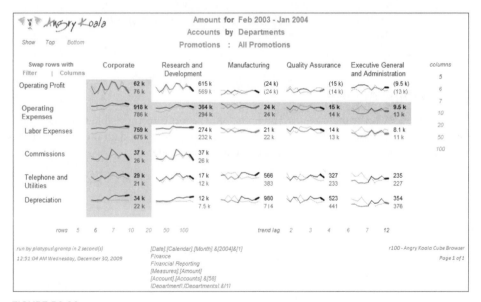

FIGURE P2-80

Anatomy of the Reports

Rather than a step-by-step approach to building the reports in this suite, let's run through the architecture and then the necessary techniques (recipes) utilized within the reports.

The reports are:

➤ r100 - Angry Koala Cube Browser

➤ r101 - Angry Koala Graph

➤ r102 - Angry Koala Driver

➤ r103 - Angry Koala Member

First, let's look at the reports and their roles. Note that the original purpose of this report suite was to show year-on-year performance, so the naming of the second comparison measure is ValueLY. But the report evolved to allow changing the lag (number of periods to show in the Australian Sparkline) so ValueLY is actually the comparison period value and is only Last Year if the lag is set to 12. If the lag is set to 3, ValueLY is actually the value 3 months ago.

 At Angry Koala we number our reports, which has been invaluable. Instead of a client calling to say. "The number doesn't look right for this month in the Sales by Territory and New Products compared to Last Year and YTD *report," it's much easier to provide assistance if you hear, "I'm having trouble with report 152." By naming a report in format r<number> - <description> you can strip out the number for the main title (just leaving the description) and have the full name in the report footer. No more confusion.*

r100 - Angry Koala Cube Browser

Angry Koala Cube Browser is the main report and is the only report directly visible to users. You can have multiple linked reports based on this physical report showing different data on rows, columns, and filters by simply creating a linked report and changing the parameters.

In this report and any linked reports based on it, users can:

➤ Change the measure.

➤ Change the date period (it can be year, quarter, month or day).

➤ Change what hierarchy to display on rows.

➤ Change what hierarchy to display on columns.

➤ Change what hierarchy to use for a filter.

➤ Change the filter value (member).

➤ Show top or bottom values (Top 10 or Bottom 10, for example, based on current measure value).

➤ Swap rows with filter.

➤ Swap rows and columns.

➤ Drill up and down the hierarchy displayed on rows.

➤ Drill up and down the hierarchy displayed on columns.

➤ Drill through to show full-sized Australian Sparkline.

➤ Change the number of rows to display.

➤ Change the number of columns to display.

➤ Change the Trend Lag (set the number of periods to display in the Australian Sparkline, for example).

Note there is a concept of "current row" or "current column." This is the Member in the row or column that is highlighted. click on the Bikes member of the Product Categories hierarchy displayed in columns; it gets highlighted and its children — Mountain Bikes, Road Bikes, and Touring Bikes — are displayed.

Figure P2-81 shows the links for the preceding actions from the Angry Koala Cube Browser to the other reports (or to itself with a new value for the parameter).

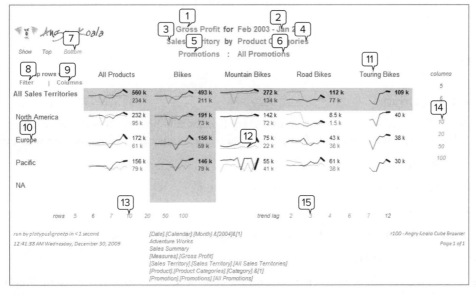

FIGURE P2-81

r101 - Angry Koala Graph

The Angry Koala Graph report is called from the Angry Koala Cube Browser report when you click on an Australian Sparkline in one of the details cells. It displays a full size version of the Australian Sparkline as shown in Figure P2-82.

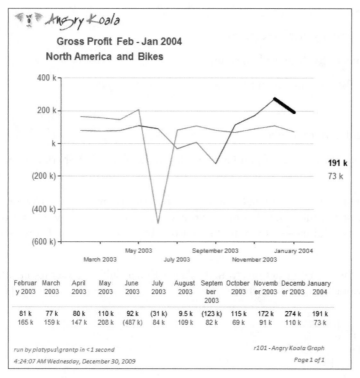

FIGURE P2-82

r102 - Angry Koala Driver

The Angry Koala Driver report is called from the Angry Koala Cube Browser report and returns a measure or a hierarchy. It is based on the Cube Metadata recipe and is called when the user wants to:

➤ Change the measure.

➤ Select a hierarchy to display on rows or columns.

➤ Select a hierarchy to filter by.

It therefore has two distinct behaviors. If the driver parameter value is `Measure`, users can:

➤ Select a cube/perspective.

➤ Select a measure from the list of measures for the cube/perspective to pass back to the Angry Koala Cube Browser.

Figure P2-83 shows how the report looks when called to select a measure.

If the driver parameter value is `Row`, `Column`, or `Filter`, users can:

➤ Select a dimension, to display its hierarchies.

➤ Choose a hierarchy to pass back to the Angry Koala Cube Browser report for the appropriate parameter: Rows, Columns or Filter.

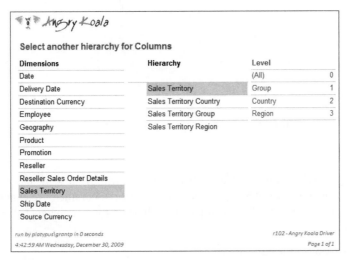

FIGURE P2-83

An example of changing the columns is shown in Figure P2-84.

FIGURE P2-84

Note that you do not hard code what report you drill back to. One of the parameters is the calling report and this allows the report to be called from different linked reports based on the Angry Koala Cube Browser.

r103 - Angry Koala Member

The Angry Koala Member report is called from the Angry Koala Cube Browser report and returns a hierarchy member. It is called when the user wants to:

➤ Select a period of time to filter the report by, such as a specific year, quarter, month or day.

➤ Select a member to filter the report by. If filtering by Product Color, for example, you could select Blue.

Figure P2-85 shows the results after a click on the + beside Q2 CY 2004; it expands to show the children: April 2004, May 2004, June 2004. If you now click on a blue Member such as May 2004, then this selection is passed back to the Angry Koala Cube Browser report.

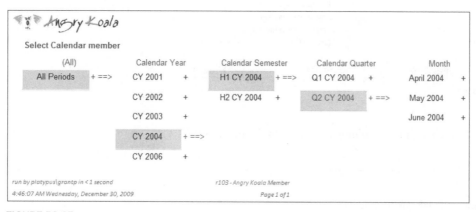

FIGURE P2-85

Behind the Scenes

Now let's look at the details of the recipes utilized that have not already been covered.

Angry Koala Cube Browser

The Angry Koala Cube Browser report is based on the Cube Browser recipe. It uses the same basic concept but extends the idea by showing the Australian Sparkline. Also added is a parameter to change rows and columns to show the bottom count instead of the top count. Here are the parameters (I have included an example default value):

➤ pCube = Sales Summary (the name of the cube or perspective)

➤ pMeasureGroup = Sales Summary (the name of the MeasureGroup)

➤ pMeasure = [Measures].[Gross Profit] (the UniqueName of the measure)

➤ pDateMbr = [Date].[Calendar].[Month].&[2004]&[4] (the UniqueName of the date member)

➤ pRowMbr = [Product].[Product Categories].[Subcategory].&[1] (the UniqueName of the member from which ascendants and children are shown on rows)

➤ pRowCount = 10 (the number of rows to show)

➤ pColMbr = [Sales Territory].[Sales Territory].[All Sales Territories] (the Unique-Name of the member from which ascendants and children are shown on columns)

➤ pColCount = 5 (the number of columns to show)

➤ pFilterMbr = [Promotion].[Promotions].[All Promotions] (the UniqueName of the member acting as filter)

➤ pLag=12 (number of periods to display in Australian Sparkline)

And two new parameters:

➤ pTopOrBottom=1 (based on the current measure show the top(1) or bottom(-1) number of rows or columns based on the RowCount or ColCount)

➤ pHightIsGoodOrBad=Good (for some Measures high values are actually bad so this allows you to reverse the meaning and therefore the colors displayed in the Australian Sparkline)

Open the dataset1 query in the r100 - Angry Koala Cube Browser report and select the parameters icon from toolbar; you'll see the list of parameters together with their default values, as shown in Figure P2-86.

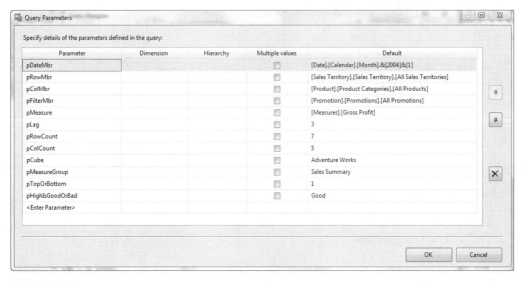

FIGURE P2-86

If you go back to the query you will find the MDX, as shown here.

The MDX is a combination of the Cube Browser and Australian Sparkline recipe MDX queries.

```
---------------------------------------------------------------------------
--
-- Angry Koala Cube Browser
--
-- Grant Paisley
-- http://angrykoala.com.au
-- 25 Jan 2010
---------------------------------------------------------------------------

WITH
-- number of points in Australian Sparkline (3 works best I think)
MEMBER [Measures].[Lag]
    AS StrToValue(@pLag)

-- The measure of interest
MEMBER [Measures].[Value]
    AS StrToValue(@pMeasure)

-- the friendly name of the measure
MEMBER [Measures].[Measure_Label]
    AS StrToValue(@pMeasure + ".Member_Name")

-- same measure value Last Year (actally depends on Lag)
MEMBER [Measures].[Value LY]
    AS StrToValue(
        "( [Measures].[Value], "
      + @pDateMbr
      + ".Hierarchy.CurrentMember.Lag("
      + Str([Measures].[Lag])
      + ") ) "
        )

-- the [Value sort] is set up to always return the value for the date hard coded
      to the last time period in the sequence
-- it is also multiplied by the value of p@TopOrBottom which has values 1 or -1 to
      give the top or bottom selection
--MEMBER [Measures].[Value Sort]
--    AS ( [Measures].[Value],
--        [Time].[by Financial Year].[Financial Month].&[2009-04-01T00:00:00]
--        )
MEMBER [Measures].[Value Sort]
    AS strToValue(
        " ( [Measures].[Value] , "
      + @pDateMbr
      + " ) * "
      + @pTopOrBottom
        )

-- Date metadata
```

```
MEMBER [Measures].[Date_Key]
    AS StrToValue(@pDateMbr + ".Hierarchy.Currentmember.Uniquename")

MEMBER [Measures].[Date_Label]
    AS StrToValue(@pDateMbr + ".Hierarchy.CurrentMember.Member_Caption")

MEMBER [Measures].[Date_Level] AS StrToValue(@pDateMbr +
    ".Hierarchy.CurrentMember.Level.Ordinal")

MEMBER [Measures].[DateLY_Key]
    AS StrToValue(
        @pDateMbr
      + ".Hierarchy.Currentmember.Lag("
      + Str([Measures].[Lag])
      + " ).Uniquename"
      )

MEMBER [Measures].[DateLY_Label]
    AS StrToValue(
        @pDateMbr
      + ".Hierarchy.CurrentMember.Lag("
      + Str([Measures].[Lag])
      + " ).Member_Caption "
      )
--[Date].[Calendar].[Month].&[2004]&[1]
--PARALLELPERIOD( [«Level»[, «Numeric Expression»[, «Member»] ] ] )


-- Row metadata

MEMBER [Measures].[Row_Key]
    AS StrToValue( @pRowMbr + ".Hierarchy.Currentmember.Uniquename" )

MEMBER [Measures].[Row_Label]
    AS StrToValue( @pRowMbr + ".Hierarchy.CurrentMember.Member_Caption" )

MEMBER [Measures].[Row_Level]
    AS StrToValue( @pRowMbr + ".Hierarchy.CurrentMember.Level.Ordinal" )

MEMBER [Measures].[Row_Level_Name]
    AS StrToValue( @pRowMbr + ".Hierarchy.Level.Name" )

MEMBER [Measures].[Row_Hierarchy_Name]
    AS StrToValue( @pRowMbr + ".Hierarchy.Name" )

MEMBER [Measures].[Row_Hierarchy_UniqueName]
    AS StrToValue( @pRowMbr + ".Hierarchy.UniqueName" )

MEMBER [Measures].[Row_Dimension_Name]
    AS StrToValue( @pRowMbr + ".Dimension.Name" )

MEMBER [Measures].[Row_Dimension_UniqueName]
    AS StrToValue(@pRowMbr + ".Dimension_Unique_Name" )
```

```
-- Column metadata

MEMBER [Measures].[Col_Key]
    AS StrToValue( @pColMbr + ".Hierarchy.CurrentMember.UniqueName" )

MEMBER [Measures].[Col_Label]
    AS StrToValue( @pColMbr + ".Hierarchy.CurrentMember.Member_Caption" )

MEMBER [Measures].[Col_Level]
    AS StrToValue( @pColMbr + ".Hierarchy.CurrentMember.Level.Ordinal" )

MEMBER [Measures].[Col_Level_Name]
    AS StrToValue( @pColMbr + ".Hierarchy.Level.Name" )

MEMBER [Measures].[Col_Hierarchy_Name]
    AS StrToValue( @pColMbr + ".Hierarchy.Name" )

MEMBER [Measures].[Col_Hierarchy_UniqueName]
    AS StrToValue( @pColMbr + ".Hierarchy.UniqueName" )

MEMBER [Measures].[Col_Dimension_Name]
    AS StrToValue( @pColMbr + ".Dimension.Name" )

MEMBER [Measures].[Col_Dimension_UniqueName]
    AS StrToValue(@pColMbr + ".Dimension_Unique_Name" )


-- Filter metadata

MEMBER [Measures].[Filter_Key]
    AS StrToValue( @pFilterMbr + ".Hierarchy.Currentmember.Uniquename" )

MEMBER [Measures].[Filter_Label]
    AS StrToValue( @pFilterMbr + ".Hierarchy.CurrentMember.Member_Caption" )

MEMBER [Measures].[Filter_Level]
    AS StrToValue( @pFilterMbr + ".Hierarchy.CurrentMember.Level.Ordinal" )

MEMBER [Measures].[Filter_Level_Name] AS StrToValue( @pFilterMbr +
    ".Hierarchy.Level.Name" )

MEMBER [Measures].[Filter_Hierarchy_Name]
    AS StrToValue( @pFilterMbr + ".Hierarchy.Name" )

MEMBER [Measures].[Filter_Hierarchy_UniqueName]
    AS StrToValue( @pFilterMbr + ".Hierarchy.UniqueName" )

MEMBER [Measures].[Filter_Dimension_Name]
    AS StrToValue( @pFilterMbr + ".Dimension.Name" )

MEMBER [Measures].[Filter_Dimension_UniqueName]
    AS StrToValue(@pFilterMbr + ".Dimension_Unique_Name" )
```

```
SELECT NON EMPTY {
 [Measures].[Lag],

 [Measures].[Date_Key],
 [Measures].[Date_Label],
 [Measures].[Date_Level],

 [Measures].[DateLY_Key],
 [Measures].[DateLY_Label],

 [Measures].[Measure_Label] ,

 [Measures].[Row_Key],
 [Measures].[Row_Label],
 [Measures].[Row_Level],
 [Measures].[Row_Level_Name],
 [Measures].[Row_Hierarchy_Name],
 [Measures].[Row_Hierarchy_UniqueName],
 [Measures].[Row_Dimension_Name],
 [Measures].[Row_Dimension_UniqueName],

 [Measures].[Col_Key],
 [Measures].[Col_Label],
 [Measures].[Col_Level],
 [Measures].[Col_Level_Name],
 [Measures].[Col_Hierarchy_Name],
 [Measures].[Col_Hierarchy_UniqueName],
 [Measures].[Col_Dimension_Name],
 [Measures].[Col_Dimension_UniqueName],

 [Measures].[Filter_Key],
 [Measures].[Filter_Label],
 [Measures].[Filter_Level],
 [Measures].[Filter_Level_Name],
 [Measures].[Filter_Hierarchy_Name],
 [Measures].[Filter_Hierarchy_UniqueName],
 [Measures].[Filter_Dimension_Name],
 [Measures].[Filter_Dimension_UniqueName],

 [Measures].[Value] ,
 [Measures].[Value LY],
 [Measures].[Value Sort]

} ON COLUMNS,

{

-- return set of date members going back pLag number of members

 (
    STRTOMEMBER(@pDateMbr)
  : STRTOMEMBER(@pDateMbr + ".lag(" +  Str([Measures].[Lag] - 1) + ")"
 )
```

```
-- show top or bottom number of members based on pColCount

*   TOPCOUNT(

--   use this code for if only want to show parent, self and children
--   STRTOSET("{"
--   + @pColMbr + ".parent, "("{"
--   + @pColMbr + ", " ("{"
--   + @pColMbr + ".children}"("{"
--   )

--   columns, show ancestors, self and children (leave a trail)

     STRTOSET(
       "{ASCENDANTS("+ @pColMbr + "), "
     + @pColMbr + ".children}"
     )

     ,StrToValue(@pColCount) -- number of columns
     ,[Measures].[Value Sort] -- current measure for last period
   )

-- show top or bottom number of members based on pRowCount

* TOPCOUNT(

--   use this code for if only want to show parent, self and children
--   STRTOSET("{"
--   + @pRowMbr + ".parent, "
--   + @pRowMbr + ", "
--   + @pRowMbr + ".children}"
--   )


-- rows, show ancestors, self and children

     STRTOSET(
       "{ASCENDANTS(" + @pRowMbr
     + "), " + @pRowMbr + ".children}"
     )

     ,StrToValue(@pRowCount)  -- number of rows
     ,[Measures].[Value Sort] -- current measure for last period
     )
   )
}
ON ROWS

-- the cube name, together with the paramater default values are the only
-- things required to point this report at a different cube

FROM_[Adventure Works]

--FROM [Risk Retention]  -- example of other cube
```

```
-- filter member

WHERE STRTOSET(@pFilterMbr)
```

To allow selecting Top or Bottom, the calculated member `[Measures].[Value Sort]` is multiplied by the `pTopOrBottom` parameter value. By multiplying the sort value by -1, this effectively reverses the `TopCount` MDX function and returns the bottom set of members. Here is the MDX snippet:

```
-- the [Value sort] is set up to always return the value for
-- the date hard coded to the last time period in the sequence
-- it is also multiplied by the value of p@TopOrBottom which
-- has values 1 or -1 to give the top or bottom selection
--MEMBER [Measures].[Value Sort] as
-- ( [Measures].[Value],
       [Time].[by Financial Year].[Financial Month].&[2009-04-01T00:00:00] )
MEMBER [Measures].[Value Sort] as
  strToValue(" (  [Measures].[Value] , " + @pDateMbr + " ) * " + @pTopOrBottom )
```

Similar to the Cube Browser, calculated measures are utilized to generated metadata for Rows, Columns, Date, and Filter members. For each you collect:

➤ Key

➤ Label

➤ Level

➤ Level_Name

➤ Hierarchy_Name

➤ Hierarchy_UniqueName

➤ Dimension_Name

➤ Dimension_UniqueName

Notice there are extra measures to display metadata for the DateLY.

```
MEMBER [Measures].[DateLY_Key]   AS
 StrToValue(@pDateMbr
        + ".Hierarchy.Currentmember.Lag("
        + Str([Measures].[Lag])
        + " ).Uniquename"
 )
MEMBER [Measures].[DateLY_Label] AS
 StrToValue(@pDateMbr
        + ".Hierarchy.CurrentMember.Lag("
        + Str([Measures].[Lag])
        + " ).Member_Caption "
)
```

This is used for the Tooltip shown in Figure P2-87 and has the following expression:

```
= Fields!Measure_Label.Value
 + " was " + FormatNumber(Last(Fields!Value_LY.Value))
 + " in " + Last(Fields!DateLY_Label.Value)
```

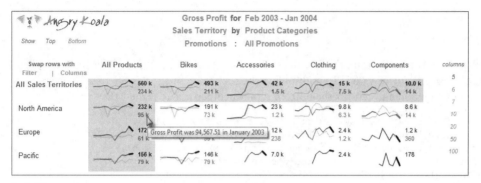

FIGURE P2-87

As shown in Figure P2-88, when you run the MDX query you see all the metadata together with the Measure value and value LY you want to display.

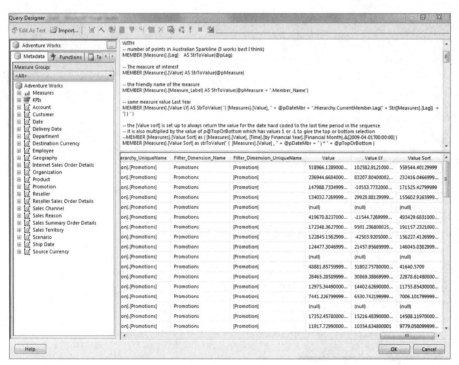

FIGURE P2-88

Report Body

The main tablix, shown in Figure P2-89, is a matrix with:

➤ columns grouped by `Col_Key` and displaying `Col_Label`

➤ rows grouped by `Row_Key` and displaying `Row_Label`

➤ the Value in the details cell (for the current measure)

➤ the ValueLY also in the details cell just below (color `DimGray`)

➤ the Australian Sparkline in the details cell

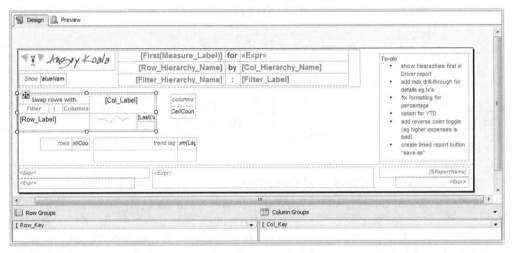

FIGURE P2-89

In the columns, similarly to the rows, the group is by `Col_Key` and sorted by the `Col_Level` (the level in the hierarchy) and within the level, descending by `Value_Sort` (see Figure P2-90).

The Value textbox has been tweaked to highlight the current member (`LemonChiffon`) for rows and columns.

The BackgroundColor is set as follows:

```
=iif(Fields!Row_Key.Value=Parameters!pRowMbr.Value, "LemonChiffon",
 iif(Fields!Col_Key.Value=Parameters!pColMbr.Value, "LemonChiffon",
 Nothing
 ))
```

On the labels for rows and columns, the same background color is set (`LemonChiffon`), but the text color is DimGray for the current member, otherwise it is Blue, indicating you can click on it to drill up and down the hierarchy.

```
=iif(Fields!Row_Key.Value=Parameters!pRowMbr.Value,
"DimGray",
"Blue")
```

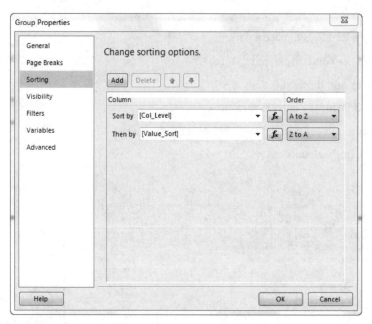

FIGURE P2-90

Restricting the Number of Rows and Columns

Restricting the number of columns or rows to display is controlled with pRowCount and pColCount. Clicking on a Blue numeric simply invokes a self-drill-through action with all parameters set as the existing value except for the Count, and that is set to the cell clicked on. See the Cube Restricting Rows recipe later in this book for an example of this.

Swap Actions

In the top left cell of the main tablix is the TablixSwap. It contains two blue cells that allow the user to swap the rows with columns or swap the rows with the filter. Again, all that happens is that a self-drill-through action takes place. See the Cube Browser recipe later in this book for details.

Titles

The titles in the report work both as titles and as places where users get to change what they see in the report. These all work identically to the Cube Browser Recipe.

Report Footer Info

To round out the report we have added some interesting information to the footer, including:

- ➤ Who ran it
- ➤ How long it took to execute
- ➤ Page numbers in 1 of *n* format
- ➤ The name of the report

This is identical to the Cube Browser recipe.

Final Thoughts

So now you have an OLAP browser. You can create user reports by creating linked reports with different parameters. Interestingly, your users can also configure the report to one they like and then just save it as a favorite in Internet Explorer.

This is also a great starting point for creating your own variation on an OLAP Cube Browser. For instance, the Angry Koala Cube Browser report uses the same basic concept as the Cube Browser but instead of showing a single measure in each data cell we show:

➤ The measure for the current period (bold)

➤ The measure for the same period in a comparison period (driven by a lag number — for example, 12 means 12 months, and so would mean the same month last year

➤ An Australian Sparkline (it has a line down under)

I think the Angry Koala Cube Browser has done a good job of implementing my three design tenets, because it allows for better use of the following:

➤ Expressions: allows generic reporting

➤ Visualization: allows better understanding of data

➤ Linking: allows easier navigation (self-calling drill-through action) and setting parameters in related reports

Finally, if you want to use the Angry Koala Cube Browser on your own Analysis Server cube, there are only three steps to follow:

➤ Edit the shared data source dsSSAS and point to your cube.

➤ In report r100, change the parameter default values to the member unique names from your cube.

➤ In the report r100 DataSet1 MDX query, change the line `asdfsd` to `dsSSAS`.

Credits and Related References

http://angrykoala.com.au/_blog/Blog

http://cubesurfer.codeplex.com

http://reportsurfer.com

http://cubesurfer.com

BULLET CHARTS

In Stephen Few's *Information Dashboard Design*, he introduced the concept of a bullet chart. It is a simple, linear chart that, while not visually stunning, has great efficacy in presenting data in an easily interpreted and quick manner. This succinctness of presentation is of the utmost importance when designing dashboards. It can be exceedingly easy to overwhelm the end user of a dashboard with too much information. Fancy and colorful gauges can be enticing elements to include in your dashboard, but report design, and especially dashboard design, is not concerned with aesthetics as it is with efficiency.

Product Versions

➤ Reporting Services 2008

What You'll Need

➤ A data source to the AdventureWorksDW2008 database named AdventureWorksDW

Designing the Report

The bullet chart is meant to be simple; therefore, the more stylistic elements that come with the default bullet chart will be stripped away. Although minimalistic in its presentation, a good deal of configuring needs to be done before a true bullet chart is created. Most of the design will take place outside of the table that the chart will eventually be placed within. Once a basic template has been created outside of the table, the chart will be placed within the table, taking its place in the detail and header rows. The final result of this recipe is shown in Figure P2-91.

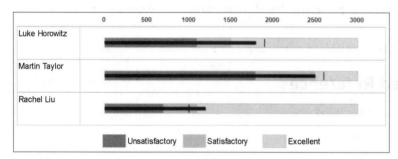

FIGURE P2-91

Before all this happens, a dataset is needed that has all of the components necessary for a bullet chart. You need values to group by within your table: an actual value, a target value, and three boundary values used to define the unsatisfactory, satisfactory, and excellent zones within the chart.

1. Add a data source for the AdventureWorksDW or AdventureWorksDW2008 sample database. Name the data source AdventureWorksDW.

2. Right-click the AdventureWorksDW data source from the Report Data pane on the far left of Report Builder and choose the Add Dataset option. Name the dataset QuarterlySalesBy-Goal, choose a Query type of text, and enter the following code into the query text area of

the window, as shown in Figure P2-92. All other options will be left as default. When you've finished, click OK to close the window.

```
SELECT
    'Luke Horowitz' AS SalesPerson
    ,1800.00 AS QuarterlySales
    ,1900.00 AS TargetSales
    ,1100.00 AS Unsatisfactory
    ,1500.00 AS Satisfactory
    ,3000.00 AS Excellent
UNION
SELECT
    'Martin Taylor'
    ,2500.00
    ,2600.00
    ,1800.00
    ,2500.00
    ,3000.00
UNION
SELECT
    'Rachel Liu'
    ,1200.00
    ,1000.00
    ,700.00
    ,1100.00
    ,3000.00
```

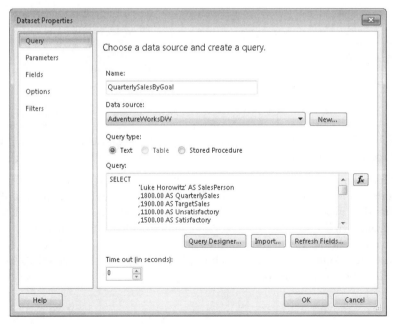

FIGURE P2-92

3. From the Insert ribbon, click the Gauge button and then click anywhere in the report design area. When the next window pops up, click the bullet graph from the linear chart options.

4. Right-click the gauge and choose Gauge Properties from the resulting menu. On the left-hand navigation menu, choose Back Fill and set the Fill Style to Solid and Color to No Color, as shown in Figure P2-93. Move down one level in the navigation menu and choose the Frame property. From here, choose None from the dropdown menu for Style.

FIGURE P2-93

5. Click the gauge to insure that the focus is on the Gauge Panel. Then from the Properties pane, assign the DataSetName value to the QuarterlySalesByGoal dataset created in Step 1. If the Properties pane is not visible, click the Properties checkbox from the View ribbon.

6. Right-click the horizontal bar at the left of the bullet chart and from the Gauge submenu choose Pointer (LinearPointer1) Properties. This is the horizontal bar component of the chart. From the Linear Pointer Properties window set the value to SUM(QuarterlySales) from the dropdown list box. Then choose Pointer Fill from the navigation bar on the left and choose the radio button labeled Solid for the Fill Style. Choose black as the color. Repeat this process for LinearPointer2, but this time choose SUM(TargetSales) as the value. The bullet chart should now look like Figure P2-94.

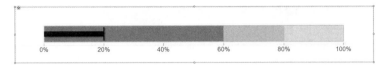

FIGURE P2-94

7. A bit more cleaning up is needed before you have a true bullet chart. Once again, right-click on the gauge and from the Gauge submenu choose Scale Properties. From the General menu, set the maximum value to MAX(Excellent), the largest value in the upper bound for our excellent range. In the Labels section, choose the Hide scale labels checkbox, and in the Major Tick Marks section choose the Hide major tick marks option.

8. Insert a table into the report design area. Give the table a header row, a detail row, and two columns. Place the SalesPerson field value in the detail row for the first column. The easiest way to do this is to hover over the textbox until the small table-like icon appears in the top right corner of the textbox. Click on this and choose SalesPerson.

9. Drag the bullet chart onto the detail row of the table in column two. This action will obscure the view of the textboxes border. To overcome this, right-click the gauge and from the Gauge sub-menu choose Gauge Panel Properties. From the Border section in the navigation bar set the Line Style to solid, Line Width to 1pt, and Line Color to Light Gray.

10. Copy the gauge in the detail row and paste it into the header of the same column. Each component of the gauge will need to be deleted with the exception of the scale. To do this, click each component and, once highlighted, right-click and choose to delete.

11. After this is complete, right-click and choose Scale Properties from the Gauge submenu. From the Labels section, uncheck the Hide scale labels checkbox, set Placement to Outside, and set Distance from scale to 10 as shown in Figure P2-95. From the Font page, change the font to a bold 26; from the Number section, change the value to Number with zero decimals; and finally, in the Major Tick Marks section uncheck Hide major tick marks. After clicking OK to exit the Linear Scale Properties window, run the report to see a table with inline gauges similar to the one in Figure P2-96.

Additionally, a legend has been included below the graph. This is recommended in order to help report users identify the visual cues that are provided in the bullet graph. The legend was made by adding a table below the graph that contains six columns and no detail rows, only a header row.

12. The background color of the first, third, and fifth columns are chosen to match those of the Linear Range values in the graph. In order to change the background colors for these columns, click the column header to highlight it; and in the Properties menu change the BackgroundColor value to Gray, Silver, and Gainsboro, respectively. For the remaining columns, click each column header, choose BorderStyle from the Properties menu, and choose None.

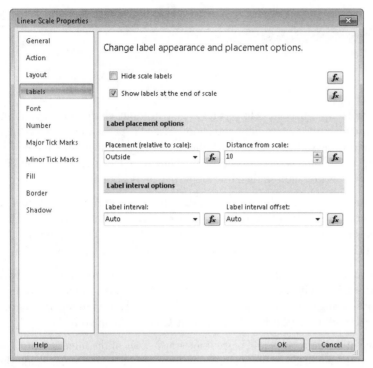

FIGURE P2-95

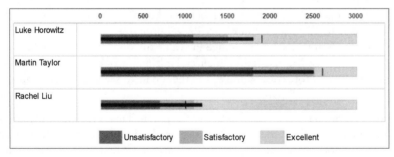

FIGURE P2-96

Final Thoughts

The great advantage of the bullet chart over similar charts, such as the bar chart, is the individuality and flexibility given to each distinct chart. Rather than have a single annotation line across the entirety of the chart area to represent a benchmark, as could be done in a bar chart, the bullet chart allows each category its own goal and its own decomposition into distinct rating categories. What it lacks in flashy exterior, it makes up for in efficiency of data visualization.

Credits and Related References

Few, Stephen. *Information Dashboard Design The Effective Visual Communication of Data.* O'Reilly Media, Inc., 2006.

How to: Bullet Charts in Reporting Services 2008 `http://blogs.adatis.co.uk/blogs/timkent/archive/2009/01/21/how-to-bullet-charts-in-reporting-services-2008.aspx`

SYNCHRONIZING GROUPS, CHARTS, AND SPARKLINES

Synchronizing groups is a common challenge. Suppose you have twenty sales people, and about half of them worked for the entire year, while a few only worked during the holiday season. When you display sparklines to show their monthly sales, you want all of the monthly sales bars to be the same size in width and be aligned to the appropriate month. Another situation is in financial reporting: suppose you have full data for each quarter in the previous year, but you only have year-to-date data for the current year. You still would like a fixed layout so that all quarters are present under the current year, regardless of whether there is already data available; you want the empty space to be preserved.

There are many more of these reporting scenarios that sometimes could be solved by using OUTER JOINS in the dataset query. However, as a report author you may desire to accomplish this simply in the report (visually) independent of the data source, which may not support the necessary query language capabilities.

This recipe explains how to synchronize inner groups in data regions, align and synchronize data visually along chart axes, and sparklines in general. The end result is shown in Figure P2-97, demonstrating synchronized trend visualizations and synchronized quarters on columns for each year.

FIGURE P2-97

Product Versions

➤ Reporting Services 2008 R2

What You'll Need

➤ AdventureWorks2008 sample database

Designing the Report

This example uses the AdventureWorks2008 sample database and a grouped query to return the sales information about products.

1. Start by designing a data source for the AdventureWorks2008 sample database.

2. Enter the following code to create a dataset query that returns product sales information by product category and subcategory, as well as by quarter and year.

```
SET DATEFORMAT mdy
SELECT
    PC.Name AS Category, PS.Name AS Subcategory,
    DATEPART(yy, SOH.OrderDate) AS OrderYear,
    'Q' + DATENAME(qq, SOH.OrderDate) AS OrderQtr,
    SUM(SOD.UnitPrice * SOD.OrderQty) AS Sales,
    PC.ProductCategoryID, PS.ProductSubcategoryID
FROM
    Production.ProductSubcategory AS PS INNER JOIN
    Sales.SalesOrderHeader AS SOH INNER JOIN
    Sales.SalesOrderDetail AS SOD ON SOH.SalesOrderID = SOD
      .SalesOrderID INNER JOIN
    Production.Product AS P ON SOD.ProductID = P.ProductID
    ON PS.ProductSubcategoryID = P.ProductSubcategoryID  INNER JOIN
    Production.ProductCategory AS PC ON PS.ProductCategoryID = PC
      .ProductCategoryID
WHERE (SOH.OrderDate BETWEEN '07/01/2002' AND '06/30/2004')
    GROUP BY DATEPART(yy, SOH.OrderDate), PC.Name, PS.Name,
    'Q' + DATENAME(qq, SOH.OrderDate),
    PS.ProductSubcategoryID, PC.ProductCategoryID
```

3. Add a matrix to display sales by categories and time intervals.

   a. Insert a new matrix using the Matrix wizard and select the sales dataset for the matrix.

   b. In Step 2 of the wizard, drag Category and Subcategory fields to the Row groups, and Year and Quarter fields to the Column groups. Drag the Sales field into the Values area. You should then have the result shown in Figure P2-98.

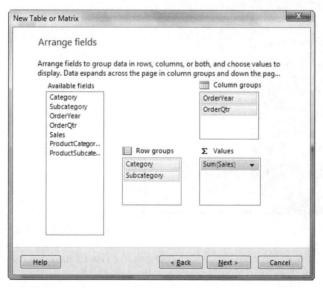

FIGURE P2-98

   c. In Step 3, select a simple layout by deselecting Show subtotals and deselecting Expand/collapse groups, and then finish the wizard.

d. You should now have a matrix on the design surface. Select the matrix, and then in the grouping pane right-click on the OrderYear group, select Add Total ⇨ Before, and merge and center the two cells in the header for the overall total and enter Sales Trend as a column label, as shown in Figure P2-99.

FIGURE P2-99

e. Select the [Sum(Sales)] cell in the matrix and specify currency formatting.

4. Add a sparkline chart to show the overall sales trend.

a. Right-click in the empty cell under the Sales Trend header and select Insert ⇨ Sparkline from the context menu, with a type of simple column for the sparkline chart.

b. Select the sparkline chart on the design surface and its data visualization panel should show on the screen.

c. Under the Values section, select the Sales field, so that the sparkline represents aggregated sales.

d. As shown in Figure P2-100, under the Category groups section, open the category group property dialog, and create a group expression and the following ascending sort expression: =Fields!OrderYear.Value & Fields!OrderQtr.Value

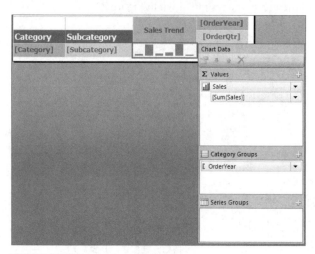

FIGURE P2-100

This concatenation will ensure the sparkline chart columns are synchronized across the combination of Years and Quarters for which data is available.

5. Preview the report for the first time.

You will notice two issues, which are resolved in the next steps.

First, the sparkline charts only show data for specific quarters with sales data, and hence there are different numbers of sparkline columns shown because product subcategories without sales in a particular year are not visually represented as gaps, which makes comparison difficult.

Second, the dataset query only returns data in the interval from Q3/2002 till Q2/2004. As a result, the matrix columns only represent those quarters. Financial reporting often requires a fixed layout structure (e.g., all quarters must be present for each year represented even if there is no data for a particular quarter).

One potential way of accomplishing these two requirements is to use an OUTER JOIN in the query. However, this may not be possible to do easily. Reporting Services 2008 R2 adds a new feature to synchronize tablix groups, as well as sparkline charts, visually. This is easy to do, and is shown in Steps 6 and 7.

Note that the synchronization for sparkline charts, horizontal axes, and so on, and tablix groups use the same underlying Group.DomainScope RDL feature added in Reporting Services 2008 R2.

6. Synchronize sparkline charts.

   a. Right-click into the sparkline series and open the Horizontal Axis Properties dialog.

   b. Select Align axes and specify the parent data region (the matrix, in our case explicitly named SalesAnalysisTablix), as shown in Figure P2-101. This way all occurrences of the charts contained within that matrix are synchronized along their horizontal axes.

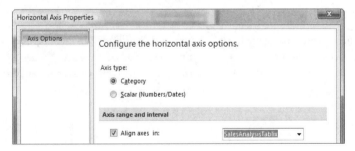

FIGURE P2-101

7. Synchronize inner matrix groups.

   a. Select the matrix, and then in the grouping pane under Column Groups select OrderQtr.

   b. In the Property grid window, locate and expand the Group properties, and set the Group.DomainScope property to the name of the matrix, SalesAnalysisTablix, as shown

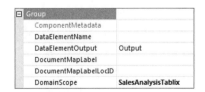

FIGURE P2-102

   in Figure P2-102. Thereby, the same number of quarters is shown under each year group present.

8. Preview the final report.

Figure P2-103 shows the final report with the yearly sales trend showing gaps for those years without sales for a particular product category. Furthermore, each year present in the sales analysis has the same number of quarters shown.

Category	Subcategory	Yearly Sales Trend	2002				2003				2004			
			Q1	Q2	Q3	Q4	Q1	Q2	Q3	Q4	Q1	Q2	Q3	Q4
Accessories	Bike Racks								$75,920.40	$60,883.20	$37,149.60	$63,084.00		
	Bike Stands								$6,996.00	$11,925.00	$8,268.00	$10,653.00		
	Bottles and Cages								$11,854.26	$15,968.16	$16,104.54	$18,659.26		
	Cleaners								$5,137.45	$4,724.37	$3,357.92	$4,949.03		
	Fenders								$7,649.04	$11,759.30	$11,583.46	$13,275.92		
	Helmets				$33,853.10	$24,870.77	$11,659.72	$25,524.15	$81,538.25	$89,595.04	$72,597.25	$101,788.71		
	Hydration Packs								$31,577.46	$27,189.52	$17,903.64	$28,254.41		
	Locks				$6,325.00	$3,780.00	$2,205.00	$3,939.00		$15.00				
	Pumps				$5,157.02	$3,226.39	$1,763.12	$3,382.31						
	Tires and Tubes								$41,940.34	$61,948.17	$61,519.46	$66,817.33		
Bikes	Mountain Bikes				$3,141,467.25	$2,837,646.75	$2,517,500.05	$2,908,658.67	$3,617,011.73	$3,808,655.50	$3,473,749.84	$4,268,134.07		
	Road Bikes				$4,930,692.78	$4,189,621.86	$3,584,254.78	$4,119,658.65	$3,844,123.56	$3,734,891.64	$3,391,876.27	$4,001,737.46		
	Touring Bikes								$3,298,006.29	$3,766,585.36	$3,414,027.38	$4,066,454.63		

FIGURE P2-103

Final Thoughts

Nesting data regions in Reporting Services is a powerful technique, which this recipe demonstrated in order to show sparklines for subsets of data as grouped in the outer data region. This recipe also demonstrated how to make this type of visual analysis more effective by synchronizing the data across individual sparklines.

Credits and Related References

A related technique is demonstrated on Sean Boon's blog titled *Building Win-Loss Sparklines in SQL Server Reporting Services 2008 R2* that may be found at: http://blogs.msdn.com/seanboon/archive/2009/11/16/building-win-loss-sparklines-in-sql-server-reporting-services-2008-r2.aspx.

PART III
Chart and Gauge Reports

- ▶ Chart Custom Color Palette

- ▶ Chart Keywords

- ▶ Column Chart with Goal Threshold Line

- ▶ Creating a Personal Report Card

- ▶ Customizing Gauges with Images

- ▶ Exception Highlighting with Gauges/Bullet Graphs

- ▶ Grouped Pie Chart Slices

- ▶ Growing Bar and Column Charts

- ▶ Histogram Chart

- ▶ Linear Regression Line

- ▶ Creating a Multi-Series Multi Y-Axis Chart

- ▶ Pareto Chart

CHART CUSTOM COLOR PALETTE

Charts use built-in predefined color palettes with 10 to 16 distinct colors. Starting with Reporting Services 2000 Service Pack 1 (SP1), you can override the default colors. To specify color values as constant or expression-based values, click the Series Style button on the appearance properties for the data value in the Edit Chart Value dialog box. You could use this, for instance, to highlight values based on a certain condition such as a minimum or maximum value within the current series.

If you don't want to define a full custom color palette, you can override the color for individual data points. Use an expression that either returns a specific color value (in order to override) or returns "Nothing," which will pick the current color from the underlying built-in color palette.

For example, suppose you want to highlight in red all data point values with negative y-values. For all the other data points, you want to apply the default colors. To do this, you would select Edit the data value and click the Appearance tab. Next you would click the Series Style button, which opens the Style Properties dialog box, and then click the Fill tab. Then you would enter the following expression in the fill color style properties:

```
=iif(Sum(Fields!Sales.Value - Fields!Cost.Value) < 0, "Red", Nothing))
```

 If you set the fill color to a constant value, this color is applied to all the data points for that data series.

The chart legend uses color fields to match the legend items to the visible data points. The legend can only show one color field per legend item (data series); hence, it shows the color of the first data point within that series. Remember this when you use expressions to dynamically determine the color of individual data points within a series; the legend item always shows the actual color of the first data point.

While the legend built into Reporting Services charts is easy to use, it lacks flexibility. For example, the legend consumes space within the chart. If the legend is placed outside the plot area and the legend grows, the chart plot area size shrinks accordingly.

You can get more flexibility and control over the legend by generating your own custom legend by using a table or a matrix. The easiest way to synchronize the colors in the chart with your custom legend is to define your own custom chart color palette. The CustomColorPalette sample report implements a custom color palette and a custom legend (see Figure P3-1).

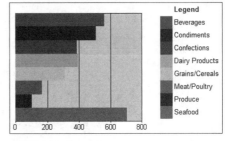

FIGURE P3-1

Product Versions

➤ Reporting Services 2000

➤ Reporting Services 2005

➤ Reporting Services 2008

What You'll Need

➤ Chart data region

➤ Business Intelligence Development Studio or Report Builder 2.0

Designing the Report

For this recipe, you'll need to open a report that contains a chart with multiple data series. To build a custom color palette, follow these steps:

1. Define the chart series groups and category groups.

By default, every chart data series has a color assigned to it. This color is based on the selected chart palette. In this example, you want to override these colors based on the series group instance values.

2. Define the custom color palette and add custom code.

The `colorPalette` variable stores the definition of our custom color palette, which has 15 distinct colors. The `count` variable keeps track of the total count of distinct grouping values in order to wrap around to the first color once you exceed the number of distinct colors in the custom color palette. The mapping hash table keeps track of the mapping between grouping values and colors. This ensures that all data points within the same data series have the same color. Later it is used to synchronize the custom legend colors with the chart colors. Enter the following code in the custom code window of the report:

```
Private colorPalette As String() = {"Green", "Blue", "Red", _
        "Orange", "Aqua", "Teal", "Gold", "RoyalBlue", _
        "MistyRose", "LightGreen", "LemonChiffon", _
        "LightSteelBlue", "#F1E7D6", "#E16C56", "#CFBA9B"}

Private count As Integer = 0

Private mapping As New System.Collections.Hashtable()

Public Function GetColor(ByVal groupingValue As String) As String

        If mapping.ContainsKey(groupingValue) Then
            Return mapping(groupingValue)
        End If

        Dim c As String = colorPalette(count Mod colorPalette.Length)

        count = count + 1

        mapping.Add(groupingValue, c)

        Return c
End Function
```

3. Call the `GetColor()` function to assign colors to data points.

Open the properties window for the chart series and set the Color property to the following expression (see Figure P3-2):

```
=Code.GetColor(Fields!Country.Value & "|" & Fields!City.Value)
```

The current series group value is passed as an argument to the `GetColor` function, which is needed to map the internal group instance value to the color value.

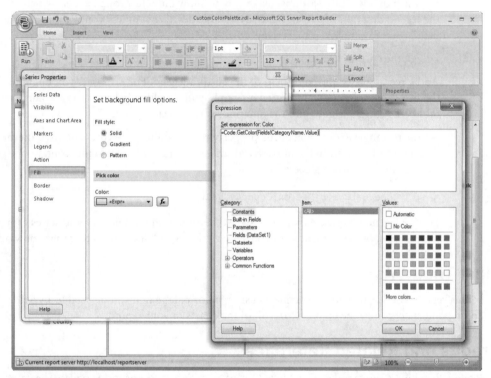

FIGURE P3-2

4. Add a chart legend.

You can use the built-in chart legend, or you can turn off the built-in chart legend and follow the steps in the next procedure to build your own custom chart legend with a table or a matrix data region.

Custom Legends

To build a custom legend, follow these steps.

1. Add a table data region to the report.

Place the table next to the chart and bind it to the same dataset as the chart.

2. Mirror the chart grouping structure in the table by adding table groups.

If the chart uses series groupings, add them to the table by adding table groups that are based on the same group expression as the one in the chart series groupings. Then add chart category groupings (if present) as inner table groups.

In general, if the chart has *m* series grouping and *n* category grouping, you add *m+n* table groups for your custom legend.

For the individual table groups, make sure to show only the group header (which will contain the legend description). Also, remove the table detail row unless you want to use the table detail rows to simulate a chart data table.

3. Design the custom legend.

Add a rectangle for the color field of the custom legend. For example, you might add it to the first table column. As indicated in Step 2, you should only have group header rows in the table. The rectangle goes into the innermost group header level.

Set the rectangle `BackgroundColor` property to the equivalent expression used on the chart data point's fill color. In the most trivial case, the expression would just contain one grouping value as in the following code:

```
=Code.GetColor(Fields!Country.Value)
```

For the legend text, use either the same expression as in the category and series group/label expressions, or experiment until you achieve the legend description text that you want.

Final Thoughts

In this recipe, you learned how to define a custom color palette that can be used to override the default colors, and synchronize the colors across all of the charts in your report.

Credits and Related References

Robert Bruckner's whitepaper, Get More Out of SQL Server Reporting Services Charts.
http://msdn.microsoft.com/en-us/library/aa964128(SQL.90).aspx

CHART KEYWORDS

Chart keywords are useful in a number of situations where you don't need to worry about the underlying calculation needed for visual elements, such as data point labels. Chart keywords are particularly practical when the same or similar complex data value calculations are needed in more than one place (for instance, data point label and data point tooltip). Furthermore, some keywords allow you to reference the value of the current series or category, which is usually hard or even impossible to accomplish through equivalent RDL expressions.

This recipe shows how to use one of the available chart keywords for data point labels and includes a table of all available keywords and explains their use.

Product Versions

➤ Reporting Services 2005 or later

What You'll Need

➤ Adventure Works DW Analysis Services sample database

Designing the Report

This example uses the AdventureWorksDW2008 for SQL Server Analysis Services 2008 sample database. The query retrieves sales data, specifically the sales reason and revenue. Figure P3-3 shows the final report, with chart data point labels automatically calculated based on `#PERCENT` keyword.

FIGURE P3-3

1. Start by designing a data source for the AdventureWorksDW2008 for Analysis Services sample databases.

2. Create a dataset query that uses the Internet Sales Amount measure with the Sales Reason hierarchy.

```
SELECT NON EMPTY { [Measures].[Internet Sales Amount] } ON COLUMNS,
NON EMPTY { ([Sales Reason].[Sales Reasons].[Sales Reason].ALLMEMBERS ) }
DIMENSION PROPERTIES MEMBER_CAPTION, MEMBER_UNIQUE_NAME ON ROWS
FROM [Adventure Works]
CELL PROPERTIES VALUE, BACK_COLOR, FORE_COLOR, FORMATTED_VALUE,
FORMAT_STRING, FONT_NAME, FONT_SIZE, FONT_FLAGS
```

3. Add a new Chart, of type simple pie, as shown in Figure P3-4.

4. Prepare the pie chart settings.

FIGURE P3-4

  a. Drag the Sales_Reason field into the category fields drop zone of the chart.

  b. Drag the Internet_Sales_Amount field into the data fields drop zone of the chart.

  c. Set the chart title to Sales by Top Sales Reasons.

  d. Open the chart properties, and set the color palette to Grayscale.

  e. Drag the legend from its default position to the bottom position so that the legend items are shown as a multi-column table inside the chart.

  f. Right-click on the chart and select Show Data Labels.

5. Setup the chart data point label.

For the data point label, you want to show the percentage for each pie slice. This can be accomplished in two ways:

  a. Use an RDL expression to specify the explicit calculation. For example,

```
=FormatPercent(Fields!Internet_Sales_Amount.Value / Sum(Fields!Internet_Sales
_Amount.Value, "Chart1"), 1)
```

  b. Use built-in chart keywords that are executed by the chart control based on the visualized data. For example,

```
#PERCENT{P1}
```

For our specific chart report example, right-click the data labels inside the pie chart, and open the "Series Label Properties" dialog. On the general page, set the label to #PERCENT{P1}, and confirm the dialog. This instructs the chart to calculate the relative percentage of the pie slice for the data point label and apply a P1 percent formatting, as defined by the .NET Framework.

This results in a chart on the design surface, as shown in Figure P3-5.

The benefit of using chart label keywords is that as a report author you don't need to worry about the underlying calculation. This is particularly practical when the same or similar complex data value calculations are needed in more than one place (e.g. data point label and data point tooltip). Note that the chart keywords can only be used for visual chart properties directly evaluated inside the chart control: Label, AxisLabel, ToolTip, LegendToolTip, LegendText, and LabelToolTip.

On the other hand, chart drill-through actions (for instance, on data points) are not visual elements of the chart, and therefore require RDL expressions as drill-through parameter values and cannot use chart keywords.

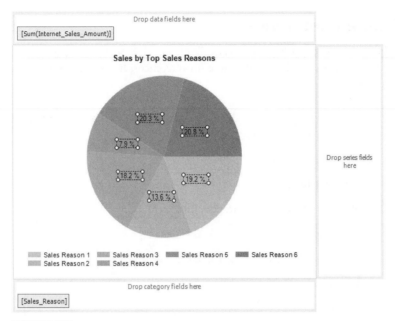

FIGURE P3-5

6. Preview the report to test the results. Figure P3-6 shows the result.

FIGURE P3-6

Final Thoughts

In most report scenarios, you don't need chart keywords to accomplish the desired visualizations. Frequently, you can also use RDL expressions to achieve similar effects. However, chart keywords can be very effective in the right situation and for sophisticated chart visualizations, so keeping their existence in the back of your mind, and having this recipe and the reference guide below, will come in handy.

Credits and Related References

A full table of available built-in chart keywords is available on MSDN at `http://msdn.microsoft.com /en-us/library/bb677551.aspx` and is included here for reference with additional information regarding format string support.

KEYWORD	REPLACED BY	APPLICABLE TO CHART TYPES	SUPPORTS FORMATTING STRING
#VALX	X value of data point	All	Yes
#VALY	Y value of data point	All	Yes
#VALY2	Y value #2 of data point	Range, Bubble	
#VALY3	Y value #3 of data point	Stock, Candlestick	
#VALY4	Y value #4 of data point	Stock, Candlestick	
#SERIESNAME	Series name	All	No
#LABEL	Data point label	All	No
#AXISLABEL	Data point axis label	Shape	No
#INDEX	Data point index in the series	All	Yes
#PERCENT	Percent of the data point Y value	All	Yes
#LEGENDTEXT	Series or data point legend text	All	No
#TOTAL	Total of all Y values in the series	All	Yes
#AVG	Average of all Y values in the series	All	Yes
#MIN	Minimum of all Y values in the series	All	Yes
#MAX	Maximum of all Y values in the series	All	Yes
#FIRST	Y value of the first point in the series	All	Yes
#LAST	Y value of the last point in the series	All	Yes

To format the keyword, enclose a .NET Framework format string in parentheses. For example, to specify the value of the data point in a ToolTip as a number with two decimal places, include the format string N2 in braces, such as #VALY{N2} for the ToolTip property on the series. For more information about .NET Framework format strings, see Formatting Types on MSDN: http://go.microsoft.com/fwlink/?LinkId=112024.

The following are examples of equivalent RDL expressions for chart keywords:

➤   #VALX: =Fields!MyField.Value

➤   #PERCENT: =FormatPercent(Fields!MyField.Value/Sum(Fields!MyField.Value, "Chart-Name"),2)

➤   #AVG, #MIN, #MAX, #FIRST, #LAST: Equivalent RDL expressions using RDL aggregate functions may not exist, specifically if chart category or series group filters or sorting are applied.

COLUMN CHART WITH GOAL THRESHOLD LINE

Chart reports are an effective way to visualize data to show trends and comparisons in a way that can help the user get real meaning from numbers. However, chart data can be meaningless without context. This example shows you how to display a column chart with a goal line so users can easily understand whether charted values are above or below an acceptable threshold. This recipe provides three versions of this report: a simple example using a SQL query to demonstrate the essentials, one with an MDX query, and a copy of the latter with a parameterized threshold and dynamically colored columns to show data points above or below the goal.

This is a report design that you can almost do with standard report design features, but it's that last little step, that last critical piece, that takes a little creativity to solve. When I was first challenged to design this report for a consulting client, I knew that it could be done but I just wasn't sure how. I grew up in Washington State in the 1970s with the legend of Bigfoot. For a while, there were Bigfoot sightings every week and everyone knew someone who claimed to have seen Bigfoot (or had seen someone who knew someone who had claimed to have seen Bigfoot). We knew he was out there in the remote wilderness but we weren't sure where. This was a little like that – the solution was out there and I just needed to find it.

This technique falls into a category known as "sleazy hacks," and I need to give credit to Chris Hays for coining that phrase in the title of his blog a few years ago. Chris is responsible for the Report Definition Language specification on the SSRS product team.

Product Versions

➤   Reporting Services 2008

What You'll Need

➤   Column, area, or line chart

➤   Experience with VB expressions

Designing the Report

This solution is more about technique than complexity. The chart you see in Figure P3-7 has some simple design features you'd expect to be fairly easy to define, but this is a little challenging to do right out of the box. In SSRS 2008, creating multi-series reports like this one, containing columns and a line, is standard fare. However, the natural behavior of all charts is that each column or line segment is plotted from the center of the data point along the axis. This means that since the lines and columns in this chart have the same range of category (X-axis) values, the line would begin in the center of the left-most column and end in the center of the right-most column instead of running from edge to edge of the chart container. In fact, no matter what the minimum and maximum values are, the chart normally provides a margin of space on each side of the axis. You'll see this, and the resolution, as we work through the report design. The final result of this recipe is shown in Figure P3-7.

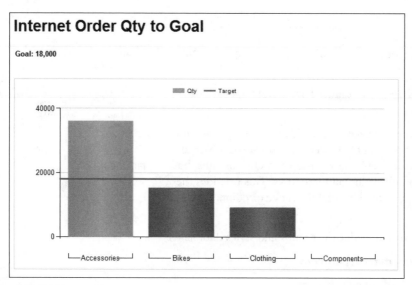

FIGURE P3-7

Let's get started. The first bit of "hack" is in the query. In order for the line to extend beyond the range of column center points, it must begin and end with lower and higher scale values than the respective column points. This means that you need to work some magic in the query and add two extra values to the scale. You will see this in the query that follows.

1. Create a new report.

2. Add a data source for the AdventureWorksDW2008 database.

3. Create a dataset and enter the following SQL script:

```sql
select
    Category as CategoryGroup
  , Qty
  , Target
  , RANK() over (order by OrderNum, Category) as OrderValue
from
(
    select Null as Category, Null as Qty, 12000 as Target, 0 as OrderNum
    union
    select
        pc.EnglishProductCategoryName as Category
      , Sum(fis.OrderQuantity) as Qty
      , 12000 as Target, 1 as OrderNum
    from
        FactInternetSales fis inner join DimProduct p
        on fis.ProductKey=p.ProductKey
        inner join DimProductSubcategory ps
        on p.ProductSubcategoryKey=ps.ProductSubcategoryKey
        inner join DimProductCategory pc
```

```
        on ps.ProductCategoryKey=pc.ProductCategoryKey
    group by pc.EnglishProductCategoryName
    union
    select Null as Category, Null as Qty, 12000 as Target, 2 as OrderNum
) as s;
```

Execute the query and view the results. They should appear as in Figure P3-8.

Notice that two fictitious rows have been added to the results on the first and last records, based on the OrderValue sort order. Notice also the lack of values for the CategoryGroup and Qty columns, but the Target column contains values in these rows. This provides the basis for the goal line to extend beyond the range of points plotted by the column chart.

	CategoryGroup	Qty	Target	OrderValue
1	NULL	NULL	12000	1
2	Accessories	36092	12000	2
3	Bikes	15205	12000	3
4	Clothing	9101	12000	4
5	NULL	NULL	12000	5

FIGURE P3-8

Next you build the chart and define the groups and series data fields.

1. Add a new chart to the report body.

2. Choose a standard column chart type.

3. Drag and drop or select the OrderValue field in the Category axis.

4. Drag and drop or select the CategoryGroup field as a second field in the category axis.

5. Click the chart in the designer to show the data field and axis field drop zones.

6. Add the Qty and Target fields to the data fields drop zone to define the data series.

7. Right-click the Target field and change the chart type for this series to a Line chart.

8. Remove the axis labels.

Cosmetic changes can be applied as appropriate. These may include the line chart weight and color. The report in the designer should look similar to Figure P3-9.

Preview the report and compare the result to Figure P3-10. You'll notice the empty columns for the OrderValue field values 1 and 5. Note how the line chart naturally extends from the center of the first column position to the center of the last. Again, the requirement is for this line to extend from margin to margin.

Don't worry about the axis labels for both of these groups. When you change the axis value range, the labels for the inner group will disappear. Before you do this, you need to show the CategoryGroup field values on the outer group instead of the numbers.

1. In the Category axis fields, edit the OrderValue group properties.

2. In the Category Group Properties dialog, set the Label property to use the CategoryGroup field. See Figure P3-11.

Now you'll work your magic on the line chart margins.

To eliminate the extra space around the chart, you'll set the left and right axis margin to be one-half of a scale value from the first and last column positions.

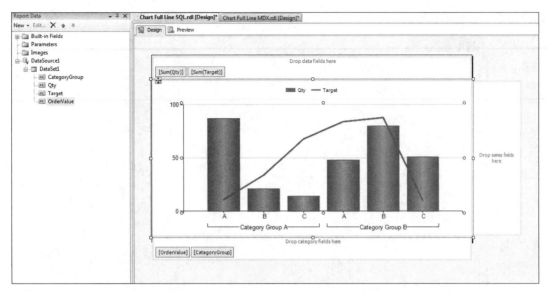

FIGURE P3-9

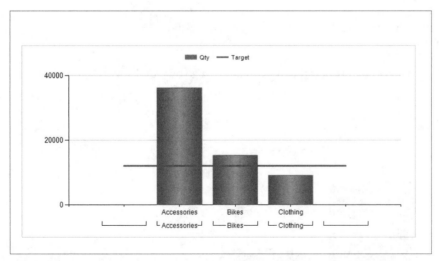

FIGURE P3-10

1. Right-click on the Category axis labels at the bottom of the chart and open the Axis Properties dialog.

2. Edit the axis scale Minimum property and set it to the following expression:

   ```
   =MIN(Fields!OrderValue.Value) + 0.5
   ```

3. Edit the axis scale Maximum property and set it to the following expression:

   ```
   =MAX(Fields!OrderValue.Value) - 0.5
   ```

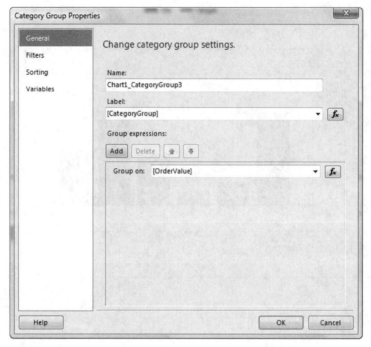

FIGURE P3-11

4. Accept these changes and preview the report, comparing your results with Figure P3-12.

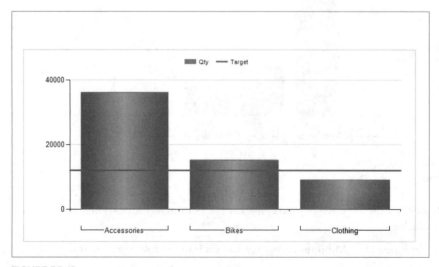

FIGURE P3-12

At this point, you have a working chart report with the essential features. The goal line, which is actually a line chart, extends from margin to margin. Even though you added extra values to the beginning and end of the axis range to make this work, now the columns fill the entire chart area.

Adding Dynamic Color

You can use a dynamic fill color to bring attention to series values that are above or below the goal line. Columns under the goal will be red and columns at or above the goal will be lime green. To enable this feature, follow these steps:

1. Click once on the chart to show the field drop zones.

2. Right-click the Qty field series and open the Series Properties dialog.

3. On the Fill page, set the Fill style property to Solid.

4. Next to the Color drop down, click the Expression button (*fx*) to open the Expression dialog.

5. Enter the following expression:

```
=IIF(Fields!Qty.Value < Fields!Target.Value, "Red", "Lime")
```

6. Close all dialogs and preview the report. It should look similar to Figure P3-13.

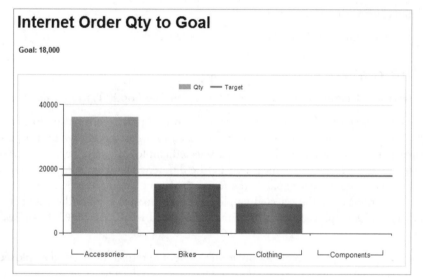

FIGURE P3-13

Final Thoughts

Charts in Reporting Services offer a lot of design flexibility and opportunities to customize the behavior and visual presentation of data. However, with these capabilities come a myriad of properties that can be a bit daunting to navigate and find in the design interface. This report design may not be quite as elusive as Bigfoot, but it does solve a specific problem and provide real business value.

When exploring new features and design patterns, I find it useful to save versions of my chart reports in different stages of development. This way I can revert to a working state if I get myself into trouble. With some practice and perhaps a few late nights of experimentation, you will develop patterns that work best for your users and the data they need to visualize.

CREATING A PERSONAL REPORT CARD

This recipe creates a personal report card report that displays an individual's performance compared with the best performer for the same performance metrics over a specific period of time. In this case, you are going to compare sales employees who are at the same hierarchical level to see how well they have performed compared to their allocated sales quota. This technique can be used to create personal report cards for any performance metrics.

Product Versions

➤ Reporting Services 2005

➤ Reporting Services 2008

What You'll Need

➤ A connection to Adventure Works cube

➤ A column chart with two data series

➤ A basic understanding of Analysis Services and MDX queries

Designing the Report

This example uses the Adventure Works cube for SQL Server 2005 or 2008 sample database.

To make this recipe easier to understand, it is broken into two parts: personal performance over a period of time, and personal performance compared to a best performer over a period of time. The first part creates a report displaying a selected employee's sales performance over a period of time where performance is measured by the difference between sales amount and target sales quota. The second part expands the first scenario by adding the best performer to the mix so you can measure the selected employee's performance against the best performer (in our case, sales employees from the same hierarchical level). Figure P3-14 shows the finished report.

For the first part of the report, let's create a simple MDX query to return the selected employee's reseller sales amount and sales target over a period of calendar years and quarters. This example uses Report Builder 2.0.

  1. Start by creating a data source for the Adventure Works DW Analysis Services OLAP database.

  2. Create a dataset MDX query using the Query Designer. Drag the following items from the left-most metadata pane to the query grid and drop them into columns from left to right:

➤ Employees attribute from the Employee dimension.

➤ Calendar Year from the Date dimension.

➤ Calendar Quarter of Year from the Date dimension.

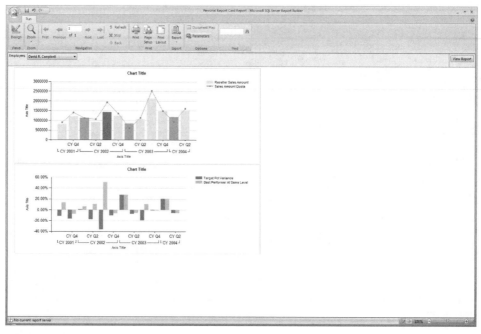

FIGURE P3-14

> ➤ Reseller Sales Amount measure.

> ➤ Sales Amount Quota measure.

3. Add a filter using the Filter pane at the top of the Query Designer.

> ➤ Drag the Department Name hierarchy from the Employee dimension to the first row of the Filter pane.

> ➤ Verify that the Equal operator is used.

> ➤ For the Filter Expression, select the Sales department to restrict data to sales employees only.

4. Add a second filter for the Employees hierarchy. This filter will also be used as a parameter.

> ➤ Drag and drop the Employees hierarchy from the Employee dimension to the second row in the Filter pane.

> ➤ Verify that the Equal operator is used.

> ➤ Leave the Filter Expression blank.

> ➤ Check the Parameter checkbox.

The parameter will be used to select the employee when a user runs the report. After you've completed these steps, the Query Designer should look like Figure P3-15.

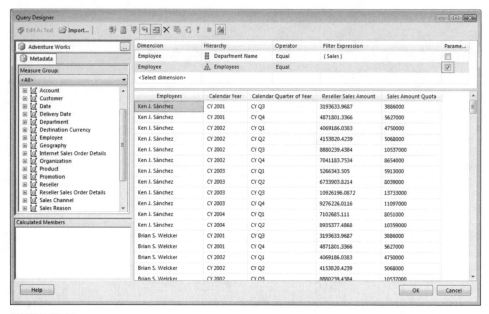

FIGURE P3-15

Now that the query is designed, let's start creating the first part of the report.

1. Add a Chart report item to the report body and select Column chart type. Resize the chart to your liking.

2. Drag the Calendar_Year and Calendar_Quarter_of_Year fields to the category field area of the chart. This will create category groups of Calendar Year and Calendar Quarter on the X-axis.

3. Drag Reseller_Sales_Amount and Sales_Amount_Quota to the data field area of the chart. This will create two data series.

At this point, the chart simply plots reseller sales amount and sales target quota data series as columns, and calendar year and calendar quarter on the X-axis. In order to display the performance of the selected employee in a more useful manner, you will change the chart type of the sales target quota data series to Line with Markers and dynamically color the reseller sales amount columns depending on their variance from the sales target. For example, if the percentage variance between reseller sales amount and sales target quota is positive (that is, reseller sales amount >= sales target quota), the data column will be colored lime; on the other hand, if the percentage variance is less than negative twenty-five percent, the column will be colored yellow; otherwise it will be colored red.

Next, update the chart to reflect the changes just mentioned. But before you begin, the report designer should look like Figure P3-16.

1. Right-click on the Sales_Amount_Quota data series and select Change Chart Type.

2. Select Line with Markers chart type.

3. Right-click on the Reseller_Sales_Amount data series and select Series Properties.

4. Select Fill page of the Series Properties dialog box and enter the following expression for Color (see Figure P3-17):

```
=switch ((Fields!Reseller_Sales_Amount.Value - Fields!Sales_Amount_Quota.Value)
/Fields!Reseller_Sales_Amount.Value > 0, "Lime",
(Fields!Reseller_Sales_Amount.Value - Fields!Sales_Amount_Quota.Value)
/ Fields!Reseller_Sales_Amount.Value < -0.25, "Red",
(Fields!Reseller_Sales_Amount.Value - Fields!Sales_Amount_Quota.Value)
/ Fields!Reseller_Sales_Amount.Value > -0.25, "Yellow")
```

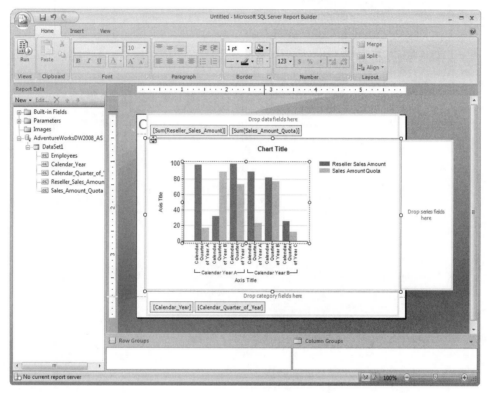

FIGURE P3-16

 In order to change the chart type for Sales_Amount_Quota data series to line with markers in SSRS 2005, go to Data Series Properties and select the Appearance tab. In the Appearance tab, check both the "Show Markers" and "Plot data as line" checkboxes. Also, in order to update the Fill property for Reseller_Sales_Amount data series in SSRS 2005, go to the data series properties and select the Appearance tab. From the Appearance tab, select the Series Style button and go to the Fill tab. From the Fill tab, select the expression button for Color and enter the expression.

Preview the report to test the results. Select employee Amy E. Alberts. As you can see in Figure P3-18, the reseller sales amount data columns change color depending on the percent variance between sales amount and sales target quota. Also, the sales target quota data series is plotted as a line with markers.

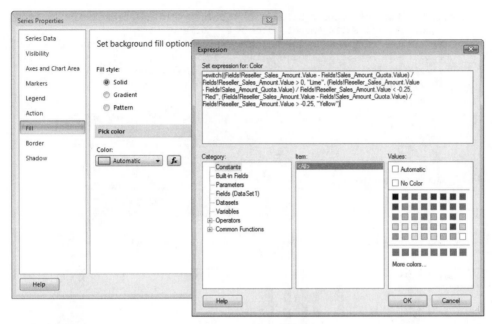

FIGURE P3-17

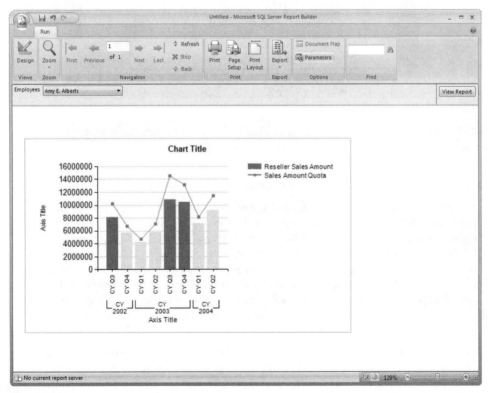

FIGURE P3-18

So, the first part of this recipe was pretty straightforward. Now, for the second part, you want to compare the performance of the selected employee with the best performer at the same level as the selected employee. In most environments, peer-to-peer comparison can be done at any level as long as the comparison is fair. In this example, you are going to compare the selected employee to the best performer on the percentage variance between reseller sales amount and sales target quota. It wouldn't be fair to compare the employees on just reseller sales amount.

For simplicity's sake, you are just going to create another dataset and chart to fulfill the requirements for this part of the recipe. The most important element of this part is creating the MDX statement for the dataset. So, let's review the MDX statement you are going to use:

```
WITH
  MEMBER [Measures].[TargetPctVariance] AS
      (([Measures].[Reseller Sales Amount])-([Measures].[Sales Amount Quota]))
    /
      ([Measures].[Reseller Sales Amount])
    ,Format_String="Percent"
  MEMBER [Measures].[BestPerformerAtSameLevel] AS
    Max
    (
      {
        StrToMember
        (@EmployeeEmployees
         ,CONSTRAINED
        ).Siblings
      }
      , ([Measures].[TargetPctVariance])
    )
SELECT
  NON EMPTY
    {
      ([Measures].[Reseller Sales Amount])
      ,([Measures].[Sales Amount Quota])
      ,([Measures].[TargetPctVariance])
      ,([Measures].[BestPerformerAtSameLevel])
    } ON COLUMNS
  ,NON EMPTY
      STRTOSET
      (@EmployeeEmployees
       , CONSTRAINED
      )*
      {
        [Date].[Calendar Year].[Calendar Year].ALLMEMBERS
      }*
      {
        [Date].[Calendar Quarter of Year].[Calendar Quarter of Year].ALLMEMBERS
      } ON ROWS
  FROM [Adventure Works]
```

In the MDX statement, you are creating two members: TargetPctVariance and BestPerformerAt-SameLevel. TargetPctVariance is the percentage variance between reseller sales amount and sales target quota. BestPerformerAtSameLevel finds the best TargetPctVariance among the employees at the same level as the selected employee using the Max MDX function. Employees at the same level are selected using the Siblings MDX member function.

After the two members are created, the select MDX statement is pretty straightforward. Along with the two members just created, you add measures Reseller Sales Amount and Sales Amount Quota to the column axis and the selected Employee (use the STRTOSET function in order to convert the employee parameter string to a set), Calendar Year, and Calendar Quarter of Year to the row axis.

Now that you have reviewed the MDX statement, let's create the dataset.

1. Right-click on the data source and select Add Dataset.

2. From the Dataset Properties dialog box, click the Query Designer button and toggle the Design Mode to text mode by clicking the Design Mode icon (⬛).

3. Copy and paste the MDX you just reviewed.

4. Add a query parameter by clicking the Query Parameter icon (⬛).

5. Enter a parameter name of EmployeeEmployees and select a Default Value of Amy E. Alberts. Leave everything else blank and click OK (see Figure P3-19).

6. Verify the MDX query by executing it in the Query Designer and click OK to close the Query Designer.

7. Click OK to close the Dataset Properties dialog box.

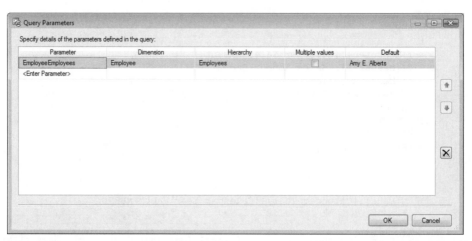

FIGURE P3-19

Now that you have created another dataset, you create a chart to display to the results.

1. Add a Chart report item to the report body and select Column chart type. Resize the chart to your liking.

2. Drag the Calendar_Year and Calendar_Quarter_of_Year fields from the second dataset to the category field area of the chart. This will create category groups of Calendar Year and Calendar Quarter on the X-axis.

3. Drag TargetPctVariance and BestPerformerAtSameLevel to the data field area of the chart.

4. Format the Y-Axis to display a percentage scale by right-clicking on the Y-Axis and selecting Axis Properties.

5. Select Number on the Axis Properties dialog box and select Percentage category and click OK (see Figure P3-20).

The report designer should look like Figure P3-21.

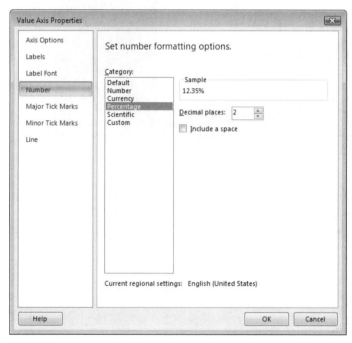

FIGURE P3-20

In order to display percentage scale on Y-Axis in SSRS 2005, go to Chart Properties. From the Chart Properties dialog box, go to Y-Axis tab and enter P2 in Format Code. Adjust the scale minimum and maximum values and major gridlines interval value according to the data.

Preview the report to test the results and select employee David R. Campbell. As you can see in Figure P3-22, both charts are displayed, with the first chart showing David's individual performance while the second chart compares David's performance with the best performer at the same level as David.

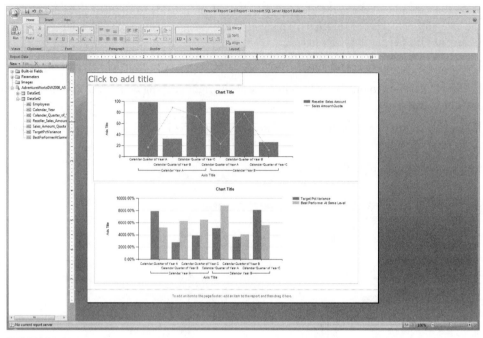

FIGURE P3-21

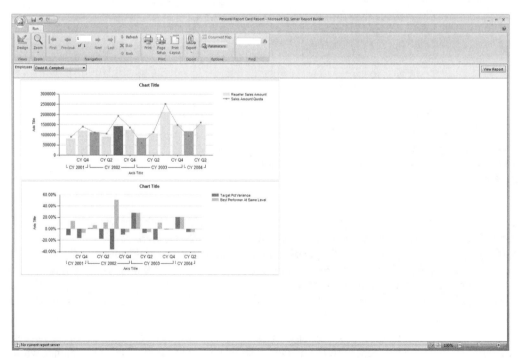

FIGURE P3-22

Final Thoughts

You can further enhance this report by adding series data labels, changing column patterns, and combining two charts into one using dual Y-axis. Combining charts may look cluttered, but in some cases, if the performance metric is common between the two charts, it may be beneficial to do so.

The technique used in this example can be used to create a personal report card report that displays an individual's performance compared with the best performer for the same performance metrics over a specific period of time. The important concept in this example is to understand the MDX that finds the best performer for the performance measure you are tracking.

CUSTOMIZING GAUGES WITH IMAGES

The addition of the Dundas components to Reporting Services has made it a very compelling platform for delivering reports with stunning data visualization. The new components include fully integrated chart and gauge elements with a variety of configurable options.

The new gauge report items offer a high level of customization, allowing the report designer to create gauges that satisfy the needs of most business requirements. There are so many properties waiting to be customized that most of us will never need to tweak them all.

We can customize gauges all the way down to the pointers and dials. An interesting option is to set the BackFrame to a custom image, whether embedded or external. This also provides an opportunity to maintain a consistent layout across your reports, especially when displaying them in dashboards.

This recipe shows how you can customize your gauge components to resemble those of a hot rod dashboard!

Product Versions

➤ SQL Server 2008 Reporting Services

What You'll Need

➤ A good-quality PNG or GIF image at 96 DPI of a custom frame for your gauge

➤ A gauge item to apply the image back frame

Designing the Report

For the purposes of this exercise, you will not delve into the details of binding the gauge to report data; thus, you only walk through the steps to set up the gauge with a customized background. Figure P3-23 shows the final output of this recipe.

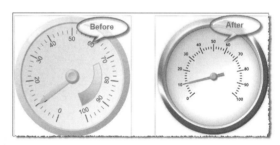

Begin by embedding the new gauge background image into the report definition. You simply need to right-click the Images item in the Report Data window and select Add Image.

FIGURE P3-23

Find the file location of your custom gauge frame image and click OK.

Now, drag and drop a new gauge item from the toolbox onto the report body. Select the Radial Gauge type, as shown in Figure P3-24, and click OK. Click inside the body of the gauge so the actual radial gauge item is selected and not the panel or another child item of the gauge.

In the Properties window for the selected gauge, expand the BackFrame section and then expand the FrameImage section. Set the Source property to Embedded and the Value property to the name of the custom image you embedded into the report on the first step, as shown in Figure P3-25.

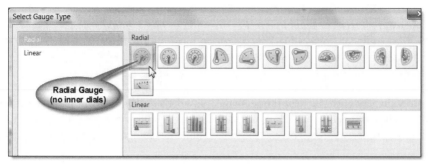

FIGURE P3-24

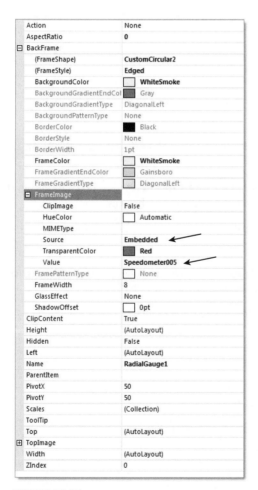

FIGURE P3-25

If you cannot see the Properties window in Report Builder, here's how to get it back on your designer view. Select the View menu option from the Ribbon menu bar. Make sure the Properties box is checked.

Your frame should now display with the new frame image. Now let's customize your gauge even further to add the final touches and deliver a slick, hot rod-style gauge! Follow the next few steps (also notice that as you change property values you can see in real-time the changes take effect on the design surface):

1. Delete the range by selecting the red gradient element (below 70 through 100 in the scale), right-click and select "Delete Range."

2. Select the scale, right-click, and choose Scale Properties. In the Properties dialog, choose the Layout section and set the following properties:
    ➤   Scale radius: 24
    ➤   Start angle: 50
    ➤   Sweep angle: 260
    ➤   Scale Bar width: 0

3. Select the Labels section and uncheck the box Rotate labels with scale. Change the Placement to Outside.

4. In the Label Font section choose Trebuchet MS, bold and 14pt size, with a Black foreground color. This will make the numbers stand out, making it easier on the eyes.

5. Change the Major Tick Marks length property to 25.

6. Click OK to save changes to the gauge scale.

7. Select the pointer arrow in the middle of the gauge, right-click, and choose Pointer Properties. Change the Needle Style option to Tapered with tail with a width of 10.

8. Choose the Pointer Fill section and make the following adjustments:
    ➤   Fill style: Gradient
    ➤   Color: Red
    ➤   Secondary Color: LightSalmon
    ➤   Gradient Style: Vertical Center

9. Choose the Cap Options section and change the following properties:
    ➤   Cap Style: Rounded with Indentation
    ➤   Cap width: 28

10. Finally, change the Cap Fill color to Silver. This ought to give the radial gauge a bold look with numbers that stand out and a beautiful red needle pointer akin to those found in automobile dashboards.

Figure P3-26 shows a before-and-after shot of the gauge item, in which a custom frame was applied, as well as your customizations to the pointer size and color, scale radius, number placement, and so on.

As you can see, you can create very realistic and appealing gauges that are sure to catch the reader's eyes.

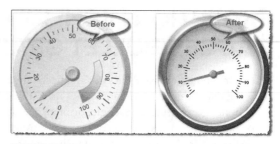

FIGURE P3-26

Final Thoughts

With a myriad of new properties and options, the new Reporting Services charting and gauging components are definitely the most customizable of any report item. In this recipe, you've seen how to access some of these properties in order to add custom images to gauges and design some eye-catching data visualizations.

Credits and Related References

Based on an original recipe from *Professional SQL Server 2008 Reporting Services* (Wrox, 2008).

EXCEPTION HIGHLIGHTING WITH GAUGES/BULLET GRAPHS

Colors and other visual cues are an effective way of quickly conveying outliers among a (typically large) set of data. This recipe demonstrates how to use a bullet graph to perform visual exception highlighting. A bullet graph features a single, primary measure (for example, sales), compares that measure to one or more other measures to enrich its meaning (for example, compared to a sales target quota), and displays it in the context of qualitative ranges of performance, such as poor, meets expectation, and exceeds expectation.

Product Versions

➤   Reporting Services 2008 or later

What You'll Need

➤   AdventureWorksDW2008 sample database

Designing the Report

This example uses the AdventureWorksDW2008 sample database. The query retrieves sales person data. Specifically, the data includes the sales person name, sales per calendar periods, and the sales quota. The final report is shown in Figure P3-27.

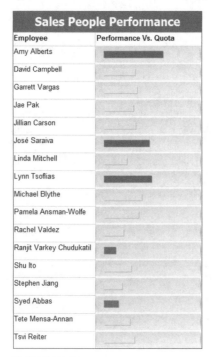

FIGURE P3-27

1. Start by designing a data source for the AdventureWorksDW2008 sample databases.

2. Enter the following select statement to create a dataset query:

```
SELECT T.CalendarYear, T.CalendarQuarter, T.MonthNumberOfYear,
    SUM(S.ExtendedAmount)as Sales,
    COALESCE(SUM(Q.SalesAmountQuota )/ COUNT(SalesAmountQuota),
    SUM(Q.SalesAmountQuota)/COUNT(SalesAmountQuota)) as Quota,
    SUM(S.ExtendedAmount)/(SUM(Q.SalesAmountQuota)/COUNT(SalesAmountQuota))
 as Within,
    E.FirstName + ' ' + E.LastName AS Employee
FROM FactResellerSales as  S
    LEFT OUTER JOIN dbo.DimDate T ON S.orderdatekey = DateKey
    JOIN dbo.DimEmployee E ON S.EmployeeKey = E.EmployeeKey
    LEFT OUTER JOIN dbo.FactSalesQuota Q on S.EmployeeKey= Q.EmployeeKey AND
    T.CalendarYear = Q.CalendarYear AND T.CalendarQuarter = Q.CalendarQuarter
GROUP BY T.CalendarYear ,T.CalendarQuarter,T.MonthNumberOfYear, E.FirstName,
    E.LastName, E.EmployeeKey
ORDER By Employee, T.CalendarYear ASC, T.CalendarQuarter ASC, T.MonthNumberOfYear
```

3. Follow these steps to create the employee table in the report:

a. Add a new textbox on the design surface and enter Sales People Performance. This will be the title of the report.

b. Add a new table beneath the title textbox and delete the third column of the table, since you need only two columns for this report.

c. Using the field selector in the table detail section of the first column, choose the Employee field. An example of a field selector icon is shown in Figure P3-28 in the right corner of the selected Employee detail textbox. A field selector simplifies referencing fields in a data region by simply selecting from the list of available dataset fields.

d. In the header area of the second column, type Sales Performance vs. Quota.

e. In the grouping pane for this table, select the Details row group and open its group properties. On the group, add a group expression based on the Employee field.

4. Next add a bullet graph.

Create a new gauge report item of type bullet graph as shown in Figure P3-29, in the empty table group cell beneath the Sales Performance vs. Quota textbox.

The resulting report layout after this step should look similar to Figure P3-30.

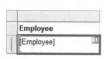

FIGURE P3-28

FIGURE P3-29

FIGURE P3-30

5. Apply the following settings to the bullet graph:

a. Select the bullet graph, open the gauge properties dialog, set the frame style to Simple and the frame style shape to Default. Click OK to exit the dialog.

b. Select the bullet graph, and then select the LinearScale as shown in Figure P3-30.

c. Right-click on the LinearScale and disable Show labels.

d. Right-click on the LinearPointer1 area shown in Figure P3-30, and open the Pointer Properties dialog.

e. On the Pointers Options page, set the pointer value to the following expression, which displays the sales performance value:

```
=Last(Fields!Within.Value) * 100
```

f. On the Pointers Options page, set the Width to 40, so that the indicator consumes more space.

g. On the Pointer Fill page, select the solid fill color option, and define an expression-based fill color like this:

```
=Switch(Last(Fields!Within.Value) * 100 < 20, "Red", Last(Fields!Within.Value)
* 100 < 50, "Yellow", Last(Fields!Within.Value) * 100 < 100, "Green")
```

With this color fill expression, you accomplish a color coding with poor sales performance being highlighted in red as less than 20% of quota, and highlighted in yellow if between 20% and 50% of the quota.

h. Optionally, select the three light/mid/dark gray linear range bars in the bullet graph and either delete them or change their color/range values. The resulting bullet graph design is shown in Figure P3-31.

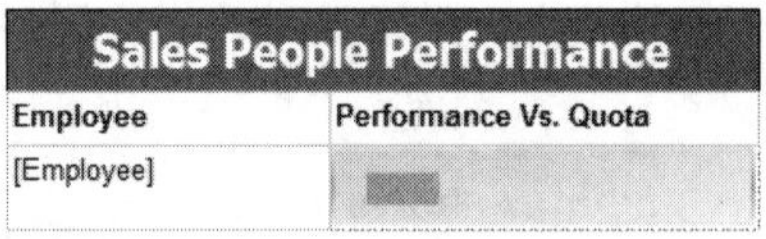

Sales People Performance	
Employee	**Performance Vs. Quota**
[Employee]	

FIGURE P3-31

6. Preview the report to test the results.

Figure P3-32 shows the current performance of sales people, highlighting exceptions as defined by the color rule in Step 5g.

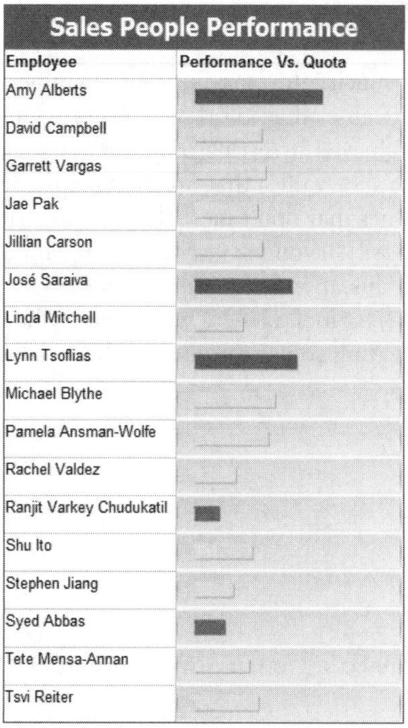

Sales People Performance

Employee	Performance Vs. Quota
Amy Alberts	
David Campbell	
Garrett Vargas	
Jae Pak	
Jillian Carson	
José Saraiva	
Linda Mitchell	
Lynn Tsoflias	
Michael Blythe	
Pamela Ansman-Wolfe	
Rachel Valdez	
Ranjit Varkey Chudukatil	
Shu Ito	
Stephen Jiang	
Syed Abbas	
Tete Mensa-Annan	
Tsvi Reiter	

FIGURE P3-32

Final Thoughts

Reporting Services 2008 added many data visualization enhancements. While one large chart with sophisticated visualizations can present information in an excellent way, this recipe shows that the combination of data regions (such as tables) and embedding charts or gauges inside a table grouping is very powerful too. Based on the tablix location where the chart or gauge is placed, it automatically is associated with the underlying data at that data region/grouping scope and the same visualization is applied to all group instances at runtime — a quick way to build a comparative visual analysis, with exceptions from the general visual trend recognizable more easily than viewing raw numbers.

Credits and Related References

You can learn more about other types of data region and chart combinations in the recipes related to Sparkline Charts.

GROUPED PIE CHART SLICES

In an effort to not inundate your report user with too much information, it is sometimes useful to limit the volume of data that you provide. To this end, rather than displaying every segment of data possible within a pie chart, much more value can be achieved by listing only the top *x* slices, those slices with values above a designated amount, or those slice values that are above a predetermined overall percentage of the whole pie chart. All other values that don't meet the pie slice criteria can be grouped into a single slice and designated as "All Others." Beyond simply providing a more readable aggregation of data, there is one more bit of utility in this approach, and that is the fact that the default color palate in Reporting Services is limited to 16 colors. If there were greater than 16 slices of segmentation in your pie chart, you would end up repeating colors for distinct slices, which can lead to confusion and loss of clarity.

Product Versions

➤ Reporting Services 2005

➤ Reporting Services 2008

What You'll Need

➤ A data source named AdventureWorksDW connecting to the AdventureWorksDW2008 database in SQL Server 2008

Designing the Report

Figure P3-33 shows the final result of this recipe.

Before completing the finished report displayed in Figure P3-33, you will first create a version of this report (shown in Figure P3-34 later in this recipe), in which the report requirements demand that the top 15 pie slices be shown individually, while the remaining slices will be grouped into a single slice. Next, you create a report where a cutoff value for pie slices is determined and all slices not meeting this criterion are lumped together, as shown in Figure P3-35.

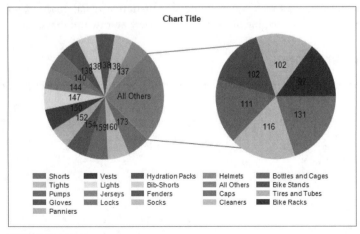

FIGURE P3-33

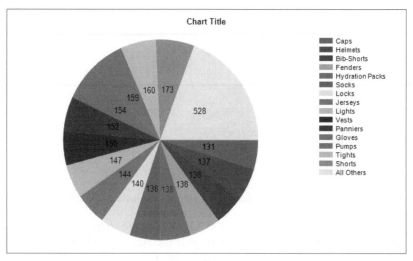

FIGURE P3-34

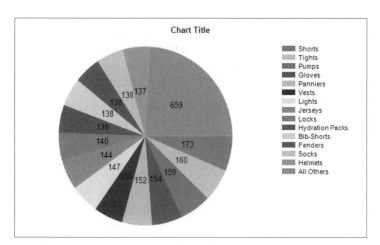

FIGURE P3-35

1. Create a new dataset named Top15AndOther using the
AdventureWorksDW data source. For the query text of the dataset, use the following code:

```
WITH Top15 AS
(
SELECT TOP 15
        COUNT(*) AS Cnt
        ,EnglishProductSubcategoryName AS ProductSubCategory
FROM FactSurveyResponse
GROUP BY EnglishProductSubcategoryName
ORDER BY COUNT(*) DESC
)
```

```
SELECT
        Cnt
        ,ProductSubCategory
FROM Top15

UNION

SELECT
        COUNT(*)
        ,'All Others' AS ProductSubcategory
FROM FactSurveyResponse FSR
WHERE NOT EXISTS
        (SELECT ProductSubCategory
         FROM Top15
         WHERE FSR.EnglishProductSubcategoryName = Top15.ProductSubCategory)
```

The common table expression Top15 selects the top 15 product subcategories from the FactSurveyResponse table in descending order so that the largest 15 of these values are selected. The result of this query is then unioned with the total count of all other product subcategories that are not present in our CTE — essentially everything else.

2.   Right-click the design area and from the Insert sub-menu choose Chart. Choose the pie chart. Drag and drop the ProductSubCategory field from the Report Data pane into the Categories box, and the Cnt field into the Values box leaving the defaulted Sum aggregation as is, and let the Series box remain empty, and press Next. Choose a style for your pie chart and press Finish.

3.   Right-click the chart area and choose the Show Data Labels option. Click the Run button on the top left corner of the Report Builder window and you will have a pie chart that is similar to the one displayed in Figure P3-34. The top 15 counts for product subcategories each have their own slice as displayed in the legend while all remaining product subcategories have been lumped together into the All Others slice.

The method just described works well for Reporting Services in SQL Server 2005 and can be adjusted for any Top X you desire, but a new feature for pie charts in Reporting Services 2008 adds further flexibility to grouping pie slices on other criteria. Rather than grouping slices on the items not included in the top X, you can choose to group all slices that do not meet a specified threshold value. This threshold can be designated as a simple value or as a percentage of the whole pie.

4.   To get started, create a new dataset named ProductSubCategoryCounts using the AdventureWorksDW data source and the following T-SQL as the query text:

```
SELECT
        COUNT(*) AS cnt
        ,EnglishProductSubcategoryName AS ProductSubCategory
FROM FactSurveyResponse
GROUP BY EnglishProductSubcategoryName
ORDER BY COUNT(*) DESC
```

5. From the Insert ribbon, choose Chart then Chart Wizard ... from the sub-menu. Using the ProductSubCategoryCounts dataset, follow the same directions in Steps 2 and 3 above to create your new pie chart.

6. Click on any portion of the pie chart and in the General section of the Properties pane expand the CustomAttributes node. (If the Properties pane is not visible click the Properties check box in the View ribbon.) For the CollectedStyle option choose SingleSlice, for CollectedThreshold type 5, set CollectedThresholdUsePercent to True, and set CollectedLegendText to "All Others." Now any slice that comprises 5 percent or less of the overall pie will be grouped into a single slice labeled All Others. The final product will appear similar to Figure P3-35.

Additionally, Reporting Services offers another option for the CollectedStyle attribute. The CollectedPie option creates another pie chart that provides detail about the collected slice in the original pie chart.

7. Change the CollectedStyle attribute to CollectedPie. Set CollectedLabel to read "All Others" and set both CollectedChartShowLabels and CollectedChartShowLegend both to True. The resulting chart is displayed in Figure P3-36.

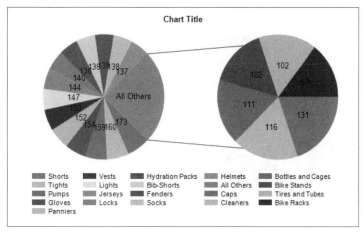

FIGURE P3-36

Final Thoughts

The three different methods used in this recipe cover the predominant methods in which pie slices can be grouped or collected. The major distinction in their implementation is that the TOP X method was really more query intensive. The grouping of all pie segments that did not meet the TOP X criterion was handled by the T-SQL that created the dataset. No special adjustments of the pie chart were needed. On the other hand, the threshold method of grouping was the opposite scenario in which our dataset query was very basic, but the grunt work was really handled by Reporting Services and its new CustomStyle attribute. While CustomStyle can conceivably create a TOP X pie chart, the amount of finagling required for the query and pie chart attributes merits the two separate methods.

GROWING BAR AND COLUMN CHARTS

You may have been in this situation before - you designed a chart based on a particular dataset and everything looks great. However, later the data volume increases, or new categories dynamically show up in your data source, and there is not enough horizontal/vertical space in the chart to show all the data or categories; unless, of course, you applied an approach to dynamically increase the height/width of the chart.

In earlier versions of Reporting Services, charts were a fixed size and you had to employ some very creative techniques to accommodate different volumes of data.

In this recipe, you learn how to create the chart shown in Figure P3-37, which grows and shrinks dynamically based on the number of data points in the report.

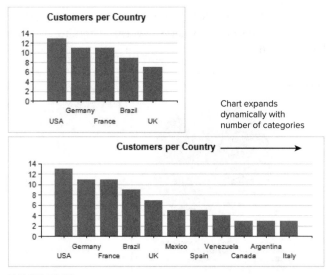

FIGURE P3-37

Product Versions

➤   Reporting Services 2008

What You'll Need

➤   Chart data region

➤   Business Intelligence Development Studio or Report Builder 2.0

Designing the Report

There are two new chart RDL properties to simplify the task of dynamically increasing chart height and width in Reporting Services 2008. The DynamicHeight and DynamicWidth properties allow you to set the height and width of your chart at runtime.

Both properties can be set to any RDL expression that evaluates to a size string at runtime, for example, ="3 in". Note the space in the size string between the numeric part and the size unit. If the properties are not specified, then the design time sizes will be applied.

The chart in this recipe dynamically increases its width based on the number of countries shown in the chart (determined by a report parameter value). To accomplish this, the DynamicWidth property of the chart is set to the following expression:

```
=(1 + Parameters!TopNCountries.Value / 2) & " in"
```

In this example, if you choose to show only the top 5 countries, the chart will have a width of $1+5/2 = 3.5$ inches. If you select the top 10 countries, the chart has a width of $1+10/2 = 6$ inches and therefore more horizontal room to draw additional categories.

The following steps walk you through implementing this in SSRS 2008.

1. Create a report with a chart that you want to dynamically resize, and a parameter to base the size on, as shown in Figure P3-38.

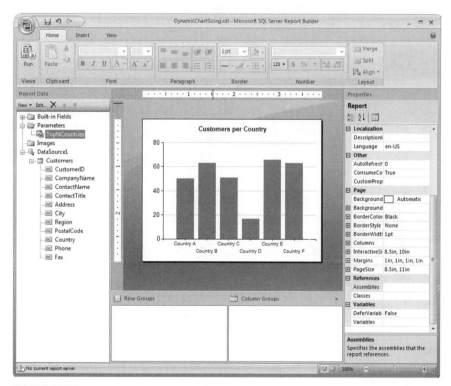

FIGURE P3-38

2. Set the DynamicWidth property of the chart as shown in Figure P3-39.

3. When you run the report, the chart will resize based on the value of the parameter. This is shown in Figure P3-40.

Select a larger value for the parameter and then click the View Report button. The chart should resize to accommodate the additional columns (see Figure P3-41).

FIGURE P3-39

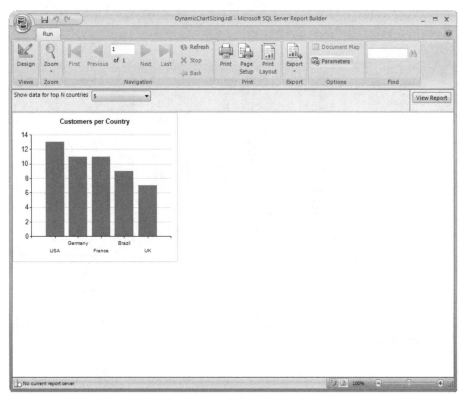

FIGURE P3-40

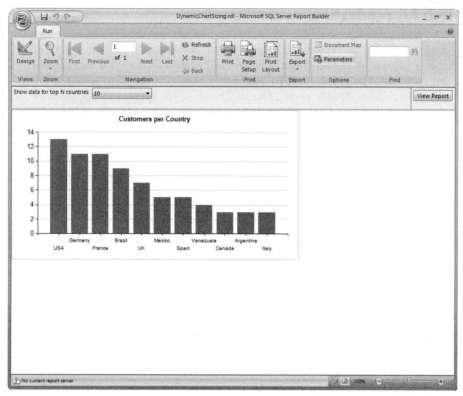

FIGURE P3-41

Final Thoughts

In this recipe, you learned how to dynamically control the width of a report using the new dynamicWidth property in Reporting Services 2008.

Credits and Related References

See Robert Bruckner's blog post, Charts with Dynamic Height or Width based on Categories/Data: http://blogs.msdn.com/robertbruckner/archive/2008/10/27/charts-with-dynamic-size-based-on-categories-or-data.aspx.

HISTOGRAM CHART

A histogram is a graphical way of presenting a frequency distribution, typically in the form of vertical columns. It shows what proportion of cases fall into each of several categories (intervals for numeric data). It is constructed by selecting a total number of intervals to be used, or by specifying a fixed width for each interval. The choice is between reducing the information sufficiently while still providing enough variability to picture the shape of the distribution.

Product Versions

➤   Reporting Services 2008

What You'll Need

➤   AdventureWorksDW sample database

Designing the Report

This example uses the AdventureWorksDW for SQL Server 2005 or 2008 sample database. The query retrieves customer demographic data, specifically the unique customer identifier and the calculated age of each customer. Figure P3-42 shows the final result.

1.   Start by designing a data source for the AdventureWorksDW or AdventureWorksDW2008 sample databases.

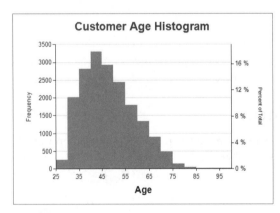

FIGURE P3-42

2.   Create a dataset query that uses the DimCustomer tables using the following code:

```
SELECT CustomerKey, BirthDate, DATEDIFF(YYYY,BirthDate,GETDATE())
as Age from AdventureWorksDW2008.dbo.DimCustomer
```

3.   Add a new Chart, of type simple column, as shown in Figure P3-43.

FIGURE P3-43

4. Prepare the chart settings as follows:

   a. Delete the legend to increase the available chart area.

   b. Drag the CustomerKey field into the category fields drop zone of the chart.

   c. Drag the Age field into the data fields drop zone of the chart.

   d. Set the chart title to Customer Age Histogram.

   e. Set the x-axis title to Age.

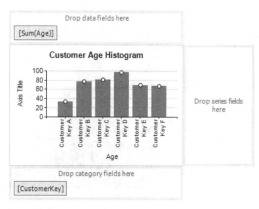

FIGURE P3-44

Figure P3-44 shows the resulting chart on the design surface.

5. Transform column chart into histogram chart.

   a. Select the chart, and then click on one of the data points, so that the Properties Window in Report Builder shows the ChartSeries properties.

   b. Apply the following settings under the CustomAttributes of the ChartSeries, as shown in Figure P3-45:

       ShowColumnAs: Histogram

       HistogramSegmentIntervalWidth: 5

The HistogramSegmentIntervalWidth setting determines the width of each segment. Setting this value to 0 results in automatic width interval calculation, using the HistogramSegmentIntervalNumber setting that can be used to configure a fixed number of intervals automatically applied over the whole dataset.

6. Preview the report to test the results.

7. Figure P3-46 shows the result of five records shown horizontally before a new row is added to the rendered layout.

CustomAttributes	ShowColumnAs=Histogra
DrawingStyle	Default
DrawSideBySide	Auto
EmptyPointValue	Average
HistogramSegmentIntervalNumber	20
HistogramSegmentIntervalWidth	5
HistogramShowPercentOnSecondary	True
LabelStyle	Auto
MaxPixelPointWidth	0
MinPixelPointWidth	0
PixelPointWidth	0
PointWidth	0.8
ShowColumnAs	Histogram
UserDefined	

FIGURE P3-45

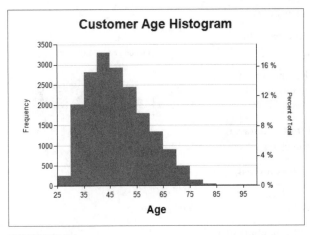

FIGURE P3-46

Final Thoughts

Histogram charts are a form of visual data binning, a data categorization technique to reduce the effects of minor data inaccuracies. Histograms show the frequency distribution of the resulting categories (how many values fall into each category). Charts in Reporting Services 2008 and later provide an easy way to automatically perform this type of statistical analysis visually in a report.

Credits and Related References

Another related technique for data categorization is a Pareto Analysis, which is discussed in the Pareto Chart recipe in this book. Additional chart and gauge layout information can be found on MSDN at http://msdn.microsoft.com/en-us/library/cc281080.aspx.

LINEAR REGRESSION LINE

One of the fantastic new features of Reporting Services in SQL Server 2008 is the capability to add a calculated series to an existing series in one of your charts. By simply right-clicking the series in design mode, a window appears that provides you with several options for calculated series. Some of the options provided are a moving average, relative strength index, Bollinger bands, and several more. One calculated series absent from the list is linear regression or trend line. Frequent users of Excel are already familiar with the capability to add trend lines to line charts in Excel, so extending that ability in Reporting Services adds a feature that some users may expect. The great strength of the linear regression line is that it can clarify sometimes ambiguous line charts and quantify the results via the slope of the line.

Product Versions

➤ Reporting Services 2000

➤ Reporting Services 2005

➤ Reporting Services 2008

What You'll Need

➤ The AdventureWorksDW sample database

Designing the Report

You will start with a line chart having a unit of time as the dependent or horizontal axis and some other measurable unit on the independent or vertical axis; in the case of this recipe, it will be dollar sales. The objective is to provide a trend line over the same time interval that provides a quantifiable generalization or trend for the series. The finished product in Figure P3-47 demonstrates the end result.

To provide a more concrete example of how the process works, a query will be provided for the dataset in this recipe. The query will report AdventureWorks' 2002 annual sales for Australia. The query script in this example has a hard-coded date range filter that can easily be parameterized.

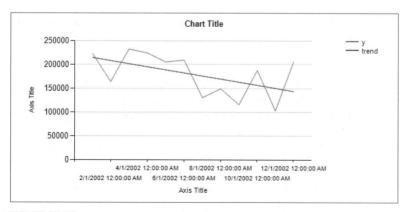

FIGURE P3-47

Instructions are provided for Report Builder 2.0 or 3.0. For the sake of compatibility, this recipe uses the 2005 version of AdventureWorksDW. This will also work with AdventureWorksDW2008 in SSRS 2008. To allow the queries to work with AdventureWorksDW2008, substitute the DimDate table for all occurrences of the DimTime table, and substitute the DateKey column for the occurrence of the TimeKey column.

1. Create a new report using Report Builder 2.0 or 3.0.

2. Add a line chart data region to the report body. Make sure the AdventureWorksDW data source is chosen and click Next.

3. From the Design a Query window click the Edit as Text button and type the following query script or paste it from the working sample report (available from the book's website on Wrox.com) and paste it in the area provided for query text.

```
DECLARE @start_month SMALLDATETIME
DECLARE @end_month SMALLDATETIME

SET @start_month = '2002-01-01'
SET @end_month = '2002-12-01';
SELECT
CAST(CONVERT(CHAR(6),DimTime.FullDateAlternateKey,112) + '01'
    AS SMALLDATETIME) AS CalendarMonth
    ,SUM(SalesAmount) AS y
FROM FactInternetSales
    INNER JOIN DimSalesTerritory
ON FactInternetSales.SalesTerritoryKey = DimSalesTerritory.SalesTerritoryKey
    INNER JOIN DimTime
        ON FactInternetSales.OrderDateKey = DimTime.TimeKey
WHERE DimSalesTerritory.SalesTerritoryKey = 9 --Australia
AND DATEPART(YEAR,DimTime.FullDateAlternateKey)
    BETWEEN DATEPART(YEAR,@start_month) AND DATEPART(YEAR,@end_month)
AND DATEPART(MONTH,DimTime.FullDateAlternateKey)
    BETWEEN DATEPART(MONTH,@start_month) AND DATEPART(MONTH,@end_month)
GROUP BY CONVERT(CHAR(6),DimTime.FullDateAlternateKey,112)
```

4. Name the new dataset AnnualSales and close the Dataset Properties dialog.

5. Click once on the chart to show the field drop zones.

6. Drag the `CalendarMonth` field and drop it into the Categories axis and then drag the `y` field and place it into the Values drop zone. Keep the `SUM` aggregate chosen for `y`.

The design area of the report should now look like Figure P3-48.

If you click the Run button on the far left of the Home ribbon to preview the report, you will see the line chart shown in Figure P3-49. It would appear that annual sales for 2002 in Australia were declining as the year progressed. The next few steps will clarify this perceived result by providing a line that generalizes the data over the year.

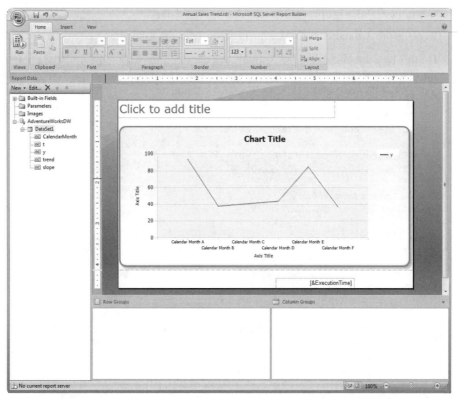

FIGURE P3-48

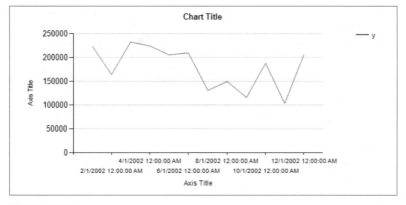

FIGURE P3-49

7. Open the Dataset Properties for the AnnualSales dataset.

8. Replace the AnnualSales dataset query script with the following query.

Do this by double-clicking the AnnualSales dataset and pasting the updated query (below) into the query text section of the Dataset Properties window. Press the Refresh Fields button and press OK to close the Dataset Properties dialog.

```
DECLARE @start_month SMALLDATETIME
DECLARE @end_month SMALLDATETIME

SET @start_month = '2002-01-01'
SET @end_month = '2002-12-01';

DECLARE @data TABLE (
CalendarMonth SMALLDATETIME,
t NUMERIC(17,7),
y NUMERIC(17,7)
);

WITH LinearRegPrep AS
(
SELECT
   CAST(
      CONVERT(CHAR(6),DimTime.FullDateAlternateKey,112) + '01'
      AS SMALLDATETIME)
   AS CalendarMonth
   ,SUM(SalesAmount) AS MonthlySalesAmount
FROM FactInternetSales
   INNER JOIN DimSalesTerritory
      ON FactInternetSales.SalesTerritoryKey =
      DimSalesTerritory.SalesTerritoryKey
   INNER JOIN DimTime
      ON FactInternetSales.OrderDateKey =
      DimTime.TimeKey
WHERE DimSalesTerritory.SalesTerritoryKey = 9 --Australia
   AND DATEPART(YEAR,DimTime.FullDateAlternateKey) BETWEEN
      DATEPART(YEAR,@start_month) AND DATEPART(YEAR,@end_month)
   AND DATEPART(MONTH,DimTime.FullDateAlternateKey) BETWEEN
      DATEPART(MONTH,@start_month) AND DATEPART(MONTH,@end_month)
GROUP BY CONVERT(CHAR(6),DimTime.FullDateAlternateKey,112)
)

INSERT INTO @data
SELECT
 CalendarMonth,
 DATEDIFF(MONTH,@start_month,CalendarMonth) AS t
 ,MonthlySalesAmount
FROM LinearRegPrep
DECLARE @intercept NUMERIC(17,7)
DECLARE @slope NUMERIC(17,7)
DECLARE @num_points INTEGER

SET @num_points = (SELECT COUNT(*) FROM @data)
```

```
--calculation of regression line slope
SET @slope =
    (
        ( SELECT @num_points*SUM(t*y) FROM @data) -
        (SELECT SUM(t)*SUM(y) FROM @data)
    )/
    (
        (SELECT @num_points*SUM(t*t) FROM @data) -
        POWER((SELECT SUM(t) FROM @data),2)
    )


--calculation of regression line intercept
SET @intercept =
    (
    (SELECT SUM(y) FROM @data) -
        (SELECT @slope*SUM(t) FROM @data)
    )/
    @num_points

SELECT
    CalendarMonth,
    t,
    y,
    (t*@slope + @intercept ) AS trend
FROM @data
```

The first thing you should note is that the common table expression in the revised query is exactly the same as in the original query. This is where the concept of reusability comes in. Even if you don't completely understand the mathematics involved in the rest of the code, the rest of the affair should involve enough plug-and-play work that even the most math-phobic developer should feel comfortable using the code within their own report.

The important thing to note about the original query is that it returns two fields: the CalendarMonth field, your x-axis, and the MonthlySalesAmount field, your y-axis. The entire objective of the additional code is to produce one more column that represents the y-axis values of a trend line over the same x-axis values of CalendarMonth. With this, you can map both of the series in your chart, getting your original line chart with a trend line superimposed over it.

Now let's take a closer look at what's happening within the code. The objective is to find an equation of a line $y = mx + b$ that best fits our data points. You may recall from middle school and high school math that the variable m represents the slope or steepness of the line, whereas the b is the y-intercept, or the point on the vertical axis where the line intersects it. Your principal interest will be slope. This value will tell you whether the data points of interest result in a negative or positive trend over the given interval of time and the degree of that rate. The process for obtaining these values is divided into two steps. The first is the calculation of the slope, which is given by

$$m = (n \sum_{i=1}^{n} t_i y_i - \sum_{j=1}^{n} t_j \sum_{k=1}^{n} y_k) / (n \sum_{l=1}^{n} t_l^2 - (\sum_{m=1}^{n} t_m)^2)$$

while the equation of the y-intercept is given by

$$b = (\sum_{i=1}^{n} y_i - m \sum_{j=1}^{n} t_j) / n$$

where n is the total number of data points, and the t_is and y_is are the components of the data point tuples (t_i, y_i).

Now that the necessary values have been computed, the last piece is to calculate the points on the regression line. This is done by applying the equation of a line to your new column t by substituting it for x in the equation $y = mx + b$. The final dataset yields the same result as the original Annual Rolling Sales query with the addition of the trend column that for each CalendarMonth gives the regression line value.

9. The AnnualSales dataset has been updated, so the trend report field can be dragged from the list of fields and dropped in the data fields drop zone of the chart area. Just as you did with the y field, keep the default value of SUM for the aggregate type.

10. On the far left of the Home ribbon, click Run. The report should now display the original line along with the regression line as in Figure P3-50.

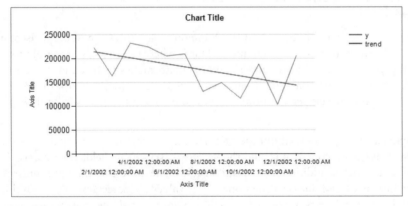

FIGURE P3-50

The beauty of the process just outlined is its portability. It begins with the exact query for which we're trying to find the regression line and then generically proceeds to calculate that line. The main consideration is that of interval of time. In this example, our discrete measure of time was at the month level. If future requirements have you measuring time at the day level, simply make that adjustment to the INSERT statement for the table valued variable's t column. That column will provide a generic measure of time by assigning each of your original time values with an integer value used in the computation of the trend column.

To parameterize the date filters for this report, remove the variable DECLARE and SET statements from the query script. You can also add a parameter in place of the hard-coded SalesTerritoryKey value. You can then customize these report parameters to meet your requirements.

Final Thoughts

A linear regression line, or trend line as it may be more commonly known, is an effective tool for demonstrating an overall trend of a time series. While the recipe above may seem a bit daunting at first, your main task in getting it to work for you is to supply a query that provides a measure of time and a value to be trended that is dependent on time — like the month and sales amount per month in this recipe. Once that is done, make sure that the column definitions and column calculation of the table variable @t reflect the interval of time you intend to trend over.

CREATING A MULTI-SERIES MULTI-Y AXIS CHART

A chart provides a way to visualize data and can convey information more effectively than lengthy lists of data. SSRS chart data region is quite flexible and packs a lot of functionality. This example will demonstrate some of that flexibility and functionality by creating a multi-series, multi Y-axis chart that will plot the data series on different chart types.

Product Versions

➤   Reporting Services 2008

What You'll Need

➤   A column chart with numeric data fields

➤   Add a third data series using a Line with Markers chart type and map it to a secondary Y-axis

Designing the Report

This example uses the AdventureWorksDW2008 for SQL Server 2008 sample database and a simple query to return the reseller sales amount, total product cost, fiscal year, and fiscal quarter. This example uses Report Builder 2.0.

1.   Start by designing a data source for the AdventureWorksDW2008 sample databases.

2.   Create the following dataset query that includes the FactResellerSales and DimDate tables.

```
SELECT
FRS.SalesAmount
, FRS.TotalProductCost
, T.FiscalYear
, T.FiscalQuarter
, 'Qtr ' + Convert(char(1),T.FiscalQuarter) as FiscalQuarterLbl
FROM dbo.FactResellerSales FRS
INNER JOIN dbo.DimDate T
   ON FRS.OrderDateKey = T.DateKey
ORDER BY T.FiscalYear, T.FiscalQuarter
```

3.   Add a Chart report item to the report body and select Column chart type. Expand the chart to your liking.

4.   Drag the FiscalYear and FiscalQuarter fields to the category field area of the chart. This creates category groups of FiscalYear and FiscalQuarter on the X-axis.

5.   Drag SalesAmount and TotalProductCost to the data field area of the chart. This creates two data series.

This simple example charts the reseller sales amount and total product cost as a column chart with fiscal year and fiscal quarter on the X-axis. In addition, the example creates a third data series for gross margin using the Line with Markers chart type and plots this series on a secondary Y-axis using a percentage number format scale.

The Report Builder should look like Figure P3-51.

Before you add the gross margin data series, preview the report and see if there is anything that needs to be modified. As you can see in Figure P3-52, every other Fiscal Quarter label is displayed by default and the label isn't very intuitive. So update the Fiscal Quarter X-axis label and change the settings so every quarter label is displayed.

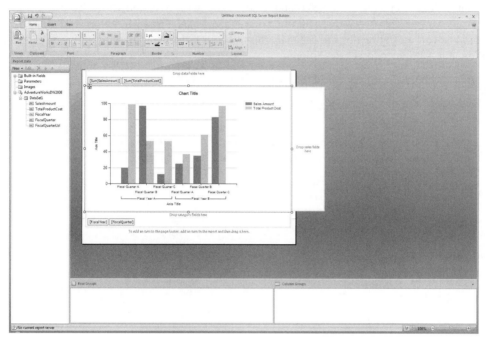

FIGURE P3-51

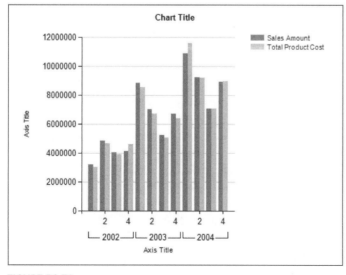

FIGURE P3-52

1. Right-click the FiscalQuarter category field and select Category Group Properties. In the Category Group Properties dialog box, change the Label dropdown to FiscalQuarterLbl field (see Figure P3-53).

2. Right-click the X-axis and select Axis Properties. In the Category Axis Properties dialog box, change the Interval to 1 (see Figure P3-54).

At this point, you have created a simple column chart report with two data series. Now you want to add a Gross Margin data series that will use a percentage scale. Gross Margin isn't a field in your dataset, but you can use expressions to calculate the value for Gross Margin. Gross Margin is defined as (SalesAmount – ProductCost)/SalesAmount.

1. Drag another SalesAmount field to the data field area of chart.

2. Right-click the newly created SalesAmount data series and select Series Properties.

3. Enter the following expression in the value field:`=(Sum(Fields!SalesAmount.Value)-Sum(Fields!TotalProductCost.Value))/Sum(Fields!SalesAmount.Value)`

4. Go to the Legend page of the Series Properties dialog box and enter a custom legend text of "Gross Margin" (see Figure P3-55).

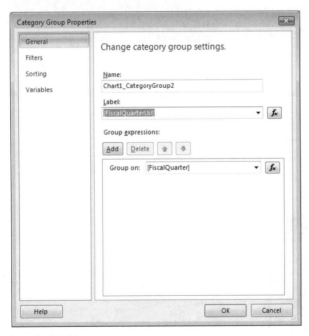

FIGURE P3-53

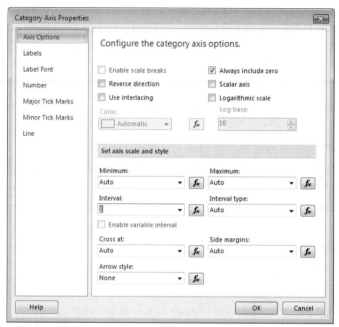

FIGURE P3-54

FIGURE P3-55

Since Gross Margin is a percentage scale, you can't use the current Y-axis scale to display Gross Margin. Instead, you need to display Gross Margin on a secondary Y-axis that has a percentage scale. Along with mapping Gross Margin to a secondary Y-axis, you will also change the chart type of the Gross Margin data series to Line with Markers to better display the Gross Margin value.

1. Go back to the Series Properties dialog box for Gross Margin data series (shown in Figure 5).

2. Select the Axes and Chart Area page of the Series Properties dialog box and select the Secondary radio button for Value Axis and click OK (see Figure P3-56).

3. Right-click on the newly added secondary Y-axis and select Axis Properties.

4. From the Number page of the Secondary Value Axis Properties dialog box, select Percentage category, 0 for decimal places and click OK (see Figure P3-57).

5. To change the chart type of Gross Margin, right-click on Gross Margin data series and select Change Chart Type.

6. Select Line with Markers chart type.

7. Preview the report to test the results.

As you can see in Figure P3-58, the chart report displays three data series with Gross Margin using a different chart type and mapped to a secondary Y-axis with a percentage scale.

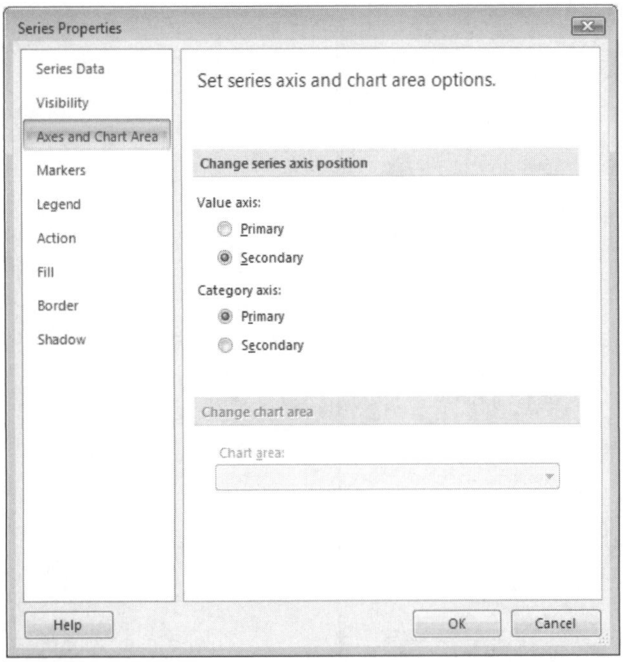

FIGURE P3-56

FIGURE P3-57

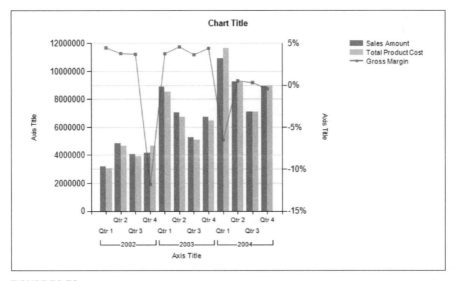

FIGURE P3-58

You can further customize the chart by adding Axis and Chart titles and changing chart types to your liking.

Credits and Related References

Robert Bruckner has a great article about SQL Server Reporting Services Charts titled "Get More Out of SQL Server Reporting Services Charts" (`http://msdn.microsoft.com/en-us/library/aa964128(SQL.90).aspx`).

PARETO CHART

A Pareto chart, named after Vilfredo Pareto, is a graphical way of highlighting the most important among a (typically large) set of factors. This type of chart contains both bars and a line graph. The bars display the values in descending order, and the line graph shows the cumulative totals (cumulative percentage) of each category, left to right.

Product Versions

➤ Reporting Services 2008 or later

What You'll Need

➤ AdventureWorksDW2008 Analysis Services sample database

Designing the Report

This example uses the AdventureWorksDW2008 for SQL Server Analysis Services 2008 sample database. The query retrieves sales data, specifically the sales reason and revenue. The final result is shown in Figure P3-59.

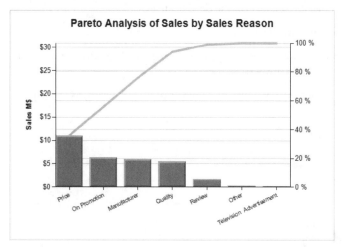

FIGURE P3-59

1. Start by designing a data source for the AdventureWorksDW2008 for Analysis Services sample databases.

2. Create a dataset query that uses the Internet Sales Amount measure with the Sales Reason hierarchy using the following code:

```
SELECT NON EMPTY { [Measures].[Internet Sales Amount] } ON COLUMNS,
NON EMPTY { ([Sales Reason].[Sales Reasons].[Sales Reason].ALLMEMBERS ) }
DIMENSION PROPERTIES MEMBER_CAPTION, MEMBER_UNIQUE_NAME ON ROWS
FROM [Adventure Works]
CELL PROPERTIES VALUE, BACK_COLOR, FORE_COLOR, FORMATTED_VALUE,
FORMAT_STRING, FONT_NAME, FONT_SIZE, FONT_FLAGS
```

3. Add a new Chart, of type simple column, as shown in Figure P3-60.

FIGURE P3-60

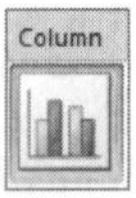

4. Prepare chart settings as follows:
   a. Delete the legend to increase the available chart area.
   b. Drag the Sales_Reason field into the category fields drop zone of the chart.
   c. Drag the Internet_Sales_Amount field into the data fields drop zone of the chart.
   d. Set the chart title to Pareto Analysis of Sales by Sales Reason.
   e. Remove the x-axis title.
   f. Right-click on the x-axis labels and open the x-axis properties. On the Labels page, select Disable auto-fit and set the label angle to -25.
   g. Set the y-axis title to Sales in M$.
   h. Increase the font size of the y-axis to 10 pt and make the font bold.
   i. Right-click on the y-axis labels, open the y-axis properties. On the Axis options page, set side margins to Disabled. On the Number page, select currency formatting, Show values in Millions, and set decimal places to 0.

   Figure P3-61 shows the resulting chart on the design surface.

5. Transform column chart into a Pareto chart.

   Select the chart, and then click on one of the data points, so that the Properties Window in Report Builder shows the ChartSeries properties.

   Apply the following settings under the CustomAttributes of the ChartSeries, as shown in Figure P3-62.

FIGURE P3-61

⊟ CustomAttributes	ShowColumnAs=Pa
DrawingStyle	Emboss
DrawSideBySide	Auto
EmptyPointValue	Average
HistogramSegmentIntervalNumbe	20
HistogramSegmentIntervalWidth	0
HistogramShowPercentOnSecond	True
LabelStyle	Auto
MaxPixelPointWidth	0
MinPixelPointWidth	0
PixelPointWidth	0
PointWidth	0.8
ShowColumnAs	Pareto
UserDefined	

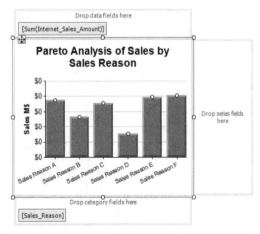

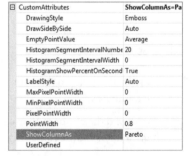

FIGURE P3-62

➤ ShowColumnAs: Pareto

➤ DrawingStyle: Emboss

Then, under the ChartSeries properties, set the BorderWidth to 3pt, which increases the Pareto line thickness.

6. Tweak the secondary Y-axis settings.

Click inside the chart area, but not on any of the data points, so that the Properties Window in Report Builder shows the Chart Area properties. Locate the ValueAxes property and click on the " ... " button as shown in Figure P3-63. This opens the settings for the primary and secondary chart y-axis. Select the secondary y-axis, set the LabelFont FontSize to 10pt, and set the Title property to an empty value.

FIGURE P3-63

7. Preview the report to test the results.

Figure P3-64 shows the result of five records shown horizontally before a new row is added to the rendered layout.

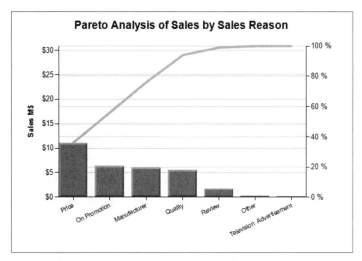

FIGURE P3-64

Final Thoughts

Pareto charts are a form of visual data categorization used to highlight the most important of a typically large set of factors. A Pareto chart shows both the frequency of occurrence as well as a cumulative percentage of occurrence, or another calculation of interest. Charts in Reporting Services 2008 and later provide an easy way to create Pareto charts to perform this type of statistical analysis in a report.

Credits and Related References

For Reporting Services 2005, Pareto charts can be implemented with expressions in certain scenarios as described in the following MSDN whitepaper under the Pareto Chart section: `http://technet.microsoft.com/en-us/library/aa964128(SQL.90).aspx`.

PART IV
Interactive Reporting

- ▶ Conditional Linking

- ▶ Drill-Through for a Multi-Level Matrix Report

- ▶ Drill-Through Report Link Breadcrumbs

- ▶ Dynamic Pivoting as a Matrix Replacement

- ▶ Using a Document Map Table for Navigation

CONDITIONAL LINKING

Real estate on a report is very valuable and it seems that today reports are expected to hold more information than ever before. Innovative ways of using space on a report have emerged but one really useful technique, conditional linking, will be explored in this recipe. The conditional link aids in the effort to reclaim valuable space on report designs by only appearing when a certain condition is met, and even then only displaying a visual indicator such as a link or icon that can be used to navigate to details.

This recipe shows how to add conditional linking that is displayed when sales exceed a certain amount. The conditional link will display a "Map It!" link alongside a globe graphic. The "Map It!" link will permit viewing a Bing map of the city that is having the sales success.

Product Versions

➤   Reporting Services 2000

➤   Reporting Services 2005

➤   Reporting Services 2008

What You'll Need

➤   Report Builder 2.0

➤   A connection to the AdventureWorks sample database

➤   A rectangle added within the City column

➤   Use of a visibility expression for the rectangle within the City column

➤   Use of a Go to URL action on a textbox within the rectangle, with URL set to an expression that creates the properly formed Bing Maps URL using report address fields

Designing the Report

This example creates a new report that uses the AdventureWorks sample database. The techniques used in this example may be used in different Reporting Services product versions; however, the specific example uses a view that is specific to the AdventureWorks SQL Server 2005 sample database and as such is not found in other versions of SQL Server sample databases, such as AdventureWorks2008.

The completed report, when run, will look like Figure P4-1.

1.   Start by designing a data source based upon the AdventureWorks sample database.

2.   Enter Conditional Linking for the Report title and format as desired.

3.   Create a dataset using the following dataset query that includes the Sales.vStoreWithDemographics view.

```
SELECT
  Sales.vStoreWithDemographics.Name
  ,Sales.vStoreWithDemographics.City
  ,Sales.vStoreWithDemographics.StateProvinceName
  ,Sales.vStoreWithDemographics.PostalCode
```

```
    ,Sales.vStoreWithDemographics.CountryRegionName
    ,Sales.vStoreWithDemographics.AnnualSales
    ,Sales.vStoreWithDemographics.AnnualRevenue
FROM
    Sales.vStoreWithDemographics
```

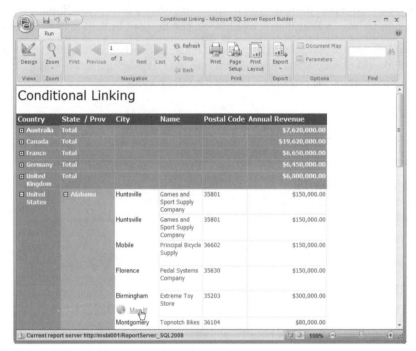

FIGURE P4-1

4. Add a table report item to the report body using the Table Wizard.

5. Add CountryRegionName and StateProvinceName to the row groups of the table.

6. Add City, Name, Postal Code, and Annual Revenue to the values of the table.

The New Table or Matrix wizard's Arrange fields options should look like Figure P4-2.

7. Set the table's layout:

a. Set the show subtotals and grand totals option to Blocked, subtotal below.

b. Enable the Expand/collapse groups option.

The New Table or Matrix Wizard's Choose the layout options should look like Figure P4-3.

8. Apply any desired style (this example uses Corporate).

The report designer should look like Figure P4-4.

9. Increase the height of the detail row to permit adding additional content below the data fields (over .56in suggested).

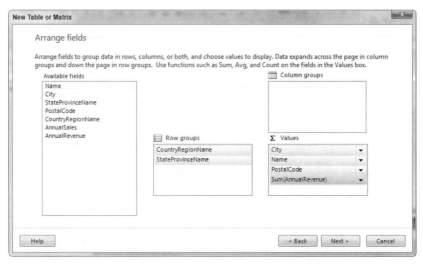

FIGURE P4-2

FIGURE P4-3

10. In the cell, remove the existing City textbox and insert a rectangle named as CityMainRectangle.

11. In the CityMainRectangle, insert the City textbox and align it to the top half of the row.

12. Within the CityMainRectangle and below the City textbox, insert another rectangle named ConditionalLinkRectangle, aligning it with the bottom half of the row.

13. Within the ConditionalLinkRectangle below the City textbox, insert any desired image (this example uses a globe) and immediately to the right of the image insert a textbox with the text value set to "Map It!".

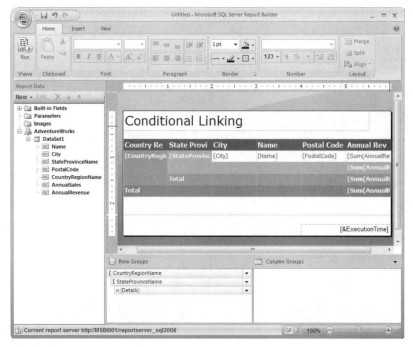

FIGURE P4-4

14. Modify the textbox added to the ConditionalLinkRectangle, adding a new "Go to URL" action setting and set the "Select URL" action property to the following expression:

```
="http://maps.msn.com/home.aspx?plce1=" &
Fields!City.Value & "," &
Fields!StateProvinceName.Value & "," &
Fields!CountryRegionName.Value &
"&regn1=" &
SWITCH(
  Fields!CountryRegionName.Value = "Australia", "3",
  Fields!CountryRegionName.Value = "Canada",   "0",
  Fields!CountryRegionName.Value = "United States",  "0",
  1=1, "1")
```

15. Modify the ConditionalLinkRectangle that contains both the "Map It!" textbox and image, adding a visibility expression that will show the ConditionalLinkRectangle and consequently show the image and "Map It!" textbox for stores having an Annual Revenue over $150,000.00 by using the following expression:

```
=IIF(Sum(Fields!AnnualRevenue.Value) > 150000, False, True)
```

The report designer should look like Figure P4-5.

The completed report, when run, looks like Figure P4-6.

During report execution, after expanding the Country Region and the State Province, notice that cities having annual revenue values exceeding $150,000.00 display the image and "Map It!" values.

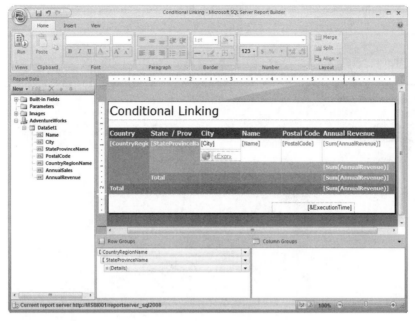

FIGURE P4-5

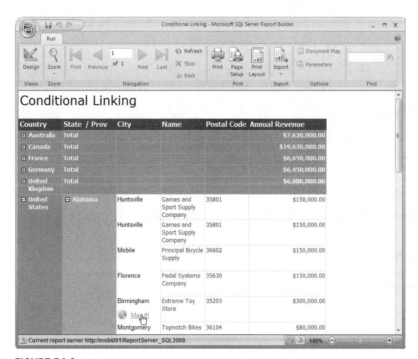

FIGURE P4-6

Click a "Map It!" value to see the city on a Bing map. Figure P4-7 shows an example.

FIGURE P4-7

Final Thoughts

This example showed how a conditional link could be added to an existing report by simply adding a rectangle to a table cell and creating a visibility expression for a desired conditional scenario.

Credits and Related References

Stephen Dvoranchik of MicroLink, LLC provided a well-thought-out implementation that is the basis for this example.

More information about building a URL for Bing maps can be found at `http://help.live.com/help .aspx?project=wl_local&market=en-us&querytype=topic&query=wl_local_proc_buildurl .htm` in the topic "Build your own URL."

DRILL-THROUGH FOR A MULTI-LEVEL MATRIX REPORT

Reporting Services offers several capabilities for providing rich, interactive reporting. One of these capabilities is to navigate to, or execute, a secondary report from the current, primary report. This type of report, commonly referred to as a *drill-through* report, is generally used to provide additional information about a particular report item or data point within the current report. For example, imagine a sales summary report that identifies each customer and total sales for the customer. Drill-through reports can be enabled on the customer records to provide related information such as contact information, or on the sales records to provide the detailed transactions that constitute the aggregate sales. The drill-through source report provides the appropriate context to the drill-through target report via report parameters.

Providing drill-through capabilities in Reporting Services is generally straightforward. On any given element, you simply enable navigation from the source report to the target report, passing the appropriate report context through report parameters. However, challenges can arise when implementing drill-through reports within matrix data regions. This recipe discusses the potential challenges of implementing drill-through reports within a multi-level matrix, provides guidance on how to address these challenges using Reporting Services 2005, and reviews the improvements in Reporting Services 2008 that facilitate, and potentially remove, these complications altogether.

Product Versions

➤ Reporting Services 2005

➤ Reporting Services 2008

What You'll Need

➤ AdventureWorks sample database

➤ AdventureWorks Sample Reports

➤ A basic understanding of drill-through reports

➤ A drill-through source report using a matrix

➤ A drill-through target report

Note that Reporting Services 2005 and 2008 each have their own, version-specific sample databases and reports. You will need the appropriate version of these samples based on the version of the product being demonstrated. You can download and install the samples from CodePlex (http://codeplex .com/SqlServerSamples).

Designing the Drill-Through Target Report

The examples demonstrated in this recipe rely on two distinct reports: the drill-through source report and the drill-through target report. For the source report, you will repurpose the Company Sales report that is provided as part of the AdventureWorks Sample Reports. This report, depicted in Figure P4-8, uses a matrix data region to display sales by product category and subcategory along the rows and by year and quarter along the columns.

When reviewing this high-level summary, a natural desire is to explore the details behind a specific cell in order to review the individual products that comprise a summarized value. This can be accomplished using a drill-through report.

		2002	2003			
			Q1	Q2	Q3	Q4
Accessories		$93,797	$15,628	$32,845	$262,613	$283,928
Bikes		$26,664,534	$6,101,755	$7,028,317	$10,759,142	$11,310,133
Clothing	Bib-Shorts	$102,183	$21,544	$43,458	$351	
	Caps	$9,467	$1,782	$2,940	$8,676	$8,519
	Gloves	$90,897	$25,692	$41,876	$26,945	$23,619
	Jerseys	$110,846	$18,205	$31,335	$173,041	$140,703
	Shorts	$49,384	$11,230	$21,424	$97,610	$84,192
	Socks	$3,173			$6,969	$6,183
	Tights	$123,871	$27,588	$51,601	$780	$244
	Vests				$81,086	$66,883
Components		$3,611,041	$459,086	$1,111,521	$2,527,699	$1,391,434

FIGURE P4-8

The remainder of this section provides guidance for creating a sample drill-through target report. Report parameters are provided to transfer the data context from the source report. The context is utilized to display all products for a given category, subcategory, year, and quarter. Please note that the instructions and figures that follow are authored using Reporting Services 2008, but should work equally well with prior versions. Any exceptions will be identified as appropriate. If you want to follow along with both 2005 and 2008, you may want to author the report first in 2005 and then simply convert it to 2008.

1. Start by opening the AdventureWorks Sample Reports solution using Business Intelligence Development Studio (BIDS).

   The default installation location is `%ProgramFiles%\Microsoft SQL Server\<version>\Samples\Reporting Services\Report Samples\AdventureWorks Sample Reports\` where `<version>` is 90 for SQL Server 2005 and 100 for SQL Server 2008. This solution contains the Company Sales report, which will be used as the drill-through source report, and a shared data source to the AdventureWorks database.

2. Add a new report named Product Detail to the solution.

3. Create a new data source named AdventureWorks that uses the AdventureWorks2008 shared data source (or simply AdventureWorks for 2005).

4. Create a new dataset named SalesDetail using the AdventureWorks data source created in the previous step.

5. Enter the following query as text into the query designer.

```
SELECT
   PC.Name AS Category
   ,PS.Name AS Subcategory
   ,P.Name AS Product
   ,DATEPART(yy, SOH.OrderDate) AS Year
   ,'Q' + DATENAME(qq, SOH.OrderDate) AS Quarter
   ,(DET.UnitPrice * DET.OrderQty) AS Sales
FROM
   Production.ProductSubcategory PS
   INNER JOIN Sales.SalesOrderHeader SOH
   INNER JOIN Sales.SalesOrderDetail DET
      ON SOH.SalesOrderID = DET.SalesOrderID
   INNER JOIN Production.Product P
      ON DET.ProductID = P.ProductID
      ON PS.ProductSubcategoryID = P.ProductSubcategoryID
   INNER JOIN Production.ProductCategory PC
      ON PS.ProductCategoryID = PC.ProductCategoryID
WHERE
   (PC.Name = @ProductCategory)
   AND (PS.Name = @ProductSubcategory)
   AND ((@Year IS NULL) OR (DATEPART(yy, SOH.OrderDate) = @Year))
   AND ((@Quarter IS NULL) OR ('Q'+DATENAME(qq, SOH.OrderDate) = @Quarter))
```

This query is based on the one provided for the Company Sales report. In fact, it is essentially the same query, except the Sales are returned by product instead of being summarized by subcategory. In addition, the query is being filtered for the data context that is provided by the source report: Product Category, Product Subcategory, Year, and Quarter. The Product Category, Subcategory, and Quarter are being matched by display name. This is not a recommended approach, but is implemented here for simplicity. In addition, both the Year and Quarter parameters accommodate null values. In this context, a null value indicates the data should not be filtered by the parameter.

6. Execute the query to ensure there are no errors. Enter the following values when you are prompted for the query parameters.

NAME	VALUE
@ProductCategory	Clothing
@ProductSubcategory	Shorts
@Year	2003
@Quarter	Q1

7. Click OK until you return to the report design surface and then save your report.

As demonstrated in Step 6, the query defined within the dataset contains embedded parameters for Product Category (@ProductCategory), Product Subcategory (@ProductSubcategory), Year (@Year), and Quarter (@Quarter). The query designer automatically detects these query parameters and creates corresponding report parameters. These report parameters are basic text fields, but are mostly sufficient for demonstration purposes. However, you need to allow null values for both the Year and Quarter parameters.

8. Modify the Year and Quarter report parameters to allow a `null` value. This is necessary in order to specify "No Quarter," as will be demonstrated later.

Next, you design the report layout to display the report parameters and the data source fields in a basic table.

1. Insert a Table data region to the body of the report design surface. This creates a simple table layout comprised of one header row, one data row, and three columns.

2. Add each field from the SalesDetail dataset to the table, placing the fields in the following order: Category, Subcategory, Product, Year, Quarter, and Sales.

3. Add a Total for Sales before the detail line, so the total appears between the header and the detail line.

4. Modify the format string of the Sales total and detail item as follows: ###,###. This will enhance the readability by rounding to the nearest whole number and providing a thousands separator.

5. Add each report parameter label and value above the table. This will help you trace the values provided by the source report. When complete, the report design surface should appear as illustrated in Figure P4-9, with some additional cleanup of the column names and spacing.

Category:	[@ProductCategory]		Year:	[@Year]	
Subcategory:	[@ProductSubcateg(		Quarter:	[@Quarter]	

Category	Subcategory	Product	Year	Quarter	Sales
					[Sum(Sales)]
[Category]	[Subcategory]	[Product]	[Year]	[Quarter]	[Sales]

FIGURE P4-9

6. Run the report to review the results. Enter the following values when you are prompted for the report parameters. Notice the total represents only the values for the first quarter (see Figure P4-10).

NAME	VALUE
Product Category	Clothing
Product Subcategory	Shorts
Year	2003
Quarter	Q1

7. Run the report again, using the value `null` for Quarter instead of Q1. Notice all available quarters within the specified years are now displayed. Compare the total displayed in Figure P4-11 to that of Figure P4-10. This is an important behavior for the drill-through report parameters, and is explored further in the remaining exercises of this recipe.

| Category: | Clothing | | | Year: | 2003 | | |
| Subcategory: | Shorts | | | Quarter: | Q1 | | |

Category	Subcategory	Product	Year	Quarter	Sales
					11,230
Clothing	Shorts	Men's Sports Shorts, M	2003	Q1	36
Clothing	Shorts	Men's Sports Shorts, M	2003	Q1	180
Clothing	Shorts	Men's Sports Shorts, S	2003	Q1	72
Clothing	Shorts	Men's Sports Shorts, L	2003	Q1	36
Clothing	Shorts	Men's Sports Shorts, M	2003	Q1	108
Clothing	Shorts	Men's Sports Shorts, S	2003	Q1	72
Clothing	Shorts	Men's Sports Shorts, S	2003	Q1	108
Clothing	Shorts	Men's Sports Shorts, M	2003	Q1	108
Clothing	Shorts	Men's Sports Shorts, S	2003	Q1	72
Clothing	Shorts	Men's Sports Shorts, M	2003	Q1	360
Clothing	Shorts	Men's Sports Shorts, M	2003	Q1	36
Clothing	Shorts	Men's Sports Shorts, S	2003	Q1	36
Clothing	Shorts	Men's Sports Shorts, M	2003	Q1	72
Clothing	Shorts	Men's Sports Shorts, S	2003	Q1	144

FIGURE P4-10

| Category: | Clothing | | | Year: | 2003 | | |
| Subcategory: | Shorts | | | Quarter: | | | |

Category	Subcategory	Product	Year	Quarter	Sales
					214,457
Clothing	Shorts	Men's Sports Shorts, M	2003	Q1	36
Clothing	Shorts	Men's Sports Shorts, M	2003	Q1	180
Clothing	Shorts	Men's Sports Shorts, S	2003	Q1	72
Clothing	Shorts	Men's Sports Shorts, L	2003	Q1	36
Clothing	Shorts	Men's Sports Shorts, M	2003	Q1	108
Clothing	Shorts	Men's Sports Shorts, S	2003	Q1	72
Clothing	Shorts	Men's Sports Shorts, S	2003	Q1	108
Clothing	Shorts	Men's Sports Shorts, M	2003	Q1	108
Clothing	Shorts	Men's Sports Shorts, S	2003	Q1	72
Clothing	Shorts	Men's Sports Shorts, M	2003	Q1	360
Clothing	Shorts	Men's Sports Shorts, M	2003	Q1	36
Clothing	Shorts	Men's Sports Shorts, S	2003	Q1	36
Clothing	Shorts	Men's Sports Shorts, M	2003	Q1	72
Clothing	Shorts	Men's Sports Shorts, S	2003	Q1	144

FIGURE P4-11

You now have a complete drill-through target report, Product Detail, to act as a companion to the drill-through source report, Company Sales. In the exercises that follow, you modify the Company Sales report to implement drill-through functionality to the Product Detail report.

Designing the Drill-Through Source Report in 2005

Reporting Services 2008 has been released for some time now, so why review the implementation of a drill-through report using Reporting Services 2005? In reality, there is a significant audience that has yet to adopt the most recent release and is still reliant on prior versions. The challenges and resolutions are distinctly different between the current and prior versions, so an in-depth review of Reporting Services 2005 is warranted.

This exercise demonstrates how to modify the Company Sales report, provided as part of the SQL Server 2005 AdventureWorks Sample Reports, in order to implement drill-through functionality from a multi-level matrix data region to the Product Detail report previously created.

1. Start by opening the AdventureWorks Sample Reports solution using BIDS.

2. Open and preview the Company Sales report. The results are shown in Figure P4-12.

In its current state, the report displays totals for the year when the quarters are collapsed, or totals for the quarter when expanded, for 2002 and 2003, respectively. This is evidenced in Figure P4-12.

Adventure Works
2002 - 2003
Sales

		2002	2003			
			Q1	Q2	Q3	Q4
Components		$3,611,041	$459,086	$1,111,521	$2,527,699	$1,391,434
Clothing	Bib-Shorts	$102,183	$21,544	$43,458	$351	
	Caps	$9,467	$1,782	$2,940	$8,676	$8,519
	Gloves	$90,897	$25,692	$41,876	$26,945	$23,619
	Jerseys	$110,846	$18,205	$31,335	$173,041	$140,703
	Shorts	$49,384	$11,230	$21,424	$97,610	$84,192
	Socks	$3,173			$6,969	$6,183
	Tights	$123,871	$27,588	$51,601	$780	$244
	Vests				$81,086	$66,883
Bikes		$26,664,534	$6,101,755	$7,028,317	$10,759,142	$11,310,133
Accessories		$93,797	$15,628	$32,845	$262,613	$283,928

FIGURE P4-12

3. Right-click the quarter group column heading to display the context menu and then click Subtotal (see Figure P4-13).

This adds a total column on the design surface to the right of the quarter group and displays a total aggregate value when the report is viewed. Next, add a drill-through action from the Sales value to the Product Detail report.

4. Right-click the Sales value field within the matrix and then click Properties from the resulting context menu (see Figure P4-14) to display the Textbox Properties dialog box.

5. From the Textbox Properties dialog box, select the Navigation tab.

6. In the section labeled Hyperlink Action, click Jump to Report and then select Product Detail from the dropdown box (Figure P4-15).

7. Use the Parameters button to identify the data context, via report parameters, to provide to the Product Detail report.

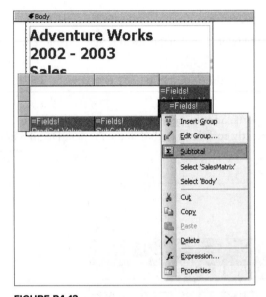

FIGURE P4-13

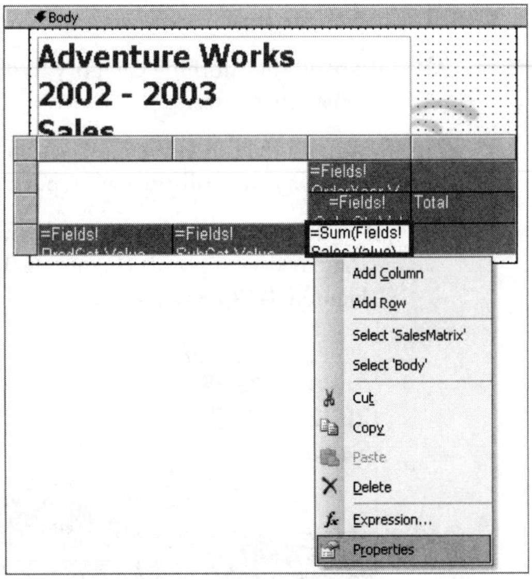

FIGURE P4-14

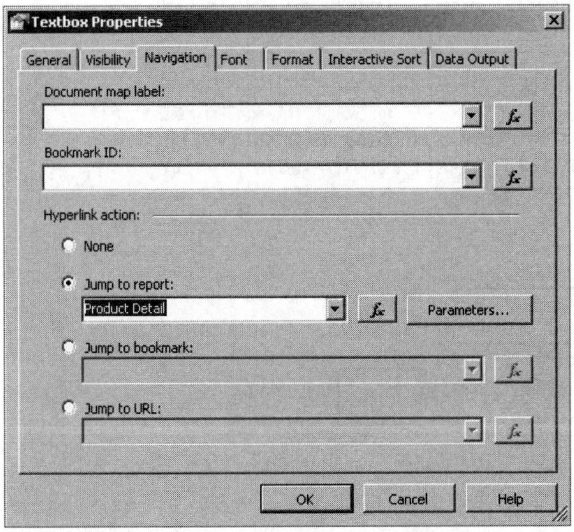

FIGURE P4-15

8. Enter the following parameter assignments:

NAME	VALUE
ProductCategory	=Fields!ProdCat.Value
ProductSubcategory	=Fields!SubCat.Value
Year	=Fields!OrderYear.Value
Quarter	=Fields!OrderQtr.Value

9. Click OK until you return to the report design surface and then preview the report.

10. Expand the Clothing category to display the related subcategories and then expand 2003 to display its quarters.

11. Click on the cell at the intersection of Clothing, Shorts and 2003, Q2 whose value is $21,424 to display the drill-through report.

The data context is preserved between reports, and the aggregate value displayed by the Company Sales report (Figure P4-16) correctly correlates to that in the Product Detail report (Figure P4-17), as expected.

Adventure Works
2002 - 2003
Sales

		2002	2003				
		Total	Q1	Q2	Q3	Q4	Total
Components		$3,611,041	$459,086	$1,111,521	$2,527,699	$1,391,434	$5,489,741
Clothing	Bib-Shorts	$102,183	$21,544	$43,458	$351		$65,353
	Caps	$9,467	$1,782	$2,940	$8,676	$8,519	$21,917
	Gloves	$90,897	$25,692	$41,876	$26,945	$23,619	$118,132
	Jerseys	$110,846	$18,205	$31,335	$173,041	$140,703	$363,284
	Shorts	$49,384	$11,230	$21,424	$97,610	$84,192	$214,457
	Socks	$3,173			$6,969	$6,183	$13,152
	Tights	$123,871	$27,588	$51,601	$780	$244	$80,212
	Vests				$81,086	$66,883	$147,968
Bikes		$26,664,534	$6,101,755	$7,028,317	$10,759,142	$11,310,133	$35,199,346
Accessories		$93,797	$15,628	$32,845	$262,613	$283,928	$595,014

FIGURE P4-16

Category:	Clothing			Year:	2003	
Subcategory:	Shorts			Quarter:	Q2	

Category	Subcategory	Product	Year	Quarter	Sales
					21,424
Clothing	Shorts	Men's Sports Shorts, M	2003	Q2	216
Clothing	Shorts	Men's Sports Shorts, M	2003	Q2	144
Clothing	Shorts	Men's Sports Shorts, L	2003	Q2	108
Clothing	Shorts	Men's Sports Shorts, S	2003	Q2	108
Clothing	Shorts	Men's Sports Shorts, M	2003	Q2	452
Clothing	Shorts	Men's Sports Shorts, L	2003	Q2	36
Clothing	Shorts	Men's Sports Shorts, M	2003	Q2	216
Clothing	Shorts	Men's Sports Shorts, S	2003	Q2	383
Clothing	Shorts	Men's Sports Shorts, S	2003	Q2	72
Clothing	Shorts	Men's Sports Shorts, M	2003	Q2	72
Clothing	Shorts	Men's Sports Shorts, L	2003	Q2	108
Clothing	Shorts	Men's Sports Shorts, M	2003	Q2	108
Clothing	Shorts	Men's Sports Shorts, M	2003	Q2	72

FIGURE P4-17

12. Now click the Total item in the same row, valued at $214,457.

The value displayed by the source report (Figure P4-18) and target report (Figure P4-19) are not consistent. A hint at the cause is evidenced in the report parameters that are provided to the target report. Even though the Total column was selected in the Company Sales report, a seemingly random value of Q1 was provided as the current data context.

		2002	2003				
		Total	Q1	Q2	Q3	Q4	Total
Components		$3,611,041	$459,086	$1,111,521	$2,527,699	$1,391,434	$5,489,741
Clothing	Bib-Shorts	$102,183	$21,544	$43,458	$351		$65,353
	Caps	$9,467	$1,782	$2,940	$8,676	$8,519	$21,917
	Gloves	$90,897	$25,692	$41,876	$26,945	$23,619	$118,132
	Jerseys	$110,846	$18,205	$31,335	$173,041	$140,703	$363,284
	Shorts	$49,384	$11,230	$21,424	$97,610	$84,192	$214,457
	Socks	$3,173			$6,969	$6,183	$13,152
	Tights	$123,871	$27,588	$51,601	$780	$244	$80,212
	Vests				$81,086	$66,883	$147,968
Bikes		$26,664,534	$6,101,755	$7,028,317	$10,759,142	$11,310,133	$35,199,346
Accessories		$93,797	$15,628	$32,845	$262,613	$283,928	$595,014

Adventure Works 2002 - 2003 Sales

FIGURE P4-18

Category:	Clothing			Year:	2003	
Subcategory:	Shorts			Quarter:	Q1	

Category	Subcategory	Product	Year	Quarter	Sales
					11,230
Clothing	Shorts	Men's Sports Shorts, M	2003	Q1	36
Clothing	Shorts	Men's Sports Shorts, M	2003	Q1	180
Clothing	Shorts	Men's Sports Shorts, S	2003	Q1	72
Clothing	Shorts	Men's Sports Shorts, L	2003	Q1	36
Clothing	Shorts	Men's Sports Shorts, M	2003	Q1	108
Clothing	Shorts	Men's Sports Shorts, S	2003	Q1	72
Clothing	Shorts	Men's Sports Shorts, S	2003	Q1	108
Clothing	Shorts	Men's Sports Shorts, M	2003	Q1	108
Clothing	Shorts	Men's Sports Shorts, S	2003	Q1	72
Clothing	Shorts	Men's Sports Shorts, M	2003	Q1	360
Clothing	Shorts	Men's Sports Shorts, M	2003	Q1	36
Clothing	Shorts	Men's Sports Shorts, S	2003	Q1	36
Clothing	Shorts	Men's Sports Shorts, M	2003	Q1	72

FIGURE P4-19

In this scenario, the desired behavior is to display and aggregate all quarters of the selected year in the Product Detail report, which can only be achieved by providing the value of null to the Quarter report parameter to indicate this parameter is irrelevant and should be ignored. The problem arises since there is a single value in the matrix that dynamically displays a different value based on the current row and column grouping, or scope.

To overcome this behavior, the parameter value passed from the source report to the target report must also have a dynamic behavior based on the current context. You can use the

Reporting Services `InScope` function to determine if the current instance of an item is within a specified scope. In this example, you want to determine if the quarter column grouping, named OrderQtr, is valid, or in scope, when the report action is invoked. If so, the user clicked a cell that intersects with a quarter; otherwise, a total value has been selected.

13. Modify the Quarter parameter associated with the report drill-through action:

```
=Iif(InScope("OrderQtr"), Fields!OrderQtr.Value, Nothing).
```

14. Preview the report and retry the drill-through action.

Compare the results of the updated drill-through result (Figure P4-20) to that of the source report (Figure P4-18). The aggregate totals now match as desired. You can scan the detail items of the report to verify multiple quarters are present. This is also evidenced by the Quarter parameter, which indicates no value was provided. You can verify that this approach continues to work for individual quarters by selecting Q1 through Q4 and reviewing the results.

Category:	Clothing			Year:	2003	
Subcategory:	Shorts			Quarter:		
Category	Subcategory	Product		Year	Quarter	Sales
						214,457
Clothing	Shorts	Men's Sports Shorts, M		2003	Q1	36
Clothing	Shorts	Men's Sports Shorts, M		2003	Q1	180
Clothing	Shorts	Men's Sports Shorts, S		2003	Q1	72
Clothing	Shorts	Men's Sports Shorts, L		2003	Q1	36
Clothing	Shorts	Men's Sports Shorts, M		2003	Q1	108
Clothing	Shorts	Men's Sports Shorts, S		2003	Q1	72
Clothing	Shorts	Men's Sports Shorts, S		2003	Q1	108
Clothing	Shorts	Men's Sports Shorts, M		2003	Q1	108
Clothing	Shorts	Men's Sports Shorts, S		2003	Q1	72
Clothing	Shorts	Men's Sports Shorts, M		2003	Q1	360
Clothing	Shorts	Men's Sports Shorts, M		2003	Q1	36
Clothing	Shorts	Men's Sports Shorts, S		2003	Q1	36
Clothing	Shorts	Men's Sports Shorts, M		2003	Q1	72

FIGURE P4-20

If you are the inquisitive type, you have probably already noticed that drill-throughs for subtotals associated with Product Category, Product Subcategory and Year do not behave as expected. You would need to apply a similar dynamic behavior to each level and parameter for comprehensive drill-through functionality. That is, you would need to dynamically check the `InScope` result for Product Category, Product Subcategory and Year as well as make appropriate logic changes to the target report to support `null` values for each of these parameters.

In this section, you learned how to provide accurate and consistent drill-through functionality for a multi-level matrix report. The following section demonstrates how this same scenario is addressed using Reporting Services 2008.

Designing the Drill-Through Source Report in 2008

With the release of Reporting Services 2008, the report rendering engine was revamped to include new report items and a more robust rendering engine. One of the most compelling of these is the introduction of the Tablix, which is a single report item that replaces the functionality provided in previous versions by the Table and Matrix report items. Although the report design user interface still provides elements named Table and Matrix, the underlying report item that implements these is the new Tablix control. While a review of the enhancements and functionality provided by the Tablix control is beyond the scope of this recipe, it is important to note the underlying change from previous versions, especially when considering the impact it has on providing drill-through functionality from a multi-level matrix report.

As with the Reporting Services 2005 example, this exercise demonstrates the implementation of drill-through functionality from the Company Sales report to the Product Detail report that you created earlier in this recipe.

1. Start by opening the AdventureWorks Sample Reports solution using BIDS. This is the same solution in which you created the Product Details report definition.

2. Open the Company Sales report (Company Sales 2008.rdl) and review the report design.

3. Use the Column Groups located at the bottom of the design surface to add a Total to the Qtr group.

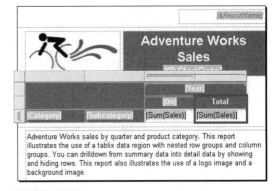

Notice a new column named Total is added to the right of the column named Qtr, as illustrated in Figure P4-21. This behavior, adding a new column header to the matrix, is reminiscent of functionality provided in Reporting Services 2005. However, unlike

FIGURE P4-21

its predecessor, the new Tablix control also creates a new cell in the body of the matrix that is used to define the specific behaviors for the group total. Compare this to Figure P4-14, which only provides a single cell that you can manipulate.

The new behavior is much more explicit, providing two distinct cells in which to define the desired behaviors instead of providing dynamic behaviors on a single cell. Next, you will add drill-through behaviors for each of these two fields.

4. Right-click the Sales cell under the Qtr column heading and then click Text Box Properties from the resulting context menu. The Text Box Properties dialog box is displayed.

5. On the Action tab, click Go to Report and then select Product Detail from the dropdown.

6. Add the following parameter assignments:

NAME	VALUE
ProductCategory	[Category]
ProductSubcategory	[Subcategory]
Year	[Year]
Quarter	[Qtr]

In this example, the report action only applies to the detail cell that is contained within the quarter column group, so the field value is always valid and there is not a need to define an expression using the InScope function as was required with Reporting Services 2005. However, the matrix cell under the quarter total does not yet have an action defined, so you implement that action next.

7. Repeat steps 4 through 6 for the Sales cell located directly beneath the Total column created in step 3, replacing the parameter value of Quarter from [Qtr] to =Nothing. This explicitly indicates a null value should be provided for the Quarter parameter, requesting the Product Detail report display all quarters for the specified year.

8. Preview the report and evaluate the drill-through results.

Figure P4-22 identifies both a detail and total cell within the drill-through source report, while Figures P4-23 and P4-24 illustrate the resulting drill-through target reports for each cell, respectively. These examples demonstrate that the core functionality behaves as anticipated. To provide a consistent and cohesive drill-through experience, similar functionality would need to be added to each appropriate level and group within the matrix: Product Category, Product Subcategory, and Year.

Adventure Works Sales
January 01, 2002 - December 31, 2003

		2002	2003				
		Total	Q1	Q2	Q3	Q4	Total
Accessories		$93,797	$15,628	$32,845	$262,613	$283,928	$595,014
Bikes		$26,664,534	$6,101,755	$7,028,317	$10,759,142	$11,310,133	$35,199,346
Clothing	Bib-Shorts	$102,183	$21,544	$43,458	$351		$65,353
	Caps	$9,467	$1,782	$2,940	$8,676	$8,519	$21,917
	Gloves	$90,897	$25,692	$41,876	$26,945	$23,619	$118,132
	Jerseys	$110,846	$18,205	$31,335	$173,041	$140,703	$363,284
	Shorts	$49,384	$11,230	$21,424	$97,610	$84,192	$214,457
	Socks	$3,173			$6,969	$6,183	$13,152
	Tights	$123,871	$27,588	$51,601	$780	$244	$80,212
	Vests				$81,086	$66,883	$147,968
Components		$3,611,041	$459,086	$1,111,521	$2,527,699	$1,391,434	$5,489,741

FIGURE P4-22

| Category: | Clothing | Year: | 2003 | | | |
| Subcategory: | Shorts | Quarter: | Q2 | | | |

Category	Subcategory	Product	Year	Quarter	Sales
					21,424
Clothing	Shorts	Men's Sports Shorts, M	2003	Q2	216
Clothing	Shorts	Men's Sports Shorts, M	2003	Q2	144
Clothing	Shorts	Men's Sports Shorts, L	2003	Q2	108
Clothing	Shorts	Men's Sports Shorts, S	2003	Q2	108
Clothing	Shorts	Men's Sports Shorts, M	2003	Q2	452
Clothing	Shorts	Men's Sports Shorts, L	2003	Q2	36
Clothing	Shorts	Men's Sports Shorts, M	2003	Q2	216
Clothing	Shorts	Men's Sports Shorts, S	2003	Q2	383
Clothing	Shorts	Men's Sports Shorts, S	2003	Q2	72
Clothing	Shorts	Men's Sports Shorts, M	2003	Q2	72
Clothing	Shorts	Men's Sports Shorts, L	2003	Q2	108
Clothing	Shorts	Men's Sports Shorts, M	2003	Q2	108
Clothing	Shorts	Men's Sports Shorts, M	2003	Q2	72
Clothing	Shorts	Men's Sports Shorts, M	2003	Q2	108

FIGURE P4-23

| Category: | Clothing | Year: | 2003 | | | |
| Subcategory: | Shorts | Quarter: | | | | |

Category	Subcategory	Product	Year	Quarter	Sales
					214,457
Clothing	Shorts	Men's Sports Shorts, M	2003	Q1	36
Clothing	Shorts	Men's Sports Shorts, M	2003	Q1	180
Clothing	Shorts	Men's Sports Shorts, S	2003	Q1	72
Clothing	Shorts	Men's Sports Shorts, L	2003	Q1	36
Clothing	Shorts	Men's Sports Shorts, M	2003	Q1	108
Clothing	Shorts	Men's Sports Shorts, S	2003	Q1	72
Clothing	Shorts	Men's Sports Shorts, S	2003	Q1	108
Clothing	Shorts	Men's Sports Shorts, M	2003	Q1	108
Clothing	Shorts	Men's Sports Shorts, S	2003	Q1	72
Clothing	Shorts	Men's Sports Shorts, M	2003	Q1	360
Clothing	Shorts	Men's Sports Shorts, M	2003	Q1	36
Clothing	Shorts	Men's Sports Shorts, S	2003	Q1	36
Clothing	Shorts	Men's Sports Shorts, M	2003	Q1	72
Clothing	Shorts	Men's Sports Shorts, S	2003	Q1	144

FIGURE P4-24

Final Thoughts

With each new release, Reporting Services provides enhancements that are relevant and impactful on the way reports are authored and designed. As demonstrated in this exercise, the introduction of the Tablix control with Reporting Services 2008 greatly simplifies the process of implementing drill-through functionality for multi-level matrix reports, making the process more intuitive and available.

Credits and Related References

TechNet: Reporting Services drill-through for a matrix report (http://blogs.technet.com/andrew/archive/2008/07/31/reporting-services-drill-through-for-a-matrix-report.aspx)

DRILL-THROUGH REPORT LINK BREADCRUMBS

If you have created multiple drill-through reports, you know that report navigation works in one direction and that some users struggle to find the best method to navigate back to a previous report, especially if there are multiple reports in the drill-through sequence. The report toolbar contains navigation controls, including a Back button for the previous report in a chain of linked reports, but many users don't find this intuitive. A common user-experience paradigm in many well-designed web applications places a series of hyperlinks at the top of a page, indicating both the path that brought the user to the page they're viewing and a path for navigating back to any page along that path. This is a breadcrumb trail of hyperlinks. Reporting Services provides a means to navigate to any other report deployed to the server but does not have any type of HTML report item that allows you to build a series of embedded hyperlinks or anchor tags.

This technique shows you how to build a series of breadcrumb hyperlinks that allow your users to see where they've been and to navigate back to any report along the trail.

Product Versions

➤   Reporting Services 2000

➤   Reporting Services 2005

➤   Reporting Services 2008

The example demonstrated in this recipe is based on Reporting Services 2008, but this technique works in earlier SSRS versions. The report design options and dialogs, however, may look a little different in earlier products.

What You'll Need

➤   A series of reports with report navigation actions

➤   A report parameter used to track the breadcrumb trail

➤   A custom code function to build an ad-hoc query

➤   A dataset used to provide breadcrumb data

➤   A matrix data region containing textbox report actions

This recipe contains a lot of detail so I recommend that you use the completed reports from the book download samples as a reference point to check and validate your own design.

Figure P4-25 shows an example of a breadcrumb trail in the report header of a detail report. Note the progressive drill-through path of reports the user opens en route to the current report.

In the production implementation of this technique, report actions can be implemented using any of the compatible report items, including textboxes, images, a grouped table, a matrix, a list, or chart data points as the report action source object. The purpose of this recipe is to demonstrate the breadcrumb technique, not the complexities of embedded report actions. As such, you will be using a simple textbox on the report body to navigate between sample reports. These reports will not have any data sources or datasets other than the one required for this technique.

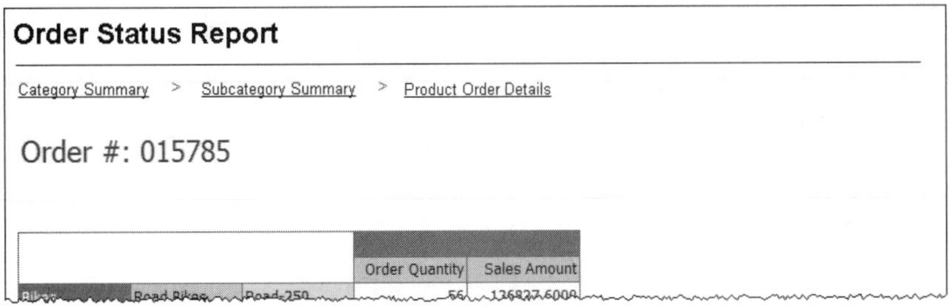

Order Status Report

Category Summary   >   Subcategory Summary   >   Product Order Details

Order #: 015785

		Order Quantity	Sales Amount

FIGURE P4-25

Designing the Report

In the end, you will have four almost identical reports designed to demonstrate the technique. You will start by designing one report with the base functionality for all reports and then create three copies of this report, rename them, and make the necessary modifications.

1. Create a new report named Breadcrumbs Report 1.

2. Drag and drop the report name from the Built-in Fields to create a title textbox and style the report header as you typically would with a large, bold font, horizontal line, and so on, as you see in Figure P4-25.

3. In the report body, about an inch or three centimeters below the line, add a textbox to use as the report action source object. The user will click this text to navigate to the next report. Add some appropriate text to this textbox to indicate that it's a link to the second report. You can see this in Figure P4-26.

[&ReportName]

Go to Report 2

FIGURE P4-26

In a more sophisticated production report, this textbox would be replaced with other report items or data regions with appropriate report actions.

A report parameter is used to pass the report navigation history to the target report. With each new report in the navigation chain, the name of that target report will be added to a comma-separated string passed in the parameter. This parameter will only be used internally and not shown to the user.

4. Add a report parameter named `callingreports`.

5. Set the parameter to accept a `null` value and set the visibility to Hidden (see Figure P4-27).

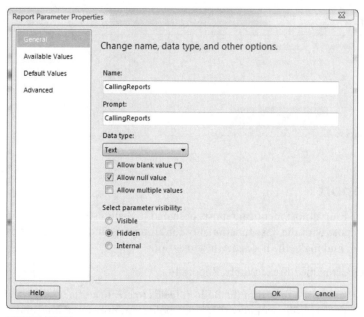

FIGURE P4-27

A dataset query will be used to drive a matrix data region to contain the report links. This query will be built using an expression and custom code function. Before you put this part into place, you must create a static query to generate the metadata for the dataset. This dataset will not actually consume any real data but must have a valid data source. Of course, a data source must have a valid connection string to satisfy this requirement.

6. Create a new dataset and name it LinksQuery.

7. Any valid shared or embedded data source may be used for this dataset because data will not actually be read from a database. Create or select a data source and select any local or remote server and any valid database. The localhost server and the Master database is used in this example.

8. For the query, type:

```
SELECT Null As Link
```

Figure P4-28 shows the Dataset Properties dialog with the query statement. This is only a temporary placeholder to generate a field object named Link. The actual query string will be generated in a custom code function and expression.

A matrix will be used to display each of the report links, each separated by a right angle bracket: >. Only the column header cells will be used in the matrix.

9. Add a matrix data region to the header area of the report body.

10. Delete the Row Group and the related rows and columns.

11. Drag the Link field to the Column Groups list to create a new group and group header.

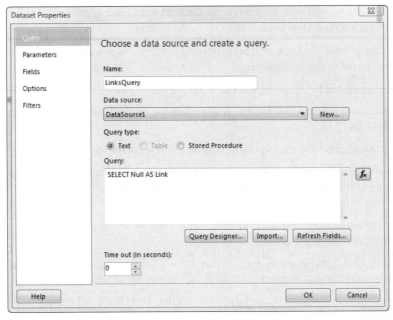

FIGURE P4-28

12. Add a new column to the right, inside the group.

13. Right-click in the header cell and Split Cells.

14. Right-click in the header cell for the new column on the right and add the following expression:

```
=IIF(Fields!Link.Value = Last(Fields!Link.Value, "LinksQuery"), "", ">")
```

15. Choose both of these cells and set the Font Color to Blue.

16. Set the text in the first cell to be underscored to make it look like a hyperlink. Compare the matrix shown in Figure P4-29 to validate your design.

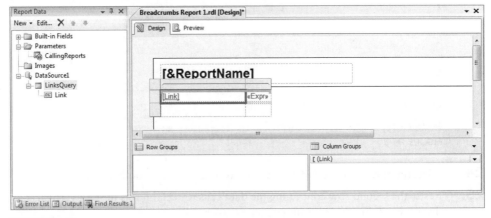

FIGURE P4-29

The Link field cell will be used to display the name of the source report and to provide a link back to it in each column instance of this cell in the matrix.

17. Right-click the cell for the Link field and choose Text Box Properties. On the Text Box Properties dialog, move to the Actions page.

18. Create a report action by choosing the radio button Go to report.

19. For the destination report, click the Expression button (*fx*) and then create an expression to reference the Link field.

20. Click OK to close and save the expression in the Expression dialog.

21. Click the Add button to add a new target report parameter. If this report has previously been created, this parameter would be available for selection. Type CallingReports in the Name column.

22. Click the Expression button (*fx*) next to the Value column and type the following (as one line) into the Expression window:

```
=IIF(IsNothing(Parameters!CallingReports.Value), Globals!ReportName,
    Parameters!CallingReports.Value & ", " & Globals!ReportName)
```

23. Close and save the expression in the Expression dialog and then use Figure P4-30 to verify these settings.

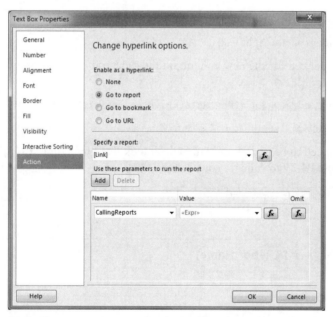

FIGURE P4-30

24. Select the entire matrix and remove all borders using the toolbar or ribbon.

25. Resize the second row containing the data cells to reclaim this unused vertical space. Reduce the height of this row to eliminate unnecessary white space.

26. Select the textbox you added back in Step 3.

This textbox will be used to navigate to another report. The following steps are identical to the previous steps for the Link cell except for the destination report.

1. Right-click the textbox and choose Text Box Properties.

2. On the Actions tab, create a report action by choosing the radio button Go to report.

3. The destination report doesn't exist yet so you will just type this value into the drop-down list. Type Breadcrumbs Report 2 into the Specify a report property.

4. Click the Add button to add a new target report parameter. If this report has previously been created, this parameter would be available for selection. Type CallingReports in the Name column.

5. Click the Expression button (*fx*) next to the Value column and type the following (as one line) into the Expression window:

```
=IIF(IsNothing(Parameters!CallingReports.Value), Globals!ReportName,
      Parameters!CallingReports.Value & ", " & Globals!ReportName)
```

6. Close and save the Expression dialog and use Figure P4-31 to verify these settings.

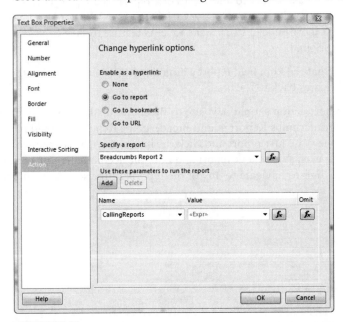

FIGURE P4-31

7. Click OK to save these settings and close the Text Box Properties dialog.

8. Edit the report properties and add the following code to the Code window:

```
Function ListToLinksSQL(List As String) As String
      Dim sTargetReport() As String
      Dim sReport As String
      Dim sOut As String
      sTargetReport = Split(List, ", ")
      For Each sReport In sTargetReport
```

```
        If sOut <> "" Then sOut &= " UNION "
        sOut &= "SELECT '" & sReport & "' AS Link"
    Next
    Return sOut
End Function
```

9. Edit the dataset properties.

10. Replace the query command text with the following expression:

```
=Code.ListToLinksSQL(Parameters!CallingReports.Value)
```

11. Save and close the report.

12. Create three copies of the Breadcrumbs Report 1, named:

- ➤ Breadcrumbs Report 2
- ➤ Breadcrumbs Report 3
- ➤ Breadcrumbs Report 4

If you are using BIDS, the easiest way to add copies of a report to the project is to select the first report in the Solution Explorer and then use Ctrl-C and Ctrl-V to copy and paste a new file, then rename it. In Report Builder 2.0, use the Save As feature to save copies of the file to the same folder as the original.

13. Modify each report so that the Link field report action targets the next report in the sequence and the last report navigates back to the first.

The Breadcrumbs Report 2 report action should navigate to Breadcrumbs Report 3. Breadcrumbs Report 3 should navigate to Breadcrumbs Report 4, and Breadcrumbs Report 4 should navigate back to Breadcrumbs Report 1. Preview the first report and click the link to navigate to the second report. Continue to follow the links on each subsequent report and note the accumulated breadcrumb links in the report header. Click any link to navigate to any of the reports in the series, as illustrated in Figure P4-32.

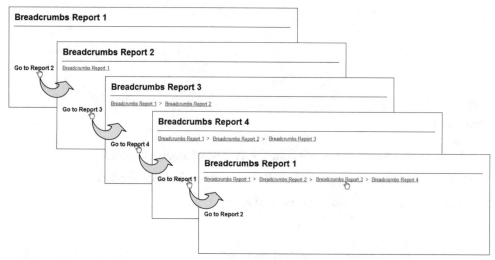

FIGURE P4-32

Final Thoughts

The breadcrumb link list is a common navigation tool, and users will intuitively know how to use it based on their experience with websites and other applications. Since Reporting Services doesn't provide a built-in mechanism for tracking navigation history, a parameter can be used to retain this information. An important point to keep in mind when you are designing reports to behave like a specific type of application (in this case, a series of active pages on a web server), is that this type of navigation will only work when reports are rendered to HTML. You may need to educate your users accordingly.

DYNAMIC PIVOTING AS A MATRIX REPLACEMENT

The Reporting Services matrix is a great tool for tabular reporting because it allows for non-static column values that are dynamically created from column and row groups. Specify what value is to be aggregated at the intersection of row and column groups, as well as the aggregate function, and the work is done for you. The weakness of this construct is that specific values that may be desired along the axis of columns may be absent if the dataset behind the matrix does not supply them. This is often the case when the column axis is a date range. This recipe will provide a solution to the problem by using a dynamically created PIVOT query that enforces the date range of the column list. The following recipe requires familiarity with the PIVOT operator. If you do not already have experience with pivoting in T-SQL, read Chapter 11 of *Beginning T-SQL with Microsoft SQL Server 2005 and 2008* (Wrox, 2008).

Product Versions

➤   Reporting Services 2005

➤   Reporting Services 2008

What You'll Need

➤   A matrix

➤   A data source for the AdventureWorksDW2008 database

Designing the Report

To provide a concrete example of the issue outlined in this recipe's introduction, take a look at the following stored procedure. It is rather simple. Taking in a product ID, a territory, and a starting month, it will return all sales for that product within each of that territory's regions for a six month range starting at the supplied starting month. Relying on the matrix to create your tabular report, you place the SalesTerritoryRegion on rows, the SalesMonth on columns, and require the sum of the OrderQuantity as the intersecting value. The result when running your report for the parameter values of product ID 587, territory group Europe, and starting month value '2003-07-01' appears as in Figure P4-33. Not quite the formatting you want to see.

Because of the scarcity of sales for this region, the months of August, October, and November are omitted from your list of columns. The strength of the matrix is that it works with whatever data you supply and takes care of the necessary formatting and aggregation. Its weakness is pretty

Sales Territory Region	Jul 2003	Sep 2003	Dec 2003
France	2	0	0
Germany	0	2	3
United Kingdom	0	0	3

FIGURE P4-33

much the same thing; it only works with what it is supplied. The following is the original query for the results shown in Figure P4-33:

```
CREATE PROCEDURE usp_Sales_By_Region
@productID SMALLINT
```

```
,@territory NVARCHAR(50)
,@startMonth SMALLDATETIME
AS
SET NOCOUNT ON;
BEGIN
SELECT
DST.SalesTerritoryRegion
,D.FullDateAlternateKey AS SalesMonth
,FRS.OrderQuantity
FROM FactResellerSales FRS
INNER JOIN DimDate D
ON FRS.OrderDateKey = D.DateKey
INNER JOIN DimSalesTerritory DST
ON FRS.SalesTerritoryKey = DST.SalesTerritoryKey
WHERE FRS.ProductKey = @productID
AND DST.SalesTerritoryGroup = @territory
AND FullDateAlternateKey BETWEEN @StartMonth AND DATEADD(month,5,@StartMonth)
END
```

To overcome this problem, you will be using the T-SQL PIVOT operator to create a cross-tab result set. The PIVOT operator will de-normalize your result set, creating repeating groups of attributes that you must explicitly specify. In this case, it will be a date range. Also required by the PIVOT operator is an aggregate function and a column to be aggregated. In effect, it does what a matrix would do for you in Reporting Services.

1. In place of the original query used for the matrix, create the stored procedure shown in the code below in the AdventureWorksDW database. This stored procedure will do the work of the original stored procedure as well as the matrix within Reporting Services. It can serve as a template for stored procedures that you will need to create within your reports.

```
CREATE PROCEDURE usp_Sales_by_Territory_Dynamic_Pivot
@productID SMALLINT
  ,@territory NVARCHAR(50)
  ,@startMonth SMALLDATETIME
AS
BEGIN

SET NOCOUNT ON;

DECLARE @sql NVARCHAR(MAX)
DECLARE @pivot_list NVARCHAR(300)
DECLARE @aliased_pivot_list NVARCHAR(350)
DECLARE @parameters NVARCHAR(100)

-- Create comma separated pivot list
SELECT
@pivot_list = ISNULL(@pivot_list + ', ','')
+ '[' + CONVERT(CHAR(10),FullDateAlternateKey,101) + '] '
FROM DimDate
WHERE FullDateAlternateKey BETWEEN @startMonth AND DATEADD(month,5,@startMonth)
AND DATEPART(Day,FullDateAlternateKey) = 1
```

```
-- Create aliased pivot list in order to have static column names for pivot table
SELECT
@aliased_pivot_list = ISNULL(@aliased_pivot_list + ', ','')
+ '[' + CONVERT(CHAR(10),FullDateAlternateKey,101) + '] AS Month_'
+ CAST(RANK() OVER(ORDER BY FullDateAlternateKey) AS NVARCHAR(2))
FROM DimDate
WHERE FullDateAlternateKey BETWEEN @startMonth AND DATEADD(month,5,@startMonth)
AND DATEPART(Day,FullDateAlternateKey) = 1

SET @sql =
N'select
SalesTerritoryRegion, ' + @aliased_pivot_list +

' from (
select DimSalesTerritory.SalesTerritoryRegion, FullDateAlternateKey, OrderQuantity
FROM FactResellerSales
INNER JOIN DimDate
ON FactResellerSales.OrderDateKey = DimDate.DateKey
INNER JOIN DimSalesTerritory
ON FactResellerSales.SalesTerritoryKey = DimSalesTerritory.SalesTerritoryKey
WHERE ProductKey = @paramProduct AND DimSalesTerritory.SalesTerritoryGroup =
   @paramTerritory
) Sales
PIVOT (SUM(OrderQuantity) FOR FullDateAlternateKey IN (' + @pivot_list + N')
) pvt'
SET @parameters = N'@paramProduct SMALLINT, @paramTerritory NVARCHAR(50)'
EXECUTE sp_executesql @sql, @parameters,
                    @paramProduct = @productID, @paramTerritory = @territory;

END
```

Before proceeding with the remaining steps in the recipe, the preceding stored procedure deserves discussion. It is quite a departure from the simplistic procedure originally used to feed our matrix, so let's look at it in detail.

There are two main obstacles in implementing your new dynamic pivoting strategy.

First, the list of values to be pivoted must be supplied dynamically based on the @startMonth parameter. Given a starting month value, a comma-separated list of all six months in the required range must be created in the format [2003-07-01], [2003-08-01], and so on.

Second, this column list must then be aliased in the outer query of the PIVOT to static values. Without this step, dataset fields will not be correctly mapped to the columns in your result set as they change from each @startMonth value to another. In other words, [2003-07-01] must be aliased as Month_1, [2003-08-01] as Month_2, and so on.

The assignment of the @pivot_list and @aliased_pivot_list variables in the code above do just this, ensuring that only month values that represent the first day of the month are chosen. If you were to print the values of the @pivot_list and @aliased_pivot_list variables above, you would get results like

[07/01/2003], [08/01/2003], [09/01/2003], . . .

and

[07/01/2003] AS Month_1, [08/01/2003] AS Month_2, [09/01/2003] AS Month_3, . . .

respectively.

One last thing to note about the stored procedure is that the `sp_excutesql` stored procedure with a definition of parameters is used to execute the dynamically built SQL statement.

By parameterizing the query, you have taken a step toward protecting your report from a SQL injection attack. This obstacle to malicious attack is especially important to implement if your report contains a single-line entry parameter that allows report users to enter any text as a value. If this parameter value is used in the construction of a dynamic SQL query, entry of a value such as `'DROP TABLE OrderDetails --` can result in some seriously unwanted consequences.

2. Create a new dataset in the report titled ResellerSalesPivot with AdventureWorksDW as the data source. Choose the Stored Procedure radio button and enter the `usp_Sales_by_Territory_Dynamic_Pivot` stored procedure above in the entry line. Navigate to the Parameters menu in the left-hand navigation bar and when prompted type the values **587** for `@productID`, **Europe** for `@territory`, and **2003-07-01** for `@startMonth`. This step is necessary in order for field metadata to be populated.

3. Associate the table to the dataset created above and expand it so that it now has seven columns. In the first header, type Sales Territory Region. Below that, in the first detail row, choose the SalesTerritoryRegion field from the dataset.

4. In the second-from-left header, where the first month's label will be, type the code provided below. This will dynamically create the column header from the `@startMonth` parameter. For the sake of space in the column header, the code truncates the month name to the first three letters of the month.

```
=Left(MonthName(Month(Parameters!startMonth.Value)),3) & " " &
   CStr(Year(Parameters!startMonth.Value))
```

5. In the next header, type the code provided below. Note that it is almost exactly like the code from Step 4 above, with the exception that the value of `@startMonth` has been incremented by one using the `DateAdd` function. Proceed in this fashion for the remaining column headers.

```
=Left(MonthName(Month(DateAdd("m",1,Parameters!startMonth.Value))),3)
   & " " &
   CStr(Year(Parameters!startMonth.Value))
```

6. In the remaining table detail row textboxes, type the expression below, substituting the numbers 1 through 6 for the "x" so that each of the fields `Month_1` through `Month_6` is represented under its correct column header.

```
=CInt(Fields!Month_x.Value)
```

7. Run the report once again with the same parameter values and note that, as shown in Figure P4-34, all months and sales quantities are now present, even entire columns of zeroes that represent an entire month where no sales exist for each region.

Sales Territory Region	Jul 2003	Aug 2003	Sep 2003	Oct 2003	Nov 2003	Dec 2003
France	2	0	0	0	0	0
Germany	0	0	2	0	0	3
United Kingdom	0	0	0	0	0	3

FIGURE P4-34

Final Thoughts

The matrix is a great tool to automate formatting of tabular data, and in most cases it can handle its designated job without issue. There are situations where sparseness of data can leave your matrix with either a non-contiguous list of columns as displayed in this recipe or just an abbreviated list of columns. By dynamically pivoting your query, you essentially do the work of the report matrix with the added advantage of forcing the inclusion of column headers that would otherwise be omitted by the matrix and create unwanted gaps.

USING A DOCUMENT MAP TABLE FOR NAVIGATION

Many advanced report design techniques may be used to provide report users an easier to understand report. The addition of a document map table to many of these advanced report designs enhances the report with a clear and easy to use navigation aid.

The document map table can be used to perform the following navigation actions on the main report:

➤ Navigate to a corresponding group section using a go to bookmark action (similar to built-in Reporting Services document map functionality)

➤ Filter the results displayed using a go to report action in conjunction with passing a parameter value

➤ Hide or show details within a specified group section by passing a parameter value

This recipe shows you how to add a custom document map that is used to filter the main report content by hiding or showing report data.

This example technique differs from the built-in Reporting Services document map functionality in that the report itself hosts a table that performs the navigation, rather than relying on the addition of a separate side pane that appears beside the report.

Product Versions

➤ Reporting Services 2000

➤ Reporting Services 2005

➤ Reporting Services 2008

What You'll Need

➤ A connection to the AdventureWorks2008 sample database

➤ An additional table based upon main report table's existing dataset

➤ A hidden report parameter

➤ A new filter to the main report table that uses the hidden report parameter as part of the value

Designing the Report

This example creates a new report using Report Builder 2.0 and the AdventureWorks2008 sample database. The AdventureWorks2008 report sample's Customer List Report may be used to compare and contrast the use of a Reporting Services built-in document map versus this example's use of a document map table for navigation.

The completed report, when run, looks like Figure P4-35.

1. Start by designing a data source based upon the AdventureWorks2008 sample database.

2. Enter "Product Catalog" for the Report title and format as desired.

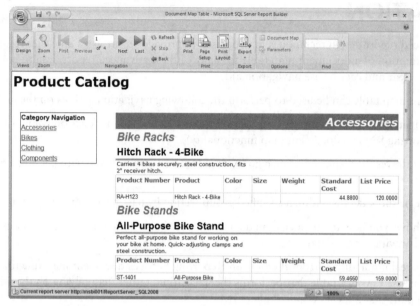

FIGURE P4-35

3. Create a ProductCatalog dataset using the following dataset query that includes the Product, ProductSubcategory, ProductCategory, ProductProductPhoto, ProductPhoto, ProductDescription, ProductModel, and ProductModelProductDescriptionCulture tables.

```
SELECT
    PS.Name AS Subcategory, PM.Name AS Model,
    PC.Name AS Category, PD.Description, PP.LargePhoto, PP.LargePhotoFileName,
        P.Name AS Product, P.ProductNumber,
    P.Color, P.Size, P.Weight, P.StandardCost, P.Style, P.Class, P.ListPrice
FROM Production.Product P INNER JOIN
    Production.ProductSubcategory PS INNER JOIN
    Production.ProductCategory PC ON PS.ProductCategoryID = PC.ProductCategoryID
        ON P.ProductSubcategoryID = PS.ProductSubcategoryID INNER JOIN
    Production.ProductProductPhoto PPP ON P.ProductID = PPP.ProductID INNER JOIN
    Production.ProductPhoto PP ON PPP.ProductPhotoID = PP.ProductPhotoID
        LEFT OUTER JOIN
    Production.ProductDescription PD INNER JOIN
    Production.ProductModel PM INNER JOIN
    Production.ProductModelProductDescriptionCulture PMPDCL
        ON PM.ProductModelID = PMPDCL.ProductModelID ON
    PD.ProductDescriptionID = PMPDCL.ProductDescriptionID
        ON P.ProductModelID = PM.ProductModelID
WHERE (PMPDCL.CultureID = 'en')
```

4. Add a table report item to the report body.

5. Add Category, Subcategory, and Model to the Row Groups of the table.

6. Add ProductNumber, Product, Color, Size, Weight, StandardCost, and ListPrice to the values of the table.

The New Table or Matrix wizard's Arrange fields options should like Figure P4-36.

FIGURE P4-36

7. Set the table's layout.

a. Set the show subtotals and grand totals option to Stepped, subtotal above.

b. Remove the Expand/collapse groups option.

The New Table or Matrix wizard's Choose the layout options should look like Figure P4-37.

8. Remove all summary values from the Category, Subcategory, and Model Row Groups.

9. Delete the Total row.

10. Insert a row above the details row using the inside group — above option.

11. Move the column labels to the new empty row above the details row.

12. Delete the row above the Category Row Group (this Row Group contained the column labels before moving or copying to row above the details row).

13. Move the Row Group textboxes to the column aligned directly over Product Number.

14. Delete the leftmost column.

15. Format the Category Row Group.

a. Set Background Color to SteelBlue.

b. Set Font to White and Verdana, 20pt, Italic, Bold.

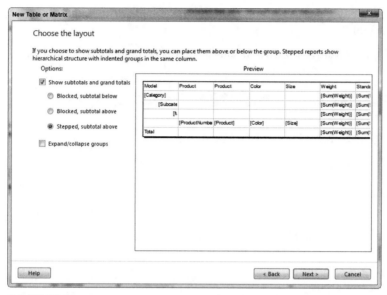

FIGURE P4-37

    c. Set Position Size to 1in, 0.4in.

    d. Set Text Align to Right.

    e. Set Border Color to LightGrey, Style to None, and Width to 1pt.

    f. Merge all the cells, forming one table width cell.

16. Format the Subcategory Row Group.

    a. Set Font to SteelBlue, Arial, 20pt, Italic, Bold.

    b. Set Border Color to LightGrey, None, 1pt.

    c. Decrease the paragraph text indentation aligning with left table edge.

    d. Merge all the cells, forming one table width cell.

17. Format the Model Row Group.

    a. Set Border Color Default to LightGrey and set Bottom to RosyBrown.

    b. Set Border Width Default to 1pt and set Bottom to 3pt.

    c. Set Border Style for Bottom to Solid.

    d. Set Font to Black, Arial, 18pt, Bold.

    e. Decrease the paragraph text indentation aligning with left table edge.

    f. Merge all the cells, forming one table width cell.

18. Format the Detail Row column headings.

    a. Set Font to Firebrick, Verdana, 11pt.

19. Insert a row between the Model Row Group and the Detail Row column headings.

20. Insert the Description field into the leftmost cell above the Product Number column heading and merge with the two cells directly to the right.

21. Change the Page Setup Orientation to Landscape and adjust column widths as desired.

The report designer should look like Figure P4-38.

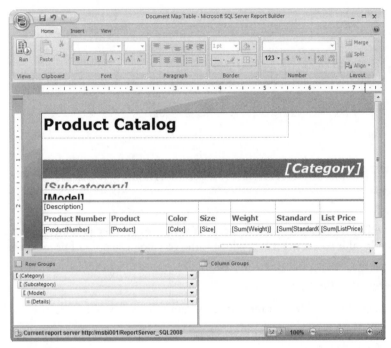

FIGURE P4-38

22. Move the existing report table right about 2 inches from the left side of the report.

23. Insert a new table with a single column to the left of the existing report table.

24. Set new table to use the same dataset as the existing report (dataset).

25. Create a New Group on the Category field and display the Category field in the Group Header.

26. Delete the detail Row Group and hide the detail column.

27. Insert another row above the Category group row and add "Category Navigation" to the textbox directly above the Category data field in order to act as a label for the navigation document map table.

28. Format this Navigation table as desired.

The report designer should look like Figure P4-39.

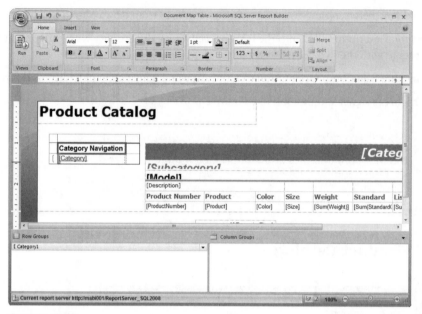

FIGURE P4-39

29. Create a new Report Parameter called `DocMap` of type `Text`. Set the parameter to `Hidden` and set the Default value to `Accessories`, which is the very first category of products in AdventureWorks.

30. Deploy the report to the report server.

31. In the Document Map Table, edit the Category data value's Textbox Properties, setting the Action options as follows:

    a. Select Go to report.

    b. In Specify a report select this same Document Map report.

    c. Add the following parameters to run the report:

        i. Set `Name` to `DocMap`

        ii. Set `Value` to `Category`

32. In the main report, edit the tablix properties to add a new filter with an expression set as `[Category] = [@DocMap]`

The completed report, when run, looks like Figure P4-40.

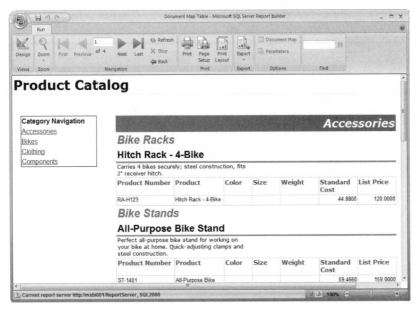

FIGURE P4-40

Final Thoughts

This example showed how a document map could be added to an existing report to permit navigation by filtering the main report. An alternative way of interacting with the main report using the document map technique would be to expand or collapse groups in order to show targeted content.

Credits and Related References

Stephen Dvoranchik of MicroLink, LLC provided a well thought out implementation used as the basis for this example.

PART V
Integrated Reporting Applications

- ► Creating a Report Server Usage Report

- ► Rotating Report Dashboard

- ► Updating Data From a Report

- ► Offline Reporting Using the Report Viewer Control

CREATING A REPORT SERVER USAGE REPORT

Over time, the number of reports in a business environment grows. This is an inevitable fact in most any medium or large organization. In the new age of self-service and user-driven reporting solutions, reports will spring up from multiple sources and, of course, the corporate IT group is charged with managing them all. In this common environment of data sprawl, most reports are duplicates of or similar to copies of others with only minor variations of sorting, grouping, and filtering features.

For IT to consolidate and optimize many reports in a business reporting platform, it must know what users are using reports and how often. It's critical to know how long different reports take to run and when the peak and lull times occur throughout the day for scheduling subscriptions and maintenance tasks.

A server usage report is an indispensible tool for wrangling out-of-control reports. With it, IT leaders can easily answer questions like:

➤ What reports are being run most often?

➤ Who is running certain reports and when?

➤ What reports have excessively long running queries?

➤ What reports don't ever get run?

➤ What similar reports may be candidates for consolidation?

Product Versions

➤ Reporting Services 2000

➤ Reporting Services 2005

➤ Reporting Services 2008

What You'll Need

➤ Connection to the ReportServer with read permission

➤ Three datasets and queries for each report section

➤ Data range parameters

Fortunately, Reporting Services gives you the ability to capture all of these important facts in the report server management databases, ReportServer and ReportServerTempDB. The following example report server usage report comes directly from the ReportServer database without first staging the data in another location. In a full, production solution where you deal with a lot of report activity and may want to analyze usage history over a long period of time, the report usage data should be transformed into a staging database.

The Report Execution Log report, shown in Figure P5-1, contains three separate report sections that each deliver a different set of statistical information. An hourly view of report server usage is an excellent tool for scheduling subscriptions and avoiding resource contention on the server. The daily view shown in Figure P5-1 is better suited for long-term usage and capacity planning.

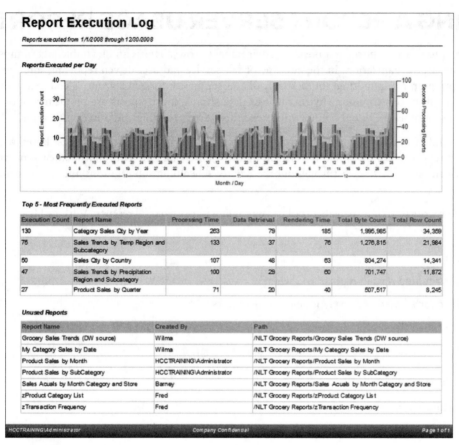

FIGURE P5-1

This report has two parameters, used to set the start and end date of the period being analyzed.

The first section at the top of the report body contains a combination column and line chart, representing the number of report executions during a day. The line chart on the same axis represents the aggregate volume of data sent from a data source.

The second section is a table listing the top five most frequently executed reports for the date selection period.

The last section shows all of the reports that were not executed during the specified period of time. This is an effective tool to find unused or seldom-used reports that can be removed or consolidated with others.

Since Reporting Services was introduced in 2003, the complexity and number of tables in the Report-Server database have increased. In SSRS 2008 R2, there are 31 tables. Only three tables are necessary to return information about report execution details, report details, and the users running reports. For the purposes of this example, the only significant difference affecting this report is that the name of the report execution log table has changed. In SSRS 2000 and 2005, the table name was ExecutionLog and in SSRS 2008 it was changed to ExecutionLogStorage.

In SSRS 2008, two views were added to the ReportServer database to simplify execution log queries and to provide backward compatibility. A view named ExecutionLog covers the ExecutionLogStorage table so references to the former table name remain to be valid in newer product versions.

Designing the Report

The three report sections are driven by three separate datasets. You will create these datasets with common parameters and then add corresponding data regions to the report.

1. Create a data source with a connection to the Report Server database on the production report server or whatever report server you need to analyze.

2. Open SQL Server Management Studio and connect a new query editor window to the ReportServer database.

 The ReportServer database can be given a different name during setup or after using the Reporting Services Configuration Manager. If it has been given a different name, substitute it in the instructions that follow.

3. Design the following query in the SSMS query editor. Note the literal dates range in the sample script. Make whatever changes to these variable assignments are needed to return a good sampling of report execution activity.

```
-- Execution Log:

-- For debugging (remove next 4 lines after pasting to dataset) --
DECLARE @DateFrom Date
DECLARE @DateTo Date
SET @DateFrom = '2008-01-01'
SET @DateTo = '2008-06-30'
-- End debugging script --

SELECT
        DATEPART(Hour, TimeStart) AS ReportYear
      , DATEPART(Month, TimeStart) AS ReportMonth
      , DATEPART(Day, TimeStart) AS ReportDay
      , DATEPART(Hour, TimeStart) AS ReportHour
      , Type
      , COUNT(Name) AS ExecutionCount
      , SUM(TimeDataRetrieval) AS TimeDataRetrievalSum
      , SUM(TimeProcessing) AS TimeProcessingSum
      , SUM(TimeRendering) AS TimeRenderingSum
      , SUM(ByteCount) AS ByteCountSum
      , SUM([RowCount]) AS RowCountSum
FROM
(
    SELECT TimeStart, Catalog.Type, Catalog.Name, TimeDataRetrieval,
  TimeProcessing, TimeRendering, ByteCount, [RowCount]
    FROM
    Catalog INNER JOIN ExecutionLog ON Catalog.ItemID =
```

```
        ExecutionLog.ReportID LEFT OUTER JOIN
    Users ON Catalog.CreatedByID = Users.UserID
    WHERE ExecutionLog.TimeStart BETWEEN @DateFrom AND @DateTo
) AS RE
GROUP BY
        DATEPART(Hour, TimeStart)
    , DATEPART(Month, TimeStart)
    , DATEPART(Day, TimeStart)
    , DATEPART(Hour, TimeStart)
    , Type
ORDER BY
        ReportYear
    , ReportMonth
    , ReportDay
    , ReportHour
    , Type
```

The results in Figure P5-2 show a record of every report execution. This includes the date and time the report request was made. All of the time-based measures are the number of milliseconds elapsed for each event.

	ReportYear	ReportMonth	ReportDay	ReportHour	Type	ExecutionCount	TimeDataRetrievalSum	TimeProcessingSum	TimeRenderingSum	ByteCountSum	RowCountSum
12	10	12	24	10	2	2	0	0	0	0	0
13	11	12	28	11	2	4	0	0	0	0	0
14	12	12	28	12	2	2	0	0	0	0	0
15	14	11	24	14	2	39	3614	3580	12442	4102567	5513
16	14	11	25	14	2	29	2979	2894	10742	3250759	4538
17	15	11	24	15	2	8	64	118	462	602196	814
18	20	11	22	20	2	94	97	852	1452	3877652	1788
19	20	11	24	20	2	40	597	1208	5986	4419617	6159
20	21	11	22	21	2	11	13	164	239	328913	263
21	21	11	24	21	2	49	777	773	3647	4407416	6811
22	22	12	30	22	2	1	50	193	100	40344	711
23	23	11	22	23	2	1	798	851	1152	3986	11

FIGURE P5-2

4. Create a new dataset named ExecutionLog. Copy and paste the query script from SSMS.

5. Delete the four debugging lines at the beginning of the script (starting with DECLARE and SET).

6. Create another dataset named Top5MostFrequent and use the following query script:

```
-- Top 5 Most Frequent:
SELECT TOP 5
        COUNT(Name) AS ExecutionCount
    , Name
    , SUM(TimeDataRetrieval) AS TimeDataRetrievalSum
    , SUM(TimeProcessing) AS TimeProcessingSum
    , SUM(TimeRendering) AS TimeRenderingSum
    , SUM(ByteCount) AS ByteCountSum
    , SUM([RowCount]) AS RowCountSum
FROM
(
    SELECT TimeStart, Catalog.Type, Catalog.Name,
```

```
            TimeDataRetrieval, TimeProcessing, TimeRendering, ByteCount, [RowCount]
        FROM
            Catalog INNER JOIN ExecutionLog ON Catalog.ItemID = ExecutionLog.ReportID
            WHERE ExecutionLog.TimeStart BETWEEN @DateFrom AND @DateTo AND Type = 2
    ) AS RE
    GROUP BY
            Name
    ORDER BY
            COUNT(Name) DESC
        , Name
```

7. Create another dataset named UnusedReports and use the following query script:

```
-- Unused Reports:
SELECT Name, Path, UserName
FROM Catalog INNER JOIN dbo.Users ON Catalog.CreatedByID = Users.UserID
WHERE Type = 2 AND
    Catalog.ItemID NOT IN
    (
        SELECT ExecutionLog.ReportID
        FROM ExecutionLog
        WHERE ExecutionLog.TimeStart BETWEEN @DateFrom AND @DateTo
    )
    ORDER BY Name
```

8. The specific report design elements and specific features may be designed according to your personal preference. Using the finished sample report as a model, build the following elements:

   a. Add a column chart based on the ExecutionLog dataset.

   b. Use the ExecutionCount field for the series value.

   c. Add two Category axis groups for the ReportMonth and ReportDay fields.

   d. If you are using SSRS 2008, add a second series using the TimeRenderingSum field. Right click on this field in the Data pane and change the chart type for this series to a line chart.

   Figure P5-3 shows the Report Builder 3.0 designer. The steps for designing the report in Report Builder 2.0 for SSRS 2008 are the same. The chart designer looks a little different but has similar functionality.

9. Add table data regions for the Top5MostFrequent and UnusedReports datasets. Style these to your liking.

10. Add appropriate report and page headers as well as textboxes to label each data region.

The execution log table rows are automatically purged after 60 days by default. This setting may be modified in Report Manager's *Site Settings* page. The setting is labeled *Remove log entries older than this number of days*. If you want to report server usage older than a few months, it's a good idea to transform this data to an archive table and use this in the query rather than the live execution log table. You can create an SSIS package to import the contents of the ExecutionLog to another table.

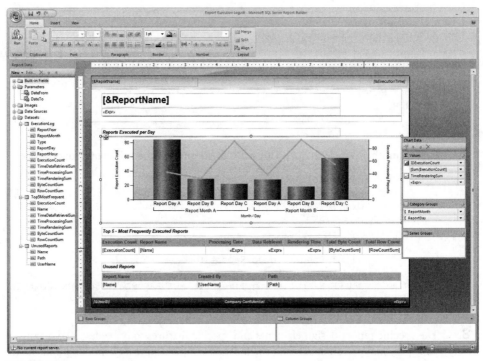

FIGURE P5-3

Final Thoughts

This report is an excellent resource for the system administrator to use to monitor the report server pulse. Using this and similar reports, you can check your report server at regular intervals to better understand the report and data source usage. If you know what reports are being run and who is running them, you have a much better chance of proactively meeting user needs and mitigating issues before they become problems.

Report solution architects and technical managers should pay attention to long-running queries, peak and idle periods, and overall server capacity and loads. Also, knowing which reports are not being used can help you remove unnecessary reports from the server and to consolidate those that can better meet more users' needs with fewer reports.

ROTATING REPORT DASHBOARD

Dashboards are a specific type of user interface that are designed in a way that permits the most important and actionable information to be displayed on a single main page. The challenge with designing dashboards is how to use the space to convey all the important content required to be viewed. One really creative solution, rotating many reports within a single report, will be explored in this recipe. The rotating reports imitate a familiar web design for advertisements that change within a confined area on a website.

This recipe shows how to add subreports to a main report and supplement with code to keep track of the next subreport to be displayed.

Product Versions

➤   Reporting Services 2000

➤   Reporting Services 2005

➤   Reporting Services 2008

What You'll Need

➤   AdventureWorks2008 sample reports or alternative reports to be called by main report subreports

➤   A set of reports that can be called from a main report using subreports

➤   A custom function to increment an integer value

➤   A textbox with an expression to increment the counter on report auto refresh by calling the custom function

➤   An expression to modify the visibility of each subreport

➤   To set the main report to auto refresh after a designated period of time

Designing the Report

This example creates a new empty report that contains subreports that are found within the Adventure-Works2008 sample reports.

The completed report, when run, will look like Figures P5-4, P5-5, and P5-6.

1.   Start by designing a report and inserting three subreports into the report body.

2.   Change the AutoRefresh report property to a value that represents the number of seconds (10, for example) that a report will display before switching to a different report.

3.   For each subreport (object) added to the report, set the report used by this report as a subreport in the subreport properties (the example uses the Company Sales 2008, Product Line Sales 2008, and Employee Sales Summary 2008 AdventureWorks 2008 sample reports).

FIGURE P5-4

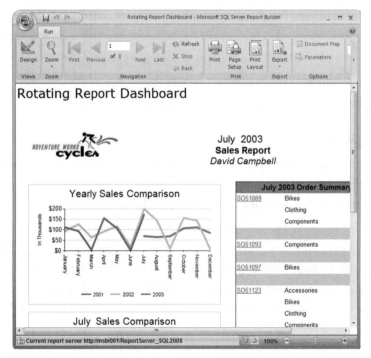

FIGURE P5-5

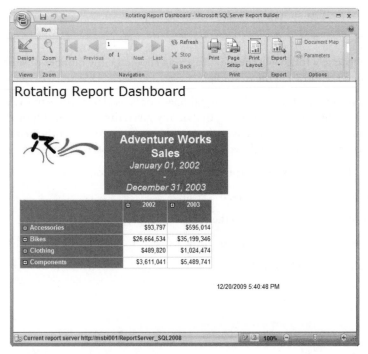

FIGURE P5-6

4. In the main hosting report's properties, enter the following IncrementCount() function code:

```
Public Shared iCount As Integer

Public Function IncrementCount() As Integer
    iCount = iCount + 1
    Return iCount
End Function
```

5. Add a textbox below the report title and before the subreports.

6. Set the textbox's value to the following expression that will increment a counter using the newly implemented IncrementCount() function code:

```
=Code.IncrementCount()
```

7. Set the textbox's visibility to hidden so that the counter value will not be visible for the report user.

8. Set the visibility of the first subreport to the following expression:

```
=IIF(Code.iCount Mod 3 = 0, false, true)
```

The number immediately following the Mod function should be the number of subreports included in the main report (3 in the example).

The number following the Mod function's equal operator is used to increment each successive subreport's visibility property ensuring that at any given time only one report will be visible. This number is zero based and as such should be set to zero (0) for the first subreport, one (1) for the second subreport, and two (2) for the third subreport.

9. Set the visibility of the second subreport to the following expression:

```
=IIF(Code.iCount Mod 3 = 1, false, true)
```

10. Set the visibility of the third subreport to the following expression:

```
=IIF(Code.iCount Mod 3 = 2, false, true)
```

The report designer should look like Figure P5-7.

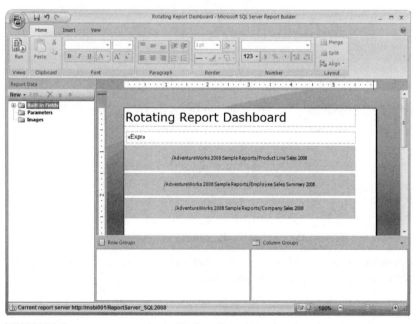

FIGURE P5-7

Final Thoughts

This example showed how a single report with auto refresh configured can display a different subreport at each refresh. The visibility of the subreports was set by an expression that evaluated the current counter, which was implemented by a custom function along with an expression on a text box.

Credits and Related References

Stephen Dvoranchik of MicroLink, LLC provided a well thought out implementation that is the basis for this example.

UPDATING DATA FROM A REPORT

It's not often that a book provides the correct method to execute a bad idea, but that is exactly what this recipe does. Allowing report users to alter data from the report itself can have so many bad effects that listing them here is not practical, but the fact is that it is possible to update, insert, or delete data from a report with a little bit of creativity and good use of parameters. I am even aware of a situation where this ability was requested by a client and implemented with great success. Even if you never have the opportunity to design reports using these techniques, this recipe is a good segue for some of the more playful examples like the Hangman and Sea Battle reports later in this book.

Product Versions

➤ Reporting Services 2000

➤ Reporting Services 2005

➤ Reporting Services 2008

What You'll Need

➤ A shared data source named AdventureWorksDW referencing either Adventure-WorksDW2005 or 2008

➤ An open mind and warranted trepidation

Designing the Report

For this recipe, you will use the DimEmployees table within AdventureWorksDW to create a report that allows the user to view personnel filtered by job title within a tablix. This report will have two parameters: A drop-down displaying the various job titles at Adventure Works and a hidden parameter that executes your update statement.

1. From SQL Server Management Studio, connect to the AdventureWorksDW2008 database and execute the stored procedures provided in the code segment below in a query window. They will respectively create the source data for the Job Title parameter, the update statement for the hidden parameter, and the source for the lone tablix within the report. There are portions of the last stored procedure that may stand out as being odd or unnecessary on the surface. You'll address this a bit later.

```
CREATE PROCEDURE [usp_Job_Titles]
AS
BEGIN
SET NOCOUNT ON;

SELECT DISTINCT Title AS JobTitle
FROM DimEmployee
ORDER BY Title ASC
END
GO

CREATE PROCEDURE usp_Update_Employee_EndDate
        @TerminatedEmployeeKey INT
```

```
          ,@JobTitle NVARCHAR(100)
AS
BEGIN
SET NOCOUNT ON;

UPDATE DimEmployee
SET EndDate = CAST(GETDATE() AS DATE), [Status] = NULL
WHERE EmployeeKey = @TerminatedEmployeeKey
END
GO

CREATE PROCEDURE [usp_Current_Employees_By_Job_Title]
          @JobTitle NVARCHAR(100)
          ,@TerminatedEmployeeKey INT
AS
BEGIN
SET NOCOUNT ON;

SELECT
          EmployeeKey
          ,FirstName
          ,LastName
          ,Title AS JobTitle
          ,StartDate
          ,EndDate
FROM dbo.DimEmployee
WHERE Title = @JobTitle AND EndDate IS NULL
          AND EmployeeKey <> ISNULL(@TerminatedEmployeeKey,-9999)
END
GO
```

2. Right-click the AdventureWorksDW data source in the Report Data menu in the far left pane in Report Builder and choose the Add Dataset option. In the Dataset Properties dialog box (see Figure P5-8) enter JobTitle for the Field Name entry and use AdventureWorksDW for the data source. For the Query Type radio box choose Stored Procedure and select usp_Job_Titles from the drop-down list box. In the Fields menu, make sure that JobTitle is pre-populated for the Field Name and Field Source. If the Field Name and Field Source entries are not pre-populated, either type them manually or go back to the Query menu and press the Refresh Fields button. Press OK to exit the Dataset Properties dialog box.

3. Create another new dataset by right-clicking the AdventureWorksDW data source and name it Employees. As you did in Step 2, choose the stored procedure radio button and select the usp_Current_Employees_By_Job_Title stored procedure. In the Parameters menu, ensure that the @JobTitle Parameter Name is mapped to the @JobTitle Parameter Value and the @TerminatedEmployeeKey Parameter Name is mapped to the @TerminatedEmployeeKey Parameter Value. All values in the Fields menu should already be populated with the Field Names EmployeeKey, FirstName, LastName, Title, StartDate, and EndDate along with their Fields Sources of the same name. If this is not the case, return to the Query menu and press the Refresh Fields button.

4. The last dataset you will create will be named TerminatedEmployee, and it will rely on the usp_Update_Employee_EndDate stored procedure. In the Parameters menu, make sure that the @TerminatedEmployeeKey Parameter Name exists with a Parameter Value of the same name. This should also be the case for the @JobTitle Parameter name. Figure P5-9 shows the configuration for this dataset's parameters. This dataset will not have any field values.

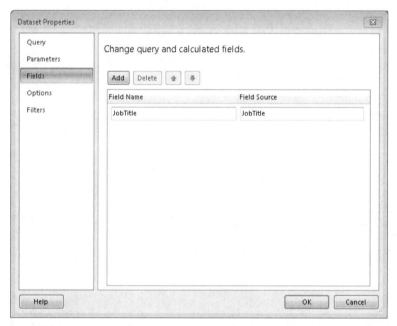

FIGURE P5-8

Now that all of your datasets are created you need to put them to use in a way that allows you to run your report as you would any other report, with the exception that this report will allow you to update the underlying data via the usp_Update_Employee_EndDate stored procedure. This is going to take some creative but not difficult use of your report parameters.

1. Make sure that the report parameter named JobTitle has a prompt name of Job Title, is of type text, and is set to be visible. In the Available Values menu in the left navigation pane of the Report Parameters Properties dialog, choose the Get values from a query radio button and choose JobTitle, JobTitle, and JobTitle for the dataset, Value field, and Label field drop-downs as shown below in Figure P5-10. Press OK to exit the Report Parameter Properties dialog box.

2. Create another report parameter with a name of TerminatedEmployeeKey, a prompt value of TerminatedEmployeeKey (this parameter will be hidden so the name does not need to be user friendly), a data type of Integer, choose to allow null values, and choose to make it hidden. In the Available values menu, choose the radio button labeled None and in the Default Values menu, choose the Specify values radio button. From here, press the Add button and enter NULL as the default value. Press OK to exit the Report Parameter Properties dialog box.

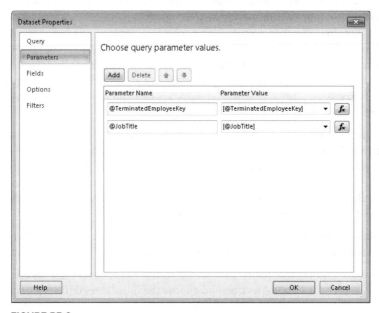

FIGURE P5-9

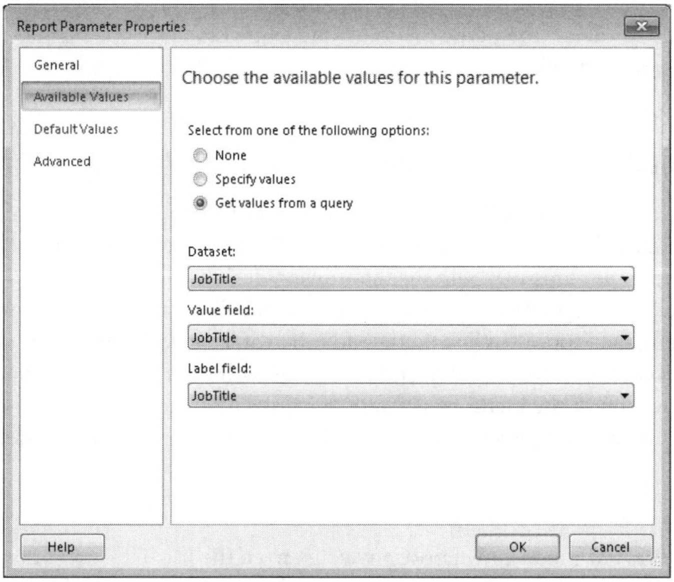

FIGURE P5-10

The report parameter TerminatedEmployeeKey is going to be the entity that updates the DimEmployee table, but you won't require any updates during the initial run of this report. In fact, there may be many occasions where the report user simply needs to view current employees and their job titles without having to terminate anyone. Because of this, you want the TerminatedEmployeeKey parameter to lay dormant — for lack of a better term. This dormancy is accomplished by making the TerminatedEmployeeKey hidden (not allowing direct user input to the parameter before report execution) and by defaulting the value of @TerminatedEmployeeKey to NULL. If the stored procedure parameter @TerminatedEmployeeKey is NULL, it will not satisfy any EmployeeKey value in the DimEmployee table, and thus no DimEmployee row will be updated.

If the TerminatedEmployeeKey parameter does not do anything initially, how do any rows ever get updated? That's where the report tablix comes in. The tablix will list all descriptive details about your employees that the usp_Current_Employees_By_Job_Title returns along with an additional column that, when clicked, reruns the report, except this execution calls the TerminatedEmployeeKey and passes in a non-null value, effectively updating the DimEmployee table and terminating the unlucky employee.

3. From the toolbox, drag and drop a table onto the report design area and give it four columns, a header row, and a details row. You do not need the footer row.

4. Click on the table to ensure that focus is set on it. From the Properties pane find the DatasetName attribute under the General section and choose the Employees dataset from the dropdown list box.

5. In the column header textboxes type the following names for the columns: Name, Title, and Start Date. The fourth column does not require a name.

6. In the text boxes for the detail row, type the following expressions for the Name, Title, and Start Date columns, respectively.

```
=Fields!LastName.Value & ", " & Fields!FirstName.Value
=Fields!Title.Value
=FormatDateTime(Fields!StartDate.Value,DateFormat.ShortDate)
```

7. In the detail row textbox for the column without a name, type the word Terminate. From the properties pane, find the Font category and expand the Font node within it. Under TextDecoration, choose Underline. This will help the report user identify this as a link to perform an action. Find the Action category in the properties pane, and click the ellipsis. From the Text Box Properties dialog that appears, click on the radio button labeled Go to report and choose the Current Employees report you are currently working within, as shown in Figure P5-11. In the parameters section of the menu, make sure that JobTitle is selected as the value for the JobTitle parameter and EmployeeKey is selected as the value for the TerminatedEmployeeKey parameter.

Click OK to exit.

8. Place the report in Preview mode and choose any value from the Job Title drop-down list box and click the View Report button. Once the report has been rendered click the Terminate link in any of the rows. The newly rendered report will now omit the employee who was chosen to terminate. In Figure P5-12 you have chosen the Tool Designer job title. Figure P5-13 displays the results of clicking the Terminate link for the Adventure Works employee Thierry D'Hers.

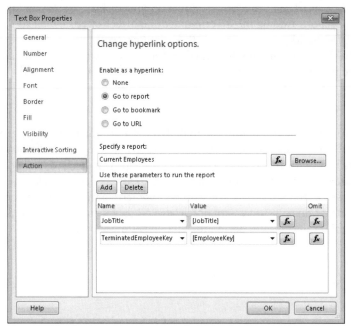

FIGURE P5-11

Name	Title	Start Date	
D'Hers, Thierry		1/11/1998	Terminate
Galvin, Janice		1/23/2001	Terminate

FIGURE P5-12

Name	Title	Start Date	
Galvin, Janice		1/23/2001	Terminate

FIGURE P5-13

You now have a working report that enables users to update the DimEmployees by simply clicking a link supplied for each of the employees' rows. Clicking this link reruns the report, and this time an explicit value is supplied to the TerminatedEmployeeKey parameter.

For the newly executed version of the report to display the updated personnel list for the chosen job title, a little trick has to be used. When you look at the usp_Current_Employees_By_Job_Title stored procedure, @TerminatedEmployeeKey looks to be extraneous. In theory, if the Terminate link is clicked then the tablix displaying employee information should be updated when the report is rerun because the DimEmployee table has been updated, but this is not the case. If the TerminatedEmployeeKey parameter were not a part of the usp_Current_Employees_By_Job_Title stored procedure, then Reporting Services would recognize that you've called the usp_Current_Employees_By_Job_Title stored procedure once again with the exact same value for the @JobTitle parameter. Instead of running a fresh instance of the report you'd get the same one again — with the employee just terminated still being displayed. It's actually a smart feature that cuts down on unnecessary processing but it yields unwanted behavior for your report. Adding the @TerminatedEmployeeKey parameter to the usp_Current_Employees_By_Job_Title stored procedure forces the stored procedure to be dependent on that parameter. This way, when the Terminate link is clicked and the report is rerun, a new call to SQL Server to execute the stored procedure is necessary because the parameters have changed.

Final Thoughts

Providing an opportunity for report users to alter the underlying data of the report they are viewing from the report itself can be a precarious situation. It can threaten data integrity, but when used effectively it opens up new possibilities for report interaction. In the recipe just covered, we went through the exercise of updating data; however, alterations can be made to just as fluently delete or insert data. The update option was chosen as the safest-case scenario because terminated employees occurred as "soft deletes," which means that no rows were actually deleted — they were just marked as no longer active. Applying tactics like this offers a safer option for these types of reports.

OFFLINE REPORTING USING THE REPORT VIEWER CONTROL

It commonly happens that managers, developers, or customers want to replace legacy, paper reports with electronic versions that have the same look and feel. Using tools or other components from SQL Server Reporting Services (SSRS), this task has just gotten that much easier.

This task can be accomplished quite easily using the combination of ASP.NET and the Microsoft Report Viewer control. In addition, we can truly reflect the power of this control through this recipe by producing an offline report or a dynamically generated report without connecting to a report server.

Product Versions

➤   Reporting Services 2005

➤   Reporting Services 2008

What You'll Need

➤   AdventureWorks2008 or 2005 Sample Database

➤   Visual Studio with Visual Web Developer

➤   Detail Report

➤   An understanding of ASP.NET and (C# or VB.NET)

➤   An understanding of Report Data sources

This recipe uses a common scenario that shows the advantages of using SSRS in an integrated solution. For example, when a technician or repair person has to come to your house or jobsite to perform a repair, the visit always ends with a receipt delivered to the customer. However, unless the charges have been agreed on beforehand, the technician may be required to handwrite the expenses and deliver a marked-up receipt. The technique developed in this recipe will generate a high quality, professional looking receipt generated on the fly and without an Internet connection.

Using the Microsoft Report Viewer control, this is entirely possible and quite simple. To use this recipe, you need to have Internet Information Services (IIS) installed and either SQL Server or SQL Server Express (the free edition of SQL Server), which for field technicians is a very common scenario. Please note that SSRS 2008 does not require IIS; however, for this example, you are integrating it with a web form application, which does require ISS. (ASP.NET Development Web Server will also work for this exercise.)

Designing the Report

1.   To get started, create a new ASP.NET Web Site Project using Visual Studio and call it AdventureWorks (see Figure P5-14).

This recipe uses Visual C#; however, it also includes code samples for Visual Basic.NET.

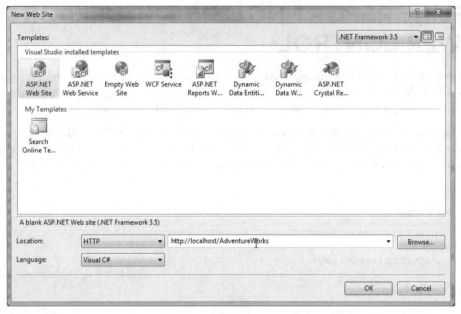

FIGURE P5-14

2. Right-click on the web project, add a new report (see Figure P5-15), and name it SalesOrderReport.rdlc.

3. Open the new report and click the link to add a new dataset.

FIGURE P5-15

This adds a new XML schema file to your solution within the App_Code folder. It is the first of two datasets to be added to your solution. The second will be called AdventureWorksLines. You add that later in this recipe.

4. Double-click the .xsd file in your solution and then right-click the design surface to add a new Data Table (see Figure P5-16).

5. Rename the dataset to AdventureWorks and add the columns shown in Figure P5-17 to your Data Table.

6. Drag a Table control from the Report Toolbox, adding the appropriate labels and formatting.

FIGURE P5-16

7. Right-click to view the properties of the table. On the first tab, you can assign the dataset to this table.

This can be done by viewing the properties of the table and, from the dropdown list on the General page, choosing the AdventureWorks dataset.

8. Drag the data columns on the design of your report and format how you like.

Unlike editing standard reports, or reports with .rdl file extensions, you don't have the option to preview the report and the data source tabs are not listed on the report. If you renamed the file and gave it an .rdl extension, then when you open the report in a standard Visual Studio Report

FIGURE P5-17

project, the data source tab and preview options would appear and you could choose to preview the report against actual data.

9. Add an additional dataset to your solution called AdventureWorksLines.

Note that, when referencing this dataset in the code, the name you will provide is Adventure-WorksDS_AdventureWorks.

10. Add a new Data Table to the dataset and add the list of columns shown in Figure P5-18.

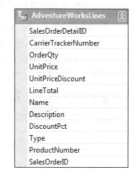

11. Add an additional table to your report and assign the data source property of the table to this dataset, formatting as necessary. This dataset will be referenced with the name AdventureWorksLinesD-S_AdventureWorksLines.

12. Once your data sources have been added to the report, drag each column onto the report, formatting as shown in Figure P5-19.

Note that the header of the report does not contain any tables, but rather four textbox controls which display a company address along with the sales order parameter.

FIGURE P5-18

What this recipe has demonstrated so far is pretty standard in terms of generating report-style invoice formats that can be used to generate receipts or just about any other type of standard document. This recipe becomes interesting during the next phase when you make the report available for use offline (that is, when it's not dependent on SSRS).

To accomplish this, there are a few prerequisites to define to make this example work. These are presented in the following section.

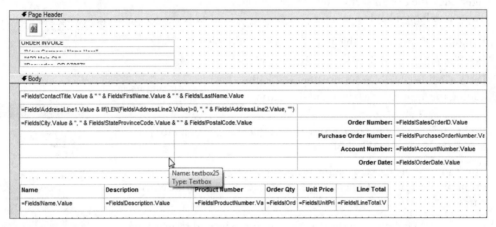

FIGURE P5-19

Computer Requirements and Prerequisites

This technique uses ASP.NET and assumes you are running IIS locally on a laptop. (ASP.NET development web server is also sufficient.) The base framework or version of ASP.NET should be at least 2.0; however, earlier versions may work as well. This technique also uses IIS 6.0 for Windows.

In addition, you will be running the database locally. The ideal software for this is SQL Express (formerly known as MSDE from the 2000 version). SQL Express is a free download from Microsoft and can easily be distributed to multiple users without licensing. The biggest limitation of SQL Express is the size limitation for user data per database. While that is not a factor with this recipe, in a production environment you would need to employ a very good data syncing architecture to ensure that your database will never get very big.

In addition to having the framework installed on the client computer, you need to include the Report View Distributable, which is also a free download from Microsoft. To obtain this download, simply open your favorite search engine and input "report viewer control download." It will likely be among the first items listed.

Finally, in order for the application to render correctly, the application pool within IIS needs to be the Classic .NET App Pool (see Figure P5-20).

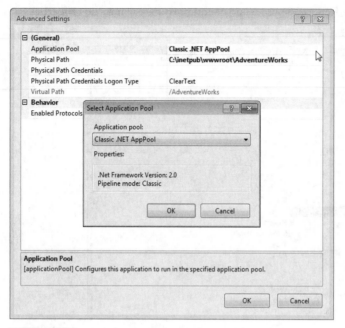

FIGURE P5-20

Wiring Up the Report

Once the requirements mentioned in the previous section are in place, you are ready to wire-up the offline reporting capability.

1. By default, the web site should include an active server page called `Default.aspx`, and in the toolbar, you should see the options shown in Figure P5-21 under your Reporting node.

2. In the design view of your page, drag the MicrosoftReportViewer control to the place of your choice.

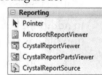

FIGURE P5-21

The HTML code it generates will look something like the following code sample. Note that when you drag the control onto the page, it will default many of the properties for you.

```
<rsweb:ReportViewer ID="ReportViewer1" runat="server" Font-Names="Verdana"
        Font-Size="8pt" Height="400px" Width="821px">
    <LocalReport DisplayName="SalesOrderDetail"
        EnableHyperlinks="True"
    </LocalReport>
</rsweb:ReportViewer>
```

Note that the display name property is set to SalesOrderDetail. When the PDF document is generated, that is what the control will use to name the file. Later you will notice that the file rendered to the screen will be named SalesOrderDetail.pdf. In addition, the local report path will be set dynamically at runtime in the code-behind. That way you can avoid directly inputting the physical path of the report and instead determine the physical path when the report is loaded.

3. In Design Mode, select the Report Viewer Control and press F4 to view the properties (see Figure P5-22).

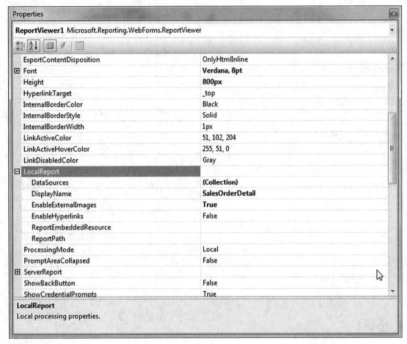

FIGURE P5-22

There are additional properties which can be set; however, the important ones include ReportPath, DisplayName, and ProcessingMode.

In addition, before you can run the application in a browser you should verify that the web configuration file has the proper reference to the Report Viewer binary.

1. Browse to the web configuration file (web.config) in your solution and open the file. Make sure the build provider shown in the following code has been added.

```
<buildProviders>
<add extension=".rdlc" type="Microsoft.Reporting.RdlBuildProvider,
    Microsoft.ReportViewer.Common, Version=9.0.0.0, Culture=neutral,
    PublicKeyToken=b03f5f7f11d50a3a"/>
</buildProviders>
```

2. In the configSections segment of web.config, add this data configuration section:

```
<section name="dataConfiguration"
type="Microsoft.Practices.EnterpriseLibrary.
 Data.Configuration.DatabaseSettings,
Microsoft.Practices.EnterpriseLibrary.Data"/>
```

3. In web.config, verify that the data source has been properly configured, as shown here:

```
<dataConfiguration defaultDatabase="AdventureWorks"/>
<connectionStrings>
```

```
<add name="AdventureWorks" providerName="System.Data.SqlClient"
connectionString=
    "data source=localhost;initial catalog=AdventureWorks;User

        ID=AdventureWorks;
            Password=pass@word1"/>
        </connectionStrings>
```

Finally, within IIS, this recipe uses the Classic .NET application pool, which has a "Classic" managed pipeline mode. This is a quick fix to allow the application to get up and running quickly.

For simplicity's sake, this technique uses Microsoft's Enterprise Library binaries and what used to be referred to as the SqlHelper class to connect to the database. These are included in the code sample for this recipe on Wrox.com.

The partial class of the web form uses some pretty basic .NET 2.0 objects, including the List<> method and grabbing the SalesOrderID from the query string. But before diving into that, let's make sure the using declarations are clearly defined.

Programming the Code-Behind

In this section you programmatically add the data to the report. By doing this at run time, you can use the appropriate business objects and you won't have to rely simply on straight T-SQL.

1. In the references section of the solution, right-click to add a reference to the aforementioned Enterprise Library binaries (data).

2. Double-click on the code-behind file and in addition to the default declarations (which have been included for you), add the following declarations:

- ➤ System.Text
- ➤ Microsoft.Practices.EnterpriseLibrary.Data;
- ➤ Microsoft.Practices.EnterpriseLibrary.Data.Sql
- ➤ System.Data.Common
- ➤ Microsoft.Reporting.WebForms

C#

```
using System;
using System.Data;
using System.Collections.Generic;
using System.Linq;
using System.Web;
using System.Web.UI;
using System.Web.UI.WebControls;
using System.Text;
using System.Data.SqlClient;
using Microsoft.Practices.EnterpriseLibrary.Data;
using Microsoft.Practices.EnterpriseLibrary.Data.Sql;
using System.Data.Common;
using Microsoft.Reporting.WebForms;
```

VB.NET

```
Imports System
Imports System.Data
```

```
Imports System.Collections.Generic
Imports System.Linq
Imports System.Web
Imports System.Web.UI
Imports System.Web.UI.WebControls
Imports System.Text
Imports System.Data.SqlClient
Imports Microsoft.Practices.EnterpriseLibrary.Data
Imports Microsoft.Practices.EnterpriseLibrary.Data.Sql
Imports System.Data.Common
Imports Microsoft.Reporting.WebForms
```

The List<> method mentioned in the previous section is part of the System.Collections. Generic namespace and allows you to pass an enumerated collection of any type of object and make it strongly typed. In this technique, you pass a collection of datasets to the report control.

Within the member declaration portion of the page, you need to define a few output parameters and byte array parameters (as shown in the following code). These parameters are required when you make the call to the report control, and the Render method will accept these output parameters.

1. Define 5 private members:

➤ Three strings: _mimeType, _encoding, and _fileNameExtension

➤ One byte array: (byte[]), _pdfDocument

➤ One integer: _salesOrderID

These members can be very easily utilized once the report control has rendered the report. For example, if you wanted to save the document to the database as an image, the byte array will be filled with the converted report.

C#

```
private int _salesOrderID;
private byte[] _pdfDocument;
private string _mimeType, _encoding, _fileNameExtension;
```

VB.NET

```
Private _salesOrderID As Integer
Private _pdfDocument As Byte()
Private _mimeType As String, _encoding As String, _fileNameExtension As String
```

2. Replace the Page_Load method with the following code.

This code will assign the private member _salesOrderID from the query string and also call the most important method, BindData.

C#

```
protected void Page_Load(object sender, EventArgs e)
{
    this.EnableViewState = true;
    this.ReportViewer1.EnableViewState = true;

    int.TryParse(Request["salesOrderID"], out _salesOrderID);
```

```
      if (!IsPostBack)
         BindData();
}
```

VB.NET

```
Protected Sub Page_Load(ByVal sender As Object, ByVal e As EventArgs)
    Me.EnableViewState = True
    Me.ReportViewer1.EnableViewState = True

    Integer.TryParse(Request("salesOrderID"), _salesOrderID)

    If Not IsPostBack Then
        BindData()
    End If
End Sub
```

The next code is called from the Page Load method. It is the BindData method that connects to the database and generates the required datasets needed to populate the report. Again, this technique uses standard practices to make efficient use of what is already available using the least amount of code possible.

3. Add the following code to create your BindData method.

Note that before you will be able to run the report, you need to create two stored procedures to provide the data and fill the datasets.

C#

```
private void BindData()
    {
        List<DataSet> dataSetList = new List<DataSet>();
        List<ReportParameter> parmList = new List<ReportParameter>();

        //create the database connection
        Database m_dbObject = DatabaseFactory.CreateDatabase();
        DbCommand dbCommand = m_dbObject.GetStoredProcCommand
          ("uspGetSalesOrderHeader");
        m_dbObject.AddInParameter(dbCommand, "@SalesOrderID",
          DbType.Int32, _salesOrderID);

        DataSet dsHeader = new DataSet();
        //assign the dataset to the ExecuteDataSet method
        dsHeader = m_dbObject.ExecuteDataSet(dbCommand);
        dsHeader.DataSetName = "AdventureWorksDS_AdventureWorks";
        dataSetList.Add(dsHeader);

        //re-assign the command to be the detail
        dbCommand = m_dbObject.GetStoredProcCommand("uspGetSalesOrderDetail");
        m_dbObject.AddInParameter(dbCommand, "@SalesOrderID",
            DbType.Int32, _salesOrderID);

        DataSet dsDetail = new DataSet();
        dsDetail = m_dbObject.ExecuteDataSet(dbCommand);
        dsDetail.DataSetName = "AdventureWorksLinesDS_AdventureWorksLines";
    dataSetList.Add(dsDetail);
        parmList.Add(new ReportParameter("LogoUrl", string.Format
```

```
                    ("http{0}://{1}/{2}AdventureWorksLogo.jpg",
                     (Request.ServerVariables["https"] == "on" ? "s" : string.Empty),
                     Request.ServerVariables["HTTP_HOST"],
                     GetDirectory(Request.ServerVariables["script_name"])))));

            if (_salesOrderID > 0)
                BindReportControl(dataSetList, "SalesOrderReport.rdlc", parmList);

    }
    public string GetDirectory(string strFullPath)
    {
        char[] delimiters = { '/', '\\' };
        int nFileName = strFullPath.LastIndexOfAny(delimiters);
        return strFullPath.Substring(0, nFileName + 1);
    }
```

VB.NET

```
Private Sub BindData()
    Dim dataSetList As New List(Of DataSet)()
    Dim parmList As New List(Of ReportParameter)()

    'create the database connection
    Dim m_dbObject As Database = DatabaseFactory.CreateDatabase()
    Dim dbCommand As DbCommand = m_dbObject.GetStoredProcCommand
      ("uspGetSalesOrderHeader")
    m_dbObject.AddInParameter(dbCommand, "@SalesOrderID", DbType.Int32,
      _salesOrderID)

    Dim dsHeader As New DataSet()
    'assign the dataset to the ExecuteDataSet method
    dsHeader = m_dbObject.ExecuteDataSet(dbCommand)
    dsHeader.DataSetName = "AdventureWorksDS_AdventureWorks"
    dataSetList.Add(dsHeader)

    're-assign the command to be the detail
    dbCommand = m_dbObject.GetStoredProcCommand("uspGetSalesOrderDetail")
    m_dbObject.AddInParameter(dbCommand, "@SalesOrderID", DbType.Int32,
      _salesOrderID)

    Dim dsDetail As New DataSet()
    dsDetail = m_dbObject.ExecuteDataSet(dbCommand)
    dsDetail.DataSetName = "AdventureWorksLinesDS_AdventureWorksLines"
    dataSetList.Add(dsDetail)

    ' Passing in the datasets, the name of the report, and a parameter list.
    ' * Any external paramaters which need to be automatically passed to the
          report the data
    ' * parameters can be handled here, such as image url's for branding
    ' *

    parmList.Add(New ReportParameter("LogoUrl", String.Format
      ("http{0}://{1}/{2}AdventureWorksLogo.jpg", (If(Request.ServerVariables
      ("https") = "on", "s", String.Empty)), Request.ServerVariables("HTTP_HOST"),
      GetDirectory(Request.ServerVariables("script_name")))))
```

```
        If salesOrderID > 0 Then
            BindReportControl(dataSetList, "SalesOrderReport.rdlc", parmList)

        End If
    End Sub
    Public Function GetDirectory(ByVal strFullPath As String) As String
        Dim delimiters As Char() = {"/"c, "\"c}
        Dim nFileName As Integer = strFullPath.LastIndexOfAny(delimiters)
        Return strFullPath.Substring(0, nFileName + 1)
    End Function
```

The `BindReportControl` method truly interacts with the Report Viewer Control. This method adds the datasets to the report and any parameters you need to set. You can do whatever you want with the output of the `Render` method, which in this case returns a byte array. As mentioned earlier, one scenario would be to add the byte array to the database and store the document, which allows the report that was generated on the technician's remote laptop to be viewed by office staff after a data sync.

4. Add the following code to create your `BindReportControl` method.

C#

```csharp
public void BindReportControl(List<DataSet> dataSetList,
    string reportName,
    List<ReportParameter> parmList)
    {
        ReportViewer1.ProcessingMode = ProcessingMode.Local;

        LocalReport localReport = ReportViewer1.LocalReport as LocalReport;

        localReport.ReportPath = reportName;

        //iterate through each dataset in the list and add them to the Report
        //Datasource
        foreach (DataSet ds in dataSetList)
        {
            ReportDataSource rDS = new ReportDataSource();
            rDS.Name = ds.DataSetName;
            rDS.Value = ds.Tables[0];
            localReport.DataSources.Add(rDS);
        }
        //any additional parameters, add them to the report here
        if (parmList != null && parmList.Count > 0)
        {
            localReport.SetParameters(parmList);
        }
        _mimeType = string.Empty;
        _encoding = string.Empty;
        _fileNameExtension = ".pdf";
        string[] streams = null;
        Warning[] warnings = null;

        _pdfDocument = localReport.Render("PDF",
            string.Empty,
```

```
                out _mimeType,
                out _encoding,
                out _fileNameExtension,
                out streams,
                out warnings);

        }
```

VB.NET

```
Public Sub BindReportControl(ByVal dataSetList As List(Of DataSet), ByVal
    reportName As String,
 ByVal parmList As List(Of ReportParameter))
        ReportViewer1.ProcessingMode = ProcessingMode.Local

        Dim localReport As LocalReport = TryCast(ReportViewer1.LocalReport,
            LocalReport)

        localReport.ReportPath = reportName

        'iterate through each dataset in the list and add them to the Report Datasource
        For Each ds As DataSet In dataSetList
            Dim rDS As New ReportDataSource()
            rDS.Name = ds.DataSetName
            rDS.Value = ds.Tables(0)
            localReport.DataSources.Add(rDS)
        Next
        'any additional parameters, add them to the report here
        If parmList IsNot Nothing AndAlso parmList.Count > 0 Then
            localReport.SetParameters(parmList)
        End If
        _mimeType = String.Empty
        _encoding = String.Empty
        _fileNameExtension = ".pdf"
        Dim streams As String() = Nothing
        Dim warnings As Warning() = Nothing


        _pdfDocument = localReport.Render("PDF", String.Empty, _mimeType, _encoding,
          _fileNameExtension, streams, _
        warnings)
    End Sub
```

5. Format the report. (This can be done directly inside the report.)

6. Render the report and view the output. The Report Viewer Control displays two formats for saving the file in the toolbox control that users can select from: Excel and PDF.

7. Use the following code to create two new stored procedures that will return the dataset queries to be passed to the report control.

```
CREATE PROCEDURE uspGetSalesOrderHeader
    @SalesOrderID int
AS
```

```
SELECT TOP 1
    Person.Contact.Title
    , Person.Contact.FirstName
    , Person.Contact.LastName
    , Person.Contact.Suffix
    , Person.Contact.EmailAddress
    , Sales.SalesTerritory.Name
    , Sales.SalesOrderHeader.OrderDate
    , Sales.SalesOrderHeader.PurchaseOrderNumber
    , Sales.SalesOrderHeader.AccountNumber
    , Person.Address.AddressLine1
    , Person.Address.AddressLine2
    , Person.Address.City
    , Person.Address.PostalCode
    , Person.StateProvince.StateProvinceCode
    , Sales.SalesOrderHeader.SalesOrderID
FROM Sales.SalesOrderHeader
    INNER JOIN
    Sales.SalesPerson
    ON Sales.SalesOrderHeader.SalesPersonID = Sales.SalesPerson.SalesPersonID
    INNER JOIN Sales.Customer
    ON Sales.SalesOrderHeader.CustomerID = Sales.Customer.CustomerID
    INNER JOIN Person.Contact
    ON Sales.SalesOrderHeader.ContactID = Person.Contact.ContactID
    INNER JOIN Sales.SalesTerritory
    ON Sales.SalesOrderHeader.TerritoryID = Sales.SalesTerritory.TerritoryID
    AND Sales.SalesPerson.TerritoryID = Sales.SalesTerritory.TerritoryID
    AND Sales.Customer.TerritoryID = Sales.SalesTerritory.TerritoryID
    INNER JOIN Person.Address
    ON Sales.SalesOrderHeader.BillToAddressID = Person.Address.AddressID
    AND Sales.SalesOrderHeader.ShipToAddressID = Person.Address.AddressID
    INNER JOIN Person.StateProvince
    ON Sales.SalesTerritory.TerritoryID = Person.StateProvince.TerritoryID
    AND Sales.SalesTerritory.TerritoryID = Person.StateProvince.TerritoryID
WHERE     (Sales.SalesOrderHeader.SalesOrderID = @SalesOrderID)
Go
CREATE PROCEDURE uspGetSalesOrderDetail
    @SalesOrderID int
AS
 SELECT
    Sales.SalesOrderDetail.SalesOrderDetailID
    , Sales.SalesOrderDetail.CarrierTrackingNumber
    , Sales.SalesOrderDetail.OrderQty
    , Sales.SalesOrderDetail.UnitPrice
    , Sales.SalesOrderDetail.UnitPriceDiscount
    , Sales.SalesOrderDetail.LineTotal
    , Production.Product.Name
    , Sales.SpecialOffer.Description
    , Sales.SpecialOffer.DiscountPct
    , Sales.SpecialOffer.Type
    , Production.Product.ProductNumber
    , Sales.SalesOrderDetail.SalesOrderID
FROM        Sales.SalesOrderDetail
```

```
        INNER JOIN Production.Product
        ON      Sales.SalesOrderDetail.ProductID = Production.Product.ProductID
        INNER JOIN Sales.SpecialOffer
        ON      Sales.SalesOrderDetail.SpecialOfferID = Sales.SpecialOffer.SpecialOfferID
        WHERE     (Sales.SalesOrderDetail.SalesOrderID = @SalesOrderID)
    go
```

The output from the invoice receipt report you just created is shown in Figure P5-23.

Open a new browser and input the following URL:

`http://localhost/AdventureWorks/default.aspx?salesOrderID=44742.`

FIGURE P5-23

Final Thoughts

This recipe demonstrates how to quickly use and extend SSRS and its components to your offline reporting needs. By designing the report in SSRS and integrating it within an ASP.NET web application, you can create professional, re-usable reports which can be used either connected or disconnected from SSRS.

PART VI
Enhanced Report Content

- ▶ Creating a Calendar Report

- ▶ Creating Mailing Labels

- ▶ Barcodes

- ▶ Currency Translation

- ▶ Custom Aggregation

- ▶ Dynamic (Conditional) Page Breaks

- ▶ Excel Worksheet Naming and Page Naming

- ▶ External Image Sources

- ▶ Language Localization

- ▶ Page Running Total

- ▶ Renderer Dependant Layout and Formatting

- ▶ Creating a Checkbox List to Show Existing Records

- ▶ Using a Checkbox List to Select and Deselect Records

- ▶ Using the Map Wizard

CREATING A CALENDAR REPORT

On occasion, someone will ask if Reporting Services contains a native month-view calendar report item, to which I have to reply "no" but it's actually not hard to do using a matrix. I've approached calendar and time reporting a few different ways in the past and the solution is generally accomplished through the presentation of the data to the report, rather than using a feature of the reporting tool. A couple of years ago, Brian Larson demonstrated the technique shown in this recipe at the PASS Global Summit and I was thoroughly impressed with his approach. He was kind enough to share this code for inclusion as a report recipe. This report produces a very functional monthly calendar with navigation controls, conditional color-coding, and drill-down details.

Product Versions

➤ Reporting Services 2000

➤ Reporting Services 2005

➤ Reporting Services 2008

What You'll Need

➤ A functional knowledge of database programming objects and TSQL query design

➤ An understanding of groups used in report design

➤ A table or matrix report

➤ Conditional expressions

Designing the Report

In this recipe, you examine a completed report and dissect all of its working components. The magic behind this reporting technique is really in the query and the rest is fairly straightforward report design. This recipe does not included step-by-step instructions to build the report from scratch, but should include sufficient details to re-construct a similar report from a working example. Figure P6-1 shows the finished report.

We'll start with the database. A backup copy of the Calendar database is provided in the book's download files at Wrox.com, along with a completed sample report. The database contains only one table named Appointments, which only has two columns: AppointmentDateTime and AppointmentDescr. Figure P6-2 shows a sampling of records in this table.

Don't you love this appointment schedule? You have to admire someone who manages to get their hair cut every other day for two weeks straight, but works out at the gym only once every few months!

To populate a matrix with each day of the month, a query must return each date as a separate record. A table-valued function is used to return every date for a given month and year by generating these rows in a loop without having to store these rows in a physical table. The function returns one row for each day of the month.

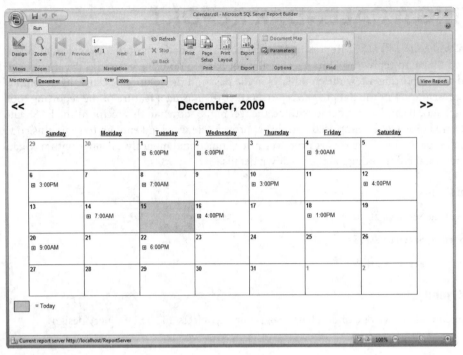

FIGURE P6-1

	AppointmentDateTime	AppointmentDescr
169	2009-08-03 17:00:00.000	School Event
170	2009-02-01 13:00:00.000	School Event
171	2009-08-01 08:00:00.000	School Event
172	2009-01-30 16:00:00.000	School Event
173	2009-01-23 08:00:00.000	Workout at Gym
174	2009-09-23 18:00:00.000	Workout at Gym
175	2009-05-21 15:00:00.000	Workout at Gym
176	2009-01-19 09:00:00.000	Workout at Gym
177	2009-09-19 17:00:00.000	Workout at Gym
178	2009-05-17 13:00:00.000	Workout at Gym
179	2009-01-15 08:00:00.000	Workout at Gym
180	2009-09-03 16:00:00.000	Workout at Gym
181	2009-05-13 07:00:00.000	Workout at Gym
182	2009-04-24 16:00:00.000	Hair Cut
183	2009-04-22 16:00:00.000	Hair Cut
184	2009-04-20 07:00:00.000	Hair Cut
185	2009-04-18 15:00:00.000	Hair Cut
186	2009-04-16 09:00:00.000	Hair Cut
187	2009-04-14 18:00:00.000	Hair Cut
188	2009-07-01 07:00:00.000	Workout at Gym
189	2009-03-01 15:00:00.000	Workout at Gym
190	2009-10-29 09:00:00.000	Workout at Gym
191	2009-06-27 18:00:00.000	Workout at Gym
192	2009-02-25 14:00:00.000	Workout at Gym
193	2009-10-25 08:00:00.000	Workout at Gym
194	2009-06-23 17:00:00.000	Workout at Gym

FIGURE P6-2

```
USE Calendar
GO

CREATE FUNCTION dbo.fn_GenerateMonth(@MonthNum int, @Year int)
RETURNS
@Month TABLE
(
    -- Add the column definitions for the TABLE variable here
    MonthDate datetime,
    DayNumber int,
    DayName varchar(12),
    DayOfWeek int,
    WeekOfMonth int,
    MonthName varchar(12)
)
AS
BEGIN
    DECLARE @MonthDate datetime
    DECLARE @WeekOfMonth int
    DECLARE @WeekFillDate datetime
    DECLARE @MonthName       varchar(12)

    SET @WeekOfMonth = 1

    -- Find the first day of the month and the month name.
    SET @MonthDate = RIGHT('0' + CONVERT(varchar(2), @MonthNum),2) + '/01/'
        + CONVERT(char(4), @Year)
    SET @MonthName = DATENAME(mm, @MonthDate)

    -- Back up to the first day of the week containing the first day of the month.
    SET @WeekFillDate = @MonthDate
    WHILE DATEPART(dw, @WeekFillDate) > 1
    BEGIN
        SET @WeekFillDate = DATEADD(dd, -1, @WeekFillDate)

        INSERT INTO
        @Month (MonthDate, DayNumber, DayName, DayOfWeek, WeekOfMonth, MonthName)
        VALUES (@WeekFillDate, DAY(@WeekFillDate), DATENAME(dw, @WeekFillDate),
                DATEPART(dw, @WeekFillDate), @WeekOfMonth, @MonthName)
    END

    WHILE MONTH(@MonthDate) = @MonthNum
    BEGIN
        IF DATEPART(dw, @MonthDate) = 1 AND DAY(@MonthDate) > 1
        BEGIN
            SET @WeekOfMonth = @WeekOfMonth + 1
        END

        INSERT INTO
        @Month (MonthDate, DayNumber, DayName, DayOfWeek, WeekOfMonth, MonthName)
        VALUES (@MonthDate, DAY(@MonthDate), DATENAME(dw, @MonthDate),
                DATEPART(dw, @MonthDate), @WeekOfMonth, @MonthName)
```

```
    SET @MonthDate = DATEADD(dd, 1, @MonthDate)
        END

        -- Finish up the week containing the last day of the month.
        SET @WeekFillDate = DATEADD(dd, -1, @MonthDate)
        WHILE DATEPART(dw, @WeekFillDate) < 7
        BEGIN
            SET @WeekFillDate = DATEADD(dd, 1, @WeekFillDate)

            INSERT INTO
            @Month (MonthDate, DayNumber, DayName, DayOfWeek, WeekOfMonth, MonthName)
            VALUES (@WeekFillDate, DAY(@WeekFillDate), DATENAME(dw, @WeekFillDate),
                    DATEPART(dw, @WeekFillDate), @WeekOfMonth, @MonthName)
        END
        RETURN
    END
    We can see the output from the function by running a simple test query in SQL
    Server Management Studio, executing this command, passing 12 for the month
     and 2009 for the year.
    SELECT * FROM dbo.fn_GenerateMonth(12, 2009)
```

The nested loop logic in the user-defined function works through several objects in the month hierarchy. First, the function logic determines the date that should appear in the top-left-most cell, which is the Sunday on or before the first day of the month. In other words, if the first of the month starts on Wednesday, that means there are three days from the prior month that must be included. Likewise, unless the end of the month falls on a Saturday, dates from the following month must be included to fill the end of the grid.

With all this information, the function is able to assign the DayName, DayOfWeek, and WeekOfMonth column values to every row — even for those that belong to adjacent months sharing the first and last weeks with the month in question. Figure P6-3 shows these column values. Note that the MonthName column is the same for every row and doesn't change for rows representing the prior and subsequent month dates (for instance, November 29 and 30 in the case of the first two rows). This column is only used in the report header title.

	MonthDate	DayNumber	DayName	DayOfWeek	WeekOfMonth	MonthName
1	2009-11-30 00:00:00.000	30	Monday	2	1	December
2	2009-11-29 00:00:00.000	29	Sunday	1	1	December
3	2009-12-01 00:00:00.000	1	Tuesday	3	1	December
4	2009-12-02 00:00:00.000	2	Wednesday	4	1	December
5	2009-12-03 00:00:00.000	3	Thursday	5	1	December
6	2009-12-04 00:00:00.000	4	Friday	6	1	December
7	2009-12-05 00:00:00.000	5	Saturday	7	1	December
8	2009-12-06 00:00:00.000	6	Sunday	1	2	December
9	2009-12-07 00:00:00.000	7	Monday	2	2	December
10	2009-12-08 00:00:00.000	8	Tuesday	3	2	December
11	2009-12-09 00:00:00.000	9	Wednesday	4	2	December
12	2009-12-10 00:00:00.000	10	Thursday	5	2	December
13	2009-12-11 00:00:00.000	11	Friday	6	2	December
14	2009-12-12 00:00:00.000	12	Saturday	7	2	December
15	2009-12-13 00:00:00.000	13	Sunday	1	3	December
16	2009-12-14 00:00:00.000	14	Monday	2	3	December
17	2009-12-15 00:00:00.000	15	Tuesday	3	3	December
18	2009-12-16 00:00:00.000	16	Wednesday	4	3	December

FIGURE P6-3

Take a close look at these column values. You now have the ability to separate row groups and column groups in a matrix based in the WeekOfMonth and the DayOfWeek values.

Joining this set of rows with the actual appointment records provides all the information necessary to populate the calendar grid in a matrix report data region.

The data source references the Calendar database using the appropriate user or application credentials. The dataset contains a left outer join between the table-valued function and the Appointments table data filtered by the month and a year.

```
SELECT
    Dates.MonthDate
  , DayNumber
  , Dates.DayName
  , Dates.DayOfWeek
  , Dates.WeekOfMonth
  , Dates.MonthName
  , Appointments.AppointmentDateTime AS ScheduledDate
  , SUBSTRING(CONVERT(char(19), Appointments.AppointmentDateTime, 100),13,7)
      AS ScheduledTime
  , Appointments.AppointmentDescr
FROM
    dbo.fn_GenerateMonth(@MonthNum, @Year) AS Dates
LEFT OUTER JOIN
    Appointments ON Dates.MonthDate = CONVERT(datetime, CONVERT(char(10),
    Appointments.AppointmentDateTime, 101))
ORDER BY
    Dates.MonthDate
```

When you run the query, you've substituted 12 for the @Month parameter and 2009 for @Year. Note that the first two rows shown in Figure P6-4 are for the last two days in the previous month.

	MonthDate	DayNumber	DayName	DayOfWeek	WeekOfMonth	MonthName	ScheduledDate	ScheduledTime	AppointmentDescr
1	2009-11-29 00:00:00.000	29	Sunday	1	1	December	NULL	NULL	NULL
2	2009-11-30 00:00:00.000	30	Monday	2	1	December	NULL	NULL	NULL
3	2009-12-01 00:00:00.000	1	Tuesday	3	1	December	2009-12-01 18:00:00.000	6:00PM	Workout at Gym
4	2009-12-02 00:00:00.000	2	Wednesday	4	1	December	2009-12-02 18:00:00.000	6:00PM	Hair Cut
5	2009-12-03 00:00:00.000	3	Thursday	5	1	December	NULL	NULL	NULL
6	2009-12-04 00:00:00.000	4	Friday	6	1	December	2009-12-04 09:00:00.000	9:00AM	Hair Cut
7	2009-12-05 00:00:00.000	5	Saturday	7	1	December	NULL	NULL	NULL
8	2009-12-06 00:00:00.000	6	Sunday	1	2	December	2009-12-06 15:00:00.000	3:00PM	Hair Cut
9	2009-12-07 00:00:00.000	7	Monday	2	2	December	NULL	NULL	NULL
10	2009-12-08 00:00:00.000	8	Tuesday	3	2	December	2009-12-08 07:00:00.000	7:00AM	Hair Cut
11	2009-12-09 00:00:00.000	9	Wednesday	4	2	December	NULL	NULL	NULL
12	2009-12-10 00:00:00.000	10	Thursday	5	2	December	2009-12-10 15:00:00.000	3:00PM	Hair Cut
13	2009-12-11 00:00:00.000	11	Friday	6	2	December	NULL	NULL	NULL
14	2009-12-12 00:00:00.000	12	Saturday	7	2	December	2009-12-12 16:00:00.000	4:00PM	Hair Cut
15	2009-12-13 00:00:00.000	13	Sunday	1	3	December	NULL	NULL	NULL
16	2009-12-14 00:00:00.000	14	Monday	2	3	December	2009-12-14 07:00:00.000	7:00AM	School Event
17	2009-12-15 00:00:00.000	15	Tuesday	3	3	December	NULL	NULL	NULL

FIGURE P6-4

Take a close look at the matrix data region in design view, shown in Figure P6-5. The design is quite simple. Rows are grouped on the WeekOfMonth field. Columns are grouped first on the MonthName.

This is just to create a header for the month. All rows returned by the query will have the same MonthName. The significant column grouping is on the DayOfWeek number, which will produce seven columns labeled with the DayName field.

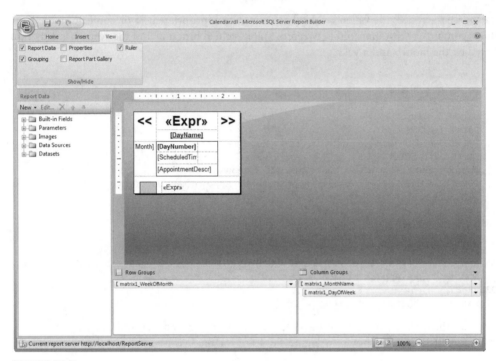

FIGURE P6-5

Note the month navigation cells in the matrix header rows. The matrix detail cell contains an embedded table. The table is used to manage multiple appointment items for each date.

The matrix data region will produce a column for each distinct DayOfWeek value and will produce a new row for each distinct WeekOfMonth value.

Some of the subtle and optional adornments are enabled through simple expressions. These include:

➤ Showing the date number for the previous and following month in gray and the current month dates in black.

➤ The current date cell is displayed with a khaki-shaded background.

➤ The description text for each appointment is hidden by default and can be displayed using the time as a toggle item to expand or collapse the description text.

A quick review of these features reveals properties that use simple expressions. The DayNumber textbox Color property is set using an expression that compares the Month value for each cell to the MonthNum parameter value. If the cell is within the selected month, the text is Black. Otherwise, it is Gray.

```
=IIF(Month(Fields!MonthDate.Value) = Parameters!MonthNum.Value, "Black", "Gray")
```

The background fill color for each cell is controlled by the BackgroundColor property of the embedded table. This property is set using an expression that compares the date value for the cell to the current date value returned by the Visual Basic.NET Now() function. If the dates are the same (and the cell represents the date for today) the background color is set to Khaki. Otherwise, it is White.

```
=IIF(Format(CDate(Max(Fields!MonthDate.Value)), "MMddyyyy")
        = Format(Now(), "MMddyyyy"), "Khaki", "White")
```

To navigate backward and forward using the double arrow "buttons" in the header, two expressions are used to alter the MonthNum and Year parameters passed in a report action. While navigating backward, it's a relatively simple task to subtract one from the current value of the MonthNum parameter, until you get to January. Likewise, navigating forward works well until you encounter December, which requires the Year parameter value to be conditionally modified as well.

For the left-most textbox, used to navigate to the previous month, the following two expressions are used:

PARAMETER	VALUE
MonthNum	`=IIF(Parameters!MonthNum.Value="01", "12", Right("0" & CStr(CInt(Parameters!MonthNum.Value)-1), 2))`
Year	`=IIF(Parameters!MonthNum.Value="01", CStr(CInt(Parameters!Year.Value)-1), Parameters!Year.Value)`

For the right-most textbox, used to navigate to the next month, the following two expressions are used:

PARAMETER	VALUE
MonthNum	`=IIF(Parameters!MonthNum.Value="12", "01", Right("0" & CStr(CInt(Parameters!MonthNum.Value)+1), 2))`
Year	`=IIF(Parameters!MonthNum.Value="12", CStr(CInt(Parameters!Year.Value)+1), Parameters!Year.Value)`

In preview, the report looks — well, it looks just like a calendar! (See Figure P6-6.)

This recipe is an excellent example of the principle I call "compounded simplicity." The techniques used to build this calendar report are not all that complicated — it's just that there are a few layers of simplicity all piled on top of each other. The reason you probably enjoy this demonstration is that it exposes the raw capability of Reporting Services in an application that it isn't specifically designed to perform.

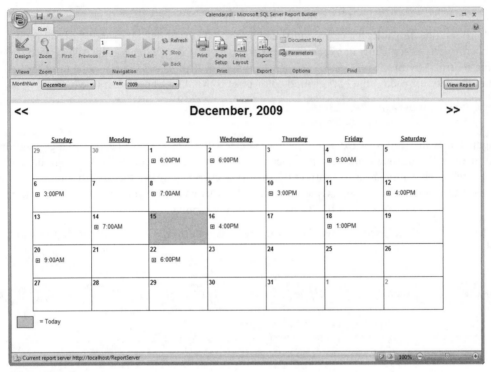

FIGURE P6-6

Final Thoughts

The most complex component of this recipe was performed by SQL Server in a table-valued user-defined function. Based on a user-specified month and year parameter, the function returns a set of rows representing all of the dates that should be included in the calendar grid. This includes the dates from the prior and subsequent months needed to fill in the ends of the calendar grid. A matrix data region groups the data on week days and week numbers to create the month grid. An embedded table displays multiple appointments per day cell. Expressions are used to conditionally format the dates that fall within the specified month and the current date cell. Navigation arrows are actually textboxes used to perform a report action and use expressions to navigate backward and forward by calculating the month and year parameter values.

Credits and Related References

Brian Larson is the author of *Microsoft SQL Server 2008 Reporting Services* (McGraw Hill Osborne Media, 2008). He is the Chief of Technology for Superior Consulting in Minneapolis, MN (http://teamscs.com), and a featured speaker at industry conferences.

Used with permission.

CREATING MAILING LABELS

Most word processing applications (Word, WordPerfect, and so on) provide the capability to create a "mail merge" from which to generate mailing labels in different formats and layouts. Mailing labels are an automated way to generate the address labels for a large number of envelopes or parcels that need to be mailed.

Reporting Services provides a few features that allow you to create mailing labels in different formats – the only thing you need to know are the exact dimensions of the label template you are targeting when printing. A common mailing label format is to use multiple columns (newspaper layout) in order to maximize the number of labels printed.

This recipe shows you how to leverage Reporting Services' multi-column layout features to create basic mailing labels, while explaining certain limitations in the rendering engine.

Product Versions

➤ All versions (examples provided in Reporting Services 2008)

What You'll Need

➤ AdventureWorksDW2008 database (or your own database and query that provides name and address data to the report)

➤ The exact template size for the labels you will use when printing (including all margins and column widths)

➤ PDF reader or Image viewer (Windows provides an image viewer that supports TIFF, JPG, GIF, and PNG)

Designing the Report

The final outcome of this recipe should be a multi-column report "perfectly" sized to fit the print layout of a mailing label template, as shown in Figure P6-7.

For the purposes of this recipe, you will utilize the Avery 5160 label template, which contains the following dimensions:

➤ Length: 2.5935"

➤ Height: 1.0000"

➤ Margins: Top 0.5", Bottom 0.5", Left 0.21975", Right 0.21975"

➤ Horizontal Spacing (gutter): 0.14000"

➤ Vertical Spacing (gutter): 0"

➤ 30 labels per sheet of letter size (8.5" x 11") paper

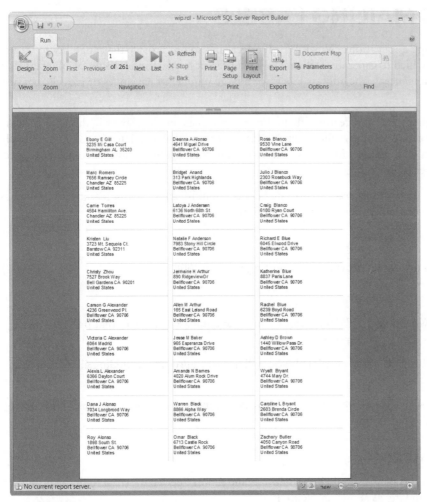

FIGURE P6-7

1. Begin by creating a new report in Report Builder, and removing all default items and the page footer from the report. You need to have a blank design surface – the report dimensions need to be very exact in order to match the labels when printing.

2. Add a new data source to the report and set its connection string to the SQL Server where the AdventureWorksDW2008 database is stored. If you are using your own database, simply choose the server and database for your own data, so you can provide your own query in the next step.

3. Add a new dataset for the data source created in the previous step. Set the query type to Text, and type the following SQL query in the command text window:

```
SELECT
        c.Title, c.FirstName, c.MiddleName, c.LastName
        , c.AddressLine1, c.AddressLine2
        , g.City, g.StateProvinceCode, g.PostalCode
        , g.EnglishCountryRegionName
FROM
        dbo.DimCustomer c
LEFT OUTER JOIN
        dbo.DimGeography g
        ON g.GeographyKey = c.GeographyKey
WHERE
        g.EnglishCountryRegionName = @Country
ORDER BY
        g.StateProvinceCode
        , g.City
        , c.LastName
```

Notice that this includes a parameter for the Country field — this will allow you to filter down the dataset to a specific country. Also, you order by State/Province, then by City, and finally, by Last Name. That seems like a reasonable way to order your labels and keep your mail person happy when processing a large case of envelopes or parcels. You should have a blank report with a dataset as shown in Figure P6-8.

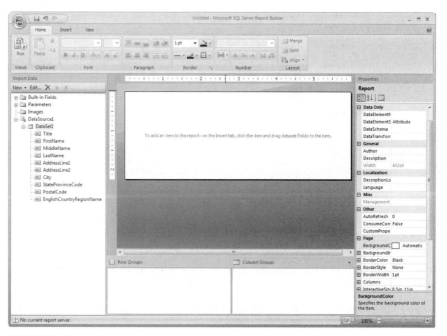

FIGURE P6-8

4.   The label template will contain three columns on a letter-size sheet of paper, so you need to set up the report size and layout for multiple columns:

a.   In the Report Properties, set the Orientation to Portrait, and Paper Size to Letter (8.5in x 11in).

b.   Set the Left and Right Margins to 0.21975in.

c.   Set the Top and Bottom Margins to 0.5in.

Click the OK button to save changes. The report properties should look as shown in Figure P6-9.

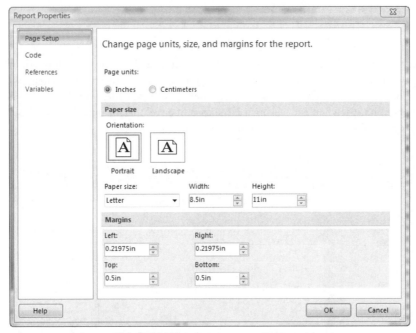

FIGURE P6-9

5.   Next, you need to set up multiple columns. The Columns and ColumnSpacing properties of the Report are not exposed via the Report Properties dialog shown in Figure P6-9. Instead, you must edit them in the Properties page for the report (if you don't see it in Report Builder, choose the View menu from the ribbon and check the Properties box to display it).

Expand the Columns node from the Properties page, and make the following edits (see Figure P6-10):

a.   Change the Columns property to 3.

b.   Change the ColumnSpacing property to 0.14in. This is the size of our label template's Horizontal Spacing gutter – the spacing between columns on the page.

Notice that the report body has been "duplicated" by the number of columns specified in the Columns property, even though you only get to work on the leftmost body template (the other ones are simply placeholders to show the designer that multiple columns will be rendered at runtime).

Since you already specified the dimensions for your label template, you might be wondering why the report is so wide, making you scroll to the right to see the multiple columns. There still are a few dimensions that you must set for the body of the report.

It's important to understand how report page sizes, body sizes, margins and column spacing relate to each other in the report. Figure P6-11 illustrates how these dimensions fit together.

From the diagram, you can then infer that the labels themselves will be the body, while the sheet of paper will be the report page. With that in mind, you will set the body dimensions according to the label size specified previously.

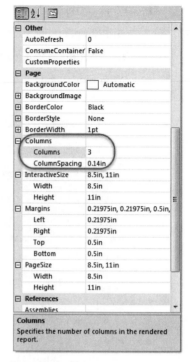

FIGURE P6-10

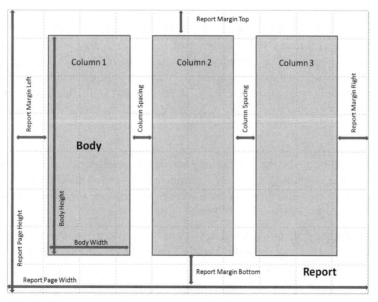

FIGURE P6-11

6. Click on the Body element, and change the following properties in the Properties window:

a. Expand the Size node and set the Width to 2.5935in.

b. Set the Height to 1in.

Your report body should now look like the diagram in Figure P6-12.

FIGURE P6-12

7. Finally, you add a data region to the body of the report, attach it to your dataset and drag data fields in for the mailing data.

In Reporting Services 2008, you can use either a List or a Table data region (both use the underlying tablix). However, if you are using an earlier version, I have found the table layout to yield more consistent results and provide a better design surface to control your formatting. I'll let you, as the report developer, decide what best fits your needs according to the requirements of your mailing label design.

I'll simply use a table with a single column and detail row, and rely on the Reporting Services 2008 rich text features of the textbox that allow you to drag and drop multiple dataset fields onto the table cell. Make sure your data region (table or list) stretches to fill 100% of the body size, without expanding it. In other words, the width and height of the data region should match that of the body. The easiest way to do this is by drawing the data region on the design surface instead of dragging it from the menu. After adding the data region to the report, double-check that your report body was not modified by the data region.

If you are using a previous version of Reporting Services, you will either use string concatenation expressions (not recommended) or use a rectangle in the cell to make the cell a free-form container for your textboxes – then you can use multiple textboxes for the dataset field, each positioned absolutely within the cell.

Here's a trick to ensure that your labels are positioned correctly within the cell: select the cell textbox and set its vertical alignment to "Middle." For some reason, Reporting Services will duplicate the data cell otherwise.

Assuming your mailing labels will require First and Last Name, Address 1 and 2, City, State, Postal Code, and Country name to be displayed, the table cell layout should look similar to Figure P6-13.

While previewing the report, keep in mind that the report viewer used in the preview of the report designer uses the Graphics Device Interface (GDI) to render the report to the screen, and because we are using multi-columns, a feature only supported in the print-oriented renderers for Reporting Services, you will only get to see the expected outcome if you click the "Print Layout" button in the preview window.

FIGURE P6-13

This leverages the print-preview renderer and not the regular preview renderer. Also, because of this limitation, a multi-column report layout is only supported in print-oriented formats: PDF, TIFF (Image), Print, and Print Preview. You cannot export and save your report to Word, so your best option is to use PDF.

The final outcome of the report in Print Layout preview is shown in Figure P6-14 (I added light gray borders to my textbox, so you can see the size of the labels).

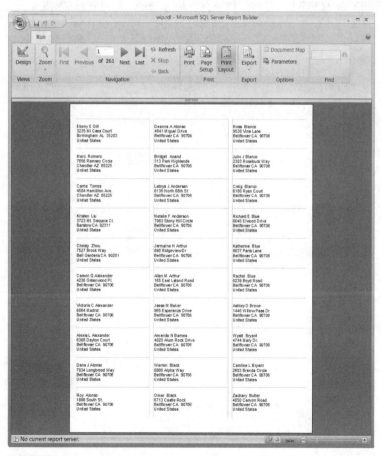

FIGURE P6-14

Final Thoughts

Reporting Services provides developers with several features to help create insightful analytical reports, as well as print-ready reports. With its multi-column capabilities, we are able to drastically change the layout of reports that target a print layout such as PDF.

This recipe showed you how to leverage the multi-column feature to create mailing labels akin to those found in Microsoft Word's mail merge feature. The compelling story, however, lies within the integration and automation possibilities. As most developers would agree, Office automation is rather complex and can be a bit frustrating at times. However, with Reporting Services' web services API, its extensibility, and rich subscription model, the task of automating the creation of mailing labels becomes much simpler.

Credits and Related References

Mailing label dimensions provided by Worldlabel.Com, Inc. (`www.worldlabel.com`).

BARCODES

Reporting Services has established itself as a solid platform for Business Intelligence reporting, leveraging OLAP with rich user interactivity capabilities. However, there's a niche group using Reporting Services for a different kind of reports: operational reporting. These types of report usually consist of real-time or near-real-time data from online transaction processing (OLTP) systems and/or operational data stores (ODS).

An example is a set of operational reports used within a distribution warehouse to provide product details such as quantities and locations. In these situations, the logistics workers generally use barcode scanners instead of having to type ID numbers to enter and retrieve product information. An operational report that contains a barcode (or a set of barcodes) is a very efficient – and less error-prone – way of keeping track of items as they move down the line to either be stored or shipped.

Although barcodes are not a built-in part of Reporting Services, there are several third-party controls available that allow you to add barcodes to your reports. These controls leverage an extensibility piece of Reporting Services called Custom Report Items (CRI). In addition, you have the option of using the good old barcode fonts (also available from third-party providers) for quick and simple report development.

This recipe shows you the pros and cons of these different approaches to using barcodes in Reporting Services, while using trial versions of custom report items and fonts. Our sample report will be a product list, where each item can be scanned via barcodes that represent its SKU number or unique identifier (in this case the primary key).

Product Versions

➤ Reporting Services 2000 (barcode fonts only)

➤ Reporting Services 2005 (limited CRI design-time support)

➤ Reporting Services 2008 and higher

What You'll Need

➤ AdventureWorks2008 (OLTP database)

➤ Business Intelligence Development Studio (BIDS) or Visual Studio 2008 (Report Builder has limited supported for CRI. (Read on for more details.)

➤ A third-party barcode CRI (we will use a trial version of the Neodynamic Barcode Professional 6.0 for Reporting Services)

➤ A third-party barcode font that supports Code 39 (you can download one for free from the web, or purchase a set of fonts with different barcode symbologies, although you only need Code 39 for this sample)

Designing the Report

Although this sample report will have a simple design, the important (and possibly more time consuming) decision is how to incorporate the barcode tags into your report designer.

There are lots of terminology and concepts to understand when dealing with barcodes. An explanation of barcode implementation and symbology is beyond the scope of this book, so it's up to you to research and learn about those details. There are plenty of resources on the web to assist with the nitty-gritty of barcode implementations.

Figure P6-15 shows the final output of this recipe using barcode fonts.

And you can see the final output using a third-party barcode CRI in Figure P6-16.

Let's start by looking at the options you have when dealing with barcodes in Reporting Services: barcode fonts and custom report items (Barcode Controls).

Fonts

A barcode font is the representation of a single symbology, which is the mapping of the message

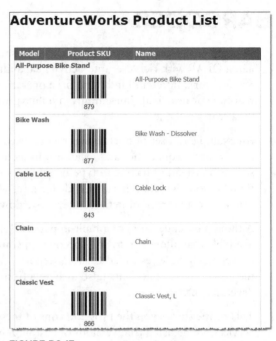

FIGURE P6-15

in a barcode. Most barcode fonts are for linear types of barcodes, as opposed to the 2D types. Linear barcode fonts can be downloaded and installed on Windows computers like any other font type and immediately become available to most of the text-editing programs which provide a font selection list (e.g., Microsoft Word).

Once a barcode font is installed in the OS, it's easy to use it in your reports: just highlight the textbox or text you want to make a barcode, then change the font type to that of the appropriate barcode font. You might see a problem with this approach, though: you only see barcodes if you have the font installed! When a user opens any word-processing document that leverages a barcode font which is not already installed, he or she will likely see "garbage" text where the barcode should be.

In other words, for a report to leverage barcode fonts, the font will need to be installed on all the Report Servers in the server farm, as well as on every end user's workstation. In large deployment scenarios, like a large enterprise, this could possibly require some coordination with multiple teams and IT to deploy the font to multiple machines.

FIGURE P6-16

Let's begin by building the report using barcode fonts. We'll use Report Builder for this exercise. Because the focus of this exercise is to show how to incorporate barcodes into reports, no detailed instruction on how to add data sources, datasets, tables, and groupings on a report are provided. It's assumed you have basic understanding of report development and design using Reporting Services.

1. Open Report Builder and create a new blank report.

2. Add a new datasource embedded into the report (not shared) which connects to your instance of SQL Server and the AdventureWorks2008 database.

3. Add a new dataset embedded into the report, which uses the data source configured in the previous step. Set the query text to the following SQL code:

```
SELECT ProductID, Name, ProductModel, CultureID
FROM Production.vProductAndDescription
WHERE CultureID = N'en'
ORDER BY Name
```

4. Insert a table data region inside the report body with three columns, which will contain the following headers respectively: Model, Product SKU, Name.

5. Bind the table to the dataset created in Step 3 by setting its Dataset Name property.

6. Add a parent Row Group to the Details group, and set its group expression the Product-Model field from the dataset.

Now you can add fields to the table's details row in order to display the data. Make sure you have a header row for the ProductModel row group.

The Product SKU column will contain the barcode. In order to show both a barcode and the actual ProductID number in the same cell, let's add a Rectangle item inside the empty cell in the details of the Product SKU column. The rectangle will act as a freeform design surface allowing us to stack textboxes inside the cell – one for the barcode, and another for the visible number.

Drag two textboxes inside the rectangle and set both textboxes' values to the ProductID field. Finally, for the first one, set its font type to the barcode font you have previously installed. In my case the font is called "Free 3 of 9 Extended," a free Code 39 barcode font found on the web (http://www.barcodesinc.com/free-barcode-font/). Also, I set the font size to 48pt, and centered it so the barcode displays at a decent size for scanning. You may have to adjust this size according to your needs for your report.

Figure P6-17 shows the report layout after creating all cells in the table and setting the barcode font type.

All that is left to do is add minor cosmetic details, such as the report title and any other changes you would like to make to the report layout. Figure P6-18 shows the finished report executed with data from AdventureWorks2008.

Custom Report Items (Barcode Components)

In Reporting Services 2000, the only way to provide report item extensibility was by creating .NET components that rendered images (as byte arrays) at runtime based on constructor arguments and instance methods.

FIGURE P6-17

So, technically, this was not a native capability of SSRS 2000, but rather a workaround that leveraged its .NET hooks to call into external assemblies. Since the report developer can add external assembly references to a report and instantiate types to be used in the custom code section of the report, it is easy for developers to create their own components.

The ability to extend the toolbox of the report designer to include custom report items (CRIs) came with version 2005 of Reporting Services. This allowed for an ecosystem of third-party components to be developed and marketed in order to fill gaps in report design with richer design-time support.

CRIs are better supported when developing reports within the BIDS environment (or Visual Studio IDE), due to its full support of .NET components and their designer views (design-time support). While there is a way to get around this limitation when using Report Builder 2.0 and 3.0, the developer loses most (if not all) of the design-time features of the CRI.

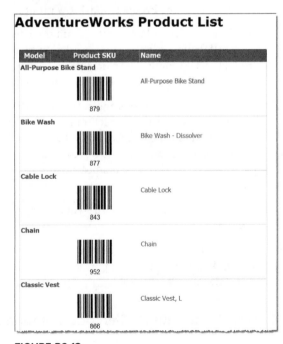

FIGURE P6-18

Unlike barcode fonts, CRIs render images at runtime, so there's no client-side deployment required for users to view barcode reports, making it a better solution for large-scale deployment with several users.

To build a report using barcode CRIs, first follow the setup and installation instructions provided by the third-party that developed the barcode control. This usually adds the control's assemblies to the .NET Global Assembly Cache for reusability, but could differ based on the control.

As mentioned previously, you'll need to use BIDS instead or Report Builder, because of the lack of CRI support in the Report Builder designer.

You can leverage the same report that you created in the instructions for the barcode fonts, since these two reports will be visually identical. The only change we'll make to the layout is to replace the textbox that displays the barcode font with the barcode report item.

1. Fire up BIDS (or Visual Studio 2008) and create a new Report Server project. Give it a name and location, then click OK. This will create the solution and project files using an empty Report Server project template

2. Right-click the Reports folder in the Solution Explorer dialog and choose Add ⇨ Existing Item. Browse to the location of the RDL that you created earlier when experimenting with barcode fonts. (If you skipped to this section, go back a page or two in this recipe and follow the steps listed under the Barcode Fonts section to create the report.)

3. Double-click the report name in Solution Explorer to open it.

4. In the cell where the barcode font was displayed, remove the entire rectangle region – which will remove both textboxes.

5. Drag and drop the Barcode Professional CRI from the toolbox into the cell. (If you are using a different CRI, follow the instructions provided by the vendor to add and configure it.)

6. Now all you need to do is configure a few properties on the Neodynamic Barcode Builder dialog for the barcode CRI. Right-click the barcode cell and choose Properties . . .

7. Set the "Value To Encode" expression to the ProductID field.

8. Choose "Code 39" in the Barcode Symbology list.

9. Check the "Use Extended Version (Full ASCII)" box – this will match with the barcode font you used earlier which is the Code 39 Extended symbology.

10. Uncheck the following boxes:

   ➤ Display Start & Stop Chars

   ➤ Calculate and Append Checksum

   ➤ Display Checksum

The resulting properties dialog for the Neodynamic Barcode Professional CRI is shown in Figure P6-19.

When you click OK you'll notice a yellow *fx* icon overlay on the top-left corner of the design-time barcode image to denote that it's data-bound, as shown in Figure P6-20.

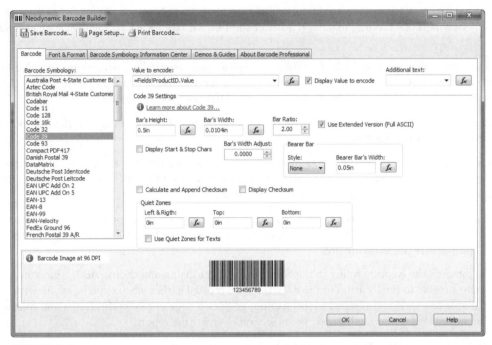

FIGURE P6-19

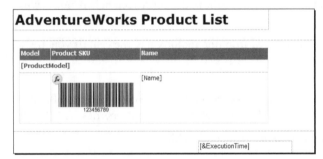

FIGURE P6-20

Now you are ready to preview your report. Each barcode that shows on the report is rendered by the CRI as an image instead of a font. This allows your report to support most export formats in Reporting Services, including PDF and Word without any extra deployment requirements for the end user. The final result is shown in Figure P6-21.

Notice the word "TRIAL" at the top of the barcode image in Figure P6-21. That is present due to trial software license restrictions. This can be resolved with the purchase of a license key from the third-party CRI software vendor.

If you are using Reporting Services 2000, you will not be able to use custom report items in this fashion. However, as a work around, most CRIs will render as images, including the Neodynamic barcode CRI used in this sample. With a little bit of .NET code, it is very simple to use the CRI and achieve similar results. Here's what you need to do.

FIGURE P6-21

1. Install the CRI component as directed by the vendor.

2. Open the report to which you wish to add the CRI barcode.

3. In the Report Properties dialog, add a new assembly reference to the Neodynamic.Reporting Services.Barcode library, and also add a new object instance of the Neodynamic.Reporting Services.Barcode class, as shown in Figure P6-22.

4. In the code dialog of the Report Properties, type in the following VB function, which takes in a string value and returns a barcode image using the Neodynamic barcode object created in Step 3. Then click OK.

```
Public Function GetBarcode(ByVal code As String) As Byte()
  barcodeCRI.Code = code
  barcodeCRI.Symbology = Neodynamic.ReportingServices.Symbology.Code39
  barcodeCRI.BarHeight = 0.5
  barcodeCRI.BarWidth = .0104
  barcodeCRI.BarRatio = 2.00
  barcodeCRI.Extended = True
  barcodeCRI.DisplayCode = True
  barcodeCRI.DisplayStartStopChar = False
  barcodeCRI.AddChecksum = False
  barcodeCRI.DisplayChecksum = False
  Return barcodeCRI.GetBarcodeImage()
End Function
```

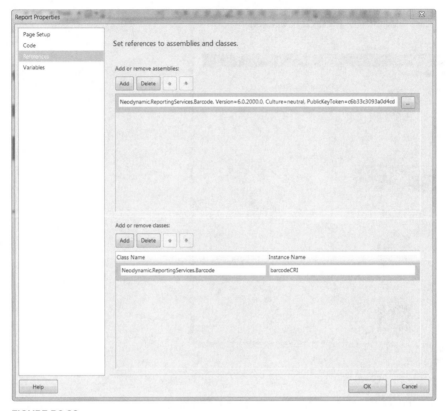

FIGURE P6-22

5. Drag and drop an Image item from the toolbox into the table cell where you want the bar-code to show, and set the following image properties (right-click and choose Properties to get to the properties window):

➤ In the General panel, set Image source to Database.

```
General > Source Field (expression):
=Code.GetBarcode(Fields!ProductID.Value.ToString())
```

➤ Also in the General panel, set MIME type to image/bmp.

➤ In the Size panel, set Display to Clip.

Figure P6-23 shows the report with both the barcode CRI and the image item leveraging the API of the barcode component library.

You may have noticed that the second row of data shows a barcode image with an invalid value when using the CRI from the toolbox, but not programmatically with an image item. There's a known bug in how Reporting Services renders CRIs and the second row of data inside a group: it always returns a NULL value instead of the expected data value!

The Neodynamic barcode CRI handles nulls by displaying a default barcode image with the number sequence "1234567890." Unfortunately, this bug will probably not be fixed until the 2008 R2 release of the product or later. In order to address this in your reports, you will either have to remove the grouping from the data region, or use the API provided by the component as shown previously.

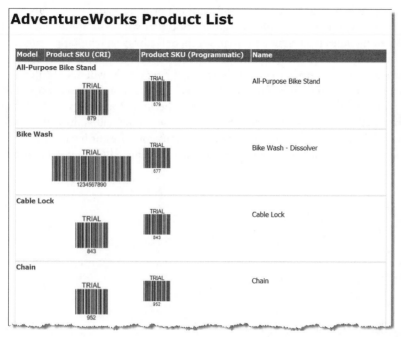

FIGURE P6-23

Final Thoughts

In this recipe you've seen how simple it can be to incorporate barcodes in your Reporting Services reports. You've experimented with two ways of dealing with barcodes: barcode fonts and custom report items.

As you design your reports, you will need to weigh the pros and cons of each approach and identify the solution that best meets your reporting requirements. There are a number of CRI vendors, such as Neodynamic, that provide mature barcoding solutions, so it's up to you to choose the best match for your needs.

Credits and Related References

What's New In Report Server Programmability (http://msdn.microsoft.com/en-us/library/cc281022.aspx)

Barcodes Inc. Free Barcode Font – Code 39 (http://www.barcodesinc.com/free-barcode-font)

Neodynamic Barcode Professional 6.0 for Reporting Services (http://www.neodynamic.com)

CURRENCY TRANSLATION

A common requirement for invoices and financial reporting is currency translation and the conversion of amount to the destination currency (and back again). SSRS doesn't provide an out-of-the-box feature for currency translation. In reality, there isn't really a single method that will work for all cases and business environments. When it comes to currency translation, there is always a temptation to simply hard-code the currency symbol or perhaps use the regional settings from the users' browser. This is an acceptable approach if the end-user or customer you are designing the report for will never differentiate currencies or have customers outside their own country. However, if this is not the case, you simply can't distinguish the currency symbol based on the users' language, because, for example, 100 United States dollars (USD) is not equal to 100 Canadian dollars (CAD). This recipe will address the needs of solution designers who will have customers in a variety of different countries or have the need to support multiple currencies. This approach or implementation may be adjusted to meet your specific requirements.

Product Versions

➤ Reporting Services 2000

➤ Reporting Services 2005

➤ Reporting Services 2008

What You'll Need

➤ A working knowledge of SQL Server and T-SQL

➤ Report Builder 2.0 (or 3.0)

Designing the Report

Figure P6-24 shows the finished report.

To get started, create a report with a data source that has a reference to a currency code and where the currency rate is stored in a relational fashion, or that allows snapshots of daily rates to be taken and the rate for that particular date to be applied.

1. Open Report Builder and create a new report. Give the report a title of "Currency Translation in SSRS."

2. Add a new report parameter called SalesOrderID, an integer value in which a null value is not allowed.

3. Double-click on the Table or Matrix icon and if you haven't created a data source connection, go ahead and create one. Otherwise, choose the connection for the AdventureWorks or AdventureWorks2008 database (See Figure P6-25).

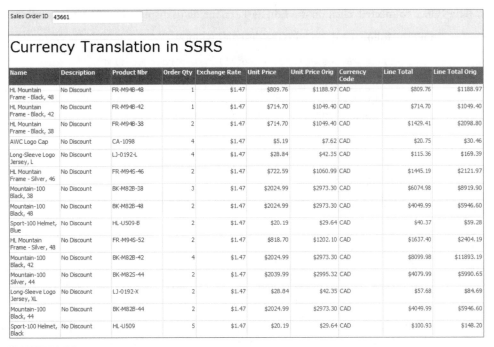

| Sales Order ID | 43661 | | | | | | | | |

Currency Translation in SSRS

Name	Description	Product Nbr	Order Qty	Exchange Rate	Unit Price	Unit Price Orig	Currency Code	Line Total	Line Total Orig
HL Mountain Frame - Black, 48	No Discount	FR-M94B-48	1	$1.47	$809.76	$1188.97	CAD	$809.76	$1188.97
HL Mountain Frame - Black, 42	No Discount	FR-M94B-42	1	$1.47	$714.70	$1049.40	CAD	$714.70	$1049.40
HL Mountain Frame - Black, 38	No Discount	FR-M94B-38	2	$1.47	$714.70	$1049.40	CAD	$1429.41	$2098.80
AWC Logo Cap	No Discount	CA-1098	4	$1.47	$5.19	$7.62	CAD	$20.75	$30.46
Long-Sleeve Logo Jersey, L	No Discount	LJ-0192-L	4	$1.47	$28.84	$42.35	CAD	$115.36	$169.39
HL Mountain Frame - Silver, 46	No Discount	FR-M94S-46	2	$1.47	$722.59	$1060.99	CAD	$1445.19	$2121.97
Mountain-100 Black, 38	No Discount	BK-M82B-38	3	$1.47	$2024.99	$2973.30	CAD	$6074.98	$8919.90
Mountain-100 Black, 48	No Discount	BK-M82B-48	2	$1.47	$2024.99	$2973.30	CAD	$4049.99	$5946.60
Sport-100 Helmet, Blue	No Discount	HL-U509-B	2	$1.47	$20.19	$29.64	CAD	$40.37	$59.28
HL Mountain Frame - Silver, 48	No Discount	FR-M94S-52	2	$1.47	$818.70	$1202.10	CAD	$1637.40	$2404.19
Mountain-100 Black, 42	No Discount	BK-M82B-42	4	$1.47	$2024.99	$2973.30	CAD	$8099.98	$11893.19
Mountain-100 Silver, 44	No Discount	BK-M82S-44	2	$1.47	$2039.99	$2995.32	CAD	$4079.99	$5990.65
Long-Sleeve Logo Jersey, XL	No Discount	LJ-0192-X	2	$1.47	$28.84	$42.35	CAD	$57.68	$84.69
Mountain-100 Black, 44	No Discount	BK-M82B-44	2	$1.47	$2024.99	$2973.30	CAD	$4049.99	$5946.60
Sport-100 Helmet, Black	No Discount	HL-U509	5	$1.47	$20.19	$29.64	CAD	$100.93	$148.20

FIGURE P6-24

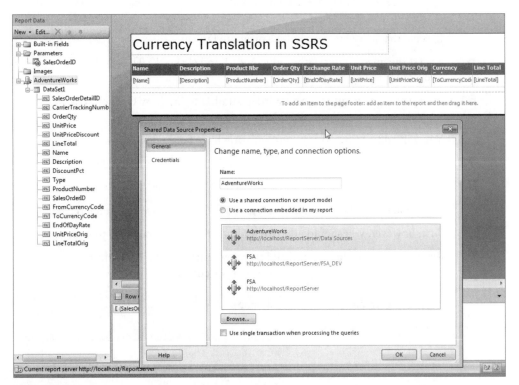

FIGURE P6-25

4. Once connected, click on the Edit as Text button to display the free-text query window.

Input the following query into the designer window.

```
SELECT      Sales.SalesOrderDetail.SalesOrderDetailID
, Sales.SalesOrderDetail.CarrierTrackingNumber
, Sales.SalesOrderDetail.OrderQty
, Sales.SalesOrderDetail.UnitPrice
, Sales.SalesOrderDetail.UnitPriceDiscount
, Sales.SalesOrderDetail.LineTotal
, Production.Product.Name
, Sales.SpecialOffer.Description
, Sales.SpecialOffer.DiscountPct
, Sales.SpecialOffer.Type
, Production.Product.ProductNumber
, Sales.SalesOrderDetail.SalesOrderID
, CR.FromCurrencyCode
, CR.ToCurrencyCode
, CR.EndOfDayRate
FROM        Sales.SalesOrderDetail
INNER JOIN Production.Product ON
Sales.SalesOrderDetail.ProductID = Production.Product.ProductID
INNER JOIN Sales.SpecialOffer ON Sales.SalesOrderDetail.SpecialOfferID =
    Sales.SpecialOffer.SpecialOfferID
INNER JOIN Sales.SalesOrderHeader ON Sales.SalesOrderHeader.SalesOrderID =
    Sales.SalesOrderDetail.SalesOrderID
LEFT OUTER JOIN Sales.CurrencyRate CR ON
CR.CurrencyRateID = Sales.SalesOrderHeader.CurrencyRateID
WHERE       (Sales.SalesOrderDetail.SalesOrderID = @SalesOrderID)
```

Execute the query and you will be prompted to enter the SalesOrderID value.

5. To test the query, enter in the value 43661 and click OK. The results will be displayed in the grid similar to Figure P6-26.

6. In the next screen, add the SalesOrderDetailID to the Row Groups area and the line total to the Values area (see Figure P6-27).

You will add additional columns once you have finished with the wizard.

7. Click the Next button to continue. Check the Show Subtotals and Grand Totals checkboxes.

8. Click the Next button and choose any style. Click Finish.

Soon, you can add the columns that give a little more meaning to the recipe.

First, however, you should add two additional fields (calculated) to your dataset.

9. Right-click on the dataset and add two new calculated fields, with the following expressions for UnitPriceOrig and LineTotalOrig, respectively:

CALCULATED FIELD	EXPRESSION
UnitPriceOrig	=Fields!UnitPrice.Value * Fields!EndOfDayRate.Value
LineTotalOrig	=(Fields!UnitPrice.Value * Fields!EndOfDayRate.Value) * Fields!OrderQty.Value

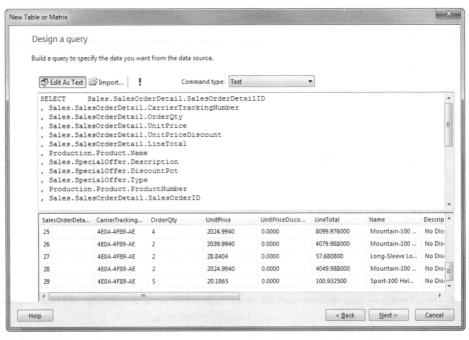

FIGURE P6-26

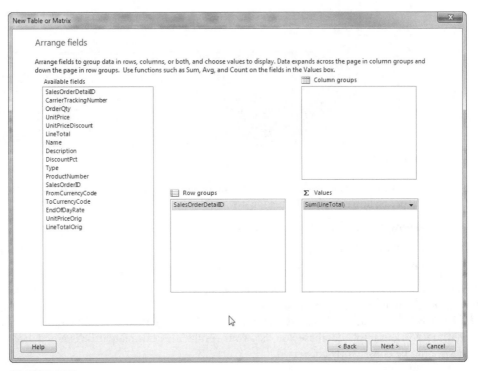

FIGURE P6-27

10. Add columns to the table for the fields mentioned in Step 9. With the table selected to show the selection handles, right-click on the last column header and add the following columns to the right:

➤ Name

➤ Description

➤ ProductNumber

➤ OrderQty

➤ EndOfDayRate

➤ UnitPrice

➤ UnitPriceOrig

➤ ToCurrencyCode

➤ LineTotal

➤ LineTotalOrig

After adding these columns and doing a little bit of formatting, you will have a detailed line item report which is similar to the one shown in Figure P6-28.

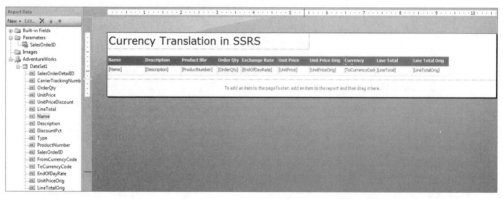

FIGURE P6-28

Note that, when adding the columns to the report, the report builder wanted to sum the currency fields; however, for this recipe it wasn't required.

You now need to format the currency cells.

11. For each one of the currency fields, right-click and view the textbox properties. Go to the Number page and select the Currency Category, shown in Figure P6-29.

At this point, you are ready to run the report. Again, when prompted, enter the SalesOrderID 43661 and the report will be displayed (as shown in Figure P6-30). The amounts were converted at a rate of 1 USD to 1.47 Canadian dollars (CAD) for this order. Note that, depending on the version of the Adventure Works sample database you use, your results may not match the example here, but the values should be consistently converted.

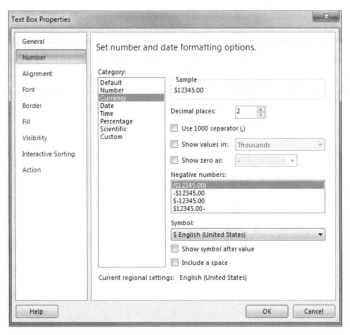

FIGURE P6-29

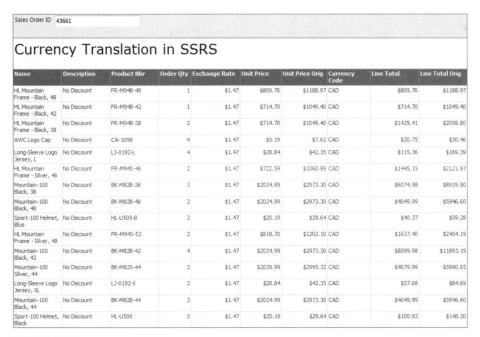

FIGURE P6-30

Final Thoughts

To accurately perform currency translation, you may need to store current and historical conversion rate information based on a recurring cycle (i.e., daily, weekly, etc.). Using calculated fields along with historical information, you are able to provide a simple yet straightforward solution to currency translation.

CUSTOM AGGREGATION

Reporting Services includes several useful aggregate functions to apply to a range or group of records. If you need to aggregate data using an aggregation or calculation not provided "out of the box," you can do this using a custom function. This recipe shows you how to add a statistical Median function to a table type report. Using the same pattern, you can apply a variety of custom business rules and apply your own calculations.

Product Versions

➤ Reporting Services 2005

➤ Reporting Services 2008

What You'll Need

➤ Table data region

➤ Fundamental Visual Basic.NET programming skills

➤ Business Intelligence Development Studio or Report Builder 2.0

Designing the Report

Of course, you can apply custom functions to practically any dataset and present the data in most any report design. In this recipe, you will create a basic table report, showing the Median value in a header row above the detail values. Both the SSRS 2005 and 2008 examples of this report use the Northwind sample database for SQL Server 2000. You can easily make the adjustment to use any other database query that returns a short range of numeric values. The Northwind database can be downloaded from the companion site for this book at Wrox.com.

Designing the Median Report in SSRS 2005

1. Create a new report in BIDS and add a data source for the Northwind sample database.

2. Create a new dataset using the following query script:

```
select * from products
```

3. Open the Report Properties dialog and then select the Code page.

4. Add the following Visual Basic.NET code to define the GetMedian and AddValue functions:

```
Dim values As System.Collections.ArrayList

Function AddValue(ByVal newValue As Decimal)
    If (values Is Nothing) Then
        values = New System.Collections.ArrayList()
    End If
    values.Add(newValue)
End Function
```

```
Function GetMedian() As Decimal
    Dim count As Integer = values.Count
    If (count > 0) Then
        values.Sort()
        GetMedian = values(count / 2)
    End If
End Function
```

5. Close and accept changes in the Report Properties dialog.

6. Add a table to the report body.

7. Drag the Product Name field into the detail row in the first column.

8. Drag the Unit Price field into the detail row in the second column.

9. Right-click the header cell in the third column and choose Expression.

10. Enter the following text in the Expression Editor. Use the IntelliSense and code completion features where available:

```
="Median Price: " & Format(Code.GetMedian(), "C2")
```

11. Close the Expression dialog and accept changes.

12. Right-click the detail cell in the third column and choose Expression.

13. Enter the following text in the Expression Editor. Use the IntelliSense and code completion features where available:

```
=Code.AddValue(Fields!UnitPrice.Value)
```

The table should appear similar to Figure P6-31.

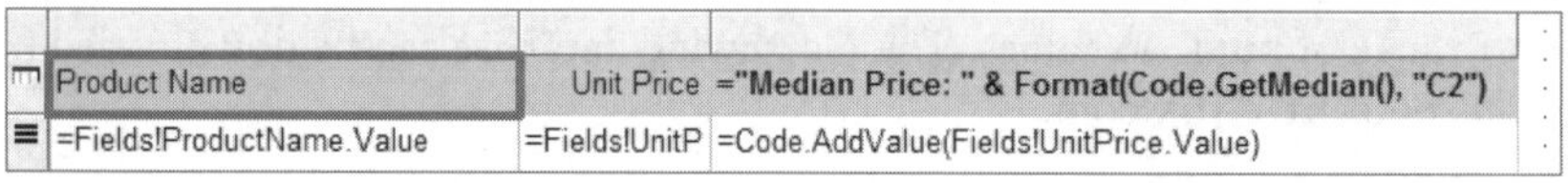

Product Name	Unit Price	="Median Price: " & Format(Code.GetMedian(), "C2")
=Fields!ProductName.Value	=Fields!UnitP	=Code.AddValue(Fields!UnitPrice.Value)

FIGURE P6-31

What happens here in SSRS 2005 is that for each instance of the detail row, the value gets passed to AddValue() and then added to the values ArrayList. A textbox in the table header then makes a call to GetMedian(), which performs a calculation on the values in the ArrayList and displays it.

It's important to note that this wasn't exactly supported in SSRS 2005 and it wouldn't even work properly in most cases. For example, if you were to add end-user sorting to the table, the processing would go through a different code path that would evaluate the headers before the details. This would mean that the GetMedian() function would be called before AddValue has a chance to add any values are added to the ArrayList. It just so happens that in this particular case, when there is no end-user sort, the details are processed first.

Whether or not it was officially supported, a number of people got this to work and are relying on this behavior. In order for the same pattern to work in SSRS 2008, the report needs to be slightly redesigned. Detailed, step-by-step, instructions are provided in the following section. Note that the pattern of using group variables outlined below is not limited to custom aggregation, but can be expanded into more complex solutions. We can show you the path and the pattern, but you will have to apply it to your unique situation. YMMV (your mileage may vary).

Implementing the Report in SSRS 2008

To work in SSRS 2008, the report needs to be slightly revamped. The custom code itself, however, doesn't have to change at all.

1. Create a new report in Report Builder 2.0 or 3.0 and add a data source for the Northwind sample database.

2. Create a new dataset using the following query script:

```
select * from products
```

3. Open the Report Properties dialog and then select the Code page.

4. Add the following Visual Basic.NET code to define the GetMedian and AddValue functions:

```
Dim values As System.Collections.ArrayList

Function AddValue(ByVal newValue As Decimal)
    If (values Is Nothing) Then
        values = New System.Collections.ArrayList()
    End If
    values.Add(newValue)
End Function

Function GetMedian() As Decimal
    Dim count As Integer = values.Count
    If (count > 0) Then
        values.Sort()
        GetMedian = values(count / 2)
    End If
End Function
```

5. Close and accept changes in the Report Properties dialog.

6. Add a table-type tablix to the report body.

7. Drag the Product Name field into the detail row in the first column. Alternatively, you can select this field from the field list in this cell.

8. Drag the Unit Price field into the detail row in the second column or select the field from the field list.

9. Right-click the header cell in the third column and choose Expression.

10. Enter the following text in the Expression Editor. Use the IntelliSense and code completion features where available:

```
="Median Price: " & Format(Code.GetMedian(), "C2")
```

11. Close the Expression dialog and accept changes.

12. Right-click the detail cell in the third column and choose Expression.

13. Enter the following text in the Expression Editor. Use the IntelliSense and code completion features where available:

```
=Code.AddValue(Fields!UnitPrice.Value)
```

At this design stage, the tablix should appear similar to Figure P6-32.

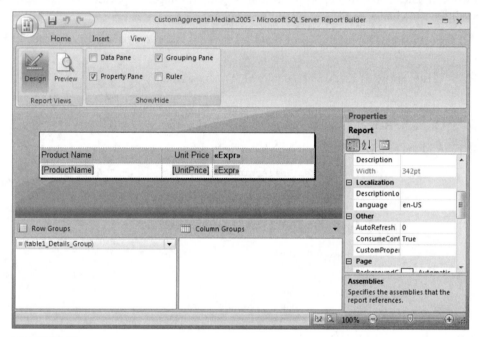

FIGURE P6-32

In on-demand processing, items are generally evaluated from the top down. This means that in order to add the values of your detail rows into the `ArrayList` from which you will calculate the Median value, you need to add a "dummy" tablix to your report with its own detail row. This row can be hidden, as it's used solely for calculation purposes. Specifically, its purpose is to make calls to the `AddValue` function to populate the `ArrayList`. So that this table can share values with the table that will be visually presented in the report, they both need to be part of the same table.

14. Add a single static row above the header row in the table. Right-click in the blue Product Name cell, and select Insert Row ⇨ Above.

15. In the newly inserted row, merge all of the cells.

Figure P6-33 displays the result.

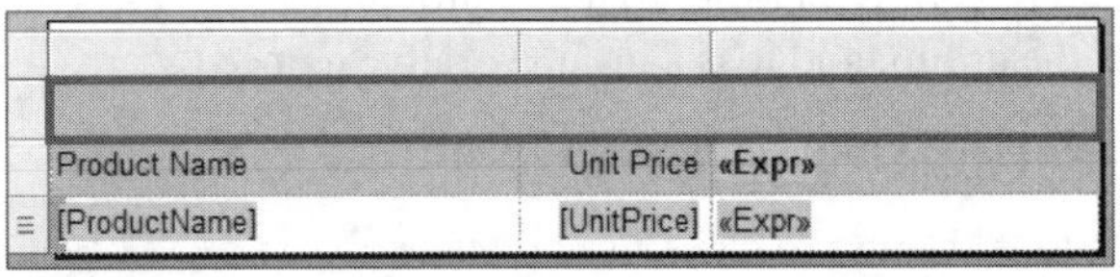

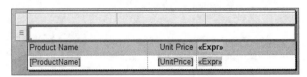

FIGURE P6-33

16. Click the new cell (as shown in Figure P6-33), and from the Insert tab on the Ribbon, select Table. Delete the top row from the newly created table, and merge the cells together, as shown in Figure P6-34.

FIGURE P6-34

17. Select the detail group for this new inner table, and set the Hidden property to True. Since this is used only for calculations, it doesn't need to be visible in the rendered output of the report (see Figure P6-35).

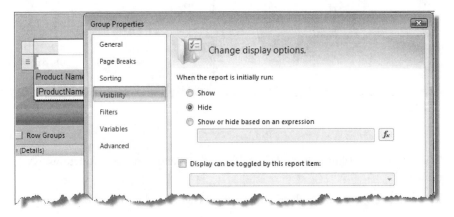

FIGURE P6-35

18. Now, you need to add the call to the `AddValues` function within the context of the nested table. As mentioned previously, a hidden textbox's value will not be evaluated due to the new on-demand processing architecture. In order to make sure the call to `AddValues` is made regardless of the visibility of the group, add it as a group variable named `GV`.

19. Add the following expression for the Value of the GV variable:

```
=Code.AddValue(Fields!UnitPrice.Value)
```

20. Verify the variable definition with Figure P6-36. Close and accept changes in the Expression and Group Properties dialogs.

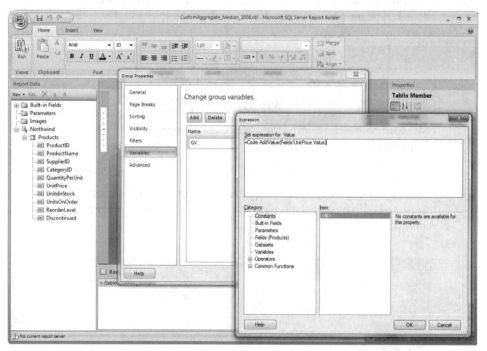

FIGURE P6-36

21. Restructure the original rows of the table so that the original row functions as a group header.

    a. Right click in the Product Name cell and select Add Group ➪ Row group ➪ Parent group.

    b. In the Tablix group dialog, enter 0 (constant value) in Group by.

    c. Select the Add group header option.

Figure P6-37 shows the Tablix group dialog.

FIGURE P6-37

22. Select the newly created group header text box (with the 0 in it), right click, and select delete column. Figure P6-38 shows the result.

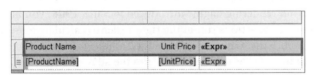

FIGURE P6-38

23. Copy the contents of the blue cells into the row below it, so that it's inside the group. Then, delete the row from which the values were copied. Re-add the blue background to the other row if you want. The report should now look like Figure P6-39.

Product Name	Unit Price	«Expr»
[ProductName]	[UnitPrice]	«Expr»

FIGURE P6-39

24. Now, in order to properly retrieve the calculated Median value, you need to add the call to `GetMedian` into a group variable for the group that contains the header where you want the value to be displayed. Select the group from the grouping pane, and add a group variable named `Median`.

25. Add the following expression for the Value of the Median variable:

```
=Code.GetMedian()
```

26. Verify the variable definition with Figure P6-40. Close and accept changes in the Expression and Group Properties dialogs.

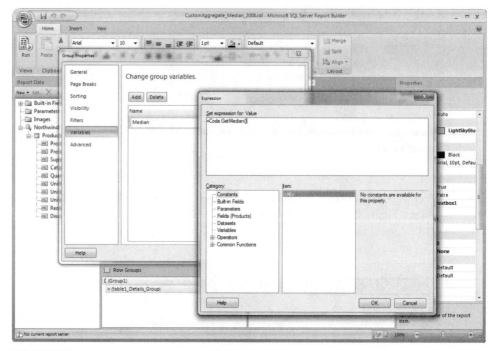

FIGURE P6-40

Final Thoughts

The SSRS 2005 implementation of this custom calculation solution was easy to visualize. However, due to optimizations in the new on-demand rendering engine introduced in SSRS 2008, you had to jump through a few more hoops to make these functions run in the right order to calculate a median value. In order to add the detail row values into the ArrayList, you added a hidden "dummy" tablix to the report with its own detail row. Each instance of this detail row ran the AddValue function, adding an item to the ArrayList, which in turn was used to calculate values in the visible table rows. Techniques like this may be used to perform specialized calculations and perform a variety of unique operations.

Credits and Related References

See Robert Bruckner's blog topic "Using Group Variables in Reporting Services 2008 for Custom Aggregation" at: http://blogs.msdn.com/robertbruckner/archive/2008/07/20/Using-group-variables-in-reporting-services-2008-for-custom-aggregation.aspx

DYNAMIC (CONDITIONAL) PAGE BREAKS

So-called logical page breaks (i.e., page breaks set on report items and groups) have a page break position property. That property cannot be set dynamically at runtime based on an RDL expression. However, it is still possible to achieve dynamic page breaks using a condition evaluated at runtime.

This recipe shows how to use the new PageBreak.Disabled property to accomplish dynamic page breaks, and then explains a second technique utilizing a dummy group.

Note that the PageBreak.Disabled technique can also be combined with the Renderer Dependant Layout and Formatting recipe later in this section of the book, to accomplish, for example, a report with automatic or explicit page breaks while viewing on the screen, but as a single Excel worksheet data export without any page breaks.

Product Versions

➤ Reporting Services 2000

➤ Reporting Services 2005

➤ Reporting Services 2008

The new PageBreak.Disabled property is available starting with Reporting Services 2008 R2.

➤ Reporting Services 2008 R2

A less flexible technique may be used in all versions of Reporting Services.

What You'll Need

➤ AdventureWorks2008 sample database

Designing the Report

This recipe uses the AdventureWorks2008 for its sample database and a grouped query to return detailed information about all products available in a product catalog. Figure P6-41 shows the finished report with varying total number of pages depending on the selected report parameter value to determine page break behavior.

1. Start by designing a data source for the AdventureWorks2008 sample databases.

2. Create a dataset query that returns product sales information by product category and subcategory, as well as by quarter and year.

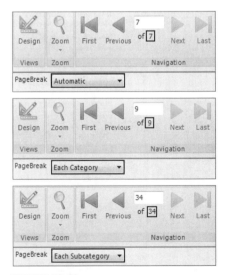

FIGURE P6-41

```
SELECT
    PC.Name AS Category, PS.Name AS Subcategory, PM.Name AS Model,
    PD.Description, PP.LargePhoto, PP.LargePhotoFileName, P.Name AS Product,
    P.ProductNumber, P.Color, P.Size, P.Weight, P.StandardCost,
    P.Style, P.Class, P.ListPrice
FROM Production.Product P INNER JOIN
    Production.ProductSubcategory PS INNER JOIN
    Production.ProductCategory PC ON PS.ProductCategoryID = PC.ProductCategoryID
        ON P.ProductSubcategoryID = PS.ProductSubcategoryID INNER JOIN
    Production.ProductProductPhoto PPP ON P.ProductID = PPP.ProductID INNER JOIN
    Production.ProductPhoto PP ON PPP.ProductPhotoID = PP.ProductPhotoID
        LEFT OUTER JOIN
    Production.ProductDescription PD INNER JOIN
    Production.ProductModel PM INNER JOIN
    Production.ProductModelProductDescriptionCulture PMPDCL ON PM.ProductModelID =
        PMPDCL.ProductModelID ON
    PD.ProductDescriptionID = PMPDCL.ProductDescriptionID ON P.ProductModelID =
        PM.ProductModelID
WHERE (PMPDCL.CultureID = 'en')
```

3. Add a table using the table wizard to display product details grouped by product category and subcategory.

   a. Insert a new table from the ribbon and use the Table wizard.

   b. In Step 1 of the wizard, chose the ProductCatalog dataset.

   c. In Step 2, group by the Category and then Subcategory. Add the following fields to the Values section: ProductNumber, Product, Size, and ListPrice into the Values section, as shown in Figure P6-42.

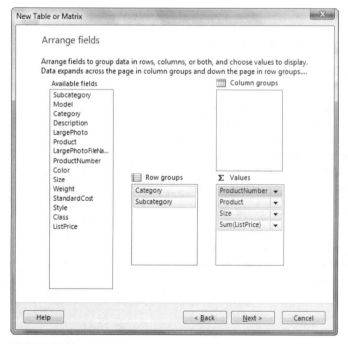

FIGURE P6-42

d. In Step 3, select a simple table layout by deselecting Show subtotals and deselecting Expand/collapse groups.

e. Finish the Table wizard.

f. Adjust the table column widths to provide enough room for the Subcategory, ProductNumber and Product fields.

g. Select the ListPrice column and apply the currency format using the $ sign button in the Number ribbon group.

4. Create a report parameter that dynamically controls what kind of page breaks the user wants.

a. Add a new report parameter called PageBreak of type Text.

b. Add a list of available values: Automatic, Category, Subcategory, as shown in Figure P6-43.

c. Set the default value to Automatic and close the parameter dialog.

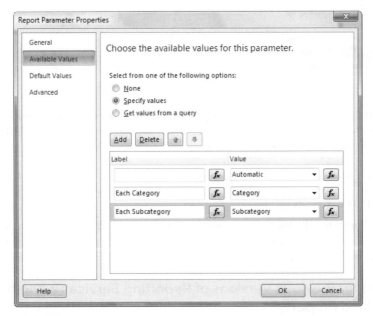

FIGURE P6-43

5. Set up dynamic page breaks for the table groups.

a. In the grouping pane under Row Groups, select the Category group. The Properties window shows the Tablix Member properties.

b.   Under the Tablix Member properties, expand the Group properties and the Page-Break properties. Set the PageBreak.Location property to Between. Set the Page-Break.Disabled property to the following expression:

```
=Not(Parameters!PageBreak.Value = "Category")
```

As a result, with the expression settings shown in Figure P6-44, the Between page break on categories is only enabled if the PageBreak report parameter is set to Category.

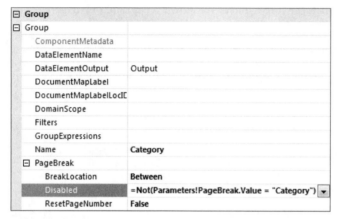

FIGURE P6-44

c.   In the grouping pane under Row Groups, select the Subcategory group and apply the equivalent settings as described in Step b, except that the PageBreak.Disabled property is set to the following expression:

```
=Not(Parameters!PageBreak.Value = "Subcategory")
```

6.   Preview the report to test the results.

After the initial preview, change the parameter to a different value and click View Report in the preview toolbar. Verify that you get the desired page break behavior, resulting in different overall number of pages, as shown in Figure P6-45.

Designing the Report for Previous Versions of Reporting Services without the PageBreak.Disabled Property

To achieve the same results with previous versions of Reporting Services requires only the following adjustment to Step 5.

5.   Set up dynamic page breaks for the table groups.

a.   Open the Table Properties dialog, go the Groups tab, and edit the Category group.

b.   On the Category group, add the following explicit sort expression based on the category value:

```
=Fields!Category.Value
```

On the category group's main page, select Page Break at End. Finally, modify the group expression to dynamically group either on a constant value (and thereby not trigger a page break in between each group instance) or for each category based on the report parameter value:

```
=iif(Parameters!PageBreak.Value = "Category", Fields!Category.Value, 1)
```

c. Edit the Subcategory group of the table and apply the equivalent settings as described in Step b, but use the following group expression:

```
=iif(Parameters!PageBreak.Value = "Category", Fields!Subcategory.Value, 1)
```

FIGURE P6-45

Final Thoughts

The enhanced PageBreak properties introduced in Reporting Services 2008 R2 are quite useful to get more fine-grained control over the report layout. This can be further combined with rendering dependent layout abilities, so that one report definition can produce optimized output for each rendering format.

That said, if your reports target earlier versions of Reporting Services, there is also the so-called dummy group technique, which may get you the desired results, despite limitations of that approach.

EXCEL WORKSHEET NAMING AND PAGE NAMING

One feature for Reporting Services that is frequently requested is the capability to define data-dependent names for worksheets when exporting to Excel.

Reporting Services 2008 R2 adds this capability through a more general feature to name pages. Those page names could be referenced in the page header and page footer from expressions through =Globals!PageName for all rendering formats. In Excel specifically however, page names determine the name of worksheets. The report item with the most top/left position on a rendered page defines the page name for a particular rendered page.

This recipe focuses specifically on naming Excel worksheets.

Product Versions

➤ Reporting Services 2008 R2

What You'll Need

➤ AdventureWorks2008 sample database

➤ Product Catalog 2008 AdventureWorks sample report

Designing the Report

The goal of this recipe is to take an existing report and modify it so that we get a particular rendering layout and formatting optimized for working with the report output in Excel, including naming of the Excel worksheets. This recipe also makes use of rendering-dependent layout, explained in more detail in the related recipe titled "Renderer Dependent Layout and Formatting." Figure P6-46 shows the final result.

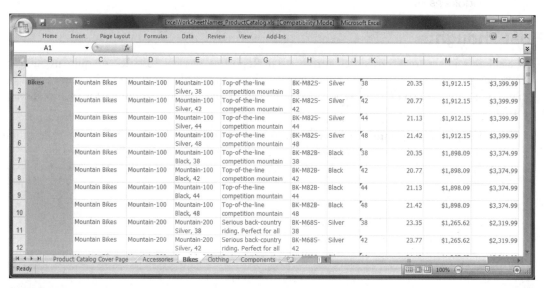

FIGURE P6-46

1. Open the Product Catalog 2008 sample report in Report Builder 3.0 of SQL Server Reporting Services 2008 R2.

   If you haven't downloaded the AdventureWorks sample reports yet from CodePlex, use the following link: http://www.codeplex.com/MSFTRSProdSamples

2. Set the page name for the cover page of the report.

   On the report design surface, select the rectangle ("Rectangle2") that contains the cover page of the product catalog report.

   In the properties grid, set the PageName property value to Product Catalog Cover Page, as shown in Figure P6-47. This will set the name of the initial page (and first worksheet on Excel export).

⊞ PageBreak	
PageName	**Product Catalog Cover Page**

FIGURE P6-47

3. Hide the product catalog details tablix for Excel export:

   a. Locate and select the overall product table ("Tablix1") near the bottom of the design surface. Select the tablix and then click the Property Pages icon in the properties grid toolbar to open the tablix properties for Tablix1.

   b. Go to the Visibility page.

   c. Use the following expression for the show or hide setting, as shown in Figure P6-48:

   ```
   =(Globals!RenderFormat.Name = "EXCEL")
   ```

   This expression will hide Tablix1 when rendered to Excel.

FIGURE P6-48

4. Make room in the report layout for an additional table.

Increase the report body height by dragging the splitter between report body and page footer.

5. Use the Table wizard to add a new table.

a. Insert a new table from the Ribbon and use the Table wizard.

b. In Step 1 of the wizard, chose the ProductCatalog dataset.

c. In Step 2, create a row group for the Category field, and add the following fields to the Values section: Subcategory, Model, Product, Description, ProductNumber, Color, Size, Weight, StandardCost, and ListPrice into the values section, as shown in Figure P6-49.

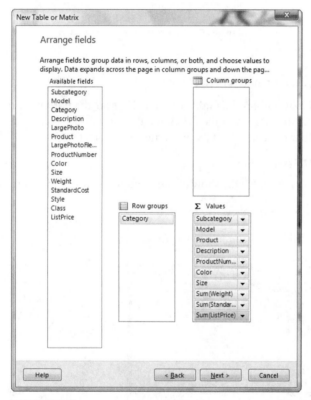

FIGURE P6-49

d. In Step 3, select a simple table layout by deselecting show subtotals and deselecting expand/collapse groups.

e. Finish the wizard.

f. Move the newly created table into the empty space at the bottom of the report page.

g. Adjust the table column widths to provide more room for fields such as Description, and decrease the width for fields such as Size and Color.

h. Select the StandardCost and the ListPrice columns of the table, and for each column apply currency formatting using the corresponding Ribbon button with the $ sign. The design surface layout should look similar to the result shown in Figure P6-50, with the new table added beneath the existing product catalog table.

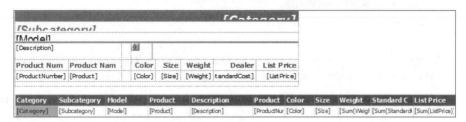

FIGURE P6-50

6. Prepare the data table to only be rendered to Excel.

a. Select the table created in the previous step and open the tablix properties dialog. In this particular case of the Product Catalog report, we do not need to add a page break before because the rectangle with the cover page already has a page break. In your specific report scenarios, you may consider adding a page break before to ensure your data table starts on a new page (and therefore on a new worksheet in Excel).

b. On the Visibility page, use the following expression for the show or hide setting:

```
=(Globals!RenderFormat.Name <> "EXCEL")
```

This expression will show the data table only when rendered to Excel, but not for any other rendering formats.

c. On the Sorting page, add the following two sort expressions in sequence so that the data table sorts the detail rows by SubCategory (ascending) and then by Model (ascending).

d. Close the table properties dialog and select the tablix member "Category1" from the grouping pane.

e. In the properties grid, expand Group and then set the PageBreak.BreakLocation to Between, and set the PageName to =Fields!Category.Value as shown in Figure P6-51.

By adding a page break in between each group instance and setting the page name to the current category, each category will create a separate worksheet when exporting the rendered report to Excel. Using this setting, each Excel worksheet will be named based on the current category of data shown on that worksheet.

7. Preview the report to test the results.

⊟ PageBreak	
BreakLocation	**Between**
Disabled	**False**
ResetPageNumber	**False**
PageName	**=Fields!Category.Value** ▾

FIGURE P6-51

Verify that when viewing the report interactively (e.g., in Report Builder Preview), you still get the original product catalog view of the report.

Then export to Excel and verify that you get the cover page, as well as four additional worksheets named by product categories. Each worksheet shows the product details under its category formatted as a simple data table, as shown in Figure P6-52.

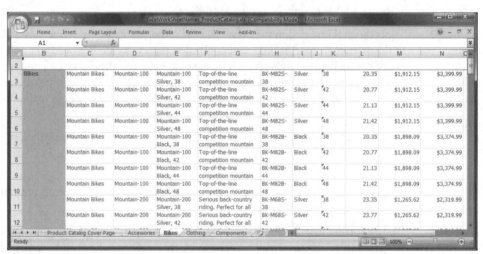

FIGURE P6-52

Final Thoughts

Reporting Services 2008 R2 adds page break enhancements that are very powerful yet could easily be overlooked. This recipe demonstrated setting names for report pages based on the current product category group value which are used as worksheet names in Excel rendering, and generating a data-oriented Excel-specific layout; unique from other rendering formats.

If you want to learn more about page break enhancements in Reporting Services 2008 R2, also take a look at the "Group Page Name Reset" and the "Dynamic Page Breaks" recipes.

EXTERNAL IMAGE SOURCES

Including images in reports is a standard, straightforward process. However, it gets a little more complicated when you need to be able to quickly and easily update the image without directly changing the image reference path within the report. Another scenario would be if you wanted to display a manipulated image (size, cropping, and so on) stored in the database, you would need to use an external image within your report. For both scenarios, a little programming creativity and the combination of SSRS and ASP.NET can make your task much less daunting.

This recipe walks you through two scenarios: creating a report that accepts a parameter and using that parameter to dynamically assign the image value as well as displaying a manipulated, cropped image within your report without directly accessing the database using ASP.NET.

Product Versions

➤ Reporting Services 2008

What You'll Need

➤ Report Builder 2.0 (or 3.0)

➤ Visual Studio with Visual Web Developer

➤ An understanding of ASP.NET and C# or VB.NET

➤ An understanding of Report Data Sources

➤ Microsoft Enterprise Library (3.0 or higher)

Designing the Report

This recipe uses the AdventureWorks2008 sample database and a grouped query to return detailed information about all products available in a product catalog. Figure P6-53 shows the finished report with both a parameterized logo for easy branding and also the product images displayed as external image sources with the dimensions being set at run-time. The product images use an ASP.NET web page to dynamically display and re-size the image.

1. Open Report Builder and connect to the report server.

2. Create a new report and add a header. From the Insert ribbon, drag an image inside the header.

3. Right-click the Parameters Folder and add a new parameter.

Note that the source of the image is External, so an external image is required for the image to display. All other image properties at this point can be left to their default values (see Figure P6-54).

FIGURE P6-53

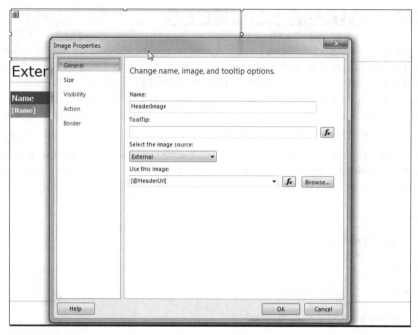

FIGURE P6-54

Name the parameter HeaderUrl, mark the parameter as hidden, and set the default value to NULL. This way, the report can be previewed without prompt or error.

4. View the expression for the image and set the value to the following:

```
=Parameters!HeaderUrl.Value
```

5. Open the Insert page in Report Builder and click the Table icon to start the Table wizard.

When prompted for a data source, create (or use an existing) connection which points to the AdventureWorks database.

6. After you have selected a connection, you will be prompted to design a query. Expand the Production folder in your database view. In the Tables folder, expand the Products folder (see Figure P6-55).

7. Select the ProductID, Name, and ListPrice columns and click the Next button.

8. Add the Name and ProductID columns to the Row groups' area and the ListPrice to the Sum Values (see Figure P6-56).

9. After clicking Next, uncheck the box to show Subtotals and Grand Totals. The Expand/Collapse Groups checkbox should be checked.

10. After clicking Next, choose your style and then click the Finish button. You will be back in the design mode of the report.

11. Now, add an additional column with a header of Product Image that will serve as the external product image.

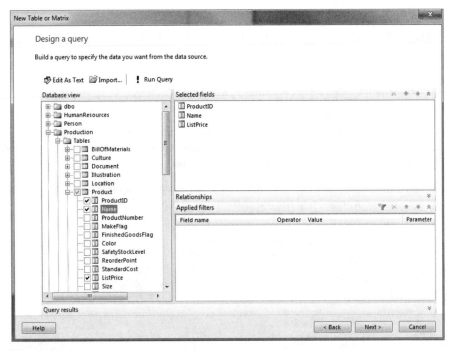

FIGURE P6-55

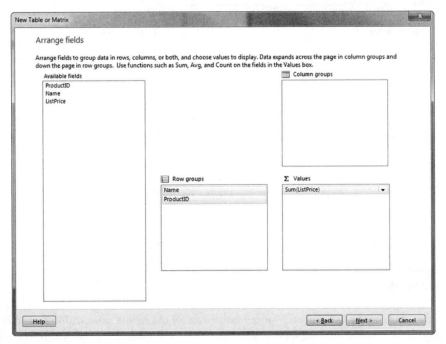

FIGURE P6-56

12. Add an additional, hidden report parameter called BaseUrl.

This will be the base portion of the URL, excluding the direct reference to the product. This again can be customized and the default value be set on a case-by-case basis. For this parameter, check the Allow Null Value checkbox.

13. Add one final, hidden report parameter, MaxSize.

This parameter will be passed to the ASP.NET web page, along with the Product ID, through the query string. This will be the maximum size of the image you want to display and the code will accept the parameter and proportionally adjust the image (width and height). The default value of this parameter should be set to 500.

14. Drag an image from the toolbar into the newly created column. Within the properties of the image, set the expression of the image to match Figure P6-57.

```
=Parameters!BaseUrl.Value & "/DisplayImages.aspx?productID=
" & Fields!ProductID.Value & "&MaxSize=" & Parameters!MaxSize.Value
```

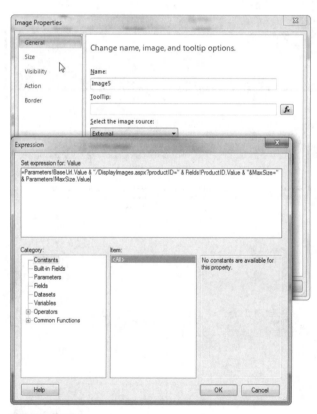

FIGURE P6-57

After clicking the OK button, you can now preview the report from within ReportBuilder. The report should look something like Figure P6-58, including the red X's for the missing images.

External Images in SSRS

Name	Product ID	List Price	Product Image
⊞ Adjustable Race		0.0000	
⊞ All-Purpose Bike Stand		159.0000	
⊞ AWC Logo Cap		8.9900	
⊞ BB Ball Bearing		0.0000	
⊞ Bearing Ball		0.0000	
⊞ Bike Wash - Dissolver		7.9500	
⊞ Blade		0.0000	
⊞ Cable Lock		25.0000	
⊞ Chain		20.2400	
⊞ Chain Stays		0.0000	
⊞ Chainring		0.0000	
⊞ Chainring Bolts		0.0000	
⊞ Chainring Nut		0.0000	
⊞ Classic Vest, L		63.5000	
⊞ Classic Vest, M		63.5000	
⊞ Classic Vest, S		63.5000	
⊞ Cone-Shaped Race		0.0000	
⊞ Crown Race		0.0000	
⊞ Cup-Shaped Race		0.0000	

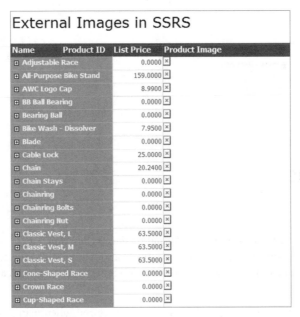

FIGURE P6-58

Saving the report will publish the report to the report server and you can now set the header and default parameters.

15. View the Properties of the report from the report server to set the parameters (see Figure P6-59).

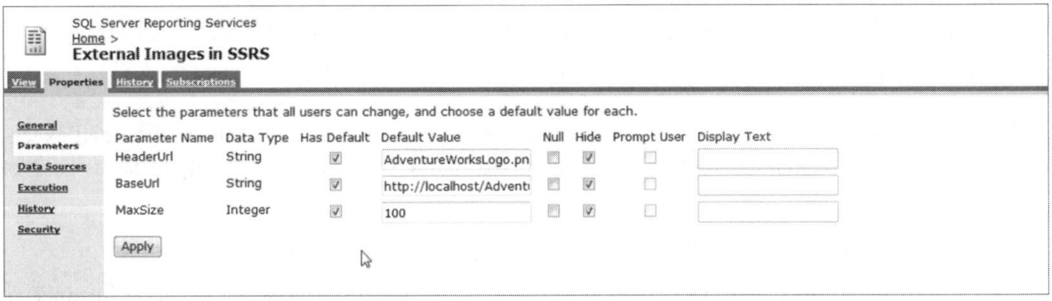

FIGURE P6-59

Before you can preview the report correctly, you will need to upload an image file for your logo. This image can be either a relative path (in which case the image would be uploaded to the report server directly) or an absolute path, which could reference a URL as the image source. At this point, if default values have been set for the parameters, the NULL checkboxes will no longer be checked.

After setting the HeaderUrl parameter, the report displays correctly with the proper branded logo (see Figure P6-60). Also note, for the MaxSize parameter, you will set the initial value to 500 and you can adjust it easily if necessary.

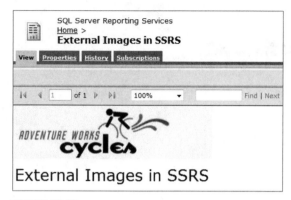

FIGURE P6-60

One of the biggest advantages you will gain from using external images within SSRS is the ability to personalize without hard-coding. The ability to parameterize reports and make them generic enough without losing quality and performance is a solid approach when designing reports which can at some point be reutilized.

However, it is important to note there is an extra configuration step required when using external images, which is configuring the unattended execution account. According to SQL Server 2008 Books Online:

> *Unattended report processing refers to any report execution process that is triggered by an event (either a schedule-driven event or data refresh event) rather than a user request. The report server uses the unattended report processing account to log on to the computer that hosts the external data source. This account is necessary because the credentials of the Report Server service account are never used to connect to other computers.*

This is very easy to accomplish, but the account used to configure or act as the unattended execution account must be kept current, meaning standard Active Directory rules apply in terms password expiration, and so on.

To configure the account, you can either use the RSCONFIG utility or do the following:

1. Start the Reporting Services Configuration tool and connect to the report server instance you want to configure.

2. Open the Execution Account Page and specify the execution account.

3. Type and re-type the password; then click Apply.

Creating the ASP.NET External Image Source

Now that you have created the report and deployed it to the report server, you can create the external image source using ASP.NET. The code samples below will be in both C# and VB.NET. You can choose the appropriate language depending on your programming background or preference.

1. Open Visual Studio.NET and create a new ASP.NET web site. The name of your virtual directory can be anything, but use AdventureWorks for this recipe.

2. Delete the initial web page provided for you (Default.aspx).

3. Add a new web page to your project and name the file DisplayImages.aspx (see Figure P6-61).

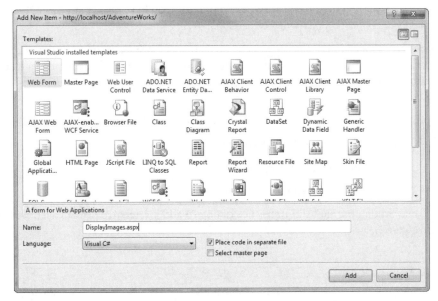

FIGURE P6-61

In the HTML Design View of this page, remove all pre-generated HTML code with the exception of the page declaration:

```
<%@ Page Language="C#" AutoEventWireup="true" CodeFile="DisplayImage.aspx.cs"
    ContentType="Image/Jpeg" Inherits="DisplayImage" %>
```

Also notice the content type of the page is changed to Image/Jpeg. This will allow the report designer and other applications to see this aspx page as a valid image source.

At this point, you need to configure your database connection string in the web configuration file.

1. Open the web.config file in your web site, and under the configSections node, add the following configuration section:

```
<section name="dataConfiguration" type="Microsoft.Practices.EnterpriseLibrary.
        Data.Configuration.DatabaseSettings,
        Microsoft.Practices.EnterpriseLibrary.Data"/>
```

2. Outside the configuration sections node group, add the following lines to configure your connection string and enable the default provider.

```
<dataConfiguration defaultDatabase="AdventureWorks"/>
<connectionStrings>
    <add name="AdventureWorks" providerName="System.Data.SqlClient"
        connectionString="data
    source=localhost;initial catalog=AdventureWorks;User ID=AdventureWorks;
    Password=pass@word1"/>
</connectionStrings>
```

In the code above, my connection string points to `localhost` (your computer) as the database server and the AdventureWorks database. You have also created a SQL `User` called `AdventureWorks` with a password of `pass@word1`.

Let's return to the code-behind of the `DisplayImage.aspx`. You are ready to wire-up the code that will accept the parameters from the query string, connect to the database to find the proper image, and finally, proportionaly adjust the image according to the MaxSize parameter, again passed in on the query string.

1. In the web site you have created, add a reference to the following three binary DLLs:

➤ Microsoft.Practices.EnterpriseLibrary.Common

➤ Microsoft.Practices.EnterpriseLibrary.Data

➤ Microsoft.Practices.ObjectBuilder

In Visual Studio, use the Add Reference dialog to add a reference to your web site (see Figure P6-62).

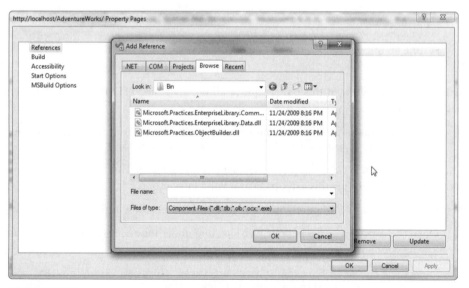

FIGURE P6-62

2. Enter the following code to add these namespaces to your web page:

- ➤ System.Drawing
- ➤ Microsoft.Practices.EnterpriseLibrary.Data.Sql
- ➤ Microsoft.Practices.EnterpriseLibrary.Data
- ➤ System.Data
- ➤ System.Data.Common
- ➤ System.Text
- ➤ System.IO

C#

```csharp
using System.Drawing;
using Microsoft.Practices.EnterpriseLibrary.Data;
using Microsoft.Practices.EnterpriseLibrary.Data.Sql;
using System.Data;
using System.Data.Common;
using System.Text;
using System.IO;
```

VB.NET

```vbnet
Imports System.Drawing
Imports Microsoft.Practices.EnterpriseLibrary.Data
Imports Microsoft.Practices.EnterpriseLibrary.Data.Sql
Imports Ssytem.Data
Imports System.Data.Common
Imports System.Text
Imports System.IO
```

3. Define two private members on your page: ProductID and MaxSize.

C#

```csharp
private int m_ProductID, m_maxSize;
```

4. In the Page_Load event of your page, add the following code snippet. This code will assign your local members from the query string and also execute the BindImage method, which will produce the image.

C#

```csharp
//allows caching based on size and product
Response.Cache.VaryByParams["maxSize;productID"] = true;

//grab and assign query string parameters
int.TryParse(Request.QueryString["productID"], out m_ProductID);
int.TryParse(Request.QueryString["maxSize"], out m_maxSize);
```

```
//clear the response buffer and set the content type
Response.Clear();
Response.ContentType = "image/gif";

//bind the image
if (!IsPostBack)
    BindImage();
```

VB.NET

```
'allows caching based on size and product
Response.Cache.VaryByParams("maxSize;productID") = True

'grab and assign query string parameters
Integer.TryParse(Request.QueryString("productID"), m_ProductID)
Integer.TryParse(Request.QueryString("maxSize"), m_maxSize)

'clear the response buffer and set the content type
Response.Clear()
Response.ContentType = "image/gif"

'bind the image
If Not IsPostBack Then
    BindImage()
End If
```

5. The `BindImage` method makes a few other calls to some additional methods noted below. This method includes code to select the `LargePhoto` from the ProductPhoto table and also includes code to re-draw the bitmap according to the specified size. Note that the T-SQL query does join the `ProductProductPhoto` and is looking at the primary image.

C#

```
private void BindImage()
{
    float width = 0;
    float height = 0;

    IDataReader reader;

    StringBuilder sb = new StringBuilder();
    sb.Append("SELECT LARGEPHOTO FROM ");
    sb.Append("Production.ProductPhoto PP ");
    sb.Append("INNER JOIN Production.ProductProductPhoto PPP ON ");
    sb.Append("PPP.ProductPhotoID = PP.ProductPhotoID ");
    sb.Append("WHERE PPP.ProductID = {0} AND PPP.[Primary] = 1");

    Database m_dbObject = DatabaseFactory.CreateDatabase();
    DbCommand dbCommand = m_dbObject.GetSqlStringCommand
        (string.Format(sb.ToString(), m_ProductID));

    byte[] imagePhoto = null;
    using (reader = m_dbObject.ExecuteReader(dbCommand))
```

```
    {
      while (reader.Read())
      {
          if (reader["LARGEPHOTO"] != null)
          imagePhoto = (byte[])reader["LARGEPHOTO"];
      }
      if (!reader.IsClosed)
          reader.Close();

    }

    if (imagePhoto != null)
    {
      System.Drawing.Image ImageObj = System.Drawing.Image.FromStream(new
      MemoryStream(imagePhoto));
      ///method to resize the image
      FitImage(ref ImageObj, m_maxSize, out width, out height);
      ///method to produce new bitmap with size
      ImageObj = GetDisplayImage(ImageObj, width, height, 100);
      ///save to output stream
      ImageObj.Save(Response.OutputStream,
      System.Drawing.Imaging.ImageFormat.Gif);
    }
}

private void FitImage(ref System.Drawing.Image obj,
        int MaxSize,
        out float Width,
        out float Height)
{

    Height = 0;
    Width = 0;
    float W, H;

    W = obj.Width;
    H = obj.Height;

    if (W > H)
    {
Width = MaxSize;
Height = (H / W) * MaxSize;
    }
    else
    {
      Height = MaxSize;
      Width = (W / H) * MaxSize;
    }
    Height = float.Parse(Height.ToString("N0"));
    Width = float.Parse(Width.ToString("N0"));
}
```

```csharp
public Bitmap GetDisplayImage
  (System.Drawing.Image image, float w, float h, int resolution)
{
    int width = 0;
    int height = 0;
    int.TryParse(w.ToString(), out width);
    int.TryParse(h.ToString(), out height);
    Bitmap bmp = new Bitmap(width, height);
    Graphics g = Graphics.FromImage(bmp);
    g.DrawImage(image, 0, 0, w, h);
    g.Dispose();
    return bmp;
}
```

VB.NET

```vbnet
  Private Sub BindImage()
      Dim width As Single = 0
      Dim height As Single = 0

      Dim reader As IDataReader

      Dim sb As New StringBuilder()
      sb.Append("SELECT LARGEPHOTO FROM ")
      sb.Append("Production.ProductPhoto PP ")
      sb.Append("INNER JOIN Production.ProductProductPhoto PPP ON ")
      sb.Append("PPP.ProductPhotoID = PP.ProductPhotoID ")
      sb.Append("WHERE PPP.ProductID = {0} AND PPP.[Primary] = 1")

      Dim m_dbObject As Database = DatabaseFactory.CreateDatabase()
      Dim dbCommand As DbCommand = m_dbObject.GetSqlStringCommand
        (String.Format(sb.ToString(), m_ProductID))

      Dim imagePhoto As Byte() = Nothing
      Using reader = m_dbObject.ExecuteReader(dbCommand)
          While reader.Read()
              If reader("LARGEPHOTO") IsNot Nothing Then
                  imagePhoto = DirectCast(reader("LARGEPHOTO"), Byte())
              End If
          End While
          If Not reader.IsClosed Then
              reader.Close()

          End If
      End Using

      If imagePhoto IsNot Nothing Then
          Dim ImageObj As System.Drawing.Image = System.Drawing.Image.FromStream
            (New MemoryStream(imagePhoto))
```

```
            '''method to resize the image
            FitImage(ImageObj, m_maxSize, width, height)
            '''method to produce new bitmap with size
            ImageObj = GetDisplayImage(ImageObj, width, height, 100)
            '''save to output stream
            ImageObj.Save(Response.OutputStream, _
                System.Drawing.Imaging.ImageFormat.Gif)
        End If
    End Sub

    Private Sub FitImage(ByRef obj As System.Drawing.Image, ByVal MaxSize As Integer, _
      ByRef Width As Single, ByRef Height As Single)

        Height = 0
        Width = 0
        Dim W As Single, H As Single

        W = obj.Width
        H = obj.Height

        If W > H Then
            Width = MaxSize
            Height = (H / W) * MaxSize
        Else
            Height = MaxSize
            Width = (W / H) * MaxSize
        End If
        Height = Single.Parse(Height.ToString("N0"))
        Width = Single.Parse(Width.ToString("N0"))
    End Sub

    Public Function GetDisplayImage(ByVal image As System.Drawing.Image, ByVal w As _
            Single, ByVal h As Single, ByVal resolution As Integer) As Bitmap
        Dim width As Integer = 0
        Dim height As Integer = 0
        Integer.TryParse(w.ToString(), width)
        Integer.TryParse(h.ToString(), height)
        Dim bmp As New Bitmap(width, height)
        Dim g As Graphics = Graphics.FromImage(bmp)
        g.DrawImage(image, 0, 0, w, h)
        g.Dispose()
        Return bmp
    End Function
```

The result of the code is a web page that acts as an image and can be created and dynamically resized. Once you re-execute the report (see Figure P6-63), the images appear and are proportionally sized. If you want to increase the size of the image, simply adjust the MaxSize parameter of the report and re-execute.

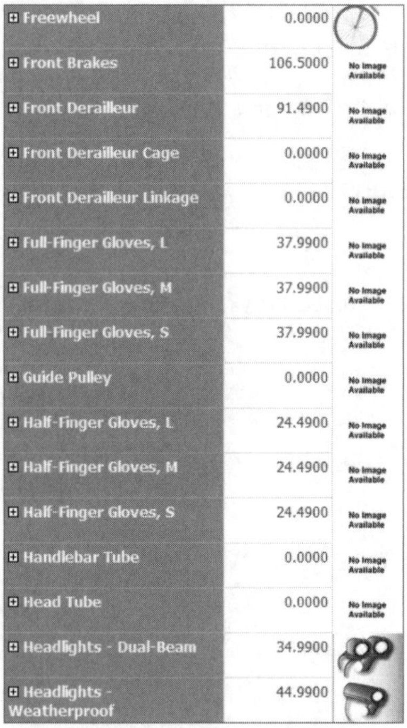

⊞ Freewheel	0.0000	
⊞ Front Brakes	106.5000	No Image Available
⊞ Front Derailleur	91.4900	No Image Available
⊞ Front Derailleur Cage	0.0000	No Image Available
⊞ Front Derailleur Linkage	0.0000	No Image Available
⊞ Full-Finger Gloves, L	37.9900	No Image Available
⊞ Full-Finger Gloves, M	37.9900	No Image Available
⊞ Full-Finger Gloves, S	37.9900	No Image Available
⊞ Guide Pulley	0.0000	No Image Available
⊞ Half-Finger Gloves, L	24.4900	No Image Available
⊞ Half-Finger Gloves, M	24.4900	No Image Available
⊞ Half-Finger Gloves, S	24.4900	No Image Available
⊞ Handlebar Tube	0.0000	No Image Available
⊞ Head Tube	0.0000	No Image Available
⊞ Headlights - Dual-Beam	34.9900	
⊞ Headlights - Weatherproof	44.9900	

FIGURE P6-63

Final Thoughts

Together, SSRS and ASP.NET can allow report developers to easily extend their reports and then increase the flexibility for further purposes or enhanced reusability. In addition, with a little programming, you can avoid the potential drawback of storing various sized images in the database. Not only can you eliminate the different versions of the image from the database, but you are able to control the size, resolution, and any other effects you wish to apply to a single image, rather than manipulating multiple versions.

LANGUAGE LOCALIZATION

At some point during your endeavors as a report designer/developer, you will run into the issue of report localization. Localization simply means that you have taken care of using lookup resources for each supported locale and culture in order to hold any static strings that will be displayed on the report; it allows you to have language and culturally aware reports. With localization, your reports should strive to be culturally aware and language-neutral so that you can truly achieve a good level of globalization.

Reporting Services provides several mechanisms that take care of certain aspects of localization. The RDL schema provides a Report Language property that can be used to set the appropriate culture and locale information that will be used to format dates, numbers, and currency. It also provides support for right-to-left languages such as Hebrew. The ReportViewer control, and most of the Report Manager UI, provides localized strings, which means that UI elements surrounding your report RDL will already be translated and formatted according to the user's current culture settings (defined by browser and OS).

Out of the box, Reporting Services, configured in native mode, supports ten languages. In SharePoint Integration Mode, you get an additional twelve.

However, you are still required to take a few additional steps in order to provide a fully localized RDL (that is, one that knows how to handle string lookups for the current culture). With the use of .NET Globalization features and a custom code assembly, you can accomplish this fairly easily.

Product Versions

➤ Reporting Services 2000

➤ Reporting Services 2005

➤ Reporting Services 2008

What You'll Need

➤ .NET class project with different resource files for each supported language, defining the static text you want the report to look up

➤ Static method that takes a key and returns a value from the current culture's resource file

➤ An RDL file that defines an external assembly reference

➤ Textbox expressions within the report body that call the external assembly

➤ Territory Sales Drilldown 2008 Report, included in the AdventureWorks 2008 Report Samples

Multi-Cultural Considerations

There are some considerations to keep in mind when following this approach. You will be using a single report RDL to display text in different languages. For tabular reports, column headers that contain static localized text will need to accommodate the longest string values among the language you plan to support; otherwise, you might encounter odd text wrapping, which can be an issue for glyph- or character-based languages such as Japanese or Chinese, where the different combination of characters implies different meanings.

If your report displays currency amounts, you need to identify whether you will be providing converted currency values. If your data stores only US dollar amounts, you may have to specify on the report the currency that is being used, or you may choose to use an external service that provides currency conversion calculations. In either case, you will want to be extremely careful about how you present this type of information and also take into consideration any latency incurred from making expensive invocations to external services.

PARAMETER PROMPT EXPRESSIONS AND THE RDCE

In early previews of Reporting Services 2008, there was a new feature that allowed the ability to apply expressions to Report parameter prompt text. While this would go hand in hand with the ability to fully localize a report and provide seamless culturally aware reports, the feature was removed in the final release version.

As in previous versions of Reporting Services, the parameter prompt text still can only hold static text, which means you cannot utilize the standard parameter toolbar to collect user input for multi-language reports without forcing all end users to understand the same language.

To address this shortcoming, developers might be forced to create multiple copies of the same report, each for a different language, which unfortunately defeats the purpose of dynamic string lookups for localization.

A feature released in Reporting Services 2008 named the Report Definition Customization Extensions (RDCE) provides hooks into the preprocessing of reports so that the developer can customize the report definition. Using the RDCE, the developer can ultimately address the parameter prompt issue by extending Reporting Services.

This is particularly interesting for report localization because it allows the custom extension to investigate values in parameters, user and locale information, and then provide a customized report definition on the fly that gets executed for that report request. More information is available at the following URL:

`http://msdn.microsoft.com/library/cc281022.aspx`

Designing the Report

The final product of this recipe will contain a Territory Sales report that uses expressions to retrieve localized static text using custom code in a .NET assembly. To show the final product, you leverage the localized Report Manager to run the report in a different locale.

Figure P6-64 shows the final product of this recipe.

FIGURE P6-64

Creating the External Resource Lookup with .NET

This section shows how you can leverage .NET Globalization and Resource files to store your static string values for multiple languages, and then how to retrieve those values from within the report body. The .NET project will provide a set of "satellite" assemblies that will contain the culturally specific resources.

The following example does not get into details of how to write code or create classes using .NET. If you need to implement this solution, you should have a certain level of experience with writing custom code.

1. In Visual Studio, create a new C# class library project (you can also write this library in your .NET language of choice) and give it the name Wrox.Localization.

2. Within your class file, add the following lines of code:

```
using System;
using System.Globalization;
using System.Resources;
using System.Reflection;

namespace Wrox.Localization
{
    public class Localizer
    {
        private ResourceManager rm;
        public string ResourceName { get; set; }
```

```
        public Localizer()
        {
            Initialize();
        }

        public Localizer(string resourceName)
        {
            this.ResourceName = resourceName;
            Initialize();
        }

        void Initialize()
        {
            string currentNs = this.GetType().Namespace;
            rm = new ResourceManager(currentNs + "." + this.ResourceName
                    , Assembly.GetExecutingAssembly());
        }

        public string GetLocalText(string key)
        {
            return rm.GetString(key);
        }

        public string GetLocalText(string key, string culture)
        {
            return rm.GetString(key, new CultureInfo(culture));
        }
    }
}
```

This defines your class with a private member, the `ResourceManager` object that will get values out of the resource files. It also defines a public method, `GetLocalText()`, with two overloads: one that takes a key and another that takes both a key and a culture name. This is important to note, because by allowing a resource name to be set as a class property, you can reuse this class for other reports, and won't need to hardcode report-specific details.

3. Next, you need to add a new resource file, named TerritorySales, to the project for each culture that you need to support.

The main resource file name does not include a culture. However, satellite resource file names for different cultures need to have the culture name appended after the resource name, but before the file extension. The naming syntax is `<Resource Name>.<Culture Name>.resx`.

For example, if the default culture file is `TerritorySales.resx`, the Chinese (Taiwan) equivalent would be `TerritorySales.zh-TW.resx`. Figures P6-65 and P6-66 show the contents of the sample resource files for both the default culture (en-US) and the French (fr-FR) culture, respectively. To include new cultures later on, just create new resource files (with Visual Studio or any text editor), and then use the `RESGEN.exe` command-line tool (if you're not using Visual Studio) or build from the IDE to compile into satellite assemblies that you can just drop into the report server's BIN folder.

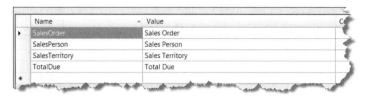

Name	▲ Value	C
▶ SalesOrder	Sales Order	
SalesPerson	Sales Person	
SalesTerritory	Sales Territory	
TotalDue	Total Due	
*		

FIGURE P6-65

Name	▲ Value	C
▶ SalesOrder	Ordre de Ventes	
SalesPerson	Vendeur	
SalesTerritory	Territoire de Ventes	
TotalDue	Total	
*		

FIGURE P6-66

Make sure that each of the resource files in the project has the Build Action property set to Embedded Resource. This tells the compiler to build each resource file in its own satellite assembly and place the file in its respective culture folder under the project's BIN folder.

4. The next step is to deploy the main assembly and the satellite assemblies to Visual Studio's PrivateAssemblies folder, as well as to the report server's BIN folder. The former allows you to execute the report in the preview window of the Report Designer, and the latter is the actual server to which the report will be deployed once it has been developed. Figure P6-67 shows all the files and folders that need to be copied over.

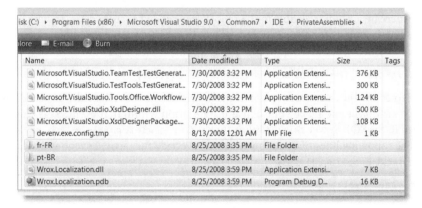

Name	Date modified	Type	Size	Tags
Microsoft.VisualStudio.TeamTest.TestGenerat...	7/30/2008 3:32 PM	Application Extensi...	376 KB	
Microsoft.VisualStudio.TestTools.TestGenerat...	7/30/2008 3:32 PM	Application Extensi...	300 KB	
Microsoft.VisualStudio.Tools.Office.Workflow...	7/30/2008 3:32 PM	Application Extensi...	124 KB	
Microsoft.VisualStudio.XsdDesigner.dll	7/30/2008 3:32 PM	Application Extensi...	500 KB	
Microsoft.VisualStudio.XsdDesignerPackage....	7/30/2008 3:32 PM	Application Extensi...	108 KB	
devenv.exe.config.tmp	8/13/2008 12:01 AM	TMP File	1 KB	
fr-FR	8/25/2008 3:35 PM	File Folder		
pt-BR	8/25/2008 3:35 PM	File Folder		
Wrox.Localization.dll	8/25/2008 3:59 PM	Application Extensi...	7 KB	
Wrox.Localization.pdb	8/25/2008 3:59 PM	Program Debug D...	16 KB	

FIGURE P6-67

5. Restart Visual Studio so the new assemblies will be loaded.

6. Next, open the Territory Sales report (found in the AdventureWorks2008 report sample project) with the BIDS report designer and add a reference to the assembly from the Report Properties window, as shown in Figure P6-68.

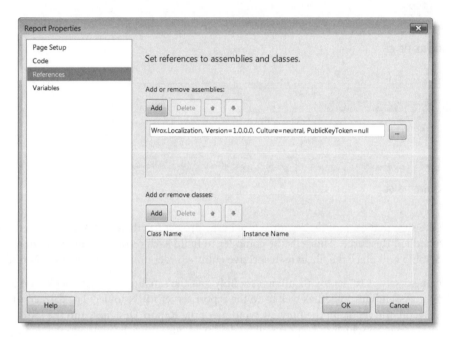

FIGURE P6-68

7. You must create a public variable in the report's embedded custom code, to which you can assign a new instance of the Localizer() object from the external assembly reference. Add the following line of code to do this:

```
Public Dim m_loc As Wrox.Localization.Localizer
```

8. In order to create the Localizer() object instance, you must override the OnInit event of the report's Code object and place your object instantiation within that event. This technique is described in the SQL Server Books Online (http://msdn.microsoft.com/library/ms152801. aspx). The following lines of code show how to override the OnInit event and create a new instance of the Localizer() class.

```
Protected Overrides Sub OnInit()
    m_loc = new Wrox.Localization.Localizer("TerritorySales")
End Sub
```

Because you used an overloaded constructor for the Localizer() class, you cannot rely on the Class Name or Instance Name options in the References window to create an object instance. This would invoke the default constructor instead, and would not let you specify the name of the resource file to use (`TerritorySales`).

Figure P6-69 shows the complete custom code section of the report with the public variable and the overridden `OnInit` event.

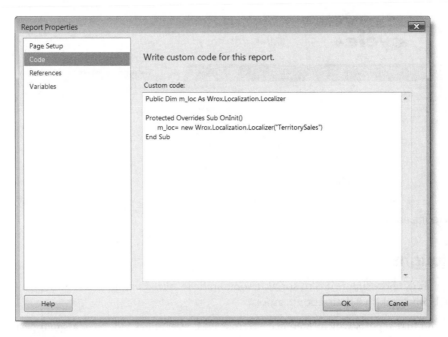

FIGURE P6-69

9. The last step is to modify the expression for each of the textboxes in the report that contain static text with a call to your custom code for the localized strings. The expression syntax should look as follows:

```
=Code.m_loc.GetLocalText("SalesTerritory")
```

The string `"SalesTerritory"` represents the key that you are retrieving from the current culture's resource assembly.

10. When you have updated all static text with lookup expressions, you can deploy your report and view the result. Figure P6-70 shows the final result of the report running in Internet Explorer with the Languages settings for the browser configured with fr-FR as the primary culture. You can see that the text strings are being retrieved correctly, and you can also see the rest of the Report Manager UI utilizing the built-in Globalization features of Reporting Services.

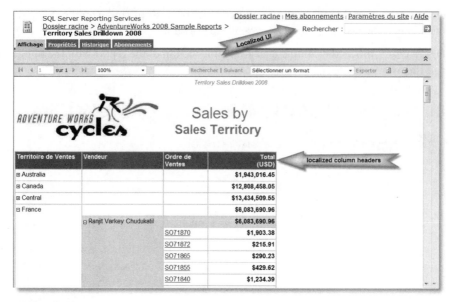

FIGURE P6-70

Final Thoughts

This recipe shows how simple it is to sprinkle some static localized text in you reports, while leveraging the .NET Framework's Globalization features.

Keep in mind that reports which reference external DLL assemblies will have a small performance penalty, which could exponentially grow if your report expression is used in a data region where the external library is called for each row of data in the report. Use your best judgment when designing your reports, and do a little benchmarking to make sure you don't create future bottlenecks.

Credits and Related References

Professional SQL Server 2008 Reporting Services. Turley, et al (Wrox, 2008).

Solution Design Considerations for Multi-Lingual or Global Deployments (Reporting Services). SQL Server 2008 Books Online (http://msdn.microsoft.com/en-us/library/ms156493.aspx).

PAGE RUNNING TOTAL

In Reporting Services it is possible to aggregate the values of textboxes in the report body visible on the current page, and display the aggregate in the page header or page footer. This so-called report item aggregate takes into account the specific textbox values that are visible on a page. If you change the page size, those aggregates may change as a result.

Prior to Reporting Services 2008 R2, however, it was nearly impossible to calculate a running total over those per-page report item aggregations. With the introduction of writable report variables, this can now be accomplished, as demonstrated in this recipe.

Product Versions

➤ Reporting Services 2008 R2

What You'll Need

➤ AdventureWorks2008 sample database

Designing the Report

This recipe uses the AdventureWorks2008 for sample database and a grouped query to return sales information about products. The final result is shown in Figure P6-71.

Note that the query also joins additional sales person and customer information. While not used directly in this recipe, that enables you to further extend the final report of this recipe so that it becomes similar to the Sales Order Detail AdventureWorks2008 sample report, but with the main difference that only one query is needed, instead of the multiple queries in the Sales Order Detail sample report.

1. Start by designing a data source for the AdventureWorks2008 sample database.

2. Create a new dataset called SalesOrder, and use the following query:

```
SELECT SOH.SalesOrderNumber, S.BusinessEntityID, S.Name
     ,SOH.SalesOrderID, SOH.SalesPersonID, SOH.TotalDue
     ,SOH.OrderDate, SOH.PurchaseOrderNumber
     ,SOH.BillToAddressID, SOH.ShipToAddressID, SOH.ShipMethodID
     ,SM.Name AS ShipMethod
     ,BA.AddressLine1 AS BillAddress1, BA.AddressLine2 AS BillAddress2
     ,BA.City AS BillCity, BA.PostalCode AS BillPostalCode
     ,BSP.Name AS BillStateProvince, BCR.Name AS BillCountryRegion
     ,SA.AddressLine1 AS ShipAddress1, SA.AddressLine2 AS ShipAddress2
     ,SA.City AS ShipCity, SA.PostalCode AS ShipPostalCode
     ,SSP.Name AS ShipStateProvince, SCR.Name AS ShipCountryRegion
     ,e.JobTitle, per.[FirstName] + N' ' + per.[LastName] AS [SalesPerson]
     ,ph.PhoneNumber, st.Name as SalesTerritory
     ,SOD.SalesOrderDetailID, SOD.OrderQty, SOD.UnitPrice
     ,CASE WHEN SOD.UnitPriceDiscount IS NULL
        THEN 0 ELSE SOD.UnitPriceDiscount END AS UnitPriceDiscount
     ,SOD.LineTotal, SOD.CarrierTrackingNumber
     ,P.Name as ProductName, P.ProductNumber
```

```
FROM [Sales].[SalesOrderHeader] SOH
INNER JOIN Sales.Customer C ON SOH.CustomerID = C.CustomerID
INNER JOIN Sales.Store S ON C.StoreID = S.BusinessEntityID
INNER JOIN Person.Address SA ON SA.AddressID = SOH.ShipToAddressID
INNER JOIN Person.StateProvince SSP ON SA.StateProvinceID
    = SSP.StateProvinceID
INNER JOIN Person.CountryRegion SCR ON SSP.CountryRegionCode
    = SCR.CountryRegionCode
INNER JOIN Person.Address BA ON SOH.BillToAddressID = BA.AddressID
INNER JOIN Person.StateProvince BSP ON BA.StateProvinceID
    = BSP.StateProvinceID
INNER JOIN Person.CountryRegion BCR ON BSP.CountryRegionCode
    = BCR.CountryRegionCode
INNER JOIN Purchasing.ShipMethod SM ON SOH.ShipMethodID = SM.ShipMethodID
INNER JOIN [Sales].[SalesPerson] sp ON sp.[BusinessEntityID]
    = SOH.[SalesPersonID]
LEFT OUTER JOIN [Sales].[SalesTerritory] st ON sp.[TerritoryID]
    = st.[TerritoryID]
INNER JOIN [HumanResources].[Employee] e
        ON SOH.[SalesPersonID] = e.[BusinessEntityID]
INNER JOIN [Person].[Person] per ON per.[BusinessEntityID]
    = sp.[BusinessEntityID]
INNER JOIN Person.PersonPhone ph ON per.[BusinessEntityID]
    = ph.[BusinessEntityID]
INNER JOIN Sales.SalesOrderDetail SOD ON SOD.SalesOrderID = SOH.SalesOrderID
INNER JOIN Production.Product P ON SOD.ProductID = P.ProductID
WHERE (SOH.SalesOrderID BETWEEN (@SalesOrderIDStart) AND (@SalesOrderIDEnd))
```

3. Set default values for the newly created report parameters.

   The query in Step 2 has two query parameters that are automatically bound to two report parameters. Open the report parameter settings for each and set the default values as follows:

   ```
   SalesOrderIDStart: 50700
   ```

   ```
   SalesOrderIDEnd: 50710
   ```

4. Add a list to the report body.

   a. Insert a list directly from the toolbar and resize it to increase its size, make room for textboxes and a table that will be inserted in a later step.

   b. Open the tablix properties of the list and set the dataset name to SalesOrder.

   c. Select the Details group of the list, and open the group properties. Add a group expression, using the SalesOrderID field.

5. Inside the list, add text boxes for the sales order header information.

   Lay out the information similar to what you see in Figure P6-72. Note that the sales order header information is not essential for the page-wise running total calculation recipe, so you could use a simpler layout or even skip this step. Also note the syntax used in Figure P6-72 for referencing data set field values are in-line with other text and formatting, [SalesOrder-Number], for example. This new syntax is part of the RichText feature added in Reporting Services 2008.

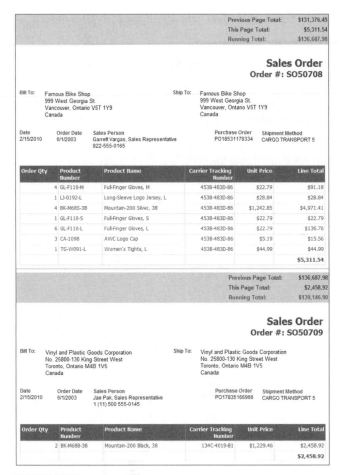

FIGURE P6-71

				Previous Page Total:	$131,376.45
				This Page Total:	$5,311.54
				Running Total:	$136,687.98

Sales Order
Order #: SO50708

Bill To: Famous Bike Shop
999 West Georgia St.
Vancouver, Ontario V5T 1Y9
Canada

Ship To: Famous Bike Shop
999 West Georgia St.
Vancouver, Ontario V5T 1Y9
Canada

| Date | Order Date | Sales Person | | Purchase Order | Shipment Method |
| 2/15/2010 | 6/1/2003 | Garrett Vargas, Sales Representative 922-555-0165 | | PO18531178334 | CARGO TRANSPORT 5 |

Order Qty	Product Number	Product Name	Carrier Tracking Number	Unit Price	Line Total
4	GL-F110-M	Full-Finger Gloves, M	453B-483D-86	$22.79	$91.18
1	LJ-0192-L	Long-Sleeve Logo Jersey, L	453B-483D-86	$28.84	$28.84
4	BK-M68S-38	Mountain-200 Silver, 38	453B-483D-86	$1,242.85	$4,971.41
1	GL-F110-S	Full-Finger Gloves, S	453B-483D-86	$22.79	$22.79
6	GL-F110-L	Full-Finger Gloves, L	453B-483D-86	$22.79	$136.76
3	CA-1098	AWC Logo Cap	453B-483D-86	$5.19	$15.56
1	TG-W091-L	Women's Tights, L	453B-483D-86	$44.99	$44.99
					$5,311.54

				Previous Page Total:	$136,687.98
				This Page Total:	$2,458.92
				Running Total:	$139,146.90

Sales Order
Order #: SO50709

Bill To: Vinyl and Plastic Goods Corporation
No. 25800-130 King Street West
Toronto, Ontario M4B 1V5
Canada

Ship To: Vinyl and Plastic Goods Corporation
No. 25800-130 King Street West
Toronto, Ontario M4B 1V5
Canada

| Date | Order Date | Sales Person | | Purchase Order | Shipment Method |
| 2/15/2010 | 6/1/2003 | Jae Pak, Sales Representative 1 (11) 500 555-0145 | | PO17835166966 | CARGO TRANSPORT 5 |

Order Qty	Product Number	Product Name	Carrier Tracking Number	Unit Price	Line Total
2	BK-M68B-38	Mountain-200 Black, 38	134C-4019-81	$1,229.46	$2,458.92
					$2,458.92

FIGURE P6-71

Sales Order
Order #: [SalesOrderNumber]

Bill To: [Name]
[BillAddress1]
[BillCity], [BillStateProvince] [BillPostalCode]
[BillCountryRegion]

Ship To: [Name]
[ShipAddress1]
[ShipCity], [ShipStateProvince] [ShipPostalCode]
[ShipCountryRegion]

| Date | Order Date | Sales Person | | Purchase Order | Shipment Method |
| [CurDate] | [OrderDate] | [SalesPerson], [JobTitle] [PhoneNumber] | | [PurchaseOrderNun | [ShipMethod] |

FIGURE P6-72

6. Add a table inside the list to represent the line item details for each sales order.

a. Create a new table using the Table wizard.

b. In Step 1 of the wizard, bind the table to the SalesOrder dataset.

c. In Step 2, do not group by any field, and just add the following fields to the Values section without using aggregation functions: OrderQty, ProductNumber, ProductName, CarrierTrackingNumber, UnitPrice, LineTotal. The result is shown in Figure P6-73.

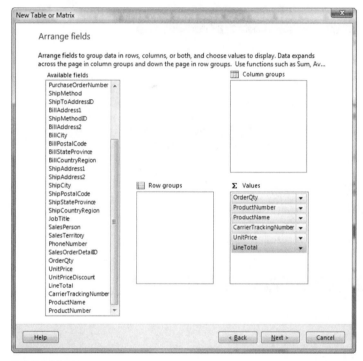

FIGURE P6-73

d. Finish the Table wizard, and then move the newly created table inside the already existing list, placing the table below the sales order header textboxes.

e. Add a table footer row to the table, and add an overall order total calculation, using the following expression:

```
=Sum (Fields!LineTotal.Value)
```

f. Rename the textbox of the total calculation to: OrderTotal and set the FontWeight to Bold. The resulting layout is shown in Figure P6-74.

Order Qty	Product	Product Name	Carrier Tracking	Unit Price	Line Total
[OrderQty]	[ProductNumber]	[ProductName]	rierTrackingNumber]	[UnitPrice]	[LineTotal]
					[Sum(LineTotal)]

FIGURE P6-74

7. Add a report variable, which is used for the running total.

Open the report properties, go the Variables page, and add a read-write report variable (make sure to uncheck the Read-Only option) called RunningTotal, and initialize it with =0.0.

8. Add custom code helper functions to be used for updating the report variable.

On the report properties, go to the Code page, and add the following custom code. Note that line breaks were added below in the code for formatting reasons; when typing in this code make sure to type the entire function declaration (the initial three lines for both functions) as one line without line breaks.

```
Public Function AddToVariable(var As
Microsoft.ReportingServices.ReportProcessing.OnDemandReportObjectModel.Variable,
ByVal increment As Double) As Double
    var.Value = var.Value + increment
    return var.Value
End Function

Public Function GetOrResetVariable(var As
Microsoft.ReportingServices.ReportProcessing.OnDemandReportObjectModel.Variable,
ByVal executeReset As Boolean)
    if executeReset then
        var.Value = 0
    end if
    return var.Value
End Function
```

9. Add a page header with textboxes to calculate the page-wise running total.

a. In the page header, add a textbox for the previous page total — that is, the current value of the RunningTotal report variable — as shown in Figure P6-75. Use the following expression for the textbox value calculation:

Previous Page Total:	«Expr»
This Page Total:	«Expr»
Running Total:	«Expr»

FIGURE P6-75

```
=Code.GetOrResetVariable(
Variables!RunningTotal, Globals!OverallPageNumber = 1)
```

b. Add a textbox for the current page total, using report item-based aggregation based on the textbox in the report body that calculates sales order totals (the textbox in the table footer in the report body is named OrderTotal):

```
=Sum(ReportItems!OrderTotal.Value)
```

c. Add a textbox for the running total, which increments the running total with the current page total and displays the resulting value:

```
=Code.AddToVariable(Variables!RunningTotal, Sum(Reportitems!OrderTotal.Value))
```

Since the report variable value has a lifetime of the current session, you have to decide whether you want the running total only to be shown when exported. In that case, you have to use a conditional expression to hide the textboxes in the page header based on the current rendering format, as shown in the Renderer-Dependent Layout and Formatting recipe (the next recipe in this book). This example performs the calculation for all rendering formats, including interactive viewing, and only resets the running total value on page 1 of the report. Consequently, if you were to navigate from page 1 to page 2 and then back again to page 1, the executed code would simply increment the report variable and lead to undesired results. This can be avoided by disabling the running total calculation for interactive rendering formats, or using a more complex data structure for the report variable, one that keeps track of totals per page and per rendering format, such as a dictionary.

10. Preview the result and then export to PDF

View all the pages of the report and note the running total calculation in the page header, as shown in Figure P6-76.

	Previous Page Total:	$131,376.45
	This Page Total:	$5,311.54
	Running Total:	$136,687.98

Sales Order
Order #: SO50708

Bill To:	Famous Bike Shop	Ship To:	Famous Bike Shop
	999 West Georgia St.		999 West Georgia St.
	Vancouver, Ontario V5T 1Y9		Vancouver, Ontario V5T 1Y9
	Canada		Canada

Date	Order Date	Sales Person		Purchase Order	Shipment Method
2/15/2010	6/1/2003	Garrett Vargas, Sales Representative		PO18531178334	CARGO TRANSPORT 5
		922-555-0165			

Order Qty	Product Number	Product Name	Carrier Tracking Number	Unit Price	Line Total
4	GL-F110-M	Full-Finger Gloves, M	453B-483D-86	$22.79	$91.18
1	LJ-0192-L	Long-Sleeve Logo Jersey, L	453B-483D-86	$28.84	$28.84
4	BK-M68S-38	Mountain-200 Silver, 38	453B-483D-86	$1,242.85	$4,971.41
1	GL-F110-S	Full-Finger Gloves, S	453B-483D-86	$22.79	$22.79
6	GL-F110-L	Full-Finger Gloves, L	453B-483D-86	$22.79	$136.76
3	CA-1098	AWC Logo Cap	453B-483D-86	$5.19	$15.56
1	TG-W091-L	Women's Tights, L	453B-483D-86	$44.99	$44.99
					$5,311.54

	Previous Page Total:	$136,687.98
	This Page Total:	$2,458.92
	Running Total:	$139,146.90

Sales Order
Order #: SO50709

Bill To:	Vinyl and Plastic Goods Corporation	Ship To:	Vinyl and Plastic Goods Corporation
	No. 25800-130 King Street West		No. 25800-130 King Street West
	Toronto, Ontario M4B 1V5		Toronto, Ontario M4B 1V5
	Canada		Canada

Date	Order Date	Sales Person		Purchase Order	Shipment Method
2/15/2010	6/1/2003	Jae Pak, Sales Representative		PO17835166966	CARGO TRANSPORT 5
		1 (11) 500 555-0145			

Order Qty	Product Number	Product Name	Carrier Tracking Number	Unit Price	Line Total
2	BK-M68B-38	Mountain-200 Black, 38	134C-4019-B1	$1,229.46	$2,458.92
					$2,458.92

FIGURE P6-76

Final Thoughts

Report variables and group variables were originally introduced in Reporting Services 2008 to enable an at-most once evaluation semantics for expressions due to the switch to the on-demand expression evaluation in Reporting Services 2008. Those variables can, however, be set only once.

Writable report variables in Reporting Services 2008 R2 can be modified as often as you want. More importantly however, those writable report variables are almost like session variables in the sense that Reporting Services provides automatic persistence throughout a user session, as well as isolation across concurrent report executions. This helps reduce the complexity of sophisticated reports (typically utilizing custom code and assemblies with complex calculations) that in previous Reporting Services releases often had to implement their own session state management and isolation for custom code variables.

RENDERER-DEPENDENT LAYOUT AND FORMATTING

One of the design principles of the Reporting Services platform is that you author a report once, and it then renders to all interactive and export formats with as much fidelity as possible (and enabled by the underlying export format). You don't need to worry how certain report items and style settings translate to HTML vs. Word vs. Excel vs. PDF. While consistent report layout and style rendering across output formats is often desired, there are reporting situations where you desire to make rendering-format decisions as well.

Reporting Services 2008 R2 introduces the ability to make layout and format decisions based on the rendering format. This recipe explains how to use this new feature in the following scenario:

➤ Use complex formatting and interactivity for onscreen display, but optimize for Excel export and post-processing with a more data oriented view.

Besides that, there are many other situations when rendering-format decisions can be useful for your reporting scenarios. For example:

➤ Add/omit text disclaimers, logos, background images, etc. when printing

➤ Disable hyperlinks when report is exported to PDF

➤ Define a particular color chart palette for all rendering formats, but use an optimized grayscale palette when using TIFF for fax, or printing

Product Versions

➤ Reporting Services 2008 R2

What You'll Need

➤ AdventureWorksDW2008 Analysis Services sample database and the Product Catalog 2008 AdventureWorks sample report

Designing the Report

The goal of this recipe is to take an existing report and modify it so that you get a particular rendering layout and formatting optimized for working with the report output in Excel, while all other rendering formats should export the report exactly as displayed on the screen. A preview of the final result appears in Figure P6-77; the report produces an Excel rendering output optimized for further data analysis, while generating a product catalog in all other rendering formats.

1. Open the Product Catalog 2008 sample report in Report Builder 3.0 of SQL Server Reporting Services 2008 R2.

If you haven't downloaded the AdventureWorks sample reports yet from CodePlex, use the following link: `http://www.codeplex.com/MSFTRSProdSamples`

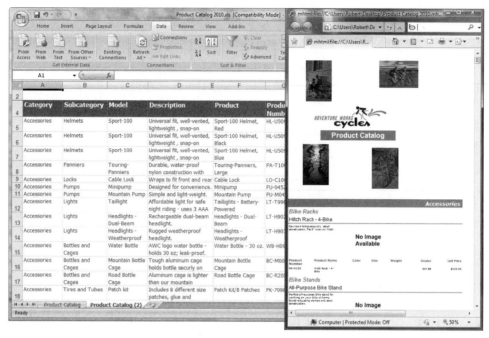

FIGURE P6-77

2. Hide the product catalog details tablix for Excel export.

Locate and select the overall product table (Tablix1) near the bottom of the design surface.

Open the tablix properties for Tablix1, go to the Visibility page, and use the following expression for the show or hide setting, as shown in Figure P6-78:

```
=(Globals!RenderFormat.Name = "EXCEL")
```

This expression will hide Tablix1 when rendered to Excel.

3. Make room in the report layout for an additional table.

Increase the report body height by dragging the splitter between report body and page footer.

4. Use the Table wizard to add a new table.

a. Insert a new table from the ribbon and use the Table wizard.

b. In Step 1 of the wizard, chose the ProductCatalog dataset.

c. In Step 2, do not group by any field; just add the following fields to the Values section: Category, SubCategory, Model, Description, Product, Product Number, Color Size, Weight, StandardCost, and ListPrice into the values section, as shown in Figure P6-79.

d. In Steps 3 and 4, just click Next and finish the wizard.

e. Move the newly created table into the empty space at the bottom of the report page.

FIGURE P6-78

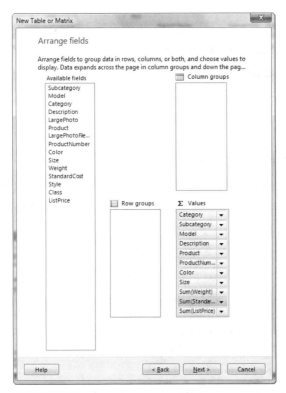

FIGURE P6-79

f. Adjust the table column widths to provide more room for fields such as description, and decrease the width for fields such as size and color.

g. Select the StandardCost and the ListPrice columns of the table, and for each column apply currency formatting using the corresponding ribbon button with the $ sign.

5. Prepare the data table to only be rendered to Excel.

a. Select the table created in the previous step, and open the tablix properties dialog.

b. In this particular case of the Product Catalog report, you do not need to add a page break of type "Before" for the tablix, because the rectangle with the cover page already has a page break. In your specific report scenarios, you may consider adding a page break before the data table to ensure that it starts on a new page (and therefore on a new worksheet in Excel).

c. On the Visibility page, use the following expression for the show or hide setting:

```
=(Globals!RenderFormat.Name <> "EXCEL")
```

This expression will show the data table only when rendered to Excel, but not for any other rendering formats.

d. On the Sorting page, add the following three sort expressions in sequence so that the data table sorts the detail rows:

```
Category (ascending)

SubCategory (ascending)

Model (ascending)
```

6. Preview the report to test the results.

Verify that when viewing the report interactively (e.g., in Report Builder Preview), the data table at the end is not visible.

When exporting to Excel, all you see is the first worksheet with the "cover page" and the second worksheet that contains the data table that enables easy post-processing of the raw data in Excel. For example, turn on Auto-Filters in Excel or perform sorting on columns.

Also note that page 1 of the report in preview and the first worksheet in Excel do have identical contents; only the rest of the report uses different layout and formatting.

Figure P6-80 shows page 3 of the report preview.

Figure P6-81 shows the Excel rendering of the same report, on the second worksheet.

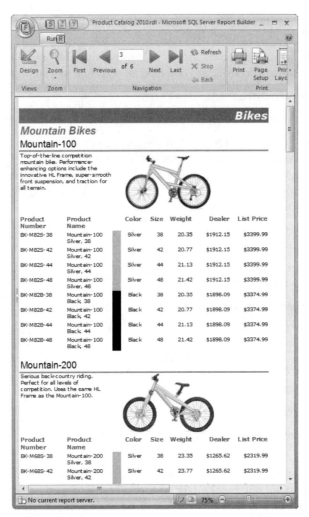

FIGURE P6-80

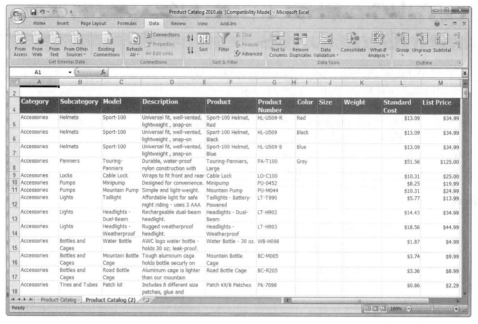

FIGURE P6-81

Final Thoughts

Reporting Services 2008 R2 adds the ability to access the name of the rendering extension as registered in the configuration file (accessible in expressions as: =Globals!RenderFormat.Name). In addition, it provides a Boolean flag (accessible in expressions as: =Globals!RenderFormat.IsInteractive) to determine whether a rendering extension is an interactive renderer (that is, not an export format or, more specifically, only Preview and HTML viewing are considered interactive renderers).

Both of those global variables can be used in layout and formatting expressions. Note that those cannot be used in data-processing-related expressions (that is, grouping, sorting, filtering, aggregation, report/group variables, subreport parameters), as those expressions are only calculated once unrelated to a specific rendering format.

CREATING A CHECKBOX LIST TO SHOW EXISTING RECORDS

A checkbox list is a familiar metaphor, used to display the state of items in a list or table. In some applications, it may allow items to be selected or modified. There are several practical uses for this style of report and this is one of two different recipes to use this checkbox list metaphor. In this example, you will see how to display a list of records with checkboxes. Items or rows that have corresponding records in another table will display a checked box and those that do not have related records will show an empty or unchecked box. With a little modification, this technique can also be used to show the state or status of different records based on data in one or multiple tables.

Product Versions

➤   Reporting Services 2000

➤   Reporting Services 2005

➤   Reporting Services 2008

What You'll Need

➤   A table data region

➤   Checked box and Unchecked box images

➤   An expression used to manipulate the image value

Designing the Report

An example of the finished report for this recipe is shown in Figure P6-82.

FIGURE P6-82

To apply this recipe, you need a query that returns a set of records from one table and corresponding values from existing records in a related table. If a related record doesn't exist, a `Null` value is returned for the corresponding column. The query shown in the code below returns a set of product names and only a `ProductKey` value for records that have Internet sales orders.

1. Add a data source to the report for the AdventureWorksDW, AdventureWorksDW2005, or AdventureWorksDW2008 sample database, depending on the version of SQL Server you are using.

2. Add a dataset to the report, using the following T-SQL query:

```
SELECT TOP 20
    DimProduct.EnglishProductName
  , MIN(FactInternetSales.ProductKey) AS ProductKey
FROM
    DimProduct LEFT OUTER JOIN FactInternetSales
    ON DimProduct.ProductKey = FactInternetSales.ProductKey
GROUP BY DimProduct.EnglishProductName
ORDER BY DimProduct.EnglishProductName
```

3. You need to capture or create two image files: an unchecked checkbox and a checked checkbox. An easy way to create these files is to open an application that displays checkbox icons in both states and use a screen capture tool to capture each of the two checkbox states to separate image files. You can use the Windows Snipping tool in Windows Vista or Windows 7 or a product like SnagIt Pro from TechSmith. Of course, you can also create your own images using MS Paint, PhotoShop, or any other graphic editing program. You can save these using any of the image formats supported by Reporting Services, including BMP, GIF, JPG, PNG, or TIF. This example uses embedded images, but the technique can be applied to external files or project resources with the appropriate modifications.

4. Save these two files with the names "checked" and "unchecked."

5. Add the files to the report as embedded images.

In Reporting Services 2000 and 2005, use the Report Properties dialog to add embedded images to a report. In Reporting Services 2008, right-click the Images folder in the Report Data window and choose Add Image.

The following table shows these two images and the corresponding properties:

IMAGE	FILE NAME	REPORT IMAGE NAME
☑	checked.gif	checked
☐	unchecked.gif	unchecked

Figure P6-83 shows a design view of the report in Report Builder 2.0. The two image files are added as embedded images and appear under the Images branch of the tree in the Report Data pane.

6. Add a table data region to the report.

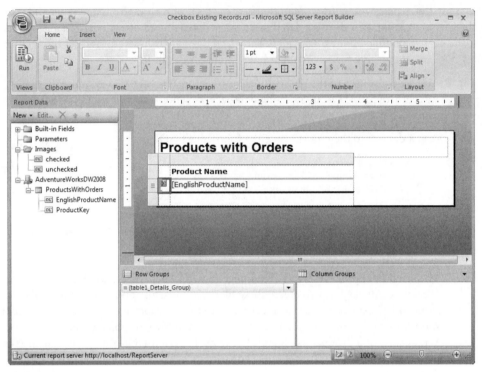

FIGURE P6-83

7. Add EnglishProductName to the second column of the detail row in the table.

8. Add an image report item to the first column of the detail row in the table.

9. Set the `Value` property of the image using the following expression:

```
=IIF(IsNothing(Fields!ProductKey.Value), "unchecked", "checked")
```

When the report is rendered, this expression is applied to the image in each row of the table. Since the query uses an outer join between the DimProduct and FactInternetSales tables, all product records in the DimProduct table are returned. Products with related sales records will return a valid `ProductKey` value from the `FactInternetSales` table, but products that have no sales will return a `Null` value for this column. The Visual Basic IsNothing function is used to make this determination and then the `IIF` function is used to return the corresponding image name based on whether a related sales record exists.

The resulting report is shown in Figure P6-84.

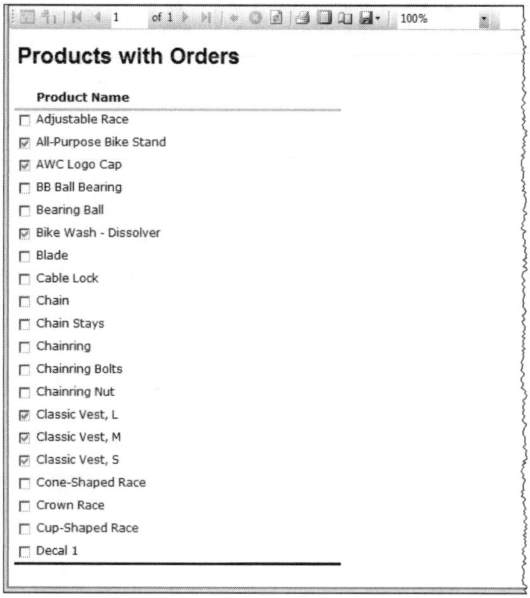

FIGURE P6-84

Final Thoughts

In this recipe, you saw how to display a checked box to indicate the state of a record, in this case when it has corresponding records in another table. This example is a simple, static view of data, but your technique can easily be modified and enhanced, as you will see in a more interactive and complex recipe titled "Using a Checkbox List to Select and Deselect Records."

USING A CHECKBOX LIST TO SELECT AND DESELECT RECORDS

In the previous recipe, "Creating a Checkbox List to Show Existing Records," you saw how to use a checkbox list to show the status of records. In this recipe, you will apply the same checkbox metaphor to create dynamic report that uses a checkbox list to select and deselect items. This technique has a variety of useful applications and may be used to pass a list of selected parameter values to another report or to modify a group of records. We want users to be able to click on a check mark icon to toggle its state from unchecked to checked and vice versa.

This recipe uses two different methods to achieve the same result. The first technique demonstrated here builds a comma-separated string of selected IDs. The other option is to write to a table to keep track of the items that users select. This works in some scenarios, but is slower and introduces more overhead. In many environments report users may not be given the necessary permissions to insert, update, or delete records using report data sources. The first option works well on a relatively small set of data.

Product Versions

➤ Reporting Services 2000

➤ Reporting Services 2005

➤ Reporting Services 2008

What You'll Need

➤ A table data region

➤ Checked box and Unchecked box images

➤ An expression used to manipulate the image value

➤ Parameters to capture the state of the selected items

Designing the Report

In "Creating a Checkbox List to Show Existing Records," you learned how to conditionally show an unchecked or checked image using a conditional expression. The visual design of this report is similar to that technique.

1. To get started, add as embedded images the same "unchecked" and "checked" graphic files used in the "Checkbox List for Existing Records" recipe.

They can be BMP, GIF, JPG, PNG or TIF files. The technique for adding images can be applied to external files or project resources with the appropriate modifications. Make sure that the report image objects are named "checked" and "unchecked." In Reporting Services 2000 and 2005, use the Report Properties dialog to do this. In Reporting Services 2008, right-click the Images folder in the Report Data window and choose Add Image.

The following table shows these two images and the corresponding properties:

IMAGE	FILE NAME	REPORT IMAGE NAME
☑	checked.gif	checked
☐	unchecked.gif	unchecked

The dataset for the report can be any query that returns a column of key values. This recipe uses product information from the AdventureWorks2008 database. If you use data from a different data source, you need to make appropriate adjustments to the query. This example has products filtered by subcategory, which is not required for this technique but is useful in keeping the result size manageable.

2. Create a new data source and a dataset, using the following query:

```
SELECT
        ProductID
    , 1 AS Selected
    , Production.ProductSubcategory.Name AS ProductSubCategoryName
    , Production.Product.ProductSubcategoryID
    , Production.Product.Name AS ProductName
    , Production.Product.ProductNumber
    , Production.Product.ListPrice
FROM
    Production.Product INNER JOIN Production.ProductSubcategory
    ON Production.Product.ProductSubcategoryID =
    Production.ProductSubcategory.ProductSubcategoryID AND
    Production.Product.ProductSubcategoryID =
    Production.ProductSubcategory.ProductSubcategoryID
```

3. Add a table data region to the report.

4. Add an image to the first column of the details row. Add the image report item to the first column of the table, as you see in Figure P6-85.

The dataset returns a derived field named Selected, which is used to indicate whether a check mark should appear on that row of the table. Otherwise, the unchecked image is used to indicate that the row is not selected.

5. For the Value property of the image, use the following expression:

```
=IIF(Fields!Selected.Value=0, "unchecked", "checked")
```

To achieve the checkbox toggling functionality, a report action is used for the image item. When clicked, the key value for that row is passed to a function to either add it to a list of selected values or to remove it from the list if it already exists. Before you can set up the actions for the image, you need a pair of functions to manage the list of selected ID values and a parameter to be used as a variable.

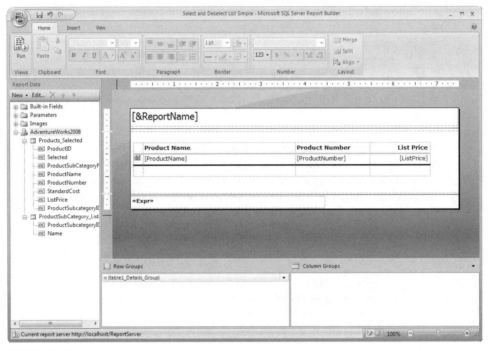

FIGURE P6-85

6. Open the Report Properties dialog and go to the Code page. You will create the two Visual Basic functions in the following block of code.

The first function is used to either add or remove an inputted value to or from a comma-separated list of values depending on whether it's already in the list. The first function calls the other two functions to maintain this list as a string.

Note that line-continuation characters (_) are added so the code fits on the printed page. You can optionally remove the underscore and the following carriage return so the code fits on a single line.

```
Function AddOrRemoveID(Selected As Boolean, ID As Integer, AllIDs As String) _
  As String
    If Selected Then
        Return RemoveSelectedID(ID, AllIDs)
    Else
        Return AddSelectedID(ID, AllIDs)
    End If
End Function

Function AddSelectedID(ID As Integer, AllIDs As String) As String
    If AllIDs = "" Then
        AllIDs =  ID.ToString()
```

```
        Else
            AllIDs &= ", " & ID.ToString()
        End If
        Return AllIDs
    End Function

    Function RemoveSelectedID(ID As Integer, AllIDs As String) As String
        Dim sIDs() As String = AllIDs.Split(",")
        Dim sID As String
        Dim sIDsOut As String = ""

        For Each sID In sIDs
            If sID.Trim() <> ID.ToString() Then sIDsOut &= sID.Trim() & ", "
        Next
          If sIDsOut.Length()>0 Then sIDsOut = sIDsOut.SubString(0, sIDsOut.Length()-2)
        Return sIDsOut
    End Function
```

With the code in place, you are ready to create and set up the parameter and then to wire-up the code and report action.

7.   Add a report parameter named ProductIDs, shown in Figure P6-86.

You will use this to store multiple values in a single string, so it's really just a scalar-valued parameter (rather than a multi-valued parameter).

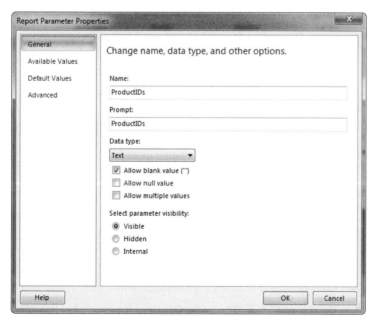

FIGURE P6-86

8.   On the General page of the Report Parameter Properties dialog (shown in Figure P6-86), allow the parameter to store a blank value and leave the rest of these properties with their default settings.

9. Move to the Default Values page, shown in Figure P6-87, and set the default value to −1.

This default value is assigned with the assumption that this will never be a valid ProductID value. You do this because the parameter needs to have a value in order for the report to run when it initially opens but you don't want any IDs to be selected.

FIGURE P6-87

10. Right-click the image report item and select Image Properties from the menu (see Figure P6-88).

11. Set the action to Go to report and then type or select the name of the current report.

12. Add a parameter and select ProductIDs from the Name list.

The purpose for this action is to re-render the report, sending it a new list of IDs in the ProductIDs parameter. The Action tab of the Image Properties dialog is shown in Figure P6-89.

13. For the Value, click the Expression button (*fx*) and call the AddOrRemoveID function that you created earlier. You will pass two arguments to the function: The Selected indicator value for the current row, and the current value of the ProductIDs parameter.

The Expression dialog containing this function call is shown in Figure P6-90.

The expression calls the AddOrRemoveID function in the report's Code class. The Selected field is a Boolean value derived in the query that indicates whether the current row has been previously selected. The ProductIDs parameter contains the comma-separated list of ProductID values from previous selections. In the first call, it will simply be an empty string.

```
=Code.AddOrRemoveID(Fields!Selected.Value, Fields!ProductID.Value,
Parameters!ProductIDs.Value)
```

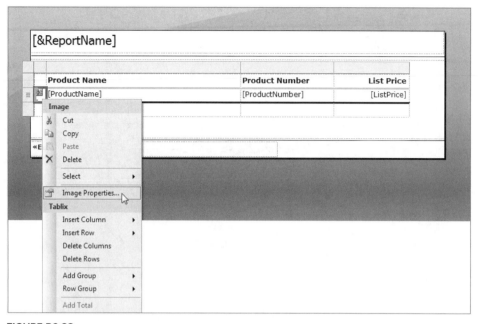

FIGURE P6-88

FIGURE P6-89

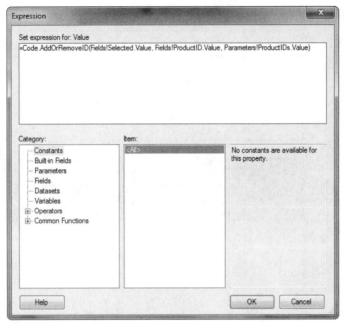

FIGURE P6-90

The final step is to replace the main dataset query with an expression. The query will have two separate SELECT statements combined using a UNION command. The first part returns the rows that have been selected and whose ProductIDs are included in the parameter. This is accomplished using a SQL IN function. The second SELECT query returns those that have not been selected and the logic is the opposite (using NOT IN).

The reason for using an expression to build the entire query string is that when using this technique, the query parser doesn't evaluate data types until the entire query is presented to the relational engine. If the @ProductIDs parameter were passed to an in-line query, the data type validation would fail because the parameter is a string and the ProductID column is an integer. This technique is useful whenever a query needs to be manipulated or prepared prior to report execution.

14. Open the Dataset Properties dialog and modify the query command string using the following expression:

```
="SELECT ProductID, 1 AS Selected," &
" Production.ProductSubcategory.Name AS ProductSubCategoryName," &
" Production.Product.Name AS ProductName, Production.Product.ProductNumber," &
" Production.Product.StandardCost, Production.Product.ListPrice," &
" Production.Product.ProductSubcategoryID" &
" FROM Production.Product INNER JOIN Production.ProductSubcategory" &
" ON Production.Product.ProductSubcategoryID =" &
" Production.ProductSubcategory.ProductSubcategoryID AND" &
" Production.Product.ProductSubcategoryID =" &
```

```
" Production.ProductSubcategory.ProductSubcategoryID AND" &
" Product.ProductID IN (" & Parameters!ProductIDs.Value & ")" &
" WHERE  Production.Product.ProductSubcategoryID ="
  & Parameters!ProductSubCategoryID.Value.ToString() &
" UNION " &
"SELECT ProductID, 0 AS Selected," &
" Production.ProductSubcategory.Name AS ProductSubCategoryName," &
" Production.Product.Name AS ProductName, Production.Product.ProductNumber," &
" Production.Product.StandardCost, Production.Product.ListPrice," &
" Production.Product.ProductSubcategoryID " &
" FROM Production.Product INNER JOIN Production.ProductSubcategory" &
" ON Production.Product.ProductSubcategoryID =" &
" Production.ProductSubcategory.ProductSubcategoryID AND" &
" Production.Product.ProductSubcategoryID =" &
" Production.ProductSubcategory.ProductSubcategoryID AND" &
" Product.ProductID NOT IN (" & Parameters!ProductIDs.Value & ")" &
" WHERE  Production.Product.ProductSubcategoryID ="
  & Parameters!ProductSubCategoryID.Value.ToString() &
" ORDER BY ProductName"
```

To test any drill-through report (whether it drills-through to another report or to itself), you'll need to deploy it to the report server first and then open it in the browser. The resulting report functions as expected.

15. Click an unchecked icon and the report will re-render with the checked icon. Click it again and the checkmark state is toggled. Figure P6-91 shows an example of this behavior.

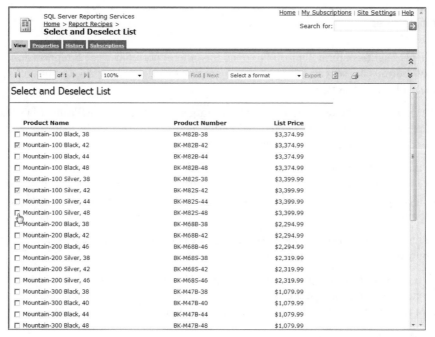

FIGURE P6-91

Using the Checkbox Report for Parameter Selection

An excellent application for this report design is to use the checkbox list report as a custom interface for selecting parameters to be passed to another report.

This question has been posed several times on the MSDN forum. Advanced report designers want to know how they can customize or replace the parameter selection bar with their own design. There are really two options: either develop a custom application and run your report exclusively in your own environment or use another report to gather the parameters.

The drill-through source version of this report has a simple modification and needs a link to open the target report.

1. Place a rectangle above the table. Optionally, you can use an embedded image to create a tiled gradient fill for the background.

2. Add a textbox to the rectangle to perform the action. Figure P6-92 shows the report with this addition.

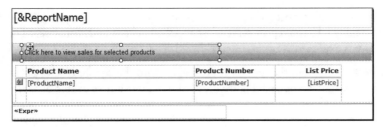

FIGURE P6-92

Clients might ask for a "button" to open the other report. Since SSRS reports don't really have buttons per se, you can just create a graphic image that looks like a button to perform the drill-through action.

The next step is quite straightforward. The target report accepts the ProductID parameter in the same format as you've prepared in this report. This can also be made to work with a standard multi-select parameter in the target report.

3. In the Action tab for the new text box, specify the target report and parameter selection just like you did on the checkbox image in this report, only the target report will be a different report whose dataset query filters data using the same parameter (see Figure P6-93 for an example).

The target report should have a single-select string type parameter. In the dataset query for the target report, simply use the T-SQL IN() function to filter records using this parameter.

After both reports have been deployed, the first report becomes a parameter input and selection menu for the second report. Use the checkboxes to select any combination of products and then use the link at the top of the report to view sales order details for the selection.

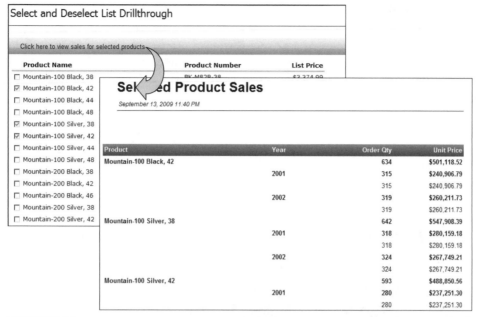

FIGURE P6-93

Final Thoughts

You can see from this example that the checkbox list report has the potential to be used for several practical purposes. You can use it to interact with itself or with other reports. Just keep in mind that it will work best when you keep the list of records to a manageable size — usually one page or less. With a little creativity you can extend this concept to add or remove content to a BI dashboard, affect other elements on the same report, process orders, manage a workflow process, launch another application, or prepare another report.

USING THE MAP WIZARD

This recipe is about showing the addresses of all your customers using the map report item introduced in Reporting Services 2008 R2 and report Builder 3.0. This technique plots address locations in the Los Angeles area. Accomplishing this requires just a few steps in Report Builder 3.0, and you don't even need to write a single expression!

Product Versions

➤   Reporting Services 2008 R2

What You'll Need

➤   Report Builder 3.0

Designing the Report

Figure P6-94 shows an example of the final map visualization of this report.

FIGURE P6-94

In this recipe, you create a map using the map wizard, and use it to display geospatial data.

1.   Start Report Builder 3.0, and create a data source connection to the AdventureWorks2008 sample database.

2.   In the Dataset Properties dialog, define a new dataset which includes geospatial data. For example:

```
SELECT
      AddressID
    , AddressLine1
    , AddressLine2
```

```
     , City
     ,StateProvinceID
     , PostalCode
     , SpatialLocation
  FROM  Person.Address
  WHERE City = 'Los Angeles'
```

Figure P6-95 shows the Dataset Properties dialog with the data source and query defined.

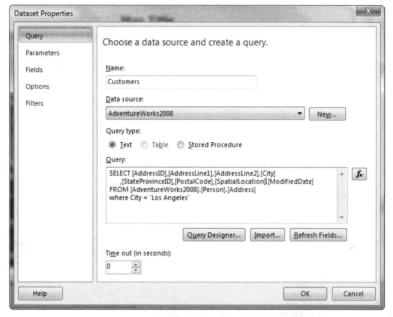

FIGURE P6-95

3. From the Report Builder 3.0 toolbar, insert a new map, using the map wizard. On the first page of the wizard, select to use a SQL Server spatial query as shown in Figure P6-96.

4. Click Next, and on the second page of the wizard, select the dataset defined in Step 2 (Customers). Then click Next.

5. Click Next to go to the third page of the wizard. There you will notice that it automatically detected that the SpatialLocation column contains geospatial data, and the wizard displays a cloud of points.

Simply select Add a Bing Maps background for this map view and you will see a backdrop for the cloud of points of the Los Angeles area, as shown in Figure P6-97. This is because the map wizard analyzes the rows contained in the dataset and their geospatial location.

6. Select Basic Marker Map as the visualization since our specific dataset doesn't contain further information about the customers (see Figure P6-98).

If we had more complex data in our dataset, such as total sales amount, we could use a bubble map, with the bubble sizes representing the relative account revenue.

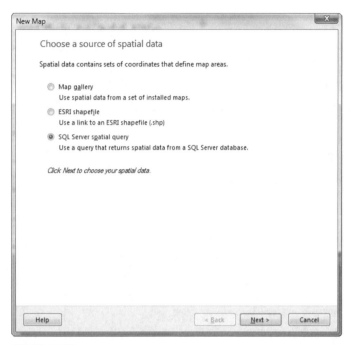

FIGURE P6-96

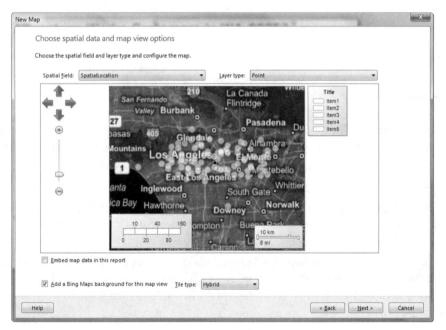

FIGURE P6-97

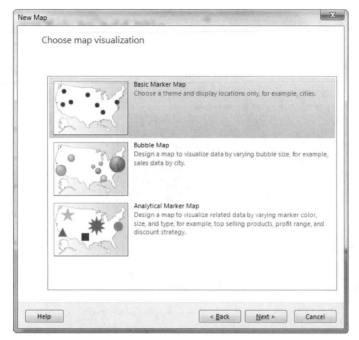

FIGURE P6-98

7. Click Next and, in the final step of the map wizard, choose the marker type and choose to display labels with each point. Note that all these settings can also be made or changed later through the map property dialogs, as well as the property grid in Report Builder. The map wizard is usually the quickest way to get started though.

You should now have a map on the design surface, as shown in Figure P6-99. You can further tweak settings of each map layer and map properties as desired.

This completes the essential design elements with a map plotting marker points for customer locations in the Los Angeles area. Of course, you can add titles, headers and other standard report embellishments to enhance and polish the design.

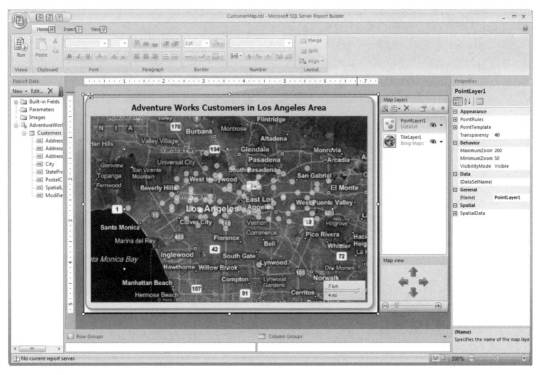

FIGURE P6-99

Final Thoughts

One of the best ways to show relationships in data is also one of the oldest: maps. Reporting Services 2008 R2 adds Map visualizations and support for geospatial data.

The map wizard is a quick way to get the initial layout of the map data done easily in a report. You can visualize your data with Bing Maps or an ESRI - shape file backdrop. Once the wizard completes, you can further tweak map settings and build fairly sophisticated and complex map visualizations using the property dialogs and property window settings.

Credits and Related References

See Robert Bruckner's blog post, RS Maps with Spatial Data and Bing Maps.
http://blogs.msdn.com/robertbruckner/archive/2009/08/11/rs-maps-with-spatial-data-and-bing-maps.aspx

PART VII
Filtering and Parameterization

- ▶ Multiple Criterion Report Filtering

- ▶ Using Multi-Value Parameters with a Stored Procedure

- ▶ Using Multi-Value Parameters with a Subscription Report

- ▶ Parameterized Top Values Report

- ▶ Cube Restricting Rows

- ▶ Creating Custom Sorting Reports

- ▶ Filtering User-Specific Report Data

MULTIPLE CRITERION REPORT FILTERING

Report design requirements may call for complex combinations of parameter values used to filter report data. Using Transact-SQL, you should be able to handle practically any advanced filtering criteria and filter the data before it reaches the report server. However, if you need to use report filtering to provide the same kinds of filtering support against data already cached by the data set query, the Report Designer has some significant limitations in this area. By employing some advanced expression logic or a little bit of custom code, practically any filtering logic can be implemented in the query or using dataset filtering within the report.

Product Versions

➤ Reporting Services 2000

➤ Reporting Services 2005

➤ Reporting Services 2008

What You'll Need

➤ Any report with multiple parameters for filtering data

➤ Solid report design skills

➤ Intermediate SQL or MDX query skills

➤ Familiarity with Visual Basic.NET expressions and custom programming

Designing the Report

Before you get started, let's briefly lay out the roadmap for this topic. The techniques for filtering data in a report range from basic to advanced, and the approach you use to solve these problems may range from simple to complex. I chat with people on the MSDN forums all the time who are trying to use very complicated and convoluted techniques to filter data and get stuck because they insist on using only one approach. For example, dynamically creating stored procedures and other database objects may require special permissions and may not work for everyone running the report. When more complex requirements take your report design efforts beyond simple, out-of-the-box features, it's important to understand the available options to solve a problem — along with the advantages and limitations for each. I recently worked with a report designer who wanted to run some complex query script in the dataset script for a report. When she previewed the report in the designer, her code was able to create and populate temporary tables, but this script wouldn't execute when the report was deployed to the server. I suggested that if she just used SELECT statements with joins, that the query would not only run more reliably but would be more efficient. When I asked why she had chosen her approach she said, "I don't know. That's just the way I've always done it." I recently had a similar experience. I was habitually building the SQL command string for a report in code and then passing the query text from a custom function through an expression. This worked, but a simple parameterized query would have worked just as well. I had found a technique that worked for me even when the best solution was easier and less complex. Lesson learned.

Having more than one technique to filter data can leave more options for being creative and finding the best approach to meet the requirement. In brief, the techniques for filtering data generally fall into these three categories:

FILTERING TECHNIQUE	DESCRIPTION	PROS AND CONS
Standard Parameterized Query	Write a SQL or MDX query in the query designer, including embedded parameter references.	This technique is the simplest, but implementing complex logic can be complicated and may not address all requirements.
Build Query String in Custom Code	Set the dataset command text to use an expression or custom code to process the parameter and filtering logic, and return the query string to the dataset.	Typically the most flexible method for handling complex parameter combinations and conditional filtering. Requires programming skills.
Dataset Filtering	Perform some or all of the filtering in the report dataset, rather than in the query, using parameter references, logical operators and expressions.	Dataset filtering offers performance enhancements and reduces server resource overhead. Standard dataset filtering features are limited but can be extended using custom code in the report.

Here, you'll see examples of all three techniques. There are three completed examples in the book downloads mentioned at the end of this recipe. For every report, you'll start with the same base query, use the same parameters, and present the results in a simple table data region. You'll build this report in stages, staring with the dataset query.

1. Create a new report with a data source for the AdventureWorks2008 relational database.

2. Add a dataset using the following query.

This query has no WHERE clause and will be the basis for all three techniques. Even if you plan to build the query string in code, you should write a simple query first to populate the fields collection of the dataset. You can then replace the command text with an expression later on.

```
SELECT
    Production.ProductCategory.Name AS ProductCategoryName
  , Production.Product.Name AS ProductName
  , Production.Product.ProductNumber
  , Production.Product.Color
  , Production.Product.StandardCost
  , Production.Product.ListPrice
FROM
    Production.ProductCategory
    INNER JOIN Production.ProductSubcategory
    ON Production.ProductCategory.ProductCategoryID =
    Production.ProductSubcategory.ProductCategoryID
```

```
INNER JOIN Production.Product
  ON Production.ProductSubcategory.ProductSubcategoryID =
Production.Product.ProductSubcategoryID
ORDER BY ProductCategoryName, ProductName
```

The report will have two parameters for filtering product records: `ProductCategory` and `PriceRange`. In this simplified example, the parameter values for both of my parameter lists are the same as the parameter label values. In a larger, production solution, you might use the key for the parameter values in place of the descriptive column values. The logic for the first parameter will be used to match a single Category value, a logical group of values, or all values. The requirement is to use a single-select parameter list rather than a multi-valued parameter. For the second parameter, you want to use named ranges of numeric values with additional logic for including all values. In each of the following tables, the first column shows the user-friendly label, and the second column shows the comparison logic.

The `ProductCategory` parameter list values are shown in the following table:

PARAMETER LABEL	PRODUCT CATEGORY FIELD MATCH
Bikes	Bikes
Components	Components
Clothing	Clothing
Accessories	Accessories
All Bike Related	Bikes OR Components
All	All rows (not filtered)

And the following table shows the `PriceRange` parameter list values:

PARAMETER LABEL	PRICE RANGE FIELD MATCH
Less than 50	<50
50 to 99	>=50 AND <100
100 to 499	>=100 AND <500
500 and higher	>=500
All	All prices (not filtered)

3. Add the ProductCategory and PriceRange parameters as Text type.

4. Use the Parameter Label text from the previous two tables to add available values for populating the parameter lists.

Each of the following three design techniques use the dataset and parameters in different ways. If you would like to follow more than one technique, you should save a separate copy of this report for each technique. Otherwise, just apply the steps for one technique.

Filtering in the Query

The SQL query language typically offers enough flexibility to handle most filtering logic. Because each of the two parameters has multiple conditions, you need to group these conditions using sets of parentheses in the WHERE clause. The following query includes all of the conditions. Indentations and line breaks separate these statements into logical groupings.

Simply replace the base query with the following script to apply this filtering technique. You can copy and paste from the download sample report to save time.

```
SELECT
    Production.ProductCategory.Name AS ProductCategoryName
, Production.Product.Name AS ProductName
, Production.Product.ProductNumber
, Production.Product.Color
, Production.Product.StandardCost
, Production.Product.ListPrice
FROM
    Production.ProductCategory
INNERJOIN Production.ProductSubcategory
    ON Production.ProductCategory.ProductCategoryID =
    Production.ProductSubcategory.ProductCategoryID
INNERJOIN Production.Product
    ON Production.ProductSubcategory.ProductSubcategoryID =
    Production.Product.ProductSubcategoryID
WHERE (
(ProductCategory.Name = @ProductCategory
OR
( @ProductCategory ='All Bike Related'
AND ProductCategory.Name IN('Bikes','Components'))
OR
( @ProductCategory ='All')
)
AND
(
( @PriceRange ='Less than 50'AND ListPrice < 50 )
OR
( @PriceRange ='50 to 99'AND ListPrice BETWEEN 50 AND 99 )
OR
( @PriceRange ='100 to 499'AND ListPrice BETWEEN 100 AND 499 )
OR
( @PriceRange ='500 and higher'AND ListPrice >= 500 )
OR
( @PriceRange ='All')
)
)
ORDER BY ProductCategory.Name, ProductName
```

This type of logic is commonplace for developers who use SQL on a regular basis. The key to combining different conditions to get the desired outcome is to group statements using sets of parentheses. Like a mathematical equation, certain statements must be resolved before others. For example, if 'All Bike Related' had been selected for the ProductCategory parameter, you'd want to include all of the records where the category is either 'Bikes' or 'Components' (think of the SQL IN function as a logical OR for each value passed in the comma-separated list). After these results are retrieved, the next condition is considered. As in this case, if the next operator is an OR, those results are added to these. If it is an AND operator, the next statement becomes a sub-selection of the first result set and fewer records may be returned.

If you have nothing but statements separated by AND operators in the WHERE clause, like additive math, there's really no requirement to use the parentheses. However, it may help to keep your sanity when you try to make sense of the code a year from now. As soon as OR logic is introduced, operational grouping becomes critical. It's important to bear in mind that even though SQL Server processes sets of records, conditional filter statements are logically processed one row at a time. Considering this may help you get your head around the logic and better understand the outcome. When debugging, consider a single row as it is processed by each condition in the WHERE clause, from the inside parentheses, out. Then consider other conditions, such as the value of parameters.

Using our example, let's say the ProductCategory parameter is 'Bikes' and the PriceRange parameter is 'Less than 50'. Now a row is evaluated with ProductCategoryName of 'Bikes' and ListPrice of $55. Consider the first section of the WHERE clause. Of course, the record passes the first condition because 'Bikes' is equal to 'Bikes'. It would also work if the ProductCategory parameter were 'All Bike Related'. But what about if the ProductCategoryparameter is 'All'? The logic in this case states that since this condition has been met, there's nothing else to check and all records pass this test, regardless of the ProductCategoryName value. This record isn't in the clear yet because of the all-mighty AND clause standing in the way. The record must still pass the ListPrice evaluation logic. The $55 record doesn't pass this test so it doesn't make the final cut.

Using Code to Build the Query String

When the query logic becomes difficult to sort out, it may be easier to use custom code to assemble a query string that is custom tailored to the parameter values. The query you will pass back to the dataset will have hard-coded filtering logic. Query languages like SQL and MDX are powerful but have some limited decision logic because they're not really programming languages. You can leverage the power of Visual Basic to write embedded functions — or any .NET language if you want to write an external assembly — to process the parameters and conditional logic, and then return an optimized query string to the dataset. I will typically use this technique when my queries get complicated.

This example handles the same logic as the previous technique, but the WHERE clause conditions will be handled using VB commands rather than SQL. To write a custom function, open the report Properties dialog and choose the Code page. There are no debugging or code formatting tools in this window. To help with debugging, I will open the Windows Forms project in Visual Studio, write and debug the code there and then paste it into this window. The following sample function takes the two report parameters as arguments and returns the entire query as a string.

```
Function BuildQuery(ProductCategoryParam As String, PriceRangeParam As String)
  As String
      Dim sQuery As String
      Dim sWhereClause As String
```

```
        sWhereClause = "WHERE "

        Select Case ProductCategoryParam
        Case "All Bike Related"
            sWhereClause &= "ProductCategory.Name IN ('Bikes', 'Components') "
        Case "All"
            sWhereClause &= "1=1"    'Return Makes AND work in next condition.
        Case ELSE
            sWhereClause &= "ProductCategory.Name = '" & ProductCategoryParam & "' "
        End Select

        Select Case PriceRangeParam
        Case "Less than 50"
            sWhereClause &= "AND ListPrice < 50 "
        Case "50 to 99"
            sWhereClause &= "AND ListPrice BETWEEN 50 AND 99 "
        Case "100 to 499"
            sWhereClause &= "AND ListPrice BETWEEN 100 AND 499 "
        Case "500 and higher"
            sWhereClause &= "AND ListPrice >= 500 "
        Case "All"
            ' Placeholder - don't do anything here.
        End Select

        sQuery = "SELECT " & vbCrLf _
    & "  Production.ProductCategory.Name AS ProductCategoryName " & vbCrLf _
    & " , Production.Product.Name AS ProductName " & vbCrLf _
    & " , Production.Product.ProductNumber " & vbCrLf _
    & " , Production.Product.Color " & vbCrLf _
    & " , Production.Product.StandardCost " & vbCrLf _
    & " , Production.Product.ListPrice " & vbCrLf _
    & "FROM " & vbCrLf _
    & "  Production.ProductCategory " & vbCrLf _
    & "  INNER JOIN Production.ProductSubcategory " & vbCrLf _
    & "  ON Production.ProductCategory.ProductCategoryID = " & vbCrLf _
    & "  Production.ProductSubcategory.ProductCategoryID " & vbCrLf _
    & "  INNER JOIN Production.Product " & vbCrLf _
    & "  ON Production.ProductSubcategory.ProductSubcategoryID = " & vbCrLf _
    & "  Production.Product.ProductSubcategoryID " & vbCrLf _
    & sWhereClause & vbCrLf _
    & "ORDER BY ProductCategory.Name, ProductName"
        Return sQuery
End Function
```

Steps for applying this technique:

1. Open the Report Properties dialog and enter the custom function into the Code window. Of course, you can copy and paste from the download sample report to save time.

2. Open the Dataset Properties and erase the original query.

3. Click the Expression (*fx*) button next to the Query box.

4. Enter the following expression:

```
=Code.BuildQuery(Parameters!ProductCategory.Value, Parameters!PriceRange.Value)
```

The Expression Builder will not help you with the custom function name, but you can use it to validate the parameters.

Filtering in the Dataset

Using the dataset filtering feature has the advantage of persisting the query results into the report instance cache and dramatically improving performance. Unfortunately, this feature doesn't offer the same level of flexibility for dealing with complex conditions. Contending with the various combinations of these and other parameter values in the confines of the Report Designer's filtering user interface would be very difficult, if not impossible, to do.

Each row of the dataset is evaluated individually. The most flexible method to handle this complexity is to write a separate Visual Basic function to handle the matching logic for each parameter and field combination. This code is called for each row. The function returns a value to be matched with a field in the row. If the values match, the row is returned. The following custom code is added to the report on the Code tab of the Report Properties dialog:

```
Function MatchProductCategory(ParamValue As String, FieldValue As String)
    As String

    Select Case ParamValue
        Case "Bikes", "Components", "Clothing", "Accessories"
            Return ParamValue
        Case "All Bike Related"
            If FieldValue = "Bikes" Or FieldValue = "Components" Then
                Return FieldValue
            End If
        Case "All"
            Return FieldValue
    End Select
End Function

Function MatchPriceRange(ParamValue As String, FieldValue As String) As Decimal
    Select Case ParamValue
        Case "Less than 50"
            If FieldValue < 50 Then Return FieldValue
        Case "50 to 100"
            If FieldValue >= 50 And FieldValue < 100 Then Return FieldValue
        Case "100 to 500"
            If FieldValue >= 100 And FieldValue < 500 Then Return FieldValue
        Case "500 and Higher"
            If FieldValue >= 500 Then Return FieldValue
        Case "All"
            Return FieldValue
    End Select
End Function
```

Using the Filters tab on the Dataset Properties dialog, as shown in Figure P7-1, executes each of the functions, matching its return value to the corresponding field.

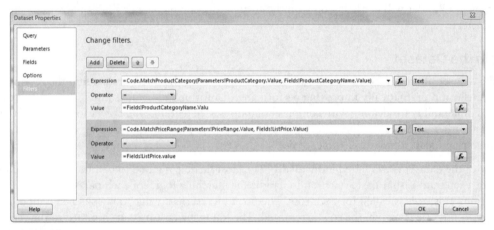

FIGURE P7-1

This technique takes all the complexity out of this simple dialog and puts it where it belongs — in program code. That environment gives you the control needed to contend with practically any set of business rules.

Samples

Three sample reports for this topic designed for Reporting Services 2008 and demonstrations of each of the techniques in this recipe are available for download from this book's website on Wrox.com. The file names are prefixed with "Advanced Filtering."

Final Thoughts

Data filtering can be performed within the dataset query or in the report. You should carefully consider the implications of using either of these techniques, as they can significantly impact performance and your ability to implement more flexible, dynamic features in an existing report design. One of the greatest advantages of the technique demonstrated in this recipe is that true programming code often handles conditional logic more effectively that a query language like T-SQL.

A "super report" meets multiple user and business requirements by applying conditional logic to the query and other report features, but this extensibility can come with a cost. Carefully consider these options when you need to design reports with more flexibility and make sure that the potential maintenance and performance costs of a more complex report design don't outweigh the savings afforded by fewer, more capable reports.

Credits and Related References

Some of this material is from the *Professional SQL Server 2005 Reporting Services*, by Paul Turley et al (Wrox 2006). A sample for SSRS 2005 is available in the sample downloads for that book on `www.wrox.com`.

USING MULTI-VALUE PARAMETERS WITH A STORED PROCEDURE

SSRS includes a multi-value parameter option that enables users to select one or more options from an embedded query. This is a simple feature, similar to the filtering format in SharePoint, which is available when building a report as a property of the parameter options. By itself, this feature provides users and developers with an advanced filtering option; however, this also presents a challenge because Reporting Services uses an array to store a multi-value parameter's value. Since T-SQL doesn't directly support arrays, passing in a string value of, for example, "1, 2, 3, 4, and 5" will cause the stored procedure to fail with a data type conversion error. This makes it difficult to pass the parameter into the T-SQL query and forces you to bring back the entire record set and do the filtering at the table level. If you are working with a simple query, this isn't too big of an issue, however, as your dataset result grows this will present a performance issue that will need to be addressed.

A better solution is to use a stored procedure and a user-defined function (UDF) to pass the array into T-SQL and keep the filtering at the T-SQL level. The function presented in this recipe allows you to pass in a string value of delimited values and splits the values by the designated delimiter. The result allows you to use a simple "IN Clausem" that will avoid the data type conversion error.

Product Versions

➤ Reporting Services 2000

➤ Reporting Services 2005

➤ Reporting Services 2008

What You'll Need

➤ An understanding of SQL Server and T-SQL

Designing the Report

An example of the finished report is shown in Figure P7-2.

To get started, add a new report and create a connection to the AdventureWorks or AdventureWorks2008 sample database.

1. Within your connection to the database or preferably within SQL Server Enterprise Manager, click the "New Query" button to execute the following code snippet.

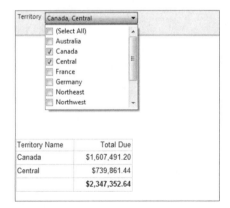

FIGURE P7-2

This code will create a new user-defined function (UDF) that will allow you to pass in a comma-separated list and split the string into individual values.

```
CREATE  FUNCTION [dbo].[fnSplitString](@text varchar(max),
@delimiter varchar(2) = ' ')
RETURNS @Strings TABLE
(
  position int IDENTITY PRIMARY KEY,
  Item varchar(max)
)
AS
BEGIN
DECLARE @index int

SET @index = -1
WHILE (LEN(@text) > 0)
  BEGIN
    SET @index = CHARINDEX(@delimiter , @text)
    IF (@index = 0) AND (LEN(@text) > 0)
      BEGIN
        INSERT INTO @Strings VALUES (@text)
          BREAK
      END
    IF (@index > 1)
      BEGIN
        INSERT INTO @Strings VALUES (LEFT(@text, @index - 1))
        SET @text = RIGHT(@text, (LEN(@text) - @index))
      END
    ELSE
      SET @text = RIGHT(@text, (LEN(@text) - @index))
    END
  RETURN
END
```

2. Enter the following code to create a new stored procedure that will utilize this function and accept a multi-value parameter. This query will return the territory and sales order information as part of the dataset, which accepts a multi-value parameter input to your query. In order to accomplish this and view the details on the territory, your query will need to join the SalesTerritory table.

```
CREATE PROCEDURE uspMultiValueReporting
   @TerritoryID varchar(200)
AS
   SELECT
     ST.[NAME], S.TOTALDUE, ST.TERRITORYID
   FROM
     SALES.SALESORDERHEADER S
     INNER JOIN SALES.SALESTERRITORY ST ON ST.TERRITORYID = S.TERRITORYID
   WHERE
     ORDERDATE BETWEEN '5/1/04' AND '6/30/04'
```

```
        AND ST.TERRITORYID IN (SELECT ITEM FROM dbo.fnSplitString
        (@TerritoryID, ','))
        ORDER BY NAME
go
```

3. Create a new dataset query that will execute the stored procedure. The command type will be Stored Procedure and the value of the field labeled Query String will be uspMultiValueReporting (see Figure P7-3).

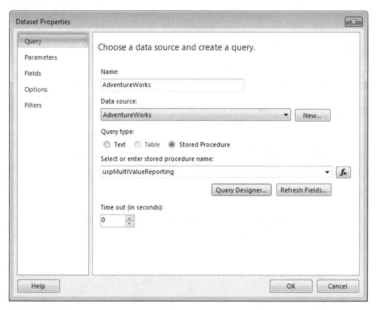

FIGURE P7-3

4. Complete the wizard and select all of the pre-generated table information and remove it. Add a new table to your report.

5. Right-click on the table and view the properties. Set the following values on the report (see Figure P7-4):

   ➤ Dataset Name: AdventureWorks.

   ➤ On the groups tab, add a new group and group by both Name and TerritoryID.

   ➤ Include Name and TotalDue columns in the detail row.

   ➤ Show the footer of the table and in the Total Due column, add a SUM of the Total-Due column.

6. Click on the data tab and add a new dataset query. This will return a list of all territories for a parameter choice. Name the dataset TerritoryList.

```
SELECT NAME, TERRITORYID FROM SALES.SALESTERRITORY ORDER BY NAME
```

FIGURE P7-4

7. Add a new report parameter called TerritoryID (see Figure P7-5) and set the following values:

- ➤ Data Type: Integer
- ➤ Prompt: Territory
- ➤ Available Values: From Query
- ➤ Default Values: From Query

In the Available values section, select the TerritoryList dataset you just created.

8. Preview the report (see Figure P7-6); you should see the drop-down list with a checkbox next to each territory.

This list will display a list of all options from your static query. By default, all of the options are selected unless you set the Default values property on the parameter option.

9. Un-check the "Select All" checkbox and this time only select a couple of the checkbox items (see Figure P7-7). Re-execute the report. This time, only the territories selected will be returned to your report.

Territory Name	Total Due
[NAME]	ium(TOTALDUE)]
	ium(TOTALDUE)]

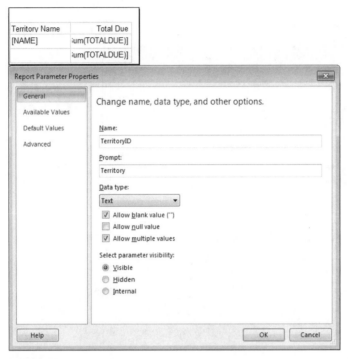

FIGURE P7-5

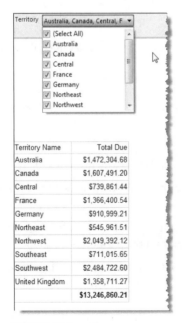

FIGURE P7-6

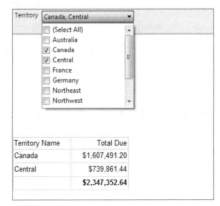

FIGURE P7-7

Final Thoughts

SSRS has introduced controls to increase usability and easily filter data within a report. This is especially true with the multi-value selection parameter option built into the report designer. However, it is up to the designer to understand exactly what is happening behind the scenes and understand both the advantages and drawbacks (if any) of using a particular control. A UDF allows you to maintain the filtering at the database level and eliminate an immediate performance concern if not using a multi-value selection parameter correctly.

USING MULTI-VALUE PARAMETERS WITH A SUBSCRIPTION REPORT

The "Using Multi-Value Parameters with a Stored Procedure" recipe demonstrated how easy it is to pass multiple values to a stored procedure using a T-SQL User Defined Function (UDF). This enabled you to maintain dataset filtering at the database level rather than directly on the report. However, it would be nice to automate this procedure and perform the same functionality for both a regular report and a subscription report. To accomplish this, this recipe shows you how to create an additional UDF — one that returns multiple values to a comma separated string. You also need to be a little creative with parameters, hiding some during the normal viewing of the report and populating others during a data-driven subscription report.

Product Versions

➤   Reporting Services 2000

➤   Reporting Services 2005

➤   Reporting Services 2008

What You'll Need

➤   An understanding of SQL Server and T-SQL

Designing the Report

This example uses the AdventureWorksDW2008 for SQL Server 2008 sample database and a simple query to return the reseller sales amount, total product cost, fiscal year, and fiscal quarter. This recipe uses a standard report project.

1.   Create a new report project and add a new report file to the project.

2.   Create a connection to either the AdventureWorks or AdventureWorks2008 data source.

3.   With SQL Server Management Studio or Query Analyzer for SQL 2000, use the following T-SQL to create a new user-defined function in your AdventureWorks database that will allow you to pass in a comma-separated list and split the string into individual values.

```
CREATE  FUNCTION [dbo].[fnSplitString](@text varchar(max),
@delimiter varchar(2) = ' ')
RETURNS @Strings TABLE
(
  position int IDENTITY PRIMARY KEY,
  Item varchar(max)
)
AS
BEGIN
DECLARE @index int

SET @index = -1
WHILE (LEN(@text) > 0)
```

```
BEGIN
  SET @index = CHARINDEX(@delimiter , @text)
  IF (@index = 0) AND (LEN(@text) > 0)
    BEGIN
      INSERT INTO @Strings VALUES (@text)
        BREAK
    END
  IF (@index > 1)
    BEGIN
      INSERT INTO @Strings VALUES (LEFT(@text, @index - 1))
      SET @text = RIGHT(@text, (LEN(@text) - @index))
    END
  ELSE
    SET @text = RIGHT(@text, (LEN(@text) - @index))
  END
RETURN
END
```

4. Create an additional user-defined function, shown in the following T-SQL, which will concatenate multiple values into a single string.

This will require a many-to-many relationship in which a single input value will return one
or many values, separated by commas. This will be used as the input parameter to your data-
driven subscription.

```
CREATE FUNCTION [dbo].[fnGetCurrenciesByRegion]
(@CountryRegionCode nvarchar(3))
RETURNS nvarchar(400)
AS
BEGIN
      DECLARE @Output nvarchar(4000)
      SET @Output = ''
      SELECT @Output = CASE @Output WHEN '' THEN CurrencyCode ELSE
            @Output + ',' + CurrencyCode END
      FROM Sales.CountryRegionCurrency
      WHERE CountryRegionCode = @CountryRegionCode

RETURN @Output
END
```

5. Enter the following code to create a new stored procedure that will use this function and
accept two multi-value parameters. You will want to return the region code, the currency
code, and the totals of the sales orders as part of your query. You will group the results in
your report. In addition, you will need to pass in two additional parameters that will only
be used during the subscription report. These values will be used in the filters if the original
@CountryRegionCode and @CurrencyCode parameters are NULL.

```
CREATE PROCEDURE uspGetSalesByCountry
@CountryRegionCode nvarchar(max) = NULL,
@CurrencyCode nvarchar(max) = NULL,
@SubscriptionCountryRegionCode nvarchar(max) = NULL,
@SubscriptionCurrencyCode nvarchar(max) = NULL
```

```
AS

SELECT DISTINCT
CONVERT(DECIMAL(13, 2), S.TOTALDUE) AS TotalSales
, CountryRegionCode
, SC.CurrencyCode
FROM
        SALES.SALESORDERHEADER S
        INNER JOIN Sales.CurrencyRate CR ON
                CR.CurrencyRateID = S.CurrencyRateID
        INNER JOIN Sales.Currency SC ON
                    SC.CurrencyCode = CR.ToCurrencyCode
        INNER JOIN Sales.CountryRegionCurrency SCRC ON
                    SCRC.CurrencyCode = CR.ToCurrencyCode
        WHERE
    ORDERDATE BETWEEN '5/1/01' AND '12/30/03'
        AND CountryRegionCode IN (SELECT ITEM FROM
        dbo.fnSplitString(COALESCE(@CountryRegionCode,
        @SubscriptionCountryRegionCode), ','))
        AND SC.CurrencyCode IN (SELECT ITEM FROM
        dbo.fnSplitString(COALESCE(@CurrencyCode,
            @SubscriptionCurrencyCode), ','))
    ORDER BY CountryRegionCode
```

6. Create a new dataset query that will execute the stored procedure. As shown in Figure P7-8, set the command type to Stored Procedure and the value of the field labeled Query string to uspGetSalesByCountry.

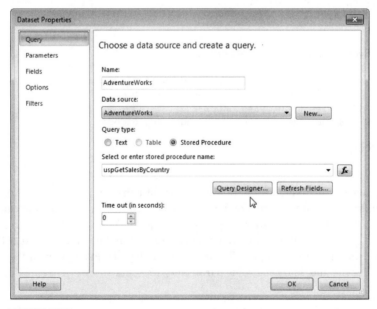

FIGURE P7-8

7. The report parameters should be added for you, but if they are not, add four new parameters for `@CountryRegionCode`, `@CurrencyCode`, `@SubscriptionCountryRegionCode`, and `@SubscriptionCurrencyCode`.

8. Add a new table to your report.

9. Right-click the table and view the properties. Set the following values on the report (see Figure P7-9):

➤ Dataset Name: AdventureWorks (you created the dataset in Step 6).

FIGURE P7-9

10. Right-click the detail row of the table and select Row Group | Group Properties and add a new group. The group properties should match Figure P7-10.

11. The columns in the detail row should include the CountryRegionCode, CurrencyCode, and TotalSales columns.

12. Right-click on the Detail Group in the Row Groups list and select Add Total | After to show the footer of the table. [Sum(TotalSales)] should now be under [TotalSales].

Your final tablix should resemble Figure P7-11.

FIGURE P7-10

13. View the Report Parameters. For each of the four parameters, check the box to allow a null value. In addition, the two parameters prefixed with subscription should also be made hidden. These parameters will not be visible to the user running the report, if applicable; however, they will be used for our data subscription.

Currency Code	Country Region Code	Total Sales
[CurrencyCode]	[CountryRegionCode]	[Sum(TotalSales)]
		[Sum(TotalSales)]

FIGURE P7-11

14. Preview the report (see Figure P7-12); you should see both parameter options, which allow null.

For the first two parameters, the country region code and currency code, you would probably want to utilize a multi-select parameter list that would present a checkbox list of values for the user to choose.

CountryRegionCode	GB,AU	☐ NULL	CurrencyCode	GBP,AUD	☐ NULL

Currency Code	Country Region Code	Total Sales
AUD	AU	$1,809,782.24
GBP	GB	$4,514,435.44
		$6,324,217.68

FIGURE P7-12

15. Deploy the report to the report server and run the report to verify.

In order to create a data-driven subscription to execute, you must be running SQL Server Agent.

16. Once you have executed the report, create a new data-driven subscription from the report (see Figure P7-13).

FIGURE P7-13

17. To create a data-driven subscription, the login credentials must be stored securely in the database. Edit your dataset and enter the proper credentials (See Figure P7-14).

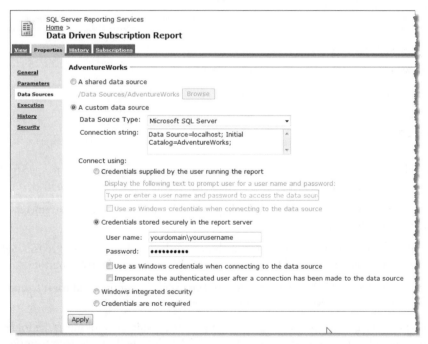

FIGURE P7-14

18. In Step 1 of the wizard, choose Windows File Share as the method of how recipients are notified.

19. In Step 2, you will be required to re-enter the credentials and store them securely in the server.

20. After completing the process of storing the credentials securely in the server, you will create a data-driven subscription, and Service Schedule Report (see Figure P7-15), specify the following command which will be used to drive the report:

```
SELECT DISTINCT
dbo.fnGetCurrenciesByRegion(CountryRegionCode) as CurrencyCode
, CountryRegionCode from Sales.CountryRegionCurrency
```

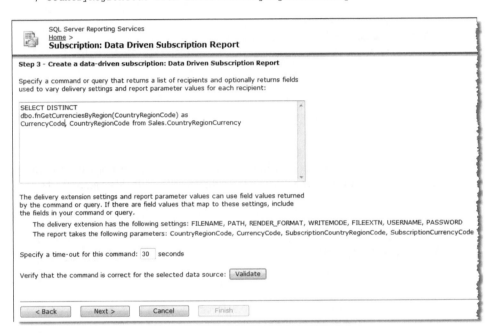

FIGURE P7-15

21. After clicking the Validate button to validate your command, click Next to specify the following delivery extension settings for Report Server FileShare. (See Figure P7-16).

22. In Step 5 of the wizard (see Figure P7-17), you will bypass the standard parameters and specify the subscription values to be used.

23. In Step 6 of the subscription wizard, you choose a schedule for the report to run. Select the option "On a schedule created for this subscription" and click the Next button.

24. In Step 7 (see Figure P7-18), set the report to run every 10 minutes and for it to end in a few days. When you are finished, click the Finish button.

25. Once the subscription has executed, you can view the results by looking at the folder and the reports the subscription produced (see Figure P7-19). You will see the subscription created reports for all country codes and for the country code FR or France, and the report lists both sales in Euros and French Francs.

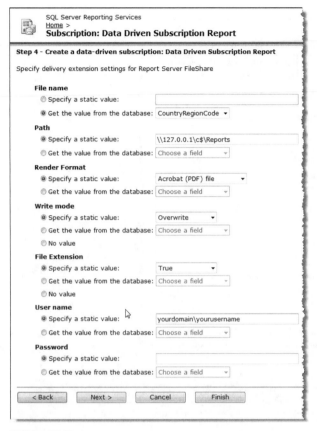

FIGURE P7-16

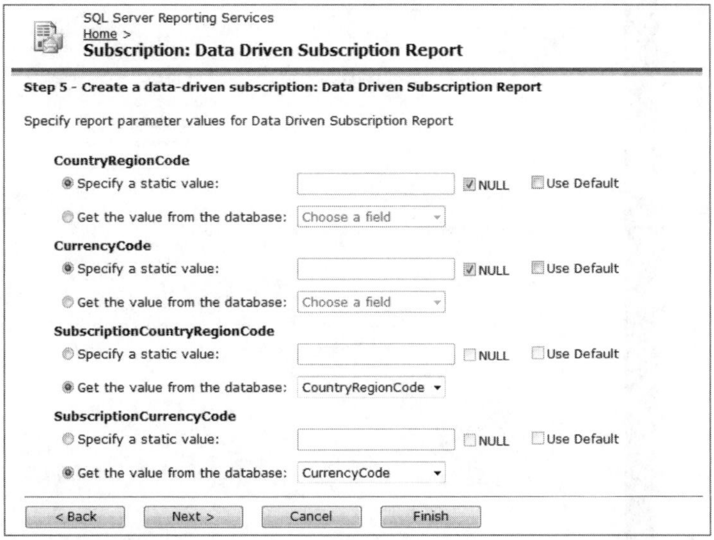

FIGURE P7-17

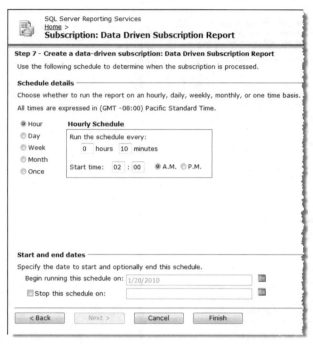

FIGURE P7-18

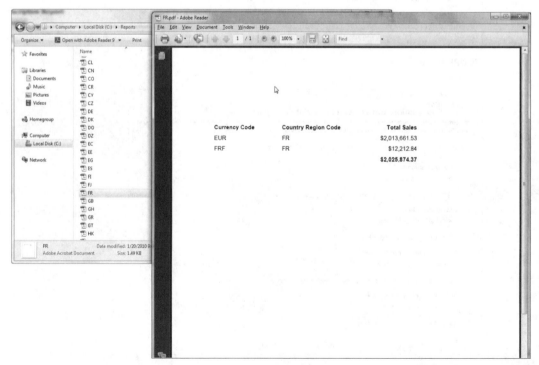

FIGURE P7-19

Final Thoughts

Subscription reporting is an important feature of SSRS. Data-driven subscription reports further enhance the benefit of delivering meaningful reports to persons within your organization on a regular basis. To increase the usability of the reports, many times the designer will need to be creative, as is the case with multi-value reporting, in order to maintain a high level of usability and also keep the overhead low. This is where the additional UDF comes into play, as it allows multiple values to be concatenated into a single string and in turn, passed into the report.

PARAMETERIZED TOP VALUES REPORT

Top ranked lists are a common type of report. In many cases, business users may want to see only a specific number of records at the top or bottom of a range, effectively reporting the best or worst items in ranked order. We see ranked lists in all types of applications to answer questions like "What are the top five best selling products?" or "Who are my five worst producing sales people?" This is a relatively simple matter using a top values or top ranked query. It may be even more useful if users could select or enter the number of items to return in the report.

Product Versions

➤   Reporting Services 2000

➤   Reporting Services 2005

➤   Reporting Services 2008

What You'll Need

➤   A query with ordered aggregate values

➤   A parameter to specify the top query value

Designing the Report

An example of the finished report is shown in Figure P7-20.

To understand the challenge, you'll start with a simple top values query in a tabular report. The query will return the top ten most profitable customers.

1.   Start by creating a new report with a data source using the AdventureWorksDW2008 or AdventureWorksDW database.

2.   Create a dataset using the following SQL query:

```
SELECT TOP 10
        DimCustomer.FirstName + ' ' + DimCustomer.LastName AS CustomerName
   , SUM(FactInternetSales.SalesAmount) AS SalesAmount
FROM
        DimCustomer INNER JOIN FactInternetSales
        ON DimCustomer.CustomerKey = FactInternetSales.CustomerKey
        GROUP BY DimCustomer.FirstName + ' ' + DimCustomer.LastName
        ORDER BY SUM(FactInternetSales.SalesAmount) DESC
```

3.   Add a table to the report and use it to show the output of this query. The report should look similar to Figure P7-21.

Add a parameter to use in place of the static top value (the number 10). Rather than adding the parameter reference to the query script and relying on the report designer to generate the report parameter, you want to manually add the parameter to the report first.

4.   Add a new report parameter and in the Report Parameter Properties dialog, name the parameter TopCustomers.

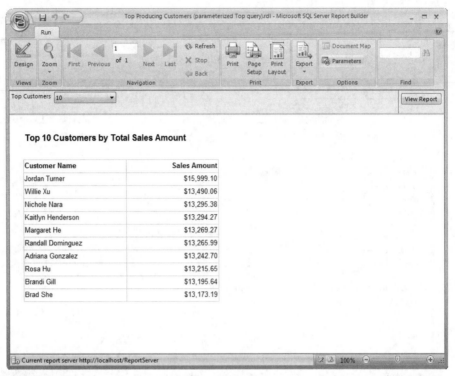

FIGURE P7-20

5. Provide an appropriate prompt and leave the rest of the properties on the General page with default values. (See Figure P7-22.)

6. On the Available Values page, enter a few integer values to be used by a user to select the number of rows to show on the report.

7. Choose Specify values.

8. Add one item for each parameter value and then for each parameter in the list, enter the same number for the Label and the Value, as you see in Figure P7-23.

9. Close the dialog and save the new parameter.

Consider the following attempt to parameterize the number of rows returned from the query results.

1. Edit the dataset query and replace the top value number 10 with the query parameter reference @TopCustomers. The query should look like this:

```
SELECT TOP @TopCustomers
        DimCustomer.FirstName + ' ' + DimCustomer.LastName AS CustomerName
    , SUM(FactInternetSales.SalesAmount) AS SalesAmount
FROM
        DimCustomer INNER JOIN FactInternetSales
        ON DimCustomer.CustomerKey = FactInternetSales.CustomerKey
        GROUP BY DimCustomer.FirstName + ' ' + DimCustomer.LastName
        ORDER BY SUM(FactInternetSales.SalesAmount) DESC
```

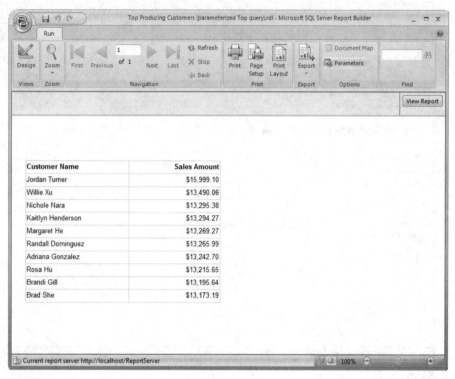

FIGURE P7-21

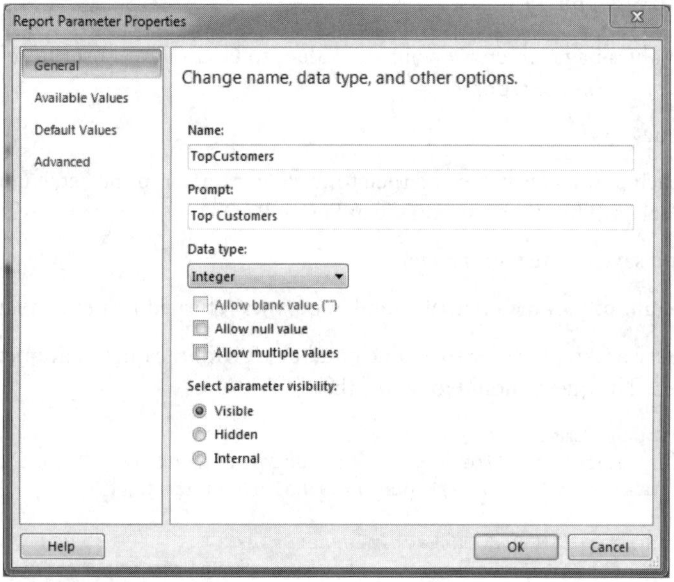

FIGURE P7-22

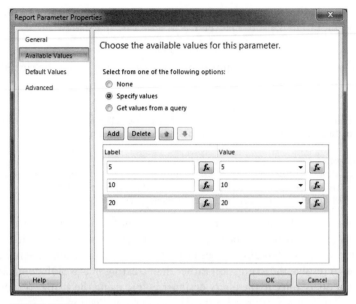

FIGURE P7-23

When you save or run the query, you will be prompted for the parameter value. Enter a value such as 5. This behavior is expected, however, the report designer will display an error after you enter this value, as you can see in Figure P7-24.

FIGURE P7-24

This query will not work because the query designer can't resolve the TopCustomerCount parameter. There are certain key words and values in a T-SQL query that cannot be parameterized, including the TOP statement. So, how do you work around this limitation?

1. On the Dataset Properties dialog, click the expression button (*fx*) next to the Query box to open the expression editor.

To deal with this challenge, the entire query is converted to a string with the parameter value concatenated into the appropriate position. String concatenation is performed using Visual Basic.NET expression code. Carriage returns may be inserted for code readability, but have no bearing on the actual string that will be presented to the data provider. Since the database engine doesn't care about line returns and extra spaces, it's not important to add these to the code, but it is important to make sure that there is at least one space between each operator and object name.

The following script returns the string equivalent of the same query with the embedded parameter value:

```
="SELECT TOP " & Parameters!TopCustomers.Value
& " DimCustomer.FirstName + ' ' + DimCustomer.LastName AS CustomerName "
& ", SUM(FactInternetSales.SalesAmount) AS SalesAmount "
& "FROM "
& " DimCustomer INNER JOIN FactInternetSales "
& " ON DimCustomer.CustomerKey = FactInternetSales.CustomerKey "
& "GROUP BY DimCustomer.FirstName + ' ' + DimCustomer.LastName "
& "ORDER BY SUM(FactInternetSales.SalesAmount) DESC"
```

When the expression is saved, the query parser may complain because a SQL statement can't start with an equal sign (=). If this happens, just accept the error and move on. It's actually fine because the field metadata has already been saved with the dataset object. After this, the designer will know to resolve the expression rather than treating it as a SQL command. It's important to run the query once in the query designer before using the string concatenation technique so the report designer can resolve the dataset Fields collection.

You'll add some header text to show the number of items the user decided to show in the report.

2. Add a textbox to the report body, above the table.

3. Right-click the textbox and add the following expression:

```
="Top " & Parameters!TopCustomers.Value & " Customers by Total Sales Amount"
```

4. Preview the report again.

5. Select a value from the parameter drop-down list and click the Run Report button on the toolbar. The report should run and return the appropriate number of rows, as seen in Figure P7-25.

For even more flexibility, create a custom function in the report properties Code window and use Visual Basic.NET code to build and return the entire query string.

Top Value Reports for Cubes

The same fundamental technique may also be applied to an MDX query. The MDX query designer, which was introduced in SSRS 2005 for reports that use SQL Server Analysis Services as a data source, has some strict restrictions about using in-line parameters. The query designer can also be unforgiving when you modify generated query script. Queries may be hand-written in the query editor text mode. In many cases, it may be easier or even necessary to assemble the query script using a Visual Basic.NET expression.

1. To apply this pattern, create a new report, similar to the one in the previous example, with a data source connecting to the AdventureWorksDW2008 Analysis Services database for SQL Server 2008 or the AdventureWorksDW database for 2005.

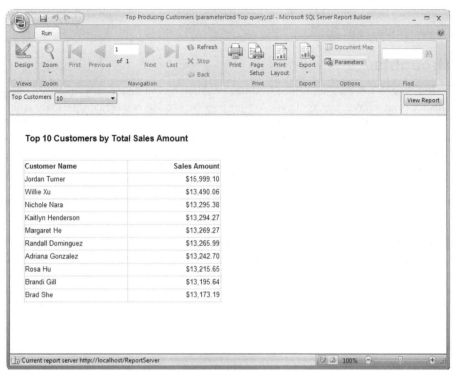

FIGURE P7-25

2. Following the same pattern as before, create a new dataset. In the MDX query designer, switch to text mode using the Design Mode button on the right-side of the toolbar, and type the following query:

```
SELECT
      {[Measures].[Internet Sales Amount]} ON COLUMNS
    , NON EMPTY TOPCOUNT([Customer].[Customer].[Customer].MEMBERS, 5
                         , [Measures].[Internet Sales Amount]) ON ROWS

FROM [Adventure Works];
```

3. Execute the query to build the dataset and Fields collection.

4. Add the TopCustomers parameter per the previous instructions.

5. In the DataSet Properties dialog, replace the query text with the following expression:

```
="SELECT "
& "{[Measures].[Internet Sales Amount]} ON COLUMNS, "
& " NON EMPTY TOPCOUNT([Customer].[Customer].[Customer].MEMBERS, "
& Parameters!TopCustomers.Value & ", [Measures].[Internet Sales Amount])
   ON ROWS "

& " FROM [Adventure Works];"
```

6.   Preview the report, select a Top Customers parameter value, and click View Report to execute the query and run the report.

Final Thoughts

You've seen how to solve an important business problem by building a custom query using an expression. This technique has many applications that may be used to resolve complex decision structures in code before assembling the SQL statement string. There are two fundamental principles that will expand your report design horizons. The first is that although query languages, like TSQL and MDX, are powerful and may be use creatively, they have their limitations. Query languages are optimized for data retrieval and manipulation, but have limited capabilities for decision structures and branching logic. True programming languages exist for this purpose and combining the strengths of both programming and query languages can often solve even the most challenging business problems.

The query designers also have limitations that can easily be circumnavigated with a little code, but typically without the aid of graphical query-building tools. As a rule, write the query in its simplest form using the design tool first and execute the query to generate the fields' metadata. After that, replace the query with script or code to handle the complexities of conditional logic and parameterization.

CUBE RESTRICTING ROWS

This recipe is another step toward the complete SSRS Cube Browser recipe that begins with the "Cube Dynamic Rows" recipe earlier in this book.

One of the challenges in creating dynamic reports is the user can accidentally request a huge amount of data. In this recipe, you take a quick look at how to add functionality for restricting the number of rows returned in a report.

Effectively, you simply use the TOPCOUNT function in MDX to restrict the number of rows returned by the query with the number of rows driven by a parameter. However, instead of the user having to select the parameter with a fiddly option box in the parameters, you will create a table in the report so users just click on the number of rows they want.

Product Versions

➤ Reporting Services 2005

➤ Reporting Services 2008

What You'll Need

➤ Ability to read MDX

Designing the Report

This solution uses custom MDX and the TOPCOUNT function to restrict the number of rows returned in a query. This technique can be utilized in any query against MDX. For this example, you start with the report created in the "Cube Dynamic Rows" recipe earlier in this book.

The final report is shown in Figure P7-26.

First, you add a parameter for the number of rows to return, and then modify the custom MDX to utilize TOPCOUNT.

1. From BIDS, copy and paste the report called Cube Dynamic Rows (highlight the report in Solution Explorer and then type CTRL+C, CTRL+V) and rename it to Cube Restricting Rows.

2. Create a string report parameter called pRowCount with a default value of 6 and the following available expression values:

LABEL	VALUE
6 Rows	6
10 Rows	10

See Figure P7-27.

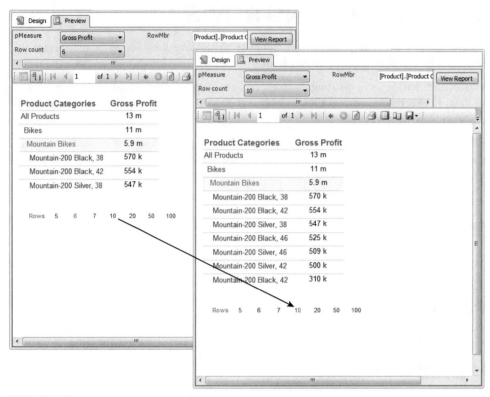

FIGURE P7-26

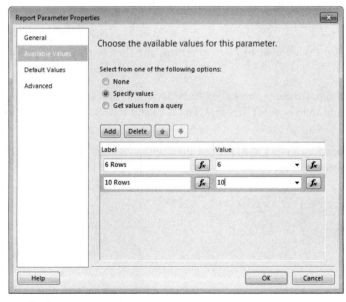

FIGURE P7-27

3.   Right click on Dataset1 and open the Query Editor. Modify the MDX by wrapping the rows code with the TOPCOUNT function:

```
-- returns the top n number of rows based on current measure
TOPCOUNT(
    -- show the current hierarachy member with its ascendants
    -- together with its children on rows
    STRTOSET(
        "{Ascendants(" + @pRowMbr + " ), "
        + @pRowMbr + ".children}"
    ) .
    ,StrToValue(@pRowCount)
    ,[Measures].[Measure_Value]
)
```

```
ON ROWS
```

4.   Click the Parameter icon in the toolbar and add pRowCount with a default value of 6. (See Figure P7-28.)

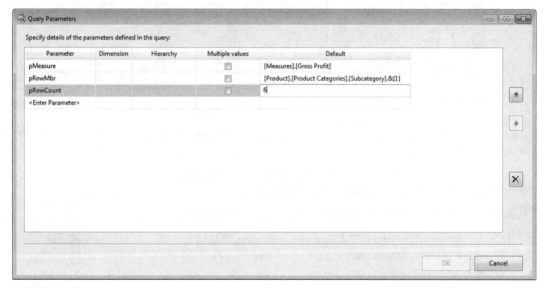

FIGURE P7-28

5.   Execute the query to check that it runs OK before returning to the data set properties. It should look like Figure P7-29.

6.   Click OK again to return to the design surface.

Your Report data should look like Figure P7-30.

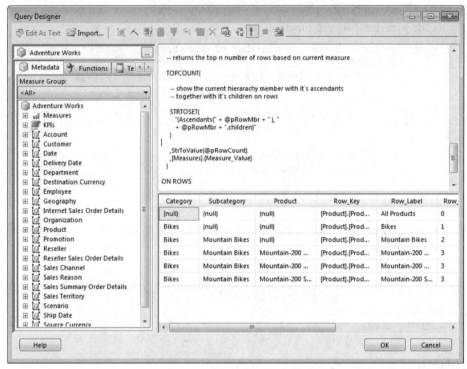

FIGURE P7-29

If you preview the report, you'll see that you can now change the number of rows displayed, as shown in Figure P7-31.

So now that you can control how many rows are returned, let's design a better way for the user to select how many rows to return.

First, you need a new dataset to produce a list of values to choose from.

1. As shown in Figure P7-32, use the following SQL query to create a new dataset called CellCount that is based on the shared datasource dsAnySQLDB:

```
Select 5 as CellCount union all
select 6 union all
select 7 union all
select 10 union all
select 20 union all
select 50 union all
select 100
```

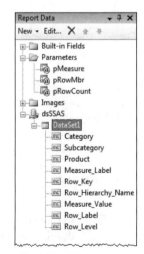

FIGURE P7-30

2. Open properties of pRowCount.

3. On the Available Values tab, change the radio button to Get values from query and select the CellCount query.

4. Set both Value field and Label field to CellCount, as shown in Figure P7-33.

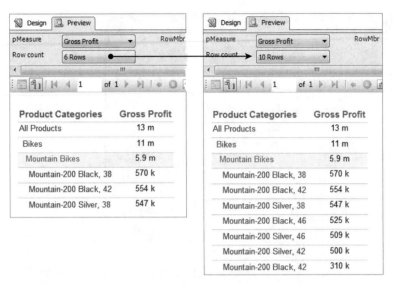

FIGURE P7-31

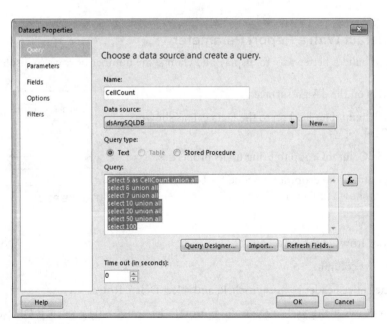

FIGURE P7-32

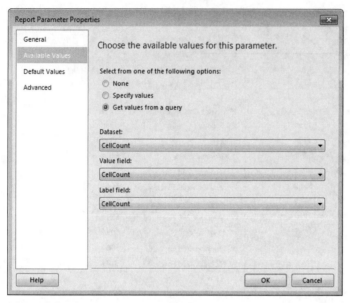

FIGURE P7-33

A Better Way to Interact With a Report Parameter

Now you are going to build a better way to display and change the number of rows to display.

1. Insert a matrix on the design surface.

2. Drag the CellCount data field on to the Data cell as shown in Figure P7-34.

3. Right click on ColumnGroup to bring up its properties.

4. Select CellCount in the drop-down value for Group expressions as shown in Figure P7-35.

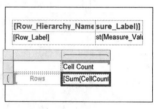

FIGURE P7-34

5. Click OK.

6. Type the word **Rows** in the Rows cell.

7. Resize the Rows column.

8. Highlight the entire header row, right-click, and select Delete Rows.

9. In the Delete Rows dialog, select the radio button Delete rows only and click OK (see Figure P7-36).

10. Reduce the width of the CellCount column.

11. Set the properties of the Rows textbox cell as follows:

   ➤ BorderStyle Default to None

   ➤ FontSize to 8pt

➤ FontColor to DimGray

➤ Alignment Horizontal to Right

12. Set the properties of the CellCount textbox cell to:

➤ BorderStyle Default to None

➤ FontSize to 8pt

➤ FontColor to Blue

➤ Alignment Horizontal to Center

Now you need to add the magic ingredients. There are two: changing the color of the CellCount textbox when it matches the pRowCount parameter to DimGray, and adding a self drill-through action. Here we go:

FIGURE P7-35

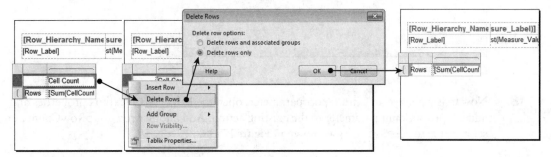

FIGURE P7-36

13. Open the CellCount textbox properties.

14. Set the Font Color according to this expression:

```
=iif(Fields!CellCount.Value = Parameters!pRowCount.Value, "DimGray", "Blue")
```

15. Add the self drill-though action by setting the Go to report radio button.

16. Set the report to the built-in function `[@ReportName]`.

17. As shown in Figure P7-37, add the required parameters (that is, the current report parameters plus the CellCount value from the cell the user clicked on, as shown in the following table):

NAME	VALUE
pMeasure	[@pMeasure]
pRowMbr	[@pRowMbr]
pRowCount	[CellCount]

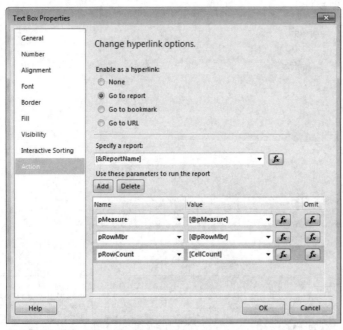

FIGURE P7-37

18. Now that you have an extra report parameter, open the Row_Label textbox properties and add the pRowCount parameter to the existing action. Add another row for pRowCount and set its value to `[@pRowCount]` as shown in Figure P7-38.

FIGURE P7-38

Note the dataset for the list of possible values for the RowCount parameter could be a real table. The advantage of this is you can change the available values in one place and have it apply across all your reports.

Another step towards the Simple SSRS OLAP browser is complete. Already users can change rows and measures (at least manually), drill up and down a cube hierarchy, and now you have added the capability for users to control the number of rows returned.

The next step is to build a way of directly interrogating the cube structure (see the "Cube Metadata" recipe earlier in this book).

Final Thoughts

You now have a way of showing information about the structure of your cubes. As developers, if we actually populate the description fields within Analysis Server, we can have up-to-date information available to our users. We could also allow a user to search for a measure by name or, on a standard report, add a help button to discover details of a dimension or measure.

In later recipes you will come back and visit this report. With some modifications, it will enable users to dynamically change the rows, columns, or filters in their user reports.

CREATING CUSTOM SORTING REPORTS

This recipe consists of a series of related report recipes that demonstrate various techniques for creating reports that enable users to dynamically modify the sort order of report content. Traditional reporting solutions typically contain several different reports with only slight differences in design. A "Super Report" is one report that replaces multiple reports by implementing dynamic features. This design pattern replaces several reports with one more capable report with features enabling custom sorting, grouping, and filtering so that one flexible report design meets the needs of many users. The techniques vary in flexibility and complexity and there are pros and cons for each. In an effort to simplify, the following list provides a brief overview of these techniques and corresponding design recipes.

> **Parameterizing Custom Sorted Queries:** This technique uses conditional logic in the dataset query to execute a conditional query, based upon a parameter selection. This is a very flexible option that can be used to address complex business requirements and complex sorting criteria.

> **Parameterizing the Order By Clause:** An optimized extension of the preceding technique, this approach is straightforward and efficiently designed. It may not offer the same level of flexibility; however, it allows users to define primary and secondary sorts without duplicating the entire dataset query.

> **Custom Sorting in Tablix Groups:** This technique places the conditional sort logic in the report rather than the query. The advantage is that sorting can be managed within table and matrix groups rather than the entire dataset query that feeds data to the report items. It may not offer the same level of control and conditional logic but it can be more efficient since the data is sorted on the report server, using cached data on the report server.

> **Using the Interactive Sort Feature:** This is the easiest sorting method to implement. It requires no conditional expressions, programming, or custom query design. Interactive Sort is a feature added in SSRS 2005 and it applies to textboxes in the table header row. You can control the group level scope of sorting but there are limitations to this feature. Small sort order direction arrows are displayed in table column headers but this interface may not be customized. Sorting is limited to only one column at a time.

> This feature is very fast and efficient due to optimizations built into the SSRS server architecture. It not only sorts on the report server data cache, but also implements client events and page level caching.

> **Creating a Custom Interactive Sort:** This technique is a custom emulation of the Interactive Sort feature that enables you to apply more explicit business rules and complex sorting logic. Sorting is implemented in the report groups using expressions, so the sorting can apply to data cached on the report server. This technique also allows you to customize the report user interface. Report actions are used to drill-through to the same report and modify parameter values used in a table, tablix, or group Sort property expression. This approach is efficient, very flexible, but takes a little more work to design.

The decision to use one technique over another should really come down to using the query or programming language best suited for the task, or perhaps the skill set of the report developer. At times this is a trade-off between the brevity of the code or script, the ease of development and the on-going cost to maintain or enhance it using available resources and developer skills. Dad always said, "When in doubt, keep it simple."

Parameterizing Custom Sorted Queries

Appropriately organizing and sorting lengthy lists of data can help users concentrate on specific sets or patterns of data and make better sense of data. Allowing users to control the sort order gives them the flexibility to view the data to their liking. This example will demonstrate the use of report parameters to control the data sort order. With this approach, the sorting work is performed by the data source and not the report processor. So, if your data source doesn't support sorting, you have to use other SSRS sorting features.

Apart from using report parameters to control the sort order, SSRS 2005 and 2008 also support Interactive Sorting. With Interactive Sorting, you can add interactive sort header text labels to tables and matrices that enable users to change the sort order of the report data. Interactive sorting is a feature of a text box in a column header and has the ability to control which part of table or matrix data region to sort (e.g. parent group, child group, or detail row), and what to sort by. However, interactive sorting is only supported by rendering formats that allow user interaction, such as HTML. Also, the sorting work is performed by the report processor, so it doesn't force a re-query and thus can be more efficient than other techniques.

In addition to Interactive Sorting, all versions of SSRS also support sorting report data using sort expressions that can be applied on data regions or groups. Sorting expressions can also be set at the category and series groups to control the sort order for data points of a chart. However, sorting report data using sort expressions isn't interactive and sorting is performed by the report processor.

Product Versions

- ➤ Reporting Services 2000
- ➤ Reporting Services 2005
- ➤ Reporting Services 2008

What You'll Need

- ➤ A table report
- ➤ An understanding of parameters and using them in data queries

Designing the Report

This example uses the AdventureWorksDW for SQL Server 2005 or 2008 sample database and a simple query that sums the reseller sales amount across sales territory, product category, subcategory, product name, and months. For the example, you are restricting your dataset to the first quarter of CY 2003. This example uses Report Builder 2.0.

The technique demonstrated in this section uses logic branching in the T-SQL script to execute one of multiple whole queries. This approach produces lengthy query script which can be more work to write and maintain than the techniques shown in later sections. However, it also allows you to isolate the query logic from one block to another, which may provide some flexibility and control.

1. Start by designing a data source for the AdventureWorksDW or AdventureWorksDW2008 sample database.

2. Create the following dataset query that includes the `FactResellerSales`, `DimDate`, `DimSalesTerritory`, `DimProduct`, `DimProductCategory` and `DimProductSubcategory` tables.

```
SELECT ST.SalesTerritoryCountry
,PC.EnglishProductCategoryName
,PSC.EnglishProductSubcategoryName
,P.EnglishProductName
,D.EnglishMonthName
,D.MonthNumberOfYear
,SUM(FRS.SalesAmount) as SalesAmount
FROM dbo.FactResellerSales FRS
    INNER JOIN dbo.DimDate D
        ON FRS.OrderDateKey = D.DateKey
    INNER JOIN dbo.DimSalesTerritory ST
        ON FRS.SalesTerritoryKey = ST.SalesTerritoryKey
    INNER JOIN dbo.DimProduct P
        ON FRS.ProductKey = P.ProductKey
    INNER JOIN dbo.DimProductSubcategory PSC
        ON P.ProductSubcategoryKey = PSC.ProductSubcategoryKey
    INNER JOIN dbo.DimProductCategory PC
        ON PSC.ProductCategoryKey = PC.ProductCategoryKey
WHERE D.CalendarYear = 2003 and D.CalendarQuarter = 1
GROUP BY ST.SalesTerritoryCountry
,PC.EnglishProductCategoryName
,PSC.EnglishProductSubcategoryName
,P.EnglishProductName
,D.EnglishMonthName
,D.MonthNumberOfYear
ORDER BY ST.SalesTerritoryCountry desc, D.MonthNumberOfYear
```

 In the AdventureWorksDW database for SQL Server 2005, the Date table is named DimTime instead of DimDate and the DateKey column is named TimeKey.

3. Add a table report item to the report body.

4. Add SalesTerritoryCountry, EnglishProductCategoryName, EnglishProductSubcategory-Name, EnglishProductName, EnglishMonthName, and SalesAmount to the data fields of the table (you may have to add additional columns in order to fit all the columns we are adding to the table).

The report designer should look like Figure P7-39.

Now that you have created the report layout, let's think about the custom sort options end users will have. For this example, you will provide users with the following four sort options:

➤ Sales Territory (desc), Month

➤ Product Category, Subcategory, Month

➤ Sales Amount (desc)

➤ Sales Territory (desc), Sales Amount (desc).

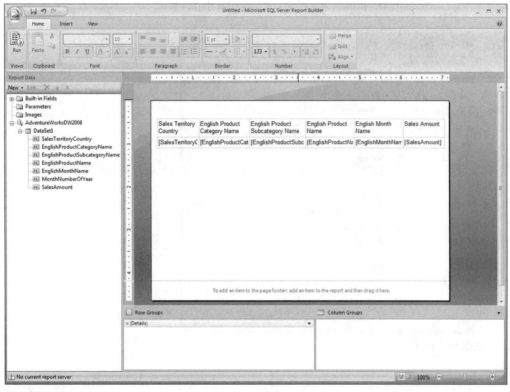

FIGURE P7-39

Let's go ahead and add the custom sort parameter.

1. Right-click on the Parameters folder and select Add Parameters.

2. In the Report Parameter Properties dialog, enter CustomSortOrder and Sort By in the Name and Prompt fields respectively (see Figure P7-40).

3. Select the Available Values page of the Report Parameter Properties dialog box.

4. Select the Specify Values radio button and add the following values by clicking the Add button (see Figure P7-41).

LABEL	VALUE
Sales Territory (desc), Month	1
Product Category, Subcategory, Month	2
Sales Amount (desc)	3
Sales Territory (desc), Sales Amount (desc)	4

5. On the Default Values page, set the default value for this parameter to 1.

6.   Click OK to close the Report Parameter Properties dialog box.

FIGURE P7-40

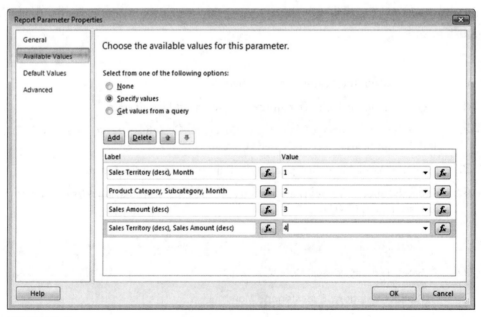

FIGURE P7-41

Now you need to take the input from the Custom Sort Order parameter and sort the data accordingly. There are a few different ways of achieving this, but for simplicity's sake, you are just going to embed logic in the query. The logic will simply sort the data based on the parameter value that was selected.

For example, if the parameter value is 1, data will be sorted on Sales Territory (desc), Month; if the parameter value is 2, data will be sorted on Product Category, Subcategory, and Month. After adding this logic, the new dataset query will look like the following query. Replace the existing dataset query with this new query.

```
IF @CustomSortOrder = 1
BEGIN
SELECT ST.SalesTerritoryCountry
  ,PC.EnglishProductCategoryName
  ,PSC.EnglishProductSubcategoryName
  ,P.EnglishProductName
  ,D.EnglishMonthName
  ,D.MonthNumberOfYear
  ,SUM(FRS.SalesAmount) as SalesAmount
FROM dbo.FactResellerSales FRS
  INNER JOIN dbo.DimDate D
    ON FRS.OrderDateKey = D.DateKey
  INNER JOIN dbo.DimSalesTerritory ST
    ON FRS.SalesTerritoryKey = ST.SalesTerritoryKey
  INNER JOIN dbo.DimProduct P
    ON FRS.ProductKey = P.ProductKey
  INNER JOIN dbo.DimProductSubcategory PSC
    ON P.ProductSubcategoryKey = PSC.ProductSubcategoryKey
  INNER JOIN dbo.DimProductCategory PC
    ON PSC.ProductCategoryKey = PC.ProductCategoryKey
WHERE D.CalendarYear = 2003 and D.CalendarQuarter = 1
GROUP BY ST.SalesTerritoryCountry
  ,PC.EnglishProductCategoryName
  ,PSC.EnglishProductSubcategoryName
  ,P.EnglishProductName
  ,D.EnglishMonthName
  ,D.MonthNumberOfYear
ORDER BY ST.SalesTerritoryCountry desc, D.MonthNumberOfYear
END

ELSE IF @CustomSortOrder = 2
BEGIN
SELECT ST.SalesTerritoryCountry
  ,PC.EnglishProductCategoryName
  ,PSC.EnglishProductSubcategoryName
  ,P.EnglishProductName
  ,D.EnglishMonthName
  ,D.MonthNumberOfYear
  ,SUM(FRS.SalesAmount) as SalesAmount
FROM dbo.FactResellerSales FRS
  INNER JOIN dbo.DimDate D
    ON FRS.OrderDateKey = D.DateKey
  INNER JOIN dbo.DimSalesTerritory ST
    ON FRS.SalesTerritoryKey = ST.SalesTerritoryKey
  INNER JOIN dbo.DimProduct P
    ON FRS.ProductKey = P.ProductKey
```

```
      INNER JOIN dbo.DimProductSubcategory PSC
         ON P.ProductSubcategoryKey = PSC.ProductSubcategoryKey
      INNER JOIN dbo.DimProductCategory PC
         ON PSC.ProductCategoryKey = PC.ProductCategoryKey
   WHERE D.CalendarYear = 2003 and D.CalendarQuarter = 1
   GROUP BY ST.SalesTerritoryCountry
     ,PC.EnglishProductCategoryName
     ,PSC.EnglishProductSubcategoryName
     ,P.EnglishProductName
     ,D.EnglishMonthName
     ,D.MonthNumberOfYear
   ORDER BY PC.EnglishProductCategoryName, PSC.EnglishProductSubcategoryName,
        D.EnglishMonthName
   END

   ELSE IF @CustomSortOrder = 3
   BEGIN
   SELECT ST.SalesTerritoryCountry
     ,PC.EnglishProductCategoryName
     ,PSC.EnglishProductSubcategoryName
     ,P.EnglishProductName
     ,D.EnglishMonthName
     ,D.MonthNumberOfYear
     ,SUM(FRS.SalesAmount) as SalesAmount
   FROM dbo.FactResellerSales FRS
      INNER JOIN dbo.DimDate D
         ON FRS.OrderDateKey = D.DateKey
      INNER JOIN dbo.DimSalesTerritory ST
         ON FRS.SalesTerritoryKey = ST.SalesTerritoryKey
      INNER JOIN dbo.DimProduct P
         ON FRS.ProductKey = P.ProductKey
      INNER JOIN dbo.DimProductSubcategory PSC
         ON P.ProductSubcategoryKey = PSC.ProductSubcategoryKey
      INNER JOIN dbo.DimProductCategory PC
         ON PSC.ProductCategoryKey = PC.ProductCategoryKey
   WHERE D.CalendarYear = 2003 and D.CalendarQuarter = 1
   GROUP BY ST.SalesTerritoryCountry
     ,PC.EnglishProductCategoryName
     ,PSC.EnglishProductSubcategoryName
     ,P.EnglishProductName
     ,D.EnglishMonthName
     ,D.MonthNumberOfYear
   ORDER BY SalesAmount desc
   END

   ELSE IF @CustomSortOrder = 4
   BEGIN
   SELECT ST.SalesTerritoryCountry
     ,PC.EnglishProductCategoryName
     ,PSC.EnglishProductSubcategoryName
     ,P.EnglishProductName
     ,D.EnglishMonthName
     ,D.MonthNumberOfYear
     ,SUM(FRS.SalesAmount) as SalesAmount
```

```
FROM dbo.FactResellerSales FRS
  INNER JOIN dbo.DimDate D
    ON FRS.OrderDateKey = D.DateKey
  INNER JOIN dbo.DimSalesTerritory ST
    ON FRS.SalesTerritoryKey = ST.SalesTerritoryKey
  INNER JOIN dbo.DimProduct P
    ON FRS.ProductKey = P.ProductKey
  INNER JOIN dbo.DimProductSubcategory PSC
    ON P.ProductSubcategoryKey = PSC.ProductSubcategoryKey
  INNER JOIN dbo.DimProductCategory PC
    ON PSC.ProductCategoryKey = PC.ProductCategoryKey
WHERE D.CalendarYear = 2003 and D.CalendarQuarter = 1
GROUP BY ST.SalesTerritoryCountry
  , PC.EnglishProductCategoryName
  , PSC.EnglishProductSubcategoryName
  , P.EnglishProductName
  , D.EnglishMonthName
  , D.MonthNumberOfYear
ORDER BY ST.SalesTerritoryCountry desc, SalesAmount desc
END
```

Preview the report to test the results.

As you can see in Figure P7-42, data is first sorted in descending order by Sales Territory Country and then in ascending order by Month.

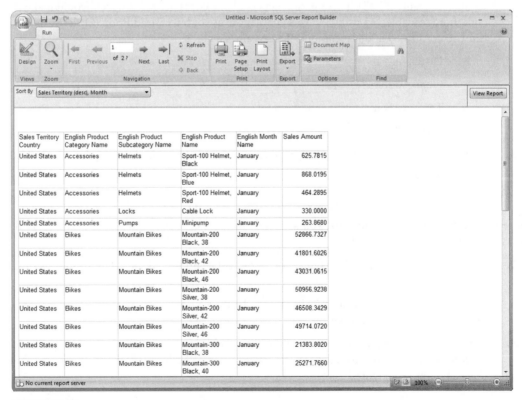

FIGURE P7-42

One of the greatest advantages of this technique is that there are very few limitations to the logic and business rules you can implement by customizing the query. This a good approach when the requirements call for sorting on multiple columns or when you need to combine sorting and filtering logic.

Any query modifications you implement will not directly impact the report user interface, which may also need to be customized using dynamic groups or conditional formatting. Although flexible, this technique doesn't take advantage of more convenient, built-in report design features like interactive sorting or instance caching. Every time a parameter value changes, the query must be executed on the database server.

Parameterizing the Order By Clause

This technique is similar to the last one, but applies conditional logic only in the Order By clause of the query. This requires less code to implement, but may not offer the same level of flexibility if the report should also be filtered using the same parameter logic. We offer this as yet another example of the same basic approach using a slightly different set of techniques.

1. Open Report Builder and create a new report.

Give the report a title of Custom Sorting with Parameters.

2. Add two new report parameters, one called OrderBy and the other called Direction.

When you create the "OrderBy" parameter, define it as an integer value with four possible values (see Figure P7-43). These parameters could be character types which would make the code more readable, but using integers enables the use of bit-wise addition (OrderBy + Direction) demonstrated in this technique. These values include:

➤ LastName - 0

➤ Email Address - 2

➤ Territory Name - 4

➤ Sales YTD - 6

3. Name the second parameter (a text parameter) Direction and add the following two values:

➤ Ascending - 0

➤ Descending - 1

Once you have created the parameters, you are ready to connect to the data source and display the information within a tablix or table.

1. Drag a table to the area inside your report. You will be prompted for a data source, as shown in Figure P7-44.

This recipe uses the AdventureWorks sample database and uses an existing, secure connection stored on the report server.

2. When prompted for the query, expand the Views folder and the vSalesPerson node. Check the following four boxes to return the Last Name, Email Address, Territory Name, and Sales YTD columns (See Figure P7-45).

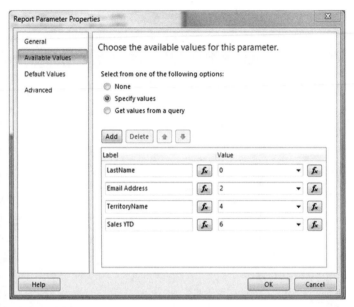

FIGURE P7-43

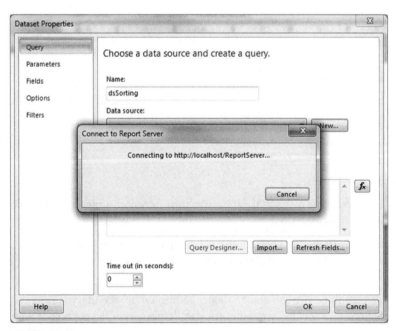

FIGURE P7-44

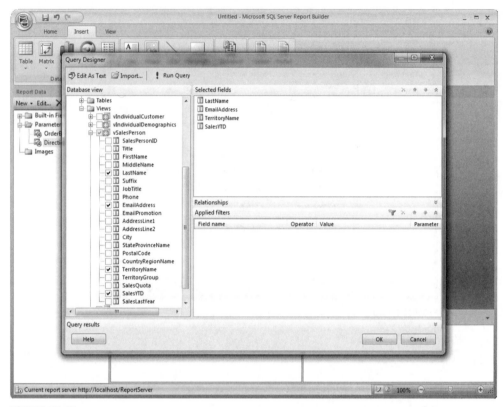

FIGURE P7-45

3. Add the following query:

```
SELECT
    Sales.vSalesPerson.LastName
    ,Sales.vSalesPerson.EmailAddress
    ,Sales.vSalesPerson.TerritoryName
    ,Sales.vSalesPerson.SalesYTD
FROM
    Sales.vSalesPerson
```

4. After you have added the query and datasource to your report, drag each of the columns to your table and format as desired.

At this point, you are ready to modify your query to accept parameters and do the sorting at the T-SQL level. This approach is powerful and useful for snapshot reporting and reports with large amounts of data.

In addition, with this technique you are able to define additional or secondary sorting options. For example, if the user chooses to sort by last name, you can define within the context of your conditional order-by clause to also sort by Sales YTD. If they choose Sales YTD as the primary sorting option, you could define another column as your secondary option.

Modify the properties of the dataset to accept parameters and do the sorting based on the parameters passed in.

Your entire query will be appended with conditional statements and will look similar to the following statement.

```
SELECT
  Sales.vSalesPerson.LastName
  ,Sales.vSalesPerson.EmailAddress
  ,Sales.vSalesPerson.TerritoryName
  ,Sales.vSalesPerson.SalesYTD
FROM
  Sales.vSalesPerson
ORDER BY
CASE @OrderBy + @Direction WHEN 0 THEN LastName ELSE NULL END ASC,
CASE @OrderBy + @Direction WHEN 1 THEN LastName ELSE NULL END DESC,
CASE @OrderBy + @Direction WHEN 2 THEN EmailAddress ELSE NULL END ASC,
CASE @OrderBy + @Direction WHEN 3 THEN EmailAddress ELSE NULL END DESC,
CASE @OrderBy + @Direction WHEN 4 THEN TerritoryName ELSE NULL END ASC,
CASE @OrderBy + @Direction WHEN 5 THEN TerritoryName ELSE NULL END DESC,
CASE @OrderBy + @Direction WHEN 6 THEN SalesYTD ELSE NULL END ASC,
CASE @OrderBy + @Direction WHEN 7 THEN SalesYTD ELSE NULL END DESC
```

The result of the query will produce the output shown in Figure P7-46.

Custom Sorting in Tablix Groups

A third approach to sorting the data is to add a sort expression within the table of your report. This technique is similar to the previous example, except as an alternative to adding the parameters to the query, you will add the conditional sorting to the table itself.

At this point, you will need to add the custom sorting to your group properties and you need to remove the OrderBy clause in the dataset from the previous query.

1. Right-click the parameters node to modify the OrderBy parameter. The value needs to be changed from a numeric format to the actual text name of each column, as shown in Figure P7-47.

2. Right click on the detail row of your tablix and view the Group Properties (see Figure P7-48).

3. Add two sort options, one for the ascending option (first option) and one for descending (second option), as shown in the following code:

    ```
    =IIf(Parameters!Direction.Value=0, Fields(Parameters!OrderBy.Value).Value,
        Nothing)

    =IIf(Parameters!Direction.Value=1, Fields(Parameters!OrderBy.Value).Value,
        Nothing)
    ```

FIGURE P7-46

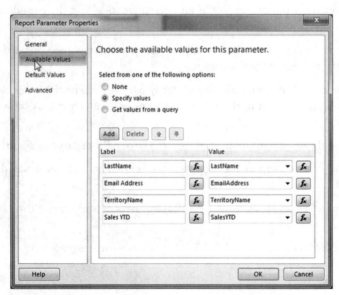

FIGURE P7-47

The Expression dialog shown in Figure P7-49 displays the code for the first sort expression.

This technique will produce the same result as the previous technique, and because the data is cached, performance is optimized since the data is not re-queried each time the report is run after the data is initially loaded and cached on the report server.

FIGURE P7-48

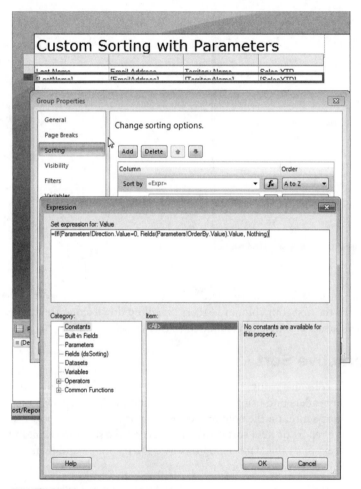

FIGURE P7-49

Using the Interactive Sort Feature

This feature was introduced in Reporting Services 2005 and made column sorting a snap. Interactive Sort is faster than other techniques when used on a relatively small result set. This is because it sorts cached data and doesn't requery the data. For larger results, it may use more server resources. As you can see in Figure P7-50, the text boxes in a table header may be used to create an interactive sort for the table. The settings are fairly self-explanatory. Sorting may be set to the current group-level scope or a specific level can be specified. Using the Interactive Sorting tab on the Text Box Properties dialog for each column header text box, check the box to enable sorting and specify a Sort By expression.

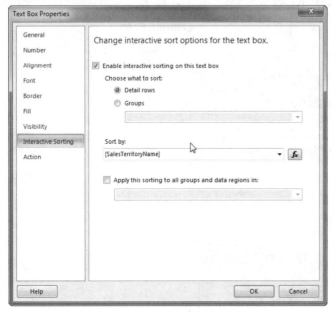

FIGURE P7-50

This is a very powerful feature with little design effort required. Figure P7-51 shows the report in preview with interactive sort enabled for the first four column headers. Small up/down icons are displayed next to each text box caption. This feature is simple but is limited to this view.

Creating a Custom Interactive Sort

As an alternative to using the built-in column sorting, you can also create a full-customized sorting experience featuring clickable column headers and using custom images and direction arrow icons to enhance user experience. Using a report action on the column header text or image, the report user clicks the column header to change the report or item sort order or to reverse the sort direction. In this example, you use the column header text in a table data region to sort by that column and then show a custom image to indicate the ascending or descending sort order.

Reporting Services for SQL Server 2000 doesn't include a specific feature for dynamic column sorting. Using parameters and report items navigation actions, text boxes and images can be made to act like hyperlinks that change parameter values, that are in turn used in expressions to customize the report behavior and user experience.

Product Versions

➤   Reporting Services 2000

Territory	Category	Sub Category	Order Qty	Line Total
Northwest	Clothing	Shorts	41	$1,097.62
Northwest	Clothing	Shorts	38	$1,196.83
Northwest	Clothing	Shorts	32	$1,007.86
Canada	Clothing	Shorts	31	$976.36
Central	Clothing	Socks	28	$113.27
Canada	Clothing	Shorts	26	$818.88
Central	Clothing	Shorts	26	$818.88
Southwest	Bikes	Road Bikes	25	$19,136.14
Southwest	Clothing	Shorts	25	$787.39
Canada	Clothing	Shorts	24	$877.67
France	Clothing	Vests	24	$796.29
Northeast	Clothing	Socks	24	$112.73
Central	Clothing	Socks	23	$108.04
Southeast	Clothing	Shorts	23	$841.10
Southwest	Clothing	Shorts	23	$841.10
United Kingdom	Clothing	Vests	23	$1,526.22
France	Clothing	Shorts	22	$804.54
Germany	Clothing	Vests	22	$729.93
Australia	Clothing	Vests	21	$696.75
Northeast	Clothing	Shorts	21	$767.97
Central	Clothing	Shorts	20	$731.40
Central	Clothing	Socks	20	$93.95
Northeast	Clothing	Socks	20	$93.95
Northeast	Clothing	Vests	20	$663.58
Northwest	Clothing	Shorts	20	$1,462.79
Southeast	Clothing	Vests	20	$663.58
Canada	Bikes	Road Bikes	19	$16,886.58
Canada	Clothing	Jerseys	19	$1,071.97
Canada	Clothing	Vests	19	$630.40
Central	Clothing	Shorts	19	$694.83
Northeast	Clothing	Shorts	19	$694.83

FIGURE P7-51

➤ Reporting Services 2005

➤ Reporting Services 2008

What You'll Need

➤ A table item presenting a columnar set of values.

➤ Table heading or group heading items used as column sort toggle items.

➤ Thumbnail images used to indicate a column's sort direction.

➤ A set of report parameters used to manage the sort column name and direction.

➤ Action expressions used to modify report parameter values.

➤ Expressions used in the table or group Sort property, using report properties.

Figure P7-52 shows a simple table with text headings, a detail row, and totals in the report footer. You can see that I've placed images in separate columns and then merged the field text boxes. I do this so the up/down arrow images appear near the column header text. These columns are merged on the detail row so the fields have enough room. Each of the three sortable columns has text with underscores to indicate that these are links. This is just a visual effect until the navigation actions are set for these text boxes.

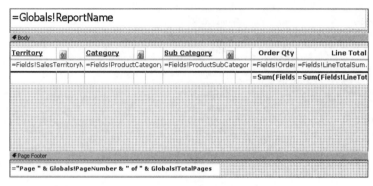

FIGURE P7-52

There are three small images embedded into the report. Figure P7-53 shows these embedded images. The no_arrow image (simply white space in the same dimensions as the arrow images) is used in place of an empty space. This is easier than changing the visibility property of the image item.

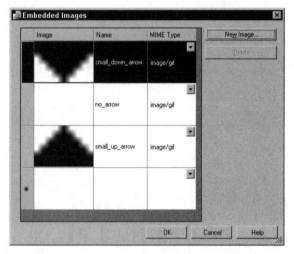

FIGURE P7-53

Just a quick aside: I have simply added the images to the cells in the table header. If you want to use transparent images over a colored or shaded background, you will need to add rectangles to the header cells and then place images in the rectangles.

Figure P7-54 shows the Report Parameters dialog with two parameters defined: `SortField` and `SortDirection`. For the report to render when it is first viewed, all parameters must have a default value. Since the parameters will be set when the user clicks the column header text, no other values need to be provided here.

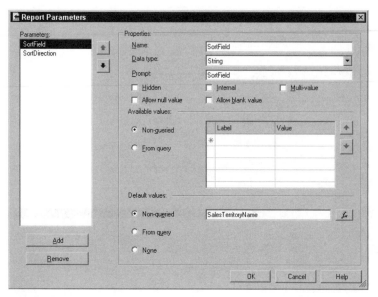

FIGURE P7-54

Set the navigation properties for each column header text box separately. When the text box is clicked, the report navigates back to itself.

Click the Parameters button on the Text Box Properties dialog Navigation tab to open the Parameters dialog shown in Figure P7-55. For each column header, the SortField parameter will be set to the name of the appropriate field and the SortDirection is set using an expression that toggles its value between Ascending and Descending.

Next to each text box, I have placed an image item. Its value will correspond to the SortDirection parameter if the SortField value matches that table column. Figure P7-56 shows the Image item Value property expression. According to this logic, if the SortField parameter value matches this table column (SalesTerritoryName), then the appropriate arrow icon will be displayed based on the SortDirection parameter value. If the SortField parameter is for another column, the "no_arrow" white space image is used.

In the Sorting properties for the table, shown in Figure P7-57, two expressions are used to test the SortDirection parameter. If the parameter value is Ascending, then the first expression (on the Ascending line) returns the field value for the field name contained in the SortField parameter. Returning an empty string ("") causes that sort expression to be ignored and enables the other (Ascending or Descending) expression.

Figure P7-58 shows the report in preview mode after clicking the first column. Note the down arrow next to the Territory column header, which indicates that this column is sorted in Ascending order.

Clicking another column causes the sort field and the sort order to change. Click the same column again to toggle the sort order for that column (see Figure P7-59).

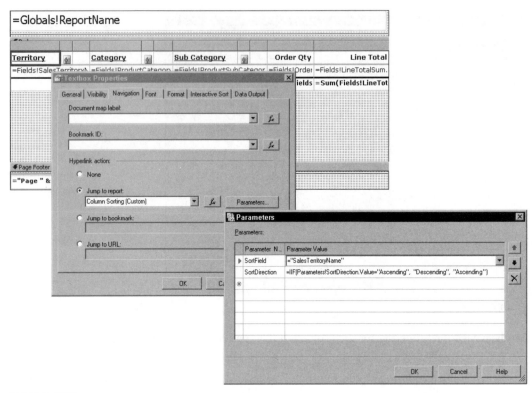

FIGURE P7-55

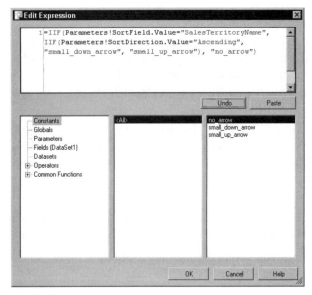

FIGURE P7-56

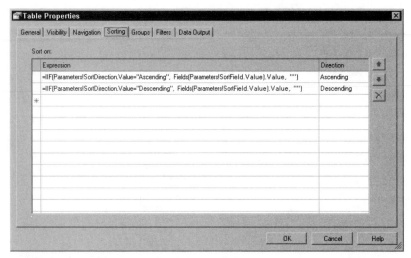

FIGURE P7-57

Column Sorting (Custom)				
Territory ▼	**Category**	**Sub Category**	**Order Qty**	**Line Total**
Australia	Accessories	Bike Racks	8	$1,728.00
Australia	Accessories	Bike Racks	3	$648.00
Australia	Accessories	Bike Racks	6	$864.00
Australia	Accessories	Bike Racks	4	$288.00
Australia	Accessories	Bike Racks	7	$504.00
Australia	Accessories	Bike Racks	1	$4,344.00
Australia	Accessories	Bike Racks	5	$720.00
Australia	Accessories	Bike Stands	1	$5,088.00
Australia	Accessories	Bottles and Cages	4	$23.95
Australia	Accessories	Bottles and Cages	6	$35.93
Australia	Accessories	Bottles and Cages	3	$26.95
Australia	Accessories	Bottles and Cages	1	$6,615.73
Australia	Accessories	Bottles and Cages	2	$11.98
Australia	Accessories	Bottles and Cages	8	$23.95
Australia	Accessories	Cleaners	2	$9.54
Australia	Accessories	Cleaners	5	$47.70
Australia	Accessories	Cleaners	1	$969.90
Australia	Accessories	Cleaners	7	$66.78
Australia	Accessories	Cleaners	3	$42.93
Australia	Accessories	Cleaners	6	$28.62
Australia	Accessories	Cleaners	4	$19.08
Australia	Accessories	Fenders	1	$4,066.30

FIGURE P7-58

Column Sorting (Custom)				
Territory	**Category**	**Sub Category** ▲	**Order Qty**	**Line Total**
Australia	Clothing	Vests	9	$342.90
Australia	Clothing	Vests	6	$457.20
Australia	Clothing	Vests	3	$228.60
Australia	Clothing	Vests	2	$228.60
Australia	Clothing	Vests	11	$1,191.08
Australia	Clothing	Vests	8	$304.80
Australia	Clothing	Vests	5	$952.50
Australia	Clothing	Vests	7	$800.10
Australia	Clothing	Vests	4	$457.20
Australia	Clothing	Vests	21	$696.75
Australia	Clothing	Vests	1	$4,800.60
Australia	Clothing	Vests	18	$597.22
Canada	Clothing	Vests	15	$995.36
Canada	Clothing	Vests	18	$597.22
Canada	Clothing	Vests	4	$1,371.60
Canada	Clothing	Vests	7	$1,333.50
Canada	Clothing	Vests	2	$533.40
Canada	Clothing	Vests	10	$1,143.00
Canada	Clothing	Vests	13	$469.21
Canada	Clothing	Vests	19	$630.40
Canada	Clothing	Vests	1	$4,216.40
Canada	Clothing	Vests	14	$4,042.46

FIGURE P7-59

Final Thoughts

Aside from choosing a technique that provides the necessary functionality, it's important to consider report performance and the impact on the data source and report server system resources in cases where queries return large data volumes.

Applying interactive sorting using the built-in feature is a fine approach for a simple report or a report not returning a lot of data. In scenarios where there may not be human interaction present or your goal is to create a report with pre-defined sorting criteria, sorting parameters that include which columns to sort by and the direction to sort them in is the way to go.

Each of these techniques has its distinct advantages and disadvantages. The interactive sort is quick and easy to design but the report user typically must be shown how to use it at least once. As an out-of-the-box feature, it's simple and efficient but may not be flexible enough to address all business requirements.

Accepting parameters with expressions to dictate the column sorting and direction is a powerful approach, as parameters can be pre-defined for subscription reports and to give the report user more control over the output of the report.

When changing sort order in the query, the data will be refreshed with each subsequent direction change and you have greater flexibility to define secondary sorts, while with the other options you may not. Finally, while sorting within the table or tablix, it is fairly easy to implement and you have the advantage of data caching with subsequent report executions, but you may not have the same level of conditional control.

Credits and Related References

The recipe titled "Creating a Custom Interactive Sort" is from *Professional SQL Server 2005 Reporting Services*, by Paul Turley et al. (Wrox, 2006). A sample for SSRS 2005 is available in the sample downloads for that book, also available at www.Wrox.com.

FILTERING USER-SPECIFIC REPORT DATA

Due to security requirements, a lot of organizations have a need to display data specific to the user accessing the report. With increasing emphasis on standards compliance, many organizations are taking the protection of private information more seriously. There are a couple of different techniques for creating user-specific reports. This example explores two techniques.

Product Versions

➤ Reporting Services 2000

➤ Reporting Services 2005

➤ Reporting Services 2008

What You'll Need

➤ A Matrix report

➤ An understanding of query parameters

➤ An understanding of report filters

Designing the Report

Creating a user-specific report requires the underlying data source to know the Domain\Username (UserID) of the user accessing the report in order to retrieve user specific data. Retrieving user-specific data requires the underlying data source to have a relationship between users and the data they have permission to view. This relationship can be defined in the underlying data source using appropriate table structures.

For instance, if an employee can only view sales data from a region he/she has access to in the relational database, there must be some relationship between the UserID and the Region. This relationship can be observed in the DimEmployee table of the AdventureWorksDW2008 sample database for SQL Server 2008 or AdventureWorksDW database for SQL Server 2005. Each employee record in the DimEmployee table contains a UserID and the related SalesTerritoryKey.

Once the underlying data source has established a relationship between the UserID and the data it has access to, it's time to think about how to display user specific data in the report. There are two ways of displaying user specific data:

➤ Use report filters to filter user-specific data based on the user accessing the report.

➤ Use query parameters to restrict data returned by the data source for the user accessing the report.

 We are assuming that the report data source uses a predefined service account, not Windows Security, to access the underlying data source.

This example demonstrates using both the options to display user specific data. You use the AdventureWorksDW for SQL Server 2005 or 2008 sample database to display sales information for the sales territories a user has access to. A simple query is used to return the reseller sales amount, sales territory, calendar year, and employee first name, last name, and UserID (loginID). This example uses Report Builder 2.0.

1. Start by designing a data source for the AdventureWorksDW2008 or AdventureWorksDW sample database.

2. Create a dataset query to include the FactResellerSales, DimSalesTerritory, DimEmployee, and DimDate tables, using the following SQL script:

```
SELECT
E.FirstName
,E.LastName
,ST.SalesTerritoryCountry
,ST.SalesTerritoryRegion
,RS.SalesAmount
,T.CalendarYear
,E.LoginID
FROMdbo.FactResellerSales RS
INNER JOIN dbo.DimSalesTerritory ST
    ON RS.SalesTerritoryKey = ST.SalesTerritoryKey
INNER JOIN dbo.DimEmployee E
    ON RS.EmployeeKey = E.EmployeeKey
INNER JOIN dbo.DimDate T
    ON RS.OrderDateKey = T.DateKey
```

 In AdventureWorksDW database for SQL Server 2005, Date table is called DimTime instead of DimDate and DateKey column is called TimeKey.

3. Add a Matrix report item to the report body.

4. Select the SalesTerritoryCountry field in the Row cell, CalendarYear field in the Column cell, and SalesAmount field in the Data cell.

At this point, you have retrieved reseller sales data for all employees. Let's preview the report to see what it looks like. As you can see in Figure P7-60, it's just a simple report that summarizes reseller sales amount for all employees over calendar year and sales territory.

Now you want to view the sales information for territories to which the user accessing the report has access. As discussed earlier, there are two possible ways of achieving this: by using report filters or by using query parameters. Let's first look at using a report filter to view user specific data.

1. Right-click on Dataset and click Dataset Properties.

2. Select Filters on the Dataset Properties and click Add to add a new filter.

3. In the newly created blank filter, select LoginID field for Expression field, Equal to Operator, and enter the User!UserID expression for Value (Figure P7-61).

4. Click OK to close the Expression and the Dataset Properties dialog box.

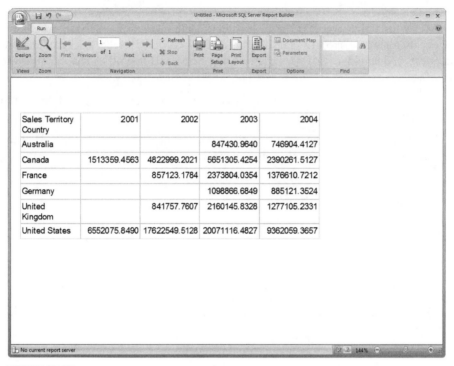

FIGURE P7-60

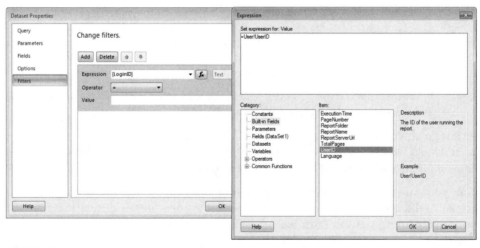

FIGURE P7-61

Reporting Services captures the Domain\Username of the user accessing the report and stores it in a global object called UserID. In the SSRS 2008 report designer and Report Builder 2.0, these objects are referred to as Built-in Fields. The filter uses the value of this object to compare the UserID of the user accessing the report to the LoginID dataset field, thus providing user specific data by filtering the data where LoginID is equal to the login name of the user accessing the report. Let's preview the report to view the results.

As you can see in Figure P7-62, the report is blank and doesn't display any data. This is the correct behavior because you are accessing the report using your credentials, and the AdventureWorks sample database doesn't have your credentials. So, there is no relationship between your credentials and the data you have access to; in other words, you don't have access to any data.

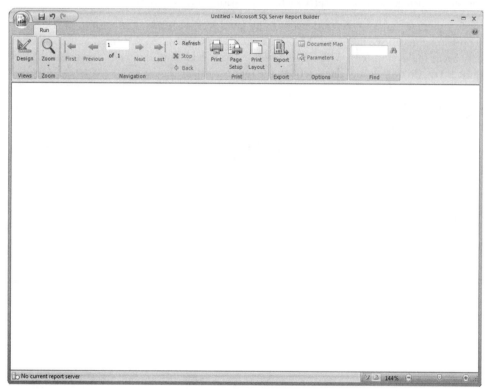

FIGURE P7-62

To validate your implementation, you need to replace one of the employee's credentials in the DimEmployee table with your credentials. This way, you should see the data the employee has access to.

1. Connect to the AdventureWorksDW database you are using for this report.

2. Replace the `LoginID` field value of an Employee with your credentials (Domain\Username). In this example, we are going to update the record where `EmployeeKey` value is equal to 285.

3. Open a new query in SQL Server Management Studio, connect to the same database as the report and run the following query:

```
updatedbo.DimEmployee
setLoginID='your credentials'
whereEmployeeKey= 285
```

Your credentials should be in the form of *Domain\Username*. If your computer isn't part of the domain, the credentials should be in the form of *ComputerName\Username*. If you would like to find out the credentials SSRS stores in the UserID global variable, drag a textbox onto the report surface, enter the User!UserID expression, and preview the report.

4. Once you have replaced the credentials of an employee with your credentials, preview the report. As you can see in Figure P7-63, the data is now restricted to United States sales territory because the employee with EmployeeKey 285 is related to United States sales territory only. If you do not see any data, refresh the report to clear the cache.

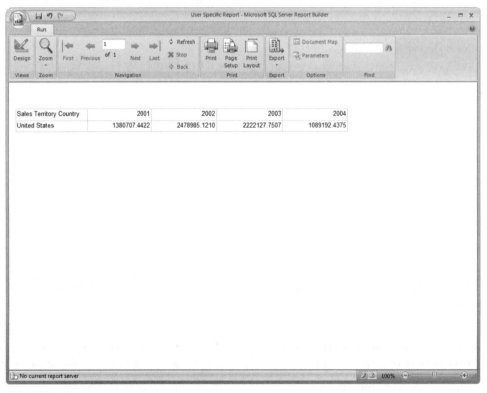

FIGURE P7-63

Now that you have created a user-specific report using report filters, let's look at the second option for achieving the same result. The second option uses query parameters to restrict data returned by the data source.

1. Right-click on Dataset and select Dataset Properties.

2. Select Filters on the Dataset Properties dialog box and delete the Filter created earlier.

3. Select Query on the Dataset Properties dialog box and update the query by inserting the following `where` clause:

```
where E.LoginID = @ReportUser
```

4. This creates a parameter called `@ReportUser`. Select Parameters on the Dataset Properties dialog box and enter the following expression for the parameter value (see Figure P7-64):

```
=User!UserID
```

5. Click OK to close the Expression and Dataset Properties dialog boxes.

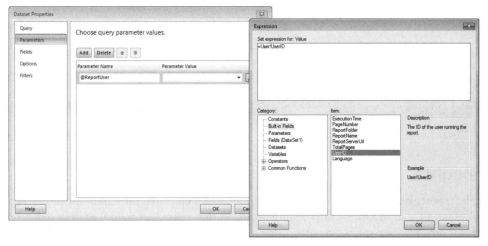

FIGURE P7-64

Again, you are using the UserID global variable to pass the Domain\Username of the user accessing the report as a parameter value for our query. This restricts data at the data-source level, as the query only returns data for the user accessing the report. It is important to understand the differences between the two options demonstrated in this example.

Preview the report to test the results. As you can see in Figure P7-65, the data is exactly the same as when you used the report filter option (see Figure P7-63).

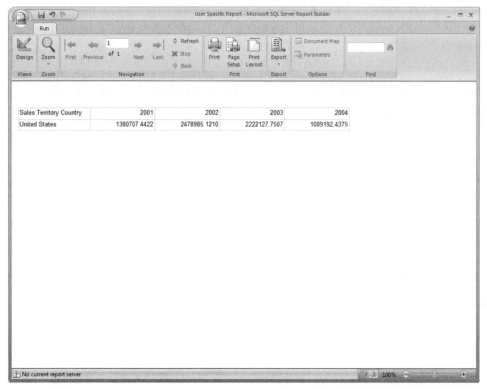

FIGURE P7-65

Final Thoughts

User-specific reports help organizations comply with increased emphasis on standards, protecting private information, and specific security requirements. In this example, you looked at two different techniques for creating user-specific reports: using report filters to filter data at the report level and using query parameters to restrict data at the data-source level. It's important to note that both techniques require the underlying data source to contain a relationship between the UserID and the data the user has permission to view. However, both techniques differ in how they filter the data, so it's also important to understand the differences between the two techniques.

PART VIII
Custom and Dynamic Data Sources

- ▶ Using a Web Service as a Data Source

- ▶ Reporting on SharePoint List Data

- ▶ Dynamics AX Report Wizard

USING A WEB SERVICE AS A DATA SOURCE

A great strength of Reporting Services is its ability to report on various kinds of information from many different types of data sources. The most common of these utilize databases of information such as SQL Server, Oracle, and Excel, among others, and are typically accessed through native interfaces or common standards such as ODBC and OLE DB.

However, it is not always possible or desirable to access the underlying database of a system or application. Over the years, a common method for transferring information across systems has emerged: Extensible Markup Language (XML). XML provides a mechanism of describing and encoding data and is generally used as a means to transfer information across heterogeneous systems, often over the Internet.

Beginning with SQL Server 2005, Reporting Services includes a built-in data processing extension for working with XML data. This *XML Data Provider* enables access to a wide variety of XML data sources such as XML documents, XML over HTTP, and XML web services. This recipe demonstrates how to use the XML data provider to access and report on information from a SOAP-based web service.

Product Versions

➤   Reporting Services 2005

➤   Reporting Services 2008

The examples demonstrated in this recipe are based on Reporting Services 2008 but this technique will work in Reporting Services 2005 as well. The report design options and dialogs may look a little different in earlier products.

What You'll Need

➤   Reporting Services configured to run in standard mode

➤   basic understanding of XML and web services

➤   An understanding of Reporting Services design concepts such as expressions and calculated fields

➤   Appropriate authorization to execute the Reporting Services web service

Designing the Report

This example utilizes the Reporting Services web service to demonstrate use of the XML data provider to report from a SOAP 1.1 compliant web service. You use the web service to retrieve a list of all report items published to the report server. You then design the report layout to display each of the report items in a hierarchal format. Figure P8-1 shows the finished report.

Before getting started, ensure you have access to the necessary Reporting Services web service. Using your web browser, navigate to the address `http://Hitachi/ReportServer/ReportService2005.asmx`, replacing `Hitachi` with the server or host name that is appropriate for your environment. The WSDL, or Web Service Description Language, for the Reporting Services web service should be displayed as shown in Figure P8-2.

Name	Type	
AdventureWorks 2008 Samples	Folder	
Data Sources	Folder	
AdventureWorks2008	DataSource	
Reports	Folder	
Company Sales 2008	Report	
Employee Sales Summary 2008	Report	
Product Catalog 2008	Report	
Product Line Sales 2008	Report	
Sales Order Detail 2008	Report	
Sales Trend 2008	Report	
Store Contacts 2008	Report	
Territory Sales Drilldown 2008	Report	
Execution Log Samples	Folder	
Data Sources	Folder	
rsexecutionlog	DataSource	
Reports	Folder	
Execution Status Codes	Report	
Execution Summary	Report	
Report Summary	Report	
Server Management Samples	Folder	
Data Sources	Folder	
master	DataSource	
Reports	Folder	

FIGURE P8-1

If you are unable to view the output as shown here, verify that the URL to your Reporting Service instance is accurate and that you have appropriate permissions to access the service. Contact your Reporting Services administrator for additional assistance if needed.

Once you have verified access to the necessary Reporting Service web service, you are ready to begin designing a report against this service. Start by creating a new report and defining an XML data source to the Reporting Services web service.

1. Create a new, blank report using Report Builder 2.0.

2. Design a new, embedded data source that uses the XML connection type.

3. In the Connection String text box, enter the URL to the Reporting Services web service: `http://Hitachi/ReportServer/ReportService2005.asmx`. Remember to replace `Hitachi` with the server or host name that is appropriate for your instance. This is shown in Figure P8-3.

4. From the Credentials tab, select Use Current Windows User.

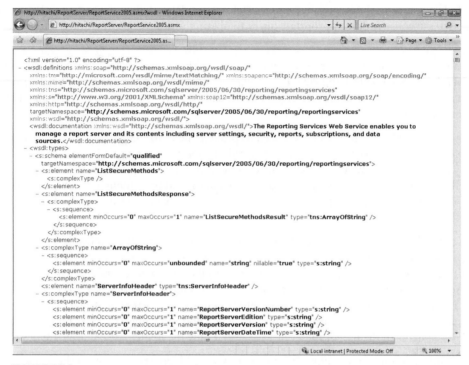

FIGURE P8-2

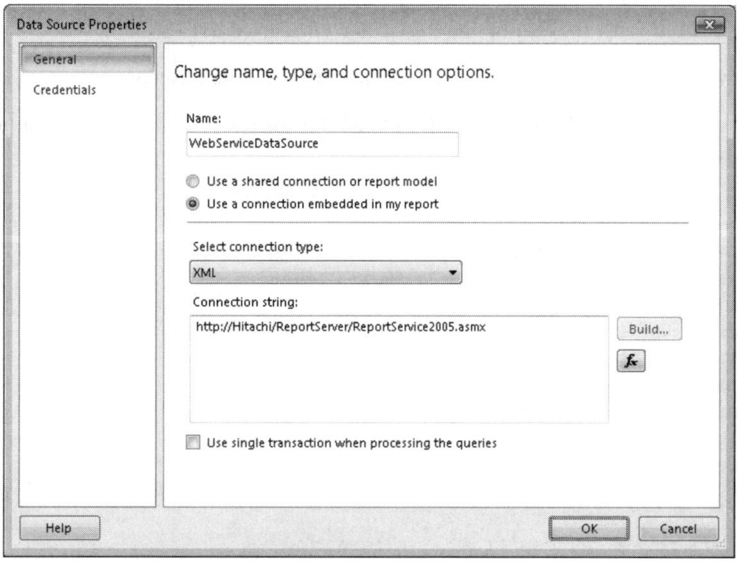

FIGURE P8-3

With the XML data source to the Reporting Services web service defined, the next task is to create an associated dataset and construct the appropriate query to obtain the desired information from this data source.

The XML data provider supports a proprietary query language that is similar to, but is distinctly different from, XPath, the XML Path Language. Reporting Services does not provide a graphical designer to support the construction of the query used by an XML data source. You are required to manually author the query yourself.

To successfully query a SOAP web service, you need to provide the XML namespace used by the service, the name of the method to execute, and the required method parameters. You could obtain this information by deciphering the WSDL, which you accessed at the start of this recipe, but this format can be reasonably complex and is generally intended to be interpreted by computers. Since this service is provided by Reporting Services, a better option is to consult the documentation available through SQL Server Books Online.

On inspection of the documentation, it is determined that the namespace for the Reporting Services web service is `http://schemas.microsoft.com/sqlserver/2005/06/30/reporting/reportingservices`. We also identify a method named `ListChildren` that returns all of the items contained within a folder on the report server. This method accepts two parameters: `Item` and `Recursive`. The `Item` parameter is required and defines the path to the parent folder of the children you want to retrieve. The second parameter, `Recursive`, is an optional parameter that accepts a Boolean value of `True` (1) if the method should list all descendants of the parent folder or `False` (0) if only the immediate children are desired.

Armed with this information, you are now able to create and configure the dataset. In the following steps, you create a dataset that queries the report server for all report items within the entire server instance.

1. Add a new dataset associated with the Reporting Services web service data source.

2. Construct the query by entering the following code as text into the query editor.

Note that the Namespace line in the following code is too long for the page, but it should be entered as one line with no breaks.

```
<Query>
  <Method Name="ListChildren" Namespace=
  "http://schemas.microsoft.com/sqlserver/2005/06/30/reporting/
    reportingservices">
    <Parameters>
      <Parameter Name="Item">
        <DefaultValue>/</DefaultValue>
      </Parameter>
      <Parameter Name="Recursive">
        <DefaultValue>true</DefaultValue>
      </Parameter>
    </Parameters>
  </Method>
  <ElementPath IgnoreNamespaces="true">*</ElementPath>
</Query>
```

This syntax may be foreign to you, but the pattern used is reasonably easy to interpret. The query takes the form of an XML fragment that identifies how to both execute the web service and process its response.

The root of the query is the appropriately named Query element. The first child element, Method, provides the information necessary to invoke the web service. The method name and web service namespace are provided via the Name and Namespace attributes, respectively. Method parameters are defined within the Parameters element, with each individual method parameter supplied within its own Parameter element. The Name attribute of the Parameter element is used to define the parameter name, while the DefaultValue child element is used to identify the value of the parameter used during method invocation, unless overridden by a corresponding report parameter. In this instance, the Item parameter indicates the root folder (/) and the Recursive parameter defaults to True, which results in all report items on the report server being returned from the web service.

The ElementPath can be used to preprocess the XML data returned by the web service. An XPath-like expression can be used to select a partial set of information contained within the overall result set. A common use of this element is to select a two-dimensional dataset from a complex hierarchal XML structure. The asterisk used in this example simply indicates that all elements should be preserved. You can reference SQL Server Books Online for more detailed information regarding the XML data provider query language.

3. Execute the query to ensure there are no errors.

4. Review the fields and data returned, which are shown in Figure P8-4. Your results will vary based on the content available to you within your instance of Reporting Services.

At this point, you should have a fully functional dataset that queries the Reporting Services web service to list all report items available on the report server. In the remaining steps, you complete the report by designing a hierarchal view of the report items.

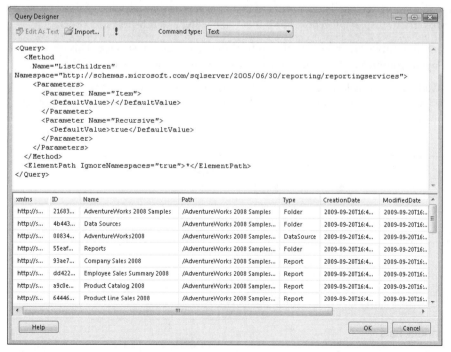

FIGURE P8-4

Reporting Services 2008 introduces a Recursive Parent property on table row groups that facilitates the display of a variable-depth, parent-child hierarchy. You can take advantage of this enhancement to easily display the visual relationship between report items. There are two fields missing from the dataset which are required to support the effective use of this feature: a Parent field, which can be used to identify the containing folder, and a Depth field, to support the visual indentation of each item.

1. Navigate to the Fields tab of the Dataset Properties Dialog.

2. Add a new calculated field to the dataset named Parent.

3. Use the following expression as the value for Parent:

    Note that the expression in the following code is too long for the page, but it should be entered as one line with no breaks.

    ```
    =Fields!Path.Value.ToString().Substring(0,
        Fields!Path.Value.ToString().LastIndexOf("/"))
    ```

    The Path field of each item contains the fully qualified path and name of the report item. The parent folder, or Parent, is derived by removing the name portion of this field value. The depth of each report item identifies the distance between the root folder and the containing parent folder. The newly created Parent field can be used to calculate this value.

4. Add another calculated field to the dataset named Depth with the following expression:

    ```
    =Fields!Parent.Value.ToString().Split("/").Length - 1
    ```

5. Click OK until you return to the report design surface.

With the addition of these two calculated fields, the dataset is complete and attention can now be turned to the report layout. This consists of a simple report that uses the aforementioned Recursive Parent property to display all report items in a table using a depth-first sort order.

1. Insert a Table data region to the body of the report design surface. This creates a simple table layout comprised of one header row, one data row, and three columns.

2. Add the Name field from the dataset to the first column of the data row in the table and the Type field to the second column of the same row. The layout should resemble the sample displayed in Figure P8-5.

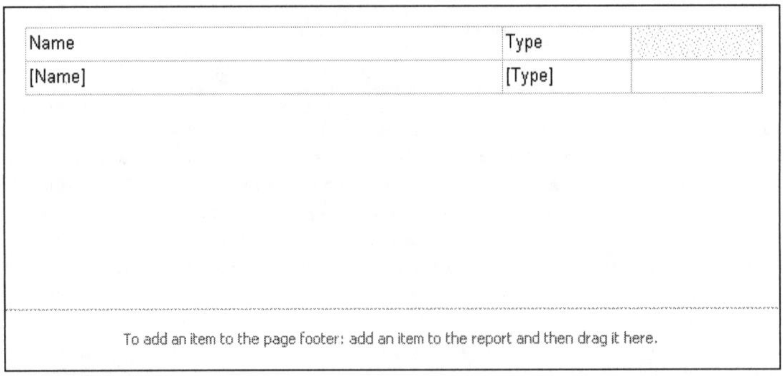

Name	Type	
[Name]	[Type]	

To add an item to the page footer: add an item to the report and then drag it here.

FIGURE P8-5

3. Open the Group Properties dialog for the Details row group.

4. From the General tab, add a new group on the Path field.

5. Click the Advanced tab and select Parent within the Recursive Parent dropdown.

6. Run the report and review the results, which are shown in Figure P8-6. The items are presented in depth-first order, although this may be difficult to discern as there is no visual clue to confirm this.

Name	Type	
AdventureWorks 2008 Samples	Folder	
Data Sources	Folder	
AdventureWorks2008	DataSource	
Reports	Folder	
Company Sales 2008	Report	
Employee Sales Summary 2008	Report	
Product Catalog 2008	Report	
Product Line Sales 2008	Report	
Sales Order Detail 2008	Report	
Sales Trend 2008	Report	
Store Contacts 2008	Report	
Territory Sales Drilldown 2008	Report	
Execution Log Samples	Folder	
Data Sources	Folder	
rsexecutionlog	DataSource	
Reports	Folder	
Execution Status Codes	Report	
Execution Summary	Report	
Report Summary	Report	
Server Management Samples	Folder	
Data Sources	Folder	
master	DataSource	
Reports	Folder	

FIGURE P8-6

7. Modify the indentation of the Name field to visually depict the hierarchal relationship with the other report items. Use the following expression to adjust the left padding according the depth of the item:

```
=(2 + 15 * Fields!Depth.Value).ToString() + "pt"
```

8. Execute the report and analyze the results. A sample of the updated output is included in Figure P8-7.

The report is now complete. You can enhance the report and overall user experience by enabling expand/collapse functionality for each of the folder items in the list, providing an Explorer-like interface for navigating the report items. This is left to you as an exercise to complete on your own.

Name	Type	
AdventureWorks 2008 Samples	Folder	
Data Sources	Folder	
AdventureWorks2008	DataSource	
Reports	Folder	
Company Sales 2008	Report	
Employee Sales Summary 2008	Report	
Product Catalog 2008	Report	
Product Line Sales 2008	Report	
Sales Order Detail 2008	Report	
Sales Trend 2008	Report	
Store Contacts 2008	Report	
Territory Sales Drilldown 2008	Report	
Execution Log Samples	Folder	
Data Sources	Folder	
rsexecutionlog	DataSource	
Reports	Folder	
Execution Status Codes	Report	
Execution Summary	Report	
Report Summary	Report	
Server Management Samples	Folder	
Data Sources	Folder	
master	DataSource	
Reports	Folder	

FIGURE P8-7

Final Thoughts

In this recipe, you were introduced to the built-in XML data processing extension for Reporting Services. You learned how to utilize this provider to retrieve data from SOAP-based web services. You can use the XML data provider and the techniques depicted in this recipe to access a wide variety of information across a wide variety of systems, including line of business systems and Internet-based applications, among others. In fact, additional recipes in this series exploit the capabilities demonstrated here to report on information stored within SharePoint lists and libraries.

Credits and Related References

MDSN: Using XML and Web Service Data Sources (http://msdn.microsoft.com/en-us/library/aa964129(SQL.90).aspx)

REPORTING ON SHAREPOINT LIST DATA

SharePoint. Now that I have your attention . . .

The marketing blitz behind SharePoint 2007 (Windows SharePoint Services (WSS) 3.0 and Microsoft Office SharePoint Services (MOSS) 2007) and SharePoint 2010 (SharePoint Foundation 2010 and SharePoint Server 2010), referred to collectively as SharePoint within this context, has spawned a significant amount of interest and activity. It seems like most of the clients I have partnered with over the past few years have had some type of strategic SharePoint initiative in the works. Whether SharePoint is seen as the answer for everything portal related or is just being used to support department-based team collaboration, the fever is spreading.

One of the great features of SharePoint is the ability to create databases of information through a simple web user interface. This is accomplished through SharePoint lists. SharePoint lists are basically equivalent to a table within a relational database management system such as SQL Server or Oracle. What makes SharePoint lists unique is their simplicity and ease of use within the SharePoint Web user interface. Any user with basic computer skills, and the proper authorization of course, can easily create new lists in SharePoint to store an assortment of information to support business activities and business processes. Couple this ease of accessibility and usability with the speed of business, and it is easy to understand how and why SharePoint lists have proliferated to support ongoing business information needs.

With more and more business information being created and stored within SharePoint, the question remains: How can a user report on this information? After all, enabling IT and business users alike with the ability to easily create "mission critical" applications in SharePoint is great, but getting data out of SharePoint is equally important. While SharePoint provides some built-in functionality for reporting, such as custom views, the Content Query Web Part, and the Data Form Web Part, the flexibility afforded by these techniques is either reasonably basic or overly complex. I enjoy mucking around with XSLT as much as the next person, but an efficient business reporting tool it is not!

In steps Reporting Services to the rescue. With its ability to connect to a myriad of data sources, Reporting Services provides the means to access information stored within SharePoint lists and then use the full featured report design capabilities to produce rich, sophisticated, and visually stimulating reports using the simple and familiar interfaces of Report Builder.

The examples demonstrated in this recipe provide guidance on how you can use Reporting Services to access and report on business information stored within SharePoint lists.

Product Versions

➤ Reporting Services 2005

➤ Reporting Services 2008*

➤ Reporting Services 2008 R2**

*Some of the examples demonstrated in this recipe are based on Reporting Services 2008 but this technique will work in Reporting Services 2005 as well. The report design options and dialogs may look a little different in earlier products.

**The last example demonstrated in this recipe demonstrates how to utilize a new data extension available with SQL Server Reporting Services 2008 R2, the *Microsoft SharePoint List Data Provider*, as an alternative approach for reporting on SharePoint list data.

What You'll Need

➤ Reporting Services configured to run in standard mode

➤ Basic understanding of XML and web services

➤ Knowledge of using web services within Reporting Services

➤ Access to a SharePoint site with the appropriate permissions

Preparing the Sample Data

Sample SharePoint list data is recommended to support the exercises presented in this recipe. While you can use the techniques presented in this recipe and modify them to work with your own list data, completing the exercises using a common set of list data ensures the consistency and accuracy of the results presented here with those that appear on your screen.

The following steps guide you through the process of creating an instance of a sample Tasks list in a SharePoint site based on the Team Site template. As each implementation of SharePoint may vary, the steps required may need to be altered slightly to align with your specific version and environment.

1. Start by navigating to your SharePoint site.

2. Select to View All Site Content from the Site Actions or Quick Launch menu.

3. Click the Create button on the toolbar of the All Site Content page to display the Create page.

4. Click the item named Tasks, located within the Tracking group as demonstrated in Figure P8-8.

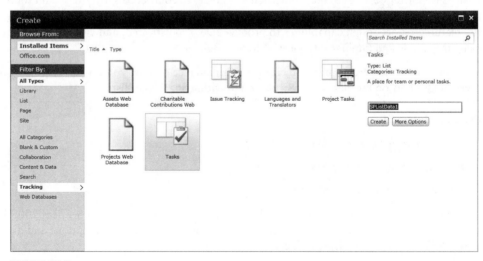

FIGURE P8-8

5. Name the list SPListData1 and click the Create button to complete the process. A new instance of a Tasks list named SPListData1 is created, as shown in Figure P8-9.

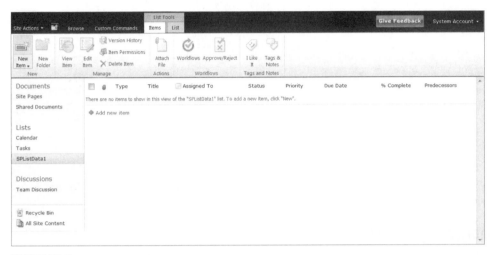

FIGURE P8-9

6. Use the New Item button on the toolbar to add sample data to the SPListData1. Add each of the following items with the specified attributes:

TITLE	STATUS	PRIORITY	% COMPLETE
SPListData1 - Task 01	Not Started	(1) High	0
SPListData1 - Task 02	Not Started	(2) Normal	0
SPListData1 - Task 03	Not Started	(3) Low	0
SPListData1 - Task 04	In Progress	(1) High	10
SPListData1 - Task 05	In Progress	(2) Normal	15
SPListData1 - Task 06	Completed	(3) Low	100

7. Take a moment to review the list and its content. The expected results are shown in Figure P8-10.

You now have sample list data in your SharePoint environment that is consistent with that used by the exercises within this recipe. In the exercises that follow, you will use various techniques to consume and display this information through Reporting Services.

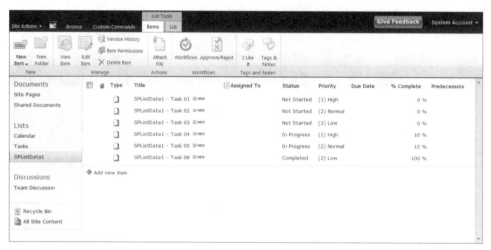

FIGURE P8-10

Designing the Report

SharePoint provides a robust set of web services that provide administrative, management, and data access capabilities for lists. Of particular interest to Reporting Services are the web services that enable the discovery and consumption of list data. SharePoint provides multiple web services for accessing list data, such as the *List Data Retrieval* web services and the *Lists* web service, among others. The first example provided here demonstrates how to consume and display information from a SharePoint list through the SharePoint Lists web service using the XML Data Provider.

The SharePoint Lists web service is accessible within each site using the URL http://<site>/_vti_bin/Lists.asmx, where <site> is the host name or path to the site where the list that contains the data you want to query is located. You can view all operations available within the Lists web service by navigating to the URL of the service in your web browser, as demonstrated in Figure P8-11.

There are many service operations available, but the one of specific interest for this example is GetListItems. The GetListItems method returns information about a list or the data within a list based on the parameters and query information provided. You can click the GetListItems link to display additional information about the available parameters (see Figure P8-12).

While not the most user-friendly documentation, the GetListItems SOAP definition identifies the following seven parameters: listName, viewName, query, viewFields, rowLimit, queryOptions, and webID. Consult SQL Server Books Online for details on each of these items.

The first parameter, listName, is used to identify which list within the site is to be acted upon. This value can either be the display name or globally unique identifier (GUID) of the list.

SharePoint lists support the concept of views, which provide a mechanism for encapsulating the data access definition and display characteristics for a list. The data access portion of the view identifies the fields to display, filter and sorting criteria, and the maximum number of rows to retrieve. You can create view definitions within a list and then utilize the viewName parameter to employ that list in your query. If a viewName is not provided, then the default view for the list is assumed. It is unfortunate and ironic that even though the parameter is called viewName, the view GUID, and not the view name, is the only supported value.

FIGURE P8-11

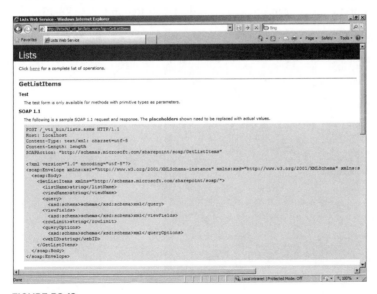

FIGURE P8-12

The `query` parameter is used to define custom filter and sorting criteria, while the `viewFields` parameter identifies the fields to select in the result set. Each of these parameters are defined using CAML, or Collaborative Application Markup Language, which is an XML-based, domain-specific language used by SharePoint to define, query, and display data. As CAML can be somewhat tedious to construct, many people often create view definitions using the web user interface and then repurpose the CAML stored behind the view for use in external products, such as Reporting Services.

The `rowLimit` parameter can be used to limit the volume of data returned from SharePoint, which is useful for paging or throttling. The `queryOptions` and `webID` parameters will not be discussed here. Please refer to SQL Server Books Online for more information.

If you have been paying close attention, you should have noticed that there is the potential for having duplicate, competing information provided by the parameters. For example, the view may identify specific fields to display and filter criteria, whereas similar but different information is provided through the `viewFields` and `query` parameters. In this instance, the view is used to define the default value for `query`, `viewFields`, and `rowLimit`; however, if explicit values for these method parameters are also included, they supersede the values provided by the view definition.

Now that you have a basic understanding of the SharePoint Lists web services, you can put that information to use. Start by creating a new report and defining an XML data source to the SharePoint Lists web service.

1. Create a new, blank report using Report Builder 2.0.

2. Design a new, embedded data source that uses the XML connection type.

3. In the Connection String text box, enter the URL to the SharePoint Lists web service: `http://Hitachi/_vti_bin/lists.asmx`. Remember to replace `Hitachi` with the server or host name that is appropriate for your instance. This is demonstrated in Figure P8-13.

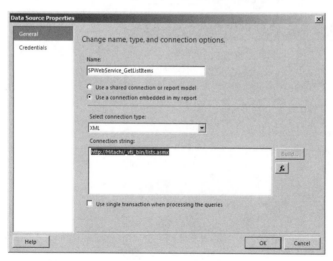

FIGURE P8-13

4. From the Credentials page, select Use Current Windows User.

5. Click OK to complete and close the Data Source Properties dialog.

You now have a connection to the Lists web services defined. The next step is to create a dataset and construct the appropriate query to execute the GetListItems method. If you are unfamiliar with the XML Data Provider or using the provider to query web services, please review the recipe entitled *Using a Web Service as a Data Source* before proceeding with the next task.

Fantastic! Now that you have a baseline understanding of consuming web services in Reporting Services and the parameters required to invoke the GetListItems method, you are ready to start building the dataset.

1. Add a new dataset associated with the GetListItems data source.

2. Construct the following query by entering the query as text into the query editor:

```
<Query>
 <SoapAction>http://schemas.microsoft.com/sharepoint/soap/GetListItems
 </SoapAction>
 <Method Namespace="http://schemas.microsoft.com/sharepoint/soap/"
         Name="GetListItems">
   <Parameters>
     <Parameter Name="listName">
       <DefaultValue>SPListData1</DefaultValue>
     </Parameter>
   </Parameters>
 </Method>
 <ElementPath IgnoreNamespaces="True">*</ElementPath>
</Query>
```

The first thing you should notice about this query is the use of the SoapAction element. If you recall from the "Using a Web Service as a Data Source" recipe, when the SoapAction element is not defined, it is derived from the Method element by combining the Namespace and Name attributes. In this instance, the inferred soap action would be http://schemas.microsoft.com/sharepoint/soap//GetListItems. Notice the double forward slash (//) before the GetListItems operation. This results from the Namespace ending in a forward slash, and the process that combines these fields always includes a new forward slash as the delimiter. Luckily, you can explicitly define the soap action to avoid this problem, which you have done here.

Next you will notice that you are only supplying the listName parameter, and you are using the list's display name over its GUID. This approach is preferred if possible, simply due to the readability and maintainability of the query. After all, Reporting Services is forcing you to author the query by hand without support of a graphical query designer (stay tuned . . . that's coming up).

And, finally, notice that you are returning all elements and attributes from the result set, allowing Reporting Services to flatten the data through auto-derivation.

3. Execute the query to ensure there are no errors. The results are displayed in Figure P8-14.

Notice that six rows are returned, which corresponds to the ItemCount column included in the result set. Review the ows_Status column and observe the last item with the value Completed. Since the query did not specify a parameter or value for viewName, the default view, All Tasks, is used and simply returns all items in the list. In the next steps you modify the query to employ the Active Tasks view, which is designed to display only tasks that have not been completed.

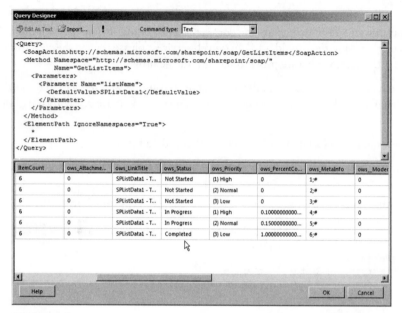

FIGURE P8-14

In order to use the Active Tasks view, you must identify it by GUID, which is somewhat counterintuitive, if not cumbersome, to acquire. If you are development savvy, then you can use the SharePoint object model to inspect the List and View objects for this information. There also exist utilities within the SharePoint community that can provide this information. For the rest of us, the GUID can be retrieved through the web user interface.

4. Navigate to the SPListData1 settings page and then click the Active Tasks view to display the Edit View page. The URL displayed in the browser's address bar contains the view GUID as the query string parameter named `View` (`&View=`).

5. Within the URL, locate the view query string parameter and extract its value. The value should be about 50 characters long and is URL encoded. In my instance the value is `%7BA50FF4C7%2D87A8%2D488C%2D9ECF%2DBD3ED436A426%7D`. The value contains occurrences of `%7B`, `%2D`, and `%7D`, which are hexadecimal encodings of special characters. You need to decode the value before it can be used in the query.

6. Replace each occurrence of `%7B` with { (open curly brace), `%2D` with - (dash), and `%7D` with } (closed curly brace). Decoding the value identified in Step 5 results in `{A50FF4C7-87A8-488C-9ECF-BD3ED436A426}`.

   Now that you are equipped with the GUID for the Active Tasks view, you can employ the Active Tasks view within your query.

7. Modify the query to include a second parameter for `viewName` as shown in bold in the following code segment. Be sure to enter the GUID retrieved from your SharePoint instance rather than the one used here.

```
<Query>
  <SoapAction>http://schemas.microsoft.com/sharepoint/soap/GetListItems
  </SoapAction>
```

```
<Method Namespace="http://schemas.microsoft.com/sharepoint/soap/"
        Name="GetListItems">
    <Parameters>
      <Parameter Name="listName">
        <DefaultValue>SPListData1</DefaultValue>
      </Parameter>
      <Parameter Name="viewName">
       <DefaultValue>{A50FF4C7-87A8-488C-9ECF-BD3ED436A426}</DefaultValue>
      </Parameter>
    </Parameters>
  </Method>
  <ElementPath IgnoreNamespaces="True">
     *
  </ElementPath>
</Query>
```

8. Execute the query again and review the results, which are shown in Figure P8-15.

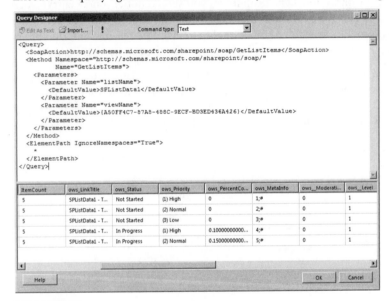

FIGURE P8-15

As expected, the single item that had a status of Completed is no longer returned, resulting in only five rows in the result set.

So that is pretty cool, but didn't I just duplicate the functionality that is natively available within SharePoint? What's the benefit?

The answer is that you can now use the full power of Reporting Services for enhanced reporting and visualizations. With just a few clicks and a minimal amount of effort, a chart like that demonstrated in Figure P8-16 can be created. Mix in some drill-down capabilities by clicking an area of the chart to see further details or an alternative perspective of the information, and you have far exceeded the capabilities afforded by the standard views in SharePoint.

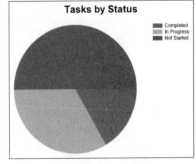

FIGURE P8-16

Designing the Report in 2008 R2

Reporting Services is an ever evolving and maturing product. Each release introduces new and exciting features and functionality to increase productivity and enhance the usability of the product, and Reporting Services 2008 R2 is no exception. While there are a great many new and exciting features available within this version, one in particular is essential to the context of this recipe: the *Microsoft SharePoint List Data Provider*.

This recipe introduces the Microsoft SharePoint List Data Provider and demonstrates its capabilities as compared to the XML Data Provider previously reviewed. Your environment will need to be equipped with SQL Server 2008 R2, Report Builder 3.0, and the sample data provided for this recipe.

1. Start by creating a new report using Report Builder 3.0.

2. Create a new data source that uses an embedded connection.

3. From the Select Connection Type dropdown, you should notice a new entry: Microsoft SharePoint List. This is a new built-in data provider introduced with Reporting Services 2008 R2 that provides specialized functionality to facilitate the consumption of SharePoint list data. Ensure this item is selected and then move to the Connection String field.

4. Enter the URL to your SharePoint site for the Connection String. Note that the path to a specific web service is not required. For example, the URL used to consume SharePoint list data using the XML Data Provider was `http://Hitachi/_vti_bin/lists.asmx`, whereas the URL for the Microsoft SharePoint List Data Provider is simply `http://Hitachi/`. This is shown in Figure P8-17.

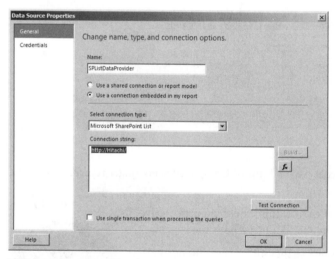

FIGURE P8-17

5. Select Use Current Windows User for the Credentials and then test the connection to ensure proper configuration.

The real benefit of the new Microsoft SharePoint List Data Provider is the addition of a graphical query designer. This new designer discovers all available lists and enables the visual composition of the query, including selection and sequencing of fields, and adding filtering criteria. You explore each of these right now.

1. Add a new dataset associated with the newly created Microsoft SharePoint List Data Provider data source.

2. Use the Query Designer button below the Query text box to display the new graphical designer. A screen shot of the designer is included in Figure P8-18.

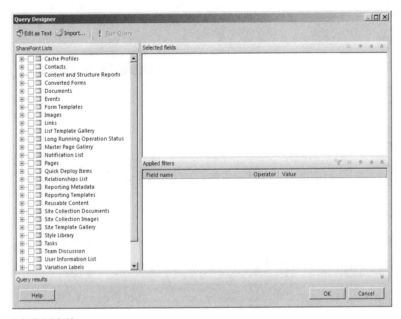

FIGURE P8-18

The SharePoint Lists window on the left of the Query Designer displays all lists and libraries that you are authorized to view. Checking the box next to the list name selects all fields from the list in the default order. Alternatively, you should expand the list node and select the specific columns of interest.

3. From the SharePoint Lists window, locate and expand the item named SPListData1.

4. Select the following columns: Title, Priority, Status, % Complete, ID, and Created By. Notice how the columns are inserted into the Selected Fields window in the upper right hand side of the Query Designer.

5. From the Selected Fields window, click the field named ID and use the Up arrow to move the field to the first item in the list.

6. Click the Add Filter button in the toolbar of the Applied Filters window in the lower right side of the Query Designer.

7.   Within the newly added filter, select Status for the Field Name, Is Not for the Operator, and Completed for the Value. Your screen should look like that depicted in Figure P8-19.

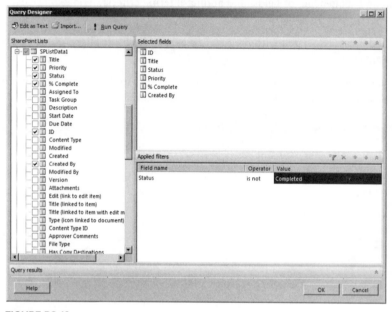

FIGURE P8-19

8.   Run the query and review the results, which are demonstrated in Figure P8-20.

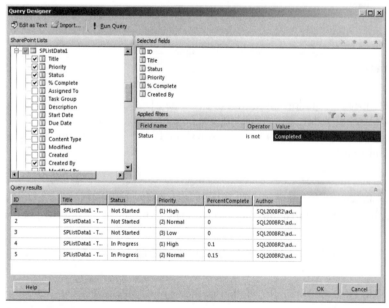

FIGURE P8-20

Do the results look familiar? They should. You have just recreated the Active Tasks view using the new Microsoft SharePoint List Data Provider available with the SQL Server 2008 R2 release. Imagine the possibilities!

Final Thoughts

This recipe introduced you to the concepts required and approaches available for accessing SharePoint list data within Reporting Services by using the built-in data providers. Web services were used to interface with SharePoint for users of Reporting Services 2005 and 2008, while the newer Microsoft SharePoint Lists Data Provider was explored as part of the Reporting Services 2008 R2 release. Both IT and the business can take advantage of these techniques to quickly and easily provide robust reporting and real business value to the SharePoint platform.

Credits and Related References

MSDN: Windows SharePoint Web Services (http://msdn.microsoft.com/en-us/library/ms479390.aspx)

MSDN: XML Query Syntax for Specifying XML Report Data (http://msdn.microsoft.com/en-us/library/ms345251(SQL.90).aspx)

TechNet: Element Path Syntax for Specifying XML Report Data (http://technet.microsoft.com/en-us/library/ms365158(SQL.90).aspx)

MSDN: Defining a Report Dataset for a Reporting Services Web Service (http://msdn.microsoft.com/en-us/library/ms345338.aspx)

DYNAMICS AX REPORT WIZARD

For those of you not familiar with Microsoft Dynamics AX (or just AX), it is a comprehensive business solution for midsize to larger organizations for those that work with and prefer common Microsoft software. Also known as an Enterprise Resource Planning (ERP) solution, AX makes it easy to manage and do business across multiple currencies and multiple continents.

Built into AX is a reporting framework that offers a variety of tools and wizards to easily create and maintain reports within AX. These report wizards, similar to the wizard used in Visual Studio, are designed to make the report more user-friendly by the modification of components. This can be done without additional coding.

Similar to many different wizards, the report wizard walks you through various different steps in order to create your report. Similar to most wizards, the goal is to dramatically reduce the time it would take you to develop the report by hand.

There are many advantages to an integrated reporting architecture within AX. One advantage is the use of template reports and the ability to utilize and leverage business objects and the AX framework directly. In addition, this allows the user to avoid directly accessing the database for your queries and potentially missing any underlying business logic.

Product Versions

➤ Reporting Services 2008

What You'll Need

➤ An understanding of data structures and relational data

➤ Dynamics AX 4.0 or 2009

➤ An understanding of Dynamics AX

Designing the Report

Figure P8-21 shows the finished report.

To get started, create a new report template you can use on your later report and any future reports you are going to create. This recipe assumes you are using an existing installation of AX and the normal setup procedures have been followed. For further assistance regarding the setup and default installation of AX, refer to online documentation by Microsoft.

1. Open AX and go to the Application Object Tree (AOT) and expand the Reports node.

2. Right-click Reports Templates and then click New Report Template.

3. Rename the Template to "FirstReportTemplate".

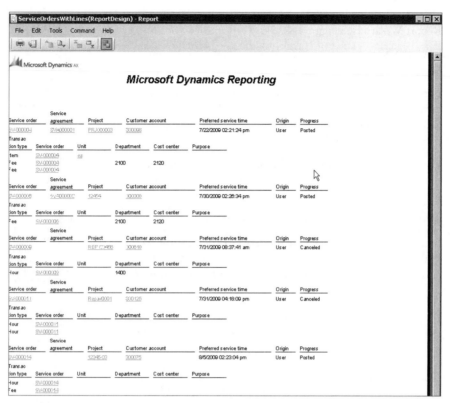

FIGURE P8-21

4. Right-click on "FirstReportTemplate" and add both a header and a footer (see Figure P8-22).

5. On the Page header, right-click and add two new controls, a bitmap and also a new text control.

6. Within the properties window, set the Text property of the text control to "Microsoft Dynamics Reporting" (See Figure P8-23) and the Image Name property of the Bitmap control.

7. Add a new text control to the footer with a default value of "Private Information Only".

8. Right-click on FirstReportTemplate and click Edit to view the design of the report. Position the controls to the desired location and the template will look similar to Figure P8-24.

You can add some information regarding your company and a branded logo to the report.

9. Save the report.

At this point you are ready to create a new report using the report wizard. Once you have created our report, you can associate this newly created template and give a consistent look and feel to the report.

10. Go to the Tools Menu ⇨ Development Tools ⇨ Wizards ⇨ Report Wizard (see Figure P8-25).

11. Click the Next button on the wizard and name your report ServiceOrdersWithLines.

For this example, you will un-check the checkbox for Auto create label. If the checkbox is not checked, the label of the fields will be displayed on the report rather than system names, tables, methods, and fields.

12. Use the Next button to go to the next step, choosing your data source. This form allows the user to choose the table(s) for the report.

13. Add the Service Orders Table to the list of selected tables.

14. Since you will want to include the service order lines as well, in the bottom left box, scroll to the service order line table and use the > box to move it to the selected tables list (see Figure P8-26).

Note that you have the option to continue to click Next and set additional properties such as sorting, layout, and so on.

15. Click the Finish button to create your report.

Once you have finished creating the report, the report will appear on the bottom of the Reports Node in the AOT. Before you preview it, let's associate the template to the report.

16. Expand the report and the designs node and select the Report Design to view the properties of the report (see Figure P8-27).

17. Use the pull down menu on the Report Template property to choose your template (see Figure P8-28).

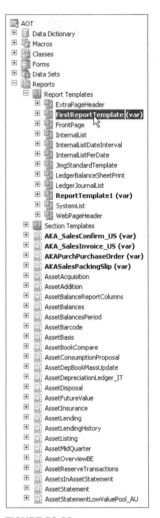

FIGURE P8-22

18. After saving the report, right-click on the report and use the Open menu option to preview the report.

A dialog box may appear asking you to specify your parameters and how you want to display the report. Inputting particular criteria for displaying the report can be done using the criteria option shown in Figure P8-29.

19. Click OK to bypass the criteria window and click OK again on the next screen to print the report to the window

The report will now be displayed on the screen. Also note that after you have created your report, you can incorporate different business logic to alter the data source or even override the fetch method to filter data.

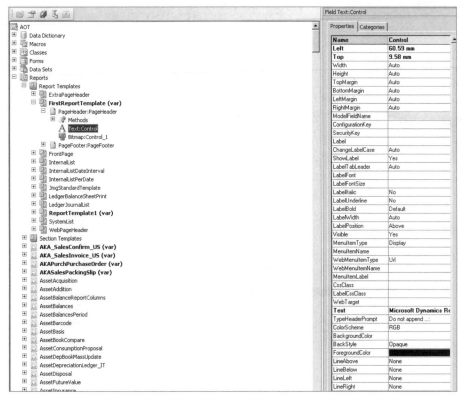

FIGURE P8-23

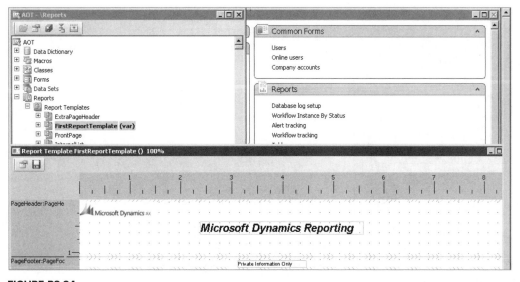

FIGURE P8-24

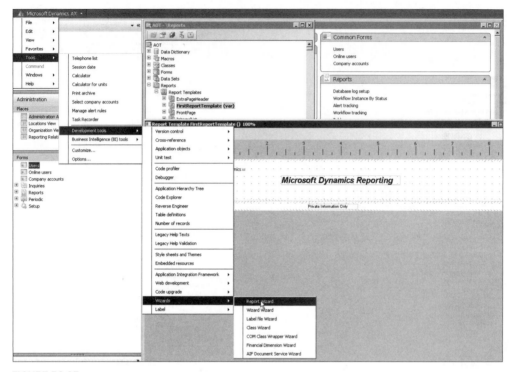

FIGURE P8-25

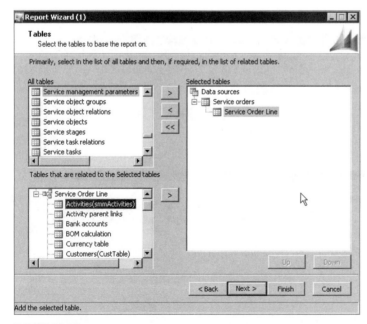

FIGURE P8-26

FIGURE P8-27

If you are unfamiliar with the concept of overriding a method, don't worry, it is pretty simple. Overriding a method in reports (or programming languages such as C# or VB.NET) allows you to overwrite a method and still execute the base or default method within your override. For example, if you wanted to override a method called Save (suppose you needed to add custom logic once the Save method has been executed), an override would allow you call the base or default method and then provide you the opportunity to wire in your logic. Instead of completely disregarding or re-writing code, overriding allows you to add to or append logic. This is an example of extending your objects rather than writing them from scratch.

Since the reports are built into the framework of the AX application, it is easy to accomplish things in addition to those this recipe shows.

For example, if you are a company that specializes in AX implementations, you may want to build a library of reports that can be used over and over again with each implementation. Customers designing or extending your reports could then add methods on top of your reports or at a higher layer, such as the Customer (CUS) layer. This promotes re-usability of your reports and further allows report designers or developers to extend, rather than re-create, reports that already exist.

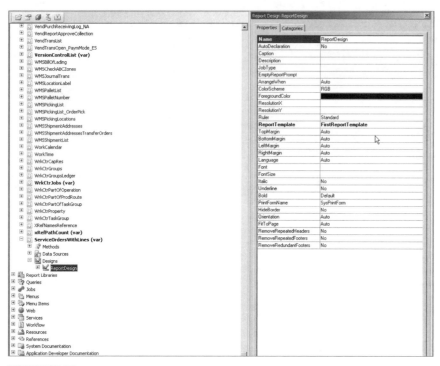

FIGURE P8-28

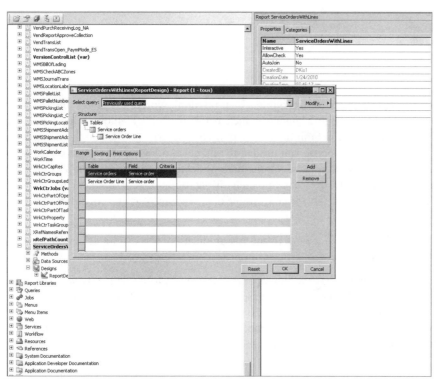

FIGURE P8-29

Figure P8-30 shows the report created in this recipe, which can then be deployed to the report server or exported as a project to a different environment.

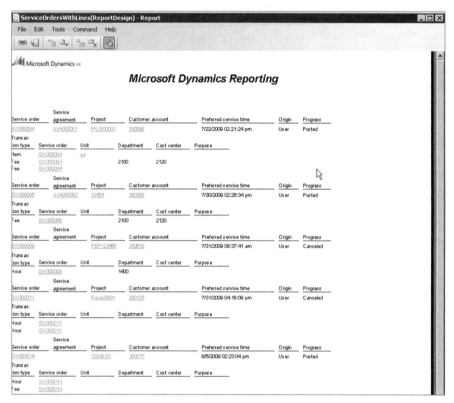

FIGURE P8-30

The output of this particular report is nothing fancy; however, it allowed you to easily create a branded report through a template and you weren't required to dive deep into the code to do so. Instead, using the report wizard you were able to quickly create a report within the AX application framework.

Final Thoughts

Microsoft Dynamics AX provides an entire enterprise solution not only for reporting, but also for managing your business across multiple continents and multiple organizations. Many smaller companies use tools such as QuickBooks or other popular accounting packages, but AX offers a solution to much larger customers and allows them to effectively work in layers and collaborate in many different areas, with integrated reporting a part of the layered architecture.

PART IX
Games

▶ Hangman Game

▶ Sea Battle Game

HANGMAN GAME

Reporting Services has the capability to build dynamic functionality into a report design. Using parameters, expressions and custom code, you can control the report behavior and customize a user's experience, enabling some interesting possibilities. This recipe shows you how some members of the SQL Server Reporting Services product team created a simple Hangman game to demonstrate report drillthrough techniques to showcase at industry conferences. This report was developed to show at the earlier "BI Power Hour" sessions at some of the regular annual conferences. Since this demonstration, several other demos have been produced for games like Mastermind, Battleship and Monopoly. The game tactics and logic rules may vary but the core techniques are the same.

If your objective is to learn game programming, there are more capable game development tools than Reporting Services. The purpose of this recipe is not so much about learning to write games using Reporting Services but to expose you to some useful techniques you can use when designing advanced reporting solutions.

Product Versions

➤ Reporting Services 2000

➤ Reporting Services 2005

➤ Reporting Services 2008

What You'll Need

➤ Images to represent the hangman's body parts

➤ Stored procedure to update database table

➤ Conditional expressions to hide and show images

➤ Hangman.rdl

➤ Hangman.bak — database backup

Techniques Demonstrated

➤ Drill-through-to-self report action

➤ Table and textbox report actions

➤ Parameterized expressions to set report item properties

➤ Using stored procedures to update data and return results

➤ Hiding and showing images based on conditional expressions

Reviewing the Report

You will not build this report from the beginning in this recipe, but you will review the inner workings of an existing report. If you would like to create a similar report from scratch, you can use this as a model.

To set up the environment and get started, follow these steps:

1. Restore the Hangman database from the provided database backup file, which is included in the book download files on Wrox.com.

2. Open the Hangman report in the BIDS or Report Builder report designer.

3. Open the embedded data source and test the connection to the Hangman database.

Figure P9-1 shows the report in design view. This is an unsophisticated design consisting of a table on the left, a textbox in the header, and a collection of six images that we'll call "Franken Jason." Each image is hidden by default and conditionally displayed based on a calculated value used to determine the number of missed guesses.

4. Preview the report.

5. Choose a letter (see Figure P9-3) as your first guess and then click the letter to see what happens.

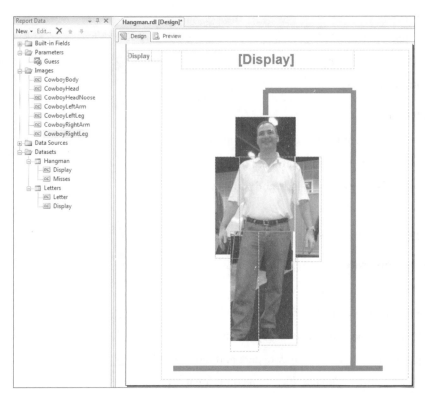

FIGURE P9-1

From childhood experience, you may recall playing this game on the chalk board, that the most common letters that appear in most English words are the vowels A, E, I, O, and U, so these are usually good first guesses. The letter E is the most commonly used letter in the alphabet.

The list of available letters is displayed in the table data region on the left side of the report. When a letter is clicked, a report action drills through to the same report passing the letter to a report parameter named Guess. When the report is re-executed after this action, the parameter is sent to a stored procedure named Puzzle, shown in the following code. This is the brains of the game and serves up the results used to hide and show the images through a dataset name Hangman.

```
CREATE PROCEDURE [Hangman].[Puzzle]
    @Guess CHAR = ''
AS
BEGIN
    DECLARE @Answer AS NVARCHAR(200)
    DECLARE @Display AS NVARCHAR(200)
    DECLARE @Index AS INT

    -- If no guess is specified, reset answer and available letters
    IF (@Guess = '')
    BEGIN
        DELETE FROM [Hangman].PuzzleStatus

        DECLARE @NumAnswers AS INT

        -- Grab a random answer
        SET @NumAnswers = (SELECT COUNT(*) FROM [Hangman].Answers)
        SET @Answer = (SELECT Answer FROM [Hangman].Answers
            WHERE AnswerNum = (FLOOR(RAND() * @NumAnswers) + 1))

        -- Replace spaces from answer in display
        SET @Display = REPLICATE('-',LEN(@Answer))
        SET @Index = CHARINDEX( ' ', @Answer)
        IF (@Index > 0)
        BEGIN
            WHILE @Index > 0
            BEGIN
                SET @Display = (STUFF(@Display, @Index, 1, ' '))
                SET @Index = (CHARINDEX(' ', @Answer, @Index + 1))
            END
        END

        INSERT INTO [Hangman].PuzzleStatus (Answer, Display, Misses)
            VALUES (@Answer, @Display, 0)

        -- Reset letters
        DELETE FROM [Hangman].Letters
        INSERT INTO [Hangman].Letters(Letter, Display) VALUES ('', 'Reset')

        DECLARE @NextChar AS NCHAR
        SET @NextChar = 'A'
        WHILE UNICODE(@NextChar) <= UNICODE('Z')
        BEGIN
            INSERT INTO [Hangman].Letters (Letter, Display)
                VALUES (@NextChar, @NextChar)
            SET @NextChar = NCHAR(UNICODE(@NextChar) + 1)
        END
    END
```

```
       -- Otherwise check for hit and remove letter from available list
   ELSE BEGIN
       DELETE FROM [Hangman].Letters WHERE Letter = @Guess

       DECLARE @Misses AS INT
       DECLARE @AnswerLen AS INT

       SET @Answer = (SELECT Answer FROM [Hangman].PuzzleStatus)
       SET @Display = (SELECT Display FROM [Hangman].PuzzleStatus)
       SET @Misses = (SELECT Misses FROM [Hangman].PuzzleStatus)
       SET @AnswerLen = LEN(@Answer)
       SET @Index = CHARINDEX(@Guess, @Answer)

       -- If guess is in answer, replace dashes in display
       IF (@Index > 0)
       BEGIN
           WHILE @Index > 0
           BEGIN
               SET @Display = (STUFF(@Display, @Index, 1, @Guess))
               SET @Index = (CHARINDEX(@Guess, @Answer, @Index + 1))
           END
       END ELSE
           SET @Misses = (@Misses + 1)

       UPDATE [Hangman].PuzzleStatus SET Display = @Display, Misses = @Misses
   END

   -- Return status
   SELECT Display, Misses FROM [Hangman].PuzzleStatus
END
```

The Puzzle stored procedure contains all of the business logic to respond to the user's letter guess, resolve a match or miss, and then update data in the PuzzleStatus table. After each guess, the Letters table is updated with only the remaining letters. This dataset uses a simple SELECT statement to return the remaining letters and display them in the corresponding table data region:

```
SELECT Letter, Display FROM Hangman.Letters
```

With each incorrect guess, the Misses field is updated with the calculated count of missed guesses. Figure P9-2 shows the expressions used to set the Hidden property for each of the images used to represent Jason's body parts.

Figure P9-3 shows the game in midplay. When the game is started, a word is selected from the Answers table and displayed with underscore placeholders at the top of the report. Click letters on the left side of the report to make a guess. Correct guesses are displayed in place of the underscores. Incorrect guesses result in one of Jason's six parts being displayed. Each letter selected, whether correct or incorrect, is removed from the list.

Using this freestyle placement of images on the report body, the image rendering will not be precise. In fact, the positioning of these images will be a bit sloppy and the images will have gaps between them and will move around a bit as more images are displayed. Improvements to the image-rendering capabilities in SSRS 2008 made it more difficult for the rendering engine to deal with overlapping images, especially for HTML and preview rendering.

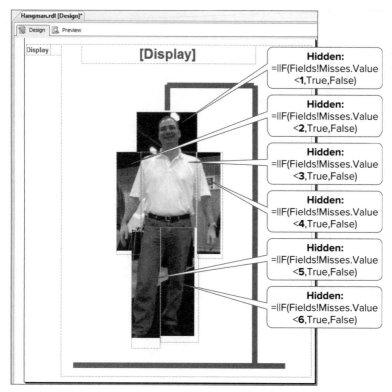

FIGURE P9-2

If you would like to take this technique to the next level, as we do next in the Sea Battle game report, use an image slicer program to chop a single hangman image into several square tiles and place them into a table grid. Tables, charts and rectangles are effective tools for controlling image placement.

Final Thoughts

This report is an excellent example of a simple drill-through-to-self technique where parameter values are passed to a subsequent report execution, processed, and used to modify the user's experience. Granted, this is not an elegant report, but the point was to keep it simple to expose the basic elements of this technique. The technique has broad business applications. Similar techniques may be used to hide and show report elements based on conditional logic, parameters, and data values.

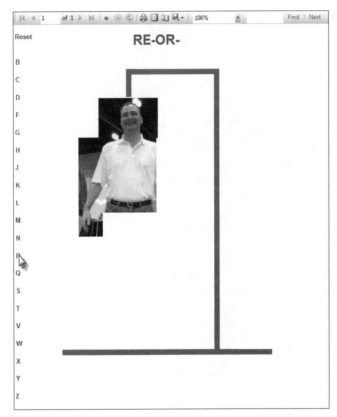

FIGURE P9-3

Credits and Related References

This demonstration report was primarily designed for the BI Power Hour sessions by Brian Welcker with help from Chris Hays. Other members of the Reporting Services product team provided input and feedback.

SEA BATTLE GAME

At annual industry conferences like the Professional Association for SQL Server (PASS) Global Summit and Microsoft TechEd, members of various Microsoft product teams participate in a session called the "BI Power Hour." This is one of the highlights of the conference where teams that contribute to the Microsoft Business Intelligence platform show off their technology in a fun way. It is about demonstrating, in perhaps unusual ways, how business intelligence and various tools of the BI stack can be useful. In past years, Reporting Services made a number of successful contributions to these events, such as Hangman, report manager as report, Etch-a-Sketch, Mastermind, an executive dashboard (Tic-Tac-Toe) and others.

This recipe is a variation of a popular multi-player game played with grids and pegs, that we shall call "Sea Battle." The goal of the game is to sink all of your opponent's ships (for example, a Battleship), before the opponent has a chance to find and sink your ships. The faster you click, the better your chances of winning.

The overall theme of the report is to demonstrate the use of interesting new data visualization features in Reporting Services 2008. It uses a chart with dynamic drill-through actions and data-point tooltips, gauges, and matrices with embedded images and other report items.

While Reporting Services was clearly not designed as a gaming platform, this demonstration of the product's flexibility brought out the competitive spirit in the SQL Server BI team. Robert Bruckner said, "When I made an initial version available for limited beta-testing on an internal report server, the news spread quickly and we immediately had more than 50 people playing, and frantically clicking on the chart's drill-through links trying to win against their human opponents. This created quite a bit of load on the report server that is also used by hundreds of other users, and provided a nice stress test scenario."

In this recipe, you will review the design elements of a working report solution, rather than build the whole thing yourself.

Product Versions

➤ Reporting Services 2008 or newer

➤ SQL Server 2008 or newer

What You'll Need

➤ SeaBattle — Start New Game.rdl

➤ SeaBattle.rdl

➤ SeaBattle.rds

➤ SeaBattle.bak - database backup

Techniques Demonstrated

➤ Drill-through-to-self report action

➤ Chart report actions

➤ Multiple parameters

➤ Parameterized expressions to set report item properties

➤ Using stored procedures to update data and return results

➤ Using custom images in charts and gauges

Reviewing the Report

To set up the environment and get started, follow these steps:

1. Restore the SeaBattle database from the provided database backup file.

2. Open the shared data source and test the connection to the SeaBattle database.

3. Using BIDS or Report Builder, deploy the data source file and both reports to the report server.

To play the game, do the following:

1. Navigate to the Report Manager or the report server using the browser.

2. Run the SeaBattle – Start New Game report. This will display a welcome message with your user name and a message prompting you to wait for another user to enter the game.

3. In a separate browser window on the same computer or from a different network location, open the same report. This time, the report will display the first user's Windows ID, prompting you to start the game.

4. If you are playing as a single user, simply use the second browser window to interact with the game report. If you have two users, refresh the first browser and begin playing the game.

5. In the large grid, located in the top-left area of the report page, click one cell at a time to try to locate and sink enemy ships. If two or more players are participating, take turns clicking the grid.

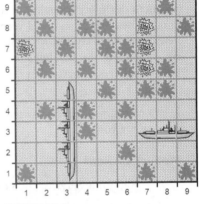

FIGURE P9-4

Figure P9-4 shows the player opponent's grid which is used to visualize hits, misses and ships that have been sunk by clicking on the cells.

A small matrix acts essentially as a data-driven grid control next to the chart to show your own ship positions and the opponent's hits and misses. The overall health status of the opponent's ships is shown using gauge report items with a custom pointer that uses an image to simulate a rising water level, as a ship sustains more and more hits (see Figure P9-5.)

Successfully sinking a ship is rewarded with an animated explosion. The really fun part is the multi-player aspect: a basic method to match up two report users so they can play against each other by simply interacting with their report on a report server.

FIGURE P9-5

How It Works

The SeaBattle report contains all the working elements for the game. Figure P9-6 shows an example of the report elements at runtime. The major components consist of a scatter chart that uses custom images to plot the position of your opponent's ships. The dataset returns a value for every position in the chart X-Y coordinates, so these data points show up as cells in a grid. The chart shows your strike misses and hits as the underlying table gets updated. This is the primary user interface. A drill-through action sends the position of each cell that you click and this action is recorded in the database, which then returns information about misses, hits and previously sunk ships.

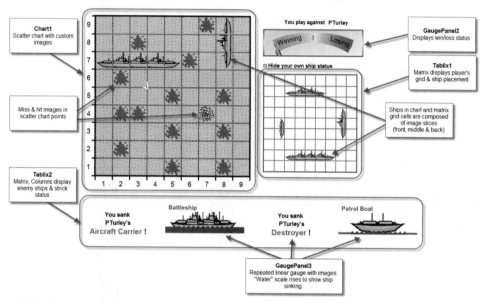

FIGURE P9-6

To the right of the opponent's grid, a gauge is used to let you know how well you're doing relative to your opponent. Below this is a matrix showing the placement of your own ships. The ship positions are generated automatically at the beginning of the game.

In the lower section of the report, a matrix is used to display the progress of enemy ship strikes and sinks. For each ship, a wave image is displayed over the top of the appropriate ship. The height of the wave is modified to show how far "down" the ship is sinking based on the number of strikes.

The following table shows all of the images embedded into the SeaBattle report. On both the opponent's grid chart report item and on your home grid, each ship is represented by individual ship sections. Different ships occupy a different number of cells composed of a front (or "bow"), back ("stern"), and zero or more middle pieces. This is the reason that the aircraft carrier looks more like an extra-long battleship. Since ships may be positioned either horizontally or vertically on the grid, two different images exist for each ship element. Four completely assembled ship images are used to display the sinking status in the lower report section.

Image	Name
	ShipFront
	ShipMid
	ShipBack
	ShipFrontVert
	ShipMidVert
	ShipBackVert
	Miss
	Hit
	AircraftCarrier
	Battleship
	Destroyer
	PatrolBoat
	Waves
	Sunk (animated image)

The startup report (SeaBattle - Start New Game) uses a dataset referencing a stored procedure called NewGame, which serves two purposes; to begin a new game and to return the current game session for the second user joining once the game has been started. Three parameters are used to track the PlayerID, which is the network user name based on the UserID report global object; a GameID, which is generated by the first user starting a game; and the PlaySolo flag, used to toggle the game between solo and multiplayer modes.

Upon close examination, the NewGame stored procedure establishes the number of players, cleans up the prior session if necessary, retrieves or derives a GameID and then returns a result set including the game and opposing player information.

```
CREATE PROCEDURE [dbo].[NewGame]
    @PlayerId NVARCHAR(50),
    @PlaySolo BIT,
    @GameId SMALLINT = 0
AS
BEGIN
    DECLARE @PrimaryPlayer AS BIT

    IF @GameId = 0 OR @GameId IS NULL
    BEGIN
        DECLARE @PlayerCount AS INT
        DECLARE @GridId AS SMALLINT

        BEGIN TRANSACTION

        SET @GameId = COALESCE((SELECT MAX(GameId) FROM MatchUp
            GROUP BY GameId HAVING COUNT(PlayerId) = 1), 0)
        SET @PlayerCount = (SELECT COUNT(PlayerId) FROM MatchUp
            WHERE GameId=@GameId)
        IF (@PlayerCount = 1 AND @PlaySolo = 0)
        BEGIN
            DECLARE @OpponentGridId AS SMALLINT
            SET @OpponentGridId = (SELECT OpponentGridId FROM MatchUp
                WHERE GameId=@GameId)
            SET @PrimaryPlayer = 0
            EXEC @GridId = [GetRandomGridLayoutId] @OpponentGridId
        END ELSE BEGIN
            SET @PrimaryPlayer = 1
            SET @GameId = COALESCE((SELECT 1+MAX(GameId) FROM MatchUp), 1)
            EXEC @GridId = [GetRandomGridLayoutId]
        END
        INSERT INTO MatchUp
            VALUES (@GameId, @PlayerId, @GridId, @PrimaryPlayer)

        -- initialize grid when primary player registers
        IF @PrimaryPlayer = 1
        BEGIN
            DELETE FROM [Grid] WHERE GameId = @GameId
            DECLARE @CountX AS SMALLINT
            DECLARE @CountY AS SMALLINT
            SET @CountX = 1
            WHILE @CountX <= 9
            BEGIN
                SET @CountY = 1
                WHILE @CountY <= 9
                BEGIN
                    INSERT INTO [Grid]
                        VALUES (@GameId, 0, @CountX, @CountY, NULL, NULL)
                    INSERT INTO [Grid]
                        VALUES (@GameId, 1, @CountX, @CountY, NULL, NULL)
                    SET @CountY = @CountY+1
                END
                SET @CountX = @CountX+1
```

```
                    END
                END

                IF @PlaySolo = 1
                BEGIN
                    -- add computer player
                    DECLARE @CompGridId AS SMALLINT
                    EXEC @CompGridId = [GetRandomGridLayoutId] @GridId
                    INSERT INTO MatchUp
                        VALUES (@GameId, 'Computer', @CompGridId, 0)
                END
                COMMIT
            END ELSE BEGIN
                SET @PrimaryPlayer = (SELECT PrimaryPlayer FROM MatchUp
                    WHERE GameId=@GameId AND PlayerId=@PlayerId)
            END

            DECLARE @OpponentId AS NVARCHAR(50)
            SET @OpponentId = (SELECT PlayerId FROM MatchUp WHERE GameId=@GameId
                AND PrimaryPlayer<>@PrimaryPlayer)
            SELECT GameId, PrimaryPlayer, @OpponentId AS OpponentId
                FROM [MatchUp]
                WHERE GameId = @GameId AND PlayerId = @PlayerId
        END
```

To initiate the game, each player's grid layout must be defined with each ship in a randomized position. As you can see, the NewGame stored procedure calls another stored procedure named GetRandomGridLayout to perform this task.

```
    CREATE PROCEDURE [dbo].[GetRandomGridLayoutId]
        @OpponentGridId SMALLINT = -1
AS
BEGIN
    DECLARE @MaxLayoutId AS SMALLINT
    SET @MaxLayoutId = (SELECT MAX(GridLayoutId) - 1 FROM ShipLocation)
    DECLARE @GridId AS SMALLINT
    SET @GridId = (SELECT 1+ROUND(@MaxLayoutId*RAND((DATEPART(ss, GETDATE()))
        + DATEPART(ms, GETDATE())* 100), 0))
    WHILE @GridId = @OpponentGridId
    BEGIN
        SET @GridId = (SELECT 1+ROUND(@MaxLayoutId*RAND((DATEPART(ss, GETDATE()))
            + DATEPART(ms, GETDATE())* 100), 0))
    END
    RETURN @GridId
END
```

When the first user opens this report, a GameID is generated and the game report waits for the first user to "log in" by running the report. When the second user runs the report, a link is displayed, prompting the users to begin game play.

Figure P9-7 demonstrates the core technique that makes these two reports work. It shows one of a few similar report actions, which drill-through and pass parameters back to the same report. This is the technique we refer to as a drill-through-to-self report action. A dataset in the report then receives these parameters and passes them to a stored procedure as the report is executed after the user clicks the link or cell.

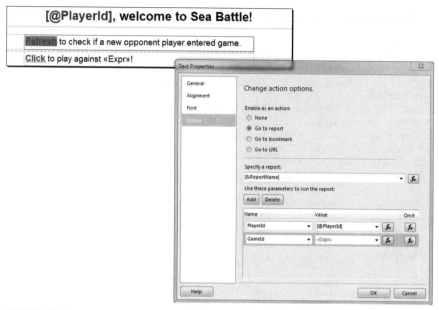

FIGURE P9-7

After the first player has entered the game, the third textbox (titled "Click to play against <player X>!") on the report is displayed using a conditional expression. To see how this works, view the Hidden property for Rectangle1 and Rectangle2 on this report. The second link is a report action that opens the game board in a report named SeaBattle.

The SeaBattle report contains two datasets named GameData and OpponentData. These are based on stored procedures named GameTurn and GameStatus, respectively. With each click of the opponent's grid, the X and Y coordinates for that cell are passed to the report as a drill-through-to-self report action. Note the parameters in the following stored procedure:

```
CREATE PROCEDURE dbo.GameStatus
    @GameId INT,
    @PrimaryPlayer BIT,
    @X SMALLINT = 0,
    @Y SMALLINT = 0
AS
BEGIN
    -- note: @X and @Y are 0 during initialization or when
    -- executing GameStatus for the opponent player
    DECLARE @GridLayoutId AS SMALLINT
    SET @GridLayoutId =
        (SELECT OpponentGridId FROM MatchUp WHERE GameId = @GameId
        AND PrimaryPlayer = @PrimaryPlayer)
```

```
DECLARE @PlayerId AS NVARCHAR(50)
SET @PlayerId =
    (SELECT PlayerId FROM MatchUp WHERE GameId = @GameId
     AND PrimaryPlayer = @PrimaryPlayer)

-- return grid and ship data
SELECT @PlayerId as PlayerName, G.X, G.Y, G.Hit,
    L.ShipId, L.ImageName, D.ShipType, D.Units AS ShipUnits,
    CASE WHEN G.X = @X AND G.Y = @Y THEN 1
    ELSE 0
    END AS LastHit,
(SELECT COUNT(G2.Hit) FROM [Grid] G2
    LEFT OUTER JOIN [ShipLocation] L2 ON (L2.X = G2.X and
        L2.Y = G2.Y and L2.GridLayoutId=@GridLayoutId)
    WHERE L2.ShipId = L.ShipId AND
        G2.GameId = @GameId AND
        G2.PrimaryPlayer = @PrimaryPlayer) AS HitUnits
FROM [Grid] G
    LEFT OUTER JOIN [ShipLocation] L ON (L.X = G.X and L.Y = G.Y
        AND L.GridLayoutId=@GridLayoutId)
    LEFT OUTER JOIN [ShipData] D ON D.ShipId = L.ShipId
WHERE G.GameId = @GameId AND
    G.PrimaryPlayer = @PrimaryPlayer
END
```

The GameTurn stored procedure is actually a wrapper around the GameStatus procedure. It accepts the same set of parameters, updates the Grid table with the current coordinate information and then executes the GameStatus procedure, which returns the updated game status information to the report.

```
CREATE PROCEDURE dbo.GameTurn
    @GameId INT,
    @PrimaryPlayer BIT,
    @X SMALLINT = 0,
    @Y SMALLINT = 0
AS
BEGIN
    IF (@X <> 0) AND (@Y <> 0)
    BEGIN
        -- update grid
        DECLARE @ClickSequenceId AS INT
        SET @ClickSequenceId = (SELECT 1+COUNT(Hit) FROM Grid
            WHERE GameId = @GameId AND PrimaryPlayer = @PrimaryPlayer)
        UPDATE [Grid]
            SET [Hit] = 1, [ClickSequenceId] = @ClickSequenceId
        WHERE GameId = @GameId AND PrimaryPlayer = @PrimaryPlayer
            AND X = @X AND Y = @Y
    END
    -- return GameStatus
    EXEC dbo.GameStatus @GameId, @PrimaryPlayer, @X, @Y
END
```

The effect of these actions is clear simply by running the report and playing the game. Although there are a few more details, the essential mechanics are simple: As each player clicks a cell on their opponent's grid, the drill-through action and subsequent GameTurn stored procedure call updates rows in the

Grid table within the SeaBattle database. Calls to the GameStatus stored procedure return ShipLocation data to determine hits and misses and ultimately sinks, wins, and losses.

Final Thoughts

This report is an impressive example of the kind of dynamic interactivity made possible with some creative report design. Many of the report design techniques exhibited in this game have also been demonstrated in other recipes. This one just puts the pieces together in a different way. Regardless of the application, the essential components are the same: report actions that send parameter values back to the same report, database procedures or programming code that processes those parameter values and then modifies report item properties to change the user's experience. In this case, a completely interactive experience was managed by storing ship positions in a database table and updating another table with information about where players clicked within a grid.

Credits and Related References

Several members of the Reporting Services product team were instrumental in creating the SeaBattle reports used in the BI Power Hour conference demonstrations.

Thanks to Robert Bruckner for gathering the details and posting information about this demonstration to his blog at http://blogs.msdn.com/robertbruckner. Robert includes some additional information about setup and optimized play.

INDEX

Symbol

= (equal sign) in SQL statement, 510

A

activity summaries, 7–8
AddOrRemoveID function, 468
AddValue function, 407
  defining, 409
Adventure Works Cycles, 21
aesthetic report design, 98
aggregate functions, 41–42
  arguments, 41
  AVG, 45
  COUNT, 45
  COUNTDISTINCT, 45
  SUM, 45
aggregation, 45, 407–414
  textbox values, 447
all-at-once reports, 3
alternate row colors, 90–92
AlternateBackgroundShading.rdl, 93
analytical reporting, 8–9
  charts, 10–14
  dashboards, 9
  interactive reports, 15–17
  matrix reports, 9–10
  pivot tables, 9–10
  scorecards, 9
anchor tags, 318
AND operator, WHERE clause, 485
Angry Koala Cube Browser, 162, 204
  Australian Sparklines and, 204
  body, 219–220
  columns, restricting, 220

Cube Browser and, 204, 210
Cube Dynamic Rows and, 204
Cube Metadata and, 204
Cube Restricting Rows and, 204
footers, 220
numbered reports, 206
r100-Angry Koala Cube Browser, 206–207
r102-Angry Koala Driver, 208–210
r101-Angry Koala Graph, 207–208
r103-Angry Koala Member, 210
rows, restricting, 220
swap actions, 220
titles, 220
Angry Koala Cube Surfer report, 182
AOT (Application Object Tree), AX, 574
App_Code folder, XML schema folder, 361
application integration, 17–18
arguments, aggregate functions, 41
ArrayList, 408
ASP.NET, 362
  Classic .NET application pool, 365
  external image source, 430–438
Australian Sparklines, 183, 185
  Angry Koala Cube Browser, 204
  characteristics, 185
  controls, 187–197
  data preparation, 187–197
  full-sized, 197–200
  pLag parameter, 187
  tables, 201–203
automation, matrix and, 330
AutoRefresh property, 349
averages, moving average, 279
Avery 5160 label template, 383
#AVG keyword, 242

AX, 574
  AOT (Application Object Tree), 574
  templates, 574
axis value, range, changing, 246
#AXISLABEL keyword, 242

B

background color, calendar reports, 381
background shading, alternate for table groups, 93–98
BackgroundColor property, 88, 238
bar charts, 65–66
  growing, 272–275
  Pareto charts, 293
Barcode Professional 6.0 for Reporting Services, 391
barcodes, 391–399
  custom report items, 393–399
  fonts, 391, 392–393
  .NET components, 393–399
  .NET Global Assembly Cache, 395
  SKU number, 391
Barcodes Inc. Free Barcode Font, 398
Battleship, 585
Beautiful Evidence (Tufte), 131
BGColor variable, 103
BI (business intelligence)
  purpose, 8–9
  strategies, 8–9
BI Power Hour, 585, 590, 591
BIDS (Business Intelligence Development Studio), 30, 306
BIN folder, 442–443
BindData method, 366, 367
BindImage method, 434
BindReportControl method, 369
Bing map service, SSRS and, 14
BMP images, 461
Body object, 39–40
Bollinger bands, 279
bookmarks, 331
Boon, Sean (blog), 138
  Building Win-Loss Sparklines in SQL Server Reporting Services 2008 R2, 232

breadcrumb link, 318–325
Bruckner, Robert
  Charts with Dynamic Height or Width based on Categories/Data, 275
  Get More Out of SQL Server Reporting Services Charts, 238, 292
  RS Maps with Spatial Data and Bing Maps, 478
  Sea Battle game, 591, 599
  Using Group Variables in Reporting Services 2008 for Custom Aggregation, 414
built-in fields, 75
built-in keywords, 240
bullet graphs
  exception highlighting, 264–267
  Few, Stephen, 222

C

CAD (Canadian dollars), 400, 404
calculated fields, 76
calculated series, adding to series, 279
calculations, RDL, 240
Calendar database, 375
  data source references, 379
calendar reports, 375–382
  date as separate record, 375
  matrix, 375
  month navigation cells, 380
  navigating, 381
CalendarMonth field, 283
CAML (Collaborative Application Markup Language), 566
cascading parameters, 74
catalogs, 6
category axis, 63
CDATE( ) function, 77
CDEC( ) function, 77
Chart Wizard, 271
charts
  bar, 65–66
  category groups, 63
  color palettes, custom, 235–238
  column, 11

keywords, 239–242
line, 11, 12–13
maps, 14–15
Pareto charts, 10
pie charts, 11
polar, 65
radar, 65
scaled grid, 12
series axis, 63
shape, 65
synchronizing, 228–232
Charts with Dynamic Height or Width based on
    Categories/Data (Bruckner), 275
check box list
  existing records, 460–463
  parameter selection, 472–473
  selecting/deselecting records, 464–473
  toggling, 465
checked/unchecked files, 464–465
CHOOSE( ) function, 77
CINT( ) function, 77
Classic .NET application pool, 365
CLR (common language runtime), 18
Code 39, 391
code-behind, offline reporting, 365–372
code completion, 409
Code Editor window, 78
collaborative portal environments, 20
color
  dynamic fill color, 249
  Gainsboro, 89
  legend, 235
  overriding, 235
    data points, 235
  values
    constant, 235
    expression-based, 235
color palette, 454
  custom, 235–238
    building, 236–237
Color property, 237
colorPalette variable, 236
column charts, 11
  goal threshold line, 244–249

growing, 272–275
histogram transformation, 277
sparklines, 131
Column Groups, 45
columns
  dynamic, 43–44
  hiding/showing, 115–120
  static, 43–44
comma-separated strings in parameters, 319,
    464
compounded simplicity, 381
conditional expressions, 76–78
conditional linking, 299–303
conditional page breaks, 415–419
conditional queries, executing, 522
continents, multiple, 574
controls in MicrosoftReportViewer, 363
converting currency, 400–406
COUNT function, 45
COUNTDISTINCT function, 45
CRI (Custom Report Items), 391
  Barcode Professional, 395
  BIDS environment, 394
  bug in rendering, 398
CRM (customer relationship management), 65
CSTR( ) function, 77
CSV (comma-separated values), 25
CSV-rendering extension, 25
Cube Browser report
  Angry Koala Cube Browser, 210
  body, 173–174
  columns, restricting, 174–175
  Cube Browser Member report, 167
  Cube Browser Metadata report, 166–167
  Cube Dynamic Rows, 167
  footer, 179–182
  linked reports, 165
  rows, restricting, 174–175
  speed, 163
  TablixSwap, 175–176
  titles, 176
    date member, 178
    hierarchy for filter, 178
    hierarchy on columns, 178

hierarchy on rows, 178
Measure, 177–178
Cube Dynamic Rows, 139–147
Cube Browser report, 167
Cube Metadata report, 139, 148–162
Cube Restricting Rows, 513
cubes
restricting rows, 513–521
structure, 521
top value reports, 510–511
cumulative percentage of occurrence, Pareto
charts, 295
currencies, multiple, 574
currency code, 400
currency translation, 400–406
currency values, language localization and, 440
CUS (Customer) layer, 579
custom assemblies, 79–80
custom code
approaches, 78
reports, 78–79
custom fields, 76
Custom Report Items (CRI), 391
CustomColorPalette sample report, 235

D

dashboards, 9
bullet graphs, 222
gauge reports, 260
rotating report dashboard, 347–351
data, updating from report, 352–358
data binning, 277
data points
color, overriding, 235
labels, 240
data regions, 134
data series, color legend, 235
data sources, 31–32
data visualization, 131
databases
Calendar, 375
samples, 21–22
Dataset Properties dialog, 320, 353

datasets, 32, 51
best practices, 36
DMVs, 149
filtering in, 487–488
LagCount, 187
parameters, 69
ProductCatalog, 101
query language, 32
date filters, parameterizing, 284
de-normalization, PIVOT operator, 326
debugging, Windows Forms, 485
DECLARE statement, 35
desktop applications, report integration, 18–19
dialogs
Dataset Properties, 320, 353
Edit Chart Value, 235
Expression, 468
Group Properties, 48
Report Parameter Properties, 525
Solution Explorer, 395
Tablix Group Properties, 46–47, 52
Tablix Properties, 126
Text Box Properties, 48
DimCustomer tables, 276
DimDate table, 280
DimEmployees table, 352
DimTime table, 280
DisplayImage.aspx, 432
distribution, histograms, 277
DMVs (Dynamic Management Views), 148
datasets, 149
DocMap, 336
document map table, navigation and, 331–336
Domain/Username (UserID), 544
dot-matrix printers, green bar reports and, 85
drill-down, 54, 55–59
multi-level grouped reports, 54
report creation, 59–60
drill-through, 54, 56–57
link breadcrumbs, 318–325
multi-level matrix reports, 305–317
OLAP browsers, 163
RDL expressions and, 240
Reporting Services 2005, 309–314

Reporting Services 2008, 314–316
reports, 60–63
reports, testing, 471
self-calling, 151
self-drill-through, 175–176
source, 57
target, 57
drop-downs, 352
Dundas components, 260
Dvoranchik, Stephen, 303, 337, 351
dynamic columns, 43–44
dynamic fill color, 249
dynamic formatting, 81
dynamic groups, 105
dynamic page breaks, 415–419
dynamic rows, 43–44
  cube dynamic rows, 139–147
Dynamics AX. See AX
DynamicWidth property, 273

E

Edit Chart Value dialog box, 235
ElementPath, 557
embedded functions, Visual Basic, 485
embedded images, 461, 538
Enterprise Library binaries, 365
Enterprise Resource Planning (ERP), 574
enumerations, 366
equal sign (=) in SQL statement, 510
ERP (Enterprise Resource Planning), 574
ESRI map objects, 14
ESRI shape files, 69
Excel-rendering extension, 26
Excel worksheet naming, 420–424
exception highlighting, 264–267
execution log table, rows, purging, 345
ExecutionLog view, 343
ExecutionLogStorage table, 342
Expression dialog, 468
Expression Editor
  opening, 89
  syntax, 75
expressions, 75–76

conditional, 76–78
functions, 77
groups, 46–47
LineTotalOrig, 402
UnitPriceOrig, 402
extensions, 23–24
external image sources, 425–438
external resource lookup, .NET and, 441–446
Extreme Reporting Services, 185

F

Few, Stephen, 222
fields
  built-in, 75
  calculated, 76
  CalendarMonth, 283
  custom, 76
  MonthlySalesAmount, 283
fills
  dynamic fill color, 249
  Gradient, 134
filtering data, 37, 331
  in datasets, 487–488
  document map and, 336
  multiple criterion, 481–489
  in queries, 484–485
  techniques, 482
  Transact-SQL, 481
  user-specific, 544–550
filters, date, parameterizing, 284
#FIRST keyword, 242
fonts, barcodes, 392–393
footers, 40–41, 53–54
  Angry Koala Cube Browser, 220
  Cube Browser report, 179–182
format
  applying, 31
  previewing, 31
FORMAT( ) function, 77
formatting
  complex, 454
  dynamic, 81
  multicolumn reports, designing, 81

numeric, 31
queries, 72–73
renderer-dependent layout and formatting, 454–459
report data, 80–81
table values, 48–51
text, 48
free-text query window, 402
frequency of occurrence, Pareto charts, 295
functions
  AddOrRemoveID, 468
  AddValue, 407
  aggregate, 41–42
  CDATE( ), 77
  CDEC( ), 77
  CHOOSE( ), 77
  CINT( ), 77
  CSTR( ), 77
  embedded, Visual Basic, 485
  expressions, 77
  FORMAT( ), 77
  GetColor( ), 237
  GetMedian, 407
  IIF, 89, 96, 462
  IncrementCount( ), 349
  InScope, 314
  INSTR( ), 77
  ISNOTHING( ), 77
  LEFT( ), 77
  MID( ), 77
  Now( ), 381
  RIGHT( ), 77
  RowNumber, 89
  RunningValue, 96
  T-SQL IN( ), 472
  table-valued, 375, 382
  TOPCOUNT, 513
  UDFs (user-defined functions), 490

G

Gainsboro, 89
GameData dataset, 597

games
  hangman, 585–590
  Sea Battle, 591–599
GameStatus stored procedure, 599
GameTurn stored procedure, 598
gauge reports, 260
gauges
  background image, report definition, 260
  binding to report data, 260
  exception highlighting, 264–267
  linear, 68
  markers, 67
  pointers, 67
  radial, 68
  ranges, 67
  scale, 67
GDI (Graphics Device Interface), 389
geographical reporting, 14–15
geospatial data, 14, 474–478
Get More Out of SQL Server Reporting Services Charts (Bruckner), 238, 292
GetColor( ) function, 237
GetListItems method, 564
GetLocalText( ) method, 442
GetMedian function, 407
  calling, 408
  defining, 409
GIF images, 461
globals, 76
go to bookmark, 331
goal threshold line in column chart, 244–249
GQE (Graphical Query Editor), 33
Gradient fill, 134
graphic editing programs, 461
graphical MDX editor, 35
graphical query designer (Microsoft SharePoint List Data Provider), 571
Graphics Device Interface (GDI), 389
green bar reports
  alternate row colors, 90–92
  designing, 86–90
  dot-matrix printers and, 85
  nested groups, 100–104
Gross Margin data series, 288, 290

Group Properties dialog, 48
Group.DomainScope RDL, 231
grouped pie chart slices, 268–271
grouped reports, 4–5
groups
  Column Groups, 45
  defining, 45–51
  definition, 55
  dynamic, 105
  expressions, 46–47
  headers, showing/hiding, 120
  multi-level grouped reports, drill-down
    and, 54
  options, 46–47
  page number resetting, 125–127
  Row Groups, 45
  sequential group index calculation, 101
  sorting in, 52–53
  synchronizing, 228–232
GUID (globally unique identifier), 564
GV variable, 412

H

hangman game, 585–590
Hays, Chris, 244, 590
  Dynamic Grouping blog entry, 99
  Greenbar Matrix blog entry, 99
  Horizontal Tables blog entry, 99
headers, 40–41, 53–54
  groups, showing/hiding, 120
  Median value, 407
hiding/showing
  columns, 115–120
  group headers, 120
hierarchical relationships, 559
hierarchies, 160
  Cube Browser Member report, 167
highlighting, exception highlighting,
  264–267
histograms, 276–278
  segment width, 277
horizontal tables, 121–124
HSB (Hue, Saturation, and Brightness), 88

HTML rendering extension, 25
HTML Viewer, 23
hyperlinks, 318
  disabling when exporting to PDF, 454

I

if-then-else functionality, 89
IIF function, 89, 96, 462
IIS (Internet Information Services), 359
image-rendering extension, 26
images
  check box list, 461
  embedded, 461, 538
  external sources, 425–438
  formats, 461
  graphic editing programs, 461
  properties, 461
  web pages acting as, 437
in-line parameters, 510
IncrementCount( ) function, 349
#INDEX keyword, 242
indexes, relative strength index, 279
Information Dashboard Design (Few),
  222
InScope function, 314
installation, samples, 21–22
INSTR( ) function, 77
IntelliSense, 409
interactive reports, 15–17
Interactive Sort, 53, 522, 523, 535
  custom, 522, 535–542
interactivity, 454
Internet Information Services (IIS), 359
intersection of lines, 283
inventory forms, 2–3
invoices, 2–3
ISNOTHING( ) function, 77
Item parameter, 556

J

joins, outer joins, 462
JPG images, 461

K

keywords, 239–242
  #AVG, 242
  #AXISLABEL, 242
  built-in, 240
  #FIRST, 242
  #INDEX, 242
  #LABEL, 242
  #LAST, 242
  #LEGENDTEXT, 242
  #MAX, 242
  #MIN, 242
  Nothing, 96
  #PERCENT, 239, 242
  #SERIESNAME, 242
  Shared, 79
  Static, 79
  #TOTAL, 242
  #VALX, 242
  #VALY, 242
  #VALY2, 242
  #VALY3, 242
  #VALY4, 242

L

#LABEL keyword, 242
labels, 6
  data points, 240
LagCount dataset, 187
language localization, 439–446
  currency values, 440
  Report Viewer control, 439
  SharePoint Integration Mode, 439
  text wrapping, 439–440
Larson, Brian, 375
  Microsoft SQL Server 2008 Reporting Services, 382
#LAST keyword, 242
layers, CUS (Customer) layer, 579
LEFT( ) function, 77
legend
  color fields, 235
  custom, 237–238
  flexibility, 235
#LEGENDTEXT keyword, 242
line charts, 11, 12–13
  margins, 246–248
  Pareto charts, 293
  sparklines, 131
line-continuation characters, 466
Line with Markers chart type, 286
linear gauges, 68
linear regression line, 279–285
lines
  intersection, 283
  slope, 283
LineTotalOrig expression, 402
link breadcrumbs, 318–325
Link field cell, 322
linked reports, Cube Browser report, 165
linking, conditional, 299–303
links, hyperlinks, 318
List < > method, 365
List Data Retrieval web services, 564
list reports, 4–5
ListChildren method, 556
Lists web service, 564
localization, 439
Localizer( ) class, 444
logical page breaks, 415
logo, 425
lookup expressions, static text, 445
lookup resources, localization and, 439
loops, nested, 378

M

mail merge, 383
mailing labels, 383–390
  columns, 386
  margins, 386
  positioning within cell, 388
  print-oriented formats, 389
manifests, 2–3
Map It link, 299–303
Map visualizations, 478

map wizard, 474–478
maps, 14–15
  map gallery, 69
margins
  line charts, 246–248
  mailing labels, 386
markers, gauges, 67
Mastermind, 585
matrix reports, 9–10, 45, 51, 326–330
  automation and, 330
  calendar reports, 375
  data supplied, 326
  item layout, 122
  multi-level, drill-through, 305–317
  populating, 375
  totals, 42–43
matrixes, horizontal tables, 121
#MAX keyword, 242
MDX (Multidimensional Expressions), 35
  query, 250–251
  Query Designer
      formatting, 72–73
      modifying, 72–73
      parameters, 70–72
  query designer, 510
  statement, 255
  TOPCOUNT function, 513
Median function, 407
Median value, header, 407
member declaration, 366
metadata, adding, 153–154
Method element, 556
methods
  BindData, 366, 367
  BindImage, 434
  BindReportControl, 369
  GetListItems, 564
  GetLocalText( ), 442
  List < >, 365
  ListChildren, 556
  overriding, 576, 579
  Page Load, 367
  Page_Load, 366
  Render, 366

MHTML (MIME-HTML), 25
MicroLink, LLC, 303, 337, 351
Microsoft Dynamics AX. See AX
Microsoft Enterprise Library binaries, 365
Microsoft SharePoint List Data Provider, 562,
    570
  graphical query designer, 571
Microsoft SQL Server 2008 Reporting Services
    (Larson), 382
MicrosoftReportViewer control, 363
MID( ) function, 77
#MIN keyword, 242
Monopoly, 585
MonthlySalesAmount field, 283
moving average, 279
MS Paint, 461
MSDN (Microsoft Developer Network), 54
MSReportServer_ConfigurationSetting class, 24
MSReportServer_Instance class, 24
multi-level grouped reports, drill-down and, 54
multi-level matrix reports, drill-through,
    305–317
multi-series, multi Y-axis charts, 286–292
multi-value parameters, 73–74
  stored procedures and, 490–495
  subscription reports, 496–505
multicolumn reports, designing, 81
multiple criterion filtering, 481–489

N

naming
  Excel worksheets, 420–424
  pages, 420–424
navigating reports, 54
  calendar report, 381
  document map and, 331–336
  summary, 62–63
navigating to URLs, 62
Neodynamic Barcode Professional 6.0 for
    Reporting Services, 391, 398
  nulls, 398
nested groups, green bar reports, 100–104
nested loops, 378

nesting data regions, 232
.NET Global Assembly Cache, 395
NOT operator, 119
Nothing keyword, 96
Now( ) function, 381
numbered reports, Angry Koala Cube Browser, 206
numeric formatting, 31

O

ODS (operational data stores), 391
Office SharePoint Server, 18
offline reporting
  code-behind, 365–372
  computer requirements, 362
  prerequisites, 362
  Report Viewer control, 359–372
OLAP browser, 163
  Angry Koala Cube Browser, 204–220
OLTP (online transaction processing), 391
on-demand processing, 410
operational data stores (ODS), 391
operational reports, 2
operators, NOT, 119
OpponentData dataset, 597
Order By clause, parameterizing, 522, 530–533
OrderValue sort order, 246
OUTER JOIN, 231
outer joins, 462
output parameters, defining, 366
overriding methods, 576, 579

P

page breaks
  dynamic (conditional), 415–419
  logical, 415
  page break position property, 415
Page Load method, 367
page naming, 420–424
page number, resetting, based on groups, 125–127
page running total, 447–453

PageBreakAtEnd, 126
PageBreak.Disabled property, 415
  previous versions of Reporting Services, 418–419
Page_Load method, 366
parameter prompt, 440
parameterizing
  custom sorted queries, 522
  date filters, 284
  logo, 425
  Order By clause, 522, 530–533
  sorted queries, 523
  top values reports, 506–512
parameters, 69–75
  cascading, 74
  check box list, 472–473
  comma-separated strings, 319
  in-line, 510
  interacting with, 518–521
  Item, 556
  list creation, 70–72
  multi-value, 73–74
    stored procedures and, 490–495
    subscription reports, 496–505
  output, defining, 366
  pLag, 187
  Recursive, 556
  report parameters, 75
  rowLimit, 566
  string parameters
    pMeasure, 140
    pRowMbr, 140
  TopCustomerCount, 509
  viewFields, 566
Parameters element, 557
Pareto, Vilfredo, 293
Pareto charts, 10, 293–296
PASS (Professional Association for SQL Server), 591
PDF-rendering extension, 26
#PERCENT keyword, 239, 242
percentage scale, 257
performance metrics, 250–259
personal report card, 250–259

PhotoShop, 461
pie charts, 11
  settings, 240
  slices, grouped, 268–271
PIVOT operator, 326
PIVOT query, 326
pivot tables, 9–10
pivoting, T-SQL, 326
pLag parameter, 187
pMeasure string parameter, 140
PNG images, 461
pointers, gauges, 67
polar charts, 65
portal content, 19–20
previewing, format, 31
process and operational support reports
  activity summaries, 7–8
  catalogs, 6
  inventory forms, 2–3
  invoices, 2–3
  labels, 6–7
  list reports, 4–5
  manifests, 2–3
  operational reports, 2
  sales orders, 2–3
  status reports, 8
  tabular reports, 4–5
  template forms, 3–4
processors, 23–24
ProductCatalog dataset, 101
ProductKey value, 461
Professional SQL Server 2005 Reporting Services
    (Turley), 489
Professional SQL Server 2008 Reporting Services
    (Turley, et al), 29, 238, 446
properties
  AutoRefresh, 349
  BackgroundColor, 88
  BackgroundColor, 238
  Color, 237
  DynamicWidth, 273
  images, 461
  PageBreak.Disabled, 415
  RecursiveParent, 558

Report Language, 439
Report object, 39
ToggleItem, 59–60
Visibility, 55–56
Properties window (Report Builder), 262
pRowMbr string parameter, 140
Puzzle stored procedure, 588

Q

queries
  conditional, executing, 522
  datasets, 32
  designing, 33–36
  filtering in, 484–485
  free-text query window, 402
  GQE (Graphical Query Editor), 33
  graphical query designer, 571
  MDX, 250–251
  OUTER JOIN, 231
  PIVOT, 326
  replacing with expressions, 470
  restricting rows returned, 513
  SOAP web services, 556
  sorted, parameterized, 522, 523
  sorting in, 51–52
  spatial queries, 475
  top values, 506
Query Analyzer for SQL 2000, T-SQL and, 496
query command string, modifying, 470
Query Designer
  formatting, 72–73
  modifying, 72–73
  parameters, 70–72
query languages, 485
  datasets, 32
  limitations, 512
query parser, 38
  data type evaluation, 470
query strings, building with code, 485–487

R

radar charts, 65
radial gauges, 68

radio buttons, Stored Procedure, 329

ranges, gauges, 67

RDCE (Report Definition Customization
Extensions), 440

RDL (Report Definition Language), 39
calculations, 240
chart height/width, 272–273
Group.DomainScope, 231

real-time data, 391

records, check box list, 460–463

Recursive parameter, 556

RecursiveParent property, 558

relative strength index, 279

Render method, 366

renderer-dependent layout and formatting,
454–459

rendering extension, accessing, 459

Report Builder, 22, 30
Properties window, 262
region-specific design wizards, 30

report caching, 24–25
CSV-rendering extension, 25
Excel-rendering extension, 26
HTML rendering extension, 25
image-rendering extension, 26
PDF-rendering extension, 26
Word-rendering extension, 26
XML-rendering extension, 25–26

Report Definition Customization Extensions
(RDCE), 440

Report Execution Log report, 341–342

report footers, 40–41

report headers, 40–41

report integration, applications, desktop,
18–19

Report Language property, 439

report localization, 439

Report Manager, 18

Report object, properties, 39

Report Parameter Properties dialog box, 525

Report Viewer control, 23
binary, referencing, 364
localization, 439
offline reporting, 359–372

Reporting Services
extensions, 23–24
processors, 23–24
samples, installation, 21–22
server availability, 23

Reporting Services 2000 Service Pack 1, 235

reports. *See also* specific report types
actionable, 18
introduction, 1
navigation, 54
parameters, 75
updating data, 352–358

ReportViewer control, 20–21

RESGEN.exe command-line tool, 442

results, filtering, 331

RGB (Red, Green, and Blue), 88

RichText, 448

RIGHT( ) function, 77

rolling comparisons, Australian Sparklines, 185

row-based reports, 4–5

Row Groups, 45, 46–47

rowLimit parameter, 566

RowNumber function, 89

rows
cube dynamic rows, 139–147
static, 43–44

RPC (Remote Procedure Call) interface, 24

RS Maps with Spatial Data and Bing Maps
(Bruckner), 478

RSCONFIG utility, 430

RunningValue function, 96

S

sales orders, 2–3

sales trends, sparklines, 131–137

samples, installation, 21–22

scale, gauges, 67

scorecards, 9

Sea Battle game, 591–599

SELECT statements, combining with UNION
command, 470

selecting/deselecting records, check box list,
464–473